SIMPLIFIED
STRUCTURED
COBOL WITH
MICROSOFT/MICROFOCUS
COBOL

SIMPLIFIED STRUCTURED COBOL WITH MICROSOFT/MICROFOCUS COBOL

DANIEL D. McCRACKEN
City College, City University of New York
New York, New York

DONALD G. GOLDEN
Cleveland State University
Cleveland, Ohio

WILEY

JOHN WILEY & SONS

New York / Chichester / Brisbane / Toronto / Singapore

Copyright ©1990 by John Wiley & Sons, Inc.

All rights reserved. Published simultaneously in Canada.

Reproduction or translation of any part of this work beyond that permitted by Section 107 or 108 of the 1976 United States Copyright Act without the permission of the copyright owner is unlawful. Requests for permission or further information should be addressed to the Permissions Department, John Wiley & Sons, Inc.

Library of Congress Cataloging in Publication Data
McCracken, Daniel D.
    Simplified structured cobol with microsoft/microfocus COBOL/
    Daniel D. McCracken, Donald G. Golden.
        p.   cm.
    1. COBOL (Computer program language) 2. Structured
    programming. I. Golden, Donald G. II. Title.
QA76.73.C25M423 1990   89-27937
005.13'3—dc20   CIP
ISBN 0-471-51407-1 (pbk.)

Printed in the United States of America

10 9 8 7 6 5 4 3 2 1

Lowry

CONTENTS

vi CONTENTS

3   DATA DIVISION ELEMENTS AND THE ARITHMETIC VERBS   29

15   FILE STORAGE DEVICES AND PROGRAMMING   411

16   CHARACTER MANIPULATION   461

APPENDIX III: PROGRAMMING STANDARDS   623

APPENDIX IV: ANSWERS TO STARRED EXERCISES   629

APPENDIX V: LOADING THE MICROSOFT COBOL COMPILER   685

INDEX   691

PREFACE

This book is for the person who wants to learn what COBOL is, the fundamentals of writing COBOL programs, how to use COBOL in typical business applications, and especially how to write COBOL programs using the Microsoft COBOL compiler. It assumes little or no previous background in programming.

Each chapter is based on one or more example programs that present the programming concepts in a framework of meaningful applications. These examples are drawn from a variety of areas in business data processing: simple inventory and payroll calculations; validation of an order from a seed catalog; preparation of sales reports; and updating sequential, indexed, and relative files, among others. In fact, more than half the book consists of example programs and the discussion of them. All programs have been run, and actual computer output is displayed for all. Where appropriate, we have shown techniques for both batch and interactive programming, and several examples present programs in both styles.

All chapters except the last one, Additional COBOL Topics, close with a set of review questions, both to reinforce the central concepts and to make the reader aware of what may need more study; answers to all review questions are given immediately following the questions. There are many exercises; answers to about half of them are given in Appendix IV. Most of the exercises call for writing partial or complete programs and are suitable for development by one person. In several chapters there are exercises of sufficient size to give you experience in developing simplified but realistic programs. Solutions to these exercises are not given, which requires that you learn to test programs for yourself to see if the results are correct.

People learn programming by writing programs. Every experienced teacher knows that the sooner students see complete programs, no matter how simple, and begin writing and running them themselves, the quicker they begin to understand what programming is all about. This book supports that fact with plentiful exercises, with chapters in which the development of a program is shown in a process of stepwise refinement, and with a chapter that shows typical steps of program debugging. The first complete program appears on page 3, and the initial chapters have exercises that can, and should, be run on your computer to help develop confidence and basic skills.

The concepts of structured programming underlie the entire presentation: only a few simple logical control structures are used, and heavy emphasis is placed on writing programs so that they are easy to understand. The importance of easy (human) readability in facilitating program checkout and maintenance is stressed throughout. The use of meaningful data and paragraph names is encouraged and illustrated. Stepwise refinement is illustrated, and techniques of structured program design are presented in a complete chapter, then demonstrated in all following chapters. In short, we have tried to make this book a guide not only to writing COBOL programs, but to writing programs for use in a business environment.

No reader need be concerned, however, that the treatment is too difficult because of the emphasis on design technique. As it is used in this book, proper design is not an advanced topic; it is simply the right way to do the job in the first place. Readers learning these methods from the outset develop habits of good programming that they can apply immediately. There is no need to develop poor programming habits and then be forced to unlearn them as your skills or work requirements increase. However, statements such as GO TO, which is used relatively little in COBOL these days, and ALTER, which is almost universally discouraged but which may be encountered when working with older programs, are presented in Chapter 20 for those readers who may need to know about them.

The material is organized so that most of the topics after Chapter 10 can be studied in any sequence that meets your individual needs, although there are a few obvious dependencies. For example, Chapter 13 (Updating Sequential Files) should be studied before Chapter 15 (File Storage Devices and Programming). On the other hand, if you want to cover the Report Writer (Chapter 17) early in your studies, you should have no trouble doing so, although it is also possible to use the book without looking at the Report Writer at all.

One of the problems that the authors faced in planning this book was choosing which microcomputer compiler to use and determining how the use of microcomputers affects the design of COBOL programs. We chose to use the Microsoft compiler primarily because we believe that this compiler is an exceptionally good one. Its flexibility in terms of being able to emulate a variety of existing COBOL compilers designed both for microcomputers and mainframes makes it suitable for use by a wide range of programmers. It can be used to develop a new library of COBOL programs, to extend or modify an existing library, or to develop programs intended for eventual use on IBM mainframe computers. In addition, the compiler's powerful but easy-to-use run-time debugger makes it particularly suitable for beginning programmers.

The approach that we have taken in presenting COBOL in this book was determined largely by what we perceive our likely audience to be. That is, we feel that the people most likely to be using COBOL on a microcomputer are either those who are developing business systems for use on microcomputers (an increasingly common activity these days); or those who are developing and testing programs that eventually will be transported and used on a mainframe computer, since the Microsoft compiler is a far superior development tool to those available on most mainframes. For the benefit of the first part of the audience, we have shown how COBOL can be used in an interactive environment, beginning with very simple I/O and becoming increasingly sophisticated, climaxing with a presentation of the Screen Section and related concepts in Chapter 12. This presentation does not simply show the format of relevant **COBOL** statements; it also discusses why interactive I/O is useful and, equally important, when it should not be used.

For the benefit of those readers whose ultimate target is the mainframe computer, we have tried to use a style that would be useful to as many readers as possible. This, of course, lead us to IBM. In general, we have presented mainframe-related features in the context of IBM's **OS/VS COBOL** and **VS COBOL II**. However, IBM has not been in the forefront of those developing **COBOL-85** compilers, so there is also material that is unique to the ANSI **COBOL-85** standard. We hope that this policy provides most readers with clear explanations of those features of **COBOL** most appropriate to their specific needs. Indeed, the vast majority of the book is quite suitable for a programmer using any microcomputer-based compiler, particularly if it is designed for IBM compatibility.

We should perhaps also mention what this book is not. It is not a replacement for Microsoft **COBOL** manuals. We have tried to present enough information about the **COBOL** language and the Microsoft **COBOL** compiler so that a reader does not have to constantly be flipping back and forth between the textbook and the Microsoft manuals, but for the serious programmer there is no substitute for having a complete set of manuals available.

New York, New York

Cleveland, Ohio

Daniel D. McCracken

Donald G. Golden

October 1989

CHAPTER 1

GETTING STARTED IN COBOL PROGRAMMING

1.1 INTRODUCTION

Computer programming is a human activity. A person who wants to use a computer to help solve a problem must develop a procedure consisting of the elementary operations that a computer is capable of carrying out. The procedure must be expressed in a language that the computer can "understand." COBOL is such a language, assuming that the computer in question is supplied with an appropriate compiler for translating from the COBOL language to the language of the particular computer. COBOL compilers are available for most computers, from microcomputers to mainframes.

It is worth pausing to emphasize that *people* have problems, whereas computers follow *procedures*. In spite of the almost-human computers that are seen so frequently on TV and in movies, a computer cannot really think or solve a problem. When we have a problem that we want to use a computer to help solve, we must first devise a precise method for solving it. The method chosen must, in principle, be something that a human being could do if given enough time. In other words, it must be absolutely clear at every stage exactly what is to be done, and the exact sequence in which operations are to be carried out. The desired sequence of actions may be expressed in many ways: in English, in some form of program design language, or as a computer program. If the procedure is not expressed as a computer program in the first place, and usually it is not, the next step is to write a computer program that carries out the processing actions of the procedure.

1.2 THE LEARNING SEQUENCE

The objective of our work together—authors and reader—is that when you have completed the study through which the text will guide you, you should be able to write COBOL programs to solve problems in your area of interest. To do that, you will need to learn three broad areas of subject matter:

1

1. The **COBOL** *language*: what it is, what constitutes a valid **COBOL** program, and some of the things that distinguish a good program from one that is not so good.
2. *Coding*: how to write a **COBOL** program, given a road map of how the computer is to do the job that is expected of it.
3. *Program design*: how to prepare the road map; that is, how to go from a statement of *what* a program is supposed to do, to a statement of *how* it is to do it.

Here is our general plan for learning these things. In the first three chapters you will learn some of the most basic things about **COBOL** and about what a program is. In the exercises for these chapters you are required to make small changes in the illustrative programs described in the chapters, and to run the modified programs. In succeeding chapters, as you learn more of the elements of **COBOL** and some of the techniques for designing **COBOL** programs, your exercises will require you to write your own programs, beginning with quite simple tasks and working up to programs that are representative (in terms of techniques used although not in size) of what working programmers do. Beginning in Chapter 4 you will be introduced to the techniques used to design programs. In the following chapters and in the case studies you will learn more and more of the procedures used to design and implement **COBOL** programs.

The point is, there is a difference between knowing what a correct program is, and being able to write one. You will find yourself saying, "I understand the programs in the book, but when I sit down to write the exercise programs I don't know where to begin." We understand! *Most* programmers feel that way to some degree, particularly when they are first learning a new language. The answer is to learn how best to go about the process of program design, to which we shall devote much attention as soon as we have covered enough material to make sense of the process.

That's the plan, in broadest outline. Now let's get started.

1.3 A SIMPLE PROGRAM

Let us begin the study of **COBOL** and of programming by considering a simple example of a program, one so short and simple that the "procedure" can be stated in a few sentences. The program required is merely to display on the CRT screen four lines giving the name and address of one of the authors, in this form:

```
Donald G. Golden
CIS Department
Cleveland State University
Cleveland, Ohio 44115
```

We will incorporate these lines into the program itself, so the program will not be required to read any data into the computer. This is totally uncharacteristic of **COBOL** programs (you will probably never write a program that does not read data), but it lets us get into the subject of programming without becoming enmeshed in certain details that beginners often find confusing.

A complete program to display these lines on the computer screen is shown in Figure 1.1. Normally line numbers will not show when you look at a program on the computer screen; we will, however, include these numbers on all program listings in this book for ease of reference.

1.4 THE FOUR DIVISIONS OF A COBOL PROGRAM

A **COBOL** program consists of four major parts, the *Identification Division*, the *Environment Division*, the *Data Division*, and the *Procedure Division*. The four divisions must appear in the program in the order just stated. The example program is extremely simple so it only uses two of the four divisions, but most programs will use all four. We see that there is a blank line between the two divisions, which is recommended practice but not strictly required; blank lines can be inserted wherever one wishes, to improve readability. The margins and indentations are discussed in Section 1.7. The Identification Division is not of much interest to us at this point so we shall postpone consideration of it until a later chapter, except to say that its basic function is, as its name implies, to identify the program.

The Procedure Division is used to tell the computer what is to be done and in what sequence. As with the words **IDENTIFICATION DIVISION**, the words **PROCEDURE DIVISION** must appear on a line by themselves, exactly as shown Figure 1.1. This Procedure Division consists of four *statements*, one on each line. A **COBOL** *sentence* consists of one or more statements followed by a period. Here we have one statement per sentence in each case, but that will not always be true. Finally, by way of preliminary definitions, **COBOL** sentences are organized into *paragraphs*. A **COBOL** paragraph consists of a paragraph name followed by a period and one or more sentences. The programs in this chapter have only one paragraph each (you may never see such a program again, certainly not in this book), but that one paragraph still should have a paragraph name. **COBOL** derives no meaning from paragraph names, which we devise to be helpful to us in understanding what paragraphs do and, when there are many of them, how they are related to each other. In fact, the first four characters of this paragraph name (**A000**) are used only to locate the paragraph within the program. The use of such prefixes will be discussed in

```
1          IDENTIFICATION DIVISION.
2          PROGRAM-ID.
3              CHAP1A.
4          AUTHOR.
5              D. GOLDEN.
6          DATE-WRITTEN.
7              AUGUST 22, 1988.
8
9          PROCEDURE DIVISION.
10         A000-WRITE-NAME-AND-ADDRESS.
11             DISPLAY 'Donald G. Golden'.
12             DISPLAY 'CIS Department'.
13             DISPLAY 'Cleveland State University'.
14             DISPLAY 'Cleveland, Ohio 44115'.
15             STOP RUN.
```

FIGURE 1.1 A complete COBOL program to print a name and address on four lines.

Chapter 4, but it should be obvious that the prefix is useful only when your programs become larger.

Every **COBOL** statement begins with a verb that says what kind of action is to be carried out. The verbs in this program are **DISPLAY** and **STOP**.

DISPLAY is a verb that tells the computer to display some text on the screen. Notice that we need one **DISPLAY** statement for each line of text that we wish to display. Although we display only very simple text in this example, the **DISPLAY** statement can do much more than this, particularly when we are writing programs for use on a microcomputer. We shall use the **DISPLAY** statement frequently in our programs, but we shall postpone a complete discussion of its capabilities until Chapter 12.

When data is given right in a **COBOL** statement, as we have done in these **DISPLAY** statements, the data item is called a *literal*. Here we have examples of *nonnumeric* literals, which must be enclosed in quotation marks as shown. **COBOL** permits using either single quotes (') or double quotes ("), but whichever you use you must use the same type of quote mark at both the start and end of the literal. For example, we could write:

```
DISPLAY 'Donald G. Golden'.
DISPLAY "CIS Department".
```

in the same program, but we could *not* write

```
DISPLAY 'Cleveland State University".
```

because the quote types do not match. (A numeric literal is not enclosed in quotes; numeric and nonnumeric literals are quite different, as we shall study in Chapter 3.)

The last statement in the program is **STOP RUN**, which simply tells the computer that we are finished and lets the computer go on to other work.

You have probably noticed that we typed all statements in upper case letters, except for the nonnumeric literals. In general, the Microsoft **COBOL** compiler is not very sensitive to the difference between upper case and lower case text, but this is not true of all **COBOL** compilers; some of the most commonly used **COBOL** compilers accept only upper case statements. Therefore, so that you will become used to this style, we will use only upper case in our programs. Since any computer that supports both upper and lower case text will accept either in nonnumeric literals, it is not necessary to restrict ourselves there.

1.5 A SLIGHTLY LARGER PROGRAM

The program in Figure 1.1 shows the basic structure of **COBOL**, but now we want to look at a program that does a bit more work and that demonstrates a few more features of the language. The program in Figure 1.2 will ask you your name, pause while you type a response, then display a simple greeting.

In this example we introduce the Data Division, which is used to define the data that the program processes and produces. In the example there is only one item of data in addition to the nonnumeric literals, the name that you type. Ordinarily, however, there will be data coming into the computer, intermediate results, and various kinds of output.

The first line of the Data Division consists of just the words **DATA DIVI-SION** followed by a period. Just as we did for the Identification Division and the Procedure Division, we must always write the line exactly this way, with nothing else on the line. The **WORKING-STORAGE SECTION** line must also be written exactly as shown. A *section* is simply part of a division; we shall learn in later chapters that there can be other sections in the Data Division, and that there can be sections in other divisions as well.

The third line of the **DATA DIVISION** describes the data item that will hold the data that you type into the computer. The **01** is called the *level number*; we shall explore that concept in Chapter 3. **USER-NAME** is the name the authors made up to identify the data item. This is quite different from words like **DATA**, **DIVISION**, **WORKING-STORAGE**, and **SECTION**, which have special meanings in the **COBOL** language and which cannot be used in any other way. Words like these are called *reserved words*. A list of **COBOL** reserved words appears in Appendix I. Notice that while most reserved words are common to all versions of **COBOL** there are variations from version to version. You must be certain that you are familiar with the reserved words for the version of **COBOL** that you are using, and you must always be careful to avoid using reserved words for any purposes other than those specified in the **COBOL** rules.

The **PICTURE X(25)** clause describes to **COBOL** what the data item looks like; it consists of 25 characters, with each character permitted to be any letter, digit, or other symbol that can be represented by your computer. If we had wanted to specify that the record would contain only letters or spaces, we would have written **PICTURE A(25)**; if we had wanted to specify numeric digits only, we would have written **PICTURE 9(25)**.[*] An item that is described with an **X** in its **PICTURE** character string, and which may therefore consist of letters, digits, or special characters, is said to be *alphanumeric*.

Part of the Procedure Division in Figure 1.2 looks familiar, but there is also some new material. The last two statements in the program (lines 18 and 19) resemble statements in our previous example. The first statement (line 15) is a **DISPLAY** statement, but with a new feature. Normally, after a **DISPLAY** statement finishes writing its text to the computer screen, the cursor automatically moves to the start of the next line. The **WITH NO ADVANCING** clause tells the computer to leave the cursor where it is, immediately following the last character written by the **DISPLAY**.

The next statement is a new statement, the **ACCEPT** statement. Just as the **DISPLAY** statement displays text on the computer screen, the **ACCEPT** statement accepts data typed at the computer keyboard. In the **DISPLAY** statement we follow the word **DISPLAY** with the text to be displayed; in the **ACCEPT** statement we must follow the word **ACCEPT** with the name of a data item that will accept the data entered at the keyboard. Notice that this *must* be a data name, not a literal, since it tells the computer where to store the data being typed. As with the **DISPLAY** statement, we are using only the simplest form of the **ACCEPT** statement. There are many other options for the **ACCEPT** statement, and we will discuss these in later chapters.

Although **USER-NAME** allows a *maximum* of 25 characters, it is not necessary to type all 25. If, for example, you type 'Mary Smith' the computer will

---

[*] Except for a detail: a numeric item in **COBOL** may not have more than 18 digits.

```
1              IDENTIFICATION DIVISION.
2              PROGRAM-ID.
3                 CHAP1B.
4              AUTHOR.
5                 D. GOLDEN.
6              DATE-WRITTEN.
7                 AUGUST 22, 1988.
8
9              DATA DIVISION.
10             WORKING-STORAGE SECTION.
11             01  USER-NAME                    PICTURE X(25).
12
13             PROCEDURE DIVISION.
14             A000-SAY-HELLO.
15                 DISPLAY 'What is your name?  ' WITH NO ADVANCING.
16                 ACCEPT USER-NAME.
17                 DISPLAY 'Hello, ' USER-NAME.
18                 DISPLAY 'How are you today?'.
19                 STOP RUN.
```

FIGURE 1.2   A **COBOL** program that accepts and displays information.

place the text you type at the *left* end of **USER-NAME** and fill the remaining 15 characters with blanks. This is called *left justification*.

The third statement in the Procedure Division is another **DISPLAY** statement, but this one uses both a literal and a data name. The **DISPLAY** statement allows you to list as many data items as you wish to have displayed on a line, either literals or data names or both, mixed in any order. The only restriction to keep in mind is that the **DISPLAY** statement does not put any spaces between items in the **DISPLAY** list, so we must explicitly include any spaces we want. For example, notice the space between the comma and the end quote in the literal on line 17. Of course, since most computer screens cannot show more than 80 characters on one line, you should also try to keep the total length of the line displayed to 80 characters or fewer.

Putting it all together then, the program does the following. First it displays a nonnumeric literal, leaving the cursor in place at the end of the line. It waits until you type a response, then it stores the data that you type in **USER-NAME**. Next, starting on a new line, it displays another literal followed by the text in **USER-NAME**, then displays a last line of text, again starting on a new line. When this is done, the run stops.

1.6 RUNNING A PROGRAM

We have now seen two complete **COBOL** programs. However, before we can use them on a computer there are several steps that need to be performed. First, you must enter them into the computer through the computer keyboard using whatever editor you have available. The program must then be translated into the language of the computer before it can be *executed*, or run.

As we said at the start of this chapter, a computer can only understand **COBOL** if it is translated into the machine language that the computer uses. The process of translating the **COBOL** *source* code that you write into the *object* code that the computer actually can understand and execute is a two-step process. First the program must be *compiled* using a **COBOL** *compile*r, then it must be *linked* to produce the code that can be executed. Since this book is not about language processors or operating systems, we will not discuss the details of how the compiling and linking processes work, or even why they must be performed. If you want your program to execute, you must go through the proper compiling and linking procedures. The details for performing compiling and linking vary considerably from machine to machine and compiler to compiler, and even limiting ourselves to the Microsoft **COBOL** compiler leaves a great deal of room for variety. For now we will simply present some very basic instructions that you can follow to run a program that you write.

As a specific example, we will use the program in Figure 1.1. We will assume that this program has been keyed into the computer and stored in a file called **CHAP1A.CBL**. You can use just about any text editor or word processor that you have available, but there are two important requirements. First, the file must be a simple ASCII text file. We will discuss in later chapters exactly what the term "ASCII" means, but for now we simply mean that there can be no hidden control text written by the editor, and that there must be a carriage return/line feed at the end of each line. If you can use the MS-DOS **TYPE** command (e.g., **TYPE CHAP1A.CBL**) and have the file print on the computer screen exactly as you typed it, your file is probably in the correct format. The second requirement is that the file extension (the part of the name after the dot) must be **CBL**, since the Microsoft **COBOL** compiler expects to see files with this extension.*

Once you have prepared the source code file, the compilation and linking process is fairly straightforward. To compile the program, type the statement:

    COBOL CHAP1A;

This tells the Microsoft **COBOL** compiler to compile the program in file **CHAP1A.CBL**. If you have no errors in your program (a topic we will discuss in depth in Chapter Eight), the compiler will print a few identifying messages on the screen and create a new file called **CHAP1A.OBJ**. You can now go on to the linking process by typing

    LINK CHAP1A;

Notice that we type only the first part of the file name, the part before the dot. If you type **CHAP1A.CBL** you will get an error message during the linking process.

The link program, called a *linker*, will produce still another file, this one called **CHAP1A.EXE**. Files with the **EXE** extension are files that can be executed, and to execute your program now you need only type

    CHAP1A

There are a few points to observe about the compile-and-link process. First, semicolons should be used at the end of the **COBOL** and **LINK** statements, and should *not* be used in the statement that executes your program; they have specific meanings and should be used only where shown. Second, remember

---

*   Actually, the compiler will accept other extensions, but this is the simplest approach for our purposes. See the Microsoft manual for further details.

that **CHAP1A** is only a name we are using for this example. You are free to use any file name you wish for your programs, providing only that you follow the requirements of the MS-DOS operating system. Although we have used the name in the **PROGRAM-ID** paragraph as the name of the program file, this is not required; there is no particular connection between the name you give your program and the name of the file in which you store that program. Third, although we have shown the statements above in upper case, this is only to make them distinctive as you read this book; MS-DOS is indifferent to the distinction between upper case and lower case.

Finally, and perhaps most important, a fair amount of preliminary work must be done before the instructions we have given you will actually work. The compiler and linker must be loaded onto your computer's hard disk and the computer must be told where to find these special programs when you call for them. Complete instructions for loading the compiler onto your computer are given in the Microsoft **COBOL** Opearting Guide. Also, an example of a basic setup technique is presented in Appendix V.

When the first sample program was run it produced this output:

```
Donald G. Golden
CIS Department
Cleveland State University
Cleveland, Ohio 44115
```

In other words, it did operate as specified. We leave the testing of the second program for the student (see Exercise 1 at the end of the chapter).

If you are in a programming course in which you will be running programs on a computer, you will probably be doing the exercises at the end of this chapter or the next. (It's not a bad idea if you are studying on your own, either.) Since you do not know enough about **COBOL** or programming yet to do anything very substantial, the exercises ask you only to make a few rather small changes in the example programs and to run the slightly modified programs. At this point, therefore, we pause to collect the information you will need to have to do those exercises, which includes the program format and the rules for forming identifiers.

1.7   THE COBOL CODING FORMAT

COBOL programs are generally entered into a computer through a terminal or computer console, frequently by the writer of the program, although many companies have data entry personnel who will type your program for you. However, whether you type your own program or someone does it for you, **COBOL** still requires that programs be written according to a special format, and it frequently is helpful to write a program out on paper before entering it into the computer. You may find it easier to check your program and make corrections on paper than at the computer, even if you are using a computer with interactive processing.

The format for **COBOL** statements was designed in the 1950s, at a time when data entry to computers was done almost entirely with punched cards. Most punched cards at the time had 80 *columns* in which characters could be punched; this is the origin of the term "columns" in the discussion that follows, and of the limit of 80 characters on a line.

Coding forms are available, with a small box for each character position in a line. Once your program has been entered into the computer, it is a simple matter to get a printed listing of it using either the editor you used to type the program or the MS-DOS PRINT command. For example, the statement

```
PRINT CHAP1A.CBL
```

will print the first example program file.

On each line of a COBOL program there are specific areas with special meanings that we must explore: sequence, continuation, Area A, Area B, and identification.

Columns 1-6 are used to number the lines in sequence, if one wishes. This capability was particularly useful when programs were commonly punched on cards. If one dropped a deck of cards, the sequence field made it possible to reassemble the deck in the proper order. Today, although the sequence field is still available in COBOL, it is commonly left blank. If you do use the sequence field, number the lines in multiples of 10 or 100, to leave room to insert new lines between old ones without having the new lines be out of order. The Microsoft COBOL compiler can be instructed to check whether lines of code are in sequence on the sequence numbers, and to give a warning if they are not.

Column 7 is used for two purposes. First, and least commonly, it is used in certain rare situations where a word or literal must be continued from a previous line in ways that would otherwise confuse the compiler. About the only circumstance where this makes any sense is the continuation of a long literal that does not fit entirely on one line. When this situation occurs, the literal is written to the end of the first line (column 72), a dash (-) is placed in column 7 of the next line, and the literal is continued beginning anywhere from column 12 on, starting with a new quote. This is sufficiently confusing and is so infrequently really necessary that most programmers avoid continuations altogether, as we shall always do.

A much more important use for column 7 is to serve as a *comment indicator*. Any program, no matter how well written, can usually benefit from comments to the reader describing what the program does and something about how it does it. These comments are ignored by the COBOL compiler and exist only to help a person trying to understand the program. To indicate that a line contains a comment, rather than a line of COBOL code, place an asterisk (*) in column 7. The COBOL compiler will then ignore everything else on the line. You can also use a slash (/) to indicate a comment line. In this case, however, when the compiler prints a listing of your program, it will skip to the top of a new page before printing the comment line.

Column 8 is the beginning of *Area A*. The names of divisions, sections, and paragraphs must begin in this area, as must FD's and 01 and 77 level entries in the Data Division (later, later!). *A statement must not begin in this area.* Column 8 is called the *A margin*.

Column 12 is the beginning of *Area B*; column 12 is called the *B margin*. Procedure Division statements may be written anywhere in this area. We shall ordinarily begin statements in column 12, unless they are subject to indentation rules that will be explained as we go along. (Indentation is used to make the program structure clearer.) The words of a statement must be separated by one or more spaces.

The B area ends in column 72. If a statement takes up too much space to fit in that area, we divide the statement after a complete word and proceed to the next line. Assuming that no word is broken in its middle—and we shall never do so—a dash in the continuation position of the next line is *not* required (and would cause an error if used). We shall never have more than one statement on a line, but one statement may—and often will—be spread over several lines.

The *identification area*, in columns 73-80, is available for anything the programmer pleases. The general idea is that it is sometimes helpful to be able to look at a program listing that has no other identifying information and find something that will tell what program this is. As with the sequence area, this area was much more useful when programs were commonly punched on cards. Some COBOL systems (compilers or source code editors) automatically insert part or all of the program name (taken either from the Identification Division or the file containing the program code) in this portion of the program listing if nothing else is written here; the Microsoft system generally ignores this field.

1.8 RULES FOR FORMING DATA-NAMES

There are many occasions when it is necessary to devise names for data items and a variety of other things in a program. The formation of these programmer-supplied names, also called *identifiers*, is subject to the following rules.

1. A data-name may contain from 1 to 30 characters.
2. The characters of which a data-name is composed must be chosen from the 26 letters of the alphabet, the 10 decimal digits, and the hyphen.
3. A data-name must contain at least one letter.
4. A data-name must not begin or end with a hyphen.
5. A data-name must not be the same as any reserved word.
6. Each data-name must be unique; that is, it must not appear in the Data Division more than once. (This rule does not apply when data-name qualification is used, as described in Chapter 10.)

It is usual practice, and strongly recommended, to devise data-names that are mnemonic; that is, that remind a reader of what the data-names stand for. Thus, we might write names such as:

```
GROSS-PAY
QUANTITY-ON-HAND
REPORT-LINE-12
W-COST-1-UNADJUSTED
45-AUTHORIZATION
```

Here are some data-names that violate the rules.

`12-56`	Does not contain a letter
`-ABC-12`	Begins with a hyphen
`ACCOUNT/RECEIVABLE`	Contains a character other than a letter, digit, or hyphen
`FILE`	This is a reserved word
`AUTHORIZED-BY-DEPARTMENT-MANAGER-OR-DELEGATE`	
	More than 30 characters

"Cute" data-names are (marginally) acceptable in programs written for exercises, but they become a hindrance to easy understandability. Using the names of friends, rock stars, sports cars, or Doonesbury characters may be amusing to you, but such names don't convey meaning about the function of the program to another reader. After using cute names a few times, you will probably discover that they don't seem so funny as they did at first, and that they are an obstacle to good communication.

1.9   A WARNING

At this time of this writing the Microsoft COBOL compiler is *extremely* sensitive to the end-of-data (EOD) mark at the end of your source program. You must be absolutely certain that every program you write in Microsoft COBOL has two characteristics:

1. There must be an EOD mark at the end of your source code.
2. The EOD mark must be on the line *following* the last line of text in your program.

The EOD mark is not visible on the computer screen, and normally you don't have to worry about it; most text editors place an EOD mark at the end of every text file automatically. However, you must be certain that you press the carriage return key following the last line of your program so that the EOD mark goes on the next line. If you have any doubts, leave one or two blank lines at the end of your program. If you leave the EOD mark at the end of the last line of code the compiler will not read this line. For a beginner, this can be a very difficult error to locate.

REVIEW QUESTIONS

1. Name the four divisions of a COBOL program.
2. Must the four divisions always appear in the same order?
3. Is it required, or only recommended, that a blank line be left between divisions?
4. What is the purpose of putting an asterisk in column 7 of a line? How does this differ from putting a slash in column 7?
5. In the program of Figure 1.2 we find the lines

```
DATA DIVISION.
WORKING-STORAGE SECTION.
01   USER-NAME           PICTURE X(25).
```

Would it be permissible to change these lines to the following?

```
DATA-DIVISION.
WORKING STORAGE SECTION.
01   USER NAME           PICTURE X(25).
```

6. What would happen if you dropped the phrase WITH NO ADVANCING from line 15 of Figure 1.2?

7. A sentence must end with a period, and putting periods where they are not called for can lead to lots of trouble. Then why is it permissible to have a period after the middle initial in this line?

```
DISPLAY 'DANIEL D. MCCRACKEN'.
```

8. What is wrong with this statement?

```
ACCEPT 'DANIEL D. MCCRACKEN'.
```

ANSWERS TO REVIEW QUESTIONS

1. Identification, Environment, Data, and Procedure.
2. Yes.
3. Recommended, but rather strongly.
4. Both an asterisk and a slash in column 7 cause the COBOL compiler to treat the line as a comment. However, a slash will cause the compiler to skip to a new page before printing the comment line in a program listing.
5. Any of these changes would trigger all kinds of error messages, some of them possibly quite misleading. It is absolutely essential to write such things exactly as shown.
6. The program would work, but the cursor would advance to a new line after asking for your name. The result would be that the question would be on one line and the answer on the next.
7. A period within a literal is part of the literal, and is not interpreted as ending the sentence.
8. You cannot have a literal in an ACCEPT statement. The ACCEPT statement takes data entered from the keyboard and stores it in a location you specify. Therefore, you must give the name of a data location, not a literal value.

EXERCISES

1. Compile, link, and execute the program shown in Figure 1.2.
2. Change the program in Figure 1.2 so that the question "How are you today?" is displayed at the end of the line that begins "Hello, ", immediately after the data displayed by USER-NAME. Before you run the program write out *exactly* what you think the line should look like when it is displayed.
3. Make the following changes in the program shown in Figure 1.2.
   a. To allow for longer names, change the PICTURE clause so that the name is 40 characters long instead of 25.
   b. Devise a new name to replace USER-NAME, and replace all occurrences of this identifier with your new name.
4. Change the literals in the program in Figure 1.1 so that it displays your name and address. If your address takes only three lines, you will of course need one less DISPLAY statement. If your name or address con-

tains an apostrophe, simply use double quotes around the literal and a single quote to represent the apostrophe. For example, you could write something like

```
DISPLAY "SEAN O'REILLY".
```

However, if instead of the Microsoft COBOL compiler you happen to be using a COBOL compiler that does not permit both double and single quote marks, you have a problem, because the computer cannot distinguish between a single quote and an apostrophe. If you write something like

```
DISPLAY 'SEAN O'REILLY'.
```

COBOL will interpret the second quote as the end of the literal and tell you that REILLY doesn't make sense at that point in a DISPLAY statement. There would likely be other error messages as well, some probably not making much sense.

CHAPTER 2

THE BASIC PROGRAM STRUCTURE

2.1 INTRODUCTION

In the previous chapter we noted that it is highly unusual for a program not to involve the reading of data, and we showed how you can pass data to a COBOL program by typing it at the computer keyboard. As it turns out, although using ACCEPT and DISPLAY statements for data input and output is frequently done in COBOL programs written for microcomputers, it is much more common for COBOL programs to read data from *files* and to write results to files. Since files are such an important part of COBOL programming, we turn immediately to an example of a program involving processing of data that comes from a simple text file rather than from the computer keyboard.

The task to be performed is simplicity itself: read a file of text and, for each line in the file, write a line of output consisting of the information read. You might wonder why we bother with files instead of just using ACCEPT and DISPLAY statements. There are two reasons. First, by putting the data in a file and reading from the file we use a relatively permanent copy of the data. That is, we can process the data more than once, we can process the data using several different programs, and we can pass data from one program to another. For example, in payroll systems an employee's hourly data (that is, the hours the employee worked during the pay period) is not entered directly into the program that produces paychecks. First, it goes into an *editing* program that checks the data for errors, making sure that each employee number is for an actual employee, that the hours worked have been keyed correctly, and so on. Pay records that are in error are usually printed on a special report, while correct data is written to a new file for further processing. It is the data in this second file that is passed along to the program that produces paychecks.

A similar situation exists with results produced by a program. If you use DISPLAY statements to show results, they are simply displayed on the computer screen, but unless you direct the computer to copy the screen to the printer the results are soon gone. If you write the output from a program to a file instead, you have a copy that can be kept as long as you wish. You can print the copy, pass it to another program, keep it for archival records, etc.

The second reason for using files is that using **ACCEPT** and **DISPLAY** as we did in Chapter 1 generally requires that you be able to interact with the program while it is running. That is, the computer asks for some data, you type it at the keyboard, the computer processes the data to produce output, and the output is displayed on the screen. However, many computers do not permit you to interact with the program once it has begun execution. Your data must be prepared entirely prior to execution, and you don't get to see any of the output until execution is complete. This mode of operation is called *batch processing*, as distinct from the *interactive processing* that we demonstrated in Chapter One. Batch processing generally makes more efficient use of the computer than interactive processing, and has the added advantage that programs can be scheduled for execution at times when the computer is not otherwise in use, such as nights and weekends. On the other hand, interactive processing allows you to correct errors immediately, see results in seconds instead or hours or even days, and make processing decisions while the program is running. Microcomputers can run programs in either batch or interactive mode, and the choice between batch and interactive is largely determined by the problem that the program is designed to solve.

In addition to the concept of files, the main thing to be learned in this chapter is the basic program structure that will be used in all programs in this book, whether we are using files or **ACCEPT** and **DISPLAY**. This basic structure—it might be called a program skeleton—will require us to understand the functioning of a new division (the Environment Division), a new section in the Data Division (the File Section), and a number of new **COBOL** verbs.

2.2 THE PROGRAM

The complete program is shown in Figure 2.1. The Identification Division is much as before but there are significant changes in the rest of the program, including the addition of a new division, the Environment Division. The basic function of the Environment Division is to define the connection between the **COBOL** program and the outside world. As we will see in later chapters, the Environment Division can be used to tell what computer the program is being compiled on, what computer it will run on, what character set is being used, and so on. The most important function of the Environment Division, however, is the one demonstrated in the example: to connect the files defined in the program to physical files residing on the disk. We shall discuss this function in more detail shortly, but first we must discuss exactly what files are.

2.3 THE DATA DIVISION

We have added a new section to the Data Division, the File Section; notice that the File Section *must* be the first section in the Data Division, ahead of the Working-Storage Section. In the File Section we must have one **FD** entry to define each file in the program. The letters **FD** were devised as an abbreviation for "file description," but you do *not* have the option of spelling them out. (**COBOL**, like other programming languages, is very rigid about its rules for spelling words and for the order in which words may appear. **COBOL** may look like English, but it definitely is not!) As you might expect, the names **TEXT-IN-**

```
 1              IDENTIFICATION DIVISION.
 2              PROGRAM-ID.
 3                  COPIER.
 4
 5              ENVIRONMENT DIVISION.
 6              INPUT-OUTPUT SECTION.
 7              FILE-CONTROL.
 8                  SELECT TEXT-IN-FILE        ASSIGN TO 'COPIER.DAT'.
 9                  SELECT LINE-OUT-FILE       ASSIGN TO 'COPIER.CPY'.
10
11              DATA DIVISION.
12              FILE SECTION.
13              FD  TEXT-IN-FILE
14                  LABEL RECORDS ARE OMITTED.
15              01  TEXT-IN-RECORD             PICTURE X(80).
16              FD  LINE-OUT-FILE
17                  LABEL RECORDS ARE OMITTED.
18              01  LINE-OUT-RECORD            PICTURE X(80).
19              WORKING-STORAGE SECTION.
20              01  OUT-OF-DATA-FLAG           PICTURE XXX.
21
22              PROCEDURE DIVISION.
23              A000-MAIN-LINE-ROUTINE.
24                  OPEN INPUT TEXT-IN-FILE
25                       OUTPUT LINE-OUT-FILE.
26                  MOVE 'NO' TO OUT-OF-DATA-FLAG.
27                  READ TEXT-IN-FILE
28                      AT END MOVE 'YES' TO OUT-OF-DATA-FLAG.
29                  PERFORM B010-PROCESS-WRITE-READ
30                      UNTIL OUT-OF-DATA-FLAG = 'YES'.
31                  CLOSE TEXT-IN-FILE
32                        LINE-OUT-FILE.
33                  STOP RUN.
34
35              B010-PROCESS-WRITE-READ.
36                  MOVE TEXT-IN-RECORD TO LINE-OUT-RECORD.
37                  WRITE LINE-OUT-RECORD.
38                  READ TEXT-IN-FILE
39                      AT END MOVE 'YES' TO OUT-OF-DATA-FLAG.
```

FIGURE 2.1. A program to read and print a text file with line numbers.

FILE and LINE-OUT-FILE are names we made up to identify the files in the program. A *file* is a collection of related data that is organized into *records*. In TEXT-IN-FILE the records are the lines of text being read by the program, and in LINE-OUT-FILE the records are the lines being printed by the program.

Each FD entry consists of a file description followed by a description of the records contained in the file. The LABEL RECORDS clause in the file description is required by COBOL; what a label record is will be described in Chapter 15. Certain other clauses may be required in the file description depending on what you are doing in the program, but we will discuss these other clauses as we need them. For now, the LABEL RECORDS clause is sufficient. Note that there is a period only at the end of the entire FD entry, following the LABEL RECORDS clause. If you put a period at the end of the first line, the COBOL compiler will get completely confused and will be unable to translate your program.

Following the **FD** entry is the description of the records contained in the file. The records in this program are very simple, with each record consisting of 80 characters. There is, of course, only one record description for each file, in spite of the fact that the files may each contain many physical lines of text. The record description only defines a *record format*; the file may contain any number of records having this format.

There is one last point to note about these entries. The words **FILE** and **RECORD**, for example, are reserved words, but they may be used as parts of data names without violating the rules for reserved words; the compiler treats a name like **TEXT-IN-FILE** as a single twelve-character name.

2.4   THE ENVIRONMENT DIVISION REVISITED

Now that we have some idea of what files are we can take a closer look at the Environment Division. The problem that we have is this: the Data Division defines the formats of the files used in the program, but it doesn't tell us which *physical* files should be used when we run the program. For example, there may be many text files on your computer's disk system. Which particular file do you want to use as input to the program, and where do you want the output to go? These are the questions that the Environment Division answers.

The Environment Division in our example contains just one section, the **INPUT-OUTPUT SECTION**, and that section contains just one paragraph, the **FILE-CONTROL** paragraph. The Environment Division can have more than one section, and the **INPUT-OUTPUT SECTION** can have more than one paragraph, but Figure 2.1 shows what is by far the most common form of Environment Division and we shall use this format for now.

The Environment Division begins with the text shown on lines 5, 6, and 7, exactly as shown, followed by one or more **SELECT** statements. There must be exactly one **SELECT** statement for each file defined in the Data Division. The name of the **COBOL** file, as defined in the Data Division, follows immediately after the word **SELECT**. The name of the *physical* file to which the **COBOL** file is being assigned is given in the **ASSIGN TO** clause. For example, the program in Figure 2.1 will read lines of text from **COPIER.DAT** and will write the same lines to the file **COPIER.CPY**.

This form of the **SELECT** statement is only one of several available in Microsoft **COBOL**. It has the advantage that it is simple to use since you can see the disk file names right in the program. Although we have only specified file names in the example, you can give a complete path name. For example,

```
'A:\INTROCOB\PROGRAM1\COPIER.DAT'
```

is a perfectly valid file specification. We can also send the output to the CRT or the printer by using the words **CON** or **PRN** instead of a path name. For example,

```
SELECT LINE-OUT-FILE        ASSIGN TO 'CON'.
```

will cause the output from the program to go to the computer screen instead of to a disk file.

The disadvantage of this format, of course, is that in order to run the program using different files it is necessary to change the source code and recompile the program. The other **ASSIGN** formats available in Microsoft **COBOL** offer considerably greater flexibility, but we will postpone further discussion of these alternatives until Chapter 15.

There is one last point to be emphasized regarding the Environment Division. One of the basic objectives in the design of the **COBOL** language was that it should be as machine-independent as possible. That is, it should be possible to take a program written on one computer and, with very few changes, run it on another computer. The people who designed **COBOL** realized, however, that it is not possible to remove *all* computer-dependent characteristics from a program. For example, the means of identifying physical files is not the same on all computers. It was decided, therefore, to restrict computer-dependent statements to the Environment Division. The result is that if you move a program from one type of computer to another it may well be necessary to make extensive changes to statements in the Environment Division, but the rest of the program should require little or no change.[*]

2.5 THE WORKING-STORAGE SECTION

The Working-Storage Section looks much like the one in Chapter One, except, of course, that the variable is different. The main difference between the File Section and the Working-Storage Section is this. The File Section defines the files and records that are used for input and output. The Working-Storage Section is used to describe information that is used by the program but that is not part of input or output and which, therefore, is not included in the **FD**s in the File Section. In this program we need to describe a data item that will be used as a *flag* to indicate whether we have yet come to the end of the text file. The word **NO** will be used to mean that we have not yet come to the end of the file, and **YES** will be used to mean that we have. Space for three characters is accordingly provided, using the **PICTURE** clause. Observe that we have written **PICTURE XXX**, which means three characters. We could also have written **PICTURE X(3)**. The choice is a toss-up in a case like this, but with **PICTURE**s describing more than three characters the parentheses form should be used.

A special word of warning: always be very sure to include the hyphen in **WORKING-STORAGE**! Most **COBOL** compilers will turn out a string of meaningless and highly confusing diagnostic error messages if the hyphen is omitted.

2.6 THE PROCEDURE DIVISION

The Procedure Division begins with an **OPEN** statement. Just as there has to be a **SELECT** clause in the Environment Division and an **FD** in the Data Division

---

[*]   Unfortunately, this works better in theory than in fact. Most compiler writers like to add a few features to *their* version of **COBOL** that are not part of the standard definition of the language, to say nothing of the fact that differences in hardware can make some types of statements or data storage work differently on different machines. To deal with this kind of problem the Microsoft **COBOL** compiler has options that can make it act like over half a dozen different common **COBOL** compilers, depending on which options you select.

for each file, so in the Procedure Division each file must be opened and later closed. The OPEN statement specifies preparatory operations for files, the exact nature of which is not of interest to us at this point. Suffice it to say that every file must be opened before it is used, in a statement that specifies whether it is an input or an output file. We have a choice whether to have the OPEN containing the names of both files or to use two separate statements, each beginning with OPEN. Choose whichever alternative seems clearer to you.

The verb in the next statement, the MOVE verb, is one that we shall use a great deal, more than any other verb, in fact. Its function is to move information from one location in the computer to another. Frequently we shall use it in the general form

MOVE data-name-1 TO data-name-2

where "data-name-1" stands for any name of data in our program, and "data-name-2" stands for some other data name in our program. We might have, for example,

`MOVE QUANTITY-ON-HAND TO OUTPUT-LINE-7`

or

`MOVE GROSS-PAY TO GROSS-PAY-EDITED`

The word MOVE sometimes carries an implication that confuses newcomers; it seems to suggest that the information is erased from the sending location and rewritten in a new location, which does *not* occur. Actually, from this viewpoint a word like COPY might be preferable, since after a MOVE *the information exists in both places*. But the word MOVE has long usage behind it and is unlikely to be changed.

The MOVE statement on line 26 is part of the scheme for reading data over and over until the end of the file is reached. We shall see how this works in a moment. Just bear in mind that as we proceed, the Working-Storage entry for OUT-OF-DATA-FLAG now contains the word NO.

2.7 THE READ VERB

The next verb, another new verb, is READ. The basic idea is simple enough. READ says to get one record from the file named. But there is a little more to it than that, because at some point we are going to attempt to read a record that isn't there, because we will have come to the end of the file. We don't know, as we write the program, how many records there will be. If the file contains four records, for instance, we want the program to execute four READs and on attempting the fifth READ to discover that all the records have been read. If there are a thousand records, we want the READ to be executed a thousand times and on attempting to read the thousand-and-first record to find out that all the records have been read. And if, through some sort of mix-up, there aren't any records in the file at all, we need to be informed of that fact on attempting the first READ in the program.

COBOL provides the facility for handling this common data processing situation with the AT END phrase of the READ statement. The way it works is this. If, when the READ verb is executed, the computer does find a record, the record is placed in storage under the record name we have provided in the FD in the Data Division; the statement (or statements) written after the AT END is not executed. On the other hand, if when the READ is executed no records remain to be read in the file, nothing is placed in file storage and whatever statement is written after AT END is carried out. What we have done here is simply to move the word YES to the OUT-OF-DATA-FLAG item in working storage. We shall see very shortly what this accomplishes.

At least one statement must be written in the AT END phrase, but there may be more than one. The AT END controls all statements between the words AT END and the end of the sentence, which is marked by a period. One example of a situation where it is useful to have more than one statement in the AT END phrase is in the first READ in a program, where we might wish not only to set a flag but also to write a message noting that there was no data to be processed.

Perhaps needless to say, one must be very careful to put the period exactly where it is supposed to be. For instance, if the period after the READ statement is omitted, all statements after the READ, until the next period, will be taken to be part of the AT END phrase, and therefore not executed so long as there is data to be read. This can be a difficult error to locate.

It is essential to understand very clearly exactly when the AT END phrase comes into play. It *does not* become active on reading the last record of a file, but rather on attempting to read a record *after* the last record of a file. Students often wonder if it wouldn't have made more sense to design COBOL so that the AT END phrase comes into play on reading the last record, as is the case with Pascal. Occasionally this could, in fact, be useful—but not very often, as it turns out. In any case, this is how COBOL works and, as with the MOVE statement, it is not likely to be changed.

2.8 THE PERFORM VERB

The PERFORM verb is one of the most powerful in the COBOL repertoire. What we are saying in this statement is that we want to carry out the instructions in another part of the program. They may be carried out just once, or a specified number of times, or—as in this case—repeatedly *until* a certain condition is true. We have two concepts here, both very important, that will be used in every program from now on, so it is important to understand them thoroughly. They are the idea of a paragraph and the idea of *conditional execution*.

2.9 THE COBOL PARAGRAPH

The first notion needing precise definition is that of a *paragraph*. A COBOL paragraph is simply a group of sentences preceded by a paragraph name. A paragraph name is defined according to the same rules that govern the formation of names for files, records, and data items—with the one additional flexibility that a paragraph name is not required to contain any letters. That is, it is permitted to consist of digits only or a combination of digits and hyphens only. This flexibility is seldom utilized in practice, however, and we shall never do so in this book. A paragraph name is required to begin somewhere in the A area, that is, in columns 8, 9, 10, or 11. We shall always begin paragraph names in column 8.

You have probably noticed that all of the Procedure Division paragraph names used in examples so far begin with a letter and three digits. Paragraph names in other divisions are all reserved words and must be written exactly as shown.* The purpose of the prefix code is to make it easier to locate a paragraph in the program listing. We shall talk more about the prefix convention in Chapter 4 when we discuss techniques of program design. For now, we will only state that if the prefix is used, paragraphs must *always* be written in sequence by prefix. For this reason prefix numbers should always be incremented in steps of at least ten to allow for the insertion of new paragraphs if the program is modified. That is, write **B010, B020, B030, . . .**, not **B001, B002, B003, . . .**.

A paragraph consists of all of the sentences from the one immediately following the paragraph name until the one just before the next paragraph name (or until the end of the program).

The only purpose in organizing statements into paragraphs that will be utilized in this book is to permit the statements to be referred to by a **PERFORM** verb.** In our program we are saying that we want the paragraph named **B010-PROCESS-WRITE-READ** to be executed (that is, performed) over and over *until* a certain condition becomes true.

This paragraph is the one that, as its name is intended to suggest, basically does all the work of this program. Whenever this paragraph is about to be executed, there will always be one record from the input file that has not yet been written. The first time the paragraph is executed, that will be the record that was brought into the computer by the first **READ**. The first thing to be done is to move that waiting record from the input area (**TEXT-IN-RECORD**) to the output area (**LINE-OUT-RECORD**). Now we say to write that record to the output file, which will be sent to the printer. Finally we read—or perhaps *attempt* to read—another record from the input file. If there is such a record, the **AT END** phrase on this **READ** has no effect, just as before. And just as before, if this **READ** encounters the situation where no more records remain, then the statement in the **AT END** phrase will be carried out.

It should be noted that when we execute a **READ**, the information coming from the input file replaces whatever was in the record area for that file in the Data Division; the previous information in the record area is no longer available, unless it had previously been stored somewhere else as well.

2.10 THE OUT-OF-DATA-FLAG

Let us summarize what happens to the contents of the data item named **OUT-OF-DATA-FLAG** as the execution of the program proceeds. First, before encountering the first **READ**, we move the word **NO** to the flag. Then, for as long as there are records being read, neither the **AT END** phrase on the first **READ** nor

---

* This is not required by COBOL, but is a convention we shall use throughout this book.
** We will learn in Chapter 20 that there is a statement called **GO TO** that is involved with paragraph names as well, but we shall have little occasion in this book to use the **GO TO** statement.

the **AT END** phrase on the **READ** that is carried out repeatedly in the performed paragraph has any effect. In other words, as long as there are records, **OUT-OF-DATA-FLAG** will continue to contain **NO**. However, whenever either **READ** encounters the end of the file—whether that be the very first time or the ten-thousandth—the word **YES** will be moved to **OUT-OF-DATA-FLAG**.

2.11 CONDITIONAL EXECUTION

Now, with one additional item of information, we can see how the whole program works. The crucial thing to know is that when the **PERFORM** statement is encountered, the condition after the word **UNTIL** is checked first, *before* performing the named paragraph. This means that if, in fact, there was *no* data to be read in the file, the **AT END** phrase on the very first **READ** will have moved **YES** to **OUT-OF-DATA-FLAG** and the paragraph named in the **PERFORM** is not executed. Instead, the statement after the **PERFORM** is executed.

Since we are ready to terminate the program we must write a **CLOSE** statement for both files. We can have a separate **CLOSE** statement for each file or, as we have done here, have one **CLOSE** statement name both files. As with the **OPEN** statement we shall not get into the details of what the **CLOSE** does, other than to say that all files must be closed before the run stops. We also observe that with **CLOSE** it is not necessary to specify whether a file is input or output.

The **STOP RUN**, as before, says that the execution of this program should stop. Observe that **STOP RUN** is not required to be the last statement in the program. It will always be the last one *executed*, in point of time, but it is not required to be—and indeed, seldom will be—*physically* the statement on the last line of the program.

2.12 ANOTHER LOOK AT THE BASIC PROGRAM STRUCTURE

This program, simple as it is, exhibits the structuring technique that will be the basis for almost all programs in this book. It is, therefore, important to understand it thoroughly, so let's try to summarize it.

A program will always begin with a group of statements right at the beginning of the Procedure Division that we will call the main line routine. Something like **A000-MAIN-LINE-ROUTINE** is suitable for its name. Schematically it will usually consist of the following operations:

Preliminary operations
PERFORM
Wrap-up operations
STOP RUN

The preliminary operations will include things such as opening files and carrying out an initial **READ** for input files. This initial **READ** has the function of checking for the possibility of a missing or empty data file and of getting the basic process started. It is, accordingly, called a *priming* **READ**. The major work of the program is carried out in the paragraph named by the **PERFORM**. Within that paragraph is a **READ** with an **AT END** phrase that sets the flag to indicate when the file has been processed completely. The setting of this flag stops repeated execution of the paragraph by virtue of the testing carried out by the PERFORM.

It is helpful to display the sequence in which the verbs of this program will be executed for several small files. Here is a complete listing of all of the verbs executed if the data file is empty.

```
OPEN
MOVE
READ (the priming READ; sets flag)
PERFORM (tests condition and does not give control to named paragraph)
CLOSE
STOP
```

It should be understood that we consider the PERFORM verb to have been "executed" even though, in this case, it did not cause the named paragraph to be carried out. The PERFORM verb was encountered and it carried out the testing, but on the basis of that testing did not call on the named paragraph. This is one form of its execution.

Here is the sequence of verb execution for a file containing one line:

```
OPEN
MOVE
READ (the priming READ; does not set flag)
PERFORM (tests condition and gives control to named paragraph)
MOVE
WRITE
READ (the performed READ; sets flag)
PERFORM (tests condition and does not give control to named paragraph)
CLOSE
STOP
```

Here is the sequence of statement execution for a file containing two lines:

```
OPEN
MOVE
READ (the priming READ; does not set flag)
PERFORM (tests condition and gives control to named paragraph)
MOVE
WRITE
READ (the performed READ; does not set flag)
PERFORM (tests condition and gives control to named paragraph)
MOVE
WRITE
READ (the performed READ; sets flag)
PERFORM (tests condition and does not give control to named paragraph)
CLOSE
STOP
```

The fundamental difference between this program and the first example in Chapter 1 is in the conditional and repeated execution of the paragraph named in the PERFORM statement. Before, to display four lines we had to put four `DISPLAY` statements in the program. Here, in the paragraph named `B010-PROCESS-WRITE-READ`, we have *one* `MOVE`, *one* `WRITE`, and *one* `READ`, all of which are executed as many times as necessary to process all of the lines in the data file. As we prepare the program we do not know—indeed, we *cannot* know—how many records there will be in the data file, but that doesn't matter. The program is designed to handle that variability correctly.

2.13   SAMPLES OF OUTPUT FROM RUNNING THE PROGRAM

This program was compiled, then run three times with three different data files. The first file consisted of one line; when the program was run with this file, it produced this line of output:

```
This file consists of one line. Unusual, but not impossible.
```

The program was next run with a different data file containing six lines, the fifth of which was entirely blank. Its output was this:

```
DONALD G. GOLDEN
CIS DEPARTMENT
CLEVELAND STATE UNIVERSITY
CLEVELAND, OHIO 44115

---FIRST CLASS MAIL---
```

(If there is any doubt in your mind, let us emphasize that a blank line is *not* the same thing as the end of the input!) Finally, the program was run with a data file of 14 lines, which produced this output:

```
Last among the essential personality traits for programming,
we might list sense of humor.  The computer
"doth make fools of us all," so that any fool without the
ability to share a laugh on himself will be unable to
tolerate programming for long.  It has been said with great
perspicacity that the programmer's national anthem is
"AAAAAHHHHH."  When we finally see the light, we see how
once again we have fallen into some foolish assumption,
some oafish practice, or some witless blunder.  Only by
singing the second stanza, "Ha Ha Ha Ha Ha," can we long
endure the role of the clown.


Gerald M. Weinberg, The Psychology of Computer Programming.
```

2.14   THE BASIC STRUCTURE AGAIN

This way of organizing the program will be the basis for just about everything we do in this book. Naturally, later programs will be much more complex than this, but you will still be able to see the same fundamental organization: a main line routine and one (or usually more) paragraphs called into play by `PERFORM`s in the main line routine. Very frequently there will be a number of levels of performed paragraphs, that is, a paragraph that has been activated by a `PERFORM` at a higher level will itself contain a `PERFORM` that activates a paragraph at a lower level. Sometimes there will be more than one input file and/or more than one output file, and there may be **ACCEPT** and **DISPLAY** statements as well. In such cases the condition for deciding when the job is finished will be more complex, but we shall learn how to write such programs so that they are not really too much harder to understand than this one. And that, of course, is a major reason for sticking with one basic structure in this way: to produce programs that are as simple as possible to understand, which makes them more likely to be correct and much easier to modify.

2.15 A CAUTION

Observe that in a **READ** statement we give the name of a *file*, whereas in a **WRITE** statement we give the name of a *record*. **COBOL** is designed this way because it is possible to read files that have several different formats of records in them, with some kind of information within the records used to let the program know which is which. When this is done, there will be a number of record descriptions following the **FD** entry. Since it is impossible to know before getting a record which format we have, **COBOL** specifies that we name the *file* in the **READ** statement. It is also possible to produce output files that have a variety of record formats, but when this happens, we can always know which kind of record it is we are writing. That is the reason for the difference between the **READ** and **WRITE** verb formats, but whether it makes sense to you or not, you have to do it! It may help to memorize the phrase "**READ** a file, **WRITE** a record."

REVIEW QUESTIONS

1. What is the difference between the File Section and the Working-Storage Section?
2. In the program in Figure 2.1, we used file names that contain the word "file" and record names that contain the word "record." Does **COBOL** make any use of that information?
3. The Data Division for the program in this chapter contains two **FD** entries. Is it essential that they be written in the order given?
4. Is it required that the Working-Storage Section come after the File Section?
5. Suppose that the program did not contain the **MOVE** statement to put **NO** in **OUT-OF-DATA-FLAG**. What would the program do?
6. Literary usage in the United States is to place a period at the end of a sentence *inside* a closing quote. What would happen if we did that in the **PERFORM** statement in this program?
7. Is the blank line between the main line routine and the performed paragraph optional or required?
8. What is the difference in the naming rules for paragraphs compared with the rules for data-names?
9. Could a paragraph consist of only one sentence?

10. Suppose an input file has only one type of record. Could we not then specify the *record* name in the **READ** statement instead of the file name?

11. Would it have been permissible to have two **CLOSE** statements naming one file each, instead of one **CLOSE** statement naming both files?

12. Is it the **OPEN** or the **CLOSE** verb that requires us to specify whether the file is **INPUT** or **OUTPUT**?

13. What would happen if you placed a period at the end of this line in the following program?

```
FD  LINE-OUT-FILE
```

ANSWERS TO REVIEW QUESTIONS

1. The File Section describes information in records coming directly into the computer from an input device such as a CRT, or going directly out of it to an output device such as a printer. The Working-Storage Section describes information that is not directly coming from or going to an input or output device. We say "not directly" because we can read information into an input file then **MOVE** it to the Working-Storage Section, or **MOVE** it from Working-Storage to an output file and then write it, if we wish.

2. Not at all. If we were to use **TEXT-IN-RECORD** as the name of a file and **TEXT-IN-FILE** as the name of a record, the **COBOL** compiler would never know the difference. This would be a silly thing to do, however, since it is very important to try to write programs that are as easy as possible for a human being to read and understand easily.

3. No. Bear in mind, however, that the **01** entry giving the name and format of the record does have to come right after the **FD** for the file in which that record appears. In other words, a complete file description consists of the **FD** line, the various clauses such as **LABEL RECORDS ARE STANDARD** and others that we shall encounter later, and all record descriptions for that file. In later programs we shall see that the complete file description can easily run to dozens of lines.

4. Yes.

5. We can never assume anything about the contents of a data item unless we have put something there. Without the **MOVE**, **OUT-OF-DATA-FLAG** would contain whatever was in that part of the computer storage before our program came into the machine. Since it is unlikely that the previous program would have left the word **YES** in that spot, the program would probably work properly, but it would be extremely unwise to get in the habit of doing things that way. (We shall learn later that there is another and slightly simpler way to give a data item an initial value, using the **VALUE** clause.)

6. The compiler would consider the literal to consist of four characters including the period, and the sentence would not have a closing period. *As it happens*, the absence of the period for sentence punctuation would not hurt *in this case*, so the program would compile without an indication of error. However, this four-character literal—including the period—

would never be equal to the three-character literal—without the period—so the program would not operate correctly. Specifically how it would work would depend on the particular COBOL compiler. With the Microsoft COBOL compiler, the program would terminate with run-time error message 146 when it tried to read past the physical end of the input file. Other systems might simply write the last line over and over, or write out meaningless garbage.

7. Optional, as blank lines always are, but strongly recommended for readability.

8. All data-names must contain at least one letter. Paragraph names have no such requirement.

9. Certainly.

10. No way. The specified formats must be adhered to in all cases, and READ statements must always name files.

11. Sure.

12. OPEN.

13. The Microsoft COBOL compiler would print compile-time error message 205-S, "RECORD missing or has zero size." This means that the compiler could not find the record definition for this file since it thought that the file description terminated at the end of the FD line.

EXERCISE

Make the following changes in the program of Figure 2.1, enter the program into the computer, and run it. Here are the changes:

1. Change the PICTURE clause for OUT-OF-DATA-FLAG so that only one character is used instead of three, then change the PROCEDURE DIVISION in the appropriate places so that Y and N are used in place of YES and NO.
2. Change the program so that there is a separate OPEN for each file and a separate CLOSE for each file.
3. Devise new names to replace TEXT-IN-FILE, TEXT-IN-RECORD, LINE-OUT-FILE, and LINE-OUT-RECORD, and replace all occurrences of these identifiers with your new names.
4. Make up a new data file so that the printed output will be something of your choice.
5. Change the name of the physical file in the first SELECT statement so that data is read from a file other than COPIER.DAT. Change the second SELECT statement so that the output file is assigned to PRINTER instead of a disk file.

In the fourth exercise in Chapter 1 we had a problem if a literal contained a quote mark. Observe that this problem does not apply in this exercise, since quotes in data do not cause the problem discussed earlier. The Irish are in business this time!

CHAPTER 3

DATA DIVISION ELEMENTS AND THE ARITHMETIC VERBS

3.1 INTRODUCTION

In Chapter 1 we learned the fundamentals of what a COBOL program looks like and in Chapter 2 the basic program structure involved in reading data, processing it, and writing results. Building on this foundation, we are now ready to put a little flesh on the program skeleton and tackle a more difficult task than those in the previous chapters.

The processing task that we shall study in this chapter has two steps. First we will read information from the keyboard and use it to build a file of data. Next we will take this file, do a bit of processing, and write one line for each input record. The information on a record describes one item in a simplified inventory control system. Each record contains a part number, a quantity on hand, a quantity received, and a unit price. For each record we are to print a line that contains all this information plus the new quantity on hand and the total value of this new quantity.

The main concepts to be studied in this chapter involve some of the basic elements of the Data Division, and the COBOL verbs for specifying arithmetic operations. There is nothing new about the basic program structure. The complete programs are shown in Figures 3.1 and 3.2. Before studying them in detail, however, let us take a quick look to get an idea of what is familiar and what is new.

Each program has four divisions (as we always do when we are using files) with no surprises in the first two. In the first program we write data to the file C03P01.INV, and in the second program we read from this file and write to CON. Recall that CON is not the name of a file, but rather is the standard name for the CRT.

The Data Division in each program contains a File Section and a Working-Storage Section as before. The presence of the 01 and 05 level numbers in the record description is new, and we shall discuss that in some detail shortly. Observe that a new convention has been employed in assigning data names in

```
1              IDENTIFICATION DIVISION.
2              PROGRAM-ID.
3                  BLD-INV.
4              DATE-WRITTEN.
5                  SEPTEMBER 1, 1988.
6
7              ENVIRONMENT DIVISION.
8              INPUT-OUTPUT SECTION.
9              FILE-CONTROL.
10                 SELECT INVENTORY-OUT-FILE          ASSIGN TO 'C03P01.INV'.
11
12             DATA DIVISION.
13             FILE SECTION.
14             FD  INVENTORY-OUT-FILE
15                 LABEL RECORDS ARE STANDARD.
16             01  INVENTORY-OUT-RECORD.
17                 05   O-PART-NUMBER              PIC X(6).
18                 05   O-QTY-ON-HAND              PIC 9(5).
19                 05   O-QTY-RECEIVED             PIC 9(4).
20                 05   O-UNIT-PRICE              PIC 9(3)V99.
21
22             WORKING-STORAGE SECTION.
23             01  W-PART-NUMBER                  PIC X(6).
24             01  W-QTY-ON-HAND                  PIC 9(5).
25             01  W-QTY-RECEIVED                 PIC 9(4).
26             01  W-UNIT-PRICE                   PIC 9(3)V99.
27
28
29             PROCEDURE DIVISION.
30             A000-MAIN-LINE-ROUTINE.
31                 OPEN OUTPUT INVENTORY-OUT-FILE.
32                 MOVE '000000' TO W-PART-NUMBER.
33                 PERFORM B010-GET-PART-DATA.
34                 PERFORM B020-LIST-INVENTORY-DATA
35                     UNTIL W-PART-NUMBER = 'ZZZZZZ'.
36                 DISPLAY ' '.
37                 DISPLAY 'RUN COMPLETED NORMALLY'.
38                 CLOSE INVENTORY-OUT-FILE.
39                 STOP RUN.
40
41             B010-GET-PART-DATA.
42                 DISPLAY 'Enter part number:       ' WITH NO ADVANCING.
43                 ACCEPT W-PART-NUMBER.
44                 DISPLAY 'Enter quantity on hand:   ' WITH NO ADVANCING.
45                 ACCEPT W-QTY-ON-HAND.
46                 DISPLAY 'Enter quantity received:  ' WITH NO ADVANCING.
47                 ACCEPT W-QTY-RECEIVED.
48                 DISPLAY 'Enter unit-price:         ' WITH NO ADVANCING.
49                 ACCEPT W-UNIT-PRICE.
50                 DISPLAY ' '.
51
52             B020-LIST-INVENTORY-DATA.
53                 MOVE W-PART-NUMBER TO O-PART-NUMBER.
54                 MOVE W-QTY-ON-HAND TO O-QTY-ON-HAND.
55                 MOVE W-QTY-RECEIVED TO O-QTY-RECEIVED.
56                 MOVE W-UNIT-PRICE TO O-UNIT-PRICE.
57                 WRITE INVENTORY-OUT-RECORD.
58                 PERFORM B010-GET-PART-DATA.
```

FIGURE 3.1 A program to build a simple inventory data file.

```
 1              IDENTIFICATION DIVISION.
 2              PROGRAM-ID.
 3                  PRT-INV.
 4              DATE-WRITTEN.
 5                  SEPTEMBER 1, 1988.
 6
 7              ENVIRONMENT DIVISION.
 8              INPUT-OUTPUT SECTION.
 9              FILE-CONTROL.
10                  SELECT INVENTORY-IN-FILE          ASSIGN TO 'C03P01.INV'.
11                  SELECT INVENTORY-OUT-FILE         ASSIGN TO 'CON'.
12
13              DATA DIVISION.
14              FILE SECTION.
15              FD  INVENTORY-IN-FILE
16                  LABEL RECORDS ARE STANDARD.
17              01  INVENTORY-IN-RECORD.
18                  05  I-PART-NUMBER                 PIC X(6).
19                  05  I-QTY-ON-HAND                 PIC 9(5).
20                  05  I-QTY-RECEIVED                PIC 9(4).
21                  05  I-UNIT-PRICE                  PIC 9(3)V99.
22
23              FD  INVENTORY-OUT-FILE
24                  LABEL RECORDS ARE STANDARD.
25              01  INVENTORY-OUT-RECORD.
26                  05  O-PART-NUMBER                 PIC X(6).
27                  05  FILLER                        PIC X(4).
28                  05  O-QTY-ON-HAND                 PIC 9(5).
29                  05  FILLER                        PIC X(3).
30                  05  O-QTY-RECEIVED                PIC 9(4).
31                  05  FILLER                        PIC X(3).
32                  05  O-UNIT-PRICE                  PIC 9(3).99.
33                  05  FILLER                        PIC X(3).
34                  05  O-NEW-QTY-ON-HAND             PIC 9(5).
35                  05  FILLER                        PIC X(3).
36                  05  O-COST                        PIC 9(6).99.
37
38              WORKING-STORAGE SECTION.
39              01  W-OUT-OF-DATA-FLAG                PIC X.
40
41              PROCEDURE DIVISION.
42              A000-MAIN-LINE-ROUTINE.
43                  OPEN INPUT INVENTORY-IN-FILE
44                       OUTPUT INVENTORY-OUT-FILE.
45                  MOVE 'N' TO W-OUT-OF-DATA-FLAG.
46                  READ INVENTORY-IN-FILE
47                      AT END MOVE 'Y' TO W-OUT-OF-DATA-FLAG.
48                  PERFORM B010-LIST-INVENTORY-DATA
49                      UNTIL W-OUT-OF-DATA-FLAG = 'Y'.
50                  CLOSE INVENTORY-IN-FILE
51                        INVENTORY-OUT-FILE.
52                  STOP RUN.
53
54              B010-LIST-INVENTORY-DATA.
55                  MOVE SPACES TO INVENTORY-OUT-RECORD.
56                  MOVE I-PART-NUMBER TO O-PART-NUMBER.
57                  MOVE I-QTY-ON-HAND TO O-QTY-ON-HAND.
58                  MOVE I-QTY-RECEIVED TO O-QTY-RECEIVED.
```

```
59          MOVE I-UNIT-PRICE TO O-UNIT-PRICE.
60          ADD I-QTY-ON-HAND, I-QTY-RECEIVED GIVING O-NEW-QTY-ON-HAND.
61          MULTIPLY O-NEW-QTY-ON-HAND BY I-UNIT-PRICE GIVING O-COST.
62          WRITE INVENTORY-OUT-RECORD.
63          READ INVENTORY-IN-FILE
64              AT END MOVE 'Y' TO W-OUT-OF-DATA-FLAG.
```

FIGURE 3.2 A program to perform a simple inventory control calculation for each record in an input file.

these programs, namely, all data names in the input record begin with the prefix **I**, all data names in the output records begin with the prefix **O**, and data names in the Working-Storage Section begin with the prefix **W**. This is one possible data naming convention, among many others, that is intended to improve understandability of a program.

Notice that instead of **PICTURE** we have used the permissible abbreviation **PIC**. The word **PICTURE** must be written so many times, many hundreds in some programs, that **COBOL** permits this abbreviation. There are a few other abbreviations of reserved words. *Only these few abbreviations are permitted.* You may not abbreviate the word **PICTURE** as **PICT**, you may not abbreviate **PER-FORM** in any way whatsoever, etc. The other new features in the **PICTURE** clause will be discussed in detail later.

The item for the **W-OUT-OF-DATA-FLAG** is only one character this time instead of three; we are going to use the letters **Y** and **N** instead of **YES** and **NO** to save a bit of space and a bit of writing.

The Procedure Division in the first program uses two new features; they relate to the way in which we get inventory data and determine when we are done adding new records to the file. In addition, although this is not a new feature, we have changed the name of the third paragraph in the Procedure Division to **B020-WRITE-INVENTORY-DATA**. The reason we have made this change is to emphasize the *function* that the paragraph performs, rather than just the sequence of operations. In all future examples we shall try to follow this convention. That is, the name of a paragraph should identify the unique function that the paragraph performs in the program, rather than just indicating what processes are carried out.

The Procedure Division in the second program contains two new verbs, **ADD** and **MULTIPLY**; we shall consider these in detail later. Also, in spite of the fact that we will be writing results on the computer screen, we are using a file and a **WRITE** statement instead of using **DISPLAY**. As we stated in Chapter Two, and as we shall demonstrate in future chapters, the **DISPLAY** statement can be very useful in writing information on the screen. However, most **COBOL** programs use files to produce reports and we want to emphasize this technique as well.

3.2 THE IDEA OF THE LEVEL STRUCTURE

The basic idea of the **COBOL** level structure is not very complicated. It is simply that we often want to be able to describe elements of data as being parts of larger groupings. In Figure 3.1, for example, we have a file named **INVENTORY-IN-FILE** containing a record name **INVENTORY-IN-RECORD**, consisting, as it happens, of 20 characters. Sometimes we want to be able to refer to the entire

20 characters of the record by that one name. At other times we want to be able to refer to the individual items themselves, one at a time.

The COBOL scheme is that the first grouping of data, which is the most inclusive, must be given the level number 01; items within that group are given higher level numbers. Here we have used 05 as the higher number, but it could have been 02 or 10 or anything else up to a maximum of 49.

To show the level structure as clearly as possible, we indent the beginnings of lines so that all entries at a given level are aligned vertically. We shall ordinarily indent by four spaces.

An item that is further subdivided is called a group item. An item that is not further subdivided is called an elementary item. For instance, the 01 level item, INVENTORY-IN-RECORD, is a group item consisting of the four 05 level elementary items shown.

It will often happen that there will be levels within levels. For instance, consider the hypothetical portion of a record description shown here:

```
01   PAYROLL-RECORD.
     05   NAME.
          10   INITIAL-1          PIC X.
          10   LAST-NAME          PIC X(20).
     05   DATE-OF-HIRE.
          10   MONTH-OF-HIRE      PIC 99.
          10   DAY-OF-HIRE        PIC 99.
          10   YEAR-OF-HIRE       PIC 99.
     05   PAY-NUMBER              PIC 9(6).
```

PAYROLL-RECORD is a group item consisting of three items at the 05 level, two of which are themselves group items. NAME, for instance, consists of two elementary items named INITIAL-1 and LAST-NAME. DATE-OF-HIRE is a group item consisting of three elementary items for the month, day, and year. PAY-NUMBER is an elementary item, since it is not further subdivided—even though it has the same level number as group items elsewhere in the record.

The meaning of this record description can be shown graphically like this:

PAYROLL-RECORD					
NAME		DATE-OF-HIRE			PAY-NUMBER
INIT	LAST-NAME	MO	DAY	YR	

```
1  2  3  4  5  6  7  8  9 10 11 12 13 14 15 16 17 18 19 20 21   22 23  24 25  26 27   28 29 30 31 32 33
```

The first elementary item in the record is INITIAL-1, which is one character and occupies character position 1 in the record. The next elementary item, LAST-NAME, is 20 characters long and occupies positions 2-21. The group item consisting of these two elementary items, NAME, occupies character positions 1-21 and is 21 characters in length. The next elementary item after LAST-NAME is MONTH-OF-HIRE; its two characters therefore occupy positions 22-23. Likewise DAY-OF-HIRE takes up positions 24-25 and YEAR-OF-HIRE, positions 26-27. The group item DATE-OF-HIRE therefore occupies positions 22-27, and is 6 characters in length. The elementary item PAY-NUMBER is in positions 28-33 and is also 6 characters long.

It is always possible to determine the character positions occupied by each group and elementary item in a record by this kind of analysis. The key idea is that the first elementary item begins in position 1, and the successive elementary items after that occupy character positions in sequence. Knowing the character positions occupied by elementary items, it is possible to establish the character positions taken up by group items.

It is instructive to note that the COBOL compiler has to go through an analysis of exactly the sort just sketched, since it must translate all data-names into references to character positions in the internal storage of the computer.

A fundamental Data Division rule says that elementary items must have PICTURE clauses and group items must not. Conceivably COBOL could have been designed to permit or require PICTURE clauses for group items, but it would have been pointless, since the compiler can always determine the size of a group item by adding up the number of characters in the elementary items of which it is composed.

Another basic rule says that group items are always considered by the compiler to be alphanumeric. Group items do not have PICTUREs, of course, so this is simply a rule of the language. This is true even if all of the elementary items in the group are numeric. The rule makes complete sense in terms of the way group items are moved, but there is no need at this time to become enmeshed in the details.

The programmer has no choice in assigning 01 as the level number for the most inclusive group item, which is the entire record. However, whether to assign the successive subdivisions the level numbers 05, 10, 15, 20, etc., as we shall do in this book, or to use 02, 03, 04, etc., or some other way, is a matter of free choice. The way we are doing it is traditional in many programming installations, presumably because at one time it was thought that programmers would occasionally want to insert new group items between existing levels when they made program modifications. It turns out that this is done very infrequently, but the pattern has caught on.

3.3 NEW PICTURE CLAUSE FEATURES

There are three new features in the PICTURE clauses for these programs, two for describing the internal representation and arrangement of data within the computer, and one for describing how information is to be prepared for output. This last is called *editing*. In the programs in Chapters 1 and 2, there was no processing of information other than to move it without change from one place in the computer to another. When this is done, each character of information is described in the PICTURE clause by the letter X. We recall that any information described with the letter X is called alphanumeric, which can include letters, digits, the character "blank," and all of the special characters (such as punctuation) that a particular computer is capable of representing. Now it is perfectly possible for an alphanumeric item, designated as such by Xs in its PICTURE clause, to consist of numeric digits only. This would be true of a United States Social Security number, for instance, so long as it is written without hyphens as it ordinarily would be in a computer. However, *any time arithmetic operations of any type are to be done on an item the item must be described as numeric*, which is done by using 9's in its PICTURE clause instead of X's. Each

9, however many there are, stands for one decimal digit. For example, the item in Figure 3.1 named **W-QTY-ON-HAND** is seen to be described as having five digits: the **9** designates numeric digits and the **5** says there are five of them. This, of course, could also have been written **99999**. The item **W-QTY-RECEIVED** has four digits. Observe that the item named **W-PART-NUMBER** is described as having six *alphanumeric* characters. Even though the part number may, in fact, be entirely numeric, as its name would seem to suggest, we never do arithmetic with it, so it is designated as alphanumeric. There are similar descriptions in **INVENTORY-OUT-RECORD**, which shows that it is by no means necessary that the elementary items within a record be all numeric or all alphanumeric.

3.4   THE ASSUMED DECIMAL POINT

We have set up this application on the assumption that the quantities involved are always whole numbers. We can have 12 hammers or 143 feet of wire, but not 63.4 pounds of lead. (This is, of course, an unrealistic assumption, made as usual to keep things simple for the time being.) But what is to be done when we have an item like price, where it is really not possible to assume that items always have prices that are whole dollars?

The answer is that we have a way of telling **COBOL** that an item is to be treated *as though* it had a decimal point in a specified position. Not an *actual* decimal point, mind you, but rather an *assumed* or *implied* decimal point. We are thinking of a typical situation where a four-character field in a file record might contain the digits 6397. We want to tell the **COBOL** compiler to treat that as if it stands for 63.97, which might be a price in dollars and cents. *This does not mean that there is a decimal point actually stored in the record.*

Common practice in writing numeric quantities that contain assumed decimal points is to write a caret (a sort of upside-down **V**) in the desired position like so:

63ʌ97

In the **COBOL** **PICTURE** clause, this assumed decimal point is represented by a **V** (presumably chosen because it looks like an upside-down caret!) which is inserted into the **PICTURE** clause in the desired position. It is very important to understand that whereas the **V** in the **PICTURE** clause takes up one character space in the **PICTURE** clause, the assumed decimal point in the data item is still *assumed: it does not take up space in the file record*. For example, in the item **O-UNIT-PRICE** in Figure 3.1, we are describing a five-digit elementary item with a decimal point assumed between the third and fourth digits to make a dollars-and-cents amount. There is no decimal point stored in the record. (In fact, it is fairly difficult in **COBOL** to read data values from file records if they contain actual decimal points.) The **COBOL** compiler, in setting up the computer program to handle this item, will take into account all of the proper decimal point considerations.

The **ACCEPT** statement, however, works a bit differently. In spite of the fact that we have used an implied decimal point in the description of **W-UNIT-PRICE** in Figure 3.1, we type the data with an actual decimal point. For example, if we have a price of $500.22, we must enter it as

500.22

If we were to type

50022

the program would interpret this as $50,022, which would cause considerable difficulty in this case because we have only allowed space for a maximum price of $999.99.

If you have a price of $10, you need only type

10

In other words, you don't need to type the leading zero, the decimal point, or the cents amount. For now, don't worry about the details of how all this works. Just remember that if you are typing numeric data for an **ACCEPT** statement, type it as you would normally write the value. The **COBOL** program will align the decimal point that you type with the assumed decimal point in the data item's picture and take care of all the other details. (However, if you are typing a dollar amount, *don't* type the dollar sign!)

3.5 THE ACTUAL DECIMAL POINT

When it comes time to print or display an item such as a dollars-and-cents amount, we do want the program to produce an actual dot on the printed listing. This is done by placing an actual decimal point in the **PICTURE** clause in the desired position. We see this in the items **O-UNIT-PRICE** and **O-COST** in Figure 3.2. When an item such as unit price is moved from **I-UNIT-PRICE** to **O-UNIT-PRICE**, the **COBOL** program will take into proper account the relationship between the assumed decimal point and the actual decimal point and put the digits of the item into the correct positions.

One more bit of information, hopefully not too confusing, and we can set aside the decimal point question for the time being. It must be understood that arithmetic can be done only on *numeric* items, by which is meant items containing only digits. The **PICTURE** for a numeric item must contain **9**'s, not **X**'s, and the **PICTURE** must *not* contain an actual decimal point. An item that contains an *actual* decimal point is *not* numeric and therefore may not be used in arithmetic operations. Thus, once **I-UNIT-PRICE** has been moved to **O-UNIT-PRICE** it is not permissible to carry out arithmetic operations on it there. Of course, it still exists as a numeric item in **I-UNIT-PRICE** and can still be used in that form in arithmetic operations.

3.6 LEADING BLANKS IN DATA

It should be realized that an item containing blanks is *not* numeric and, therefore, cannot be used in arithmetic operations. This means that, in general, leading zeros in values in input records (i.e., records in files used for input) *cannot be replaced by blanks*, unless appropriate measures are taken in the Procedure Division as discussed in Chapter 16. Although some versions of **COBOL** will accept leading blanks, in other versions failure to heed this advice will cause the program to fail, with not-very-helpful messages on the order of "data exception." Key in all of those leading zeros in data files!

3.7 THE FILLER ITEM

It commonly happens that we need to describe characters in a record that we never refer to by name. Sometimes these are positions that are to contain blanks, as in our case. Sometimes they are elementary items that will receive information when something is moved to the group of which they are a part. In any event, they do describe character positions within the record and are counted in determining how many characters the record contains, but they do not have a name, and therefore cannot be referenced except as part of the group item that contains them.

In our situation all that is involved is that when we print the line for each inventory item, we don't want the individual numbers bunched up together, but rather want some blank spaces between them. The amount of space to be provided is a decision of the person who designs the format of the output report. These decisions depend on questions of making the printing fit a preprinted form, general questions of pleasing appearance, and the like. We see that in this program four spaces have been provided in one place and three in others.

The insertion of FILLER characters implies nothing whatsoever about the contents of those characters. In our case, it *may not* be assumed that those positions will automatically be blank. We shall take care of that question later, in the Procedure Division, and we shall see in Chapter 6 how it might have been done with a VALUE clause in the Working-Storage Section of the Data Division.

FILLER is a COBOL reserved word, not a programmer-supplied data-name. The word FILLER accordingly can, and usually does, appear many times in a program, since it is not subject to the uniqueness rule that applies to data-names.

COBOL-85

In COBOL-85 the word FILLER actually can be omitted. Thus, for example, in this version of COBOL we can write the definition of INVENTORY-OUT-RECORD as follows:

```
01   INVENTORY-OUT-RECORD.
     05   O-PART-NUMBER            PIC X(6).
     05                            PIC X(4).
     05   O-QTY-ON-HAND            PIC 9(5).
     05                            PIC X(3).
     05   O-QTY-RECEIVED           PIC 9(4).
     05                            PIC X(3).
     05   O-UNIT-PRICE             PIC 9(3).99.
     05                            PIC X(3).
     05   O-NEW-QTY-ON-HAND        PIC 9(5).
     05                            PIC X(3).
     05   O-COST                   PIC 9(6).99.
```

This is *exactly* equivalent to the version shown in Figure 3.2 and either approach may be used.

END COBOL-85

3.8   THE MAIN LINE ROUTINES

The main line routine in both programs is similar to that of the program in Chapter 2, with relatively minor differences. In all three programs we open files, initialize data, get the first data item, perform a processing paragraph until we run out of data, close files, and stop the run. This pattern will be used repeatedly with minor variations throughout the book, and for the most part we will make no further comments about it.

3.9   PROCESSING IN THE FIRST PROGRAM

The details of processing in this program involve two new concepts. To begin with, the input data does not come from a file, but we need more than a single value before we can start processing the data. Rather than writing all the **DISPLAY** and **ACCEPT** statements to accomplish this directly in the main paragraph (and having to repeat them in the processing paragraph!) we collect the statements needed to get all the data for an inventory item into one paragraph, **B010-GET-PART-DATA**, then perform that paragraph wherever we need to. This allows us to treat the code needed to get the data almost as though it were a single **READ** statement.

The code for paragraph **B010-GET-PART-DATA** is a straightforward extension of the technique we used in Chapter 1. We use **DISPLAY** with the **NO ADVANCING** option to write a *prompt* to the screen, then use an **ACCEPT** statement to get the response from the keyboard. After we have read all the data for an item, we display an extra blank line to separate the displays for consecutive items. This is done simply by displaying one character on the line, the literal ' '.

There is an important difference between accepting data from a keyboard and reading it from a file, and this brings us to the second new concept in this program. When we read data from a file, we know when we have reached the end of the file because the **AT END** condition is raised in the **READ** statement. However, there is no corresponding concept with the **ACCEPT** statement so we must write our own code to signal the end of the input data.

The basic technique is simply to select a special data value to indicate an "end of file." In Figure 3.1 the value that we use is a part number of all Z's. We could have used any value we want, with only two requirements. First, the value should easily be typed and remembered; you don't want the user to have to go through a major exercise in cryptography to be able to terminate processing. Second, the value we use should not be one that could also be a valid data value.

There are two points to keep in mind when using this technique. First, we must initialize the flag variable, **W-PART-NUMBER** in this example, to some value other than the special flag value. In the example we used **000000** but we could have used any value other than **ZZZZZZ**. Second, there is an important difference between using a data flag to indicate end of data and using the **AT END** clause in the **READ** statement. When the **AT END** condition is raised, no record has been read and the data values in memory remain unchanged. In our current example, even after we enter a value of **ZZZZZZ** for the part number, we must still enter values for quantity on hand, quantity received, and unit price before the program terminates the processing loop. We don't have to use meaningful values (e.g., we could enter zeroes for the last three items), but we must give some legal value.

The processing paragraph itself, B020-WRITE-INVENTORY-DATA, really doesn't contain any new concepts, other than the fact that we are moving several data items from Working-Storage to fields in the output record, instead of just moving an input record to the output record. The rest of the paragraph resembles the processing paragraph in Chapter 2.

3.10   THE PROCESSING IN THE SECOND PROGRAM

The processing paragraph in the program in Figure 3.2 involves a number of new features, the most important of which are the verbs for specifying arithmetic, ADD and MULTIPLY in this program. First, however, there are certain preliminary operations.

The first of these is a MOVE statement that puts spaces (blanks) in all character positions of the output record. SPACES is a new type of reserved word called a *figurative constant*. When the COBOL compiler encounters this word, it supplies as many of the character *blank* as there are characters in the receiving item. We have designated the entire record in this case, which happens to contain room for 51 characters. Observe incidentally that this is a *group* MOVE, which places blanks in all 11 of the elementary items in the group item. (The FILLER items are considered to be elementary items since they have PICTUREs, even though they cannot be referred to by name.)

The purpose of moving spaces to this record is to get blanks into all of the FILLERs. This is necessary because, as we noted previously, setting aside storage locations in the FILLER items does not tell us anything about what those positions will contain. With many compilers, if we do not move spaces to this record those positions would contain whatever was left there by the program that used the computer before this one. By sheerest accident that might happen to be blanks, but it would be foolish to assume so. Without this MOVE statement, our printed output would accordingly contain miscellaneous garbage in the positions between fields that should have been blank. As it happens, the Microsoft COBOL compiler initializes Working-Storage data to blanks unless you specify otherwise, but this is *not* typical of most COBOL compilers! In particular, the IBM mainframe compilers do not initialize data storage. Don't count on the compiler doing your work for you!

The processing of an input record begins with moving the four items in the record to their desired positions in the output record that will later be written. There is nothing new about this except that when the unit price is moved from the input record to the output record, editing is performed: an actual decimal point is inserted into the dollars-and-cents unit price.

3.11   THE ADD STATEMENT

Now we come to something quite new, a statement that calls for two numbers to be added, in this statement:

```
ADD I-QTY-ON-HAND, I-QTY-RECEIVED GIVING O-NEW-QTY-ON-HAND.
```

This means: form the sum of **I-QTY-ON-HAND** and **I-QTY-RECEIVED**, and place that sum in **O-NEW-QTY-ON-HAND**. Neither **I-QTY-ON-HAND** nor **I-QTY-RECEIVED** is changed by this action. The comma is entirely optional; the action of the statement would be exactly the same without it. It may be used as one wishes if it is thought to improve readability. Many programmers never use the optional commas, however, since they are an additional source of possible error and since they are sometimes hard to distinguish from periods in printed listings.

(There is much more to be said about the **ADD** statement. We shall devote considerable time to the different forms of this verb and the other arithmetic verbs after seeing how the rest of the program works.)

3.12 THE MULTIPLY STATEMENT

The **MULTIPLY** statement that comes next computes the total cost of the new amount of inventory on hand for this item. As with the **ADD** statement, neither of the quantities in this computation is changed as a result. We shall see shortly that this is true when any of the arithmetic verbs are used with the **GIVING** option.

It should be noted that we are making an assumption about the relative size of the quantities that go into this multiplication. According to the input **PICTURE**s, the largest possible quantity on hand is 99999 and the largest possible unit price is 999.99. If both of these maximum sizes occurred for any inventory item, then their product—the total cost for that item—would be $99,998,000.01. That would lead to a problem because in the Data Division for **O-COST** we specified only six digits before the decimal point, not eight. Some **COBOL** compilers will accordingly produce a warning message indicating the possibility that high order digits can be lost in this multiplication.

However, it is reasonable to assume that the two factors in the multiplication would not both take on the maximum sizes for any one inventory item. An item that the company would stock in very large quantity would tend to have a low unit price, and conversely an item with a high unit price would tend to be stocked in low quantities. The assumption made in setting up this program is that the total cost of any one inventory item will never exceed $999,999.99. So long as that assumption is justified, the compiler's warning message about the possibility of lost digits need not concern us. Naturally, such assumptions must not be made casually. If we were talking about IBM's stock of microcomputers, for example, this would presumably be a very bad assumption.

This completes the processing that is done by this program, so we may proceed to write the record that has now been developed, get another input record, and repeat the process.

3.13 THE OUTPUT

The two programs were run with a small sample of data and, after the second program was run, produced the following output:

123456	00012	0003	010.00	00015	000150.00
123459	11111	0022	001.00	11133	011133.00
234567	00005	0006	340.44	00011	003744.84
23AAX4	00400	0148	001.54	00548	000843.92
23AAX5	00023	0012	433.00	00035	015155.00

Looking at any one line, we see that the value in column 2 plus the value in column 3 equals the value in column 5; this is the result of the statement

```
ADD I-QTY-ON-HAND, I-QTY-RECEIVED GIVING O-NEW-QTY-ON-HAND
```

Also, the value in column 6 on any line is the product of the values in columns 4 and 5, resulting from

```
MULTIPLY O-NEW-QTY-ON-HAND BY I-UNIT-PRICE GIVING O-COST
```

Thus we see that the arithmetic was carried out as desired.

It is always necessary to compare at least a few typical results with hand-calculated values to establish that the program has no obvious errors.

As soon as we have learned the necessary techniques, in Chapter 7, we shall see how to handle a number of matters that would normally be done a bit differently. Ordinary practice would include at least column headings, the deletion of leading zeros, and the provision of appropriate dollar signs and commas to improve readability. We shall also see that it will ordinarily be unusual to do arithmetic on an item after it has been moved to an output record, which is legal in this case only because we did not perform the normal action of replacing leading zeros with blanks.

3.14   GENERAL FORMATS FOR COBOL STATEMENTS

A good deal of flexibility is available in writing many of the COBOL statements, but there are rules that must be followed with great care. It is accordingly necessary for the programmer to be able to determine readily exactly how a given statement may be written. This need is answered by a way of showing the available options that is called the *general format*. Here, for example, is the format for the form of the ADD statement that we have just used.

$$
\underline{\text{ADD}} \quad \left\{ \begin{array}{l} \text{identifier-1} \\ \text{literal-1} \end{array} \right\} \left\{ \begin{array}{l} \text{identifier-2} \\ \text{literal-2} \end{array} \right\} \left[\begin{array}{l} \text{identifier-3} \\ \text{literal-3} \end{array} \right] \ \cdots
$$

$$
\underline{\text{GIVING}} \ \text{identifier-m} \ [\underline{\text{ROUNDED}}] \ [\text{identifier-n} \ [\underline{\text{ROUNDED}}] \ ] \ \cdots
$$

$$
[\text{ON} \ \underline{\text{SIZE}} \ \underline{\text{ERROR}} \ \text{imperative-statement}]
$$

We shall consider this carefully after discussing a number of conventions that are used in writing all such formats.

1. All words printed entirely in capital letters are reserved words. All such words have preassigned meanings in COBOL and, as we have noted earlier, may not be used in any other way. In a general format, words in capital

letters represent an actual occurrence of those words. That is, nothing else may be substituted for them. Reserved words must be spelled exactly as shown. They must not be abbreviated unless an abbreviation is specifically permitted, and plurals of words must not be used unless the plural is specifically allowed.

2. All underlined reserved words are required unless the portion of the format containing them is itself optional. These words are *key words*. If any such word is missing or incorrectly spelled, it is an error and the program cannot be compiled correctly. Reserved words not underlined may be included or omitted at the option of the programmer. These words are used only for the sake of readability and are called *optional words*. However, if they are used, they must be spelled correctly.

3. The characters +, -, <, >, and =, when appearing in formats, are required although they are not underlined.

4. All punctuation and other special characters (except certain symbols discussed below) represent the actual occurrence of those characters. Punctuation is essential where it is shown. Additional punctuation can sometimes be inserted according to rules specified elsewhere. The comma in our **ADD** statement is an example of additional punctuation.

5. Words that are printed in lowercase letters represent information to be supplied by the programmer. In the case of the **ADD** format, in place of identifier-1 we are to write the name of a data item such as **I-QTY-ON-HAND**, and in place of literal-1 we could write 12.6 or 2 or any other number as needed.

6. In order to facilitate references to them in describing the format, some lowercase words are followed by a hyphen and a digit or letter. This modification does not change the meaning of the word. For example, in our **ADD** format identifier-1, identifier-2, identifier-3, etc., are all simply identifiers that are to be supplied by the programmer. It is also not to be inferred by this convention that the identifiers are required to be different. It would be perfectly legitimate to write a statement such as

       ADD HOURLY-USAGE, HOURLY-USAGE GIVING USAGE-LIMIT.

This would have the result of putting two times **HOURLY-USAGE** into **USAGE-LIMIT**.

7. Square brackets [ ] are used to indicate that the enclosed item may be either used or omitted depending on the requirements of the particular program. When two or more items are stacked within brackets, one or none of them may be used. In the format at hand, for example, either identifier-3 or literal-3 may be used, or neither. In the **ADD** statement in our program we used neither.

8. Braces { } enclosing vertically stacked items indicate that exactly one of the enclosed items must be chosen. For example, immediately after the word **ADD** one must write either an identifier or a literal and following that one must again write an identifier or a literal. This is simply a precise way of stating the fairly obvious fact that there must be at least two things to be added. One is *not* permitted to write a statement such as

       ADD GROSS-PAY GIVING STARTING-VALUE

in an attempt to get the same effect as a **MOVE**.

9. The ellipsis ... indicates that the immediately preceding unit may occur once or any number of times in succession. A *unit* means either a single lowercase word or a group of lowercase words and one or more reserved words included in brackets or braces. In the ADD format the ellipsis means that we could have identifier-4 or literal-4, identifier-5 or literal-5, etc.

3.15 BACK TO THE ADD STATEMENT

Now that we have explored the symbolism to be used in presenting the options available in writing COBOL statements, let us return to the case at hand, the ADD verb. Here it is again, for easy reference, and this time we identify it as Format 2, since in fact it is one of two ways of writing an ADD, and the one that is usually given second in reference manuals.

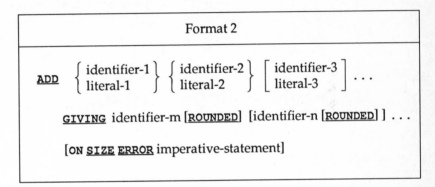

We see that the word ADD is underlined, meaning that it must be present; that is only reasonable since all COBOL statements must begin with a verb that specifies the action to be performed. Then we have braces enclosing identifier-1 and literal-1; this means that we must make a choice from those two possibilities. Similarly, braces tell us that we must choose between an identifier and a literal for what to write next. Note that braces mean that we are forced to pick one of the items enclosed; we do not have the option of writing neither. The square brackets enclosing identifier-3 and literal-3, however, give us precisely that option: *if we wish to write additional operands*, then the choice once again is between an identifier and a literal. The ellipsis indicates that the previous unit, in this case the choice indicated by the square brackets, may be repeated as many times as desired. What this means is that we may add up as many identifiers and/or literals as we please, simply writing their names or values before the word GIVING. Since the word GIVING is underlined, it too is required in this format of the ADD.

3.16 THE ROUNDED OPTION

Observe that the key word ROUNDED is optional in the ADD statement, since it appears in square brackets. When used, this applies to a situation where the sum has more decimal places than are provided in the item to which the sum is being sent. This, of course, would not be an oversight (hopefully!), but a deliberate design decision. In our program, for example, management might specify that the cost was to be reported in whole dollars. To accomplish this we would write the **PICTURE** for **O-COST** with no digits to the right of the actual decimal point, and then use the **ROUNDED** option on the **MULTIPLY** verb. Then if the cost turns out to have a cents figure of 49 or less, the cents are dropped and the dollar is left unchanged. If the cents figure comes out to 50 or greater, the cents are still dropped but the dollar amount is increased by 1. This is all that rounding means.

3.17   THE ON SIZE ERROR OPTION

This option permits us to make provision for the possibility that the addition will produce a quantity too large to fit in the space provided for it. If we write this option, we are free to put any sort of statement(s) we wish in the place shown as imperative-statement. This statement could stop the program, or terminate processing of this record after writing an error message, or could call for almost anything we please.

The **ON SIZE ERROR** option is seldom used because there are usually better ways to deal with the problem that it is designed to handle. As we shall learn, it is strongly recommended practice to check input data extensively for validity. If this has been done, the programmer will seldom be in any doubt about whether a result is going to fit in the space provided.

3.18   THE FORMAT 1 ADD

The form of the **ADD** statement that we have just studied is usually listed second in reference manuals. (There is also a third format, the **ADD CORRESPONDING**, but this is seldom used.) The other permissible form of the **ADD** statement is as shown here.

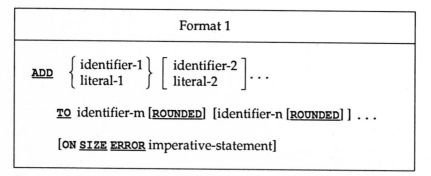

This means to form the sum of all of the quantities listed, including the original value of identifier-m, with the sum replacing the previous value of identifier-m. The difference between the **ADD TO** and **ADD GIVING** forms, therefore, is that with the **ADD TO** the original value of identifier-m is included in the sum, whereas with **ADD GIVING** it is not. If more than one identifier appears after the word **TO**, then the meaning is that the sum of all of the quantities before the word **TO** is added to each of these others separately.

Identifiers appearing in arithmetic statements must always be elementary items. (This does not apply to ADD CORRESPONDING and SUBTRACT CORRESPONDING, but as noted previously these will seldom be used.)

Examples of the ADD statement

	Before				After			
	A	B	C	D	A	B	C	D
ADD A TO B	3	6			3	9		
ADD A, B TO C	1	4	7		1	4	12	
ADD A, B TO C, D	1	4	7	22	1	4	12	27
ADD A, B GIVING C	1	4	7		1	4	5	

COBOL-85

3.19   THE FORMAT 2 ADD IN COBOL-85

In COBOL-85 Format 2 has been extended to eliminate an error which occurred commonly in earlier versions of COBOL. This extension allows you to insert "TO identifier-m" before the word GIVING; the resulting format is shown below. In this format the values of all literals and identifiers preceding the word TO are added together. The total is then added to the literal or identifier between TO and GIVING; the result is stored as the new value of identifier-m, identifier-n, etc. Since the word TO is not underlined it may be omitted, in which case this version of the Format 2 ADD reduces to the older version.

```
            Format 2 - COBOL-85

ADD   { identifier-1 }  ...  TO  { identifier-2 }
      { literal-1    }           { literal-2    }

GIVING identifier-m [ROUNDED] [identifier-n [ROUNDED] ] ...

[ON SIZE ERROR imperative-statement]
```

Examples of the extended format 2 ADD statement

	Before				After			
	A	B	C	D	A	B	C	D
ADD A TO B GIVING C	1	4	7		1	4	5	
ADD A, B TO C GIVING D	1	4	7	22	1	4	7	12

END COBOL-85

3.20 THE SUBTRACT STATEMENT

The two formats for the **SUBTRACT** statement are as shown below.

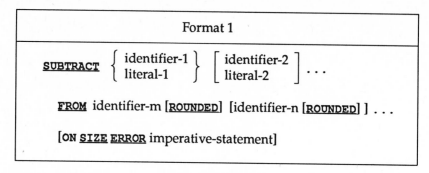

Format 1

$$\underline{\text{SUBTRACT}} \left\{ \begin{array}{l} \text{identifier-1} \\ \text{literal-1} \end{array} \right\} \left[\begin{array}{l} \text{identifier-2} \\ \text{literal-2} \end{array} \right] \ldots$$

FROM identifier-m [**ROUNDED**] [identifier-n [**ROUNDED**]] . . .

[ON **SIZE ERROR** imperative-statement]

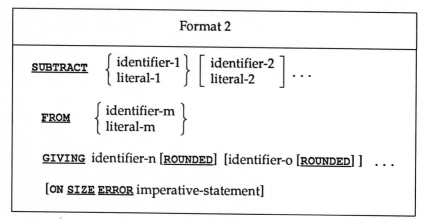

Format 2

$$\underline{\text{SUBTRACT}} \left\{ \begin{array}{l} \text{identifier-1} \\ \text{literal-1} \end{array} \right\} \left[\begin{array}{l} \text{identifier-2} \\ \text{literal-2} \end{array} \right] \ldots$$

$$\underline{\text{FROM}} \left\{ \begin{array}{l} \text{identifier-m} \\ \text{literal-m} \end{array} \right\}$$

GIVING identifier-n [**ROUNDED**] [identifier-o [**ROUNDED**]] . . .

[ON **SIZE ERROR** imperative-statement]

In Format 1 the values of all literals or identifiers preceding the word **FROM** are added together and this total is then subtracted from the value of identifier-m and from the value of identifier-n (if stated), etc. The result of the subtractions are then stored as the new values of identifier-m, identifier-n, etc.

In Format 2 the values of all literals or identifiers preceding the word **FROM** are added together, and this total is subtracted from the value of literal-m or identifier-m. The result of the subtraction is then stored as the new value of identifier-n, and, if specified, identifier-o, and so on.

Examples of the SUBTRACT statement

	Before				After			
	A	B	C	D	A	B	C	D
SUBTRACT A FROM B	5	9			5	4		
SUBTRACT A, B FROM C	1	4	15		1	4	10	
SUBTRACT A FROM B GIVING C	1	4	15		1	4	3	
SUBTRACT A, B FROM C GIVING D	1	4	15	22	1	4	15	10
SUBTRACT A, B FROM C, D	1	4	15	22	1	4	10	17
SUBTRACT 3 FROM A	12				9			
SUBTRACT A, B FROM 22 GIVING C	2	3	47		2	3	17	

3.21   THE MULTIPLY STATEMENT

The MULTIPLY statement also comes in two forms, with and without the word GIVING.

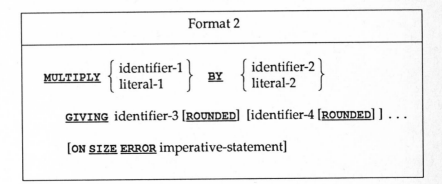

```
┌─────────────────────────────────────────────────────────────┐
│                          Format 1                             │
├─────────────────────────────────────────────────────────────┤
│                                                               │
│             ┌ identifier-1 ┐                                  │
│   MULTIPLY  ┤              ├                                  │
│             └ literal-1    ┘                                  │
│                                                               │
│     BY  identifier-2 [ROUNDED] [identifier-3 [ROUNDED] ] ...  │
│                                                               │
│     [ON SIZE ERROR imperative-statement]                      │
│                                                               │
└─────────────────────────────────────────────────────────────┘
```

```
┌─────────────────────────────────────────────────────────────┐
│                          Format 2                             │
├─────────────────────────────────────────────────────────────┤
│                                                               │
│             ┌ identifier-1 ┐        ┌ identifier-2 ┐          │
│   MULTIPLY  ┤              ├   BY   ┤              ├          │
│             └ literal-1    ┘        └ literal-2    ┘          │
│                                                               │
│     GIVING identifier-3 [ROUNDED] [identifier-4 [ROUNDED] ] ..│
│                                                               │
│     [ON SIZE ERROR imperative-statement]                      │
│                                                               │
└─────────────────────────────────────────────────────────────┘
```

When Format 1 is used, the value of identifier-1 (or literal-1) is multiplied by the value of identifier-2. The value of identifier-2 is then replaced by the product. If identifier-3 is present, the value of identifier-1 or literal-1 is multiplied by identifier-3 and the result placed in identifier-3, and so on. (It may seem to some readers as though normal English usage would suggest that the product should replace the value of identifier-1, but this is not so.)

When the GIVING form is used, Format 2, the value of identifier-1 (or literal-1) is multiplied by the value of identifier-2 (or literal-2) and the product is placed in identifier-3, identifier-4, etc. Identifier-2 is unchanged.

Examples of the MULTIPLY statement

	Before				After			
	A	B	C	D	A	B	C	D
MULTIPLY A BY B	2	4			2	8		
MULTIPLY A BY B, C	2	4	6		2	8	12	
MULTIPLY A BY B GIVING C	2	4	17		2	4	8	
MULTIPLY A BY B GIVING C, D	2	4	17	20	2	4	8	8
MULTIPLY 4 BY A	3				12			
MULTIPLY A BY 6 GIVING B	3	4			3	18		

Notice in the sixth example that there is a literal after the word **BY**. This is acceptable because the **GIVING** clause places the result of the multiplication in B. We could *not*, however, write the fifth example as

```
MULTIPLY A BY 4
```

because we would be trying to place the result in the literal 4!

3.22 THE DIVIDE STATEMENT

This verb has three formats, which are as shown below.

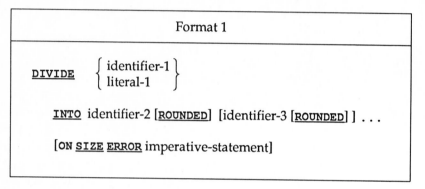

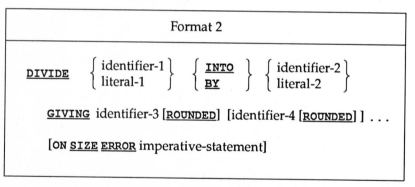

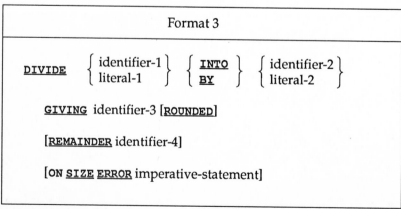

In Format 1 the value of identifier-1 or literal-1 is divided into the value of identifier-2, and the value of identifier-2 is replaced by the value of the quotient. If identifier-3 is present, identifier-1 or literal-1 is divided into the value of identifier-3 and the quotient is placed into identifier-3, and so on.

In Format 2 the value of identifier-1 (or literal-1) is divided into or by the value of identifier-2 (or literal-2). The quotient is stored in identifier-3, identifier-4, etc.

In Format 3 the value of identifier-1 (or literal-1) is divided into or by the value of identifier-2 (or literal-2). The quotient is stored in identifier-3 and the remainder is optionally stored in identifier-4. The remainder is defined as the result of subtracting the product of the quotient and the divisor from the dividend. If the ROUNDED option is also specified, the quotient is rounded after the remainder is determined. The REMAINDER option is seldom used.

Examples of the DIVIDE statement

	Before				After			
	A	B	C	D	A	B	C	D
DIVIDE A INTO B	3	15			3	5		
DIVIDE A INTO B, C	3	15	21		3	5	7	
DIVIDE A INTO B GIVING C	3	15	4		3	15	5	
DIVIDE A INTO B GIVING C, D	3	15	4	6	3	15	5	5
DIVIDE A BY B GIVING C	24	12	19		24	12	2	
DIVIDE 2 INTO A	18				9			
DIVIDE A BY 3 GIVING B	24	2			24	8		
DIVIDE A BY B GIVING C REMAINDER D	19	7	0	0	19	7	2	5
DIVIDE A BY B GIVING C REMAINDER D	7	19	0	0	7	19	0	7

3.23   THE HANDLING OF ALGEBRAIC SIGNS

COBOL makes provision for handling signed quantities correctly. That is, if two negative quantities are multiplied, the product is positive; if two quantities having different signs are added, the effect is that of a subtraction, etc.

3.24   MOVING NUMERIC QUANTITIES

Whenever a numeric quantity is placed in an elementary item, either as a result of an arithmetic operation or in a simple MOVE, certain rules govern what is done when the quantity being sent is not the same size as the receiving field.

1. If the receiving field has fewer positions to the right of the decimal point than the item being sent, the extra digits are simply dropped and no warning is given. Thus, if we sent the quantity 1234.567 to a field described by

    PICTURE 9999.99

the stored result would be 1234.56. Notice that there is *no* automatic rounding; the 7 is simply dropped.

2. If the receiving field has more positions to the right of the decimal point than the item being sent, zeros are supplied. Thus, if the quantity 1234.567 is sent to a field described by

    PICTURE 9999.9999

    the result will be 1234.5670.

3. If the receiving field has more positions to the left of the decimal point than the item being sent, then again zeros are supplied. Thus, if the quantity 1234.567 is sent to a field described by

    PICTURE 9(6).999

    the result will be 001234.567.

4. For the case where the receiving field has fewer positions to the left of the decimal point than the item being sent, we have to distinguish between the case where this is the result of a **MOVE** and where it is the result of an arithmetic operation.

    a. On a **MOVE**, the extra digits simply are dropped. Thus if the quantity 1234.567 is sent to a field described by

        PICTURE 99.999

        the result will be 34.567. In this case some compilers will give a warning that significant digits can potentially be lost, but the program will be compiled. If we ignore the compiler's warning and run the program, no additional warning will be given when significant digits are actually lost. Except in highly unusual cases, this will be a very serious error. That is why it is so important to be certain that any assumptions about maximum sizes of results are justified.

    b. For an arithmetic result, the precise outcome is not easily predicted; that is, it will certainly be wrong, but the value that will be placed in the receiving field depends on the exact nature of the arithmetic calculation. Again, the compiler may issue a warning, but if the warning is ignored, there will be no notification of the problem when the program is run. If there can be legitimate questions about the assumptions on the sizes of results, we have an occasion for the use of the **ON SIZE ERROR** option.

3.25 THE HANDLING OF DECIMAL QUANTITIES IN ARITHMETIC OPERATIONS

The **COBOL** compiler automatically takes care of most of the problems having to do with decimal points. For example, if two numbers to be added do not have the same number of digits after their decimal points, **COBOL** will provide for correctly aligning the quantities before adding. Similarly, the results of arithmetic operations are stored with proper allowance for the relationship between the decimal point location of the result and the decimal point location shown in the Data Division for the item where that result is stored. (In almost all cases in a discussion such as this, we are talking about *assumed* decimal points. Data items involved in arithmetic operations *must not* have actual decimal points. The result of an arithmetic operation may be placed in an elementary item that has an actual decimal point, if the GIVING form of the arithmetic statements are used, but such a data item may not be used in any further arithmetic.)

COBOL-85

However, in COBOL-85, the edited result may be moved back to a numeric field and the data is converted back to numeric format. For example, suppose we have three fields defined as follows:

```
01  A      PIC 99V9.
01  B      PIC 99.9.
01  C      PIC 99V9.
```

If we move A to B, then move B to C, the results will be as follows.

| | Before | | | After | | |
	A	B	C	A	B	C
MOVE A TO B.	12ᴧ3	00.0	00ᴧ0	12ᴧ3	12.3	00ᴧ0
MOVE B TO C.	12ᴧ3	12.3	00ᴧ0	12ᴧ3	12.3	12ᴧ3

We must emphasize that this will work only in COBOL-85! In earlier versions of COBOL, moving B to C will cause an error; in these versions it is not possible to "unedit" numeric data.

END COBOL-85

It is not quite sufficient, however, to say simply "COBOL will take care of the decimal point," and forget about the subject. The problem is that in setting up the Data Division we have to know in complete detail what the various quantities are going to look like. This is particularly true with regard to providing enough space for the maximum size that any arithmetic result could assume. Let us accordingly study this subject a little more closely.

3.26 DECIMAL LOCATION IN ADDITION AND SUBTRACTION

Addition and subtraction do not present too much of a problem. The COBOL compiler arranges to align decimal points automatically if the quantities involved do not have the same number of digits after the decimal point. This may involve extra operations for the computer, which will sometimes slow things down, but the change in speed is usually too small to measure and in any case we are not concerning ourselves about such efficiency considerations for now.

Elaborate rules can be devised for determining the maximum size of the result of an addition or subtraction, but the following procedure is recommended. Simply write down all of the operands in the form of all 9's, with decimal points properly aligned, and perform the addition using pencil and paper or a pocket calculator. The result will be the biggest number you could ever get. Naturally, if any of the numbers being added are negative, or if we are talking about a subtraction of numbers having the same sign, then the result will be smaller than that. And as noted in connection with the program in Figure 3.1, we may know something about the application that will tell us that the result just could never be that large.

3.27 THE DECIMAL LOCATION ON MULTIPLICATION

The situation with regard to multiplication is a little more complicated than for addition and subtraction, but not much. The rule is this: the product of multiplying two factors has as many digits to the right of the decimal point as the sum of the number of digits to the right of the decimal point in the two factors, and likewise it may have as many digits to the left of the decimal point as the sum of the number of digits to the left of the decimal point in the two factors. That is a mouthful but it is not really too difficult to understand. Consider, for example, the multiplication of 12.345 by 9.87. One of the factors has three digits after the decimal point and the other has two, so the result will have five. One of the factors has two digits before the decimal point and the other one has one, so the product will have three. The product of these two numbers is, in fact, 121.84515.

It must be understood, or course, that we are talking about the *maximum possible* size of results. For instance, if a number is described in the Data Division as having four digit positions before the decimal point, but the actual number has three leading zeros, then of course there will be leading zeros in the product. Somewhat similarly, if we multiply 1.23 by 2.3 the rule tells us that the product *could* have two digits to the left of the decimal point, but the *actual* product is 2.829. This does not mean that the rule is wrong, however, since the rule speaks about *maximum* possible sizes. If we multiply 7.89 by 6.7, then we get 52.863, a product that does indeed have two digits to the left of the decimal point.

3.28 DECIMAL LOCATION ON DIVISION

Division is an altogether different story for two fundamental reasons having to do with mathematics and not COBOL. The first is that the quotient of two numbers does not necessarily have a finite decimal representation. The simplest example is the division of 1 by 3, the result of which cannot be represented exactly in any finite number of decimal digits, but only as a string of as many 3's as we wish to write following the decimal point. The second problem is that it is not possible to state the maximum size of a quotient without knowing both the maximum value of the dividend and the minimum value of the divisor. For example, suppose we have a dividend described by

    PICTURE 9999V99

a divisor described by

    PICTURE 99V99

and a quotient described by

    PICTURE 99999.999

Now, if we do this division

$$\frac{0412.58}{55.11}$$

the stored result will be 00007.486. No problem. But consider this division

$$\frac{7359.10}{00.34}$$

The result this time is 27648.260, which just barely fits in the space allocated for the quotient. And if we do this division

$$\frac{6359.10}{00.05}$$

the result is 127182.000, and there is insufficient room to store the result.

Mathematically, the extreme case of this problem is in the attempt to divide by zero. If we really don't know anything about what the possible number of sizes is, we have to take the largest possible dividend and the smallest possible divisor and provide space for the quotient that would result. In many cases this is far too conservative and will result in considerable wasted space. Again, the proper approach is to know as much as possible about the data and either test your data to be sure your assumptions are justified, using techniques shown in following chapters, or else use the ON SIZE ERROR option.

REVIEW QUESTIONS

1. In the programs in Figures 3.1 and 3.2 we used prefixes (I, O, and W) to designate the nature of the data items (input, output, and Working-Storage, respectively). Do these prefixes have any meaning in COBOL?

2. You are given that each of the three parts of a date takes up two digits, and that regular and overtime hours are both three digits with one place after the assumed decimal point. Is this a legal Data Division structure for these items?

```
01  PAY-DATA-RECORD.
    05  PAY-DATE.
        10  MONTHS          PIC 99.
        10  DAYS            PIC 99.
        10  YEARS           PIC 99.
    05  HOURS.
        10  REGULAR-HOURS   PIC 99V9.
        10  OT-HOURS        PIC 99V9.
```

3. How many characters are there in the record described by these Data Division entries?

```
01  DATA-RECORD.
    05  ONE                 PIC X(10).
    05  TWO.
        10  THREE           PIC XXX.
        10  FOUR            PIC XXXX.
    05  SIX.
        10  SEVEN.
            15  EIGHT       PIC XXX.
            15  NINE        PIC X.
        10  TEN             PIC XX.
```

4. Consider the following illustrative portion of a Data Division:

```
01  FIRST.
    05  SECOND              PIC XX.
    05  THIRD.
        10  FOURTH          PIC X(10).
        10  FIFTH           PIC X(12).
    05  SIXTH               PIC X.
```

Name the group items and the elementary items. Is it possible for a group item to be a part of a more inclusive group?

5. An elementary item may be numeric, alphabetic, or alphanumeric. What can you say about group items?

6. Can a data item having a level number of 01 be an elementary item?

7. The letter **v** for an assumed decimal point and a decimal point itself representing an actual decimal point both take up space in a **PICTURE** clause. Do they also both describe a character that takes up space in the data items to which they refer?

8. Could **FILLER** ever be used as the name of a data item in the Procedure Division? We understand that **FILLER** is a reserved word, but if it occurred only once in the Data Division, could we not refer to that data item by that name **FILLER**?

COBOL-85

In **COBOL-85** you need not use the word **FILLER** at all. Could you then use it as a data name?

END COBOL-85

9. Locate errors in these Data Division entries.

```
a.  01  SAM               PIC X(20).
        05  JOE           PIC X(12).
        05  BILL          PIC X(8).
```

```
b.  01  DAN.
        05  TOM           PIC X(20).
            10  ONCE      PIC X(10).
            10  TWICE     PIC X(10).
        05  RACHEL        PIC X(30).
```

```
c.  01  JUNE
        05  GINI          PIC X(10)
        05  CINDY         PIC X(23)
```

10. How many characters are there in the record described by these entries?

```
01  GEORGE.
    05  BETTY             PICTURE X(3).
    05  GLORIA            PICTURE XX.
    05  LIZ.
        10  ED            PICTURE X(12).
        10  LEO           PICTURE X(8).
    05  NAN.
        10  LEN           PICTURE X.
        10  ZEB           PICTURE XX.
```

11. Suppose a program contains the following statement:

    `ADD REGULAR-HOURS OVERTIME-HOURS GIVING TOTAL-HOURS`

    If you are told the values of `REGULAR-HOURS` and of `OVERTIME-HOURS` before execution of this statement, but not the value of `TOTAL-HOURS`, can you tell exactly what the statement will do?

12. Suppose you are given the following statement:

    `SUBTRACT A, B, C FROM D GIVING E`

    Write a formula that expresses what will be placed in `E` in terms of the values of the other four data items.

13. What is wrong with this statement?

    `ADD A TO B GIVING C`

14. For each statement, fill in the "after" positions for items that have a "before" entry.

	Before				After			
	A	B	C	D	A	B	C	D
ADD A TO B	12	14						
ADD A, B TO C	1	2	14					
ADD A B TO C D	2	4	6	10				
ADD A, B, C TO D	1	2	3	4				
ADD A B C GIVING D	1	2	3	4				
ADD 12 TO A	13							
SUBTRACT A FROM B	2	8						
SUBTRACT A FROM B GIVING C	1	2	12					
SUBTRACT A, B FROM C	1	2	12					
SUBTRACT A, B FROM C GIVING D	1	2	12	39				
SUBTRACT 5 FROM A	8							
SUBTRACT A FROM 35 GIVING B	25	99						
MULTIPLY A BY B	6	3						
MULTIPLY A BY B GIVING C	6	3	29					
MULTIPLY 4 BY A GIVING B	5	21						
DIVIDE A INTO B	2	12						
DIVIDE A INTO B GIVING C	2	12	23					
DIVIDE A BY B GIVING C	12	4	98					
DIVIDE A BY 12 GIVING B	36	7						
DIVIDE A BY B GIVING C REMAINDER D	23	7	8	6				

ANSWERS TO REVIEW QUESTIONS

1. None whatever. Experienced programmers recommend such conventions, but they are for the benefit of human readers (including the writer) of the program, not the COBOL compiler.

2. Yes.

3. 23.

4. The group items are FIRST and THIRD; the elementary items are SECOND, FOURTH, FIFTH, and SIXTH. A group item certainly can be part of a larger group. THIRD is such a case.

5. Group items are always treated as if they are alphanumeric. That statement can be misleading, however, since the elementary items *within a group* can be numeric.

6. Certainly, so long as it is not further subdivided. In the program in Chapter 2, for example, we read an entire record and printed all the contents. The entire record was described by

    PICTURE X(80)

    making the contents of the record one elementary item.

7. Absolutely not. An assumed decimal point is *assumed*, not stored explicitly! This has a crucial bearing on such things as alignment of operands for arithmetic operations, but an assumed decimal point does not exist as a character in the data item.

8. No way. A practical problem is that ordinarily the word FILLER will appear many times, so the COBOL compiler would have no way of knowing which one you meant. But in any event, this is illegal.

COBOL-85

This is true in COBOL–85, as well as older versions of COBOL, even if you do not use the word FILLER more than once. It is still a reserved word and may not be used as a data name.

END COBOL-85

9. a. SAM, as a group item, must not have a PICTURE!
   b. Ditto for TOM.
   c. There are no periods after the entries.

10. Twenty-eight, the sum of the number of characters in each of the PICTURE clauses.

11. Certainly. Using the GIVING option, the previous value of the data item named after the word GIVING is simply replaced by the result of the arithmetic operation.

12. E = D - (A + B + C)

    The point is that in any SUBTRACT the values of all of the items before the word FROM will first be added together and then that result subtracted from the value of the item named after the word FROM. This is true whether or not the GIVING option is used.

13. This is actually a trick question, because the answer depends on which version of COBOL you are using, or which compiler options you have set in Microsoft COBOL. In COBOL-85 the statement is perfectly acceptable. In most other versions of COBOL, however, the GIVING option does not permit the TO. (But even some of the older compilers simply issue a warning, then compile as though the TO were not there.)

14.

	Before				After			
	A	B	C	D	A	B	C	D
ADD A TO B	12	14			12	26		
ADD A, B TO C	1	2	14		1	2	17	
ADD A B TO C D	2	4	6	10	2	4	12	16
ADD A, B, C TO D	1	2	3	4	1	2	3	10
ADD A B C GIVING D	1	2	3	4	1	2	3	6
ADD 12 TO A	13				25			
SUBTRACT A FROM B	2	8			2	6		
SUBTRACT A FROM B GIVING C	1	2	12		1	2	1	
SUBTRACT A, B FROM C	1	2	12		1	2	9	
SUBTRACT A, B FROM C GIVING D	1	2	12	39	1	2	12	9
SUBTRACT 5 FROM A	8				3			
SUBTRACT A FROM 35 GIVING B	25	99			25	10		
MULTIPLY A BY B	6	3			6	18		
MULTIPLY A BY B GIVING C	6	3	29		6	3	18	
MULTIPLY 4 BY A GIVING B	5	21			5	20		
DIVIDE A INTO B	2	12			2	6		
DIVIDE A INTO B GIVING C	2	12	23		2	12	6	
DIVIDE A BY B GIVING C	12	4	98		12	4	3	
DIVIDE A BY 12 GIVING B	36	7			36	3		
DIVIDE A BY B GIVING C REMAINDER D	23	7	8	6	23	7	3	2

EXERCISES

*1. A record named ACCOUNTS consists of three elementary items named RECEIVABLE, PAYABLE, and PAST-DUE, each of which is a dollars-and-cents amount with five digits before the assumed decimal point. Write Data Division entries describing this record.

* Answers to starred exercises will be found in Appendix IV at the end of the book.

2. A record named **INVENTORY** consists of elementary items named **ON-HAND** and **ON-ORDER**, each of which contains five digits before the assumed decimal point and three digits after, together with a 25-character alphanumeric item named **DESCRIPTION**. Write Data Division entries describing this record.

*3. Here is the description of an input record. Its name is **ALPHA-INPUT**. The first item in the record is a group item, named **A**, consisting of a four-character item named **B** and a five-character item named **C**. Next after **A** is a six-character elementary item named **D**, and finally a seven-character elementary item named **E**. All characters are alphanumeric. Write suitable Data Division entries describing the record.

4. Here is the description of an input record. The name of the record is **INPUT-RECORD**. The first 10 characters make up an alphanumeric data item named **A**. The next 8 characters make up a numeric data item named **B**. The next 9 characters make up an alphanumeric item named **C**, that is further divided into a three-digit numeric item named **D**, a two-digit numeric item named **E**, and a four-digit item named **F**. The last 53 characters make up an alphanumeric item named **G**. Write a suitable Data Division entry for this record.

*5. An output record named **NORMAL-LINE-OUT** contains the following:
   A three-character alphanumeric item named **IDENT**, followed by space for three blanks (which would be inserted by a **MOVE SPACES TO NORMAL-LINE-OUT** statement in the Procedure Division).
   A group item named **COSTS**, consisting of elementary items named **OUTGOING** and **RETURNING**, each of which is a dollars-and-cents amount with a maximum size of 9999.99. These items are to be printed with decimal points, and each is to be followed by space for two blanks.
   An elementary item named **TOTAL-MILES**, which has five numeric digits without a decimal point.
   Write suitable Data Division entries describing this record.

6. An output record named **ERROR-LINE-OUT** contains the following fields.
   NAME, which consists of **INITIAL-1** and **INITIAL-2**, each one character followed by space for one blank, and **LAST-NAME**, which is 20 characters, followed by space for four blanks.
   REST-OF-RECORD, which is 43 alphanumeric characters.
   Write suitable Data Division entries.

*7. Refer to the schematic representation of a record shown at the top of the next page. The essential information about each elementary item is as follows:

PREFIX	2 letters
BIN-NUMBER	4 digits
QTY	6 digits
DOLLARS	7 digits with 2 assumed decimal places
DESCRIPTION	15 alphanumeric characters
WHERE-MADE	1 letter
MFG-PURCH	1 digit
HI-LO-USAGE	1 digit
QOH	5 digits

Write a complete record description entry.

Level

	INVENTORY							
01								
05	PART		YTD-USAGE		DESCRIPTION	CODES			QOH
10	PREFIX	BIN-NUMBER	QTY	DOLLARS		WHERE-MADE	MFG-PURCH	HI-LO-USAGE	

8. Refer to the schematic representation of the record shown below. The essential information about each elementary item is as follows:

DEPT	2 letters
PERSON	5 digits
RATE	5 digits, 4 decimal places
SEX	1 letter
MONTH	2 digits
DAY-NO	2 digits
YEAR	2 digits
GROSS	6 digits, 2 decimal places
SS-TAX	3 digits, 2 decimal places
WITHHOLDING	6 digits, 2 decimal places
PENSION	5 digits, 2 decimal places

Write a complete record description.

Level

	PAYROLL									
01										
05	EMPLOYEE		RATE	SEX	SERVICE-DATE			YTD			
10	DEPT	PERS			MONTH	DAY-NO	YEAR	GROSS	SS-TAX	WITHHOLDING	PENSION

*9. Write a description, in words, of the record represented by the following Data Division structure. How many characters are there in the record?

```
01   PREMIUM-LINE-1.
     05   POLICY-NUMBER        PIC X(7).
     05   FILLER               PIC X(3).
     05   AMOUNTS.
          10   PREMIUM         PIC 9(4).99.
          10   FILLER          PIC XX.
          10   DIVIDEND        PIC 9(4).99.
          10   FILLER          PIC XX.
          10   INTEREST        PIC 9(4).99.
          10   FILLER          PIC XX.
          10   AMOUNT-DUE      PIC 9(4).99.
          10   FILLER          PIC XX.
```

10. Write a word description of the record represented by the following Data Division structure. How many characters are there in the record?

```
01   PREMIUM-LINE-2.
     05   NUMBER-OF-MONTHS     PIC XX.
     05   FILLER               PIC XX.
     05   DATE-DUE.
          10   MONTH-DUE       PIC XX.
          10   FILLER          PIC X.
          10   DAY-DUE         PIC XX.
          10   FILLER          PIC X.
          10   YEAR-DUE        PIC XX.
     05   FILLER               PIC X(38).
     05   LOAN-BALANCE         PIC 9(5).99.
```

*11. State in words what these statements do.

   a. ADD R, S TO T.

   b. ADD R, S GIVING T.

   c. SUBTRACT A, B, C FROM D.

   d. SUBTRACT A, B, C FROM D GIVING E.

   e. MULTIPLY 12.3 BY FACTOR-9.

   f. DIVIDE M INTO N.

   g. DIVIDE M INTO N GIVING Q ROUNDED.

12. State in words what these statements do.

   a. ADD X TO Y.

   b. ADD X, Y GIVING Z.

   c. SUBTRACT G, H FROM P.

   d. SUBTRACT G, H FROM P GIVING Q.

   e. MULTIPLY FACTOR-1 BY FACTOR-2 ROUNDED.

   f. MULTIPLY MONTHLY-USAGE BY 12 GIVING YEARLY-USAGE.

   g. DIVIDE 12 INTO YEARLY-USAGE GIVING MONTHLY-USAGE.

   h. DIVIDE 24 INTO TOTAL-HOURS GIVING DAYS REMAINDER HOURS.

*13. Write single arithmetic statements that will have the effect of carrying out each of the following actions.

   a. Add the values of JAN, FEB, and MAR, and place the sum in 1-QUARTER.

   b. Add the values of YEAR-1 and YEAR-2, with the sum replacing the value of YEAR-2.

   c. Add 13.45, the value of ABC, and the value of DEF, with the sum going to DEF.

   d. Same as c., except that the sum goes to GHI.

   e. Decrease the value of Q-1 by 12.

   f. Form the sum of Y-88 and Y-89, and subtract that sum from the value of YEARS.

   g. Multiply the value of FINAL-TOTAL by the value of RATE-ADJUSTMENT, with the rounded product being placed back in FINAL-TOTAL.

  h. Multiply the value of MONTHLY-USAGE by 12, with the product placed in YEAR-TOTAL.

  i. Multiply the value of MILES-PER-HOUR by the value of HOURS, to get the value of DISTANCE.

  j. Divide the value of YEAR-TOTAL by 12, to get the value of MONTHLY-AV-ERAGE.

  k. Divide the value of MACHINE-UTILIZATION by the value of OVERLAP-FACTOR, with the rounded quotient replacing the previous value of MACHINE-UTILIZATION.

  l. Divide the value of TOTAL-TIME by 60; place the quotient in HOURS and the remainder in MINUTES.

14. Write arithmetic statements to carry out the following actions.

  a. Place the sum of the values of REG-HOURS and OT-HOURS in TOTAL-HOURS.

  b. Increase the value of Q-1 by 12.

  c. Add the values of MON, TUES, WED, THUR, and FRI; place the sum in WEEK.

  d. Add the value of MON-1, MON-2, and MON-3; place the sum in MON-3.

  e. Subtract 69.3 from the value of FACTOR-3.

  f. Add the values of QTY-1 and QTY-2, subtract that sum from QTY-3, and place the final result in FINAL-VALUE.

  g. Add 39 to the sum of the values of F-6 and F-8, subtract that sum from F-10, and place the result in F-10.

  h. Multiply the values of OT-HOURS by 1.5 and place the product in TEMP-STORAGE.

  i. Multiply the value of S and Y and place the product back in S.

  j. Divide the value of SUMMATION by the value of N and place the quotient in AVERAGE, rounded.

  k. Divide the value of KW-USAGE by 1.2, with the quotient replacing the previous value of KW-USAGE.

  l. Divide the value of AMOUNT by 5; place the quotient in NICKELS and the remainder in PENNIES.

*15. In each part of this exercise you are given an arithmetic statement and a PICTURE clause for each item entering into the arithmetic.
Find the PICTURE clause for RESULT that will permit the largest possible result to be placed in RESULT, without wasting space.

```
ADD A B GIVING RESULT.

    05   A        PICTURE 99V9.
    05   B        PICTURE 9(3)V99.

MULTIPLY A BY B GIVING RESULT.

    05   A        PICTURE 9(3).
    05   B        PICTURE 99V9.

MULTIPLY A BY 12.34 GIVING RESULT.

    05   A        PICTURE 9(3)V9(4).
```

16. Same as Exercise 15.

```
ADD A B GIVING RESULT.

    05  A        PICTURE 9(3)V99.
    05  B        PICTURE 9V9.

MULTIPLY A BY B GIVING RESULT.

    05  A        PICTURE 9V9(3).
    05  B        PICTURE 9(3)V9(3).
```

*17. You are given a data file. Each record in the file contains payroll information about one employee, in the following format:

Columns 1-5	Identification number
Columns 6-8	Hours worked, to tenths of an hour
Columns 9-12	Pay rate, in dollars and cents

Write a program that will read the data records, compute the employee's pay (hours multiplied by rate), and print the following information on a line for each worker:

Positions 1-5	Identification number
Positions 9-12	Hours worked, with a decimal point
Positions 16-20	Pay rate, with a decimal point
Positions 24-30	Pay, with a decimal point

Be sure to blank out the **FILLER** positions between items in the output.

Your program is to include all four divisions, and you should compile it and run it with sample data. Compare your results with hand-calculated test cases.

Instead of reading the payroll information from a data file you may wish to use **ACCEPT** and **DISPLAY** statements to get the data, as was done in Figure 3.1. Actually, you ought to try this program using both techniques so that you get experience with both. If you write the program using the structure shown in the example programs, the changes needed to go from one version of the program to the other are fairly simple, and you should become equally familiar with reading data from files and from the keyboard.

18. You are given a data file with records containing this information:

Columns 1-7	Identification number
Columns 8-10	Hours worked on Monday, to tenths of an hour
Columns 11-13	Hours worked on Tuesday
Columns 14-16	Hours worked on Wednesday
Columns 17-19	Hours worked on Thursday
Columns 20-22	Hours worked on Friday
Columns 23-25	Hours worked on Saturday

Write a program that will read these records, and for each record compute the total hours worked and the average hours worked (the total divided by 6). For each record, a line is to be printed giving the following information:

Positions 1-7	Identification number
Positions 12-15	Total hours worked, with a decimal point
Positions 17-21	Average hours worked, to hundredths of an hour

EXERCISES **63**

Be sure to blank the positions between items in the output line. Use rounding on the average. Compile and run your program with illustrative data.

As in Exercise 17, you may wish to try this once reading the input data from a file, and once using **ACCEPT** and **DISPLAY** to read it from the keyboard.

19. (This exercise is suitable for use as a small project.)

Assume you are developing a sales and inventory report for the National Widget Corporation. Input records for the report have the following format:

Columns 1-5	product code (alphanumeric)
Columns 6-30	product description (alphanumeric)
Columns 31-35	sales for three weeks ago
Columns 36-40	sales for two weeks ago
Columns 41-45	sales for last week
Columns 46-50	inventory level
Columns 51-57	selling price in dollars and cents

For each record in this inventory you are to produce a line on the report that shows all of the data in the record. In addition, you are to calculate and print several pieces of information. First, the company would like to have a forecast of next week's sales. (All sales figures are recorded in units sold.) Basically, this is calculated as an average of the past three weeks' sales. However, since it is assumed that current data is more likely to reflect current sales conditions than older data, the company uses a *weighted* average. That is, if **WEEK1** represents the sales for three weeks ago and **WEEK3** represents the sales for last week, then the forecast is computed as

forecast = (**WEEK1** + 2×**WEEK2** + 3×**WEEK3**) / 6

The result is to be rounded to the nearest unit.

In addition to the forecast for next week's sales you are to compute the current value of each item in inventory. An item's value is defined to be the quantity in inventory times the selling price of the item.

Finally, the company wants to know the average value of an item in inventory. This is defined to be the total value of all items divided by the number of different products in the warehouse. The average product value is to be printed at the end of the report.

The headings shown on the sample report below are for explanation only and you need not produce any headings in your program. However, each column should be separated from the following column by a blank space.

Prod Code	Product Description	3 wk Sales	2 wk Sales	Last week Sales	Curr Inv	Product Price	F'cst Sales	Product Value
AA123	SNOW BLOWER	00002	00000	00005	00022	00299.95	00003	0006598.90
BB345	LAWN CHAIR	01050	02577	00933	09515	00017.50	01501	0166512.50
AVERAGE VALUE								0086555.70

CHAPTER 4

PROGRAM DESIGN

4.1 INTRODUCTION

Developing a computer program requires two steps: first, you must plan what the program is to do and how it is to do it; second, you translate this plan into the actual program. Although you may not believe it now, writing the program is the easier of the two tasks. Unfortunately, it is not possible to skip the planning step. At some point you *must* decide how the program is to work. If you don't do it before you start writing the COBOL code, you will find yourself doing it while you try to write the program. The result will be a program that is harder to write, harder to debug, and much more complicated than one that is carefully designed in advance.

Teaching all of the techniques for designing large programs is beyond the scope of this book. Our objective in this chapter is simply to present the basic tools of program design. You will be introduced to *hierarchy charts*, which are used to design the overall structure of a program, and *pseudocode*, which lets you define what each part of the program is to do. We will discuss the basic method for designing a program and show an example of how a simple program might be designed. Keep in mind that we have not yet covered enough COBOL to actually *implement* all of the programs we will design. This doesn't matter! Eventually you will learn the necessary COBOL, and in any case the design techniques you will learn are independent of the language used to write the program.

4.2 PROGRAM FUNCTION

We begin the design of a program by recognizing that every program performs a *function*, or task. Therefore, we must try to think about a program in terms of this function, *not* in terms of the detailed steps that must be performed to carry out the function. This is not a natural way for a beginner to think about a program. At this point you are very likely overwhelmed by the complexities of what you have learned about COBOL, to say nothing of what will be covered in the remainder of this book. When you start to think about how to write a program such as the one presented in Chapter 3, you are likely to start with something like "Well, first I have to read a record. Now what do I do with it? Oh yes, I had better go back and open the files I need...." This approach is very natural and quite common. It really has only one serious flaw—it won't work! Even if you have been able to design your first few programs this way (and you may already have run into trouble!), it will become harder and harder to use this method as your programs become larger and more complex. Although you may get the program working eventually, it will take longer and produce a much more complicated program than if you do it the right way. So let's begin by remembering that we want to think in terms of the *functions* that a program performs, and go on to see how we can put these functions down on paper.

4.3 HIERARCHY CHARTS

If programmers could picture the operation of an entire program all at once, the task of writing a program would be simple. Unfortunately, the human mind is capable of dealing with only a limited number of concepts at one time, and research has shown that this limit runs between five and nine concepts, depending on the person and the difficulty of each concept. If you try to deal with a problem that has more factors than this, you start to forget about parts of the problem and to make mistakes in your solution; the more factors you try to deal with at one time the more mistakes you make. Unfortunately, most computer programs involve many more than nine factors, which leads us to a serious conflict. On the one hand, we cannot deal with all of the factors necessary to develop most programs. On the other hand, we *must* be able to deal with large problems if programming is to be a useful activity.

The solution to this conflict is to divide the original problem into several smaller problems, which, if carried out correctly, solve the original problem. We don't have to decide how the smaller problems will be solved yet; that can be done later on. Right now all we must do is be certain that *if* the smaller problems can be solved, then we will have solved the original problem. Later on we can worry about how to solve each of the smaller problems. For example, if I were to try to plan my day minute by minute from the time I wake up in the morning until the time I go to sleep at night, I probably wouldn't have too much success. I would omit details, then remember things that I had to do earlier, make corrections to my schedule, and so on. Instead, I can start by listing major activities like this:

1. Shower
2. Get dressed
3. Have breakfast
4. Go to office
5. Check mail
6. Review output from last night's computer runs
7. Continue design of sales report program

.
.
.

If I wanted to, I could go on to divide each of these activities into still smaller tasks. For example, I could divide "have breakfast" into "pour juice, prepare cereal, make coffee, . . . ," and I could further divide one of these steps into the detailed activities required, for example, to make coffee. In a similar manner, instead of trying to understand all of the details needed to make a typical program work, we divide the program into the major tasks required to accomplish the basic function of the program, then as necessary divide each of these tasks into smaller tasks, and so on. At each stage, we don't have to decide exactly how to carry out the tasks, we are listing; we only need to be certain that, if we get the proper tasks listed then the program will accomplish the original task. Eventually we will have the program broken down into a number of tasks, each of which is small enough that we can deal with it.

In order to keep track of these tasks and how they relate to each other, we use a hierarchy chart. (You may find hierarchy charts referred to elsewhere by other names, such as *structure charts*. The style may vary slightly but the concept is the same.) For example, Figure 4.1 shows part of a hierarchy chart that documents the daily activities listed above.

This hierarchy chart tells us that the daily schedule consists of the activities "shower," "get dressed," and so on, and that the activity "have breakfast" consists of three more detailed activities. Notice that we can show lower levels of detail for one activity without showing them for all activities. If we wished, we could show lower levels of detail for preparing cereal and making coffee.

4.4 A HIERARCHY CHART FOR A SIMPLE PROGRAM

We are ready now to develop a simple hierarchy chart for a program. The particular program we are going to design is the one shown in Figure 3.2. We begin the design by considering just what task this program is trying to ac-

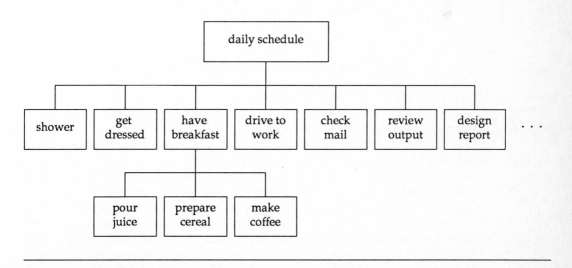

FIGURE 4.1 Hierarchy chart of day's schedule.

complish. Basically, the function of the program is to produce an inventory report. This function, then, becomes the top box, or *module*, of the hierarchy chart.

```
┌─────────────┐
│  PRODUCE    │
│  INVENTORY  │
│  REPORT     │
└─────────────┘
```

The next question is, what tasks must be performed in order to produce the inventory report? Keep in mind that we aren't at all concerned with the details of the COBOL code that must be written to carry out these tasks. Suppose all of the inventory records were printed on three-by-five-inch cards, and the report was to be computed by hand and written on a printed form, one line for each item in inventory. How would you describe what had to be done to produce the report?

Your description would probably go something like this: "First I get an inventory record. I copy the part number, quantity on hand, quantity received, and unit price to the report. Then I compute the new quantity on hand and put it on the report, and finally I compute the value of the item and write it on the report. When I'm done with this, I repeat the whole process for the next inventory record."

If you look at this description, you can see that producing the inventory report consists of four tasks:

1. get the next inventory record;
2. copy the item data to the report;
3. compute the new quantity on hand (QOH);
4. compute the item value.

Notice that we have not shown any of the details of how these tasks are performed. We have not, for example, shown that task 3 is the result of an addition. All we are trying to do at this point is describe the *function* of the task. Later we will tell how the task is actually carried out.

Based on this list of tasks we can now expand the hierarchy chart for the program, producing the version shown in Figure 4.2.

At this point we should review the hierarchy chart to see if there are any details that we have forgotten. In this case, there is one more task that we should add that did not show up in the manual preparation of the report. That task is writing the report record. When we described the manual activities, we assumed that each piece of data was being written by hand in its proper place on the report form. In COBOL, of course, we must use a WRITE statement. The final version of the hierarchy chart is shown in Figure 4.3. Each module contains a *brief* (a few words) statement of the function that the module performs, including a *precise verb* that tells what the major action of the module is, such as *get, copy, compute,* or *write*.

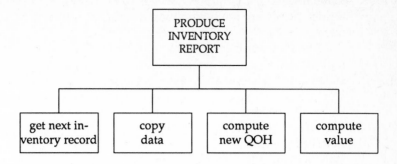

FIGURE 4.2   Expanded version of a hierarchy chart for an inventory report program.

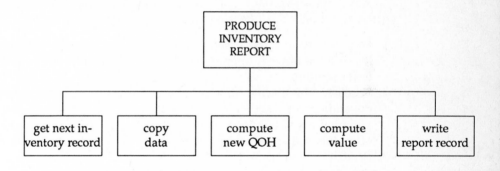

FIGURE 4.3   Final version of a hierarchy chart for an inventory control program.

We have one question left to resolve in preparing hierarchy charts. When do we *stop* adding more levels of detail? In this example that was no problem because the tasks being performed were very simple. In more complicated programs, however, the problem is not so easily resolved. Is it necessary, for example, to continue until each module consists of only one COBOL statement? The answer is, No! We can stop adding more detail when the lowest level of modules describes basic tasks. In some cases each of these tasks may consist of only one COBOL statement. More likely, a task will represent an entire paragraph containing a number of statements. The main requirement is that you must be able to visualize clearly how the task is to be carried out.

4.5   CONTROL OF EXECUTION

Although a hierarchy chart will show you what functions a program must perform to accomplish its basic task, it will not show the order in which these functions must be performed, whether some functions are performed repeatedly, or what details are actually carried out to accomplish each function. The tool that we shall use to specify in detail what each module actually does is called *pseudocode*. The name is meant to suggest that the notation of pseudocode is similar to program code such as COBOL; but the "pseudo" part of the name means that although there are similarities, the two are not identical. In particular, we are not bound by the rules for writing COBOL statements and, in fact, are free to use abbreviations and ordinary English where appropriate.

The statements in a COBOL program (and in the pseudocode specifications for a COBOL program) can be divided into two basic types. First, there are the statements such as READ, DISPLAY, ADD, MOVE, etc., which carry out the detailed work of the program. Second, there are statements such as PERFORM and others we shall encounter shortly that control the execution of the program. For example, in Figure 3.2, the PERFORM statement in paragraph A000-MAIN-LINE-ROUTINE controls whether paragraph B010-LIST-INVENTORY-DATA and the statements inside this paragraph get executed. In most programs, the control statements are by far the most important of the two types. If the control statements are designed correctly, the remainder of the program can be written in a fairly straightforward manner. If the control structure of a program is poorly designed, no amount of effort will produce a good program.

Any computer program, whether in COBOL or some other language, can be written using only the following three types of control structures:

1. *Sequence.* This is the basic mode of operation of any program. Unless specified otherwise, operations are carried out from top to bottom in the order written.
2. *Selection.* This means to select one of two alternative courses of action, depending on whether some condition is true or not. For example, in planning my schedule for the day I might say "If I have to visit a client's office today, then I will drive to work; if not, then I will take the bus."
3. *Iteration.* This means to perform some action repeatedly until a stated condition terminates the repetition. For example, in Figure 3.2 paragraph B010-LIST-INVENTORY-DATA is performed repeatedly until we run out of inventory records. As is the case in this program, the number of "repeats" can be zero.

There is also a fourth type of structure that is frequently used, called the *case* structure. The case structure is actually just a special type of selection, so it is sometimes omitted from pseudocode specifications. However, since COBOL-85 includes a statement that supports the case structure, we shall include the structure here.

4. *Case.* This means to perform one of several alternative actions, depending on the value of some variable. For example, a delivery service might charge $7.50 for a delivery within 5 miles of the center of town, $10 for a delivery over 5 miles but within 10 miles, and $1/mile for deliveries over 10 miles.

4.6 PSEUDOCODE STRUCTURES

As in COBOL itself, the sequence structure requires no special notation. It is simply a series of statements written one after the other.

The selection structure is indicated by an IFTHENELSE pseudocode statement. For example, the selection statement given above would be written as:

```
IF have to visit client's office THEN
    drive to work
ELSE
    take bus to work
ENDIF
```

The interpretation of this statement is fairly simple. If the condition specified between IF and THEN is true, execute the statement (or statements) between THEN and ELSE. If the condition is false, execute the statement(s) between ELSE and ENDIF. Optionally, the word ELSE and the statements following it may be omitted. In this case if the condition following IF is false, we do nothing and go on to the next statement.

The ENDIF part of the IFTHENELSE statement is very important, especially if there are several statements following ELSE, since the word ENDIF defines very clearly where the entire structure ends. This is particularly important if one of the statements to be executed is itself an IFTHENELSE structure. Consider the following example.

```
IF employee is salaried THEN
    set gross-pay to weekly-salary
ELSE
    set base-pay to hours-worked x pay-rate
    IF hours-worked are greater than 40 THEN
        set overtime-pay to 1.5 x pay-rate x (hours-worked - 40)
    ELSE
        set overtime-pay to zero
    ENDIF
    set gross-pay to base-pay + overtime-pay
ENDIF
```

The use of the ENDIFs makes clear where each IF structure terminates.

We also want to call your attention to the format of the structure. The words ELSE and ENDIF are aligned under the IF, and the action statements are indented. Following this format makes the pseudocode much easier to read than if we wrote it something like this:

```
IF have to visit client's office THEN drive to work ELSE take bus to work ENDIF
```

The meaning of the statement hasn't changed, but the ease of understanding certainly has!

For the iteration structure, we shall take into account the fact that in COBOL iteration is expressed with the PERFORM...UNTIL statement, and we shall use a similar format, PERFORM-UNTIL, in our pseudocode. Just as we use the ENDIF to show explicitly the end of the scope of influence of the IF structure, we shall use an ENDPERFORM for the same function with iteration. The statements controlled by the PERFORM-UNTIL will be indented and shown right in the same place as the PERFORM-UNTIL. Although this is not the same as the COBOL **PERFORM...UNTIL** statement, it matches common program design usage. The following example shows the PERFORM-UNTIL structure in use:

```
move 'N' to flag
get record; at end move 'Y' to flag
PERFORM-UNTIL flag = 'Y'
    process record
    get record; at end move 'Y' to flag
ENDPERFORM
```

The case structure has numerous formats in general program design, so we shall again borrow from **COBOL** and use a format based on the equivalent statement in **COBOL-85**. For example, the evaluation of the delivery service fee described above could be written as follows:

```
EVALUATE distance from center of town
    WHEN less than or equal to 5 miles
        fee is $7.50
    WHEN more than 5 miles but less than or equal to 10 miles
        fee is $10
    WHEN more than 10 miles
        fee is $1/mile
ENDEVALUATE
```

The EVALUATE structure begins with an expression following the word EVALUATE, and contains a series of WHEN clauses, each of which begins with a possible value for the expression. We evaluate the expression, then compare this value to each of the values in the WHEN clauses. If we find a value that matches the current value of the expression, the statement or statements following the WHEN value are executed and we go on to the next statement. At most, one WHEN clause is executed in the structure. If none of the values in WHEN clauses matches the current value in the expression, no action is taken and the EVALUATE statement is ignored.

The EVALUATE structure has two optional features that are not shown in this example. First, we can have more than one value in each WHEN clause. Second, we can follow the *last* WHEN clause with the word OTHERWISE. In this case, if no WHEN clause is executed, the statement(s) following OTHERWISE will be executed. For example, consider the following specification for evaluating a student's standing in a class:

```
EVALUATE quiz-grade
    WHEN 10
        class-standing is excellent
    WHEN 8 or 9
        class-standing is above-average
    WHEN 5 or 6 or 7
        class-standing is average
    WHEN 3 or 4
        class-standing is below-average
    OTHERWISE
        class-standing is failing
ENDEVALUATE
```

With the EVALUATE structure, as with the IF and PERFORM structures, we have an END word, in this case ENDEVALUATE, to mark the end of the scope of the structure.

4.7 SPECIFICATION OF THE INVENTORY REPORT PROGRAM

We are now ready to complete the design of the inventory report program by providing pseudocode specifications for each of the modules on the hierarchy chart. In many cases each module is treated as though it were a separate paragraph in a **COBOL** program. In this case, however, each second-level module will consist of only a few statements, so we shall treat the entire second level as a single "paragraph."

We begin with the basic specifications for the top module, "PRODUCE INVENTORY REPORT." This module reads an inventory record, then for every inventory record in the file it processes the record and reads another record. So far, the specifications to perform this task look like the following:

```
Read an inventory record; at end move 'Y' to flag
PERFORM-UNTIL flag = 'Y'
    process the inventory record
    read an inventory record; at end move 'Y' to flag
ENDPERFORM
stop
```

Next we expand the design by replacing the "process" statement, which really doesn't tell much about what the program is to accomplish, with the names of the remaining modules on the hierarchy chart:

```
Read an inventory record; at end move 'Y' to flag
PERFORM-UNTIL flag = 'Y'
    copy data
    compute new quantity on hand
    compute value
    write report record
    read an inventory record; at end move 'Y' to flag
ENDPERFORM
stop
```

Finally, we can complete the specification by replacing the names of the processing modules with pseudocode that tells what each module is to do:

```
Read an inventory record; at end move 'Y' to flag
PERFORM-UNTIL flag = 'Y'
    move spaces to output record
    move part-number to output record
    move qty-on-hand to output record
    move qty-received to output record
    move unit-price to output record
    compute new qty-on-hand as the sum of the qty-on-hand and
        the qty-received
    compute value by multiplying the new qty-on-hand
        by the unit-price
    write report record
    read an inventory record; at end move 'Y' to flag
ENDPERFORM
```

For all practical purposes the specification of the inventory report program is now complete. If you wish, you may add statements to open and close the input and output files, and to set the initial value of the flag to 'N'. These changes are left as an exercise for the student.

We do, however, wish to show an enhancement to this program to demonstrate how various types of control structures can be combined in a specification. Let us assume that it is possible to have a quantity-received of zero. In this case, we will leave the qty-received and new qty-on-hand fields of the output record blank, and we will compute the value as the product of the old qty-on-hand and the unit price. If the qty-received is greater than zero, the revised program is to produce the same results as the original one. The pseudocode for this enhanced program is as follows:

```
Read an inventory record; at end move 'Y' to flag
PERFORM-UNTIL flag = 'Y'
   move spaces to output record
   move part-number to output record
   move qty-on-hand to output record
   move unit-price to output record
   IF qty-received > 0 THEN
      move qty-received to output record
      compute new qty-on-hand as the sum of the qty-on-hand
           and the qty-received
      compute value by multiplying the new qty-on-hand
           by the unit-price
   ELSE
      compute value by multiplying the old qty-on-hand
           by the unit-price
   ENDIF
   write report record
   read an inventory record; at end move 'Y' to flag
ENDPERFORM
stop
```

We have not yet studied the COBOL statements necessary to implement this enhanced program, but the meaning of the pseudocode should still be clear. If necessary, study the example until you understand what the revised program will do when we write it. We will study the required COBOL code in the following chapter.

4.8 PROGRAMMING STANDARDS

Up to now your primary objective with any COBOL programs you have written is simply to get the program to work, and at this stage in your education that is not an unreasonable objective. However, you must now begin to look ahead to the time when you will be writing COBOL programs for an employer. What is acceptable for a beginner is not acceptable in the workplace!

The classroom environment is not a very realistic one as far as programming is concerned. In most of your programming assignments you will be writing relatively small programs (even if they don't seem small at the time), you will be working alone, and you will need to get your programs to work only *once;* after that neither you nor anyone else will look at it again. In the typical work environment, your programs may be thousands of lines long, you will likely be working on a team with other programmers, and the programs you write will be in use for years and may very well be modified by other programmers long after you have gone on to other work. In this type of environment it is vital that programs be written to be as clear and readable as possible. Consider the plight of the poor programmer who is awakened at 2 a.m. to come into the office to fix a program that blew up, and whose output *must* be available for a 9 a.m. management meeting! (What if that programmer is *you?*)

We made a start in developing good programs when we studied techniques for designing programs instead of just letting them happen. Another important step toward creating good software is to write the COBOL code according to standards. The objective of programming standards is not to make your program look exactly like everyone else's. There is plenty of room for individuality of technique, and it is highly unlikely that any two people will produce exactly the same program for a given problem. However, if you hold to a standard style in your programs, it becomes much easier for someone else to read your code and follow what you are trying to do.

In Appendix III you will find suggested COBOL programming standards. The basic goal of these standards is to promote a style of coding that makes the code as easy to read as possible. These standards are not unique, and you may wish to modify them or use other standards entirely. In any case, remember that the function of programming standards is to make your code readable; making sure that the code *means* something is another problem entirely.

We recommend this point of view: if your program can't be understood by another human being, you may as well not have written it.

One part of the suggested programming standards that may require special explanation is the use of prefixes such as A000 or B010 in paragraph names. These prefixes serve two purposes. First, they indicate the relative position of a paragraph in a hierarchy chart of the program. A paragraph beginning with A is on level one, a paragraph beginning with B is on level two, and so on. Second, since paragraphs are *always* written in prefix-number sequence in the program, the prefix makes it much easier to find a paragraph when you are trying to read a program. This may not mean much to you yet, since the programs you have encountered up to now only contain two or three paragraphs, but consider the problem of trying to find a paragraph quickly when your program contains twenty or thirty paragraphs! (That is intended to sound large to you; in "real life," programs of hundreds of paragraphs are routine, and programs of thousands of paragraphs are not rare.)

4.9 SUMMARY

In this chapter you have learned five new concepts:

1. Programs must be *designed*, not just thrown together;
2. Every program performs a *function*, every paragraph in the program performs a specific task that is part of this function, and the design of the program should be based on these tasks;
3. A *hierarchy chart* is a tool that is used to document the tasks that a program performs and their relationship to each other;
4. *Pseudocode* is used to specify the way in which each task, or *module*, on a hierarchy chart performs its function;
5. Programs should be written to be as readable as possible by other people, and to help achieve this goal they should be written following *standards*.

We have used these concepts in developing the programs in the first three chapters, and we will continue to demonstrate techniques for designing and writing good COBOL code throughout the remainder of this book.

REVIEW QUESTIONS

1. What are the two basic program design tools introduced in this chapter? Describe the function of each.

2. Name the four basic control structures that were described in the chapter and state the function of each.

3. Why do we need program design aids? Why can't we simply sit down and start writing the COBOL code directly?

4. What is wrong with the following hierarchy chart?

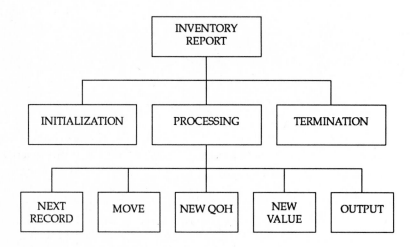

5. What, if anything, is wrong with the following pseudocode?

```
EVALUATE flag
    WHEN 'Y'
       write "The flag is set to 'Y'."
    OTHERWISE
       write "The flag is not set to 'Y'."
ENDEVALUATE
```

6. Are the following pseudocode statements equivalent?

```
EVALUATE amount
    WHEN greater than zero
       add amount to positive-total
    WHEN less than zero
       add amount to negative-total
    WHEN equal to zero
       write "The amount is zero."
ENDEVALUATE
```

```
    IF amount > zero THEN
       add amount to positive-total
    ELSE
       IF amount < zero THEN
          add amount to negative-total
       ELSE
          write "The amount is zero."
       ENDIF
    ENDIF
```

7. What, if anything, is wrong with the following pseudocode?

```
move 'N' to flag
read an input record; at end move 'Y' to flag
PERFORM-UNTIL flag = 'Y'
    IF record is a sales record THEN
       move the seller's name to the output record
       move the sale amount to the output record
       write the output record
    read an input record; at end move 'Y' to flag
ENDPERFORM
```

8. What is the reason for using programming standards?

ANSWERS TO REVIEW QUESTIONS

1. Hierarchy charts and pseudocode. The hierarchy chart defines the structure of the program in terms of the basic functions the program performs and the relationship of these functions to each other, and the pseudocode defines the detailed actions required to perform each function.

2. *Sequence.* The basic top-to-bottom mode of operation of any program or program specification.
   Selection. Choose between two alternative actions depending on whether some condition is true or false.
   Iteration. Repeat an action until some condition becomes true.
   Case. Choose one of several alternative actions depending on the value of a variable or expression.

3. We need design aids because the human mind cannot deal with all of the factors that are needed to write a typical program. If you try to keep more than nine or ten concepts in mind at the same time, you will forget details and make mistakes. The design tools help the programmer break a program into manageable pieces.

4. The module names don't tell anything about the functions of the modules, and most of the names don't specify an action. The name of a module should always consist of a brief (a few words) statement that describes the action that the module is to perform.

5. The statement is perfectly correct, although it is more common to use an IFTHENELSE structure if you are only choosing between two alternatives.

6. Yes.

7. The ENDIF, which should follow the write statement, is missing. From the indentation we assume that what the PERFORM-UNTIL loop was intended to do is to process the current record, then read a new record, repeating until flag becomes equal to 'Y'. However, as the specifications stand the read statement inside the PERFORM-UNTIL is within the scope of the IF statement and will only be executed if the record is a sales record. If a program written according to these specifications ever encountered a record other than a sales record, the read would not be executed and the program would loop forever (or until someone or some part of the operating system stopped its execution).

8. Programming standards are used to improve program readability. Standards generally prohibit coding styles that lead to overly complex code, and they make it easier for a programmer to read programs written by other people in his/her organization.

EXERCISES

*1. Write pseudocode statements to carry out the following operations.
   a. Add 1 to an item named LEGAL-ADULT if AGE is 18 or greater.
   b. Print STOCK-ITEM if PART-1-A contains the letter S.
   c. Add 1 to BIG if SIZE-A is greater than 800; add 1 to LITTLE if SIZE-A is less than or equal to 800.
   d. If the item in NAME-A is greater than the item in NAME-B, move the contents of NAME-A to TEMPORARY; if the item in NAME-A is less than the item in NAME-B, move the contents of NAME-B to TEMPORARY; if the two are equal, move either of them to TEMPORARY.
   e. If the value of the item named HOURS-WORKED is *anything but* 40, print "NON-STANDARD HOURS".

2. Write pseudocode statements to carry out the following operations.
   a. Add 1 to an item named MAJOR-BILLING if ACCOUNT-TOTAL is greater than 1000.00.
   b. Determine whether the value of the item named FINAL-BILL is greater than 999.99 and, if so, print "SPECIAL APPROVAL REQUIRED".
   c. If the item named CODE-A contains the characters AB47Z, move the characters APPROVED to the item named APPROVAL.
   d. Move zero to SIGNAL if MEASUREMENT is zero, and move 1 to SIGNAL if MEASUREMENT is not zero.
   e. Print "CODE-A IS INVALID" if CODE-A contains anything but letters and spaces.

3. Each student in a class has a grade record containing the student's name (contained in a field named STUDENT-NAME) and three examination grades named GRADE-1, GRADE-2, and GRADE-3. For each student, the three grades are to be added and their sum divided by 3, giving the

---

* Answers to starred exercises will be found in Appendix IV at the end of the book.

average grade. If the average grade is 65 or more, the word **PASS** is to be placed in the item named **FINAL-GRADE**; otherwise, the word **FAIL** is to be placed in **FINAL-GRADE**. In either case a record containing the student's name, all three grades, and the contents of **FINAL-GRADE** are to be printed. After all students have been graded, a count of the number of passing students and a count of the number of failing students are to be printed. Design a program to produce this grade report. Show both a hierarchy chart and a pseudocode for every module.

*4. Suppose that a salesperson's commission is based on a **PRODUCT-CODE**, as follows.

PRODUCT-CODE	Commission Formula

1
$0.15 \times$ **SALE-PRICE**
2
$0.40 \times ($**SALE-PRICE** $-$ **BASE-PRICE**$)$
3
$0.10 \times$ **BASE-PRICE** $+ 0.50 \times ($**SALE-PRICE** $-$ **BASE-PRICE**$)$
4
$\$25 + 0.05 \times$ **BASE-PRICE**
5
$\$75$

For every sale there is a **SALE-RECORD** containing **SELLER** (the salesperson's name), **PRODUCT-CODE**, **SALE-PRICE**, and **BASE-PRICE**. Design a program that reads all sales records and, for each record, writes a record containing the salesperson's name, the product code, sale price, base price, and commission. If **PRODUCT-CODE** is anything but 1, 2, 3, 4, or 5, set the commission to zero and add the message **"ERRONEOUS PRODUCT CODE"** to the end of the output record, following the normal fields.

5. Each record in a data file has the following format.

Columns 1-5:	Cost center code
Columns 6-11:	Budgeted expense, dollars
Columns 12-17:	Actual expense, year to date, dollars

Design a program that reads such a file and, for each record, prints a line giving the information read together with a comment **EXCEEDS BUDGET** if the actual expense is greater than the budgeted amount.

*6. Each record in a file contains an alphanumeric identification in columns 45-50 and a gross pay in dollars and cents in columns 70-76. A city tax is to be computed for each, the tax being 4% of the amount (if any) over $2000. For each record, a line is to be printed containing the input data and the computed tax. Design a suitable program.

7. Each record in a file contains an alphanumeric identification in columns 40-47 and a total price in columns 31-36 in dollars and cents. For each record a discount is to be computed and printed, along with the input data. The discount is 2% if the amount is over $1000, and zero if it is not. Design a suitable program.

*8. A file contains records having the following format:

Columns 1-8	IDENT	Alphanumeric
Columns 9-15	DOLLARS	9(5)V99
Columns 16-80	OTHER-INFO	Alphanumeric

The contents of each record are to be listed; the amount in the DOLLARS field from each record should be added to a total (which is initially set to zero); when the end of the file is detected, this total should be printed. Design a suitable program.

9. Extend the program of Exercise 8 as follows. First, any record in which the dollar amount is zero should not be printed. Second, you are to keep a count of the number of records having a zero dollar amount and the number having a nonzero amount; both of these counts should be printed on the final total line, together with their sum (the total number of records), and the average of the nonzero amounts (which is the total of the dollar amounts divided by the number of nonzero records).

CHAPTER 5

COBOL STRUCTURE STATEMENTS

5.1 INTRODUCTION

In Chapter 4 we introduced some of the techniques used to design COBOL programs. In particular, we looked at the basic control structures: sequence, selection, iteration, and case. In this chapter we present COBOL statements that correspond to these structures. The sequence structure, of course, requires no special statement since it represents simply the standard order in which COBOL statements are executed, but each of the other control structures has a COBOL statement that implements that structure. We shall examine each of these statements, beginning with the IF statement.

5.2 THE IF STATEMENT

The IF statement, which is very similar to the pseudocode IF structure, is used to specify that a condition is to be evaluated and to specify what is to be done for each outcome of the evaluation. The most common format of the statement is this:

```
IF  condition
       statement-1
ELSE
       statement-2.
```

In this format the *condition* is usually a test of the relationship between two items. For example, we can have IF statements with conditions like these:

```
IF HOURS-WORKED IS GREATER THAN 40.0

IF CODE-1 = '2'

IF QTY-ON-HAND IS LESS THAN REORDER-QTY
```

We shall study the possible types of relation conditions after getting an idea of the general nature of the `IF` statement.

Following the condition comes a statement of what is to be done when the condition is true. This can be any COBOL statement or group of statements. Continuing with the examples above, we might have:

```
IF HOURS-WORKED IS GREATER THAN 40
    PERFORM OVERTIME-ROUTINE
    MOVE 'X' TO OVERTIME-FLAG

IF CODE-1 = '2'
    MOVE NAME-AND-ADDRESS TO PAGE-AREA-1

IF QTY-ON-HAND IS LESS THAN REORDER-QTY
    PERFORM REORDER-ROUTINE
    MOVE ORDER-QTY TO QTY-ON-ORDER
    ADD 1 TO ORDER-RECORD-COUNT
```

Next comes the word `ELSE` followed by a statement(s) specifying what is to be done when the condition is not true. We might have:

```
IF HOURS-WORKED IS GREATER THAN 40
    PERFORM OVERTIME-ROUTINE
    MOVE 'X' TO OVERTIME-FLAG
ELSE
    PERFORM NORMAL-TIME-ROUTINE
    MOVE SPACES TO OVERTIME-FLAG.

IF CODE-1 = '2'
    MOVE NAME-AND-ADDRESS TO PAGE-AREA-1
ELSE
    MOVE NAME-AND-ADDRESS TO PAGE-AREA-2.

IF QTY-ON-HAND IS LESS THAN REORDER-QTY
    PERFORM REORDER-ROUTINE
    MOVE ORDER-QTY TO QTY-ON-ORDER
    ADD 1 TO ORDER-RECORD-COUNT
ELSE
    SUBTRACT TRANSACTION-QTY FROM QTY-ON-HAND.
```

Finally, there is a period. The position of the period is crucial! Since this format of the `IF` statement has nothing that corresponds to the ENDIF of the IF pseudocode structure, there *must* be a period at the end of the `IF` statement and there *must not* be a period anywhere else in the `IF` statement.

The general format of the `IF` statement has been shown with the components written on separate lines. Actually, the COBOL compiler will permit the parts to be written on one line if they will fit. However, we shall always write `IF` statements with their parts on different lines, with indentation of the statements that are controlled by the decision, to make the meaning of the program easier to understand. `IF` statements are of central importance in most programs, and it is worthwhile doing anything we can to make their meaning and operation as clear as possible.

Here is another example of a complete `IF` statement:

```
IF W-GROSS-PAY IS GREATER THAN W-EXEMPTION-TOTAL
    SUBTRACT W-EXEMPTION-TOTAL FROM W-GROSS-PAY
        GIVING W-TAXABLE
    MULTIPLY W-TAXABLE BY C-TAXRATE GIVING W-TAX ROUNDED
ELSE
    MOVE ZERO TO W-TAX.
```

This statement comes from a program that we shall be studying in the next chapter. It determines whether the gross pay for a worker is greater than his or her exemption. If this condition is true, then the worker has tax to pay, which we proceed to calculate with the arithmetic statements shown, and the statement shown after the **ELSE** is not executed. On the other hand, if the worker's gross pay is not greater than the exemptions, then he or she is not required to pay tax and we set the tax to zero (note the new figurative constant **ZERO**). In this case the statements before the **ELSE** are not executed.

The format of the **IF** statement is, as you have probably noticed, almost identical to that of the IF pseudocode structure. The major difference between the two is that the pseudocode IF terminates with ENDIF, while the **COBOL IF** simply terminates with a period. If the operations to be performed by the **IF** statement are complicated, then the **COBOL** code required to execute them can also become extremely complicated. In this case we can write the **IF** statement as in the following example:

```
IF HOURS-WORKED IS GREATER THAN 40
    PERFORM OVERTIME-ROUTINE
ELSE
    PERFORM NORMAL-ROUTINE.
```

There is now only one statement to be executed for the true path and only one for the false path. These happen to be **PERFORM** statements, which would call into play complete paragraphs.

Observe here the use of the **PERFORM** statement in a new form, without the **UNTIL** phrase. This means to carry out the named paragraph exactly once. The paragraphs **OVERTIME-ROUTINE** or **NORMAL-ROUTINE** might contain complex code, but by moving this code away from the **IF** statement we have achieved two results. First, we can focus our attention on designing each of the paragraphs separately, without having to worry about how one paragraph relates to the other or about how either paragraph relates to the **IF** statement. Second, we can put periods at the end of every statement in the paragraphs, which we could not do if the code were part of the **IF** statement, since the only period permitted in an **IF** statement is at the end of the statement. As we shall see in later examples, this can simplify the **COBOL** code considerably.

5.3   THE IF STATEMENT WITHOUT AN ELSE

Sometimes it happens that we have something to be done when a condition is true, but when that condition is false no other action is required. In this case we have two choices. The first is simply to omit the word **ELSE** and the statement(s) following it altogether. When the condition is true, the statement(s) will be executed and when the condition is false, they will not be.

The second choice is to write **ELSE NEXT SENTENCE**, which has exactly the same effect. Some people recommend this form as promoting clarity in complex programs. However, we shall simply omit the **ELSE** in this situation.

5.4 THE COMPLETE GENERAL FORMAT OF THE IF STATEMENT

The general format shown at the start of Section 5.2 for the **IF** is actually a condensation, for the sake of simplicity in a first look. Here is the complete general format of the statement:

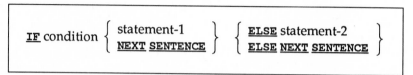

We see that **NEXT SENTENCE** may be written for the true path as well as the false path. This has little point for the kind of **IF** statement we shall be considering for the next few chapters, but is occasionally useful. Observe in this format that the choice between **ELSE** statement-2 and **ELSE NEXT SENTENCE** is in braces, not square brackets. Under the rules for general formats that were given in Chapter 3, this would seem to mean that we must pick one of the two and that we cannot omit both. The format is given this way to make it apply to the more complex **IF** statements that will be taken up later. The general format (in a reference manual) is accompanied by a statement that the words **ELSE NEXT SENTENCE** may be omitted if they immediately precede the period at the end of the sentence. Here is an example of an **IF** statement without an **ELSE** phrase:

```
IF TRANSACTION-CODE = '1'
    PERFORM ADDITION-ROUTINE.
```

Here is another example of an **IF** statement without an **ELSE**, based on the program that will be discussed in the next chapter:

```
IF I-HOURS-WORKED IS GREATER THAN 40
    SUBTRACT 40 FROM I-HOURS-WORKED GIVING W-OVERTIME-HOURS
    MULTIPLY 0.5 BY W-OVERTIME-HOURS
    MULTIPLY W-OVERTIME-HOURS BY I-PAYRATE
        GIVING W-OVERTIME-PAY ROUNDED
    ADD W-OVERTIME-PAY TO W-GROSS-PAY.
```

This says to test whether the hours-worked item is greater than 40. If so, the four statements shown are carried out; otherwise, the calculations are not carried out.

5.5 THE IMPORTANCE OF THE PERIOD IN AN IF STATEMENT

It is of crucial importance that the period of an **IF** statement appear *exactly where it is intended* because, unlike the IF pseudocode structure, the **COBOL IF** statement has nothing that corresponds to ENDIF. Suppose, for example, that in the last example we absentmindedly put a period at the end of the **SUBTRACT** statement. That would tell the **COBOL** compiler that the end of the **IF** statement had been reached. The effect would be to make the execution of the **SUBTRACT** conditional, but the two **MULTIPLY** verbs and the **ADD** would not be controlled by the **IF** and would, in fact, *always* be carried out. The pseudocode corresponding to the two different statements is shown in Figure 5.1 and Figure 5.2.

Obviously, the misplaced period destroys the intended effect of the program. This error can sometimes be rather difficult to locate. It is not possible for the compiler to flag this error, which has nothing to do with the rules of COBOL; the erroneous program would be entirely legal—it would just not do what we wanted it to do.

Leaving off the period at the end of an IF is also disastrous. This has the effect of making everything that was supposed to *follow* the IF, up to the next period, part of the IF statement. Occasionally this error will create an illegal program that can be caught by the compiler, but in most cases not. The results of this error can also be difficult to diagnose.

Similar comments apply to the period at the end of the READ statement. If there are several statements in the AT END phrase, placing a period after any except the last will remove the statement(s) after the period from control of the AT END. Omit the period following the AT END phrase, and all statements up to the next period will be part of the AT END and, therefore, will be executed only on detecting the end of the file.

It is also essential to be careful about a READ statement within an IF. The problem is that there is no way to indicate that the end of the statements in the AT END phrase has been reached other than by writing the period at the end of the sentence. What this means, in short, is that if a READ appears in an IF, everything in the rest of the sentence will be considered part of the AT END phrase of the READ. If this is not what is desired, the READ must be put into a separate paragraph and executed with a PERFORM.

```
IF the hours-worked exceeds 40 THEN
        set overtime-hours to hours-worked - 40
        multiply overtime-hours by 0.5
        set overtime-pay to overtime-hours times payrate
        add overtime-pay to gross-pay
ENDIF
```

FIGURE 5.1   Pseudocode corresponding to correct IF statement.

```
IF the hours-worked exceeds 40 THEN
        set overtime-hours to hours-worked - 40
ENDIF
multiply overtime-hours by 0.5
set overtime-pay to overtime-hours times payrate
add overtime-pay to gross-pay
```

FIGURE 5.2   Pseudocode corresponding to erroneous IF statement.

5.6   RELATION CONDITIONS

We have been using relation conditions in programming since Chapter 2, where we had a statement

```
PERFORM B010-PROCESS-WRITE-READ
     UNTIL OUT-OF-DATA-FLAG = 'YES'.
```

The part of this statement following the UNTIL is a simple example of a relation condition. (We see in this PERFORM, incidentally, that conditions appear in statements other than the IF.) Now we need to be more precise about the concept of a relation condition, which we have used intuitively so far.

The general format of a relation condition is:

$$
\left\{\begin{array}{l}\text{identifier-1}\\\text{literal-1}\\\text{arithmetic-expression-1}\end{array}\right\}\ \text{relational-operator}\ \left\{\begin{array}{l}\text{identifier-2}\\\text{literal-2}\\\text{arithmetic-expression-2}\end{array}\right\}
$$

We see that a relation condition involves a comparison between two items. The first is called the *subject* and the second the *object*. For example, in the relation condition

```
IF MORE-DATA-FLAG = 'NO'
```

MORE-DATA-FLAG is the subject, the equal sign is the relational operator, and the alphanumeric literal 'NO' is the object. Both subject and object may be either identifiers, literals, or arithmetic expressions (see Chapter 20). One combination is not permitted, however, and that is the comparison of two literals. Since literals never change value, such a relation condition would either be always true or always false, which means that it would not really be conditional. For example, the relation condition

```
IF 12 IS GREATER THAN 10
```

would always be true, making the test pointless, so this kind of comparison is not allowed.

5.7 RELATIONAL OPERATORS

There are three relational operators that may be used in forming relation conditions. These are used to determine whether the object is greater than, less than, or equal to the object. The permissible ways of writing these relational operators are shown in the following table.

Relational operator	Meaning
IS [NOT] GREATER THAN IS [NOT] >	Greater than or not greater than
IS [NOT] LESS THAN IS [NOT] <	Less than or not less than
IS [NOT] EQUAL TO IS [NOT] =	Equal to or not equal to

COBOL-85

COBOL-85 supports two additional operators:

Relational operator	Meaning
IS GREATER THAN OR EQUAL TO IS >=	Not less than
IS LESS THAN OR EQUAL TO IS <=	Not greater than

As you can see from the meaning of these new operators, they do nothing that could not be done with the older operations. They simply provide a more natural (and occasionally shorter) way of expressing certain relations.

END COBOL-85

We see that the words IS, THAN, and TO are always optional, and that the word NOT may be used if it is desired to reverse the effect of a comparison. The two forms of each relational operator are equivalent so that, for instance, we have complete freedom either to write IS GREATER THAN or the symbol >, which means the same thing. The mathematical symbols may not be familiar or comfortable to some programmers or it may be felt desirable to keep the program as close to ordinary English as possible. We shall use both forms.

Every relational operator must be preceded by and followed by a space.

5.8 THE COLLATING SEQUENCE

The comparison of numeric items determines which of two numbers is larger; this involves no new concepts. The comparison of two nonnumeric items, however, requires that we know how the computer treats such items. Is the digit 7 "more" or "less" than the letter K? Mathematically the question has no meaning, but such tests are very commonly required in data processing, and we must know how our computer operates. The question is answered by knowing the *collating sequence* for the machine; that is, the sequence in which the computer will rank characters, from smallest to largest, in a relation test.

With regard to certain types of nonnumeric comparisons, all computers work the same way. Letters of the alphabet are compared according to their ordinary alphabetic sequence; the character "blank" (space) is less than any letter. Unfortunately, however, computers are not all the same with regard to other types of nonnumeric comparisons. For instance, in some computers the numeric digits are considered to be smaller than the letters, but in others it is just the reverse. It is necessary for you to know how the particular computer you are using operates.

Almost all computers use one of two common collating sequences: ASCII (American Standard Code for Information Interchange, pronounced "AS-key"), or EBCDIC (Extended Binary-Coded-Decimal Interchange Code, pronounced "EB-cee-dick"). These collating sequences are shown in the following table, along with the most common names for the characters.

	ASCII			EBCDIC	
1.		space			space
2.	!	exclamation point	¢		cent sign
3.	"	double quote	.		period, decimal point
4.	#	number sign, pound sign	<		less-than sign
5.	$	dollar sign	(		left parenthesis
6.	%	percent sign	+		plus sign
7.	&	ampersand	|		vertical bar
8.	'	apostrophe, single quote	&		ampersand
9.	(	left parenthesis	!		exclamation point
10.	)	right parenthesis	$		dollar sign
11.	*	asterisk	*		asterisk
12.	+	plus sign	)		right parenthesis
13.	,	comma	;		semicolon
14.	-	minus sign, hyphen	¬		logical not
15.	.	period, decimal point	-		minus sign, hyphen
16.	/	slash	/		slash
17.	0-9	digits	,		comma
18.	:	colon	%		percent sign
19.	;	semicolon	_		underscore
20.	<	less-than sign	>		greater-than sign
21.	=	equal sign	?		question mark
22.	>	greater-than sign	:		colon
23.	?	question mark	#		number sign, pound sign
24.	@	at sign	@		at sign
25.	A-Z	uppercase letters	'		apostrophe, single quote
26.	[	left bracket	=		equal sign
27.	\	reverse slash, backslash	"		double quote
28.	]	right bracket	a-z		lowercase letters
29.	^	caret	A-Z		uppercase letters
30.	_	underscore	0-9		digits
31.	`	grave accent			
32.	a-z	lowercase letters			
33.	{	left brace			
34.	|	vertical bar			
35.	}	right brace			
36.	~	tilde			

These collating sequences are given in *ascending* sequence. For example, a blank (space) is smaller than any other character in either of the sequences, while the digit 9 is the largest EBCDIC character and the tilde (~) is the largest ASCII character. In general, microcomputers use ASCII characters while IBM mainframes use EBCDIC. A few mainframes and minicomputers use other characters sets, and if you use a computer that does use a different character set, you will need to obtain the collating information from an appropriate reference manual. In many applications it is not essential to know the details of the collating sequence so long as we can be assured—as we are—that any given computer will always perform comparisons the same way. In fact, in many current **COBOL** compilers (such as the Microsoft **COBOL** compiler) you can set the collating sequence to be anything you want.

It is often necessary to compare nonnumeric items that are not of the same length. When this is done, the effect is as though the shorter item had additional blanks on its right to make it the same length as the longer. This simply means that normal alphabetization rules apply. For example, the name **DAN** is considered "smaller" than the name **DANFORTH**.

5.9 CLASS CONDITIONS

The relation condition that we have presented so far is only one of four types of conditions, all of which we shall find useful. We now consider the *class condition*, which determines whether the contents of a data item are alphabetic or numeric. The general format is:

$$
\text{identifier IS [\underline{NOT}]}
\left\{
\begin{array}{l}
\underline{\text{NUMERIC}} \\
\underline{\text{ALPHABETIC}}
\end{array}
\right\}
$$

Class conditions are used primarily to test input data. The full story would get us into the question of representation of information inside the computer, which we shall consider more fully in Chapter 10; for now we will simply say that the numeric class test cannot be used with an alphabetic item (only **A**s in its **PICTURE**) and the alphabetic test cannot be used on a numeric item (only **9**s in its **PICTURE**). Either one may be used with an alphanumeric item (**X**s in its **PICTURE**).

The purpose of this test is to be sure that items that are supposed to be numeric do in fact contain only digits, and that items that are supposed to be alphabetic contain only letters. For the purpose of a class test, an item is considered to be numeric if it consists of nothing but digits. In particular, if it contains any blanks it is *not* numeric. This, in fact, is one of the most common uses of the class test: to determine whether an input item contains blanks where the user may have intended zeros. In the absence of appropriate corrective measures that we shall consider in later chapters, this condition can cause the program to abort (that is, stop unexpectedly), since arithmetic generally cannot be done on items containing blanks.

A program's exact response will vary depending on the computer and compiler being used. For example, some IBM compilers will treat blanks in a numeric item as zeros for arithmetic so long as there is not a blank in the rightmost digit position; if the entire item is blank, however, using it in arithmetic will abort the program. The Microsoft **COBOL** compiler, on the other hand, generally will treat numeric items containing blanks as though they contained zero. It is inadvisable to rely on such quirks in compilers, however. The same characteristics that allow the IBM compilers to treat most blanks as zeros also cause them to treat letters as digits, but give meaningless results if the data is used for arithmetic operations.

An item is considered to be alphabetic only if it consists of nothing but letters and spaces. Here, in other words, the character "space" is considered to be part of the alphabet. We shall have less occasion to use this test.

COBOL-85

Since **COBOL-85** recognizes the distinction between lowercase and uppercase letters, it supports two additional tests, **ALPHABETIC-LOWER** and **ALPHABETIC-UPPER**. The format for the class conditions with these additions is as shown here:

$$\text{identifier IS [\underline{NOT}]} \begin{Bmatrix} \underline{\text{NUMERIC}} \\ \underline{\text{ALPHABETIC}} \\ \underline{\text{ALPHABETIC-LOWER}} \\ \underline{\text{ALPHABETIC-UPPER}} \end{Bmatrix}$$

The **ALPHABETIC-LOWER** and **ALPHABETIC-UPPER** tests are used in the same way as the **ALPHABETIC** test. However, **ALPHABETIC-LOWER** is true only if the identifier contains nothing but "a" through "z" or blank, and **ALPHABETIC-UPPER** is true only if the identifier contains nothing but "A" through "Z" or blank. **ALPHABETIC** will accept either lowercase or uppercase.

END COBOL-85

As the formats show, any of the class condition tests may be reversed by use of the word **NOT**.

5.10 COMPOUND CONDITIONS

It often happens that we wish to combine several conditions in one test. Did the employee work more than 40 hours *and* is he or she on the weekly payroll? Is the first item *or* the second item nonnumeric?

Very complex compound conditions can be built up following rules that we shall examine later. We shall also consider at a later time how it is sometimes possible to simplify the way that compound conditions are written. For now, we restrict ourselves to just two types of compound conditions, those in which the simple conditions are connected by OR and those in which the simple conditions are connected by AND.

5.11 THE LOGICAL OPERATOR OR

A compound condition made up of two or more simple conditions connected by the logical operator OR is true if any one or more of the simple conditions is true. For example, consider this statement

```
IF      ACCOUNT-AGE IS GREATER THAN 90
        OR CREDIT-CODE = '6'
        PERFORM CREDIT-ROUTINE.
```

The true path on this IF statement (PERFORM CREDIT-ROUTINE) will be taken if either condition is true or if both are.

We shall ordinarily use indentation, as illustrated here, to align corresponding items vertically, but this is a matter of programming style, not COBOL requirements. In fact, it is permissible to write a compound condition all on one line—but at the expense of ease of understanding.

5.12 THE LOGICAL OPERATOR AND

A compound condition made up of two or more simple conditions connected by the logical operator AND is true if *all* of the simple conditions are true. For example, we might write

```
IF      HOURS-WORKED IS NUMERIC
        AND HOURS-WORKED IS LESS THAN 80
        AND HOURS WORKED IS GREATER THAN ZERO
        PERFORM NORMAL-PROCESSING
ELSE
        PERFORM HW-ERROR-PROCESSING.
```

This compound condition is true if and only if all three of the simple conditions are satisfied.

5.13 THE PERFORM...UNTIL STATEMENT

The pseudocode structure PERFORM-UNTIL is, of course, implemented in COBOL by the PERFORM...UNTIL statement. We have used this statement in several examples in preceding chapters and have discussed it in connection with these examples, so no extensive explanation is required here. However, we do wish to emphasize the fact that the condition that follows UNTIL is tested *before* the named paragraph is executed. This is very important in determining how many times a loop will be executed. For example, consider the following COBOL code, where the dots indicate other statements that do not concern us in this discussion:

```
        MOVE 1 TO COUNT.
        PERFORM B010-PROCESS
            UNTIL COUNT = 10.
            .
            .
            .

    B010-PROCESS.
        ACCEPT WORK-DATA.
        DISPLAY COUNT  '.  '  WORK-DATA.
        ADD 1 TO COUNT.
```

Paragraph **B010-PROCESS** will be executed *nine* times, not ten. When **COUNT** becomes equal to ten after execution of the **ADD** statement, the **PERFORM** statement finishes execution of **B010-PROCESS**, then tests the **UNTIL** condition to determine whether to execute the paragraph again. Since this happens *before* the tenth execution of **B010-PROCESS**, the loop terminates before the tenth execution of the paragraph.

If you have any question in your mind about how this works, try it out with paper and pencil. Make one column to show the current value of **COUNT** and one column to count the number of times **B010-PROCESS** has been executed. Mark down the initial value of **COUNT** in the first column, then trace through the code, following the sequence of steps the computer would take in executing the loop. Each time you enter **B010-PROCESS** make a mark in the second column, and each time you get to the **ADD** statement write down the new value of **COUNT** in the first column. This technique of "playing computer" can be a very useful tool in trying to understand exactly what a program is doing as loops execute. One useful tactic: test that the loop works correctly for zero executions and for one execution; if it does, you have greatly increased your confidence that it will work correctly for any other number of executions.

In any case, it is absolutely essential that you know exactly how many times any loop will be executed. One good building block is to be positive that you understand clearly how the **PERFORM** statement works.

5.14 THE CASE STRUCTURE

Most versions of **COBOL** have no statement that corresponds directly to the CASE structure. However, we can accomplish the same results using other **COBOL** statements. Although there are several ways in which this can be done, the simplest makes use of what is called a *nested* **IF**. This refers to an **IF** statement in which the statement following **ELSE** is itself an **IF** statement. The appropriate format can best be demonstrated by means of an example.

Suppose we are designing part of a payroll system for a company whose employees work in one of four departments. As part of the payroll reporting, we want to determine how much of the total payroll is to be charged to each department. Therefore, after we have computed the gross pay for an employee we will add the amount to a total for the department in which the employee works. The pseudocode for this process is as follows:

```
EVALUATE department number
    WHEN 1
        add gross pay to dept-1-total
    WHEN 2
        add gross pay to dept-2-total
    WHEN 3
        add gross pay to dept-3-total
    WHEN 4
        add gross pay to dept-4-total
    OTHERWISE
        the department number is in error
ENDEVALUATE
```

COBOL code to implement this structure looks like the following:

```
IF      DEPT-NBR = 1
    ADD GROSS-PAY TO DEPT-1-TOTAL
ELSE IF DEPT-NBR = 2
    ADD GROSS-PAY TO DEPT-2-TOTAL
ELSE IF DEPT-NBR = 3
    ADD GROSS-PAY TO DEPT-3-TOTAL
ELSE IF DEPT-NBR = 4
    ADD GROSS-PAY TO DEPT-4-TOTAL
ELSE
    PERFORM X100-DEPT-NBR-ERROR.
```

Observe the structure of this example carefully. What we have done is to insert an **IF** statement as the action to be executed in the false path of another **IF** statement, and repeat this process of nesting the **IF** statements for each additional case. The condition of each **IF** statement tests the CASE variable against a different value, and the final **ELSE** takes care of the **OTHERWISE** action. We can also write a compound condition if two or more case values require the same action, as in the following example:

```
IF      DEPT-NBR = 1 OR DEPT-NBR = 2
    ADD GROSS-PAY TO DEPT-1-2-TOTAL
ELSE IF DEPT-NBR = 3
    ADD GROSS-PAY TO DEPT-3-TOTAL
ELSE IF DEPT-NBR > 3 AND DEPT-NBR < 100
    ADD GROSS-PAY TO OTHER-TOTAL
ELSE
    PERFORM X100-DEPT-NBR-ERROR.
```

In general, nested **IF** statements tend to be a source of trouble in COBOL and must be used with care. However, they do provide a simple way of implementing the case structure if you are careful to follow two rules:

1. Use the conditional phrase after an **IF** only to test values for the case variable, such as "IF DEPT-NBR = 1 OR DEPT-NBR = 2".
2. Use only simple, unconditional statements for the case actions. In particular, *never* use an **IF** statement for one of the action statements. If it is necessary to execute an **IF** statement as part of a case action, set up a separate paragraph and use the case action to **PERFORM** the paragraph.

We will discuss the use of nested **IF** statements again in Chapter 8. For now, we will restrict the use of the nested **IF** to implementation of the CASE structure.

COBOL-85

5.15 END STATEMENTS IN COBOL-85

Up to this point, although we have presented some new features of COBOL-85, the differences between COBOL-85 and earlier versions of COBOL have been relatively minor. With the introduction of structure statements, however, we encounter enhancements that are perhaps the *major* difference between COBOL-85 and its predecessors.

We mentioned before that although the conditional structure terminates with an ENDIF, COBOL has no such statement to terminate the IF statement. What we have not emphasized, however, is how serious a problem this can be. For example, consider the following pseudocode:

```
set counter to 0
PERFORM-UNTIL counter = 10
    IF rec-code = 'A'
            read data record; at end set flag to 'Y'
            add 1 to counter
            process the record
    ENDIF
ENDPERFORM
```

You might be tempted to use this code to implement this specification:

```
MOVE ZERO TO COUNTER.
PERFORM B010-PROCESS
    UNTIL COUNTER = 10.
.
.
.
B010-PROCESS.
    IF REC-CODE = 'A'
        READ DATA-FILE
            AT END MOVE 'Y' TO FLAG
        ADD 1 TO COUNTER
        PERFORM C050-PROCESS-RECORD.
```

Unfortunately, as we indicated in Section 5.5, this would produce an error. The program would continue to execute B010-PROCESS until the end of file was reached, then would keep on executing the paragraph causing an error when the computer tried to read the nonexistent records following the end of the file. The problem is that the IF statement cannot contain a period until the end of the statement, and the AT END clause does not terminate *until* a period is encountered. Therefore, COUNTER is incremented only when the AT END phrase is executed. Furthermore, C050-PROCESS-RECORD will not be executed for any record until the end of file is reached, since it is part of the AT END clause.

This type of problem occurs frequently in older versions of COBOL and has no clean solution. COBOL-85, however, introduces END phrases to terminate statements such as IF and PERFORM, and to terminate phrases such as the AT END phrase in the READ statement. The use of these END phrases is always optional, so any code we have shown up to now is still valid in COBOL-85. However, there are situations where the use of an END phrase can clarify and simplify your program.

5.16 THE READ STATEMENT WITH END-READ

The problem we encountered trying to implement the previous example occurred because we had no way of terminating the AT END phrase of the READ statement without also terminating the entire IF statement. In COBOL-85 we can write the paragraph as follows:

```
B010-PROCESS.
    IF REC-CODE = 'A'
        READ DATA-FILE
            AT END MOVE 'Y' TO FLAG
        END-READ
        ADD 1 TO COUNTER
        PERFORM C050-PROCESS-RECORD.
```

This is an accurate implementation of the pseudocode specification given for the problem. The COBOL compiler can tell that the AT END action terminates with the END-READ phrase, and executes the ADD statement regardless of whether or not the end of file has been reached. This new feature of the READ statement is very useful in implementing certain types of programs. It is typical of the END phrases in COBOL-85 in that it allows you to specify clearly where a conditional statement or phrase ends and the next statement begins.

5.17 THE ARITHMETIC VERBS WITH END PHRASES

Just as the READ statement has a conditional phrase, AT END, so the arithmetic statements (ADD, SUBTRACT, MULTIPLY, and DIVIDE) have a conditional phrase, the ON SIZE ERROR phrase. As you might expect, COBOL-85 has an END phrase for each of these statements. For example, we can change the previous example to the following:

```
B010-PROCESS.
    IF REC-CODE = 'A'
        READ DATA-FILE
            AT END MOVE 'Y' TO FLAG
        END-READ
        ADD 1 TO COUNTER
            ON SIZE ERROR MOVE 'Y' TO ERROR-FLAG
        END-ADD
        PERFORM C050-PROCESS-RECORD.
```

In this example, the program will read a record from DATA-FILE, add 1 to COUNTER, then perform C050-PROCESS-RECORD. If the end of the file is encountered in the READ, FLAG is set to 'Y'. If a size error is detected as a result of the ADD, ERROR-FLAG is set to 'Y'. In any case, however, all three statements are executed any time REC-CODE is equal to 'A'.

Just as there is the END-ADD phrase for the ADD statement, so there is END-SUBTRACT, END-MULTIPLY, and END-DIVIDE for the other arithmetic statements. Their formats are very similar to that of the ADD and END-ADD and, although we will demonstrate the use of these END-STATEMENTS in future examples, we will not show the complete formats here.

5.18 THE IF STATEMENT WITH END-IF

The format of the IF statement in COBOL-85 is as follows.

$$
\text{\underline{IF} condition-1 THEN}
\left\{
\begin{array}{l}
\{\text{statement-1}\}\ \dots \\
\text{\underline{NEXT} \underline{SENTENCE}}
\end{array}
\right\}
\left\{
\begin{array}{l}
\text{\underline{ELSE}} \ \{\text{statement-2}\}\ \dots\ [\text{\underline{END-IF}}] \\
\text{\underline{ELSE} \underline{NEXT} \underline{SENTENCE}} \\
\text{\underline{END-IF}}
\end{array}
\right\}
$$

The major difference between this format of the IF statement and the format shown in Section 5.4 is the addition of the END-IF phrase. This enhancement of the IF statement makes its structure identical to that of the pseudocode IF structure, which greatly improves the flexibility and readability of the statement. The use of END-IF delimits the scope of all statements within the IF very clearly, and makes it easier to change a program without causing errors. The real advantage of this capability comes when we use nested IF statements for something other than implementing the case structure. However, we will defer detailed discussion of the nested IF until Chapter 8.

There is one more change in the COBOL-85 version of the IF statement, the word THEN after the condition. Since the THEN is not underlined, it is not required and, in fact, has no effect on the meaning of the IF statement. However, some programmers feel that its use improves the readability of the IF statement. We will generally not use THEN in an IF statement, if only to maintain compatibility with earlier versions of COBOL.*

5.19 THE PERFORM STATEMENT WITH END-PERFORM

Frequently, when you design a program, you will specify a module that, in addition to other statements, contains a simple iteration specification. When this is implemented in COBOL, however, it has always been necessary to create a separate paragraph because the PERFORM statement would execute only named paragraphs. With the addition of the END-PERFORM phrase in COBOL-85, it is now possible to execute many loops "in-line," without creating a new paragraph. For example, consider the following pseudocode specification:

```
set counter to zero
PERFORM-UNTIL counter = 10
    add 1 to counter
    display counter on screen
ENDPERFORM
```

In COBOL-85 we can implement this as

```
MOVE ZERO TO COUNTER.
PERFORM UNTIL COUNTER = 10
    ADD 1 TO COUNTER
    DISPLAY COUNTER
END-PERFORM.
```

* *Some* earlier versions of COBOL accept the use of THEN in the IF statement, but this is by no means universal.

There are two restrictions on the use of the END-PERFORM. First, you cannot specify the name of a paragraph to be performed (between PERFORM and UNTIL) *and* specify in-line code and END-PERFORM as well. You must choose one or the other. Second, if you use in-line code, the END-PERFORM phase is *not* optional.

5.20   THE EVALUATE STATEMENT

In addition to improving the control structure of COBOL by adding the END phrases, COBOL-85 has added a new statement that implements the case structure directly instead of through other statements. This new statement is the EVALUATE statement (hence the name for our pseudocode structure), and a simplified version of its format is as shown.

```
EVALUATE  { identifier-1  }
          { expression-1  }

  {       { TRUE                                                                              }
  {       { FALSE                                                                             }
  { WHEN  {        { identifier-2            }  { THROUGH } { identifier-3            }        }
  {       { [NOT]  { literal-2               }  { THRU    } { literal-3               }        }
  {       {        { arithmetic-expression-1 }             { arithmetic-expression-2 }        }

       imperative-statement-1  }  ...

  [WHEN OTHER imperative-statement-2]  [END-EVALUATE]
```

Even this version of the EVALUATE statement, which is simplified considerably over the complete statement, is quite a bit to handle, so let's look at a few examples to see what this really means. The COBOL statements that correspond to the examples of the EVALUATE pseudocode structure in Section 4.6 (page 72) are shown in Figures 5.3 and 5.4.

These examples of the EVALUATE statement show how the statement is used much more clearly than does the statement format. In both examples, we have specified an identifier after the word EVALUATE; this is the *selection*

```
EVALUATE DIST-FROM-TOWN
    WHEN 0 THRU 5
        MOVE 7.50 TO FEE
    WHEN 5 THRU 10
        MOVE 10.00 TO FEE
    WHEN OTHER
        MOVE DIST-FROM-TOWN TO FEE
END-EVALUATE.
```

FIGURE 5.3 EVALUATE statement corresponding to first CASE example in Chapter 4.

```
EVALUATE QUIZ-GRADE
    WHEN 10
        MOVE 'EXCELLENT' TO CLASS-STANDING
    WHEN 8 THRU 9
        MOVE 'ABOVE-AVERAGE' TO CLASS-STANDING
    WHEN 5 THRU 7
        MOVE 'AVERAGE' TO CLASS-STANDING
    WHEN 3 THRU 4
        MOVE 'BELOW-AVERAGE' TO CLASS-STANDING
    WHEN OTHER
        MOVE 'FAILING' TO CLASS-STANDING
END-EVALUATE.
```

FIGURE 5.4 **EVALUATE** statement corresponding to second CASE example in Chapter 4.

subject. Following each occurrence of **WHEN** we have specified either a single value or a range of values; these are the *selection objects*. The program computes the current value of the selection subject, then compares it to each of the selection objects in turn. If the value of the selection subject matches the value(s) specified by a selection object, then the statement following the selection object is executed. (Of course, although these examples show only one imperative statement for each selection object, you can have a series of imperative statements just as in **PERFORM**.) If no selection object matches the value of the selection subject, the **WHEN OTHER** statement is executed. If no **WHEN OTHER** phrase is specified, the **EVALUATE** statement causes no action. In any case, no more than *one* **WHEN** statement will be executed. If more than one selection object would match the value of the selection subject, only the statement following the *first* selection subject to make the match is executed.

Notice that the format of the **EVALUATE** statement includes the words **TRUE** and **FALSE**. These are two new reserved words whose values match the values that can be taken by a conditional expression such as "**AMOUNT > 1000**". **TRUE** and **FALSE** are *not* general purpose constants and may *not* be used in any statement except **EVALUATE**. The following example shows how these values might be used.

```
EVALUATE DIST-FROM-TOWN > 10
    WHEN TRUE
        MULTIPLY DIST-FROM-TOWN BY 2 GIVING FEE
    WHEN FALSE
        MOVE 12.50 TO FEE
END-EVALUATE.
```

Of course, this example could also be written as

```
IF DIST-FROM-TOWN > 10
    MULTIPLY DIST-FROM-TOWN BY 2 GIVING FEE
ELSE
    MOVE 12.50 TO FEE
END-IF.
```

Rather than going through more examples here, we shall wait to demonstrate the use of **EVALUATE** and the other **COBOL-85** enhancements throughout the following chapters.

END COBOL-85

REVIEW QUESTIONS

1. What is the function of the period in the `IF` statement?

2. What does `NEXT SENTENCE` accomplish?

3. What happens if you omit the `ELSE` part of an `IF` statement? Will you get an error?

4. Is there more than one category of condition?

5. What is the function of the relation condition?

6. List the relational operators. Your answer will depend on whether or not you are using `COBOL-85`. Give the answer for your version.

7. What is the collating sequence of a computer? What is its function?

8. What will these statements do?

   a.
   ```
   PERFORM NORMAL-SALE
        UNTIL  COLUMN-1 = '6'
           OR COLUMN-2 = '7'
           OR COLUMN-7 = 'A'.
   ```

   b.
   ```
   PERFORM LO-EQUAL-ROUTINE
        UNTIL KEY-1 > PREVIOUS-KEY-1.
           OR TRANS-EOF = 'Y'
   ```

   c.
   ```
   READ TRANSACTION-FILE
        AT END WRITE MESSAGE-RECORD-5
              MOVE 'Y' TO TRANSACTION-EOF-FLAG.
   ```

   d.
   ```
   READ TRANSACTION-FILE
        AT END WRITE MESSAGE-RECORD-5.
              MOVE 'Y' TO TRANSACTION-EOF-FLAG.
   ```

9. Point out any errors in syntax in the following `IF` statements, that is, any violations of the rules for writing legal `COBOL` statements, without regard for what the statements might mean.

   a.
   ```
   IF A = B
        WRITE EQUAL-RECORD.
   ELSE
        WRITE UNEQUAL-RECORD.
   ```

   b.
   ```
   IF HOURS-WORKED IS GREATER THAN 40
        SUBTRACT 40 FROM HOURS-WORKED GIVING OT-HOURS
        MULTIPLY 0.5 BY OT-HOURS.
        ADD OT-HOURS TO HOURS-WORKED.
   ```

   c.
   ```
   IF 24.0 GREATER THAN 37.0
        MOVE 'STRANGE' TO COMMENT-1.
   ```

   d.
   ```
   IF A IS LESS THAN B MOVE X TO Y ELSE
   MOVE X TO Z.
   ```

   e.
   ```
   IF ON-HAND IS
                        LESS            THAN
   REORDER-POINT ADD 1 TO ORDER-COUNT MOVE REORDER-QTY TO
   RECORD-AREA-6 WRITE ORDER-RECORD
   ELSE
        WRITE NORMAL-LINE.
   ```

10. Name two figurative constants.

11. Each record in a payroll file is supposed to contain either a **c**, an **H**, or an **s** in field 8. Any other character would give erroneous results. Would the following **IF** statement correctly check for the possibility of error?

```
IF      FIELD8 IS NOT EQUAL TO 'C'
    OR FIELD8 IS NOT EQUAL TO 'H'
    OR FIELD8 IS NOT EQUAL TO 'S'
    PERFORM X100-BAD-FIELD8.
```

12. Given the following code, how many records would be written to the output file?

```
        MOVE 1 TO COUNT.
        PERFORM D010-WRITE
            UNTIL COUNT = 100.
        .
        .
        .

   D010-WRITE.
        WRITE OUTPUT-RECORD.
        ADD 1 TO COUNT.
```

13. How many records would this code write to the output file?

```
        MOVE 1 TO COUNT.
        PERFORM D010-WRITE
            UNTIL COUNT = 100.
        .
        .
        .

   D010-WRITE.
        WRITE OUTPUT-RECORD.
        ADD 2 TO COUNT.
```

ANSWERS TO REVIEW QUESTIONS

1. The period marks the end of the **IF** statement. If you omit the period, everything following the **IF** statement becomes part of the **IF** statement.

2. It does nothing, which sometimes is precisely what you want to do. For example, if you want to perform some action if the **IF** condition is false but do nothing if the condition is true, writing **NEXT SENTENCE** for the "true action" will produce the result you need.

3. Omitting the **ELSE** part of an **IF** statement will certainly not cause an error. It simply means that if the condition is false, you don't want the computer to do anything.

4. Yes. So far we have encountered the *class* condition and the *relation* condition. Eventually we shall study four categories of conditions.

5. The relation condition compares two values. These values may be identifiers, literals, or arithmetic expressions (but you can not compare two literals).

6. The relational operators are:

```
IS GREATER THAN                     >
IS NOT GREATER THAN                 NOT >
IS LESS THAN                        <
IS NOT LESS THAN                    NOT <
IS EQUAL TO                         =
IS NOT EQUAL TO                     NOT =
```

If you are using **COBOL-85**, you also have

```
IS GREATER THAN OR EQUAL TO         >=
IS LESS THAN OR EQUAL TO            <=
```

7. The collating sequence of a computer is the order in which it will rank characters in a comparison. It is used to determine the value of a comparison in a relation condition.

8. a. The paragraph named **NORMAL-SALE** will be performed repeatedly until any one or more of the relations shown is true.

   b. If the program could be compiled, the paragraph named **LO-EQUAL-ROUTINE** would be performed until **KEY-1** is greater than **PREVIOUS-KEY-1**; but the period at the end of this relation, which presumably is not intended, makes the next line illegal. No **COBOL** statement begins with **OR**.

   c. A record from the file named **TRANSACTION-FILE** is read. If this is the end of file, two statements are carried out, writing a message and setting the flag.

   d. A record from the file named **TRANSACTION-FILE** is read. If this is the end of file, a message is written. Unconditionally, the end of file flag is set. Presumably the extra period after the first relation is unintended, but the resulting sequence of statements is completely legal from the standpoint of the **COBOL** rules. The end of file flag will be set after reading the first record, and succeeding statements will presumably stop program execution before processing the first record. *The compiler could not give any warning!*

9. a. A statement beginning with the word **IF** and ending with the first period is syntactically legal. However, the first period makes the material beginning with **ELSE** syntactically illegal.

   b. Presumably the period at the end of the **MULTIPLY** is unintended, but there are no syntactic errors here. The **SUBTRACT** and the **MULTIPLY** would be conditional but the **ADD** would always be performed.

   c. A relation condition may not compare two literals.

   d. This is syntactically legal according to the rules of **COBOL**. The fact that the **IF** statement is written on two lines instead of four violates the programming standards followed in this text, but no **COBOL** rules are broken.

   e. This also contains no syntactic errors. The point here is to demonstrate how very difficult it can be to read programs that do not follow sensible conventions about the form in which statements are written.

10. SPACES, ZERO.

11. X100-BAD-FIELDS would *always* be performed. FIELD8 cannot possibly be equal to all three of C, H, and S on any one record, so at least two of the simple conditions connected by the ORs would always be true. This error, which is very common, is probably the result of confusion between the rather loose usage of the words "and" and "or" in English usage and the very precise way the logical operators AND and OR are used in COBOL.

The desired result can be obtained by replacing the ORs in the statement with ANDs, or perhaps more understandably, writing

```
IF    FIELD8 IS EQUAL TO 'C'
   OR FIELD8 IS EQUAL TO 'H'
   OR FIELD8 IS EQUAL TO 'S'
      NEXT SENTENCE
ELSE
      PERFORM X100-BAD-FIELD8.
```

12. 99. Since the UNTIL condition is tested *before* D010-WRITE is executed, the 100th record is never written. A better way to write this type of code is to change the first line to

```
MOVE ZERO TO COUNT
```

This makes COUNT a count of how many records have actually been written, rather than having it indicate which record is *going* to be written.

13. The code would continue forever (or until some other condition terminated the program). COUNT is initially set equal to 1, and since the paragraph adds 2 each time it is executed, COUNT always has an odd value. Therefore, it will never be equal to 100, which is even. The point is that you must be very careful when designing a loop that it is always possible to reach the termination condition.

EXERCISES

*1. Write statements to carry out the following operations.

a. Add 1 to an item named LEGAL-ADULT if AGE is 18 or greater.

b. Perform a paragraph named D050-PROCESS-STOCK-ITEM if PART-1-A contains the letter S.

c. Add 1 to BIG if SIZE-A is greater than 800 and add 1 to LITTLE if SIZE-A is less than or equal to 800.

d. If the item in NAME-A is greater than the item in NAME-B, move the contents of NAME-A to TEMPORARY; if the item in NAME-A is less than the item in NAME-B, move the contents of NAME-B to TEMPORARY; if the two are equal, move either of them to TEMPORARY.

e. If the value of the item named HOURS-WORKED is *anything but* 40, perform C035-NON-STANDARD.

f. Perform the paragraph named X020-BAD-CODE if CODE-X contains anything but digits.

* Answers to starred exercises will be found in Appendix IV at the end of the book.

2. Write statements to carry out the following operations.

   a. Add 1 to an item named **MAJOR-BILLING** if **ACCOUNT-TOTAL** is greater than 1000.00.

   b. Determine whether the value of the item named **FINAL-BILL** is greater than 999.99 and, if so, perform the paragraph named **D035-SPECIAL-APPROVAL**.

   c. If the item named **CODE-A** contains the characters **AB47Z**, move the characters **APPROVED** to the item named **APPROVAL**.

   d. Move zero to **SIGNAL** if **MEASUREMENT** is zero, and move 1 to **SIGNAL** if **MEASUREMENT** is not zero.

   e. Perform the paragraph named **C055-REGULAR** if the value of **HOURS-WORKED** is exactly 40.0.

   f. Perform the paragraph named **Y030-BAD-CODE** if **CODE-A** contains anything but letters and spaces.

*3. Given the appropriate Data Division entries, write statements that will move either **REORDER-QTY** or zero to **ORDER-AMOUNT**, depending on whether the sum of **ON-HAND** and **ON-ORDER** has or has not fallen below **REORDER-POINT**.

4. Three examination grades are named **GRADE-1**, **GRADE-2**, and **GRADE-3**. The three are to be added and their sum divided by 3, giving the average grade. If the average grade is 65 or greater, the word **PASS** is to be placed in the item named **FINAL-GRADE**; otherwise the word **FAIL** is to be placed in **FINAL-GRADE**. Write appropriate statements.

*5. Suppose that a salesperson's commission is based on a **PRODUCT-CODE**, as follows:

PRODUCT-CODE	Commission Formula
1	0.15 × SALE-PRICE
2	0.40 × (SALE-PRICE - BASE-PRICE)
3	0.10 × BASE-PRICE + 0.50 × (SALE-PRICE - BASE-PRICE)
4	$10.00 + 0.05 × BASE-PRICE
5	$35.00

Given **PRODUCT-CODE**, **SALE-PRICE**, and **BASE-PRICE**, write statements to compute **COMMISSION**. If **PRODUCT-CODE** is anything except 1, 2, 3, 4, or 5, move zero to **COMMISSION** and move **X** to **BAD-PRODUCT-CODE-FLAG**.

6. Given **ANNUAL-EARNING**, write statements that will compute **TAX** according to the following table.

ANNUAL-EARNINGS	TAX
Not over $5000	Zero
Over $5000 but not over $15,000	2% of the amount over $5000
Over $15,000	$200 plus 5% of the amount over $15,000

Exercises 7 - 12 all require you to write programs. In each of these exercises the data used by the program is presented in terms of an input data file. However, we recommend that you try writing each program twice, once using a data file as described in the problem, and once using **ACCEPT** and **DISPLAY** statements. That is, use **DISPLAY** statements to write prompts to the computer screen, and use **ACCEPT** statements to read the data from the keyboard. Use the style we have shown in previous chapters; do not simply **ACCEPT** a formatted data record.

*7. Each record in a data file has the following format:

Columns 1-20	Name
Columns 21-25	Blank
Columns 26-27	Years of service

Write a program to read the data file, print the data from each record and, if the years of service are greater than 40, write the comment **AN ABC COMPANY VETERAN**.

8. Each record in a data file has the following format:

Columns 1-5	Cost center code
Columns 6-11	Budgeted expense, dollars
Columns 12-17	Actual expense, year to date, dollars

Write a program that will read such a file and, for each record, print a line giving the input data together with a comment **EXCEEDS BUDGET** if the actual expense is greater than the budgeted amount.

*9. Each record in a data file contains an alphanumeric identification in columns 45-50 and a gross pay in dollars and cents in columns 70-76. A city tax is to be computed for each, the tax being 2% of the amount (if any) over $2000. For each record, a line is to be printed containing the input data and the computed tax. Write a suitable program.

10. Each record in a data file contains an alphanumeric identification in columns 40-47 and a total price in columns 31-36 in dollars and cents. For each record a discount is to be computed and printed, along with the input data. The discount is 2% if the amount is over $1000, and zero if it is not. Write a suitable program.

*11. Read a file whose records have the following format:

Columns 1-8	IDENT	Alphanumeric
Columns 9-15	DOLLARS	9(5)V99
Columns 16-80	OTHER-INFO	Alphanumeric

The contents of each record are to be listed with three blanks between fields. The amount in the DOLLARS field from each record should be added to a total (that is initially set to zero); when the end of the file is detected, this total should be printed.

If you read data using an **ACCEPT** statement, enter only **IDENT** and **DOLLARS**; do not bother with **OTHER-INFO**.

12. Extend the program of Exercise 11 as follows. First, any record in which the dollar amount is zero should not be printed. Second, keep a count of the number of records having a zero dollar amount and the number having a nonzero amount; both of these counts should be printed on the final total line, together with their sum (the total number of records), and the average of the nonzero amounts (which is the total of the dollar amounts divided by the number of nonzero records).

13. (This exercise extends the project-level Exercise 19 in Chapter 3.)
Assume that the inventory record has been modified as follows:

Columns 1-5	product code
Columns 6-30	product description
Columns 31-35	sales for three weeks ago
Columns 36-40	sales for two weeks ago
Columns 41-45	sales for last week
Columns 46-50	inventory level
Columns 51-57	selling price in dollars and cents
Columns 58-62	standard inventory level

The standard inventory level for a product is the ideal number of units that the company would like to have in stock for that product. (This may be changed at any time by management, such as for seasonal products.) If a product's inventory level has fallen below the standard level, then the company needs to order more of the product from their supplier. The quantity to be ordered is determined by the following function:

reorder qty = predicted sales + (standard level - inventory)

where "predicted sales" is the sales predicted for the following week (see Exercise 3.19), "standard level" is the standard inventory level for the product, and "inventory" is the current inventory level for the product.

Modify the program of Exercise 3.19 so that if the inventory level of a product has fallen below the standard inventory level, the program will calculate the quantity to be ordered and print a message on the report. The message should consist of the word REORDER, followed by a single space, then the reorder quantity. The standard inventory level should also be printed, between the columns for current inventory and selling price. Here is a sample of the revised report:.

Prod Code	Product Description	3 wk Sales	2 wk Sales	Last week Sales	Curr Inv	Std Inv	Product Price	F'cst Sales	Product Value	
AA123	SNOW BLOWER	00002	00000	00005	00022	00025	00299.95	00003	0006598.90	REORDER 00006
BB345	LAWN CHAIR	01050	02577	00933	09515	08500	00017.50	01501	0166512.50	
	AVERAGE VALUE								0086555.70	

14. (This exercise is suitable for a small project.)
Write a program that uses records in a payroll file to produce a payroll report. The payroll records have the following format:

Column 1	not used
Column 2-6	employee number
Column 7-11	department number
Column 12-17	not used
Column 18-21	hours worked; numeric, 2 decimals
Column 22-25	base pay rate; numeric, 2 decimals
Column 26-27	municipality code

For each employee compute the employee's gross pay as hours worked times base pay rate for the first 37.5 hours, then base rate times 1.5 times hours worked in excess of 37.5 hours. For example, if an employee worked 41.50 hours with a base pay rate of $10.00 the gross pay would be $435.00 ($375 for the first 37.5 hours, plus $60 for the remaining 4 hours).

In addition to computing the employee's gross pay you are to compute the employee's deductions. Deductions consist of federal tax (25% of gross pay), state tax (5% of gross pay), and city tax. City tax varies depending on where the employee lives; this is coded in the "municipality code" field. Using the municipality code, city tax is calculated as follows:

Municipality	Tax
03	1.50% of gross pay
07	2.00%
15	5.25%
23	3.75%
77	2.50%

The employee's net pay is the gross pay minus the sum of all deductions. Print a report showing the following information for each employee:

Column 1-5	employee number
Column 8-12	hours worked
Column 15-19	base pay rate
Column 22-28	gross pay
Column 31-37	federal tax
Column 40-45	state tax
Column 48-53	city tax
Column 56-62	net pay

All decimal fields should show the actual decimal point.

CHAPTER 6

A SIMPLE PAYROLL PROGRAM

6.1 INTRODUCTION

In the preceding chapters we showed how to design a program, then introduced the COBOL statements that implement the basic control structures. It is now time to see these tools used in a complete program. We shall design an illustrative program, then show code that implements the design. Finally, we shall make some revisions to the program, first changing the design specifications, then changing the program.

6.2 REQUIREMENTS OF THE PROGRAM

The function of the program is to accept payroll data for workers in a company. We are required to compute the gross pay, tax, and net pay for each worker and to print a line for each. The basic program structure—that is, a main line routine and a performed paragraph that is executed for each record—is the same as in previous chapters. However, within the performed paragraph we shall perform lower-level paragraphs to carry out details, and shall have IF statements that determine whether there is overtime pay to be calculated and whether the worker has any taxable income.

The input to the program consists of five pieces of information for each employee:

1. payroll number (5 alphanumeric characters);
2. name (20 alphanumeric characters);
3. hours worked to tenths (three digits);
4. hourly pay rate with three decimals (five digits);
5. number of dependents (two digits).

For each employee we are required to carry out the following calculations. The number of hours worked is to be multiplied by the pay rate, giving gross pay. If the person worked more than 40 hours, time-and-a-half is to be paid for hours over 40. The employee is allowed an exemption of $50.00 for each dependent; if the gross pay is greater than the total of the exemptions, a tax of 21% is assessed against the taxable amount (the difference between gross pay and the total of exemptions). A line is to be printed for each employee, giving all of the input data and calculated results. The format in which the results are to be presented may be seen in the sample output in Figure 6.4.

6.3 DESIGNING THE PROGRAM

We begin the design process by determining what the major functions of the program are. The basic function of the program is to *produce payroll calculations*. This can be accomplished if we can *calculate the payroll for one employee*, then do this repeatedly for all employees. Based on the program requirements given in Section 6.2, we have the following functions that must be performed for an employee:

1. Get payroll data for one employee;
2. Compute gross pay (including overtime pay);
3. Compute exemptions;
4. Compute tax;
5. Compute net pay;
6. Print output line.

From these functions we can produce the hierarchy chart that is shown in Figure 6.1. You may wish to add modules to open and close the files, subordinate to the main module.

The next design step is to write pseudocode specifications for each module. These are shown in Figure 6.2.

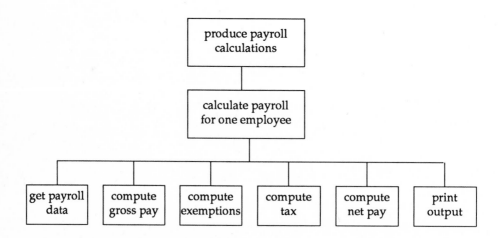

FIGURE 6.1 Hierarchy chart for a payroll program.

PRODUCE PAYROLL CALCULATIONS:
open file(s)
set payroll-number to zero
get payroll data for one employee
PERFORM-UNTIL payroll-number = 99999
    calculate payroll for employee
    get payroll data for one employee
ENDPERFORM
close file(s)

CALCULATE PAYROLL FOR EMPLOYEE:
compute gross-pay
compute exemptions
compute tax
compute net pay
print output line

GET PAYROLL DATA FOR ONE EMPLOYEE:
get payroll-number
IF payroll-number is not equal to 99999 THEN
    get employee-name
    get hours-worked
    get pay-rate
    get number-dependents
ENDIF

COMPUTE GROSS PAY:
gross-pay = hours-worked x pay-rate
IF hours-worked is greater than 40 THEN
    overtime-hours = hours-worked - 40
    multiply overtime-hours by 0.5
    overtime-pay = overtime-hours x pay-rate
    add overtime-pay to gross-pay
ENDIF

COMPUTE EXEMPTIONS:
exemptions = 50.00 x number-dependents

COMPUTE TAX:
IF gross-pay is greater than exemptions THEN
    tax = 0.21 x (gross-pay - exemptions)
ELSE
    tax = 0
ENDIF

COMPUTE NET PAY:
net-pay = gross-pay - tax

PRINT OUTPUT LINE:
move payroll-number, employee-name, hours-worked, pay-rate,
        number-dependents, gross-pay, tax, and net-pay
        to output-record
print output-record

FIGURE 6.2 Pseudocode specifications for a payroll program.

We must emphasize that it is *not* necessary to go into this level of detail when designing most programs. Most of the modules defined in Figure 6.2 will be implemented by only one or two lines of **COBOL** and can certainly be written in-line, without creating a separate paragraph for each module. In fact, *all* of the modules on the bottom level of the hierarchy chart can be implemented as in-line code (see Exercise 6.3). However, we will show each module as a separate paragraph in the program to emphasize the modularity and the relationship between the hierarchy chart and the final program.

Observe that the higher level modules emphasize control of execution and the overall logic of the program, while the lower level modules show the details of computation. This division of activity is common in most programs. In the higher levels we concentrate on *when* things are done, and leave the details of *how* they are done for lower levels. The payroll program itself is shown in Figure 6.3.

```
1          IDENTIFICATION DIVISION.
2          PROGRAM-ID.
3              PAYROLL1.
4          DATE-WRITTEN.
5              SEPTEMBER 9, 1988.
6
7          ENVIRONMENT DIVISION.
8          INPUT-OUTPUT SECTION.
9          FILE-CONTROL.
10             SELECT REPORT-FILE          ASSIGN TO 'C06P01.REP'.
11
12         DATA DIVISION.
13         FILE SECTION.
14         FD  REPORT-FILE
15             LABEL RECORDS ARE STANDARD.
16         01  REPORT-RECORD.
17             05  O-PAYROLL-NUMBER    PIC X(5).
18             05  FILLER              PIC XX.
19             05  O-NAME              PIC X(20).
20             05  FILLER              PIC XX.
21             05  O-HOURS-WORKED      PIC 99.9.
22             05  FILLER              PIC XX.
23             05  O-PAYRATE           PIC 99.999.
24             05  FILLER              PIC XX.
25             05  O-DEPENDENTS        PIC 99.
26             05  FILLER              PIC XX.
27             05  O-GROSS-PAY         PIC 999.99.
28             05  FILLER              PIC XX.
29             05  O-TAX               PIC 999.99.
30             05  FILLER              PIC XX.
31             05  O-NET-PAY           PIC 999.99.
32
33         WORKING-STORAGE SECTION.
34         01  C-EXEMPTION         PIC 99V99     VALUE 50.00.
35         01  C-TAXRATE           PIC V999      VALUE    .210.
36         01  W-DEPENDENTS        PIC 99.
37         01  W-EXEMPTION-TOTAL   PIC 999V99.
38         01  W-GROSS-PAY         PIC 999V99.
39         01  W-HOURS-WORKED      PIC 99V9.
40         01  W-NAME              PIC X(20).
41         01  W-NET-PAY           PIC 999V99.
```

```
42        01  W-OVERTIME-HOURS          PIC 99V9.
43        01  W-OVERTIME-PAY            PIC 999V99.
44        01  W-PAYROLL-NUMBER          PIC X(5)          VALUE '00000'.
45        01  W-PAYRATE                 PIC 99V999.
46        01  W-TAX                     PIC 999V99.
47        01  W-TAXABLE                 PIC 999V99.
48
49        PROCEDURE DIVISION.
50        A000-PRODUCE-PAYROLL-CALC.
51            OPEN  OUTPUT REPORT-FILE.
52            PERFORM C010-GET-PAYROLL-DATA.
53            PERFORM B010-CALC-EMP-PAYROLL
54                UNTIL W-PAYROLL-NUMBER = '99999'.
55            CLOSE REPORT-FILE.
56            STOP RUN.
57
58        B010-CALC-EMP-PAYROLL.
59            PERFORM C020-COMPUTE-GROSS-PAY.
60            PERFORM C030-COMPUTE-EXEMPTIONS.
61            PERFORM C040-COMPUTE-TAX.
62            PERFORM C050-COMPUTE-NET-PAY.
63            PERFORM C060-PRINT-OUTPUT.
64            PERFORM C010-GET-PAYROLL-DATA.
65
66        C010-GET-PAYROLL-DATA.
67            DISPLAY 'Enter payroll number:'          AT 0101
68                WITH BLANK SCREEN.
69            ACCEPT W-PAYROLL-NUMBER                   AT 0127.
70            IF W-PAYROLL-NUMBER IS NOT EQUAL TO '99999'
71                DISPLAY 'Enter employee name:'        AT 0201
72                ACCEPT W-NAME                         AT 0227
73                DISPLAY 'Enter hours worked:'         AT 0301
74                ACCEPT W-HOURS-WORKED                 AT 0327
75                DISPLAY 'Enter pay rate:'             AT 0401
76                ACCEPT W-PAYRATE                      AT 0427
77                DISPLAY 'Enter number dependents:'    AT 0501
78                ACCEPT W-DEPENDENTS                   AT 0527
79            ELSE
80                DISPLAY 'Run Terminated'              AT 0301.
81
82        C020-COMPUTE-GROSS-PAY.
83            MULTIPLY W-HOURS-WORKED BY W-PAYRATE
84                    GIVING W-GROSS-PAY ROUNDED.
85            IF W-HOURS-WORKED IS GREATER THAN 40
86                SUBTRACT 40 FROM W-HOURS-WORKED GIVING W-OVERTIME-HOURS
87                MULTIPLY 0.5 BY W-OVERTIME-HOURS
88                MULTIPLY W-OVERTIME-HOURS BY W-PAYRATE
89                        GIVING W-OVERTIME-PAY ROUNDED
90                ADD W-OVERTIME-PAY TO W-GROSS-PAY.
91
92        C030-COMPUTE-EXEMPTIONS.
93            MULTIPLY C-EXEMPTION BY W-DEPENDENTS
94                    GIVING W-EXEMPTION-TOTAL.
95
96        C040-COMPUTE-TAX.
97            IF W-GROSS-PAY IS GREATER THAN W-EXEMPTION-TOTAL
98                SUBTRACT W-EXEMPTION-TOTAL FROM W-GROSS-PAY
99                    GIVING W-TAXABLE
100               MULTIPLY C-TAXRATE BY W-TAXABLE GIVING W-TAX ROUNDED
101           ELSE
102               MOVE ZERO TO W-TAX.
```

```
103
104            C050-COMPUTE-NET-PAY.
105                SUBTRACT W-TAX FROM W-GROSS-PAY GIVING W-NET-PAY.
106
107            C060-PRINT-OUTPUT.
108                MOVE  SPACES                  TO REPORT-RECORD.
109                MOVE  W-PAYROLL-NUMBER        TO O-PAYROLL-NUMBER.
110                MOVE  W-NAME                  TO O-NAME.
111                MOVE  W-HOURS-WORKED          TO O-HOURS-WORKED.
112                MOVE  W-PAYRATE               TO O-PAYRATE.
113                MOVE  W-DEPENDENTS            TO O-DEPENDENTS.
114                MOVE  W-TAX                   TO O-TAX.
115                MOVE  W-GROSS-PAY             TO O-GROSS-PAY.
116                MOVE  W-NET-PAY               TO O-NET-PAY.
117                WRITE REPORT-RECORD.
```

FIGURE 6.3 A program to calculate weekly pay, including overtime.

6.4 THE VALUE CLAUSE IN THE WORKING-STORAGE SECTION

It frequently happens that data items in Working-Storage need to be loaded into a computer with specified initial values. We recall that it is impossible to know what a location in computer storage contains unless we specifically put something there. In past programs we have done this by means of MOVE statements in the Procedure Division. However, in many cases that is a bit awkward, and an alternative method has been provided, the VALUE clause.

In order to give a starting value to a data item in the Working-Storage section, we follow its PICTURE clause with the word VALUE and a literal. This literal value is assigned to the data item when the program is first loaded into storage. If the item is numeric, the literal must be numeric, that is, written without quotes. For example, in our program we give the data item C-TAXRATE the numeric value .210, written without quotes. If the item is nonnumeric, then a nonnumeric literal—with quotes—is required. In our program, the data item W-PAYROLL-NUMBER is given the nonnumeric value '00000'.

VALUE clauses should be written for elementary items only. Although they can be used on group items, doing so tends to decrease program flexibility and tends to be a source of errors as well. Therefore, in this book we use VALUE items only on elementary items. Observe, too, that VALUE clauses may be written for items in Working-Storage only; they may not be used this way on File Section items.

The value given to a Working-Storage item by a VALUE clause may be changed later by a Procedure Division statement, if the programmer wishes. In the program shown, the value for the payroll number certainly will be changed as the program executes.

The first two items in Working-Storage are never changed by the program. These items, the tax rate and the exemption rate, could have been replaced by numeric literals wherever they are used in the Procedure Division. However, if we had done that, it would be necessary to search through the entire Procedure Division looking for numbers that need to be changed every time the tax laws change. By creating the Working-Storage entries, we only need to change the two VALUE clauses to install any tax changes. Since the items never change in the Procedure Division they are called constants, and we suggest this by using a prefix of **c** in their names.*

We strongly urge adherence to this rule: no Procedure Division literals! Zero and one, used to initialize and increment counters, are a permissible exception, as is 100 when used to convert from a fraction to a percentage, and *possibly* a very few others. For anything else, the voice of experience says: make named constants out of them. "Constants" have an uncanny way of not staying constant very long! No magic numbers! (A "magic number" is a constant appearing in the Procedure Division without any explanation of what it is. Pity the poor maintenance programmer!)

It is important to realize that a value is given to a Working-Storage item by a **VALUE** clause *only at the time the program is loaded into the computer.* If this value is changed later by a Procedure Division action, there is no way to get the **VALUE** clause to "do its job" again—at least not until the program is run from scratch again. If the item must be returned to its initial value after having been changed, a Procedure Division statement must be provided to do that.

6.5   THE PROCEDURE DIVISION

The main module for this program is essentially the same as the one we have studied previously, with the slight difference that we perform a paragraph to get the data for the first employee instead of coding a **READ** statement directly in the module. In the paragraph executed by the **PERFORM...UNTIL** we compute the gross pay and the exemptions, then compute the tax. Finally, we compute the net pay, print the input data and results, and get the data for the next employee.

The structure of this paragraph is simple, easy to code, and easy to understand, because we used **PERFORM** statements to execute all of the calculation details. Of course, it is not really necessary to use **PERFORM** statements in a program as simple as this one, and we did so only to emphasize the structure of the program. In actual practice, if a module contains only a few lines of code, it is not usually coded as a separate paragraph.

Paragraph **C010-GET-PAYROLL-DATA** gets the data needed to process one employee. We have taken advantage of the opportunity presented by this new program to introduce a slightly more sophisticated version of **ACCEPT** and **DISPLAY**. We will discuss these new formats in a moment, but for now simply assume that they work more or less as before. However, because we are using **ACCEPT** statements to get data instead of a **READ** statement, we need to define an end of data flag. In this case, it is an employee number of 99999. Notice that we now can use the **IF** statement to improve on the technique used in Chapter Three. If the employee number is 99999 we don't bother reading the remaining data for this "employee."

* The Microsoft **COBOL** compiler supports a special type of Working-Storage entry whose value *cannot* be changed. However, since this type of entry is unique to Microsoft **COBOL** we will not use it in our examples.

The next paragraph computes the employee's gross pay. We begin by multiplying the hours worked by the worker's pay rate to get a "provisional" gross pay. It is provisional because if the **IF** statement established that the worker put in more than 40 hours, this gross pay figure must be adjusted upward.

We have already seen the **IF** statement in the examples in Chapter 5. The specification for this program requires that any hours beyond 40 are to be paid for at the rate of one-and-one-half times the normal pay rate. There are various ways to arrange this calculation. The way that is used here is to get the number of overtime hours by subtracting 40 from the hours worked, and then to multiply the difference by 0.5 to get what might be called the premium hours. When this number is multiplied by the pay rate, we have the overtime premium, which is then added to the gross pay. Regardless of the number of hours that the employee worked, the gross pay in dollars and cents is now in the item named **W-GROSS-PAY**.

The following paragraph computes the total exemption for the employee by multiplying the number of dependents by the exemption allowed for each dependent. As we mentioned in the previous section, we have used a data name, **C-EXEMPTIONS**, to represent the exemption rate rather than coding the actual value in the **MULTIPLY** statement. This has two advantages. First, it presents a descriptive name to indicate what values are being multiplied, rather than just showing the "magic" number 50.00. Second, if the exemption rate changes, it is much easier to change the value clause in the Data Division than to search through the Procedure Division looking for "50.00".

After we have computed the exemptions we compute the tax. If the gross pay exceeds the exemptions, the employee owes tax, so we subtract the total exemption from the gross pay to get the amount of the pay that is taxable, then multiply that amount by the tax rate to get the tax; notice that we round the multiplication to the nearest cent. Of course, if no tax is owed we simply set the tax to zero. Once we have the tax, we compute the net pay by subtracting the tax from the gross pay.

The final paragraph begins by moving spaces to the output record, moves the input data and computed results to their locations in the output record, and writes the output record.

6.6 A NEW VERSION OF ACCEPT AND DISPLAY

One of the advantages of using microcomputers for data entry is that it is possible to use very sophisticated techniques for handling screen I/O. We will discuss these techniques in detail in Chapter 12, but at this point we want to introduce just a few simple options to suggest what can be done.

We begin with the **DISPLAY** statement on lines 67 and 68. Up till now, whenever we have used a **DISPLAY** statement the text being displayed is simply written on the next line of the screen, beginning in column 1. Depending on whether or not we use the **WITH NO ADVANCING** clause, the cursor either remains at the end of what is displayed or advances to the start of the next line. When we reach the bottom of the screen, any output already on the screen scrolls up one line to make room for the new text.

The new format of the **DISPLAY** statement causes two changes in this technique. First, we can position the cursor anywhere we want on the screen by means of the **AT** clause. Second, by using the **WITH BLANK SCREEN** clause, we can blank out whatever is on the screen before displaying the new text.

The **AT** clause consists of the word **AT** followed by a four-digit number. The first two digits represent a line number, normally from 1 to 25, and the last two digits represent a column number, normally from 1 to 80.* The cursor is positioned to this point on the screen before any output is displayed. Although we use constants in this example, the cursor position can also be specified by an integer variable defined as **PIC X(4)**.

The **AT** clause can also be used on an **ACCEPT** statement. For example, the statement on line 69 will position the cursor at column 27 of row 1 before accepting data. Notice that this means we do not have to include spaces at the end of the prompt text in the **DISPLAY** statement. The **AT** clause automatically positions the cursor wherever we wish.

The result of these changes is that when we use the program we see the following results. First, the screen blanks out and the prompt for the payroll number is written immediately in the upper left-hand corner. After we supply the number, the prompt for the employee name is written on the second line of the screen, also beginning in column 1. Because all the **ACCEPT** statements start in column 27, all our responses are aligned under each other. As soon as we enter the number of dependents and press the Return key, the screen clears and the prompt for the next employee number is displayed in the upper left-hand corner.

A result which is not at all obvious from the program is that if your program is written in Microsoft **COBOL**, it now responds differently to keyed input!** Writing an **ACCEPT** statement that uses any options beyond the basic format shown in Chapter 1 causes the compiler to generate much more sophisticated code. One of the first changes you will notice is that when you reach the right end of an input field—for example, after typing the fifth digit of the payroll number—a symbol appears in the lower right-hand corner of your screen. If you try to type more characters in the field, the computer beeps and an error message is displayed at the bottom of your screen.

You will notice several changes when you enter numeric data such as hours worked and pay rate. For one thing, the computer will not let you enter invalid data! If you try to type a nonnumeric character in a numeric field, the computer will beep and display an error message at the bottom of the screen, and the character you typed will not be accepted. Remember, this error checking is all handled automatically by the **ACCEPT** statement; you need only write what is shown in Figure 6.3.

One minor limitation of the extended **ACCEPT** statement is that numeric fields must be treated more like fixed format data than with the basic **ACCEPT**.

---

* If you are using a screen with enhanced graphics, so that you have more than 99 lines or more than 99 columns, you can use a six-digit number. In this case the first three digits indicate the row and the last three indicate the column. In any case, the number must have either four digits or six digits.

** The precise way in which the program responds can be altered by making changes to the compiler. We will discuss some of the more common options in Chapter 12 .

For example, if you want to enter a pay rate of $8.75, you should type "08750", not "8.75". The results of typing a decimal point in a numeric field are not always what you expect, so remember to type the data as though it were a field in an input record. By way of compensation, however, the computer will prompt you for data, showing exactly how many digits should be typed. You should experiment with the new ACCEPT operations, using either the program in Figure 6.3 or one of your own.

6.7 THE OUTPUT OF THE FIRST VERSION OF THE PROGRAM

The program was compiled and run with sample data. Figure 6.4 contains the output it produced. The text over each column was not produced as part of the program; it was inserted in this listing to identify the data.

Payroll Number	Name	Hrs	Pay Rate	Nbr Dep	Gross Pay	Tax	Net Pay
12345	Thos H. Kelly	20.0	05.350	00	107.00	022.47	084.53
12401	Henry Jensen	40.0	07.500	01	300.00	052.50	247.50
12511	Nancy Kahn	40.0	07.500	03	300.00	031.50	268.50
26017	Jane Milano	10.0	06.875	03	068.75	000.00	068.75
26109	Peter W. Sherwood	40.0	10.000	05	400.00	031.50	368.50
26222	George M. Mulvaney	41.0	10.000	05	415.00	034.65	380.35
27511	Ruth Garrison	50.0	10.000	04	550.00	073.50	476.50
28819	Leo X. Butler	40.1	10.000	02	401.00	063.21	337.79
29000	Anne Henderson	40.2	10.000	03	403.00	053.13	349.87
29001	Julia Kipp	40.3	10.000	01	404.00	074.34	329.66
88888	Ima Testcase	99.9	99.999	99	979.87	006.27	973.60

FIGURE 6.4 Output from the payroll calculation program.

Looking at the first line, we see that Kelly worked 20.0 hours at a pay rate of $5.35 per hour, earning a gross pay of $107.00. He claimed no dependents, so his entire gross pay was taxable at the 21% rate, for a tax of $22.47. His net pay was thus $84.53. Jensen earned $300.00 for his week's work; after subtracting his $50.00 exemption, the remaining $250 was taxable, for a tax of $52.50 and a net pay of $247.50. Milano worked only 10 hours, and did not earn enough to have any taxable amount. The tax is accordingly zero, and her gross and net pay are equal.

The first worker in this sample to earn overtime is Mulvaney: he received $10 per hour for the first 40 hours, and 1.5 times that rate for the one hour over 40, for a gross pay of $415.00. The next employee, Garrison, received time-and-a-half for 10 hours.

Look closely at the results for Butler, however. He worked 40.1 hours; at $10 per hour that would give him $401.00, plus overtime. The overtime is 0.1 hours. This is multiplied by 0.5, giving 0.05. This is multiplied by the pay rate, which ought to give $0.50, for a total pay of $401.50. So, why did the program print $401.00? The answer is the automatic dropping of digits in the multiplication of W-OVERTIME-HOURS by 0.5, which should have given 00.05—but the PICTURE for this item is 99V9. The last digit is simply dropped, without rounding. Adding ROUNDED would not be much of a solution since the stored result would then be 00.1, resulting in an overpayment of 50 cents. The proper solution is to write PICTURE 99V99. The second version of the program, shown later in the chapter, incorporates this change; the results of that program for Butler are correct.

The last "worker," Ima Testcase, was placed there to demonstrate the consequences of not having enough space to the left of the decimal point. (By the way, notice that we had to give Ima an employee number of 88888 rather than 99999.) The 99.9 hours at $99.999 per hour with overtime should result in a gross pay of $12,984.87, but at various points in the calculation the items are too small for the intermediate and final results to be stored. Digits were dropped at different stages and in obscure ways, so that there is no obvious relationship between the correct results and what was printed.

Some compilers will produce a warning message for this program such as: "An intermediate result or a sending field might have its high order digit position truncated." Others, such as the Microsoft compiler, issue no warning at all. In any case, if a warning is ignored on the assumption that no worker would ever earn more than $999.99 in one week, the program will produce nonsense when such a case is tried. We shall consider in later chapters what can be done to guard against this situation and to take appropriate action if it occurs, either because of correct input that does not match our assumptions or because of bad data.

6.8 THE PAYROLL CALCULATION WITH OVERTIME—VERSION TWO

The program we have just studied has a number of limitations which will have to wait to be remedied until the next chapter, when we shall learn how to present the results in a fashion that is easier to read and use. However, it also has an important advantage in that invalid data *cannot* be entered into the program. That is, although a data value may not be what we intended to type, we will never have nonnumeric data in a numeric field.

Unfortunately, this is not true if we read the same data from an input file instead of from ACCEPT statements, and this is just what we must do in many programs. If the program does not use interactive input it is easily disrupted by bad data; just one nonnumeric character in any field that has been described as supposedly being entirely numeric, and the program will have serious problems. On some computers it will blow up, frequently giving no meaningful notification as to the cause of the termination; if this happens, subsequent good records will not be processed. Even worse, the program may continue to run but produce erroneous results with no indication that an error has occurred. (To get some idea of the problem involved in detecting this kind of error, consider the fact that Butler is not the only employee whose gross pay is short by 50 cents. Did you spot the second error when you first looked at Figure 6.4?) This is hardly an acceptable state of affairs. Therefore, if we revise the program for use in a batch environment, we must seek ways to detect these conditions and handle them more gracefully. In general, a good programmer is a firm believer in Murphy's Law: Anything that can go wrong, will (especially with data)! A correctly written program should *never* permit an erroneous calculation or abnormal termination due to incorrect data.

6.9 REVISING THE PROGRAM SPECIFICATIONS

Basically, the changes that we want to make to the program are these. First, we want to read the payroll data in batch mode from an input file. Second, if any data entered into the program contains an error, we want to display an error message that will tell the user that a problem exists. We will assume that input consists of one record for each employee, with the following format:

Columns 1-5	Payroll number	X(5)
Columns 6-25	Name	X(20)
Columns 26-28	Hours worked	99V9
Columns 29-31	Not used	
Columns 32-36	Hourly pay rate	99V999
Columns 37-38	Number of dependents	99

Remember, if a record read from the payroll file contains errors in any of the data fields, we will print an error message on the report and go on to the next record; otherwise, we process the record just as in the original version of the program. In other words, instead of simply getting the next payroll record to process, we want to get the next *valid* payroll record. Any errors we find can be corrected later by retyping the record in the data file. (This is similar to real payroll systems, in which the process of detecting and correcting errors usually is separate from the process of calculating employees' pay.)

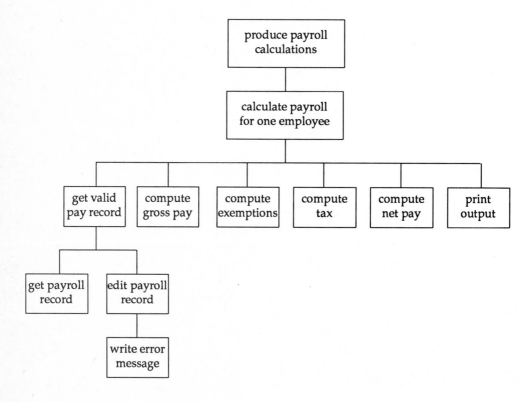

FIGURE 6.5 Hierarchy chart for revised payroll program.

To incorporate these changes into the program, we change the hierarchy chart as shown in Figure 6.5. Notice that the design changes are fairly simple; most of the changes involve COBOL code rather than design. The module labeled "get valid pay record" does more than just read the next record from the payroll file. After it reads the record, it *edits* the data fields in the record to check for invalid data; if one or more bad fields are found, the edit module writes an error message and the entire process must be repeated for the next record, or until the end of file is encountered. The pseudocode for the module is shown in Figure 6.6.

The module begins by setting the valid record flag to N, in effect saying, "No, we do not yet have a valid payroll record." It will continue looking for a valid record until it finds one, or until it runs out of records in the payroll file. To find a valid record, the module first gets a record from the payroll file. If the end of file was not encountered, the module edits the record just read. If the edit module detects errors it prints a message; otherwise, it sets the valid record flag to Y. If neither the valid record flag nor the end of file flag have been set to Y, the loop will be repeated; otherwise, the loop terminates and we have either a valid record or the end of the file.

The module "get valid pay record" serves the same same function as the module "get payroll data" did in the first version of the program. The next module, "edit payroll record," requires that we decide what the editing should involve. In this case, we will simply test every numeric field to make sure that it actually contains only numeric data. Although the employee payroll number is defined as alphanumeric, notice in Figure 6.4 that it actually contains only numeric values. Therefore, we shall also test the payroll number for nonnumeric data.

The last new module, "write error message," will require some new concepts when we write the COBOL code, but conceptually there is nothing difficult in the design. The pseudocode specification of these last few modules, therefore, is left as an exercise (see Exercise 6.1). The revised payroll program is shown in Figure 6.7.

```
GET VALID PAY REC:
set valid-rec-flag to 'N'
PERFORM-UNTIL valid-rec-flag = 'Y' or eof-flag = 'Y'
      get payroll-record
      IF eof-flag = 'N' THEN
            edit payroll-record
      ENDIF
ENDPERFORM
```

FIGURE 6.6 Pseudocode for revised payroll input module.

```
1              IDENTIFICATION DIVISION.
2              PROGRAM-ID.
3                  PAYROLL2.
4              DATE-WRITTEN.
5                  SEPTEMBER 9, 1988.
6
7              ENVIRONMENT DIVISION.
8              INPUT-OUTPUT SECTION.
9              FILE-CONTROL.
10                 SELECT PAYROLL-FILE       ASSIGN TO 'C06P02.DAT'.
11                 SELECT REPORT-FILE        ASSIGN TO 'C06P02.REP'.
12
13             DATA DIVISION.
14             FILE SECTION.
15             FD  PAYROLL-FILE
16                 LABEL RECORDS ARE STANDARD.
17             01  PAYROLL-RECORD.
18                 05  I-PAYROLL-NUMBER      PIC X(5).
19                 05  I-NAME               PIC X(20).
20                 05  I-HOURS-WORKED       PIC 99V9.
21                 05  FILLER               PIC X(3).
22                 05  I-PAYRATE            PIC 99V999.
23                 05  I-DEPENDENTS         PIC 99.
24                 05  FILLER               PIC X(42).
25
26             FD  REPORT-FILE
27                 LABEL RECORDS ARE STANDARD.
28             01  REPORT-RECORD            PIC X(69).
29
30             WORKING-STORAGE SECTION.
31             01  NORMAL-OUTPUT-LINE.
32                 05  O-PAYROLL-NUMBER     PIC X(5).
33                 05  FILLER               PIC XX.
34                 05  O-NAME               PIC X(20).
35                 05  FILLER               PIC XX.
36                 05  O-HOURS-WORKED       PIC 99.9.
37                 05  FILLER               PIC XX.
38                 05  O-PAYRATE            PIC 99.999.
39                 05  FILLER               PIC XX.
40                 05  O-DEPENDENTS         PIC 99.
41                 05  FILLER               PIC XX.
42                 05  O-GROSS-PAY          PIC 999.99.
43                 05  FILLER               PIC XX.
44                 05  O-TAX                PIC 999.99.
45                 05  FILLER               PIC XX.
46                 05  O-NET-PAY            PIC 999.99.
47
48             01  ERROR-RECORD.
49                 05  BAD-DATA             PIC X(38).
50                 05  FILLER               PIC X(4)         VALUE SPACES.
51                 05  ERROR-MESSAGE        PIC X(27)
52                     VALUE 'INVALID DATA IN THIS RECORD'.
53
54             01  C-EXEMPTION              PIC 99V99        VALUE 50.00.
55             01  C-TAXRATE                PIC  V999        VALUE  .210.
56             01  W-EXEMPTION-TOTAL        PIC 999V99.
57             01  W-GROSS-PAY              PIC 999V99.
58             01  W-NET-PAY                PIC 999V99.
59             01  W-OUT-OF-RECORDS-FLAG    PIC X            VALUE 'N'.
```

```
60        01  W-OVERTIME-HOURS          PIC  99V99.
61        01  W-OVERTIME-PAY            PIC 999V99.
62        01  W-TAX                     PIC 999V99.
63        01  W-TAXABLE                 PIC 999V99.
64        01  W-VALID-RECORD-FLAG       PIC X.
65
66        PROCEDURE DIVISION.
67        A000-PRODUCE-PAYROLL-CALC.
68            OPEN  INPUT PAYROLL-FILE
69                 OUTPUT REPORT-FILE.
70            PERFORM C010-GET-VALID-PAY-REC.
71            PERFORM B010-CALC-EMP-PAYROLL
72                UNTIL W-OUT-OF-RECORDS-FLAG = 'Y'.
73            CLOSE PAYROLL-FILE
74                  REPORT-FILE.
75            STOP RUN.
76
77        B010-CALC-EMP-PAYROLL.
78            PERFORM C020-COMPUTE-GROSS-PAY.
79            PERFORM C030-COMPUTE-EXEMPTIONS.
80            PERFORM C040-COMPUTE-TAX
81            PERFORM C050-COMPUTE-NET-PAY.
82            PERFORM C060-PRINT-OUTPUT.
83            PERFORM C010-GET-VALID-PAY-REC.
84
85        C010-GET-VALID-PAY-REC.
86            MOVE 'N' TO W-VALID-RECORD-FLAG.
87            PERFORM D010-VALID-RECORD-LOOP
88                UNTIL    W-VALID-RECORD-FLAG = 'Y'
89                    OR W-OUT-OF-RECORDS-FLAG = 'Y'.
90
91        C020-COMPUTE-GROSS-PAY.
92            MULTIPLY I-HOURS-WORKED BY I-PAYRATE
93                     GIVING W-GROSS-PAY ROUNDED.
94            IF I-HOURS-WORKED IS GREATER THAN 40
95               SUBTRACT 40 FROM I-HOURS-WORKED GIVING W-OVERTIME-HOURS
96               MULTIPLY 0.5 BY W-OVERTIME-HOURS
97               MULTIPLY W-OVERTIME-HOURS BY I-PAYRATE
98                       GIVING W-OVERTIME-PAY ROUNDED
99               ADD W-OVERTIME-PAY TO W-GROSS-PAY.
100
101       C030-COMPUTE-EXEMPTIONS.
102           MULTIPLY C-EXEMPTION BY I-DEPENDENTS
103                   GIVING W-EXEMPTION-TOTAL.
104
105       C040-COMPUTE-TAX.
106           IF W-GROSS-PAY IS GREATER THAN W-EXEMPTION-TOTAL
107              SUBTRACT W-EXEMPTION-TOTAL FROM W-GROSS-PAY
108                  GIVING W-TAXABLE
109              MULTIPLY C-TAXRATE BY W-TAXABLE GIVING W-TAX ROUNDED
110           ELSE
111              MOVE ZERO TO W-TAX.
112
113       C050-COMPUTE-NET-PAY.
114           SUBTRACT W-TAX FROM W-GROSS-PAY GIVING W-NET-PAY.
115
116       C060-PRINT-OUTPUT.
117           MOVE SPACES               TO NORMAL-OUTPUT-LINE.
118           MOVE I-PAYROLL-NUMBER      TO O-PAYROLL-NUMBER.
119           MOVE I-NAME               TO O-NAME.
120           MOVE I-HOURS-WORKED        TO O-HOURS-WORKED.
```

```
121                MOVE  I-PAYRATE          TO  O-PAYRATE.
122                MOVE  I-DEPENDENTS       TO  O-DEPENDENTS.
123                MOVE  W-TAX              TO  O-TAX.
124                MOVE  W-GROSS-PAY        TO  O-GROSS-PAY.
125                MOVE  W-NET-PAY          TO  O-NET-PAY.
126                WRITE REPORT-RECORD FROM NORMAL-OUTPUT-LINE.
127
128           D010-VALID-RECORD-LOOP.
129                PERFORM E010-GET-PAYROLL-RECORD.
130                IF W-OUT-OF-RECORDS-FLAG = 'N'
131                     PERFORM E020-EDIT-PAYROLL-RECORD.
132
133           E010-GET-PAYROLL-RECORD.
134                READ PAYROLL-FILE
135                     AT END MOVE 'Y' TO W-OUT-OF-RECORDS-FLAG.
136
137           E020-EDIT-PAYROLL-RECORD.
138                IF        I-PAYROLL-NUMBER IS NOT NUMERIC
139                     OR   I-HOURS-WORKED   IS NOT NUMERIC
140                     OR   I-PAYRATE        IS NOT NUMERIC
141                     OR   I-DEPENDENTS     IS NOT NUMERIC
142                     MOVE PAYROLL-RECORD TO BAD-DATA
143                     WRITE REPORT-RECORD FROM ERROR-RECORD
144                ELSE
145                     MOVE 'Y' TO W-VALID-RECORD-FLAG.
```

FIGURE 6.7   A program to calculate weekly pay, including overtime, for all employee records in an input file; provides some validation of the input.

6.10   THE REVISED PROGRAM—THE WRITE FROM OPTION

The revised version of the program requires that we be able to produce either of two rather different output records, one for a normal line and one for an error line. This problem can be handled in any of several ways; we have chosen the one that will prove most convenient in the applications of later chapters. The technique is to provide, in the File Section, for a record consisting of just one long elementary item, REPORT-RECORD. The name of the record is accordingly the name of this one item. Within the Working-Storage Section we provide space to set up the two types of records that we are required to be able to write, NORMAL-OUTPUT-LINE and ERROR-RECORD. (ERROR-RECORD is not subdivided into data fields, as are the input record and the normal output record, because some kinds of errors—such as omitting one character early in the record—would make the output more difficult to read than if it is simply printed in an unbroken string. Therefore, we shall simply print invalid input records in the field BAD-DATA.) Within the Procedure Division we make the decision as to which one is to be printed and on the basis of that decision move the information from the input record to the appropriate output record, in the Working-Storage Section.

At this point it is not possible simply to say WRITE, because nothing has been placed in the record *in the File Section*. We must either move the chosen record from the Working-Storage Section to the File Section, using a group MOVE followed by a WRITE, or else use the WRITE FROM option. We have

```
WRITE REPORT-RECORD FROM ERROR-RECORD.
```

where **REPORT-RECORD** is the name of the record in the File Section and **ERROR-RECORD** is the name of the record in the Working-Storage Section. The effect of this statement is *exactly* the same as if we had written

```
MOVE ERROR-RECORD TO REPORT-RECORD.
WRITE REPORT-RECORD.
```

6.11   THE DATA DIVISION

Aside from the changes described in the previous section, there are four changes in the Data Division. First, we have have dropped the input data fields from the Working-Storage Section and created an appropriate file and record definition in the File Section. (We have, of course, also added a **SELECT** statement to the **FILE-CONTROL** paragraph in the Environment Division.) Second, we have added an end of file flag, **W-OUT-OF-RECORDS-FLAG**, and used a **VALUE** clause to initialize it to **N**. Third, we have added the flag **W-VALID-RECORD-FLAG** to the Working-Storage Section; this flag is to be used in editing the input payroll record. We have not initialized the flag with a **VALUE** clause because it is always initialized at the start of **C010-GET-VALID-PAY-REC**. Finally, the **PICTURE** for **W-OVERTIME-HOURS** has been changed to **99V99**, to take care of the problem with overtime calculation noted in the first version of the program.

6.12   THE PROCEDURE DIVISION

This version of the program has several more levels of code than the first version, corresponding to the additional levels of hierarchy shown in the hierarchy chart. There are two structural differences between the actual program and the hierarchy chart, however. First, we were forced to create a separate paragraph, **D010-VALID-RECORD-LOOP**, because **COBOL** requires the paragraph for the **PERFORM** statement. Second, although we showed "write error message" as a separate module on the hierarchy chart, we simply wrote it as in-line code in the program. These changes emphasize the fact that although the hierarchy chart is used as a guide in designing the program, it should not be treated as a straitjacket. Certain changes in the structure of the program are mandated by the requirements of **COBOL**, while others can be made to simplify the program code.

Compare the final structure of the program to the hierarchy chart and the revised pseudocode, then compare the revisions to the specifications and code for the first version of the program. Be sure that you understand what changes were made, why they were made, and what design principles were used.

6.13   THE OUTPUT OF THE SECOND VERSION OF THE PROGRAM

This version of the program was compiled and run, using the same sample data as before with some erroneous records added. The output it produced is shown in Figure 6.8. As in Figure 6.4 the headings were added to aid readability, and were not produced by the program.

Payroll Number	Name	Hrs	Pay Rate	Nbr Dep	Gross Pay	Tax	Net Pay
12345	Thos H. Kelly	20.0	05.350	00	107.00	022.47	084.53
12401	Henry Jensen	40.0	07.500	01	300.00	052.50	247.50
12511	Nancy Kahn	40.0	07.500	03	300.00	031.50	268.50
UILKMB.	R. Brooks	400	0575002	INVALID	DATA	IN THIS	RECORD
26017	Jane Milano	10.0	06.875	03	068.75	000.00	068.75
12	4Kay Deluccia	400	0600004	INVALID	DATA	IN THIS	RECORD
26109	Peter W. Sherwood	40.0	10.000	05	400.00	031.50	368.50
26222	George M. Mulvaney	41.0	10.000	05	415.00	034.65	380.35
26500A.	W. Enwright	40	0545001	INVALID	DATA	IN THIS	RECORD
27511	Ruth Garrison	50.0	10.000	04	550.00	073.50	476.50
28819	Leo X. Butler	40.1	10.000	02	401.50	063.32	338.18
28820D.	X. Iannuzi	450	4.50003	INVALID	DATA	IN THIS	RECORD
28821K.	L. Ng, Jr.	350	450003	INVALID	DATA	IN THIS	RECORD
28822Daniel Reiner		350	045000C	INVALID	DATA	IN THIS	RECORD
28822L.	E. Simon	388	06000 3	INVALID	DATA	IN THIS	RECORD
2883QA.	Real Bad-one	3 8	4.5KJXX	INVALID	DATA	IN THIS	RECORD
7HGV6GARBAGE-CASE-1		..M.,M.,M.,M.		INVALID	DATA	IN THIS	RECORD
NJI9GARBAGE-CASE-2		GV 6 46	8 H	INVALID	DATA	IN THIS	RECORD
GARBAGE-CASE-3		----------++++++,M		INVALID	DATA	IN THIS	RECORD
29000	Anne Henderson	40.2	10.000	03	403.00	053.13	349.87
29001	Julia Kipp	40.3	10.000	01	404.50	074.45	330.05
88888	Ima Testcase	99.9	99.999	99	984.87	007.32	977.55

FIGURE 6.8 Output from the revised payroll calculation program.

Note that Butler's overtime pay is now correctly computed, so we have solved that problem. Ima Testcase, on the other hand, is still wrong; we will have to take that case up again later.

The records that triggered the error messages have a variety of types of bad data—blanks for zeros, alphabetic characters, special characters. Observe the payroll number for B. R. Brooks: UIKLM is what you get on some data entry keyboards if you forget to hold down the numeric key while trying to enter 12567. The record with the name A. Real Bad-One contains errors in all four fields that are checked, to demonstrate that the compound condition does respond to one *or more* of the simple conditions.

Three records with the name Garbage-Case were inserted as a matter of policy. The objective of running test data is to detect any possible errors in the program. This means that we must make certain that erroneous data items are detected and dealt with, and that valid data items are processed correctly. We encountered a case of this second type of error in the first version of the program when we realized that certain overtime pay was not being calculated correctly. In this test run we are primarily concerned with detecting errors in input data. The problem with this type of error checking is to try to anticipate every conceivable error that could occur, which is impossible. In a small attempt to force out errors that we might not have thought of, we put in some test cases consisting of random data, just to satisfy ourselves that the program will indeed reject bad data. In this program it is hard to see how we might have overlooked types of bad data, but these random tests sometimes can turn up errors we have missed.

This is not to say that program testing is merely a matter of putting in random data and seeing what happens. It is absolutely necessary to determine that the program does produce correct results for cases that have been calculated by hand, and that it specifically rejects all the kinds of bad data that it is designed to check for. We suggest a small amount of testing with random data only because of the difficulty of anticipating all of the strange things that can happen. In any case, however, you must be certain that you know what results to expect for every input record. If you don't know how the program *should* process a record, you can't tell if the results are wrong.

We shall consider the requirements of error handling and bad data throughout the remainder of the book, but since it is an important part of data processing you should be thinking about it in testing *all* of your programs.

REVIEW QUESTIONS

1. What is the purpose of editing input data?
2. Is the **VALUE** clause used correctly in each of the following examples?

   a. `01   COUNTER          PIC 9(3) VALUE ZERO.`

   b. `01   FLAGS                      VALUE SPACES.`
       `     05   EOF-FLAG    PIC X.`
       `     05   ERR-FLAG    PIC X.`

   c. `01   COUNTERS.`
       `     05   GOOD-RECS   PIC 9(3) VALUE SPACES.`
       `     05   BAD-RECS    PIC 9(3) VALUE SPACES.`

3. Is it acceptable to use *only* randomly chosen data values as test values? Explain your answer.
4. What two classes of errors should testing try to detect?
5. The program of Figure 6.7 contains a deviation from our usual punctuation standards. Can you find it?
6. What is the difference between the following alternatives:

   a. `ACCEPT DATA-FIELD AT 0545.`

   b. `ACCEPT DATA-FIELD AT 005045.`

ANSWERS TO REVIEW QUESTIONS

1. To be certain that a program does not try to process data that was entered with errors. Obviously there are limits to this objective. The program will probably not be able to tell that you meant to enter 3 when you typed 2, but it can tell if there is, for example, nonnumeric data in a field that should be numeric.
2. a. Yes.
   b. Yes, but we do not recommend using the **VALUE** clause at the group level.

c. No. The constant following **VALUE**, whether it is a figurative constant or a literal, must be compatible with the **PICTURE** of the variable. In this case we are trying to initialize a numeric variable with a nonnumeric value.

3. No. Randomly chosen test data may be used to try to catch errors that you had not thought of in planning your tests, but the bulk of the test cases should be planned carefully to test specific actions in the program.

4. The first class consists of errors that occur when valid data is processed and the program gives incorrect results. Example: the incorrect processing of overtime pay in the first version of the payroll program. The second class consists of errors that occur when the program tries to process invalid data, such as nonnumeric values in a numeric field.

5. The third **PERFORM** statement in **B010-CALC-EMP-PAYROLL** does not have a period. Hard to see, isn't it? What if that had been syntactically legal but logically incorrect?

6. None, really. In both versions the cursor moves to line 5, column 45 of the screen, then waits for you to type a value for **DATA-FIELD**. The six-digit cursor location used in version b is intended for screens that have more than 80 characters per line or more than 25 lines per screen, but it works perfectly well on standard screens (or in the upper left-hand part of larger screens).

EXERCISES

1. Write the pseudocode for the "edit" and "write" modules in Figure 6.5.

*2. Write a simple program that lets you try out the way in which the compiler handles data, particularly numeric data, in **ACCEPT** statements with the **AT** clause. You should test things like:

- what happens if you try to type too many characters?
- what happens if you type nonnumeric data in a numeric field?
- if a field already has a value, does the **ACCEPT** statement display anything *before* you type a new value?
- what happens if you type a decimal point in a numeric field? try typing it before you reach the **v** in one example, at the **v** in a second example, and after the **v** in a third example;
- what happens if you don't type leading zeroes in a numeric field?
- what happens if you press Return before you fill the entire field?
- what happens if you press the backspace key in the middle of a field? how about the cursor-left key?

*3. Rewrite the program in Figure 6.3 so that all C-level paragraphs are coded in-line; i.e., the program should consist only of paragraphs **A000-PRODUCE-PAYROLL-CALC** and a revised version of **B010-CALC-EMP-PAYROLL**.

4. Rewrite the program in Figure 6.7 so that all paragraphs below the B-level *except* those needed for **PERFORM** loops are recoded as in-line code.

---

*   Answers to starred exercises will be found in Appendix IV at the end of the book.

*5. Modify the program of Figure 6.3 so that it produces a final line at the end of the report, giving the total number of employees processed.

6. Modify the program of Figure 6.7 so that it produces a final line at the end of the report, giving the number of good records processed and the number of records in which errors were detected.

*7. If you are using a version of **COBOL** that supports in-line **PERFORM** statements (e.g., **COBOL-85** or IBM VS COBOL II), modify the program of Figure 6.7 to eliminate paragraph **D010-VALID-RECORD-LOOP** by rewriting the **PERFORM** statement in **C010-GET-VALID-PAY-REC** as an in-line **PERFORM**. Try to eliminate **E010-GET-PAYROLL-RECORD** and **E020-EDIT-PAYROLL-RECORD** as well by using the appropriate **END** statements.

8. (The next two exercises are suitable for small projects.)

Modify the program in Exercise 13 of Chapter 5 to meet the following new specifications.

Assume that inventory records may contain errors. Edit the data as follows:

1. The first two characters of the product code must be alphabetic;
2. The last three characters of the product code must be numeric;
3. All three sales fields must be numeric;
4. Both current inventory and standard inventory levels must be numeric;
5. Selling price must be numeric;
6. No item's inventory value should exceed $2,000,000.00.

If a record is found to be in error, do not print the product in the normal format. Instead, print the record image with a simple error message similar to the format shown in Figure 6.8.

9. Modify Exercise 14 of Chapter 5 according to the following new specifications.

The payroll system is now required to handle both salaried and hourly employees. For this reason the payroll record has been modified as follows:

Column 1	pay code; H for hourly, s for salaried
Column 2-6	employee number
Column 7-11	department number
Column 12-17	for hourly employees the field contains zero; for salaried employees the field contains the weekly salary; numeric, 2 decimals
Column 18-21	for salaried employees the field contains zero; for hourly employees the field contains the hours worked; numeric, 2 decimals
Column 22-25	for salaried employees the field contains zero; for hourly employees the field contains the base pay rate; numeric, 2 decimals
Column 26-27	municipality code

For salaried employees gross pay is simply the weekly salary. Deductions and net pay are calculated as in Exercise 5.14 for all employees.

Assume that payroll records may contain errors. A valid record must meet the following requirements:

1. The pay code must be **H** or **S**;
2. The employee number must be numeric;
3. The first character of the department number must be alphabetic;
4. The last four characters of the department number must be numeric;
5. The salary of a salaried employee must be numeric;
6. The salary of a salaried employee must not exceed $3000;
7. The hours worked for an hourly employee must be numeric;
8. The hours worked for an hourly employee must not exceed 80 hours;
9. The base pay rate of an hourly employee must be numeric;
10. The municipality code must be 03, 07, 15, 23, or 77.

If a payroll record is in error do not perform any calculations on it. Instead, print the record and a simple error message using the general format shown in Figure 6.8.

CHAPTER 7

PICTURES AND RELATED TOPICS

7.1 INTRODUCTION

We begin this chapter with a study of the full power of the **PICTURE** clause, which finds heavy use in preparing output so that it is pleasing in appearance and convenient to use. Most of this discussion will apply whether the data in question is being displayed on a screen or printed on a page. Therefore, whether we talk about displayed output or printed output, we will assume that the discussion applies to both unless we specifically state otherwise.

We will also look at the payroll program again and use the program to introduce several other topics; for example, level **77** and **88** entries in the Data Division, and obtaining the current date for use in the program. Finally, we will discuss how to read numeric data that has arithmetic signs.

7.2 THE PICTURE CLAUSE

A **PICTURE** clause, consisting of the word **PICTURE** or **PIC** and an appropriate character string, is required for all elementary items with a very few exceptions that will be discussed in later chapters. The character string in a **PICTURE** clause describes to the **COBOL** compiler two related but somewhat different aspects of an elementary data item.

- It conveys information about the form in which the data item is stored inside the computer. For example, if a **PICTURE** clause contains only **9**s, the compiler knows that the item is expected to be numeric and is capable of being used in arithmetic operations. If such an item contains a **V**, designating an assumed decimal point, the compiler takes that information into account in setting up decimal point alignment for any computations involving the item. If the item contains **X**s or **A**s, the compiler knows that it is not numeric and that arithmetic will therefore never be done using it.

- It conveys information about the external representation of an item that receives values from input or that is sent to output. For example, if an item in an input record is described with **PICTURE 999**, we (and the **COBOL** compiler) know that when typed at a terminal the item takes up exactly three characters, and by inspecting the PICTURE clauses for the rest of the record, we can tell exactly *where* in the record those three characters will be located. If the PICTURE clause for an item that will be displayed contains a decimal point, then a decimal point will appear at that point in the visual representation of the item.

All items described in the Data Division have an internal representation within the computer. All items in the File Section of the Data Division either come from input or go to output. Items in the Working-Storage Section may receive values that have first been read into the File Section; they may be sent to output, also through the File Section; or they may be intermediate results of computations and never see the light of day in the outside world.

All of this needs to be said in order to provide a basis for distinctions we will have to make in what follows, as we talk about the movement of data within a computer and the preparation of results for visual output.

Let us now consider in detail the various characters that may be used in PICTURE clauses and something about how they may be combined.

7.3 THE SYMBOL S IN A PICTURE CHARACTER STRING

The symbol s is used in a PICTURE character string to indicate the presence of a sign on a numeric data item. This is called an *operational sign*. It has nothing whatever to do with the ways in which a sign may be represented in typed input or displayed output, which we shall study later. A numeric item that has an s in its PICTURE character string is allowed to be either positive or negative, whereas an item without an s in its PICTURE character string is always positive. When the s is used, it must be the leftmost character in the PICTURE.

Experienced COBOL programmers often put an s in the PICTURE string for numeric items even if they know that the items should never be negative. For one thing, it saves having to make a decision for each numeric item as to whether or not the item should be signed. For another, if an error occurs in the program, or if the program specifications change, it is much easier to spot a negative result that should be positive than to figure out why an item that is always positive has the wrong value. We shall ordinarily put a sign on numeric items in programs from now on. For example, in the program shown later in the chapter, we have two numeric constants that are entered as items in Working-Storage. Neither would have any meaning as a negative number, yet we still make them signed numbers by the use of the s in the PICTURE clauses:

```
PIC S99V99 VALUE +50.00.
PIC SV999  VALUE +.210.
```

An important characteristic of the operational sign is that it takes no additional space in memory. For example, the following PICTUREs take exactly the same amount of memory:

```
PICTURE S999V99.
PICTURE  999V99.
```

7.4 THE ALLOWABLE SIZE OF A PICTURE CHARACTER STRING

A PICTURE character string may not contain more than 30 characters. This will be far more than adequate for all but very unusual circumstances, in which case the field might have to be defined as two separate data items. It should be understood clearly that *this limitation applies to the* PICTURE *character string itself,* not to the item described by the character string. For instance, this PICTURE character string

    PICTURE X(71).

contains 5 characters but describes an item that takes 71 characters. On the other hand, the character string here

    PICTURE S999V99.

contains 7 characters but describes an item that has only 5, since the s and the v do not describe character positions in the representation of the item.

Quite apart from the number of characters in its PICTURE character string, remember that a numeric item may not have more than 18 digits in it.

7.5   THE PICTURE CHARACTER STRING FOR EDITING

The PICTURE clause, as we have just discussed it and in most of the ways we have used it thus far in the book, provides information to the compiler about how to set up storage for data. It describes how many characters there are, where an assumed decimal point is, and something about the kind of internal representation to be used. A PICTURE character string for *editing* goes a considerable step further: applied to an item that receives a value as a result of a MOVE or an arithmetic operation, it specifies action to be taken when the object program is run. The precise nature of the action taken depends on the value of the data item. Editing, in this context, refers to the preparation of data for displaying or printing in a more easily readable form than the way it appears in storage, and to the insertion of dollar signs, commas, etc.

Editing actions, which may refer to elementary items only, must refer to a *receiving area*, that is, a data item that receives data as the result of a MOVE statement or an arithmetic statement. In a statement such as MOVE A TO B, A is called a *sending item* and B is called a *receiving item*. The editing that is called for by an editing PICTURE clause takes place at the time the object program is run, when a data value is transmitted to the item by a MOVE statement or an arithmetic statement with a GIVING phrase.

Most editing actions in COBOL are applied to numeric data, but some limited editing can be done on nonnumeric items. Thus, in a statement such as MOVE A TO B, if the PICTURE string for B specifies editing, then A must almost always be numeric. In any event, after editing the resulting item will automatically be an alphanumeric item whether a value was placed there by a MOVE or by an arithmetic statement. *Further arithmetic cannot be done on an edited item.*

COBOL-85
_____

Ordinarily, once an item has been edited it is not possible to "unedit" the data. However, COBOL-85 allows you to MOVE data from an edited field to an unedited field (containing only 9s, v, and s in its PICTURE), in which case the result is once more numeric and can be used in arithmetic.

_____

END COBOL-85

7.6 THE SYMBOL Z IN A PICTURE CHARACTER STRING

The character **z** specifies suppression of leading zeros. (A leading zero is one that does not have a nonzero digit to the left of it. Thus, the number 00102 contains two leading zeros.) Whenever the character in the data item corresponding to a **z** in the picture contains a leading zero, the data character is replaced by a space. If all character positions of the data item correspond to **zs** in the **PICTURE** character string, and the item in fact contains all zeros, then the edited item will be blank.

Examples

SENDING ITEM		RECEIVING ITEM	
PICTURE	SAMPLE DATA	PICTURE	EDITED RESULT
9(5)	12345	ZZ999	12345
9(5)	01234	ZZ999	1234
9(5)	00001	ZZ999	001
9(5)	00000	ZZ999	000
9(5)	10023	ZZ999	10023
9(5)	10000	ZZ999	10000
9(5)	00010	Z(5)	10
9(5)	00000	Z(5)	

7.7 THE SYMBOL $ IN A PICTURE CHARACTER STRING

A single dollar sign (or other currency symbol as appropriate) as the leftmost character of a **PICTURE** character string specifies that a dollar sign should be placed in the edited item *in that position*. This is generally called a *fixed dollar sign*.

Examples

SENDING ITEM		RECEIVING ITEM	
PICTURE	SAMPLE DATA	PICTURE	EDITED RESULT
9(4)	1234	$9(4)	$1234
9(4)	0023	$9(4)	$0023
9(4)	0023	$ZZ99	$ 23
9(4)	0004	$ZZ99	$ 04
9(4)	0050	$Z(4)	$ 50
9(4)	0000	$Z(4)	$

Observe the blank in the space for the edited item on the last line. This is correct: for the PICTURE shown, a zero sending item produces all blanks.

Zero suppression with a floating dollar sign is specified by placing a dollar sign in each leading position to be zero suppressed; the rightmost character suppressed will be replaced by a dollar sign in the edited result. Zero suppression with the floating dollar sign is specified only if *more than one* dollar sign is written.

To avoid truncation of the sending item, the PICTURE character string for floating dollar sign insertion must contain space for all of the characters of the sending item *plus one position for the dollar sign*. Thus, in the example above and in those that follow, the four-character sending items are sent to receiving items having five-character pictures.

Examples

SENDING ITEM		RECEIVING ITEM	
PICTURE	SAMPLE DATA	PICTURE	EDITED RESULT
9(4)	0123	$$999	$123
9(4)	0002	$$999	$002
9(4)	1234	$(5)	$1234
9(4)	0000	$$$99	$00
9(4)	0000	$(5)	
9(4)	0102	$$$99	$102

7.8   THE COMMA IN A PICTURE CHARACTER STRING

When a comma is written in a PICTURE character string, it will be inserted in the position shown without loss of digits from the sending data item. If all characters to the left of the comma(s) in the sending data item are zeros, and zero suppression is called for, the comma(s) will be replaced by space(s).

Examples

SENDING ITEM		RECEIVING ITEM	
PICTURE	SAMPLE DATA	PICTURE	EDITED RESULT
9(6)	123456	999,999	123,456
9(6)	000078	999,999	000,078
9(6)	000078	ZZZ,ZZZ	78
9(6)	000000	ZZZ,ZZZ	
9(6)	001234	ZZZ,ZZZ	1,234
9(6)	000123	ZZZ,ZZZ	123
9(6)	000030	ZZ,9999	0030

7.9 THE DECIMAL POINT IN A PICTURE CHARACTER STRING

This is one feature of the editing PICTURE that we have already seen, beginning in Chapter 3. When a decimal point is written in a PICTURE character string, it is inserted into the position shown without loss of digits from the sending data item. This, as we have discussed, is an *actual* decimal point, which occupies a character position in the edited result. An item may never contain more than one decimal point, actual or assumed.

When data from a sending item is moved to a receiving item for which the PICTURE character string contains a decimal point, the assumed decimal point of the sending item is taken into account. That is, the sending value is placed in the receiving item with the actual decimal point in the receiving item aligned with the assumed decimal point in the sending item. This may cause insertion of zeros in the edited result, as shown in the third example. If the receiving item is smaller than the sending item, the decimal point alignment may also cause *truncation, without any warning whatever*! This is shown in the fourth example. Carets denote assumed decimal points in the sending items.

Examples

SENDING ITEM		RECEIVING ITEM	
PICTURE	SAMPLE DATA	PICTURE	EDITED RESULT
9(4)V99	1234ˬ56	9(4).99	1234.56
99V9(4)	01ˬ2345	99.9(4)	01.2345
9V9(5)	1ˬ23456	99.9(6)	01.234560
99V9(4)	12ˬ3456	9.999	2.345
99V9(4)	00ˬ0123	99.9(4)	00.0123
99V9(4)	10ˬ0000	99.9(4)	10.0000

It is entirely possible to combine different types of editing in one PICTURE clause. For example, zero suppression may be combined with decimal point insertion. A very common operation combines floating dollar sign insertion, conditional comma insertion, and decimal point insertion. A few of the possibilities are illustrated in the following examples.

Examples

SENDING ITEM		RECEIVING ITEM	
PICTURE	SAMPLE DATA	PICTURE	EDITED RESULT
9(4)V99	0100ˬ00	ZZZ9.99	100.00
9(4)V99	0041ˬ09	ZZZ9.99	41.09
9(6)V99	123456ˬ78	$ZZZ,ZZ9.99	$123,456.78
9(6)V99	000044ˬ44	$ZZZ,ZZ9.99	$ 44.44

9(6)V99	000000‸01	$ZZZ,ZZ9.99	$ 0.01
9(6)V99	123456‸78	$$$$,$$9.99	$123,456.78
9(6)V99	012000‸00	$$$$,$$9.99	$12,000.00
9(6)V99	000012‸00	$$$$,$$9.99	$12.00
9(6)V99	000000‸12	$$$$,$$9.99	$0.12
9(6)V99	000000‸00	$$$$,$$9.99	$0.00

7.10 THE SYMBOL - (MINUS SIGN) IN A PICTURE CHARACTER STRING

The symbol **s** in a PICTURE character string designates an *operational* sign. An operational sign is not counted in determining the number of characters in an item, and we need not concern ourselves with the way it is represented inside the computer. A display sign, on the other hand, which has to do only with data items intended for output, does take up space.

If a single minus sign is written as the first or last character of a PICTURE clause and if the data item is negative, a display minus sign will be inserted into the edited item where written. If the data item is positive or if it is unsigned, a space is inserted into the same position.

None of this says anything about how signed quantities are represented when typed into a record at a terminal. We will delay this topic for a bit, and simply assume that the signs have somehow been placed in the data items, perhaps as the result of an arithmetic operation. In the examples that follow, the operational sign of the sending item is represented by a plus or minus sign over the rightmost character.

Examples

SENDING ITEM		RECEIVING ITEM	
PICTURE	SAMPLE DATA	PICTURE	EDITED RESULT
S999	12$\bar{3}$	-999	-123
S999	12$\bar{3}$	999-	123-
S999	12$\overset{+}{3}$	-999	123
S999	12$\overset{+}{3}$	999-	123
S999	00$\bar{0}$	-999	000
S999	00$\overset{+}{0}$	999-	000

It is possible to combine the operations of zero suppression and sign insertion by writing more than one minus sign at the beginning of a PICTURE clause. When this is done, the rightmost character suppressed will be replaced by a minus sign in the edited result if the sending item is negative. As with the floating dollar sign, be sure to allow one extra position in the receiving field for the sign itself.

Examples

SENDING ITEM		RECEIVING ITEM	
PICTURE	SAMPLE DATA	PICTURE	EDITED RESULT
S9(4)	123$\bar{4}$	---99	-1234
S9(4)	001$\bar{2}$	----9	-12
S9(4)	001$\overset{+}{2}$	----9	12
S9(4)	000$\bar{8}$	---99	-08
S9(4)	000$\overset{+}{0}$	---99	00
S9(4)	000$\overset{+}{0}$	-----	
S9(4)	001$\bar{2}$	-----	-12

7.11 THE SYMBOL + (PLUS SIGN) IN A PICTURE CHARACTER STRING

If a single plus sign is written as the first or last character of a PICTURE character string, a display plus sign is inserted into the edited item where written if the data item is positive; if the data item is negative, a minus sign is inserted. If the sending item has no sign (that is, if its PICTURE character string does not contain an S), it is considered to be positive.

Examples

SENDING ITEM		RECEIVING ITEM	
PICTURE	SAMPLE DATA	PICTURE	EDITED RESULT
S9(5)	1234$\bar{5}$	+9(5)	-12345
S9(5)	1234$\overset{+}{5}$	+9(5)	+12345
S9(5)	1234$\bar{5}$	9(5)+	12345-
S9(5)	1234$\overset{+}{5}$	9(5)+	12345+
S9(5)	0000$\overset{+}{0}$	+9(5)	+00000
S9(5)	0000$\bar{0}$	9(5)+	00000-
S9(5)	0012$\bar{3}$	+Z(4)9	- 123

Zero suppression may be combined with the insertion of a floating plus or minus sign by placing a plus sign in each leading position to be suppressed. The rightmost character suppressed will be replaced by a plus sign if the sending item is positive or has no sign, and by a minus sign if the sending item is negative. As with the floating minus sign, this applies only if more than one plus sign is written.

Examples

SENDING ITEM		RECEIVING ITEM	
PICTURE	SAMPLE DATA	PICTURE	EDITED RESULT
S9(4)	$\overset{+}{1234}$	+++99	+1234
S9(4)	$\overset{+}{0023}$	+++99	+23
S9(4)	$\overset{-}{0023}$	+++99	−23
S9(4)	$\overset{+}{0004}$	+++99	+04
S9(4)	$\overset{+}{0000}$	+(5)	

7.12 THE SYMBOLS CR AND DB IN A PICTURE CHARACTER STRING

The combination CR and DB, for credit and debit, may appear *only as the rightmost two characters* of a PICTURE character string. If the sending item is negative, the edited result will contain whichever of these pairs of symbols is written. If the sending item is positive or has no sign, these symbols will be replaced by spaces. Although it might seem reasonable, it is not possible to get both CR and DB from one picture, such as CR if negative and DB if positive. If output so labeled is required, it can be managed, but only by some additional effort including an IF statement in the Procedure Division.

Examples

SENDING ITEM		RECEIVING ITEM	
PICTURE	SAMPLE DATA	PICTURE	EDITED RESULT
S9(4)	$\overset{+}{1234}$	9(4)CR	1234
S9(4)	$\overset{-}{1234}$	9(4)CR	1234CR
S9(4)	$\overset{-}{0002}$	9(4)DB	0002DB
S9(4)	$\overset{-}{0002}$	Z(4)CR	2CR
S9(4)	$\overset{+}{0000}$	Z(4)CR	

We may summarize the actions for the various types of display signs for positive and negative data as follows:

PICTURE characters	Edited result if data is positive	Edited result if data is negative
-	blank	-
+	+	-
CR	2 blanks	CR
DB	2 blanks	DB

7.13   THE CHARACTER * (ASTERISK) IN A PICTURE CHARACTER STRING

The asterisk in a PICTURE character string is used for check protection, to make it difficult for numbers to be altered fraudulently by inserting leading digits. (For this reason, the asterisk is frequently referred to as the *check protect character*.) The action with this symbol is a combination of insertion and zero suppression. Any leading zero in the sending item that corresponds to an asterisk in the picture is replaced by an asterisk in the receiving item. This is different from the various floating insertion symbols that we have seen previously, where only the rightmost character suppressed is replaced by the symbol. Here *all* suppressed characters are replaced. If only asterisks or other suppression characters are used and the data item is zero, the edited result will be all asterisks except for an actual decimal point.

Examples

SENDING ITEM		RECEIVING ITEM	
PICTURE	SAMPLE DATA	PICTURE	EDITED RESULT
9(4)	1234	**99	1234
9(4)	0023	**99	**23
9(4)	0000	**99	**00
9(4)	0000	****	****
9(4)	0080	***9	**80
9(4)	0080	**99	**80
9(4)	0080	*999	*080

7.14   THE CHARACTER 0 (ZERO) IN A PICTURE CHARACTER STRING

The character zero in a PICTURE character string is a straight insertion symbol. It causes a zero to be inserted into the corresponding position in the receiving item without loss of characters from the sending item.

Examples

SENDING ITEM		RECEIVING ITEM	
PICTURE	SAMPLE DATA	PICTURE	EDITED RESULT
9(4)	1234	990099	120034
9(4)	1234	099990	012340
9(4)	0012	ZZZZ0	120
9(4)	1234	$$,$$9.00	$1,234.00
9(4)	0080	$$,$$9.00	$80.00

7.15 THE CHARACTER B IN A PICTURE CHARACTER STRING

The character **B** causes the insertion of a space (blank) in the corresponding position of the receiving item without loss of characters from the sending data item.

The insertion of blanks will more often be useful than the insertion of zeros. The next-to-last line of the following examples, for instance, shows a Social Security number, written without spaces as it would normally appear in file storage, and grouped in the ordinary way in the edited result by the insertion of blanks. Note that since the dash (-) is *not* an insertion character, we cannot use the **PICTURE** clause to print the Social Security number in the format 999-99-9999. We can obtain this format, but we will have to wait until Chapter 16 to learn the technique.

Examples

SENDING ITEM		RECEIVING ITEM	
PICTURE	SAMPLE DATA	PICTURE	EDITED RESULT
9(6)	123456	99BBB9999	12 3456
X(6)	ABCDEF	XXBBBXXXX	AB CDEF
999	123	90B90B90	10 20 30
X(9)	123456789	999B99B9999	123 45 6789
X(7)	FTBAKER	XBXBX(5)	F T BAKER
X(7)	DANIELD	X(6)BX	DANIEL D
X(7)	DONALDG	X(6)BX	DONALD G

7.16 THE CHARACTER / (SLASH) IN A PICTURE CHARACTER STRING

The character / in a **PICTURE** character string is still another insertion symbol. It is used primarily for printing the date in numeric format, but may actually be used in any **PICTURE**. It causes no loss of characters from the sending item.

Examples

SENDING ITEM		RECEIVING ITEM	
PICTURE	SAMPLE DATA	PICTURE	EDITED RESULT
9(6)	103188	99/99/99	10/31/88
9(6)	070488	99/99/99	07/04/88
9(6)	070488	Z9/99/99	7/04/88
X(8)	JMWILSON	X/X/X(6)	J/M/WILSON
X(8)	MMDDYY	XX/XX/XX	MM/DD/YY

7.17 THE CHARACTER P IN A PICTURE CHARACTER STRING

The character **P** in a **PICTURE** character string is used differently from the characters we have just seen. It does not cause editing of the data field; instead, it is used to *scale* numeric data for use in calculations. Suppose, for example, that a company is preparing a sales report for management. If the company is large, the sales figures are generally not reported to the last cent, but are shown to the nearest thousand dollars for ease of comparison. If we have the following code, the value stored in **SALES-87** is 075, not 075000, but for arithmetic operations it is still treated as 75,000.

```
01  SALES-87        PIC 999PPP.
    .
    .
    .
    MOVE 75000 TO SALES-87.
```

The character **P** may be placed in a **PICTURE** character string only at the beginning of the string or at the end of the string. If the string begins with **P**, then the decimal point is assumed to be immediately to the left of the first **P**; optionally, an **S** and a **V** may appear to the left of the first **P**. In each of the following pairs, the pictures are equivalent.

```
PIC  PPP999.
PIC  VPPP999.

PIC  SPP9(5).
PIC  SVPP9(5).
```

If the **PICTURE** character string ends with **P**, the decimal point is assumed to follow the last **P**; optionally, **V** may follow the last **P**. For example, **99PPP** is equivalent to **99PPPV**.

The character **P** does *not* take up space in memory, but it *does* count as one digit in determining the maximum size (18 digits) of numeric items. For example, **SVP(10)99** only takes up *two* characters in memory, but represents a *twelve* digit number. Each position represented by a **P** in a **PICTURE** character string is considered to contain the value zero.

Examples

SENDING ITEM		RECEIVING ITEM	
PICTURE	SAMPLE DATA	PICTURE	EDITED RESULT
999PPP	075	ZZZ,ZZ9	75,000
PPP999	075	9.9(6)	0.000075
PPP999	075	9.9(5)	0.00007
9(6)	150000	999PPP	150
9(6)	123456	999PPP	123
V9(6)	‸001234	PP99	12

The data given for the first three sending items in these examples shows what the items would look like if you could somehow look directly at the computer's memory, but not how the sending items were initialized. As the edited output for the receiving items shows, the first sending item (for example), has a value of 75,000 *not* 75. To initialize this sending item it would be necessary to use a statement such as the following:

```
MOVE 75000 TO SENDING-ITEM-1.
```

Likewise, to initialize the second sending item we might use a statement such as this:

```
MOVE 0.000075 TO SENDING-ITEM-2.
```

Remember: the **P** character in a **PICTURE** character string does not affect the value stored in the data item, it simply allows **COBOL** to save space by not storing leading or trailing zeros in memory.

7.18   A SUMMARY OF PICTURE RULES

Here is a summary of rules governing the use of the **PICTURE** clause.

1. A **PICTURE** character string may not contain more than 30 characters.
2. A **PICTURE** character string may contain no more than one sign designation and no more than one actual or assumed decimal point. (This does not contradict the principle of floating sign insertion; multiple plus signs or multiple minus signs are considered as *one* "sign designation.")
3. A numeric literal or an operand in any arithmetic operation may not exceed 18 digits, including any digits represented by the character **P**. All **PICTURE** character strings, whether for editing or not, must reflect this restriction—although in practical commercial applications it would be extremely unusual to have any occasion to exceed this limit. (For example, in 18 digits you could represent a number several orders of magnitude greater than the Gross National Product of the United States.)
4. An edited item may at a later time become a sending item. This would usually happen through movement of the group item of which the edited item is one of the elementary items, but it may occasionally happen that an edited item becomes a sending elementary item. When this is done, it must be remembered that *edited items are always nonnumeric and may not be used in arithmetic.* Also, the edited item—which is now alphanumeric—may not be moved to a receiving item that calls for further numeric editing. In other words, for purposes of arithmetic or further editing, an edited item should be treated as though its **PICTURE** contained only **X**s.

COBOL-85

5. In **COBOL-85** only, an edited numeric item may be de-edited by moving it to a numeric item.

END COBOL-85

6. Zero suppression may not be employed more than once in one PICTURE character string. For example, the following PICTURE is illegal.

   PICTURE Z9/Z9/99

   However, one type of zero suppression may be combined with other types of insertion, such as the insertion of space.

7. The PICTURE character string for a receiving item must provide enough space for the largest number that is expected to be placed there. This, of course, is true whether or not editing is involved. It is mentioned here because when a floating dollar sign is used, one of the dollar signs is an insertion character and the rest stand for digits. The dollar sign for insertion must be considered in determining the amount of space required. For instance, if the PICTURE character string for a sending item were 9999 and we sent it to a receiving item having a PICTURE of $$$$, some compilers will warn us of a possible truncation of high order digits: after using one dollar sign for insertion, we have provided only three characters for the possible four nonzero digits of the sending item.

8. The insertion of zeros, blanks, and slashes are the only editing operations that may be applied to alphabetic and alphanumeric items as well as to numeric items.

One final reminder on two matters that beginners frequently forget: one cannot do arithmetic on an edited item, and one cannot do any editing on group items.

7.19 COMBINING EDITING OPERATION

We have already seen that it is possible to combine editing operations in one PICTURE character string. Figure 7.1 shows a variety of applications of the PICTURE clause, including a number that combine operations.

SENDING ITEM		RECEIVING ITEM	
PICTURE	SAMPLE DATA	PICTURE	EDITED RESULT
9(6)	123456	$ZZZ,ZZZ.99	$123,456.00
9999V99	123456	$ZZZ,ZZZ.99	$ 1,234.56
9(4)V99	000123	$ZZZ,ZZZ.99	$ 1.23
9(4)V9(2)	000006	$ZZZ,ZZZ.99	$ .06
9(4)V99	000123	$$$$,$$$.99	$1.23
9(4)V99	000000	$$$$,$$$.99	$.00
9(4)V99	000000	$$$$,$$$.$$	
9(6)	102030	$ZZZ,ZZZ.ZZ	$102,030.00

9(6)	000100	$$$$,$99.99	$100.00
9(6)	000008	$$$$,$99.99	$08.00
9(4)V99	123456	$***,***.99	$**1,234.56
9(4)V99	000123	$***,***.99	$******1.23
9(4)V99	000098	$***,***.99	$*******.98
9(4)V99	000000	$***,***.99	$*******.00
9(4)V99	000000	$***,***.**	********.**
9(5)V9	001234	$$$$,$$$.99	$123.40
9(4)V99	000123	Z,ZZZ.ZZ	1.23
9(4)V99	000123	Z,ZZZ,ZZZ.ZZ	1.23
9(6)	123456	-999999	123456
S9(6)	12345$\overline{6}$	-9(6)	-123456
S9(6)	00012$\overline{3}$	-9(6)	-000123
S9(6)	00012$\overline{3}$	-(6)9	-123
S9(6)	00012$\overline{3}$	9(6)-	000123-
S9(6)	00012$\overline{3}$	Z(6)-	123-
9(6)	123456	+9(6)	+123456
S9(6)	12345$\overline{6}$	+9(6)	-123456
S9(6)	00001$\overline{2}$	+(6)9	-12
S9(4)V99	00123$\overline{4}$	$*,***.99CR	$***12.34CR
S9(4)V99	00123$\overline{4}$	$*,***.99DB	$***12.34DB
S9(4)V99	00123$\overline{4}$	$$,$$$.99CR	$12.34CR
S9(4)V99	00000$\overline{0}$	$$,$$$.99CR	$.00CR
S9(4)V99	00000$\overline{0}$	$$,$$$.$$CR	
9(6)	001234	ZZZBBB999	1 234
9(6)	123456	9B(4)9(5)	1 23456
X(6)	ABCDE5	XXBXXXBBX	AB CDE 5

FIGURE 7.1 Examples of the actions of a variety of editing PICTUREs.

7.20   THE PAYROLL CALCULATION WITH OVERTIME - VERSION THREE

We now take up still another version of the payroll calculation that we studied in Chapter 6. There are two new requirements for the program. First, the printed output must include headings over the columns before the first output; the format of these headings is shown in the sample output in Figure 7.5. Second, the numeric quantities in the body of the report are to be edited. Leading zeros are to be suppressed and dollar amounts are to have a floating dollar sign inserted.

We begin as always with a program design. Figure 7.2 shows the revised hierarchy chart, based in the first program in Chapter 6.

There is only one change in this chart: a module has been added, directly subordinate to the main module, which will print column headings before any other processing is done. The rest of the changes will affect the **COBOL** code but do not show up in the design. For convenience, the pseudocode for the program is reproduced in Figure 7.3, with the slight changes required for the column headings.

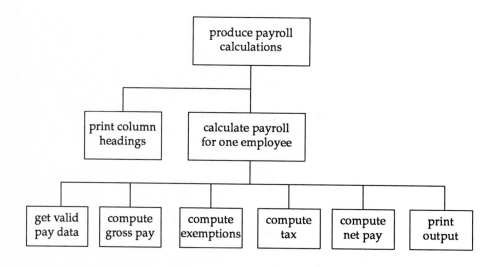

FIGURE 7.2   Hierarchy chart for third version of payroll program.

```
PRODUCE PAYROLL CALCULATIONS:
open file(s)
print column headings
set payroll-number to zero
get payroll data for one employee
PERFORM-UNTIL payroll-number = 99999
     calculate payroll for employee
     get payroll data for one employee
ENDPERFORM
close file(s)


PRINT COLUMN HEADINGS:
get today's date
print date line
print heading text lines


CALCULATE PAYROLL FOR EMPLOYEE:
compute gross-pay
compute exemptions
compute tax
compute net pay
print output line


GET PAYROLL DATA FOR ONE EMPLOYEE:
get payroll-number
IF payroll-number is not equal to 99999 THEN
     get employee-name
     get hours-worked
     get pay-rate
     get number-dependents
ENDIF


COMPUTE GROSS PAY:
gross-pay = hours-worked x pay-rate
IF hours-worked is greater than 40 THEN
     overtime-hours = hours-worked - 40
     multiply overtime-hours by 0.5
     overtime-pay = overtime-hours x pay-rate
     add overtime-pay to gross-pay
ENDIF


COMPUTE EXEMPTIONS:
exemptions = 50.00 x number-dependents


COMPUTE TAX:
IF gross-pay is greater than exemptions THEN
     tax = 0.21 x (gross-pay - exemptions)
ELSE
     tax = 0
ENDIF
```

COMPUTE NET PAY:
net-pay = gross-pay - tax

PRINT OUTPUT LINE:
move payroll-number, employee-name, hours-worked, pay-rate,
        number-dependents, gross-pay, tax, and net-pay
    to output-record
print output-record

FIGURE 7.3 Pseudocode specifications for version three of the payroll calculation program.

As you can see, the changes from the previous version are slight. Most of what needs to be done to meet the revised specifications will show up in the COBOL program rather than in the design.

7.21 THE PAYROLL PROGRAM

A revised payroll program is shown in Figure 7.4. It includes several new features, the first of which is illustrated at the beginning of the Working-Storage Section. Any time we have elementary items in Working-Storage that we do not wish to organize into any larger group, we may indicate this fact by using a special level number, 77. Level 77 entries, if any, are generally placed at the start of the Working-Storage Section. Earlier versions of COBOL required this placement and, although the requirement does not exist in current versions of the language, the convention is often still followed. In any case, level 77 items must begin in the A margin.

As a practical matter, there is really no strong incentive to use a level 77 entry, which does nothing that cannot be done by using an elementary item at level 01. Nevertheless this feature is used in many existing programs and the reader should be aware of it. To show it in action, we have placed all of the items used for temporary storage, as well as the two constant items, into level 77 entries in this program. The only advantage you may find in using level 77 items is that in some computers they will use slightly less space than the same item written as level 01. Also, bear in mind that level 77 entries may not be used in the File Section.

```
1        IDENTIFICATION DIVISION.
2        PROGRAM-ID.
3            PAYROLL3.
4        DATE-WRITTEN.
5            SEPTEMBER 16, 1988.
6
7        ENVIRONMENT DIVISION.
8        INPUT-OUTPUT SECTION.
9        FILE-CONTROL.
10           SELECT REPORT-FILE        ASSIGN TO 'C07P01.REP'.
11
12       DATA DIVISION.
13       FILE SECTION.
14       FD  REPORT-FILE
15           LABEL RECORDS ARE STANDARD.
16       01  REPORT-RECORD            PIC X(75).
17
```

```
18          WORKING-STORAGE SECTION.
19          77  C-EXEMPTION                PIC  S99V99     VALUE +50.00.
20          77  C-TAXRATE                  PIC   SV999     VALUE +.210.
21          77  W-DEPENDENTS               PIC 99.
22          77  W-EXEMPTION-TOTAL          PIC S999V99.
23          77  W-GROSS-PAY                PIC S999V99.
24          77  W-HOURS-WORKED             PIC 99V9.
25          77  W-NAME                     PIC X(20).
26          77  W-NET-PAY                  PIC S999V99.
27          77  W-OVERTIME-HOURS           PIC  S999V99.
28          77  W-OVERTIME-PAY             PIC S999V99.
29          77  W-PAYROLL-NUMBER           PIC 9(5).
30              88  END-OF-DATA                            VALUE 99999.
31          77  W-PAYRATE                  PIC 99V999.
32          77  W-TAX                      PIC S999V99.
33          77  W-TAXABLE                  PIC S999V99.
34          77  W-TODAYS-DATE              PIC 9(6).
35
36          01  HEADING-LINE-1.
37              05  FILLER                 PIC X(26)
38                  VALUE 'PAYROLL CALCULATION REPORT'.
39              05  FILLER                 PIC X(41)       VALUE SPACES.
40              05  REPORT-DATE            PIC 99/99/99    VALUE ZERO.
41
42          01  HEADING-LINE-2.
43              05  FILLER                 PIC X(42)
44                  VALUE 'NUMBER        NAME          HOURS   RATE '.
45              05  FILLER                 PIC X(29)
46                  VALUE ' DEP   GROSS      TAX      NET'.
47
48          01  PAYROLL-LINE.
49              05  O-PAYROLL-NUMBER       PIC X(5).
50              05  O-NAME                 PIC BBX(20).
51              05  O-HOURS-WORKED         PIC BBZ9.9.
52              05  O-PAYRATE              PIC BBZ9.999.
53              05  O-DEPENDENTS           PIC BBZ9.
54              05  O-GROSS-PAY            PIC BB$$$9.99.
55              05  O-TAX                  PIC BB$$$9.99.
56              05  O-NET-PAY              PIC BB$$$9.99.
57
58
59          PROCEDURE DIVISION.
60          A000-PRODUCE-PAYROLL-CALC.
61              OPEN OUTPUT REPORT-FILE.
62              PERFORM B010-PRINT-COLUMN-HEADINGS.
63              PERFORM C010-GET-PAYROLL-DATA.
64              PERFORM B020-CALC-EMP-PAYROLL
65                  UNTIL END-OF-DATA.
66              CLOSE REPORT-FILE.
67              STOP RUN.
68
69          B010-PRINT-COLUMN-HEADINGS.
70              ACCEPT W-TODAYS-DATE FROM DATE.
71              MOVE W-TODAYS-DATE TO REPORT-DATE.
72              WRITE REPORT-RECORD FROM HEADING-LINE-1.
73              MOVE SPACES TO REPORT-RECORD.
74              WRITE REPORT-RECORD.
75              WRITE REPORT-RECORD FROM HEADING-LINE-2.
76              MOVE SPACES TO REPORT-RECORD.
77              WRITE REPORT-RECORD.
```

```
 78             MOVE SPACES TO REPORT-RECORD.
 79             WRITE REPORT-RECORD.
 80
 81         B020-CALC-EMP-PAYROLL.
 82             PERFORM C020-COMPUTE-GROSS-PAY.
 83             PERFORM C030-COMPUTE-EXEMPTIONS.
 84             PERFORM C040-COMPUTE-TAX.
 85             PERFORM C050-COMPUTE-NET-PAY.
 86             PERFORM C060-PRINT-OUTPUT.
 87             PERFORM C010-GET-PAYROLL-DATA.
 88
 89         C010-GET-PAYROLL-DATA.
 90             DISPLAY 'Enter payroll number:'        AT 0101
 91                 WITH BLANK SCREEN.
 92             ACCEPT W-PAYROLL-NUMBER                 AT 0127.
 93             IF NOT END-OF-DATA
 94                 DISPLAY 'Enter employee name:'     AT 0201
 95                 ACCEPT W-NAME                       AT 0227
 96                 DISPLAY 'Enter hours worked:'      AT 0301
 97                 ACCEPT W-HOURS-WORKED               AT 0327
 98                 DISPLAY 'Enter pay rate:'          AT 0401
 99                 ACCEPT W-PAYRATE                    AT 0427
100                 DISPLAY 'Enter number dependents:' AT 0501
101                 ACCEPT W-DEPENDENTS                 AT 0527
102             ELSE
103                 DISPLAY 'Run Terminated'           AT 0301.
104
105         C020-COMPUTE-GROSS-PAY.
106             MULTIPLY W-HOURS-WORKED BY W-PAYRATE
107                     GIVING W-GROSS-PAY ROUNDED.
108             IF W-HOURS-WORKED IS GREATER THAN 40
109                 SUBTRACT 40 FROM W-HOURS-WORKED GIVING W-OVERTIME-HOURS
110                 MULTIPLY 0.5 BY W-OVERTIME-HOURS
111                 MULTIPLY W-OVERTIME-HOURS BY W-PAYRATE
112                         GIVING W-OVERTIME-PAY ROUNDED
113                 ADD W-OVERTIME-PAY TO W-GROSS-PAY.
114
115         C030-COMPUTE-EXEMPTIONS.
116             MULTIPLY C-EXEMPTION BY W-DEPENDENTS
117                     GIVING W-EXEMPTION-TOTAL.
118
119         C040-COMPUTE-TAX.
120             IF W-GROSS-PAY IS GREATER THAN W-EXEMPTION-TOTAL
121                 SUBTRACT W-EXEMPTION-TOTAL FROM W-GROSS-PAY
122                         GIVING W-TAXABLE
123                 MULTIPLY C-TAXRATE BY W-TAXABLE GIVING W-TAX ROUNDED
124             ELSE
125                 MOVE ZERO TO W-TAX.
126
127         C050-COMPUTE-NET-PAY.
128             SUBTRACT W-TAX FROM W-GROSS-PAY GIVING W-NET-PAY.
129
130         C060-PRINT-OUTPUT.
131             MOVE SPACES                 TO PAYROLL-LINE.
132             MOVE W-PAYROLL-NUMBER       TO O-PAYROLL-NUMBER.
133             MOVE W-NAME                 TO O-NAME.
134             MOVE W-HOURS-WORKED         TO O-HOURS-WORKED.
135             MOVE W-PAYRATE              TO O-PAYRATE.
136             MOVE W-DEPENDENTS           TO O-DEPENDENTS.
```

```
137              MOVE  W-TAX              TO  O-TAX.
138              MOVE  W-GROSS-PAY        TO  O-GROSS-PAY.
139              MOVE  W-NET-PAY          TO  O-NET-PAY.
140              WRITE REPORT-RECORD FROM PAYROLL-LINE.
```

FIGURE 7.4 A program to calculate weekly pay, including overtime, for all employee records in an input file; provides some validation of the input. Headings are printed and output fields are edited.

7.22   LEVEL 88 ENTRIES

A level **88** entry makes it possible to give a name to a value or set of values for an elementary item anywhere in the Data Division. This name, more precisely called a *condition name*, may then be used anywhere that a condition is required in writing Procedure Division statements.

All of this is much easier to present through an example than through abstract descriptions. Consider the definitions on lines 29 and 30 of the program. In the version in Chapter 6, we gave W-PAYROLL-NUMBER an initial value of zero, then tested it for a value of 99999 using a PERFORM statement with an UNTIL phrase that read

```
UNTIL W-PAYROLL-NUMBER = '99999'.
```

In the current version we use the level **88** entry on line 30 to give a name to the value 99999. An obvious name is END-OF-DATA. Then in the Procedure Division we write

```
PERFORM B020-CALC-EMP-PAYROLL
        UNTIL END-OF-DATA.
```

The effect is exactly the same as what we did in Chapter 6 except that the new form is perhaps easier to read. Naturally, it is easier to read *only if we take the trouble to devise meaningful names*. This condition could also be named **XQ13G**; the program would work correctly but program readability would take a giant step backward.

We should note, by the way, that we have made two other changes in W-PAYROLL-NUMBER. First, we changed its definition from PIC X(5) to PIC 9(5). This will cause the program to reject any nonnumeric data in the ACCEPT statement on line 92. Second, we removed the VALUE clause from line 29. This has nothing to do with the level 88 entry on the following line; the logic of the program simply does not require initializing the payroll number.

A level **88** entry may have, besides the name of the condition it defines, only a VALUE clause. It *must not* have a PICTURE clause. On the other hand, the elementary item to which a level **88** item refers *must* have a PICTURE clause; it may or may not have a VALUE clause, as circumstances dictate. The elementary item to which the condition name refers may be a level **77** item, but it may also be at any other level. For example, we could have defined the payroll data in the program as follows:

```
01   PAYROLL-DATA.
     05   W-PAYROLL-NUMBER         PIC 9(5).
          88  END-OF-DATA                        VALUE 99999.
     05   W-NAME                   PIC X(20).
     05   W-HOURS-WORKED           PIC 99V9.
     05   W-PAYRATE                PIC 99V999.
     05   W-DEPENDENTS             PIC 99.
```

In fact, a condition name may even be associated with a group item; we shall discuss this usage in Chapter 11. Whether a condition name relates to a group item or an elementary item, it must follow directly behind the definition of the item whose values it describes.

Level **88** entries are permitted in both the File Section and the Working-Storage Section of the Data Division. It is only in level **88** entries that **VALUE** clauses are permitted in the File Section.

Finally, a level **88** entry may specify not only a single value but also a range of values, as suggested in the following example:

```
05   PRODUCT-CODE          PIC X.
     88 HOUSEWARES                   VALUE 'A' THRU 'F'.
     88 AUTOMOTIVE                   VALUE 'G' THRU 'Q'.
     88 DRY-GOODS                    VALUE '7'.
     88 NOTIONS                      VALUE '8' 'J' 'R' THRU 'W'
                                           '1' THRU '4'.
```

We should mention that some programmers dislike the use of condition names because reference to a name such as **AUTOMOTIVE**, for example, in the Procedure Division does not document the fact that the *field* being examined is **PRODUCT-CODE**. This is a valid point and not to be ignored. Nonetheless, we can argue that the term **AUTOMOTIVE** tells the reader what the program is looking for more effectively than simply testing if the **PRODUCT-CODE** is in the range **G** through **Q**. In the end, the deciding factor should be one of the basic rules of programming: write the program in the way that conveys the most information to a human reader.

7.23 THE PROGRAM OUTPUT

There are two basic changes in the output for this version of the payroll program. First, we have headings at the start of the output, and second, the numeric data values have been edited for easier reading. The changes in the program code begin with two new entries in the Working-Storage Section, **HEADING-LINE-1** and **HEADING-LINE-2**. These structures will be printed at the start of the Procedure Division to create the heading text. Basically, there is nothing new about the structures. Their elementary fields have been initialized with text using **VALUE** clauses, just as we did with the constants in the previous version of the program. Notice that it is not necessary to define a heading line as a single elementary item; we can break it up into pieces in a structure in whatever manner is most convenient.

PAYROLL-LINE is almost the same as **REPORT-RECORD** in Chapter 6, except that we have changed the numeric **PICTURE**s to suppress leading zeros and insert floating dollar signs where appropriate. We have also used the **B** insertion character to put blank spaces between columns instead of having to use **FILLER** entries. This method works equally well; the choice between the two is a matter of personal preference.

In the beginning of the Procedure Division we have added a statement to **PERFORM** the module that prints the column headings, and renumbered the **CALC-EMP-PAYROLL** paragraph to make sure that the paragraph prefixes remain in ascending sequence. Of course, we could have placed the new paragraph after **CALC-EMP-PAYROLL** and given it the **B020** prefix, but the order shown is more in keeping with the hierarchy of the program, and it is generally not wise to bend the structure of a program to fit the convenience of the moment.

Paragraph **B010-PRINT-COLUMN-HEADINGS** begins with an **ACCEPT** statement, but with a slightly different format from what we have seen before. When we follow the data name with the **FROM DATE** phrase, the statement obtains the date from the computer and stores it in the identifier. There are two other options similar to the **DATE** option, and the format of the **ACCEPT** statement for all these options is as shown:

The identifier may be any data item whose format is consistent with the particular data source chosen. **DATE** gives the current date in the form **YYMMDD** (year, month, day), and has the implicit format **9(6)**; for example, July 4, 1981 is given as 810704. **DAY** contains the year and day of the year in the form **YYDDD**, and has the implicit format **9(5)**; July 4, 1981 is expressed as 81185. **TIME** contains the time of day in the form **HHMMSSHH** (hours, minutes, seconds, hundredths of a second), and has the implicit format **9(8)**. For example, 30 seconds after 3:45 p.m. is expressed as 15453000. (Note the use of the 24-hour clock.)

The data names **DATE, DAY,** and **TIME** are reserved words that may be used only with the **ACCEPT** statement. You could *not*, for example, write

```
MOVE TIME TO TIME-OF-DAY.
```

COBOL-85

COBOL-85 provides a fourth data source, **DAY-OF-WEEK**. **DAY-OF-WEEK** has the implicit format **9**, and its value is an integer between 1 and 7 whose value represents the current day of the week; Monday is day 1, and Sunday is day 7. For example, if a program were run on July 4, 1990, **DAY-OF-WEEK** would have the value 3, representing Wednesday.

END COBOL-85

Notice that **DATE** presents the date in the order year, month, and day, and that we have not changed this order in moving the data into **REPORT-DATE**. There are several ways in which we could have reordered the data fields into the more familiar month/day/year sequence, but for now we will leave the order unchanged. The reason we accepted the date into **W-TODAYS-DATE** instead of accepting it directly into **REPORT-DATE** is to get the slashes edited into the field. The **ACCEPT** verb treats **DATE** as though it were a character field and performs no editing.

PAYROLL CALCULATION REPORT   88/10/26

NUMBER	NAME	HOURS	RATE	DEP	GROSS	TAX	NET
12345	Thos. H. Kelly	20.0	5.350	0	$107.00	$22.47	$84.53
12401	Henry Jensen	40.0	7.500	1	$300.00	$52.50	$247.50
12511	Nancy Kahn	40.0	7.500	3	$300.00	$31.50	$268.50
12567	B. R. Brooks	40.0	5.750	2	$230.00	$27.30	$202.70
26017	Jane Milano	10.0	6.875	3	$68.75	$0.00	$68.75
12004	Kay Deluccia	40.0	6.000	4	$240.00	$8.40	$231.60
26109	Peter W. Sherwood	40.0	10.000	5	$400.00	$31.50	$368.50
26222	George M. Mulvaney	41.0	10.000	5	$415.00	$34.65	$380.35
26500	A. W. Enwright	40.0	5.450	1	$218.00	$35.28	$182.72
27511	Ruth Garrison	50.0	10.000	4	$550.00	$73.50	$476.50
28819	Leo X. Butler	40.1	10.000	2	$401.50	$63.32	$338.18
28820	D. X. Iannuzi	45.0	4.500	3	$213.75	$13.39	$200.36
28821	K. L. Ng, Jr.	35.0	4.500	3	$157.50	$1.58	$155.92
28822	Daniel Reiner	35.0	4.500	3	$157.50	$1.58	$155.92
28822	L. E. Simon	38.8	6.000	3	$232.80	$17.39	$215.41
22831	A. Real Bad-One	38.0	4.500	0	$171.00	$35.91	$135.09
70006	GARBAGE-CASE-1	0.0	0.000	0	$0.00	$0.00	$0.00
70007	GARBAGE-CASE-2	0.0	0.000	0	$0.00	$0.00	$0.00
70008	GARBAGE-CASE-3	0.0	0.000	0	$0.00	$0.00	$0.00
29000	Anne Henderson	40.2	10.000	3	$403.00	$53.13	$349.87
29001	Julia Kipp	40.3	10.000	1	$404.50	$74.45	$330.05
88888	Ima Testcase	99.9	99.999	99	$984.87	$7.32	$977.55

FIGURE 7.5 Illustrative output of the program in Figure 7.4.

The remainder of B010-PRINT-COLUMN-HEADINGS holds no surprises. Notice that in order to print blank lines we had to move SPACES into REPORT-RECORD before writing it. There is a better way to do this, which we shall discuss in Chapter 9.

Other than these changes, and the use of a level 88 item in C010-GET-PAYROLL-DATA, the current version of the payroll program is exactly the same as the first one in Chapter 6. It was run with the test data that was use for the program in Figure 6.7, and produced the output shown in Figure 7.5. Of course, several of the input values were found to be in error. The program would not, for example, accept alphabetic values for the payroll number. Where possible we made reasonable corrections to the bad data fields. For records such as the garbage cases, we simply assumed that all data was invalid and substituted zeroes. Compare this report to the one shown in Section 6.13. Quite an improvement!

It is clear that we have accomplished our objectives. The report heading appears at the top of the report, with the current date on the first line and descriptive text over each column. The numeric fields, except for the payroll number, have had leading zeros suppressed; and the fields that represent dollar amounts have dollar signs preceding each amount. However, the last line, for Ima Testcase, is still in error; the fact that the numbers look prettier doesn't alter the fact that they are wrong! We will learn how to deal with this last problem in the next chapter.

7.24 READING SIGNED DATA

We have one last topic to consider relating to data pictures: How do we read signed numeric data from a field in a record? There is no problem if we are getting the data using an **ACCEPT** statement; we type the data with a leading sign and the computer does everything else for us. If we are reading data from a field in a record, however, the situation is different. If we simply define a numeric item with an operational sign, such as **S999**, the sign is assumed to be stored *within* the numeric field, generally associated with the rightmost digit. This makes no difference within the computer (after all, as long as the compiler knows where the sign is, it usually doesn't make any difference to us what the details are), but it becomes immensely important when we need to type a negative number to be entered into the computer as data.

In earlier versions of **COBOL** the problem could be resolved fairly easily. Since data was entered on punched cards, you could simply type *both* the digit and the sign in the same column on the card. This technique doesn't work too well with a computer terminal.

You might consider using the display sign, + or -, but this really isn't a good solution either. The main problem is that the treatment of display signs in input records is not consistent from compiler to compiler. The Microsoft compiler treats a display sign as a separate character on input and reads the data correctly. For example, suppose we had an input record defined as

```
01  INPUT-DATA.
    05  AMOUNT-1        PIC -9(5)V99.
    05  AMOUNT-2        PIC +9(5)V99.
    05  REST-OF-RECORD  PIC X(50).
```

and we read the record

```
-0050095-2039950...
```

The fields **AMOUNT-1** and **AMOUNT-2** will take on the values -500.95 and -20,399.50, respectively. Although you can't do arithmetic on **AMOUNT-1** or **AMOUNT-2** (because they contain display signs, not operational signs), the compiler will allow you to move the fields to Working-Storage fields which do contain operational signs and do arithmetic there.

Unfortunately, what works reasonably well for Microsoft **COBOL** will not work with other compilers. For example, another popular microcomputer **COBOL** compiler will not even compile a program that tries to move a field like **AMOUNT-1** to a field with an operational sign, since this involves "unediting" numeric data. The IBM mainframe compiler will compile a program containing the definition of a record such as **INPUT-DATA** (but not if you try to move the fields to ones with operational signs), but produces an error termination when it actually tries to *read* the input records. In other words, regardless of what the actual results might be, they usually aren't what you want!

The proper solution to the problem is to use the **S** picture in combination with a new clause, the **SIGN** clause. For example, suppose we want to read a record for a retail sales operation. This record contains the date, the customer's name and address, and a transaction amount. If the transaction represents a sale, the amount is positive, but if the transaction is for returned merchandise, then the amount is negative. The following structure definition could be used for this record:

```
01   TRANSACTION-RECORD.
     05   TR-DATE              PIC 9(6).
     05   TR-NAME              PIC X(20).
     05   TR-STREET-ADDR       PIC X(20).
     05   TR-CITY              PIC X(10).
     05   TR-STATE             PIC XX.
     05   TR-ZIP               PIC 9(5).
     05   TR-AMOUNT            PIC S9(4)V99
                               SIGN IS TRAILING SEPARATE.
```

The **SIGN** clause tells the compiler that the sign is to be treated as a separate character which, in this example, follows the amount field. This means that the **TR-AMOUNT** is a *seven*-character item: 4 digits before the decimal point, an implied decimal point (which takes no space), 2 digits after the decimal point, and a sign. We could, for example, type **TRANSACTION-RECORD** as

```
891231AJAX CORPORATION    123 MAIN STREET     MIDDLETOWNOH44999009998-
```

The complete format for the **SIGN** clause is

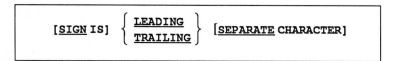

If the **SEPARATE** phrase is omitted, the sign is stored within the item and the **s** character does not occupy a separate position in the computer; this is essentially the situation that normally exists, when no **SIGN** clause is used. However, if the **SEPARATE** phrase is present, the sign is treated as a separate character, either preceding or following the number, depending on whether **LEADING** or **TRAILING** is used.

REVIEW QUESTIONS

1. Fill in the edited result column for each of the following.

SENDING ITEM		RECEIVING ITEM	
PICTURE	SAMPLE DATA	PICTURE	EDITED RESULT
9(6)	000123	ZZZ,999	
9(6)	000008	ZZZ,999	
9(6)	123456	ZZZ,ZZZ.00	
9(4)V99	123456	ZZZ,ZZZ.ZZ	
9(4)V99	001234	$$,$$9.99	
9(4)V99	000078	$$,$$9.99	
9(4)V99	000078	$Z,ZZ9.99	
S9(4)V99	000078 (+)	$Z,ZZ9.99CR	

S9(4)V99	04567̄8	$Z,ZZ9.99CR
S9(6)	12345̄6	-999,999
S9(6)	12345⁺6	-999,999
S9(6)	12345⁺6	+999,999
S9(6)	12345̄6	+999,999
S9(6)	12345̄6	----,--9
S9(6)	00012⁺3	----,--9
S9(6)	00123⁺4	++++,++9
9(6)	123456	99B99B99
9(6)	123456	99/99/99
9(6)	001234	Z(6)0
9(6)	000092	ZZZ,ZZZ00
999PPP	123	9(8)
X(6)	123ABC	XBXBXBBXXX
X(6)	123ABC	X/X/X//XXX

2. For each of the following entries, supply the character that is used in a PICTURE character string to designate the function.

   a. Assumed decimal point.
   b. Actual decimal point.
   c. Zero suppression without insertion of any other character.
   d. Numeric digit.
   e. Alphanumeric character.
   f. Alphabetic character.
   g. Zero suppression and check protection.
   h. Presence of a sign.
   i. Zero suppression with floating dollar sign insertion.
   j. Credit.
   k. Debit.
   l. Scale factor.

3. True or false:

   a. An assumed decimal point takes up no space in storage and is therefore not counted in determining the size of an item.
   b. A display decimal point takes up no space in storage and is therefore not counted in determining the size of an item.

c. A scale factor (character **P**) takes up no space in storage and is therefore not counted in determining the size of an item.

d. Given the following Data Division entry

```
05  FIELD-R         PICTURE X(5).
```

we could legally write

```
ADD 3 TO FIELD-R.
```

e. Given the following Data Division entry

```
05  FIELD-X         PICTURE 999.
```

we could legally write

```
MOVE 'ABC' TO FIELD-X.
```

f. **PICTURE 99,99Z.99** could be used to zero-suppress a field up to and including the decimal point.

4. Which of the following may appear more than once in a **PICTURE** clause?
   a. Actual decimal point.
   b. Assumed decimal point.
   c. Dollar sign.
   d. Scale factor.
   e. Comma.
   f. Sign designation.
   g. Minus sign.
   h. Plus sign.

5. Identify any errors in the following **PICTURE** character strings.
   a. `99.99.99`
   b. `99,99,99`
   c. `-Z,ZZ9.99CR`
   d. `$$$Z.99`
   e. `ZZZ,ZZ9.Z9`
   f. `$**,***.99`
   g. `+++,$$$.99`
   h. `999,PPP,999`

6. For each of the following, supply a **PICTURE** clause that could produce the edited results from the data shown. There will not, in most cases, be just one correct answer, since you will not know how other data might be treated. On the first entry, for example, the **PICTURE** could be **Z9.9999** or **ZZ.9999** and give the same result with the data shown.

SENDING ITEM		RECEIVING ITEM	
PICTURE	SAMPLE DATA	PICTURE	EDITED RESULT
99V9(4)	013579		1.3579

99V9 (4)	011111	001.11110
9 (6)	000000	
9 (6)	000001	1
9 (4) V99	000123	$ 01.23
9 (4) V99	000123	$1.23
9 (4) V99	001234	$***12.34
9 (6)	000005	$5.00
S9 (6)	000014 (+)	*****14+
S9 (6)	000014 (+)	+ 14
S9 (6)	000014 (−)	14CR
S9 (6)	000014 (+)	+14
S9 (6)	000014 (−)	014−
S9 (6)	009876 (+)	+9,876
S9 (4) V99	012345 (−)	$123.45DB
S9 (4) V99	123456 (+)	$1,234.56+
S9 (4) V99	000123 (−)	$****1.23−
X (6)	USARMY	U S ARMY
9 (6)	123456	1,23,456
9 (6)	123456	123 4560

7. Identify errors in each of the following.

```
a.  05  SALARY-CODE.
        88  MONTHLY         PIC X VALUE '1'.
        88  WEEKLY          PIC X VALUE '2'.
        88  SPECIAL         PIC X VALUE '3'.
        88  ERROR-CODE      PIC X VALUE '0' '4' THRU '9'.
b.  01  CODES.
        77  CODE-1          PIC X.
        77  CODE-2          PIC X.
c.  01  FLD-9       PIC -9(5) SIGN IS LEADING SEPARATE.
d.  77  TODAYS-DATE     PIC Z9/99/99.
            .
            .
            .
        ACCEPT TODAYS-DATE FROM DATE.
```

8. In Section 7.22 we said that it was not necessary to give an initial value to the payroll number. Why is this true?

ANSWERS TO REVIEW QUESTIONS

1.

SENDING ITEM		RECEIVING ITEM	
PICTURE	SAMPLE DATA	PICTURE	EDITED RESULT
9(6)	000123	ZZZ,999	123
9(6)	000008	ZZZ,999	008
9(6)	123456	ZZZ,ZZZ.00	123,456.00
9(4)V99	123456	ZZZ,ZZZ.ZZ	1,234.56
9(4)V99	001234	$$,$$9.99	$12.34
9(4)V99	000078	$$,$$9.99	$0.78
9(4)V99	000078	$Z,ZZ9.99	$ 0.78
S9(4)V99	000078⁺	$Z,ZZ9.99CR	$ 0.78
S9(4)V99	045678⁻	$Z,ZZ9.99CR	$ 456.78CR
S9(6)	123456⁻	-999,999	-123,456
S9(6)	123456⁺	-999,999	123,456
S9(6)	123456⁺	+999,999	+123,456
S9(6)	123456⁻	+999,999	-123,456
S9(6)	123456⁻	----,--9	-123,456
S9(6)	000123⁺	----,--9	123
S9(6)	001234⁺	++++,++9	+1,234
9(6)	123456	99B99B99	12 34 56
9(6)	123456	99/99/99	12/34/56
9(6)	001234	Z(6)0	12340
9(6)	000092	ZZZ,ZZZ00	9200
999PPP	123	9(8)	00123000
X(6)	123ABC	XBXBXBBXXX	1 2 3 ABC
X(6)	123ABC	X/X/X//XXX	1/2/3//ABC

2. a. v

   b. .

   c. z

    d. 9

    e. X

    f. A

    g. *

    h. S

    I. $

    j. CR

    k. DB

    l. P

3. a. True.

    b. False.

    c. True. The scale factor affects the number of *digits* the item represents, but not the amount of space the item occupies.

    d. False. Arithmetic may not be done on alphanumeric items.

    e. False. Alphanumeric data may not be stored in a numeric item.

    f. False. Zero suppression applies only to *leading zeros*, so if a picture has both 9s and Zs, the Zs must be to the left of any 9s.

4. a. May not appear more than once, since decimal point alignment would be ambiguous.

    b. Ditto.

    c. More than one dollar sign specifies floating dollar sign.

    d. Any number may be written, but must be either at the left end of the picture or the right end.

    e. Any number may be written.

    f. Only one permitted.

    g. More than one calls for floating sign insertion.

    h. Ditto.

5. a. A decimal point may not appear more than once in a PICTURE character string.

    b. No error.

    c. A PICTURE string may not have both a minus sign and CR or DB.

    d. Only one form of zero suppression is permitted in one PICTURE character string.

    e. A 9 may not precede a Z which, if permitted, would describe separate zero suppression operations within one item.

    f. No error.

    g. Two different floating string characters are not permitted in the same PICTURE character string.

    h. The scale factor must be at one end or the other of the PICTURE character string, not in the middle.

6.

SENDING ITEM		RECEIVING ITEM	
PICTURE	SAMPLE DATA	PICTURE	EDITED RESULT
99V9(4)	013579	Z9.9(4)	1.3579
99V9(4)	011111	999.9(5)	001.11110
9(6)	000000	ZZZ,ZZZ	
9(6)	000001	ZZZ,ZZZ	1
9(4)V99	000123	$Z,Z99.99	$ 01.23
9(4)V99	000123	$$,$$9.99	$1.23
9(4)V99	001234	$*,**9.99	$***12.34
9(6)	000005	$$$$,$$9.00	$5.00
S9(6)	000014 (+)	***,**9+	*****14+
S9(6)	000014 (+)	+ZZZ,ZZ9	+ 14
S9(6)	000014 (−)	ZZZ,ZZ9CR	14CR
S9(6)	000014 (+)	++++,++9	+14
S9(6)	000014 (−)	ZZZ999−	014−
S9(6)	009876 (+)	++++,+++	+9,876
S9(4)V99	012345 (−)	$$,$$9.99DB	$123.45DB
S9(4)V99	123456 (+)	$$,$$9.99+	$1,234.56+
S9(4)V99	000123 (−)	$*,**9.99−	$****1.23−
X(6)	USARMY	XBXBX(4)	U S ARMY
9(6)	123456	9,99,999	1,23,456
9(6)	123456	0999B9990	0123 4560

7. a. The elementary item to which a level **88** entry refers must have a **PICTURE** clause; a level **88** entry itself must not have a **PICTURE**.

b. Level **77** entries cannot be parts of group items.

c. If the **SIGN** phrase is used, the **PICTURE** character string must contain an operational sign character, not a display sign character.

d. The **ACCEPT** statement simply moves the contents of **DATE** into the identifier, **TODAYS-DATE** in this case, so the editing implied by the **Z** and the slashes in the picture would not be performed.

8. Because the first thing the program does after printing the column headings is to execute paragraph **C010-GET-PAYROLL-DATA**, which begins by getting a new payroll number. Any previous value is ignored.

EXERCISES

*1. In each of the five parts of this exercise you are given four sending items, a **PICTURE** character string that describes all of them, and corresponding edited receiving items. For each part write a **PICTURE** clause for the receiving area that would edit the sending items as shown.

    a. 9(5)

```
12345      12345
01234       1234
00123        123
00012        012
```

    b. 9(6)

```
012345     $12345
000123       $123
000001         $1
000000
```

    c. 9(4)V99

```
012345     $123.45
000123     $  1.23
000001     $  0.01
000000     $  0.00
```

    d. S9(4)

```
  +
1234      +1234
  -
0012       -12
  +
0004        +4
  +
0000
```

    e. S9(5)

```
01462       1   462
00192       0   192
10004      10   004
98765      98   765
```

2. Same as Exercise 1.

    a. S999

```
  +
123      123
  -
123     -123
  -
002      -2
  +
000       0
```

    b. 9(4)V99

```
123456     1,234.56
001234        12.34
000123         1.23
000012         0.12
```

* Answers to starred exercises will be found in Appendix IV at the end of the book.

c. 9(4)

```
1234    1234.00
0012      12.00
0001       1.00
0000       0.00
```

d. 999V99

```
12345    $123.45
00012    $***.12
00001    $***.01
00000    ****.**
```

e. 9(4)

```
1234    $1234
0123    $123
0012    $12
0001    $01
```

*3. Study the input record format shown and the printed output produced from it for sample data. Supply the PICTURE clauses for I-RECORD and O-DETAIL-LINE that would properly describe such a record and produce such output. On the output provide five blank spaces between columns.

Input record format:

Columns 1-5	Customer Number	numeric
Columns 6-25	Customer Name	
Columns 6	First Initial	
Columns 7-25	Last Name	
Columns 26-31	Amount of Sale	dollars and cents; negative for refund
Columns 32-37	Product Code	mixed letters and numbers
Columns 38-79	Blanks	
Columns 80	Record Code	A-Z

Sample output:

```
12 345    J DOE            $1,012.09    CD149A    S
23 456    R ROE               $4.79-    PQ276C    R
34 567    J SMITH              $.84      CX726X    S
```

```
01  I-RECORD.
    05  I-CUST-NO
    05  I-CUST-NAME
    05  I-AMT-SALE
    05  I-PROD-CODE
    05  FILLER
    05  I-RECORD-CODE

01  O-DETAIL-LINE.
    05  O-CUST-NO
    05  FILLER
    05  O-CUST-NAME
    05  FILLER
    05  O-AMT-SALE
    05  FILLER
    05  O-PROD-CODE
    05  FILLER
    05  O-RECORD-CODE
```

(Suggested by Professor Stuart J. Travis, Ferris State College.)

4. Supply PICTURE clauses for the following record format.

Record format:

Columns 1-5	Cust No.	numeric only
Columns 6-65	Cust. Address	
Columns 6-25	Name	
Columns 26-45	Street Address	
Columns 46-65	City and State	
Columns 66-72	Amount of Sale	
Columns 73-79	Not Used	
Columns 80	Code	A-Z only

```
01   DATA-RECORD.
     05   CUST-NO
     05   CUST-ADDRESS
          10   NAME
          10   STREET
          10   CITY
     05   SALE-AMT
     05   FILLER
     05   REC-CODE
```

In the following two exercises you are given a File Section description of a number of sending items that are to be edited for printing in a specified format. The format required is described and a sample of the described output is shown. You are to prepare the entries, including all necessary PICTURE clauses, for a record named OUTPUT-LINE. You are not required to write any Procedure Division entries, but it is assumed that for each exercise there would be MOVE statements of the form

```
MOVE ITEM TO ITEM-OUT
```

for each item to be printed.

*5. (See general description above.) The output goes on a preprinted form (see next page), so decimal points are not required and most items are to be printed without spaces between adjacent fields. Specifically, the items from ID-NUMBER through REFERENCE have no spaces between them. Between REFERENCE and GROSS there is one blank space, between GROSS and DISC-OR-DEDUC there is one, and between DISC-OR-DEDUC and AMOUNT-PAYABLE there are two.

```
01   INPUT-RECORD.
     05   ID-NUMBER          PIC X(6).
     05   REQUISITION        PIC X(6).
     05   FUND               PIC X(4).
     05   DEPARTMENT         PIC X(4).
     05   B                  PIC XX.
     05   PURCHASE-ORDER     PIC X(6).
     05   REFERENCE          PIC X(18).
     05   GROSS              PIC 9(5)V99.
     05   DISC-OR-DEDUC      PIC 999V99.
     05   AMOUNT-PAYABLE     PIC 9(5)V99.
```

ANYVILLE UNIVERSITY					DETACH THIS STUB BEFORE CASHING				E 431861	
REFERENCE		FUND	DEPT	B	P. O. NUMBER	YOUR REFERENCE	GROSS	DISCOUNT OR DEDUCTIONS	AMOUNT	
NUMBER	REQ.									
508397		0100	2104	02		HONORARIUM	250 00	0 00	250 00	

Please direct any correspondence regarding this payment to ACCOUNTS PAYABLE, BUSINESS OFFICE, ADMINISTRATIVE SERVICES BLDG.
2810 University Place, Gotham City, XX 12345 OR TELEPHONE 212-345-6789

```
01   OUTPUT-LINE.
     05   ID-NUMBER-OUT
     05   REQUISITION-OUT
     05   FUND-OUT
     05   DEPARTMENT-OUT
     05   B-OUT
     05   PURCHASE-ORDER-OUT
     05   REFERENCE-OUT
     05   FILLER
     05   GROSS-OUT
     05   FILLER
     05   DISC-OR-DEDUC-OUT
     05   FILLER
     05   AMOUNT-PAYABLE-OUT
```

6. (See general description before Exercise 5.) The output goes on a pre-printed form, but of a different design with more room. There are eight items to be printed; the number of blank spaces between them, reading from left to right, are two, three, two, two, one, one, and one. The item named LEASE-BEGAN consists of five characters including the slash. Zero suppression is to be applied only to the three dollar amounts, which are to have decimal points inserted but not dollar signs.

```
01   INPUT-RECORD.
     05   LEASE-BEGAN          PIC X(5).
     05   LEASE-TERM           PIC XX.
     05   PAYABLE              PIC X.
     05   DESCRIPTION          PIC X(21).
     05   LEASE-NUMBER         PIC X(5).
     05   CURRENT-RENT         PIC 999V99.
     05   SALES-TAX            PIC 99V99.
     05   CURRENT-AMT-DUE      PIC 999V99.

01   OUTPUT-LINE.
     05   LEASE-BEGAN-OUT
     05   FILLER
     05   LEASE-TERM-OUT
     05   FILLER
     05   PAYABLE-OUT
```

```
05   FILLER
05   DESCRIPTION-OUT
05   FILLER
05   LEASE-NUMBER-OUT
05   FILLER
05   CURRENT-RENT-OUT
05   FILLER
05   SALES-TAX-OUT
05   FILLER
05   CURRENT-AMT-DUE-OUT
```

Lease began	Lease term	Payable	Equipment Description	Lease Number	Current Rent	Sales Tax	Current Amount Due
08/87	36	M	PHOTOCOPIER	38459	162.43	13.40	175.83

*7. Prepare a hierarchy chart and pseudocode to design a program that will prepare an accounts receivable report, then write a program to implement your design.

The input consists of records having the following format:

Columns 1-5	Customer number
Columns 6-25	Customer name
Columns 26-30	Invoice number
Columns 31-36	Invoice date
Columns 37-42	Invoice amount in dollars and cents, with an assumed decimal point

The problem is to produce a report with page and column headings of the following form. (You may ignore the requirement to limit the number of detail lines; come back to this after you have studied the ADVANCING clause and line spacing.)

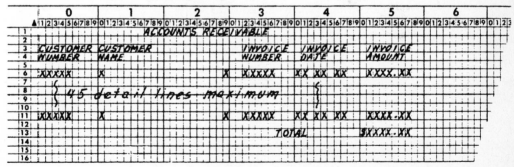

The report is to start with the 5 lines (including blanks) of the heading, as shown. As the accounts receivable records are read and printed, a final total of the invoice amounts is to be accumulated. When the last record has been read, this total should be printed following the body of the report.

Here is sample input for the exercise:

```
12810AMERICAN CAN        1122311238715746  8
12810AMERICAN CAN        1233612308704090  2
21654APPLEBEE MFG.       0985201058803300  0
22873BAKER TOOL          1245311268705769  0
24251C.F.B. FREIGHT      1334201068813007  6
```

For this input, the program should produce the following output.

ACCOUNTS RECEIVABLE

CUSTOMER NUMBER	CUSTOMER NAME	INVOICE NUMBER	INVOICE DATE	INVOICE AMOUNT
12810	AMERICAN CAN	11223	11 23 87	1574.68
12810	AMERICAN CAN	12336	12 30 87	409.02
21654	APPLEBEE MFG.	09852	01 05 88	330.00
22873	BAKER TOOL	12543	11 26 87	576.90
24251	C.F.B. FREIGHT	13342	01 06 88	1300.76

| | | | TOTAL | $4,191.36 |

(Adapted, by permission of the author, from Joan K. Hughes, *PL/I Programming*. New York: Wiley, 3rd edition, 1985.)

8. Design (hierarchy chart and pseudocode) and implement a program to produce proof totals for a weekly payroll.

    You are given a file whose records have the following format.

Column 1	Record Type 1 = regular pay 2 = overtime pay 3 = bonus pay 4 = other pay
Columns 2-6	Employee Number (numeric)
Columns 7-11	Earnings in dollars and cents, with an assumed decimal point.

    The goal is to produce four totals, one for each type of earnings. For each type of earnings, the program is to print a count of the number of records of that type. For instance, the total for regular earnings consists of the sum of the earnings amount on all records having the record type of 1.

    The printer layout should be as follows:

Here is some sample data:

```
11111118542
21111101465
11111229011
21111201200
11111340000
31111308000
41111450000
11111538065
11111642000
21111612376
41111601000
11111729999
11111868011
31111910500
```

For this input, the program should produce this output:

```
PROOF TOTALS FOR WEEKLY PAYROLL

REGULAR          7      $2,656.28

OVERTIME         3        $138.41

BONUS            2        $185.00

OTHER            2        $510.00
```

(Adapted, by permission of the author, from Joan K. Hughes, *PL/I Programming*. New York: Wiley, 3rd edition, 1985.)

*9. Modify the program in Figure 7.4 so that it treats the data as invalid and prints the message GROSS PAY SUSPICIOUSLY LARGE if the computed gross pay exceeds $600.

*10. Modify the program in Figure 7.4 so that at the end of the listing, it produces a count of the total number of employees processed, the total of the gross pay for all employees, the total of the tax for all employees, and the total of the net pay for all employees.

*11. A United States company pays taxes in 10 different states. In a certain tax summarization program it is desired to be able to write statements like

```
IF ALABAMA
        PERFORM D010-ALABAMA-TAX-COMP.
```

rather than

```
IF STATE-CODE = '01'
        PERFORM D010-ALABAMA-TAX-COMP.
```

Show how this can be accomplished.

12. Continuing with Exercise 11, suppose that the 50 states are to be referenced in three categories:

   a. Those that have a condition name consisting of their name, of which there are only 4: California, Michigan, Illinois, and Florida;

   b. Any of the other 6 states to which the company pays taxes, referred to by a condition name of OTHER-STATE;

   c. Any of the other 40 states, referred to by INVALID-STATE.
   Show how this can be accomplished.

*13. All of the examples of the actions of various PICTURE characters were produced by COBOL programs. Write a program to produce the examples in Section 7.7.

14. Same as Exercise 13, except write the program to produce the examples in Section 7.10. Be sure to include code that will write the sign of each sending item above the item, as shown in the examples.

CHAPTER 8

DEBUGGING

8.1 INTRODUCTION

By now you have probably discovered that it is almost impossible to write a program, in COBOL or any other language, without making *some* kind of error. The objective of this chapter is to study various types of errors that occur in a COBOL program, and to find ways of dealing with them.

Errors in COBOL programs can be divided into two types: *compile-time* and *run-time*. Recall that the function of the COBOL compiler is to take the *source code* that you write and turn it into *machine code*, also called *object code*, that can be executed by the computer. (This is a slight simplification, since linking is needed to create the actual machine code that the computer executes, but we can ignore this for our purposes.) Compile-time errors are those that occur during the compilation process, that is, errors in your COBOL code that are detected by the COBOL compiler. Run-time errors are those that occur when the program executes. In other words, you have written a syntactically correct COBOL program but it doesn't produce the proper results. An example of this type of error is the output produced for Ima Testcase in the payroll program of the previous chapters. The program compiled correctly and executed, but the results for this test case were incorrect.

The methods we use for dealing with the two types of errors are completely different. Compile-time errors are detected by the COBOL compiler, which produces a message indicating that an error has been made and where it is located in the program. The general nature of this type of error is always the same: something you have written does not obey the rules of COBOL. The problem is simply a matter of determining why the code is illegal, then correcting it.

Run-time errors are generally much more difficult to deal with. In the first place, the computer frequently will not tell you that an error has occurred. (Consider the first version of the payroll program; it ran and produced output, and nothing the computer did informed us that part of the output was incorrect.) We must learn how to tell if the output the computer produces is invalid. However, even if the computer does tell you that *something* has gone wrong, it usually does not do a very good job of telling you exactly what caused the problem and where the error is located in the program. It is your job as the programmer to find the answers to these questions, then determine how to correct the problem.

8.2   THE EFFECT OF PROGRAM DESIGN ON DEBUGGING

The best way to fix program errors is not to put them in the program in the first place. Although this may seem to be a rather sarcastic comment ("Of course I don't want to put errors into my program!"), the intent is quite serious. The place to start debugging a program is with the design. If the design of the program is clear and logical, and if the specifications are complete and free of errors, then the program will probably not have serious problems. However, no amount of work will make a good program from a poor design. *If you don't understand how to solve the problem, the computer won't figure it out for you!*

We discussed the basics of program design in Chapter 4, and now we see more of the motive for the techniques used. It is not sufficient simply to produce a program; we must be able to develop a program that works correctly, with a minimum of debugging, and (as we shall see throughout the book) that can be modified with a minimum amount of effort. The design techniques presented in Chapter 4 serve this goal.

What we did not stress in Chapter 4, however, is the need to review the design for completeness and accuracy. Do not expect that the first attempt at designing a program will be the final attempt. One rarely creates an acceptable design with the first try. After you create the initial versions of the hierarchy chart and pseudocode, review them carefully to make sure that they say what you want them to; that is, if you write a program precisely to those specifications, will it do what it should? In all likelihood you will realize that you have forgotten something or made some kind of error, or simply that there is a better structure for the design. This is not unreasonable. It is necessary to study a problem repeatedly until you learn enough about it to be able to design a good program. The more effort you put into the program design, the more you will understand the problem, and the more likely that your program will be free of serious errors.

8.3   PROGRAMMING STYLE

A good design is not all that is necessary to develop a good program. The coding style that is used in writing a program also affects the number of errors to be found in the program, which is why in our example programs we use the coding standards given in Appendix III. The objective of these standards is to present the program in such a way as to make its statements as clear as possible to the reader. We have mentioned some of these standards in previous chapters and will continue to mention coding technique wherever it is appropriate. Remember: the easier it is for you to read what you have written, the less likely you are to miss errors in the code.

Once the program has been entered into the computer, begin your error checking by getting a printed listing of the program; you may use the print capabilities of your editor, the PRINT command of DOS, or whatever other printing tools you have on your computer. Although the listing should be used to check for simple typing errors, its main purpose is to give you a clean, readable version of the program that can be studied for design errors; you will find that a printed listing is much easier to study than a relatively limited screen display. In particular, verify that the structure of the program matches the structure of the hierarchy chart, and that this structure is a logical one. One of the most important program characteristics to check for is to make certain that each paragraph performs a single, well-defined function. For example, suppose we modified the payroll program in Figure 6.7 slightly so that it counts the number of valid records processed (see Exercises 5 and 6 in Chapter 6). We *could* accomplish this by changing paragraphs **E010-GET-PAYROLL-RECORD** and **E020-EDIT-PAYROLL-RECORD** as follows:

```
E010-GET-PAYROLL-RECORD.
    READ PAYROLL-FILE
            AT END MOVE 'Y' TO W-OUT-OF-RECORDS-FLAG.
    ADD 1 TO VALID-RECORD-COUNT.
E020-EDIT-PAYROLL-RECORD.
    IF      I-PAYROLL-NUMBER IS NOT NUMERIC
        OR  I-HOURS-WORKED   IS NOT NUMERIC
        OR  I-PAYRATE        IS NOT NUMERIC
        OR  I-DEPENDENTS     IS NOT NUMERIC
        MOVE PAYROLL-RECORD TO BAD-DATE
        WRITE REPORT-RECORD FROM ERROR-RECORD
        SUBTRACT 1 FROM VALID-RECORD-COUNT
    ELSE
        MOVE 'Y' TO W-VALID-PAYROLL-RECORD.
```

There are two problems with this code, however. First, each paragraph performs two or more unrelated activities. The activities performed by **E010-GET-PAYROLL-RECORD**, reading a record and incrementing the counter, have nothing to do with one another since one involves getting the next record (valid or not) and the other is related only to valid records. The statements performed in **E020-EDIT-PAYROLL-RECORD** when the condition is true all relate to processing an *invalid* record, except for the **SUBTRACT** statement that is related to processing *valid* records. The task of counting the number of valid records is split over two paragraphs, and the part in each paragraph doesn't really make much sense where it is.

The second basic problem with this version of the program is simply that it will give incorrect results. If the value of **VALID-RECORD-COUNT** is printed at the end of the program, it will not give an accurate count of the number of valid records. The precise nature of the error is left as an exercise (see Exercise 1 at the end of this chapter).

A much better solution to the problem is the following:

```
B020-CALC-EMP-PAYROLL.
    PERFORM C020-COMPUTE-GROSS-PAY.
    PERFORM C030-COMPUTE-EXEMPTIONS.
    PERFORM C040-COMPUTE-TAX.
    PERFORM C050-COMPUTE-NET-PAY.
    PERFORM C060-PRINT-OUTPUT.
    ADD 1 TO VALID-RECORD-COUNT.
    PERFORM C010-GET-VALID-PAY-REC.
```

This approach is based on the fact that counting the number of valid records is related to processing those records, which is controlled by paragraph **B020-CALC-EMP-PAYROLL**. The first version tried to associate counting *valid* records with reading *any* record, then found it necessary to fudge the count when an invalid record was detected, and still did not arrive at an error-free solution. In general you will find that the more closely related the statements in a paragraph are, and the more you place the actions needed to carry out a function in the same paragraph, the more likely you are to have a well-designed program without major errors.

8.4 NESTED IF STATEMENTS

There are several statements or structures in **COBOL** that cause a disproportionately large number of programming problems, particularly for beginning **COBOL** programmers. One of the ways to minimize errors in a **COBOL** program is to avoid using these statements or, if they must be used, to be aware of the problems they can cause.

The first of these "dangerous" constructions that we will look at is the nested **IF**. We have already encountered the nested **IF** in Section 5.14 as a means of implementing the case structure. We now want to see some of the uses of the nested **IF** beyond this one format, and to learn the dangers that the structure presents. Most of the problems that we will discuss apply only to versions of **COBOL** prior to **COBOL-85**. If you are using **COBOL-85**, read the remainder of this section to see how nested **IF** statements are used, but remember that the problems we will be discussing can usually be cured with the **END-IF** phrase.

Recall that a nested **IF** exists when one of the actions of an **IF** statement is itself an **IF** statement. In the following discussion we will use the letter **c** to stand for a Condition, and the letter **s** to stand for a Statement. There will generally be one or more of each, so we shall number them. Thus, we might write

```
IF C1
    IF C2
        S1.
```

to stand for a simple nested **IF** statement such as

```
IF ACCOUNT-NO IS EQUAL TO PREVIOUS-ACCT-NO
    IF DISTRICT IS EQUAL TO PREVIOUS-DISTRICT
        PERFORM C040-PROCESS-DETAIL-RECORD.
```

Another statement that could be represented by the same shorthand is

```
IF HOURS-WORKED IS EQUAL TO 40
    IF REGULAR-PAY
        MOVE 'X' TO NORMAL-PROCESSING-FLAG.
```

In other words, **c1** and **c2** can be any conditions, including condition names from **88** level entries (such as **REGULAR-PAY**). Furthermore, any time we indicate one statement, by writing **s**, any number may be written. Thus the skeleton above would also describe

```
IF A = B
   IF C = D
      MOVE 'X' TO ABCD-FLAG
      PERFORM D055-BOTH-EQUAL.
```

It is always possible to represent the logic of a nested **IF** by one or more simple **IF**s having compound conditions. The statement just given, for example, has exactly the same effect as

```
IF A = B AND  C = D
   MOVE 'X' TO ABCD-FLAG
   PERFORM D055-BOTH-EQUAL.
```

The more complex nested **IF** statements that we shall study later, if translated to unnested form, become many **IF**s, sometimes with very complicated compound conditions. The choice between nested **IF**s vs. simple **IF**s with compound conditions is, to a certain extent, a matter of taste. However, remember that you should always try to make the program as straightforward and readable as possible.

Here is a slightly more complicated nested **IF**:

```
IF C1
   IF C2
      S1
   ELSE
      S2.
```

When written without the nested **IF**, it becomes these two statements:

```
IF C1 AND C2
   S1.
IF C1 AND NOT C2
   S2.
```

This is a good place to mention once again the crucial importance of putting the periods of **IF** statements in the right place. For instance, if the first period in the two unnested **IF**s just shown were omitted, the result would be syntactically correct, but it would represent altogether different logic. The pseudocode for the statements above is shown in Figure 8.1, while the pseudocode for the statements without the first period is shown in Figure 8.2.

The "true" path for the first decision in Figure 8.2 will be taken only if **C1** and **C2** are both true. But if this is the case, it cannot also be the case that **C1** is true and **C2** is false--so **S2** would never be executed. (A "smart" compiler would be able to detect that **S2** is *dead code*, meaning that it can never be reached, but most compilers are not that sophisticated.)

```
IF C1 and C2 THEN
    S1
ENDIF
IF C1 and not C2 THEN
    S2
ENDIF
```

FIGURE 8.1 Pseudocode for correctly written **IF** statements.

```
IF C1 and C2 THEN
    S1
    IF C1 and not C2 THEN
        S2
    ENDIF
ENDIF
```

FIGURE 8.2. Pseudocode for incorrectly written IF statements.

It might be argued that without the period after the first **IF** the indentation of the **COBOL** code is wrong, since then the second **IF** is controlled by the first **IF** and ought to be indented. This, of course, is true, but we must always remember that the compiler knows nothing about indentation rules. These are of great importance for clarity of communication between human beings, but the compiler takes no information from them. In fact, even deeply nested **IF**s may all be written on one line if the data names are short enough. That is not an intelligent way to write code, but it is legal.

An alternate way to write statements such as the ones above is to use a separate paragraph for the nested **IF**. For example, we could write

```
IF C1
    PERFORM NESTED-PARA.
    .
    .
    .

NESTED-PARA.
    IF C2
        S1
    ELSE
        S2.
```

This approach has the advantage that we don't have to worry about omitting the first period, but this comes at the cost of splitting the function to be performed over two paragraphs, which might be pages apart on the listing. Again, within limits, the decision is largely a matter of personal taste and clarity in a specific situation.

Now consider the following **IF** statement, and the matching pseudocode:

```
    COBOL                 PSEUDOCODE

IF C1                  IF C1 THEN
    IF C2                  IF C2 THEN
        S1                     S1
    ELSE                   ELSE
        S2                     S2
ELSE                       ENDIF
    S3.                ELSE
                           S3
                       ENDIF
```

Here each **IF** has a matching **ELSE**. The next step in this progression is to have decisions on both branches of the first decision:

```
        COBOL                PSEUDOCODE

IF C1                   IF C1 THEN
    IF C2                   IF C2 THEN
        S1                      S1
    ELSE                    ELSE
        S2                      S2
ELSE                        ENDIF
    IF C3               ELSE
        S3                  IF C3 THEN
    ELSE                        S3
        S4                  ELSE
                                S4
                            ENDIF
                        ENDIF
```

We have now reached a level of complexity where it is necessary to have rules telling us exactly what is meant by certain forms of nested **IF** statements. The first rule governing the meaning of nested **IF**s is this:

Rule 1: Every statement within a nested **IF** is controlled by the most recent **IF** or **ELSE**.

Here is an **IF** statement where this rule causes no problem:

```
        COBOL                PSEUDOCODE

IF C1                   IF C1 THEN
    S1                      S1
    IF C2                   IF C2 THEN
        S2                      S2
    ELSE                    ELSE
        S3                      S3
ELSE                        ENDIF
    S4                  ELSE
                            S4
                        ENDIF
```

On the true path from the **C1** decision we have first an unconditional statement, then another decision. This is perfectly legal.

Here is an **IF** statement that is also legal but that does not do what is suggested by the indentation. Notice the difference between the two specifications. (The heading INDENTATION PSEUDOCODE is meant to suggest that this is what the **COBOL** codes *looks* like it means, as contrasted with what it really means, as shown in the column headed ACCURATE PSEUDOCODE.)

```
        COBOL           INDENTATION          ACCURATE
                        PSEUDOCODE           PSEUDOCODE

IF C1               IF C1 THEN           IF C1 THEN
    IF C2               IF C2 THEN           IF C2 THEN
        S1                  S1                   S1
    ELSE                ELSE                 ELSE
        S2                  S2                   S2
    S3                  ENDIF                    S3
ELSE                    S3                   ENDIF
    S4              ELSE                 ELSE
                        S4                   S4
                    ENDIF                ENDIF
```

The presumed intention of the indentation in the **COBOL** code is that the action should be as shown in the column headed INDENTATION PSEUDOCODE. The idea is that if **C1** is true, then **S3** is always carried out, regardless of the outcome of the **C2** decision. This is done easily in **COBOL-85** by using the **END-IF** phrase in a manner identical to that shown in the pseudocode. However, in earlier versions of **COBOL** that do not have the **END-IF**, Rule 1 specifies that each statement is controlled by the most recent **IF** or **ELSE**. This means that to describe the action of **COBOL** correctly, **S3** should have been indented exactly the same as **S2**. Regardless of the indentation, however, the action of the **COBOL** statement written will be as shown by the pseudocode in the column marked ACCURATE PSEUDOCODE. **S3** will be carried out only on the false path of **C2**.

This is not an unsolvable problem. One simple solution is to make a performed paragraph out of the **C2** decision. Now the scope of the inner **IF** is contained completely within a performed paragraph; all that appears in the outer **IF** is a **PERFORM**. Statement **S3** can follow this **PERFORM** with no problems as to which **IF** controls it; the outer **IF** does. The code, in skeleton form, would be like this:

```
IF C1
      PERFORM INNER-IF-PARAGRAPH
      S3
ELSE
      S4.
   .
   .
   .

INNER-IF-PARAGRAPH.
   IF C2
      S1
ELSE
      S2.
```

It is very important in interpreting the meaning of **IF**s to know which **IF** goes with which **ELSE**. This is true even if there is an **ELSE** for every **IF**, and it is made even more urgent by the fact that **COBOL** does not require every **IF** to have an **ELSE** path. The meaning of a nested **IF** in this regard is governed by the following rule:

Rule 2: Each **ELSE** in a nested **IF** is matched with the most recent **IF** that does not already have an **ELSE**.

The simplest violation of Rule 2 is shown in this example:

COBOL	INDENTATION PSEUDOCODE	ACCURATE PSEUDOCODE
IF C1	IF C1 THEN	IF C1 THEN
IF C2	IF C2 THEN	IF C2 THEN
S1	S1	S1
ELSE	ENDIF	ELSE
S2.	ELSE	S2
	S2	ENDIF
	ENDIF	ENDIF

The indentation suggests the interpretation shown in the column headed INDENTATION PSEUDOCODE, with the **ELSE** matching the first **IF**. Rule 2, however, states that the actual meaning is that of the column headed ACCU-RATE PSEUDOCODE. Once again this is an error in the semantics of COBOL (the *meaning* of the statement), not an error in the *syntax* (the rules for writing a correct COBOL statement). The statement as written will be compiled without diagnostic error indications, since in fact it breaks no rule of COBOL; it simply doesn't do what the programmer wanted.

Happily this problem has an easy solution, the NEXT SENTENCE feature. At any point in an IF statement where there is nothing to be done and we wish simply to "escape" from the logic of the IF, we may write NEXT SENTENCE. In the example just shown, this permits us to write:

```
IF C1
    IF C2
        S1
    ELSE
        NEXT SENTENCE
ELSE
    S2.
```

The effect is now precisely what is suggested by the indentation.

It occasionally will happen that a set of nested IFs will require no action when the IF conditions are true, but will call for various actions on each of the ELSE paths. In this case we can use the NEXT SENTENCE feature where we would otherwise execute a statement controlled by the "true" path of the innermost IF.

It is possible to write IF statements that are nested as deeply as one wishes, certainly deeper than is generally advisable from the viewpoint of clarity. Consider the following example:

```
IF C1
    S1
    IF C2
        IF C3
            S2
        ELSE
            S3
    ELSE
        S4
        IF C4
            S5
        ELSE
            S6.
```

This example shows the danger that a very complex, deeply nested IF can present, namely that it is easily subject to misinterpretation. Since the compiler can give us no help with semantic errors that are not also syntactic errors, serious mistakes can sometimes go undetected. This suggests that great care should be exercised in determining that nested IFs really do what they are supposed to do, and it also suggests some kind of common sense limit on how complex such statements should be allowed to become. It is difficult to say what constitutes "too complex" but, as a general indication, we suggest that the last example is too error-prone for safety.

We cannot ignore the fact that some programs require complex condition testing simply because of the nature of the problems they deal with. What we can do, however, is to present the code in a manner that is less prone to error than deeply nested **IF**s. For instance, the example above could be written as shown here:

```
IF C1
    PERFORM D010-NESTED-FUNCTION-1.
    .
    .
    .

D010-NESTED-FUNCTION-1.
    S1.
    IF C2
        PERFORM E010-NESTED-FUNCTION-2
    ELSE
        PERFORM E020-NESTED-FUNCTION-3.
    .
    .
    .

E010-NESTED-FUNCTION-2.
    IF C3
        S2
    ELSE
        S3.

E020-NESTED-FUNCTION-3.
    S4.
    IF C4
        S5
    ELSE
        S6.
```

Of course, in a real program the paragraph names for the inner functions would indicate the task that each function is to perform. If the statements being executed, such as **S1** and **S4**, are complex, this approach to coding the program can be much easier to write correctly than trying to create a deeply nested **IF**. Remember, no one gives extra points (or bonuses!) for writing a program with fewer paragraphs. Clarity and correctness are what count.

8.5 OTHER COMMON CODING PROBLEMS

Although the **IF** statement is one of the largest sources of errors in **COBOL**, there are other statement structures that are also common trouble spots. One of these, which we have mentioned before, comes from the fact that conditional clauses in **COBOL** statements can be terminated only by a period. If the conditional clause occurs in the middle of an **IF** statement, which *must not* have a period before its end, we have a problem. Countless hours of debugging time have been spent trying to figure out why code such as the following does not work as expected:

```
MOVE ZERO TO COUNTER.
MOVE 'N' TO EOF-FLAG.
READ INPUT-FILE
        AT END MOVE 'Y' TO EOF-FLAG.
PERFORM B035-PROCESS-RECORD
    UNTIL EOF-FLAG = 'Y'.
    .
    .
    .
```

```
B035-PROCESS-RECORD.
    PERFORM C020-EDIT-RECORD.
    IF EDIT-FLAG = 'Y'
        WRITE OUTPUT-LINE FROM ERROR-MESSAGE
        READ INPUT-FILE
            AT END MOVE 'Y' TO EOF-FLAG
        ADD 1 TO COUNTER
    ELSE
        PERFORM C030-PROCESS-VALID-RECORD
        READ INPUT-FILE
            AT END MOVE 'Y' TO EOF-FLAG.
```

After the program is executed, COUNTER will have a value of 0 or 1—
depending on which READ triggers the AT END—not the number of invalid
records detected. The problem, of course, lies with the first READ statement in
B035-PROCESS-RECORD. Since there is no period following the AT END clause of
this statement, the ADD statement is treated as part of the AT END action and is
executed only once, when the end of file is detected.

Another common error involving the READ statement occurs in code such
as this:

```
MOVE ZERO TO RECORD-COUNT.
MOVE 'N' TO EOF-FLAG.
PERFORM B010-PROCESS-RECORD
    UNTIL EOF-FLAG = 'Y'.
    .
    .
    .

B010-PROCESS-RECORD.
    READ INPUT-FILE
        AT END MOVE 'Y' TO EOF-FLAG.
    ADD 1 TO RECORD-COUNT.
    PERFORM C050-PROCESS-DATA.
```

This program will produce two errors. First, RECORD-COUNT will indicate
one more record than is actually in the input file. Second, an erroneous record
will be processed in C050-PROCESS-DATA. The problem here is that while the
AT END clause signals the end of file, processing still continues within B010-
PROCESS-RECORD. That is, even when the end of file is detected, the ADD and
PERFORM statements are still executed.

There are two cures for this problem. First, a priming record can be read in
the driver paragraph before the PERFORM...UNTIL statement, and the READ
can be moved to the end of B010-PROCESS-RECORD. This means that the AT
END action is executed just before the PERFORM...UNTIL statement tests to see
whether the loop condition is true, thereby ensuring that no action takes place
inside the loop after the end of file. The second cure involves changing B010-
PROCESS-RECORD as follows:

```
B010-PROCESS-RECORD.
    READ INPUT-FILE
        AT END MOVE 'Y' TO EOF-FLAG.
    IF EOF-FLAG = 'N'
        ADD 1 TO RECORD-COUNT
        PERFORM C050-PROCESS-DATA.
```

Now the **ADD** and **PERFORM** are executed only if the end of file has not yet been detected.

Still another common error involving the **READ** statement occurs when the program attempts to read a record even after the end of file has been encountered. Consider the following example. We want to read a maximum of ten records, but stop processing if the end of file is encountered first.

```
MOVE ZERO TO COUNTER.
MOVE 'N' TO EOF-FLAG.
PERFORM B010-PROCESS-RECORD
    UNTIL EOF-FLAG = 'Y'  AND  COUNTER = 10.
    .
    .
    .

B010-PROCESS-RECORD.
    READ INPUT-FILE
            AT END MOVE 'Y' TO EOF-FLAG.
    IF EOF-FLAG = 'N'
        ADD 1 TO COUNTER
        PERFORM C010-PROCESS-DATA.
```

What we wanted to say was that the loop should terminate either if the end of file was reached or the counter was equal to ten. What the code actually says is that the loop will continue until *both* these conditions occur. If the input file contains anything but ten records, the program will attempt to read past the end of the file, generally with fairly disastrous results. While this is one example of how a program might try to read past the end of a file, it is certainly not the only way the problem might occur. Be certain in every program that detecting an end of file will actually cause the program to stop reading from that file.

The example above demonstrates another common **COBOL** error, confusing the use of **AND** and **OR** in a compound condition. Remember that a compound condition using **AND** is true only if *all* of its components are true, while a compound condition using **OR** is true if *any* of its components are true. In the example, what was desired was that the loop should terminate if either of the conditions **EOF-FLAG = 'Y'** or **COUNTER = 10** are true; what was written required that both the conditions must be true to stop the loop.

A very serious type of **COBOL** error involves a particular misuse of the **PERFORM** statement. Since Chapter 4, when we introduced the use of hierarchy charts in program design, we have always used the **PERFORM** statement in such a way that a module on one level of the chart always performed a module on a lower level of the chart. If this approach is followed consistently, we avoid violating one of the restrictions on the use of the **PERFORM** statement: the paragraph named in the **PERFORM** statement cannot be the paragraph containing the **PERFORM** statement. In other words, a statement such as the following is illegal:

```
B010-PROCESS-DATA.
    PERFORM B010-PROCESS-DATA.
```

Although some **COBOL** compilers will detect an error this obvious and generate a warning, many (including the Microsoft compiler) will not. Further more, the restriction on the use of the **PERFORM** actually goes farther than this.

The complete form of the restriction is this: the paragraph named in a PERFORM statement may not be the paragraph containing the PERFORM statement, nor may the PERFORM statement perform any paragraph that results in a PERFORM of the original paragraph. For example, the following code is illegal:

```
PARA-1.
    PERFORM PARA-2.

PARA-2.
    PERFORM PARA-3.

PARA-3.
    PERFORM PARA-1.
```

This type of procedure is called *recursive*. In languages like Pascal, recursion is legal and often useful for solving the types of problems best attacked with such languages. However, in COBOL recursive programming is illegal. If you use the design techniques we have shown in this book, it is unlikely you will need to use recursion. In any case, it is not supported by COBOL and will cause an error sooner or later. Unfortunately, the error frequently occurs in such a way that the cause is not obvious.

The last common error we wish to mention is one we have already discussed. It occurs when a program tries to execute with data containing errors, such as nonnumeric data in a (supposedly) numeric field. This type of error sometimes will cause abnormal program termination, but more commonly simply gives results that are incorrect, and not always obviously so. It is vital that your program validate any input data that could contain errors, if at all possible. Most commonly this involves testing numeric fields to be certain that their contents actually are numeric. Other times it will involve testing data to be certain that it is within an acceptable range, or that a value can be found on a list of legal values. The exact nature of the validation will depend on the program and the data involved, but it must be done. There is no excuse for a program that "blows up" because of invalid input data.

We should add two warnings, however. First, it is not always necessary that data validation and data processing be done in the same program. For example, in a payroll system one might wish to validate the payroll records in one program, then process the valid records in a second program. This gives the people who use the program an opportunity to correct errors before payroll checks are actually produced. The second warning is that there are some fields that cannot be edited by a program. For example, it is difficult to come up with a formula for validating a person's name without rejecting names that are perfectly correct; the name "John P. O'Malley, Jr." is correct, but contains several nonalphabetic characters. This simply means that you should validate the fields that you can, but not force validation on those fields that can't be edited.

The errors that we have discussed in this section are common COBOL errors, but they are certainly not the only errors you may encounter. We will discuss other potential errors as we present new material; in the remainder of this chapter we discuss ways of locating and dealing with various general types of errors.

8.6 COMPILE-TIME ERRORS

COBOL compilers are designed to identify code that is not legal COBOL (syntax errors). Of course, no two compilers use exactly the same format for reporting these errors. In some cases, the error messages are displayed in the middle of a program listing, immediately following the line(s) of code containing the error(s). In other cases, all error messages are printed at the end of the program listing along with line or statement numbers to identify the code in error. In still other cases, with microcomputers in particular, the compiler may not create a program listing at all, relying on your ability to use a source code editor to look at the program. The following discussion will be based on an example run using the Microsoft COBOL compiler. Obviously the messages used by this compiler are not universal, and you may need to adapt the following material if you are using a different compiler.

8.7 AN EXAMPLE OF COMPILE-TIME ERRORS

The payroll program presented in Chapter 7 (Figure 7.4) intentionally was modified to create syntax errors. Because of the seriousness of some of these errors, the COBOL compiler was not able to produce an object program. It is instructive to examine the diagnostic error messages in Figure 8.4 to see how they can help in developing a correct program. Naturally, no other compiler would give *exactly* this list of messages. Nevertheless, readers not using this compiler will find the following discussion useful, since the general principles are valid even though details differ.

```
1          IDENTIFICATION DIVISION.
2          PROGRAM-ID.
3              PAYROLL4.
4          AUTHOR.
5              D. GOLDEN.
6          DATE-WRITTEN.
7              OCTOBER 3, 1988.
8          *
9          *    THIS PROGRAM CONTAINS MANY DELIBERATE ERRORS.
10         *    A CORRECT VERSION OF THE PROGRAM IS SHOWN IN FIGURE 8.5.
11         *
12
13         ENVIRONMENT DIVISION.
14         FILE-CONTROL.
15             SELECT PAYROLL-FILE      ASSIGN TO 'C06P02.DAT'.
16             SELECT REPORT-FILE       ASSIGN TO C07P01.REP.
17
18         DATA DIVISION.
19         FILE SECTION.
20         FD  PAYROLL-FILE.
21             LABEL RECORDS ARE STANDARD.
22         01  PAYROLL-RECORD.
23             05  I-PAYROLL-NUMBER     PIC X(5).
24             05  I-NAME               PIC X(20).
25             05  I-HOURS-WORKED       PIC 99V9.
26             05  FILLER               PIC X(3).
27             05  I-PAYRATE            PIC 99V999.
28             05  I-DEPENDENTS         PIC 99.
29             05  FILLER               PIC X(42).
30
```

```
31      FD   REPORT-FILE
32           LABEL RECORDS ARE STANDARD.
33      01   REPORT-RECORD              PIC X(75)          VALUE SPACES.
34
35      WORKING STORAGE SECTION.
36      77   C-EXEMPTION               PIC S99V99         VALUE +50.00.
37      77   C-TAXRATE                 PIC   SV999        VALUE   +.210.
38      77   W-EXEMPTION-TOTAL         PIC S999V99.
39      77   W-GROSS-PAY               PIC S999V99.
40      77   W-NET-PAY                 PIC S999V99.
41      77   W-OUT-OF-RECORDS-FLAG     PIC X              VALUE N.
42           88  OUT-OF-RECORDS                           VALUE 'Y'.
43      77   W-OVERTIME-HOURS          PIC   S99V99.
44      77   W-OVERTIME-PAY            PIC S999V99.
45      77   W-TAX                     PIC S999V99.
46      77   W-TAXABLE                 PIC S999V99.
47      77   W-TODAYS-DATE             PIC   9(6).
48      77   W-VALID-RECORD-FLAG       PIC X.
49           88  VALID-RECORD                             VALUE 'Y'.
50
51      01   HEADING-LINE-1.
52           05  FILLER                PIC X(26)
53               VALUE 'PAYROLL CALCULATION REPORT'
54           05  FILLER                PIC X(41)          VALUE SPACES.
55           05  W-TODAYS-DATE         PIC 99/99/99       VALUE ZERO.
56
57      01   HEADING-LINE-2.
58           05  FILLER                PIC X(42)
59               VALUE 'NUMBER        NAME              HOURS   RATE   '.
60           05  FILLER                PIC X(29)
61               VALUE ' DEP   GROSS      TAX      NET'.
62
63      01   NORMAL-OUTPUT-LINE.
64           05  O-PAYROLL-NUMBER      PIC X(5).
65           02  O-NAME                PIC BBX(20).
66           05  O-HOURS-WORKED        PIC BBZ9.9.
67           05  O-PAYRATE             PIC BBZ9.999.
68           05  O-DEPENDENTS          PIC BBZ9.
69           05  O-GROSS-PAY           PIC BB$$$9.99.
70           05  O-TAX                 PIC BB$$$9.99.
71           05  O-NET-PAY             PIC BB$$$9.99.
72
73      01   ERROR-RECORD.
74           05  BAD-DATA              PIC X(38).
75           05  FILLER                PIC X(4)           VALUE SPACES.
76           05  ERROR-MESSAGE         PIC X(27)
77               VALUE 'INVALID DATA IN THIS RECORD'.
78
79
80      PROCEDURE DIVISION.
81      A000-PRODUCE-PAYROLL-CALC.
82          OPEN  INPUT PAYROLL-FILE.
83                OUTPUT REPORT-FILE.
84          PERFORM B010-PRINT-COLUMN-HEADINGS.
85          PERFORM C010-GET-VALID-PAY-REC.
86          PERFORM B020-CALC-EMP-PAYROLL
87                UNTIL OUT-OF-RECORDS.
88          CLOSE PAYROLL-FILE
89                REPORT-FILE.
90          STOP RUN.
91
```

```
 92          B010-PRINT-COLUMN-HEADINGS.
 93              ACCEPT W-TODAYS-DATE FROM DATE.
 94              MOVE W-TODAYS-DATE TO REPORT-DATE.
 95              WRITE REPORT-RECORD FROM HEADING-LINE-1.
 96              MOVE SPACES TO REPORT-RECORD.
 97              WRITE REPORT-RECORD.
 98              WRITE REPORT-RECORD FROM HEADING-LINE-2.
 99              MOVE SPACES TO REPORT-RECORD.
100              WRITE REPORT-RECORD.
101              MOVE SPACES TO REPORT-RECORD.
102              WRITE REPORT-RECORD.
103
104          B020-CALC-EMP-PAYROLL.
105              PERFORM C020-COMPUTE-GROSS-PAY.
106              PERFORM C030-COMPUTE-EXEMPTIONS.
107              PERFORM C040-COMPUTE-TAX.
108              PERFORM C050-COMPUTE-NET-PAY.
109              PERFORM C060-PRINT-OUTPUT.
110              PERFORM C010-GET-VALID-PAY-REC.
111
112          C010-GET-VALID-PAY-REC.
113              MOVE 'N' TO W-VALID-RECORD-FLAG.
114              PERFORM D010-VALID-RECORD-LOOP
115                  UNTIL    VALID-RECORD
116                      OR OUT-OF-RECORDS.
117
118          C020-COMPUTE-GROSS-PAY.
119              MULTIPLY I-HOURS-WORKED BY I-PAYRATE
120                      GIVING W-GROSS-PAY ROUNDED.
121              IF I-HOURS-WORKED IS GREATER THAN 40
122                  SUBTRACT 40 FROM I-HOURS-WORKED GIVING W-OVERTIME-HOURS
123                  MULTIPLY 0.5 BY W-OVERTIME-HOURS
124                  MULTIPLY W-OVERTIME-HOURS BY I-PAYRATE
125                      GIVING W-OVERTIME-PAY ROUNDED
126                  ADD W-OVERTIME-PAY TO W-GROSS-PAY.
127
128          C030-COMPUTE-EXEMPTIONS.
129              MULTIPLY C-EXEMPTION BY I-DEPENDENTS
130                      GIVING W-EXEMPTION-TOTAL.
131
132          C040-COMPUTE-TAX.
133              IF W-GROSS-PAY IS GREATER THAN W-EXEMPTION-TOTAL
134                  SUBTRACT W-EXEMPTION-TOTAL FROM W-GROSS-PAY
135                      GIVING W-TAXABLE.
136                  MULTIPLY C-TAXRATE BY W-TAXABLE GIVING W-TAX ROUNDED
137              ELSE
138                  MOVE ZERO TO W-TAX.
139
140          C050-COMPUTE-NET-PAY.
141              SUBTRACT W-TAX FROM W-GROSS-PAY GIVING W-NET-PAY.
142
143          C060-PRINT-OUTPUT.
144              MOVE SPACES              TO NORMAL-OUTPUT-LINE.
145              MOVE I-PAYROLL-NUMBER    TO O-PAYROLL-NUMBER.
146              MOVE I-NAME              TO O-NAME.
147              MOVE I-HOURS-WORKED      TO O-HOURS-WORKED.
148              MOVE I-PAYRATE           TO O-PAYRATE.
149              MOVE I-DEPENDENTS        TO O-DEPENDENTS.
150              MOVE W-TAX               TO O-TAX.
151              MOVE W-GROSS-PAY         TO O-GROSS-PAY.
152              MOVE W-NET-PAY           TO O-NET-PAY.
153              WRITE REPORT-RECORD FROM NORMAL-OUTPUT-LINE.
154
```

```
155          D010-VALID-RECORD-LOOP.
156              READ PAYROLL-FILE
157                  AT END MOVE 'Y' TO W-OUT-OF-RECORDS-FLAG
158              IF NOT OUT-OF-RECORDS
159                  PERFORM E020-EDIT-PAYROLL-RECORD.
160
161          E020-EDIT-PAYROLL-RECORD.
162              IF       I-PAYROLL-NUMBER IS NOT NUMERIC
163                  OR   I-HOURS-WORKED   IS NOT NUMERIC
164                  OR   I-PAYRATE        IS NOT NUMERIC
165                  OR   I-DEPENDENTS     IS NOT NUMERIC
166                  MOVE PAYROLL-RECORD TO BAD-DATA
167                  WRITE REPORT-RECORD FROM ERROR-RECORD
168              ELSE
169                  MOVE 'Y' TO W-VALID-RECORD-FLAG.
```

FIGURE 8.3 A modification of the payroll program. *This program contains many deliberate errors.*

Remember as you study the errors described in Figure 8.4 that the program basically is well-designed. The only errors in the program are of the type that might be created in entering the program into a computer.

Each message consists of three lines. The first line is the image of the COBOL statement on which the error was detected, preceded by the number of the line on which the statement occurs in your program. The second line in the error message consists of an error code, followed by a row of asterisks which terminates under the part of the COBOL statement that caused the error; and the third line gives the text of the message. The error code consists of a number, which identifies the message so you can look it up in the Microsoft Error Messages Manual, and a letter. The letter, which may be I, W, E, S, or U, indicates how serious the error is. I stands for Information, and simply indicates something in the program of which you may need to be aware. W stands for Warning. A warning indicates that there may be a problem in the code even though it is syntactically correct. E indicates an Error in your code, but one which the compiler might be able to fix. That is, the compiler will make assumptions about what you intended and try to continue processing your program. S indicates that you have a Severe error in your code. Programs with error messages I through E can probably be executed, although the results might not be correct. However, programs with severe errors generally cannot be executed at all. A code of U indicates an Unrecoverable error and is produced during program execution rather than during compilation. When this type of error is encountered, program execution stops.

We see that the very first message here, for line 16, refers to a problem with the SELECT statement for REPORT-FILE. Obviously, the problem occurs because we "forgot" to put the required quote marks around the name of the file to which REPORT-FILE is assigned. As a result the compiler thinks that the statement ends with the first period. REP is interpreted as a paragraph name because it doesn't match any reserved word in the Environment or Data Divisiions. Since the compiler cannot identify the file, it will not be able to compile the program.

The second error, on line 21, actually occurs because of the extra period at the end of line 20. Because the compiler doesn't know how to interpret a LABEL RECORDS clause except as part of an FD, a severe error message is produced.

```
Microsoft (R) COBOL Optimizing Compiler Version 3.00

COBOL software by Micro Focus
Copyright (C) Microsoft Corporation 1984,1988.  All rights reserved.
Copyright (C) Micro Focus Ltd. 1984,1988.  All rights reserved.

    16     SELECT REPORT-FILE          ASSIGN TO C07P01.REP.
**209-S**********************************************************          **
**    PROCEDURE DIVISION missing or unknown statement
    21     LABEL RECORDS ARE STANDARD.
**205-S*********                                                          **
**    RECORD missing or has zero size
    35 WORKING STORAGE SECTION.
**209-S*******                                                            **
**    PROCEDURE DIVISION missing or unknown statement
    41 77  W-OUT-OF-RECORDS-FLAG     PIC X            VALUE N.
**  44-S*******************************************************            **
**    Literal expected
    54     05  FILLER                PIC X(41)        VALUE SPACES.
**  14-E******                                                            **
**    Period missing. Period assumed.
**  27-S******                                                            **
**    Number too large
    66     05  O-HOURS-WORKED        PIC BBZ9.9.
**225-S******                                                             **
**    Level hierarchy wrong
    83          OUTPUT REPORT-FILE.
**301-S***************                                                    **
**    Unrecognized verb
    93     ACCEPT W-TODAYS-DATE FROM DATE.
**   5-S***********************                                           **
**    User-name  not unique
    94     MOVE W-TODAYS-DATE TO REPORT-DATE.
**   5-S**********************                                            **
**    User-name  not unique
   137     ELSE
**302-S*********                                                          **
**    IF....ELSE or scope-delimiter mismatch
   157          AT END MOVE 'Y' TO W-OUT-OF-RECORDS-FLAG
**  12-S***************************************************                **
**    Operand  is not declared
* Checking complete - errors found
```

FIGURE 8.4 The diagnostic messages produced when the program of Figure 8.3 was processed by the Microsoft COBOL compiler.

The missing hyphen in WORKING-STORAGE was mentioned in Chapter 2 as being a potential source of lots of problems. In this particular case the situation actually is not too bad. The message for line 35 occurs because the compiler cannot identify the start of the Working-Storage Section. (That hyphen really is critical!) Since user-defined sections can be used in the Procedure Division— we won't have any need for these sections until Chapter 18—the compiler considers the possibility that we are actually in the Procedure Division but that you forgot to write the Procedure Division statement. On the other hand, we might still be in the Data Division, in which case the compiler has no idea what the statement on line 35 is all about. In any case, the Microsoft compiler handles this situation better than some other **COBOL** compilers; a similar program run under a different compiler caused that compiler to generate over two dozen extraneous error messages!

The error on line 41 occurred because we omitted the quote marks around the **N** in the **VALUE** clause. As the message says, the compiler expected a literal at the end of the clause, not what appears to be a variable name.

Writing a compiler is a difficult task, and writing diagnostic routines to anticipate *every* possible error in a source program is virtually impossible. This is said in apology for the fact that error messages are not always obviously related to the error that produced them. For example, the first error message for line 54 is fairly clear, although the omitted period actually should be on the preceding line, line 53. The second message, however, bears no obvious relationship to the code at hand. This message is actually related to the problem that occurs if you use a number of more than 18 digits. Since there are no numeric fields on line 54, the message is irrelevant here. You might take comfort, however, from the fact that inserting the period in its proper place causes both error messages to vanish.

The message on line 66 obviously is caused by the fact that the level number on line 65 is 02 rather than 05. The fact that **NORMAL-OUTPUT-LINE** begins with a level 05 entry followed by a level 02 entry is strange, but not actually illegal in **COBOL**. What causes the problem is that fact that the third entry is level 05 again. This indicates that **O-NAME** is the start of a group item and that **O-HOURS-WORKED** is the first entry in that group. However, **O-NAME** has a **PICTURE** clause and **PICTURE** clauses can only be written for elementary items. Thus, we are defining **O-NAME** both as a group item and an elementary item at the same time. This is what triggered the error message.

The first error in the Procedure Division is found on line 83. Since we typed a period at the end of line 82, the compiler thinks we are starting a new statement on line 83; of course, **OUTPUT** is not a valid **COBOL** verb.

The next two errors, on lines 93 and 94, occur because we typed **W-TODAYS-DATE** on line 55 where we should have typed **REPORT-DATE**. The result is that **W-TODAYS-DATE** is defined twice, and **REPORT-DATE** is not defined at all. The mistake in the Data Division did not trigger an error message because what we did is not actually a syntactic error. It is permissible to have the same data name in two different group items--which leads to the subject of data qualification, to be discussed in Chapter 10. Notice, however, that this produces *two* errors on line 94, in spite of the fact that there is only *one* error message. The problem with **W-TODAYS-DATE** masks the fact that **REPORT-DATE** is undefined. This type of problem, while perhaps regretable, is not uncommon, and means that frequently you will have to compile a program several times to catch all the errors in it.

Missing or extra periods are a very common problem for beginners (and sometimes for experienced **COBOL** programmers as well). The error on line 137 occurs because we have an extra period at the end of line 135. In spite of what the indentation implies, the **MULTIPLY** statement on line 136 is *not* part of the **IF** statement on line 133. This is no problem as far as the compiler is concerned, but the program would not run the way we expected it to even if we could get it to compile. Fortunately, however, the **ELSE** on line 137 has no **IF** statement to be matched with so we get an error.

A related situation occurs on line 157. The missing period at the end of the line means that the following **IF** statement is part of the **AT END** phrase, which is not at all what we want. However, the error message that appears is not caused by this mistake! Because we had an error in the declaration of **W-OUT-OF-RECORDS-FLAG** (line 41) this variable is not recognized as a valid operand in the **MOVE** statement on line 157. If we correct this error without noticing the missing period, the compiler will not tell us about it!

8.8   RUN-TIME ERRORS

The **COBOL** compiler helps you find syntax errors in your program at compile time. Unfortunately, even a program that is syntactically correct may contain errors that appear when it runs. These run-time errors show up in two different ways. First, a run-time error may cause abnormal program termination; this is also known as an *abend*. An abend typically occurs when the computer hardware can detect an abnormal condition. For example, if you attempt to perform a division by zero, most computers will detect the error and terminate the program.

Although it may be difficult to track down the cause of an abend, at least you know that an error has occurred. The second type of run-time error simply produces results that look valid but are logically or arithmetically incorrect. Not only do you have the problem of determining the cause of this type of error, you must first detect that the error has occurred!

8.9   PROGRAM TESTING

The first step in dealing with run-time errors is to test the program *thoroughly* to locate all bugs. Testing does *not* mean just running one set of test data, then assuming that everything is okay if no abend occurs. Testing a program is not a casual activity and, especially for large programs, requires careful planning. The testing activity can be divided into two types of testing which, for historical reasons, are called *black box* testing and *white box* testing. Black box testing involves testing a program based solely on the specifications of the problem it is supposed to solve. For example, the payroll program is supposed to perform certain calculations based on data found in records having a predefined format. To do black box testing on the payroll program we would try to list all the possible mistakes that could occur in the input data, then run tests to see what the program would do if it actually encountered such data. This is essentially what we did in Chapter 6.

White box testing involves studying the program source code, then using our knowledge of how the program is actually written to try to find more weaknesses. For example, if you notice that a **READ** statement was written without an **AT END** clause you might try running the program with no records in the input file. This approach gives you an idea of what the basic objective of testing really is: to make a program fail! When you test a program you are not trying to prove that it works. You can run test files for years and they won't prove that the program works; after all, the very next test might find an error. The only thing that a well-designed test can really accomplish is to locate another error. Eventually, if you are unable to locate more errors, you can stop testing the programs. (This doesn't necessarily mean that there aren't any more errors in the program. It means only that you haven't found them.)

If circumstances will permit it, one of the most effective ways of locating errors is to swap programs with a colleague. You try to find the errors in your friend's program, and your friend tries to find the errors in yours. The difficulty in finding errors in your own program is that you know what it is *supposed* to do, which makes it hard for you to see what it *really* does, which may be quite different. This psychological blindness to mistakes doesn't apply in the same way in reading another person's program.

Many commercial programming organizations take this principle a step further. Each programmer is required to present his or her program to a small group of colleagues, simply explaining what the program does and how it does it. Such a presentation is called a *walkthrough*. The colleagues, who are seeing the program with a fresh view, can often spot mistakes or unwarranted assumptions that the writer would have caught only with much greater effort.

Whether in the formal structure of a walkthrough or just getting a friend to help, you will be surprised how often you will see your own mistake as you try to explain your logic and your coding to someone else. It happens all the time: you ask a friend to help with your program, start to explain it, suddenly see the problem, and exclaim, "Gee, thanks for your help!" The friend can only laugh and say, "You're welcome!"--he or she hadn't even started to get an idea of what you were doing!

One final word on testing: you must examine the output from your tests *carefully* to determine whether the results of the run contain errors or not. There are far too many times when a programmer, either novice or professional, declares a program ready for use, only to have someone later point out blatant inconsistencies in the output. For example, consider the payroll program. Suppose you have modified the program to print total net pay for the company, and the value printed is $890.28. Is this reasonable? The sample data contains 11 valid records (including the record for Ima Testcase), whose values appear to average around three hundred dollars. Obviously then, the total payroll should be about $3300. Clearly our result is unreasonable, and the printed value seems to indicate that a leading digit has been dropped.

If our test run had printed a net payroll of $2912.73, it would not be immediately obvious whether this was correct or not, although in light of our rough estimate it seems a bit low. In any case, there is no obvious indication as to what the error actually is, if indeed there is an error. What we must do is to add the individual net pay amounts with a pocket calculator, then compare this total with the computer's output. If this is done, you will find that the total net pay should be $3890.28, so we have dropped $977.55. Does this amount give any clue as to where the error lies? The general conclusion is clear. Not only is it necessary to examine the results of your test runs in detail, you must know what to expect from these tests. If you have not calculated what the results *should* be, you can't really tell if they are wrong.

8.10   DEBUGGING AIDS

Once you detect an error in a COBOL program, you must locate the cause of the error. COBOL contains several statements that can assist you in this process, and we shall discuss these debugging aids in the next few sections. We will finish the chapter with a discussion of one of the major reasons for using the Microsoft COBOL compiler for software development: its run-time debugging tool.

Actually, the first and most important debugging aid is not a feature of COBOL; it is *you*. There is no magic technique, no wonderful tool in any programming language that will automatically find the cause of an error. You must begin the debugging process by *thinking* about the error and its possible causes. For example, in the payroll errors we discussed in the previous section, a study of the nature of the error should give you several clues as to the cause of the problem. If the amount printed is almost correct but has one or more leading digits omitted, look for a field that is too small for the result placed in it. If the total was close to the correct value but a bit short of it, see if the missing amount is equal to the net pay for one of the employees. You may also find the reverse situation; the total may be too high, with the excess equal to the pay for an employee. In either case, if you can detect the case, or cases, which contributed to the error you have made a good start in locating the bug.

Whatever the nature of an error and whatever the cause, the responsibility for finding the cause rests with *you*. You may choose to use some of the COBOL debugging aids for help, but the most these aids can do is provide you with supplementary data. Analyzing and interpreting these results require human action. After all, if you wrote the program you know more about it than anyone else. It is not a mysterious box whose contents are unknown. Think about the program's structure and what functions each part performs, then try to determine how these functions might relate to the symptoms of the error.

8.11   THE ON SIZE ERROR PHRASE

One of the basic steps in locating a program error is to determine if intermediate calculations are producing unexpected results. You will recall from the discussions of arithmetic operations in earlier chapters that a result that is too large for its receiving field will normally be truncated, with no warning of the loss of data. This, for example, is the cause of the errors in the payroll program for Ima Testcase. We can detect this type of truncation in arithmetic operations by using the ON SIZE ERROR phrase.

The ON SIZE ERROR phrase was mentioned in Chapter 3. It may optionally be used with any of the arithmetic verbs (and, as we shall see later, with the COMPUTE statement). Its effect is very similar to the AT END phrase on a READ: if the condition arises, then the statement(s) in the ON SIZE ERROR phrase are executed. If the condition does not arise, they are ignored. The condition that the program is directed to test for is the existence of an arithmetic result that is too large to fit into the space provided for it. In the payroll program, for example, we allowed for a week's gross pay that can be no larger than $999.99. We have already seen that if the data values are such as to generate an amount larger than this, the program produces gibberish.

The rules of **COBOL** permit any *imperative* statement to be written in an **ON SIZE ERROR** phrase. An imperative statement is defined as one that specifies *unconditional* action. This obviously excludes the **IF** statement, but it also excludes the **READ** (since its **AT END** phrase is conditional), and it excludes any arithmetic operation that has an **ON SIZE ERROR** phrase.

COBOL-85

As with any conditional phrase or statement, **COBOL-85** provides **END** phrases for the arithmetic verbs to be used with the **ON SIZE ERROR** phrase. The following example shows how this might be used:

```
IF VALID-RECORD-FLAG = 'Y'
    ADD AMOUNT TO TOTAL-AMOUNT
        ON SIZE ERROR MOVE 'Y' TO SIZE-ERROR-FLAG
    END-ADD
    READ INPUT-FILE
        AT END MOVE 'Y' TO EOF-FLAG
    END-READ
END-IF.
```

There is an **END** phrase for each of the arithmetic verbs: **END-ADD**, **END-DIVIDE**, **END-MULTIPLY**, and **END-SUBTRACT**. In each case the format is the same as in the example.

END COBOL-85

There is one common type of arithmetic truncation which, unfortunately, will not create a size error. This is truncation that occurs as a result of a **MOVE** statement. For example, consider the following code:

```
77   FLD-1              PIC 9(5)V999.
77   FLD-2              PIC Z(4).99.
         .
         .
         .
     MOVE FLD-1 TO FLD-2.
```

The **MOVE** statement will truncate the leftmost and rightmost digits of **FLD-1** with no warning whatever, nor is it possible to **ROUND** the result in **FLD-2**. Although some compilers may give a warning that truncation of the leading digit might occur, basically it is the responsibility of the programmer to be aware of this problem and guard against it.

8.12   A REVISED VERSION OF THE PROGRAM

A revised version of the payroll program is shown in Figure 8.5. In this version, if the on size error condition arises, the entire record will be rejected from further processing and the notice "gross pay suspiciously large" will be printed. There are several changes you should study. First, an error flag was added to tell of the size error condition that was detected. Also, **ERROR-RECORD** was changed to eliminate the text of the message, and two new structures were added for the two possible error messages. In the Procedure Division,

B020-CALC-EMP-PAYROLL and **C020-COMPUTE-GROSS-PAY** were modified to test and set the size error flag. Notice that it is not necessary to test for a size error on all arithmetic statements, only where there is a possibility of overflowing the receiving field.

```
1        IDENTIFICATION DIVISION.
2        PROGRAM-ID.
3            PAYROLL4.
4        DATE-WRITTEN.
5            OCTOBER 7, 1988.
6
7        ENVIRONMENT DIVISION.
8        INPUT-OUTPUT SECTION.
9        FILE-CONTROL.
10           SELECT PAYROLL-FILE       ASSIGN TO 'C06P02.DAT'.
11           SELECT REPORT-FILE        ASSIGN TO 'C08P02.REP'.
12
13       DATA DIVISION.
14       FILE SECTION.
15       FD  PAYROLL-FILE
16           LABEL RECORDS ARE STANDARD.
17       01  PAYROLL-RECORD.
18           05  I-PAYROLL-NUMBER      PIC X(5).
19           05  I-NAME                PIC X(20).
20           05  I-HOURS-WORKED        PIC 99V9.
21           05  FILLER                PIC X(3).
22           05  I-PAYRATE             PIC 99V999.
23           05  I-DEPENDENTS          PIC 99.
24           05  FILLER                PIC X(42).
25
26       FD  REPORT-FILE
27           LABEL RECORDS ARE STANDARD.
28       01  REPORT-RECORD             PIC X(75).
29
30       WORKING-STORAGE SECTION.
31       77  C-EXEMPTION               PIC  S99V99   VALUE +50.00.
32       77  C-TAXRATE                 PIC    SV999   VALUE +.210.
33       77  W-EXEMPTION-TOTAL         PIC S999V99.
34       77  W-GROSS-PAY               PIC S999V99.
35       77  W-NET-PAY                 PIC S999V99.
36       77  W-OUT-OF-RECORDS-FLAG     PIC X         VALUE 'N'.
37           88  OUT-OF-RECORDS                      VALUE 'Y'.
38       77  W-OVERTIME-HOURS          PIC  S99V99.
39       77  W-OVERTIME-PAY            PIC S999V99.
40       77  W-SIZE-ERROR-FLAG         PIC X.
41           88  NO-SIZE-ERROR                       VALUE 'N'.
42       77  W-TAX                     PIC S999V99.
43       77  W-TAXABLE                 PIC S999V99.
44       77  W-TODAYS-DATE             PIC 9(6).
45       77  W-VALID-RECORD-FLAG       PIC X.
46           88  VALID-RECORD                        VALUE 'Y'.
47
48       01  HEADING-LINE-1.
49           05  FILLER                PIC X(26)
50               VALUE 'PAYROLL CALCULATION REPORT'.
51           05  FILLER                PIC X(41)     VALUE SPACES.
52           05  REPORT-DATE           PIC 99/99/99  VALUE ZERO.
53
```

```
54          01   HEADING-LINE-2.
55               05   FILLER                    PIC X(42)
56                    VALUE 'NUMBER           NAME           HOURS   RATE '.
57               05   FILLER                    PIC X(29)
58                    VALUE ' DEP  GROSS        TAX       NET'.
59
60          01 NORMAL-OUTPUT-LINE.
61               05   O-PAYROLL-NUMBER     PIC X(5).
62               05   O-NAME               PIC BBX(20).
63               05   O-HOURS-WORKED       PIC BBZ9.9.
64               05   O-PAYRATE            PIC BBZ9.999.
65               05   O-DEPENDENTS         PIC BBZ9.
66               05   O-GROSS-PAY          PIC BB$$$9.99.
67               05   O-TAX                PIC BB$$$9.99.
68               05   O-NET-PAY            PIC BB$$$9.99.
69
70          01   ERROR-RECORD.
71               05   BAD-DATA             PIC X(38).
72               05   FILLER               PIC X(4)          VALUE SPACES.
73               05   ERROR-MESSAGE        PIC X(30)
74                    VALUE 'INVALID DATA IN THIS RECORD'.
75
76          01   MESSAGE-1                  PIC X(30)
77               VALUE 'INVALID DATA IN THIS RECORD'.
78          01   MESSAGE-2                  PIC X(30)
79               VALUE 'GROSS PAY SUSPICIOUSLY LARGE'.
80
81
82          PROCEDURE DIVISION.
83          A000-PRODUCE-PAYROLL-CALC.
84              OPEN INPUT  PAYROLL-FILE
85                    OUTPUT REPORT-FILE.
86              PERFORM B010-PRINT-COLUMN-HEADINGS.
87              PERFORM C010-GET-VALID-PAY-REC.
88              PERFORM B020-CALC-EMP-PAYROLL
89                  UNTIL OUT-OF-RECORDS.
90              CLOSE PAYROLL-FILE
91                    REPORT-FILE.
92              STOP RUN.
93
94          B010-PRINT-COLUMN-HEADINGS.
95              ACCEPT W-TODAYS-DATE FROM DATE.
96              MOVE W-TODAYS-DATE TO REPORT-DATE.
97              WRITE REPORT-RECORD FROM HEADING-LINE-1.
98              MOVE SPACES TO REPORT-RECORD.
99              WRITE REPORT-RECORD.
100             WRITE REPORT-RECORD FROM HEADING-LINE-2.
101             MOVE SPACES TO REPORT-RECORD.
102             WRITE REPORT-RECORD.
103             MOVE SPACES TO REPORT-RECORD.
104             WRITE REPORT-RECORD.
105
106         B020-CALC-EMP-PAYROLL.
107             PERFORM C020-COMPUTE-GROSS-PAY.
108             IF NO-SIZE-ERROR
109                 PERFORM C030-COMPUTE-EXEMPTIONS
110                 PERFORM C040-COMPUTE-TAX
111                 PERFORM C050-COMPUTE-NET-PAY
112                 PERFORM C060-PRINT-OUTPUT
```

```
113                ELSE
114                    MOVE PAYROLL-RECORD TO BAD-DATA
115                    MOVE MESSAGE-2 TO ERROR-MESSAGE
116                    WRITE REPORT-RECORD FROM ERROR-RECORD.
117                PERFORM C010-GET-VALID-PAY-REC.
118
119        C010-GET-VALID-PAY-REC.
120            MOVE 'N' TO W-VALID-RECORD-FLAG.
121            PERFORM D010-VALID-RECORD-LOOP
122                UNTIL    VALID-RECORD
123                    OR OUT-OF-RECORDS.
124
125        C020-COMPUTE-GROSS-PAY.
126            MOVE 'N' TO W-SIZE-ERROR-FLAG.
127            MULTIPLY I-HOURS-WORKED BY I-PAYRATE
128                    GIVING W-GROSS-PAY ROUNDED
129                    ON SIZE ERROR MOVE 'Y' TO W-SIZE-ERROR-FLAG.
130            IF NO-SIZE-ERROR
131                IF I-HOURS-WORKED IS GREATER THAN 40
132                    SUBTRACT 40 FROM I-HOURS-WORKED
133                        GIVING W-OVERTIME-HOURS
134                    MULTIPLY 0.5 BY W-OVERTIME-HOURS
135                    MULTIPLY W-OVERTIME-HOURS BY I-PAYRATE
136                        GIVING W-OVERTIME-PAY ROUNDED
137                    ADD W-OVERTIME-PAY TO W-GROSS-PAY
138                        ON SIZE ERROR MOVE 'Y' TO W-SIZE-ERROR-FLAG.
139
140        C030-COMPUTE-EXEMPTIONS.
141            MULTIPLY C-EXEMPTION BY I-DEPENDENTS
142                    GIVING W-EXEMPTION-TOTAL.
143
144        C040-COMPUTE-TAX.
145            IF W-GROSS-PAY IS GREATER THAN W-EXEMPTION-TOTAL
146                SUBTRACT W-EXEMPTION-TOTAL FROM W-GROSS-PAY
147                    GIVING W-TAXABLE
148                MULTIPLY C-TAXRATE BY W-TAXABLE GIVING W-TAX ROUNDED
149            ELSE
150                MOVE ZERO TO W-TAX.
151
152        C050-COMPUTE-NET-PAY.
153            SUBTRACT W-TAX FROM W-GROSS-PAY GIVING W-NET-PAY.
154
155        C060-PRINT-OUTPUT.
156            MOVE SPACES            TO NORMAL-OUTPUT-LINE.
157            MOVE I-PAYROLL-NUMBER  TO O-PAYROLL-NUMBER.
158            MOVE I-NAME            TO O-NAME.
159            MOVE I-HOURS-WORKED    TO O-HOURS-WORKED.
160            MOVE I-PAYRATE         TO O-PAYRATE.
161            MOVE I-DEPENDENTS      TO O-DEPENDENTS.
162            MOVE W-TAX             TO O-TAX.
163            MOVE W-GROSS-PAY       TO O-GROSS-PAY.
164            MOVE W-NET-PAY         TO O-NET-PAY.
165            WRITE REPORT-RECORD FROM NORMAL-OUTPUT-LINE.
166
167        D010-VALID-RECORD-LOOP.
168            PERFORM E010-GET-PAYROLL-RECORD.
169            IF NOT OUT-OF-RECORDS
170                PERFORM E020-EDIT-PAYROLL-RECORD.
171
```

```
172        E010-GET-PAYROLL-RECORD.
173            READ PAYROLL-FILE
174                AT END MOVE 'Y' TO W-OUT-OF-RECORDS-FLAG.
175
176        E020-EDIT-PAYROLL-RECORD.
177            IF    I-PAYROLL-NUMBER IS NOT NUMERIC
178               OR I-HOURS-WORKED   IS NOT NUMERIC
179               OR I-PAYRATE        IS NOT NUMERIC
180               OR I-DEPENDENTS     IS NOT NUMERIC
181            MOVE PAYROLL-RECORD TO BAD-DATA
182            MOVE MESSAGE-1 TO ERROR-MESSAGE
183            WRITE REPORT-RECORD FROM ERROR-RECORD
184            ELSE
185                MOVE 'Y' TO W-VALID-RECORD-FLAG.
```

FIGURE 8.5 A revised payroll program utilizing the ON SIZE ERROR test.

When this version of the program was run with the data file used before, the output shown in Figure 8.6 was produced. Observe that we have finally found a way of detecting the error for Ima Testcase.

```
PAYROLL CALCULATION REPORT                                  88/10/07

NUMBER         NAME              HOURS  RATE   DEP  GROSS     TAX       NET


12345  Thos H. Kelly            20.0   5.350   0  $107.00   $22.47   $84.53
12401  Henry Jensen             40.0   7.500   1  $300.00   $52.50  $247.50
12511  Nancy Kahn               40.0   7.500   3  $300.00   $31.50  $268.50
UILKMB. R. Brooks        400   0575002     INVALID DATA IN THIS RECORD
26017  Jane Milano              10.0   6.875   3   $68.75    $0.00   $68.75
12  4Kay Deluccia         400   0600004     INVALID DATA IN THIS RECORD
26109  Peter W. Sherwood        40.0  10.000   5  $400.00   $31.50  $368.50
26222  George M. Mulvaney       41.0  10.000   5  $415.00   $34.65  $380.35
26500A. W. Enwright       40   0545001     INVALID DATA IN THIS RECORD
27511  Ruth Garrison            50.0  10.000   4  $550.00   $73.50  $476.50
28819  Leo X. Butler            40.1  10.000   2  $401.50   $63.32  $338.18
28820D. X. Iannuzi       450   4.50003     INVALID DATA IN THIS RECORD
28821K. L. Ng, Jr.       350    450003     INVALID DATA IN THIS RECORD
28822Daniel Reiner       350   045000C     INVALID DATA IN THIS RECORD
28822L. E. Simon         388   06000 3     INVALID DATA IN THIS RECORD
2883QA. Real Bad-one     3 8   4.5KJXX     INVALID DATA IN THIS RECORD
7HGV6GARBAGE-CASE-1      ..M.,M.,M.,M.     INVALID DATA IN THIS RECORD
  NJI9GARBAGE-CASE-2     GV 6 46  8  H      INVALID DATA IN THIS RECORD
     GARBAGE-CASE-3 ----------++++++,M     INVALID DATA IN THIS RECORD
29000  Anne Henderson           40.2  10.000   3  $403.00   $53.13  $349.87
29001  Julia Kipp               40.3  10.000   1  $404.50   $74.45  $330.05
88888Ima Testcase        999   9999999    GROSS PAY SUSPICIOUSLY LARGE
```

FIGURE 8.6 Illustrative output of the program in Figure 8.5.

8.13 RUN-TIME DEBUGGING AIDS

Once an error has been identified in a program, either an abend or incorrect results, the next step is to locate the bug that caused the error. Begin by studying the nature of the error, the structure of the program, and the COBOL source code. If this is not sufficient to locate the bug, the next step is to look at the results of preliminary calculations that lead to the final output. For example, in the payroll program we now see that the calculated results for Ima Testcase are incorrect, but this may give you no idea of what caused the error. It might be that the data values were read incorrectly (although this is unlikely considering the fact that the program worked correctly for all the other test cases), or there might be a calculation or logic error at any of several steps. What we would like to be able to do is see the step-by-step operation of the program as it processes the data.

One way we could accomplish this is to set up a new output record in Working-Storage, then use it to print the data values we need to see. This has several flaws, however. First and most obvious is the effort of setting up an output record, particularly one that is flexible enough to show the variety of data fields that need to be studied. The second problem is that the error may involve an incorrect format for an output data field; if we repeat the same format in the new record we have accomplished nothing. Last, and perhaps most important, is the fact that on many computers an abend will destroy as much as several pages of output waiting to be printed.

Fortunately, COBOL provides more effective ways of showing intermediate data. In the next two sections we will look at statements in COBOL that commonly are used in debugging, and following this we will look at ANIMATOR, a debugging tool for use with the Microsoft COBOL compiler.

8.14 THE DISPLAY STATEMENT AS A DEBUGGING AID

The first debugging aid we will look at is a statement we are already familiar with, the DISPLAY statement. The value of the DISPLAY statement is that it allows us to print any combination of literals and variables without the need of setting up formal output records in the File Section. For example, look at paragraph C020-COMPUTE-GROSS-PAY in Figure 8.7.

The DISPLAY output for Ima Testcase is shown in Figure 8.8. By comparing this output with the code in paragraph C020-COMPUTE-GROSS-PAY, we can see how the output shown in previous chapters was computed. Truncation at each of several steps (A, D, and E) leads to the final incorrect result.

Using the DISPLAY statement to show this output has several advantages over using a WRITE statement. First, of course, it is much easier to set up a DISPLAY than to set up a WRITE. Not only does the WRITE statement necessitate defining a new record, but the data to be printed must be moved to the output fields; the DISPLAY statement allows us to print *any* data, even data defined in the Working-Storage Section. Second, the DISPLAY statement shows the data *exactly* as it appears in the computer's memory. This avoids any error that may be caused by an incorrect PICTURE in the output record. Finally, because of the way in which DISPLAY statements are processed by the computer, an abend will not affect output from a DISPLAY unless it occurs while the DISPLAY statement itself is being executed.

```
C020-COMPUTE-GROSS-PAY.
    MULTIPLY I-HOURS-WORKED BY I-PAYRATE
            GIVING W-GROSS-PAY ROUNDED.
    DISPLAY 'A:   (GROSS PAY) ', W-GROSS-PAY.
    IF I-HOURS-WORKED IS GREATER THAN 40
        SUBTRACT 40 FROM I-HOURS-WORKED GIVING W-OVERTIME-HOURS
        DISPLAY 'B:   (OVERTIME HOURS) ', W-OVERTIME-HOURS
        MULTIPLY 0.5 BY W-OVERTIME-HOURS
        DISPLAY 'C:   (OVERTIME HOURS) ', W-OVERTIME-HOURS
        MULTIPLY W-OVERTIME-HOURS BY I-PAYRATE
                GIVING W-OVERTIME-PAY ROUNDED
        DISPLAY 'D:   (OVERTIME PAY) ', W-OVERTIME-PAY
        ADD W-OVERTIME-PAY TO W-GROSS-PAY.
    DISPLAY 'E:   (GROSS PAY) ', GROSS-PAY.
```

FIGURE 8.7 The paragraph to compute gross pay, taken from Figure 8.5 and modified to display intermediate results.

Notice in the example above that we began each DISPLAY statement with a literal containing a letter followed by the name of the variable being displayed. Because the DISPLAY statement gives no indication of what data is being printed, or where in the program the statement is located, the literal serves two purposes. First, it tells us *which* DISPLAY statement is responsible for producing a particular line of output; second, it identifies the data being printed. If you omit this information you may find yourself staring at a page of numbers with no easy way to match them to specific statements in your program. Further, although the example for the payroll problem showed output for only one test record, in an actual run the DISPLAY output would be printed for *every* record in the input file. In addition to the data we showed, you might wish to display the employee number so that you know which record is being processed.

Before concluding this section we should emphasize that the operation of the DISPLAY statement varies considerably if you are running a program on a microcomputer or on a mainframe. On microcomputers DISPLAY is used extensively to write output to the computer screen, and it appears in many programs. On mainframes, however, DISPLAY output is limited primarily to use as a debugging tool. As a general rule, programs intended for use on a mainframe, even if they are being developed and tested on a microcomputer, should use DISPLAY statements only for diagnostic output.

```
A:   (GROSS PAY) 98990
B:   (OVERTIME HOURS) 5990
C:   (OVERTIME HOURS) 2995
D:   (OVERTIME PAY) 99497
E:   (GROSS PAY) 98487
```

FIGURE 8.8. DISPLAY output for "Ima Testcase" from the paragraph shown in Figure 8.7.

8.15 THE TRACE STATEMENT

Although the **TRACE** statement is not a standard **COBOL** statement, it is available in many compilers, including the Microsoft compiler and the IBM OS/VS compiler. When the **TRACE** mode is enabled, the **COBOL** program will automatically print the name of every paragraph as it is executed, which allows you to follow the execution of the program paragraph by paragraph. **TRACE** mode is turned on by executing the statement **READY TRACE**; it is turned off by executing **RESET TRACE**. The names of the paragraphs are printed on the same default file used by **DISPLAY**. Figure 8.9 shows code to turn on **TRACE** at the start of the payroll program and turn it off at the end. Figure 8.10 shows the trace output for Ima Testcase.

Some programmers, especially beginning **COBOL** programmers, look on the **TRACE** statement as the solution to all their debugging problems. They seem to feel that if only they stare at the **TRACE** output long enough it will tell them what is wrong with their program. In point of fact, the **TRACE** tells you nothing that you can't discover using the **DISPLAY** statement, and it produces *much* more output. Although a trace of the program will tell you *where* the execution went, it will not tell you *why* it went there, which is usually much more important. Most of the time, careful use of **DISPLAY** statements will give you the most useful information with the least amount of output, which is really what you need in order to understand the program. However, if you do decide to use **TRACE**, use **READY TRACE** and **RESET TRACE** very carefully to turn on the trace only where you think the problem is located. If you simply enable the **TRACE** mode at the start of the program, you may have so much output you can't separate the useful information from the junk.

8.16 THE ANIMATOR PROGRAM

Along with the Version 3.0 **COBOL** compiler, Microsoft provides a debugging tool called *ANIMATOR*. This is a program which gives you the ability to watch your **COBOL** program as it executes. You can see the order in which statements are executed, check the values of selected variables as execution

```
PROCEDURE DIVISION.
A000-PRODUCE-PAYROLL-CALC.
    READY TRACE.
    OPEN INPUT PAYROLL-FILE
        OUTPUT REPORT-FILE.
    PERFORM B010-PRINT-COLUMN-HEADINGS.
    PERFORM C010-GET-VALID-PAY-REC.
    PERFORM B020-CALC-EMP-PAYROLL
        UNTIL OUT-OF-RECORDS.
    CLOSE PAYROLL-FILE
        REPORT-FILE.
    RESET TRACE.
    STOP RUN.
```

FIGURE 8.9 Driver paragraph to turn **TRACE** on and off in payroll program.

```
B010-PRINT-COLUMN-HEADINGS
C010-GET-VALID-PAY-REC
D010-VALID-RECORD-LOOP
E010-GET-PAYROLL-RECORD
E020-EDIT-PAYROLL-RECORD
B020-CALC-EMP-PAYROLL
C020-COMPUTE-GROSS-PAY
C030-COMPUTE-EXEMPTIONS
C040-COMPUTE-TAX
C050-COMPUTE-NET-PAY
C060-PRINT-OUTPUT
C010-GET-VALID-PAY-REC
D010-VALID-RECORD-LOOP
E010-GET-PAYROLL-RECORD
```

FIGURE 8.10   Output from **TRACE** for a file containing one payroll record.

progresses, skip quickly past parts of the program which are of no interest in the debugging process, and generally monitor your program as you learn what is causing a particular error. In this section we will present some of the basic functions of ANIMATOR, using the payroll program as an example. We will pretend that we have no idea why the results for Ima Testcase are incorrect, and we will use ANIMATOR to solve the problem. We assume that the payroll program is stored in the file **PAYROLL.CBL**.

To prepare your program for execution by ANIMATOR you must first compile it with the ANIM option. For example, to prepare the payroll program for ANIMATOR you would type

COBOL PAYROLL ANIM;

Notice that you do not use the .CBL part of the file name.

It is not necessary to link a program which is being controlled by ANIMATOR, so you do not execute the LINK step. In fact, since you do not need to use LINK, you can make the compilation process slightly more efficient by writing

COBOL PAYROLL ANIM,NUL;

which tells the compiler not to bother generating the code used for the linking process. Instead, the compiler generates two files, **PAYROLL.INT** and **PAYROLL.IDY**, which are used by ANIMATOR.

After you have compiled your program, begin execution of ANIMATOR by writing

ANIMATE PAYROLL

For our example program, the first thing you would see after the file is loaded is the screen shown in Figure 8.11.

Note the underline under the **o** in line 77; this indicates the position of the cursor. This line would also be highlighted on your screen, but we have no effective way to indicate highlighting. A number of the characters at the bottom of the screen, which we have shown with shading, would also be highlighted.

```
75 PROCEDURE DIVISION.
76 A000-PRODUCE-PAYROLL-CALC.
77     OPEN INPUT PAYROLL-FILE
78          OUTPUT REPORT-FILE.
79     PERFORM B010-PRINT-COLUMN-HEADINGS.
80     PERFORM C010-GET-VALID-PAY-REC.
81     PERFORM B020-CALC-EMP-PAYROLL
82          UNTIL OUT-OF-RECORDS.
83     CLOSE PAYROLL-FILE
84          REPORT-FILE.
85     STOP RUN.
86
87 B010-PRINT-COLUMN-HEADINGS.
88     ACCEPT W-TODAYS-DATE FROM DATE.
89     MOVE W-TODAYS-DATE TO REPORT-DATE.
90     WRITE REPORT-RECORD FROM HEADING-LINE-1.
91     MOVE SPACES TO REPORT-RECORD.
92     WRITE REPORT-RECORD.
93     WRITE REPORT-RECORD FROM HEADING-LINE-2.
94     MOVE SPACES TO REPORT-RECORD.
95     WRITE REPORT-RECORD.
```

```
Animate PAYROLL                         Level=01 Speed=5 Ins Caps Num Scroll
F1=help F2=view F3=align F4=exchange F5=where F6=look-up  F9/F10=word-</> Escape
Step Go Zoom next-If Perform Reset Break Env Query Find Locate Text Do 0-9=speed
```

FIGURE 8.11 The initial ANIMATOR screen image for the payroll program.

The three menu lines at the bottom of the screen provide information about the program and give prompts regarding the options we have at this point. The information line, the first of the three lines, tells us that we are in the main (Animate) menu and that we are testing the program in the file **PAYROLL**. The words Ins, Caps, Num, and Scroll tell whether we are in insert or overwrite mode for typing, and whether the Caps Lock, Num Lock, and Scroll Lock keys have been pressed. We will discuss the meaning of Level and Speed as we go along.

At this point you should experiment with the various cursor movement and control keys. If you have not already done so, load a program into ANIMATOR and see how the screen compares to Figure 8.11. Try pressing the insert key and watch what happens to Ins on the information line, then try typing a few characters in both insert and overwrite mode to see the difference between the two.

Most of the cursor keys have the expected effect. The arrow keys move the cursor left or right, up or down. The Home key moves the cursor to column 8 (the A margin) of the current line, while End moves the cursor to the right end of the line. However, if you press Home twice in a row, the cursor will go first to the start of the current line, then to the start of the top line on the screen. Pressing Home a third time will move the cursor to the beginning of the file. You can accomplish this last movement in one step simply by pressing the Ctrl and Home keys simultaneously. The End key can be used in a similar fashion to move toward the end of the program.

On the next line you can see the use of each of the function keys. F1 will access a help screen which shows different information depending on the menu you are looking at. F3 helps you scroll through the program by moving the display so that line on which the cursor is located becomes the third line from the top of the screen. F5 moves the cursor from any location in the program to the start of the next statement to be executed. If you want to move the cursor to the start of a specific line, press F6 then type the number of the line to which you wish to move. Finally, F9 and F10 move the cursor one word back and one word forward, respectively. We will discuss the use of F2, as well as the commands on the third menu line, as we go through the payroll example; the use of F4 is beyond the scope of this discussion.

We can start debugging the payroll program by executing a few program statements. Each time we press S (Step), the next highlighted statement is executed and the cursor moves to the next statement scheduled for execution. If we press S once, the **OPEN** statement is executed and the cursor moves to the start of line 79. If we press S again, the cursor moves to line 88, the first statement in **B010-PRINT-COLUMN-HEADINGS**.

We could continue to step through **B010-PRINT-COLUMN-HEADINGS** by pressing S repeatedly. However, we can accomplish the same thing automatically by pressing G (Go). If you are trying ANIMATOR with a sample program of your own, press G to enter the Go mode and watch the cursor advance through the statements. As the program executes, press any number key from 0 to 9 (preferably not the number 5). When you press the number key, two things happen. First, the number by the Speed indicator on the information line changes to match the number you pressed. Second, the speed of execution either increases or decreases depending on which number you selected. At speed 0 there is about a minute between statements and you have plenty of time to study a statement before the next one is executed. At speed 9, the highlight moves so rapidly that you can barely follow the statements being executed. At any time you can press a different number to change the speed of execution, or press the Escape key to suspend the Go mode. Of course, you can also change the execution speed *before* you begin simply by selecting a speed other than 5 before you press G.

We could continue to follow the program execution line by line, using either Step or Go. However, we know that nothing interesting is going to happen until execution enters **B020-CALC-EMP-PAYROLL**. In other words, everything up to that point works so why bother watching it? What we will do instead is move the cursor to the start of line 100, then type B to enter the Breakpoint menu. The screen will resemble Figure 8.12.

Breakpoints are places in the program where execution stops automatically so that we can look at intermediate results. The first two lines of the breakpoint menu are much the same as for the main menu, but the third line shows different options. We can use Set to set a break point at the current cursor location, Unset to clear the breakpoint at the current cursor location, or Cancel-all to clear all breakpoints in the program. For now, we want to set a new breakpoint so we press S for Set; this automatically returns us to the main menu. Notice that although the cursor is at the start of line 100, the line is not highlighted; only the next statement to be executed is highlighted.

At this point we could press G to re-enter Go mode, but the whole point of setting the breakpoint is that we don't need to see the first part of the program execute. Therefore, we press Z to enter the Zoom mode. In this mode the program executes just as it would under normal execution (although perhaps a bit slower), and all we see is the normal computer screen.

```
 80        PERFORM C010-GET-VALID-PAY-REC.
 81        PERFORM B020-CALC-EMP-PAYROLL
 82            UNTIL OUT-OF-RECORDS.
 83        CLOSE PAYROLL-FILE
 84            REPORT-FILE.
 85        STOP RUN.
 86
 87 B010-PRINT-COLUMN-HEADINGS.
 88        ACCEPT W-TODAYS-DATE FROM DATE.
 89        MOVE W-TODAYS-DATE TO REPORT-DATE.
 90        WRITE REPORT-RECORD FROM HEADING-LINE-1.
 91        MOVE SPACES TO REPORT-RECORD.
 92        WRITE REPORT-RECORD.
 93        WRITE REPORT-RECORD FROM HEADING-LINE-2.
 94        MOVE SPACES TO REPORT-RECORD.
 95        WRITE REPORT-RECORD.
 96        MOVE SPACES TO REPORT-RECORD.
 97        WRITE REPORT-RECORD.
 98
 99 B020-CALC-EMP-PAYROLL.
100        PERFORM C020-COMPUTE-GROSS-PAY.
```

```
Break-points On-count=unset                    Level=01 Speed=5 Ins Caps Num Scroll
F1=help F2=view F3=align F4=exchange F5=where F6=look-up F9/F10=word-</> Escape
Set Unset Cancel-all Examine If Do On-count
```

FIGURE 8.12 The Animator Breakpoint Menu.

When the program reaches the start of statement 100, execution stops and we see a screen similar to the one shown in Figure 8.11, with two changes. First, statement 100 is near the top of the screen and is highlighted since it is the next statement to be executed. Second, at the bottom of the screen we see the additional message

Break-point encountered

to tell us why the program halted.

Notice also that the Level indicator shows 02. This is because we are now in a paragraph that was called from the main program. In other words, the Level indicator generally corresponds to levels on the hierarchy chart. If we look at the Level indicator while ANIMATOR is executing a C-level paragraph it will indicate level 03, and so on.

We might want to look at the data that the program is about to process to make sure that everything looks all right. We do this by pressing Q to get the Query menu. The main body of the program is unchanged, but the menu at the bottom of the screen now shows the following:

```
Query-data                                     Level=02 Speed=5 Ins Caps Num Scroll
F1=help F2=view F3=align F4=exchange F5=where F6=look-up F9/F10=word-</> Escape
Cursor-name Enter-name Repeat Monitor-off Dump list
```

The data item whose contents we want to examine is **I-PAYROLL-NUMBER**. If this name appeared near the current cursor location, we would only need to place the cursor anywhere on the name, then press C to select the name at the cursor location as the name to be queried. However, since **I-PAYROLL-NUMBER** is not located conveniently nearby, we type E so that we can enter the name. The menu changes to a new sub-menu and we enter the name of the variable we want to query, as shown below:

```
Query-data                                 Level=02 Speed=5 Ins Caps Num Scroll
F1=help F2=clear                                                        Escape
Enter name [+ offset] or hex literal address
i-payroll-number                                                              ]
```

When we press Return, the menu changes once again and we see the following display:

```
Query:    I-PAYROLL-NUMBER               Level=02 Speed=5 Ins Caps Num Scroll
F1=help F2=clear F3=hex F4=monitor                      ↑↓ up/down data
F7=containing F8=contained F9=same level                ↲   Alt      Escape
12345]
```

with the value of **I-PAYROLL-NUMBER** shown at the bottom of the screen.

At this point we have several options. If we press F2, the value of **I-PAYROLL-NUMBER** is erased and we can type in any new value that we want. Pressing F3 will change the display so that the value of the field is shown in hexadecimal rather than in character. (This will mean much more after we get to Chapter 10.) F4 allows us to monitor the value of **I-PAYROLL-NUMBER** as the program executes. If we press F4, the value of **I-PAYROLL-NUMBER** remains at the bottom of the screen when we return to the main menu, and as we continue execution of the program the value in the display changes each time **I-PAYROLL-NUMBER** is changed. We are restricted, however, to monitoring one variable at a time.

Function keys F7, F8, and F9 are useful for examining related elements in a data structure. If we press F7, the display changes so that we see the contents of the structure containing **I-PAYROLL-NUMBER**. If **I-PAYROLL-NUMBER** were itself a structure, we could press F8 and see the first element contained in that structure. Finally, we can press F9 to see the next element at the same level as **I-PAYROLL-NUMBER**, which in this example would be **I-NAME**. To get back to **I-PAYROLL-NUMBER** from **I-NAME**, press F7 to get to the start of **PAYROLL-RECORD**, then press F8.

We might as well look at the entire record, so we press F7. We notice two changes in the menu display. First, the data name is now **PAYROLL-RECORD**; second, the value shown at the bottom of the screen is now the entire payroll record.

```
Query:    PAYROLL-RECORD                 Level=02 Speed=5 Ins Caps Num Scroll
F1=help F2=clear F3=hex F4=monitor                      ↑↓ =up/down data
F7=containing F8=contained F9=same level                ↲   Alt      Escape
12345Thos H. Kelly      200    0535000]
```

So that we can see the program output as it is produced, we modified the **SELECT** statement for **REPORT-FILE** so that the file is assigned to 'CON' instead of to a disk file. If we press F2 from the main menu, the screen display changes to show the normal program output screen. Pressing any key while in View mode returns us to the ANIMATOR screen.

Clearly, ANIMATOR can be very helpful in tracing the execution of a program and in examining data values as execution proceeds. However, it is also clear that it will take a while to reach the record we are interested in, even if we only stop at the breakpoint to see which record is about to be processed. What we really would like to do is to continue until the program is about to process record 88888, *then* stop.

We do this with a *conditional breakpoint*. We press ESCape to leave the query menu (bringing us back to the main menu), then press B to enter the breakpoint menu. We press U to Unset the unconditional breakpoint at statement 100, then we press I to enter the If sub-menu. This menu asks us to enter a condition which determines when the breakpoint is to be activated. The condition that we enter can be any valid **COBOL** condition. Each time the program reaches the statement at which the breakpoint is set (statement 100 in the example), the condition that we specify is tested. If the condition is true, execution stops just as it did with an unconditional breakpoint. If the condition is false, execution continues without pausing. To set a breakpoint for the last data record, we test to see if **I-PAYROLL-NUMBER** is equal to 88888; the menu looks like the following:

```
Break-points On-count=unset                      Level=02 Speed=5 Ins Caps Num Scroll
F1=help F2=clear                                                            Escape
Enter condition:
i-payroll-number=88888                                              ]
```

We press ESCape to return to the main menu, then press Z to enter Zoom mode. Execution continues until the program reaches the last record in the payroll file. At this point, execution stops at statement 100 and we see the message

```
Break-point encountered      i-payroll-number=88888
```

We know that the program is ready to process the data for Ima Testcase, so we step execution using the S key until the cursor is at the start of statement 116. The program has just completed the first calculation for this record, the **MULTIPLY** on lines 114-115, and we want to see if **W-GROSS-PAY** contains the proper result. We move the cursor to the name **W-GROSS-PAY** (pressing F9 twice will do the job nicely), then press Q for the query menu, and C for cursor select. The value that appears at the bottom of the screen shows us that **W-GROSS-PAY** has the value +989.90. Since **W-GROSS-PAY** is the product of **I-HOURS-WORKED** and **I-PAYRATE**, which have the values 99.9 and 99.999, the value of **W-GROSS-PAY** should be 9989.9001! The cause of the problem is obvious. **W-GROSS-PAY** is too small to hold the result of the multiplication so the fractional part is rounded to two digits, which causes no problem, and the integer part is *truncated*, which causes a serious problem indeed.

If we continue to step through the program, we can see that the next arithmetic statement subtracts 40 from 99.9 giving a value of 59.90 for **W-OVER-TIME-HOURS**, which is correct; and that the **MULTIPLY** on line 118 gives a value of 29.95, which is also correct. However, the next step multiplies 29.95 by 99.999 which should give a value of 2994.97. Since **W-OVERTIME-PAY** only has three digits before the decimal point, the result is again truncated. If we query the value of **W-OVERTIME-PAY**, we see the following result:

```
Query:   W-OVERTIME-PAY                          Level=03 Speed=5 Ins Caps Num Scroll
F1=help F2=clear F3=hex F4=monitor                        ↑↓ =up/down data
F7=containing F8=contained F9=same level                   ↵  Alt              Escape
994.97+]
```

When we add this truncated value to the (incorrect) value for **W-GROSS-PAY**, we should get a result of 1984.87. However, if we step through the **ADD** statement on line 121, then query **W-GROSS-PAY** once more, we see that the result has been truncated again giving a final value for **W-GROSS-PAY** of 984.87. The causes of the erroneous results for Ima Testcase are now clear and we can correct them in either of two ways. First, we could add **SIZE ERROR** clauses to the appropriate statements, as described in Section 8.11, and print error messages. Second, we could increase the sizes of **W-GROSS-PAY** and **W-OVERTIME-PAY** to accept the larger values. Either approach is acceptable and your choice depends on how you want the program to work.

Obviously, we have not presented a complete discussion of all the options in ANIMATOR. However, most of the remaining commands relate to locating statements in the program and determining how much detail is shown. We recommend that you read the Microsoft manual to learn more about the advanced features of ANIMATOR, but for our purposes what have have covered is sufficient. Remember the basic procedure for using ANIMATOR: use Step, Go, or Zoom to execute statements in the program, use conditional and unconditional Breakpoints to stop execution at points of interest, and use Query to look at important data values. The ability of ANIMATOR to let you decide as the program is executing what you wish to look at provides a very flexible and powerful debugging tool.

REVIEW QUESTIONS

1. In what way is program design related to program errors?
2. How does programming style affect the likelihood of finding errors in a program?
3. Does the indentation of the following nested **IF** statements correspond to the way a **COBOL** compiler would interpret the statements?

```
a.  IF C1
        S1
        IF C2
            S2
        ELSE
            IF C3
                S4
    ELSE
                S5.
```

```
b.  IF C1
        IF C2
            IF C3
                S1
            ELSE
                S2
        ELSE
            S3
    ELSE
        S4.
```

```
c.  IF C1
        S1
    ELSE
        IF C2
            S2
        ELSE
            S3.
```

```
d.  IF C1
        S1
        IF C2
            S2
        ELSE
            S3
        S4
    ELSE
        S5.
```

```
e.  IF C1
        IF C2
            S1
        ELSE
            IF C3
                S2
            ELSE
                S3
    ELSE
        S4.
```

4. Rewrite each of the following nested **IF** statements as several unnested **IF** statements, some of which have compound conditions; that is, use **AND** and **NOT** operators.

```
a.  IF C1
        IF C2
            S1
        ELSE
            S2
    ELSE
        S3.
```

```
b.  IF C1
        IF C2
            IF C3
                S1
            ELSE
                NEXT SENTENCE
        ELSE
            S2.
```

```
c.  IF C1
        S1
        IF C2
            NEXT SENTENCE
        ELSE
            S2.
```

   d. IF C1
             IF C2
                   S1
             ELSE
                   IF C3
                         S2
                   ELSE
                         NEXT SENTENCE
         ELSE
               S3.

5. The following program, based on an example we shall study in the next chapter, contains nine syntactic errors, all of which were diagnosed by a compiler, and two very serious punctuation errors that were not diagnosed because they did not create syntax errors. Find the errors. (There are also two missing statements, neither of which caused an error.)

```
1     IDENTIFICATION DIVISION.
2     PROGRAM-ID.
3         FINDERRS.
4
5     DATE-WRITTEN.
6         NOVEMBER 15, 1988.
7
8     ENVIRONMENT DIVISION.
9     INPUT-OUTPUT SECTION.
10    FILE-CONTROL.
11        SELECT INPUT-FILE           ASSIGN TO 'INPUT'.
12        SELECT REPORT-FILE          ASSIGN TO 'REPORT'.
13
14    DATA DIVISION.
15
16    FD  INPUT-FILE
17        LABEL RECORDS ARE STANDARD
18    01  INPUT-RECORD.
19        05  ACCOUNT-NUMBER          PIC X(5).
20        05  ACCOUNT-DOLLARS         PIC 9(5)V99.
21        05  FILLER                  PIC X(68).
22
23    FD  REPORT-FILE
24        LABEL RECORDS ARE STANDARD.
25    01  REPORT-RECORD               PIC X(132).
26
27    WORKING-STORAGE SECTION.
28
29    01  FLAGS.
30        05  MORE-DATA-REMAINS-FLAG.
31            88  MORE-DATA-REMAINS             VALUE 'YES'.
32            88  NO-MORE-DATA-REMAINS          VALUE 'NO'.
33
34    01  LINE-AND-PAGE-COUNTERS.
35        05  LINE-NUMBER             PIC S99   VALUE +1.
36        05  PAGE-NUMBER             PIC S999  VALUE +1.
37
38    01  SAVE-ITEM.
39        05  PREVIOUS-ACCOUNT-NUMBER PIC X(5).
40
41    01  TOTALS.
42        05  ACCOUNT-TOTAL           PIC S9(6)V99 VALUE ZERO.
43        05  FINAL-TOTAL             PIC S9(6)V99 VALUE ZERO.
44
```

```
45          01   DETAIL-LINE.
46               05   ACCOUNT-NUMBER-OUT      PIC Z(4)9.
47               05   FILLER                  PIC X(3).
48               15   ACCOUNT-TOTAL-OUT       PIC $$$$,ZZ9.99.
49               05   FILLER                  PIC X(8).
50               05   FINAL-TOTAL-OUT         PIC $$$$,$$9.99.
51
52          01   HEADING-LINE.
53               05   FILLER                  PIC X(48)
54                    VALUE 'ACCOUNT     TOTAL            FINAL TOTAL      PAGE.
55               05   PAGE-NUMBER-OUT         PIC Z(6)9.
56
57          PROCEDURE DIVISION.
58          A000-PREPARE-SALES-REPORT.
59              OPEN INPUT-FILE
60                   REPORT-FILE.
61              READ INPUT-FILE
62                  AT END MOVE NO TO MORE-DATA-REMAINS-FLAG.
63              IF MORE-DATA-REMAINS
64                  MOVE ACCOUNT-NUMBER TO PREVIOUS-ACCOUNT-NUMBER
65                  PERFORM B010-PROCESS-INPUT-RECORD
66                      UNTIL NO-MORE-DATA-REMAINS-FLAG
67                  PERFORM B020-FINAL-TOTAL-PROCESSING.
68              CLOSE INPUT-FILE
69                   REPORT-FILE.
70
71          B010-PROCESS-INPUT-RECORD.
72              IF ACCOUNT-NUMBER IS NOT EQUAL TO PREVIOUS-ACCOUNT-NUMBER
73                  PERFORM C010-PROCESS-ACCOUNT-TOTAL
74              ADD ACCOUNT-DOLLARS TO ACCOUNT-TOTAL
75                                      FINAL-TOTAL
76              READ INPUT-RECORD
77                  AT END MOVE 'NO' TO MORE-DATA-REMAINS-FLAG.
78
79          B020-FINAL-TOTAL-PROCESSING.
80              PERFORM C010-PROCESS-ACCOUNT-TOTAL.
81              MOVE SPACES TO DETAIL-LINE.
82              MOVE FINAL-TOTAL TO FINAL-TOTAL-OUT.
83              PERFORM C020-LINE-OUT.
84
85          C010-PROCESS-ACCOUNT-TOTAL.
86              MOVE SPACES TO DETAIL-LINE
87              MOVE PREVIOUS-ACCOUNT-NUMBER TO ACCOUNT-NUMBER-OUT
88              MOVE ACCOUNT-TOTAL TO ACCOUNT-TOTAL-OUT
89              PERFORM C020-LINE-OUT
90              MOVE ACCOUNT-NUMBER TO PREVIOUS-ACCOUNT-NUMBER
91              MOVE ZERO TO ACCOUNT-TOTAL
92
93          C020-LINE-OUT.
94              IF LINE-NUMBER EQUALS 1
95                  MOVE PAGE-NUMBER TO PAGE-NUMBER-OUT
96                  WRITE REPORT-RECORD FROM HEADING-LINE
97                  MOVE SPACES TO REPORT-RECORD
98                  WRITE REPORT-RECORD
99                  MOVE 2 TO LINE-NUMBER
100                 ADD 1 TO PAGE-NUMBER.
101             WRITE REPORT-RECORD FROM DETAIL-LINE.
102             IF LINE-NUMBER = 66
103                 MOVE 1 TO LINE-NUMBER
104             ELSE
105                 ADD 1 TO LINE-NUMBER.
```

6. A programmer has stated that the purpose of testing a program is to prove that it contains no errors. Do you agree with this statement? Explain your answer.

7. Which of the following statements describes what happens as a result of an arithmetic statement that includes the **SIZE-ERROR** phrase, when a size error occurs.

a. The run is terminated and the words **SIZE-ERROR** are printed.

b. A partial result is stored and then the truncated high order digits are saved in a special storage location.

c. Nothing is stored and the imperative statements in the **SIZE-ERROR** phrase are executed.

d. The receiving field is enlarged to accommodate the high order digits.

e. None of the above.

ANSWERS TO REVIEW QUESTIONS

1. A well-designed program will have few, if any, serious program errors. Conversely, a poorly designed program is likely to contain serious problems and, even if they are fixed, the program will probably continue to cause maintenance problems throughout its lifetime.

2. If a program is written in a style that makes the code easy to read, it is easier to spot typing errors, simple logic errors, and so on. If the code is hard to read, these errors can slip by even the most careful checking.

3. Statements **b**, **c**, and **e** are correct. The second **ELSE** in statement **a** violates the rule that an **ELSE** matches the most recent **IF** that does not already have an **ELSE**; the second **ELSE** accordingly should be indented to match **IF C3**. In statement **d** the indentation of **S4** violates the rule that every statement is controlled by the most recent **IF** or **ELSE**; it should be aligned with **S3**.

4. a.
```
IF C1 AND C2
    S1.
IF C1 AND NOT C2
    S2.
IF NOT C1
    S3.
```

b.
```
IF C1 AND C2 AND C3
    S1.
IF C1 AND NOT C2
    S2.
```

c.
```
IF C1
    S1.
IF C1 AND NOT C2
    S2.
```

d.
```
IF C1 AND C2
    S1.
IF C1 AND NOT C2 AND C3
    S2.
IF NOT C1
    S3.
```

5. The program contains the following syntactic errors, as listed below:
   1. Missing period on line 17; this causes error messages for lines 18 - 21, 23, 59, 64, 72, 74, and 90.
   2. No **PIC** clause on line 30; two error messages for line 34, one for line 66.
   3. Incorrect level number on line 48;
   4. No closing quote mark on line 54; several error messages for line 54 and 55, one for line 95.
   5. **NO** not in quotes on line 62;
   6. Record specified instead of file in **READ** on line 76;
   7. **OUT** is spelled with a zero, not the letter **O**, on line 83;
   8. No period at end of paragraph on line 91; error message for line 93;
   9. **EQUALS** (line 94) is not a **COBOL** reserved word.

The **FILE SECTION** statement is missing, but did not cause an error.

```
Microsoft (R) COBOL Optimizing Compiler Version 3.00

COBOL software by Micro Focus
Copyright (C) Microsoft Corporation 1984,1988. All rights reserved.
Copyright (C) Micro Focus Ltd. 1984,1988. All rights reserved.

    18 01   INPUT-RECORD.
**207-S**                                                          **
**    FD, CD or SD qualification syntax error
    19     05   ACCOUNT-NUMBER          PIC X(5).
**206-S******                                                      **
**    01 or 77 level required
    20     05   ACCOUNT-DOLLARS         PIC 9(5)V99.
**206-S******                                                      **
**    01 or 77 level required
    21     05   FILLER                  PIC X(68).
**206-S******                                                      **
**    01 or 77 level required
    23 FD  REPORT-FILE
**205-S**                                                          **
**    RECORD missing or has zero size
    34 01   LINE-AND-PAGE-COUNTERS.
**217-S**                                                          **
**    Preceding item at this level has zero length
**217-S**                                                          **
**    Preceding item at this level has zero length
    48     15   ACCOUNT-TOTAL-OUT       PIC $$$$,ZZ9.99.
**225-S******                                                      **
**    Level hierarchy wrong
    54            VALUE 'ACCOUNT    TOTAL           FINAL TOTAL       PAGE.
**  4-E********************************************************************  **
**    Continuation character expected. End of literal assumed.
    55     05   PAGE-NUMBER-OUT         PIC Z(6)9.
** 14-E******                                                      **
**    Period missing. Period assumed.
**  7-E******                                                      **
**    VALUE literal too large. Literal truncated.
** 27-S******                                                      **
**    Number too large
```

```
*       INPUT-FILE
**244-S**********                                                  **
**    FD missing for file INPUT-FILE
    59      OPEN INPUT-FILE
** 11-S*******************                                         **
**    Reserved word missing or incorrectly used
    62          AT END MOVE NO TO MORE-DATA-REMAINS-FLAG.
** 14-S**********************                                      **
**    Invalid operand
    64          MOVE ACCOUNT-NUMBER TO PREVIOUS-ACCOUNT-NUMBER
** 12-S***************************                                 **
**    Operand is not declared
    66              UNTIL NO-MORE-DATA-REMAINS-FLAG
** 12-S*********************************************               **
**    Operand is not declared
    72      IF ACCOUNT-NUMBER IS NOT EQUAL TO PREVIOUS-ACCOUNT-NUMBER
** 12-S********************                                        **
**    Operand is not declared
    74      ADD ACCOUNT-DOLLARS TO ACCOUNT-TOTAL
** 12-S***********************                                     **
**    Operand is not declared
    76      READ INPUT-RECORD
** 12-S********************                                        **
**    Operand is not declared
    90      MOVE ACCOUNT-NUMBER TO PREVIOUS-ACCOUNT-NUMBER
** 12-S***********************                                     **
**    Operand is not declared
    93 C020-LINE-OUT.
** 29-S*************                                               **
**    Not a data name
    94      IF LINE-NUMBER EQUALS 1
** 54-S************************                                    **
**    Class name required
    95          MOVE PAGE-NUMBER TO PAGE-NUMBER-OUT
** 12-S*******************************************                 **
**    Operand is not declared
*     C020-LINE-OUT
**348-S*************                                               **
**    Procedure name C020-LINE-OUT undeclared
*     C020-LINE-OUT
**348-S*************                                               **
**    Procedure name C020-LINE-OUT undeclared
* Checking complete - errors found
```

Finding the punctuation errors and the second missing statemnt are left as an exercise. (See Exercise 2.)

6. This is not the objective of testing. Unless we are able to run test cases that cover *all possible paths through the program,* an activity that would take years even for relatively small programs, we cannot *prove* that a program is correct through testing. A more reasonable goal of testing is to find the errors in the program. If, after a thorough job of testing, we can find no more errors we can say that there are probably no *major* errors left in the program.

7. c.

EXERCISES

*1. The first example in Section 8.3 contains a bug. Identify the bug and modify the code shown to correct the error. Do not rewrite the entire example--just modify to code shown, doing as little as necessary to make the correction.

*2. Correct the syntactic errors identified for Review Question 5, then use ANIMATOR to locate the punctuation and other processing errors. If you think you have determined what the errors are just from studying the program listing, use ANIMATOR to verify your opinion.

COBOL-85

3. If you are using **COBOL-85**, insert **END-IF** phrases in parts **a** and **d** of Review Question 3 so that the indentation matches the way a **COBOL** compiler would interpret the statements.

END COBOL-85

*4. Write a nested **IF** statement that will do the following. A marital status code has level **88** entries defining condition names **SINGLE**, **MARRIED**, **DIVORCED**, and **WIDOWED**. Depending on the value of the code, it is necessary to perform **D010-SINGLE-ROUTINE**, **D020-MARRIED-ROUTINE**, **D030-DIVORCED-ROUTINE**, or **D040-WIDOWED-ROUTINE**. If the code is not any of these, **D050-ERROR-ROUTINE** should be performed. Assume that for the employee group involved, the most common status is married, then single, then divorced, and the least frequent is widowed; write the statement so that it is as efficient as possible in view of these frequencies.

5. A certain company manufactures electric motors in the range of 1 to 99 horsepower. Three different departments are involved, and a nested **IF** statement must choose an appropriate order routine according to the following table:

If the value of **HORSEPOWER** is:	PERFORM:
Less than 1	D040-ERROR-ROUTINE
At least 1 but less than 5	D010-DEPT-23-ORDER
At least 5 but less than 20	D020-DEPT-26-ORDER
At least 20 but less than 100	D030-DEPT-39-ORDER
100 or over	D040-ERROR-ROUTINE

(This can be done with one nested **IF** containing no **AND**s.)

*6. Write a nested **IF** statement that performs a routine **E050-EXCESSIVE-PAY-POSSIBLE** if any one of the following conditions is true:

The value of **SALARY-CODE** is **W** and **GROSS-PAY** is greater than **500**.
The value of **SALARY-CODE** is **S** and **GROSS-PAY** is greater than **1400**.
The value of **SALARY-CODE** is **M** and **GROSS-PAY** is greater than **4500**.

Perform **X030-ERROR-ROUTINE** is **SALARY-CODE** is not **W**, **S**, or **M**.

* Answers to starred exercises will be found in Appendix IV at the end of the book.

7. Write a nested **IF** statement to carry out one of four routines according to the following combinations of the value of the two items named **FLD-1** and **FLD-2**:

FLD-1	A	A	A	B	Anything but **A** or **B**
FLD-2	1	2	Anything but **1** or **2**	3	Doesn't matter
PERFORM:	A-1-RTN	A-2-RTN	ERROR-RTN	A-3-RTN	ERROR-RTN

*8. Modify the program in Exercise 7 of Chapter 7 to print an error message if the total of the invoice amounts overflows the total field. The program should continue to run until all data has been processed, and the error message should be printed once, in place of the normal total.

9. Modify the program in Exercise 8 of Chapter 7 so that if any of the total fields overflows, an error message is printed for that field in place of the total at the end of the output. The overflow could occur for none of the fields, one of the fields, etc., and only the affected totals should show the error message.

CHAPTER 9

CONTROL BREAKS

9.1 INTRODUCTION

The primary topic for this chapter is the processing of a file that is in sequence on some control field in each record, building a report that is organized according to the changes in that field. A change from one control group to the next is called a *control break*, hence the title of the chapter. Because the data file must be in sequence for this processing to work correctly, the data in a control break program is usually stored in a file, then sorted before the program is run. Although it is possible to key data directly into the program and have it sorted as the program executes, the technique for doing so will not be discussed until Chapter 18. Therefore, the examples in the current discussion will all use batch files for input.

The vehicle for this study will be an application of broad general interest. Starting with a file of sales data that is in ascending sequence, we are to produce a summary of the data by region, seller, and account. The techniques involved in processing such a file are of fundamental importance (they will concern us in future chapters as well), and summarization is a basic computer application. The program will be developed in two stages, starting first with a simpler task.

In the course of this study we also examine several new COBOL features. The first is the content of the Identification Division, which is much simpler and shorter than the Data and Procedure Divisions and which does not require a great deal of effort. The second is the use of techniques that allow us to skip lines between lines of output in a printed report and to skip to the top of a new page. We will present some additional examples of debugging, and discuss the handling of requests for program modification.

9.2 THE SALES STATISTICS APPLICATION

Suppose we have an input file of information about the previous month's sales of some company. The company has a number of sales regions; within each region there are a number of salespeople; each salesperson handles a number of accounts. We are required to produce a sales summary that shows the total

REGION	TOTAL	SALESPERSON	TOTAL	ACCOUNT	TOTAL	FINAL TOTAL	PAGE	1
				20	$17.00			
				24	$36.00			
				27	$184.00			
		1	$237.00					
				17	$26.00			
				24	$266.90			
		2	$292.90					
				10	$87.50			
				16	$54.75			
		12	$142.25					
1	$672.15							
				40	$50.12			
				41	$105.99			
		4	$156.11					
				44	$1,594.14			
		39	$1,594.14					
2	$1,750.25							
				30	$1,180.94			
				35	$69.26			
				38	$157.43			
				49	$45.00			
				60	$1,234.56			
				78	$276.02			
		15	$2,963.21					
3	$2,963.21							
						$5,385.61		

FIGURE 9.1 Illustrative output of a program to produce three-level control totals.

sales for the entire company for the month, the total sales for each region, the total sales for each salesperson, and the total sales for each account. Figure 9.1 indicates the general layout of the report that we are to produce and helps to clarify the hierarchical nature of the data organization.

When faced with a programming task that is too complex for us to solve in a single step, we can approach it by first determining if there is a related but simpler task that we can do. Once we have found a workable approach to the simpler job, we can build on that foundation to complete the task we really want to accomplish. In the assignment for this chapter, an obvious simplification is to deal first with only one level of control totals rather than three.

Suppose that the input file for a one-level version of our program is this:

ACCOUNT	AMOUNT
20	$ 12
20	18
20	4
24	72
27	40
27	26
27	218
27	2
27	82

We see that there are three transactions for account 20, totaling $34. Account 24 has only one transaction, so its account total is just the $72 for that one transaction. Account 27 has five transactions for a total of $368. The final total is for all transactions, which is also equal to the sum of all account totals.

The purpose of the program is to prepare summary totals from the input file of such transactions. The output of the program that we shall develop for this one-level version, given this input file, would be as follows:

```
ACCOUNT          TOTAL        FINAL TOTAL        PAGE        1

   20            $34.00
   24            $72.00
   27           $368.00
                                474.00
```

9.3   SEQUENTIAL FILE PROCESSING

It is certainly possible to prepare summaries of this type when the transactions appear in random order, although the program might get rather cumbersome if we were dealing with 30,000 accounts instead of only three. In this chapter, however, we are assuming a file in which the records appear in ascending sequence on the account numbers contained in them. For our example file this means that, since 20 is the smallest account number, all the transactions for that account must appear together at the beginning of the file; since 24 is the next larger account number, its transaction must appear next; all of the transactions for account 27 must appear at the end of the file. We don't care at all what the order of the transactions is within any one account number; reverse the first two transactions, for instance, and the program should produce the same result.

It is not to be expected that the sales records will already be in proper ascending sequence on the account number. Getting the records into sequence requires a preliminary operation called sorting, which is done with an appropriate program. We shall learn in Chapter 18 how this can be done by using the COBOL verb SORT.

The value of knowing that the records appear in ascending sequence is that we are able to write a program that never has to deal with more than two transaction records at any one time. After getting the process started, by a method that we shall investigate shortly, we always ask whether the transaction just read has the same account number as the transaction before this one. If not, then the previous transaction was the last one (or the only one) for an account number group, and we can produce the group's total. When we discover that the account number for the transaction just read is different from the account number of the previous transaction, we have what is called a *control break*. If the account number for the current transaction is the same as that for the previous one, then there is nothing to be done except add the dollar amount for this transaction to the account total. This contrasts sharply with what the situation would be if the transactions could arrive in random sequence. Then we would have to keep a separate total for each account number, since it would be impossible to print any of the totals until reaching the end of the file; there would be no way of knowing until then that any of the account groups was complete. The extra storage required could present a problem, especially on small computers, if the number of account groups was large. Of course, we would gain the advantage of not having to sort the transactions into ascending sequence before doing the process.

Sequentially and randomly accessed files both have their place, depending primarily on the needs of the application. After studying the use of sequentially accessed files in Chapters 9 and 13, we shall study randomly accessed files in Chapter 15, where trade-offs between the two will be considered more fully.

9.4 A PROGRAM DESIGN FOR THE ONE-LEVEL VERSION

We begin the design of this program by looking at the structure of the two files being processed, the data file and the report file. Each file consists of individual records—account records for the data file and lines of print for the report file—but this doesn't really help us very much. What does help is to observe that both files contain sets of records for account groups. In the input file the account group consists of one or more records having the same account number; in the report file an account group is just one line. The basic task of the program, therefore, is to process account groups until all groups have been processed, then produce a final total. Processing an account group is simple: all we have to do is add the amount on the current record to the group total. The tricky part is to determine when we have reached the end of a group, and to initialize a new account group. The hierarchy chart for the program is shown in Figure 9.2, and the basic pseudocode is in Figure 9.3.

The basic structure of this design follows the structure of the data files. In the main program we execute a priming READ, then process account groups until we run out of data, at which time we print the final total. At this level we are not really concerned with what an account group is or what the individual

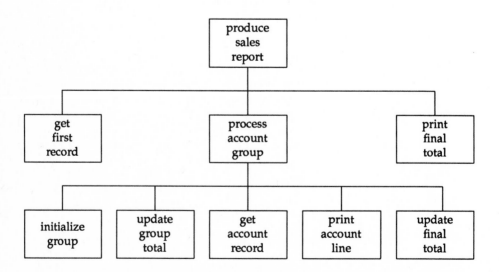

FIGURE 9.2 Hierarchy chart for a one-level control break program.

```
PRODUCE SALES REPORT:
open files
set final total to zero
set more-data-flag to 'Y'
get account record; at end set more-data-flag to 'N'
PERFORM-UNTIL no more data
     process account group
ENDPERFORM
print final total
close files


PROCESS ACCOUNT GROUP:
initialize account group
PERFORM-UNTIL
          current account number is not equal to previous account number
               or
          no more data
     update account total
     get account record; at end set more-data-flag to 'N'
ENDPERFORM
print account line
update final total


INITIALIZE ACCOUNT GROUP:
set account total to zero
set previous account number to account number of current record
```

FIGURE 9.3. Basic pseudocode for one-level control break.

input records look like. However, if the input file is empty, the program will not process any account groups, which is what we would want.

In any program such as this, which processes successive data groups, the most difficult task usually is dealing with the end of one group and the start of the next. We would like to have a general technique for this situation, one that does not require special handling for special cases. The basic approach we will use is to have two variables, one to identify the group to which the *current* record (the one we are working with now) belongs, and one to identify the group to which the *previous* record (the one we just finished with) belongs.

As long as these two variables have the same value, everything is easy; we simply continue processing the current data group. When the variables have different values, however, we know that we are at the end of one group and the start of another. We terminate the current group, then start the new one. In the pseudocode for PROCESS ACCOUNT GROUP, this means that we terminate the PERFORM-UNTIL loop, print the account line, and update the final total. This completes the old group, and we go through the PERFORM-UNTIL loop of PRODUCE SALES REPORT once more (assuming there is still more data).

Up to this point, nothing in the pseudocode has changed the value of previous account number. Now, however, we begin execution of PROCESS ACCOUNT GROUP again, which requires that we execute INITIALIZE ACCOUNT GROUP. Here we set the total for the new group to zero, then take the account number of the record we just read and save it as the previous account number. We are now ready to process the new data group.

Notice that each time we start a group, the record we use as the first record of the group is the one that was read when we *ended* the previous group.

There are two special groups to deal with: the first group in the file and the last group in the file. The last group is easy. Both PERFORM-UNTIL loops will terminate when an end-of-file is encountered, so we simply print the final total, close the files, and stop the run. The first group is a bit more complex because there is no previous group to start it off. We can solve this problem rather easily, however, by reading a priming record before we start the main PERFORM-UNTIL loop in PRODUCE SALES REPORT. This record becomes the current record that is used to set the previous account number in INITIALIZE ACCOUNT GROUP.

This technique is very general, and can easily be adapted to any system where the input file is structured as a sequence of data groups.

The hierarchy chart and pseudocode imply that the program should have about nine modules (although we have not actually shown the pseudocode for all). In point of fact, we shall not actually use this many paragraphs in the COBOL program. Most of the modules are very simple and are coded in-line. The code for the program is shown in Figure 9.4. This listing has a slightly different format from most of the listings in this book. It is taken directly from the output produced by the LIST option of the Microsoft COBOL compiler, whereas the other program listings are taken from program files with line numbers added by the authors. We show the Microsoft listing simply to show what you normally would see if you request a listing from the compiler.

```
Microsoft COBOL Version 3.00      L2.0 revision 053 12-Feb-89 14:57 Page 1
*                                 C09P01.CBL
*
*
 1 IDENTIFICATION DIVISION.
 2 PROGRAM-ID.
 3      ONELEVEL.
 4 AUTHOR.
 5      D. GOLDEN.
 6 INSTALLATION.
 7      CLEVELAND STATE UNIVERSITY.
 8 DATE-WRITTEN.
 9      FEBRUARY 12, 1989.
10 DATE-COMPILED. 12-Feb-89 14:57.
11 SECURITY.
12      NON-CLASSIFIED.
13*
14*      THIS PROGRAM PRODUCES A SIMPLE ONE-LEVEL SUMMARY REPORT FOR A
15*      SALES ACCOUNTING SYSTEM
16*
17
18 ENVIRONMENT DIVISION.
19 INPUT-OUTPUT SECTION.
20 FILE-CONTROL.
21      SELECT ACCOUNT-FILE          ASSIGN TO "C09P01.ACC".
22      SELECT REPORT-FILE           ASSIGN TO "C09P01.REP".
23
24 DATA DIVISION.
25 FILE SECTION.
26
```

```
27 FD   ACCOUNT-FILE
28      LABEL RECORDS ARE OMITTED.
29 01   ACCOUNT-RECORD.
30      05   ACCOUNT-NUMBER           PIC X(5).
31      05   SALE-AMOUNT              PIC 9(5)V99.
32      05   FILLER                   PIC X(68).
33
34 FD   REPORT-FILE
35      LABEL RECORDS ARE OMITTED.
36 01   REPORT-RECORD                 PIC X(132).
37
38 WORKING-STORAGE SECTION.
39
40 77   ACCOUNT-TOTAL                 PIC S9(6)V99.
41 77   FINAL-TOTAL                   PIC S9(6)V99.
42 77   LINE-NUMBER                   PIC S99.
43 77   MORE-DATA-FLAG                PIC X.
44      88   NO-MORE-DATA                              VALUE 'N'.
45 77   PAGE-NUMBER                   PIC S999.
46 77   PREVIOUS-ACCOUNT-NUMBER       PIC X(5).
47
48 01   DETAIL-LINE.
49      05   ACCOUNT-NUMBER-OUT       PIC Z(4)9.
50      05   FILLER                   PIC XXX.
51      05   ACCOUNT-TOTAL-OUT        PIC $$$$,$$9.99.
52      05   FILLER                   PIC X(8).
53      05   FINAL-TOTAL-OUT          PIC $$$$,$$9.99.
54
55 01   HEADING-LINE.
56      05   FILLER                   PIC X(48)
57      VALUE 'ACCOUNT    TOTAL            FINAL TOTAL        PAGE'.
58      05   PAGE-NUMBER-OUT          PIC Z(6)9.
59
60 PROCEDURE DIVISION.
61 A000-PREPARE-SALES-REPORT.
62      OPEN   INPUT ACCOUNT-FILE
63             OUTPUT REPORT-FILE.
64      MOVE ZERO                     TO FINAL-TOTAL.
65      MOVE 55                       TO LINE-NUMBER.
66      MOVE 'Y'                      TO MORE-DATA-FLAG.
67      MOVE ZERO                     TO PAGE-NUMBER.
68      READ ACCOUNT-FILE
69             AT END MOVE 'N' TO MORE-DATA-FLAG.
70      PERFORM B010-PROCESS-ACCOUNT-GROUP
71             UNTIL NO-MORE-DATA.
72      MOVE SPACES TO DETAIL-LINE.
73      MOVE FINAL-TOTAL TO FINAL-TOTAL-OUT.
74      PERFORM X010-LINE-OUT.
75      CLOSE ACCOUNT-FILE
76             REPORT-FILE.
77      STOP RUN.
78
79 B010-PROCESS-ACCOUNT-GROUP.
80      MOVE ZERO TO ACCOUNT-TOTAL.
81      MOVE ACCOUNT-NUMBER TO PREVIOUS-ACCOUNT-NUMBER.
82      PERFORM C010-PROCESS-ACCOUNT-RECORD UNTIL
83             ACCOUNT-NUMBER IS NOT EQUAL TO PREVIOUS-ACCOUNT-NUMBER
84             OR NO-MORE-DATA.
85      MOVE SPACES TO DETAIL-LINE.
86      MOVE PREVIOUS-ACCOUNT-NUMBER TO ACCOUNT-NUMBER-OUT.
87      MOVE ACCOUNT-TOTAL TO ACCOUNT-TOTAL-OUT.
```

```
 88        PERFORM X010-LINE-OUT.
 89        ADD ACCOUNT-TOTAL TO FINAL-TOTAL.
 90
 91 C010-PROCESS-ACCOUNT-RECORD.
 92        ADD SALE-AMOUNT TO ACCOUNT-TOTAL
 93        READ ACCOUNT-FILE
 94               AT END MOVE 'N' TO MORE-DATA-FLAG.
 95
 96 X010-LINE-OUT.
 97        ADD 1 TO LINE-NUMBER.
 98*              SEE IF WE ARE AT THE END OF THE PAGE
 99*              IF SO, PRINT A NEW PAGE HEADING
100        IF LINE-NUMBER IS GREATER THAN 55
101            ADD 1 TO PAGE-NUMBER
102            MOVE PAGE-NUMBER TO PAGE-NUMBER-OUT
103            WRITE REPORT-RECORD FROM HEADING-LINE
104                    AFTER ADVANCING PAGE
105            MOVE SPACES TO REPORT-RECORD
106            WRITE REPORT-RECORD
107                    AFTER ADVANCING 2 LINES
108            MOVE 4 TO LINE-NUMBER.
109        WRITE REPORT-RECORD FROM DETAIL-LINE
110                AFTER ADVANCING 1 LINE.
111
* Microsoft COBOL Version 3.00        L2.0 revision 053
* (C)Copyright Microsoft Corp 1984, 1988
```

FIGURE 9.4 A program to produce one-level control totals for a sales accounting system.

You may not have noticed that in Figure 9.4 there is no period after the ADD statement on line 92. Since neither the ADD nor the READ is subordinate to a conditional statement, they were simply carried out in order. With only one period at the end of the paragraph, this became a one-sentence paragraph with two statements in it, instead of a two-sentence paragraph, each with one statement. Under these conditions, the missing period is completely legal and, in fact, causes no trouble.

We do not recommend taking advantage of this flexibility, however. It is better to learn good habits and stick with them. The omission was intended to demonstrate—to some readers at least—how difficult it can be to "see" an omission that, when it is later pointed out, is perfectly obvious. Here the omission triggered no diagnostic messages and caused no trouble. The problem is that things like this will sometimes trigger no diagnostic messages but will cause a great deal of trouble.

9.5 THE IDENTIFICATION DIVISION

This program contains several new features, beginning with a full-scale Identification Division, the only one that appears in the book. The Identification Division is by far the simplest of the four divisions of a COBOL program. We shall be able to cover its various entries rather briefly.

The Identification Division is considered to be organized into paragraphs with paragraph names. PROGRAM-ID, for example, is a paragraph name. The balance of a paragraph is supposed to be written according to the rules for the formation of sentences and paragraphs that apply elsewhere in a COBOL program. However, the Microsoft compiler will accept almost anything that is written within a paragraph in the Identification Division as a comment entry. That means that since the compiler takes no meaning from it, anything at all may be written there.

A few simple rules cover the syntax of the Identification Division.

1. The PROGRAM-ID entry is the only entry that should always be present, although even this entry is actually optional with the Microsoft compiler. For many other compilers, the entry in this paragraph becomes the name by which the compiler and other components of the operating system refer to the program. For example, if you are writing programs for an IBM mainframe compiler the name in the PROGRAM-ID paragraph should be eight characters or less and should begin with a letter, since these are the rules the IBM operating system uses for forming program names. In Microsoft COBOL, the program is identified by the name of the file containing the source code, so the PROGRAM-ID is not really necessary. However, you should get into the habit of using the PROGRAM-ID to maintain compatibility with other compilers.
2. All other entries in the Identification Division always are optional. If present, however, they must be written in the order shown in this program. The paragraph names must be spelled correctly.
3. If the Date-Compiled entry is present, it is normal to leave the paragraph empty because the compiler replaces any written comments with the date on which the compilation was done in any case. For example, the program in Figure 9.4 was compiled just before 3 p.m. on February 12, 1989.

We see in this entry that the compiler has inserted the compilation date on the same line as the paragraph name. Recall from Chapter 1 that the first sentence of any paragraph in a COBOL program is permitted to begin on the same line as a paragraph name, but that in the interest of readability and maintainability we never exercise that option in this book.

It is common for any installation to have simple rules as to what should be written in the Identification Division. Besides the required program identification, it is usual to include the author's name and the date compiled. The latter is useful when, as frequently happens, there are multiple versions of a program in existence and it becomes important to know whether you have the latest one.

Although all entries shown in the program are supported by COBOL-85, the COBOL-85 standard has specified that all paragraphs in the Identification Division *except* the PROGRAM-ID paragraph will be deleted whenever the *next* standard is issued. Although this may not be for several years, COBOL programs frequently have a lifetime of well over a decade, so you may want to start using alternatives to these "comment" paragraphs now.

9.6 COMMENTS

The alternative to using the optional entries in the Identification Division is demonstrated in the four lines following the Security paragraph. These lines are *comment lines*. As we mentioned in Chapter 1, a comment line is a line beginning with an asterisk in column 7. Comments are ignored by the compiler and may be placed anywhere in the program that you wish to include a note to the reader. If you place a slash ("/") in column 7, the line is still treated as a comment, but the printer will skip to the top of a new page before printing that line when the compiler prints a listing of the program.

It is common to place a comment at the end of the Identification Division to give a brief statement of what the program is to do. Comments are frequently used in the Procedure Division to explain a particularly tricky piece of code, or in the Data Division to document the use of data fields. Although many programs can benefit from the use of thoughtfully placed comments, we recommend sparing use of them since a well-written program ought to be largely self-documenting; too many comments can hide the actual code.

9.7 THE CONTROL OF LINE SPACING

The next new feature of **COBOL** demonstrated by this program involves several different parts of the program. In the programs up to this point we have taken no special measures to control the vertical spacing of lines on printed output. The result has been to get an automatic single spacing of all lines, with no attention paid to where one page stops and the next one begins.

Often this is not adequate. Sometimes we wish to guarantee that a line of column headings will be printed at the top of a new page; other times we may wish to double or triple space; on rare occasions we may wish to suppress spacing and print two lines in the same position. **COBOL** makes provision for all of these operations in a fairly simple way that we now investigate.

9.8 THE COMPLETE WRITE STATEMENT

Two types of options are available in using the **WRITE** statement. We have already seen how to utilize the **WRITE FROM** capability and now we look into the **ADVANCING** feature. Here is the complete general format of the **WRITE** verb as it is used for the kind of files we know about thus far:

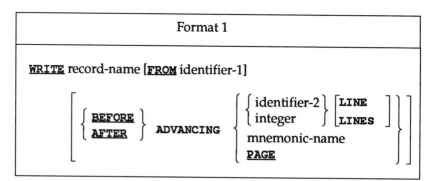

We see that it is possible to specify that the printing of a line take place either before or after actions having to do with the vertical positioning of the paper and, therefore, the printing. We might say, for instance,

```
WRITE OUTPUT-RECORD AFTER ADVANCING 2 LINES.
```

This would mean to double-space before printing the line specified by `OUT-PUT-RECORD`. We might also say

`WRITE MESSAGE-LINE AFTER ADVANCING NUMBER-OF-LINES LINES.`

This would mean to space as many lines as the current value of the item named `NUMBER-OF-LINES`.

The number of lines is allowed to be *zero*. When this is done, the printer is not advanced at all and the line prints in the same position as the previous line. The facility may be used to print the same line twice and gain a bold-faced effect, or it may be used to obtain underlining.

In general, if *any* of the `WRITE` statements for a file employ the `ADVANCING` option, then *all* `WRITE` statements for that file should have it. This is because, on some computers, the only way that the compiler can tell whether to format output as normal data or whether to format it for writing to a printer is by the presence or absence of the `ADVANCING` clause. In Microsoft `COBOL`, if you use the `ADVANCING` clause on some write statements for a file but omit it on others, the statements with no `ADVANCING` clause act as though you had written

`WRITE OUTPUT-RECORD AFTER ADVANCING 0 LINES.`

In other words, the output from this `WRITE` statement will overwrite the output from the previous `WRITE` statement. This means that if you use the `ADVANCING` option to get spacing to the top of the page or for any other purpose, then you should also use it when you want normal single-spacing, even if this occasionally requires you to write things like

`WRITE OUTPUT-RECORD AFTER ADVANCING 1 LINE.`

A word of caution is in order at this point. Although `COBOL` allows you to use both `BEFORE ADVANCING` and `AFTER ADVANCING` for the same file (that is, sometimes write one and sometimes the other), it is generally not advisable to do so. The program will work, but the results of this type of mixing are not always what you might expect. If you must mix the two options on the same file, do so with care.

The option mnemonic-name refers to names that we may apply to certain hardware functions that are built into the mechanisms that control spacing in printers. The primary example is moving the paper so that the next line will print at the top of a new page. All computer printers provide this•feature, but the exact details of how it is specified vary from one machine to the next. The specification of aspects of a program that depend on the nature of the equipment is precisely the function of the Environment Division. We shall not go into the details here, other than to say that if you work with programs from other computers, particularly older programs, you will observe that entries in the `SPECIAL-NAMES` paragraph in the Environment Division are used to provide mnemonic ("aiding the memory") names for controlling page ejects.

A much easier way to accomplish the same result is to use the `PAGE` option. Thus, for example, the phrase

`AFTER ADVANCING PAGE`

on line 104 causes the printer to skip to the top of a new page before printing `HEADING-LINE`.

All of the variations of the `ADVANCING` feature we shall ordinarily need are illustrated in our program. When a heading is to be written, the heading line employs the form `AFTER ADVANCING PAGE`. To get two blank lines between the heading line and the first detail line we place spaces in the output record and then write that blank line with the **AFTER ADVANCING 2 LINES** option. Finally, detail lines are written with the **AFTER ADVANCING 1 LINE** form.

9.9 THE CARRIAGE CONTROL CHARACTER

With a number of **COBOL** compilers (IBM in particular), when the **ADVANCING** option is used it is necessary to provide space for one extra character at the beginning of each record to be printed. This is called the *carriage control character*, because it controls the part of a mainframe printer (the carriage) that advances the paper. We are not required to place anything in this character position; that is done as a consequence of whatever is written in the **ADVANCING** phrase. Indeed, if we do place anything in the carriage control character, it is overwritten by the action of the **ADVANCING** phrase. The character that is placed there by the object program is not printed but is, instead, used to control the line spacing on the printer.

There are three points about which you should be very clear. First, the carriage control character is not a standard **COBOL** feature and is only used on some compilers. In particular, the Microsoft **COBOL** compiler does not require a carriage control character and you should not leave space for one unless you expect your program to be moved to an IBM mainframe. Second, if you are using a computer that does require a carriage control character, the **ADVANCING** phrase will *always* use the first character of the output record for the carriage control character. If you don't allow space for this character, then the first character of your output data will be overwritten. Finally, whatever computer you are using, if you don't use the **ADVANCING** option on the **WRITE** statements for a file, then don't leave space for a carriage control character; it is only used by the **ADVANCING** phrase.

9.10 PRINTING HEADINGS

The need to print headings in a report is a very common one, and the code used in Figure 9.4 is typical. The problem we have to deal with is simple. Because we only want a certain number of lines on a page (55 in this example), we count the lines each time an output line is written. When this count exceeds our limit, we skip to a new page, print the heading, print the detail line, and reset the line counter. While we could update the line counter and test for the end of the page every place in the program that we write an output record, this would add quite a bit to the size of the program and would be prone to error. It is much simpler to have a single paragraph that does all the work, then perform this paragraph whenever we want to print a line. Notice, however, that **X010-LINE-OUT** can write records only from **DETAIL-LINE**. If, as in the payroll program, we had to write several different records to the report, it would be necessary to move the record to **DETAIL-LINE** before performing **X010-LINE-OUT**.

Paragraph **X010-LINE-OUT** has an **X** prefix instead of **C** or **D** because the paragraph is not part of the main structure of the program. Since it may be performed from any level of the hierarchy to accomplish the task of printing a line of output, it is considered to be a utility paragraph and is given a prefix code outside the normal hierarchical sequence.

9.11 DESIGN OF THE THREE-LEVEL VERSION

The full problem that we set out to solve involves three levels of control totals. What is called the *major* level is a summary by sales region. Within each region there are several salespeople; salesperson is called the *intermediate* level; finally, each salesperson has several accounts and this is called the *minor* level. To summarize each level, input records for this version must contain the region number, the salesperson number, the account number, and the dollar amount of the sale.

The sales records are required to be in sequence (after a preliminary sort) on all three control fields. Thus all the records must be in ascending sequence on region number, the major control. Within any one region, all the records in that group must be in sequence on salesperson number, the intermediate control. For any one salesperson, all the records in that group must be in sequence on account number, the minor control. The records can be put into order on three control fields this way with just one sort, as we shall learn in Chapter 18.

The logic of the three-level program we must now develop, as shown in Figure 9.5, will be a bit more complex than that of the one-level program we studied at the start of this chapter. Somehow, the program must handle each level of control break properly. If there has been a break on the minor control, for example, it must produce a minor total but not a major or intermediate one. If there has been a break on the intermediate control, it must produce minor and intermediate totals but not a major one. Finally, if there has been a break on the major control, it must produce all three totals.

Much of the logic of this version of the program is the same as or very similar to that for the one-level version. This similarity, of course, is the reason it is worthwhile approaching the full job in two steps as we have done.

Notice that the bottom three levels of the chart are almost identical. Module names are slightly different, and the lowest level contains an extra module, but the similarities in structure are strong. Basically, this structure states that to produce the sales report, we must process all regions within the company, then print the final total; to process a region, we must process all sellers within the region, then print the region total; to process a seller, we must process all accounts for the seller, then print a seller total; and to process an account, we process all sales records for that account, then print the account total.

What does not show up on the hierarchy chart is how we know when we have finished processing a group. In the one-level case this was easy; if the account number changed, we were starting a new group. In the three-level case things are a bit more tricky. For example, suppose a salesperson moved from one region to another during the month. Then the seller number for two consecutive records is the same, but the region numbers are different. This means that we have finished both the seller group and the region group. The technique for dealing with this problem is to realize that a control break for a level occurs not only when the group number for that level changes, but also if the group number for any higher level changes.

The pseudocode for this program is shown in Figure 9.6.

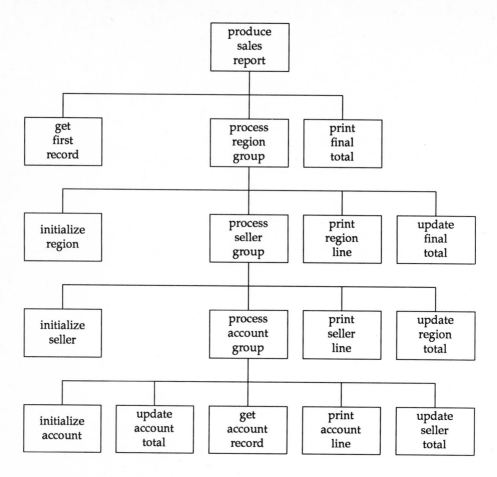

FIGURE 9.5 Hierarchy chart for a three-level control break program.

Again observe the similarities between the module specifications. Except for the control variable involved, the **PROCESS** specifications are all essentially the same, as are the **INITIALIZE** specifications. Using these specifications as a basis, we can easily produce the program shown in Figure 9.7.

```
PRODUCE SALES REPORT:
open files
set final-total to zero
set more-data-flag to 'Y'
get account record; at end set more-data-flag to 'N'
PERFORM-UNTIL no-more-data
    process region group
ENDPERFORM
print final-total
close files
```

PROCESS REGION GROUP:
initialize region group
PERFORM-UNTIL
          current region number is not equal to previous region number
                or
          no-more-data
      process seller group
ENDPERFORM
print region line
update final-total

PROCESS SELLER GROUP:
initialize seller group
PERFORM-UNTIL
          current seller number is not equal to previous seller number
                or
          current region number is not equal to previous region number
                or
          no-more-data
      process account group
ENDPERFORM
print seller line
update region-total

PROCESS ACCOUNT GROUP:
initialize account group
PERFORM-UNTIL
          current account number is not equal to previous account number
                or
          current seller number is not equal to previous seller number
                or
          current region number is not equal to previous region number
                or
          no-more-data
      update account total
      get account record; at end set more-data-flag to 'N'
ENDPERFORM
print account line
update seller-total

INITIALIZE REGION GROUP:
set region-total to zero
set previous region number to region number of current record

INITIALIZE SELLER GROUP:
set seller-total to zero
set previous seller number to seller number of current record

INITIALIZE ACCOUNT GROUP:
set account-total to zero
set previous account number to account number of current record

---

FIGURE 9.6   Basic pseudocode of the logic for a three-level control break.

```
1          IDENTIFICATION DIVISION.
2          PROGRAM-ID.
3              THREELVL.
4          AUTHOR.
5              D. GOLDEN.
6          DATE-WRITTEN.
7              FEBRUARY 12, 1989.
8          *
9          *   THIS PROGRAM PRODUCES A SIMPLE THREE-LEVEL SUMMARY REPORT FOR
10         *   A SALES ACCOUNTING SYSTEM
11         *
12
13         ENVIRONMENT DIVISION.
14         INPUT-OUTPUT SECTION.
15         FILE-CONTROL.
16             SELECT ACCOUNT-FILE          ASSIGN TO "C09P02.ACC".
17             SELECT REPORT-FILE           ASSIGN TO "C09P02.REP".
18
19         DATA DIVISION.
20         FILE SECTION.
21
22         FD  ACCOUNT-FILE
23             LABEL RECORDS ARE OMITTED.
24         01  ACCOUNT-RECORD.
25             05   REGION-NUMBER           PIC X(5).
26             05   SELLER-NUMBER           PIC X(5).
27             05   ACCOUNT-NUMBER          PIC X(5).
28             05   SALE-AMOUNT             PIC 9(5)V99.
29             05   FILLER                  PIC X(58).
30
31         FD  REPORT-FILE
32             LABEL RECORDS ARE OMITTED.
33         01  REPORT-RECORD               PIC X(133).
34
35         WORKING-STORAGE SECTION.
36
37         77  LINE-NUMBER                 PIC S99.
38         77  MORE-DATA-FLAG              PIC X.
39             88   NO-MORE-DATA                           VALUE 'N'.
40         77  PAGE-NUMBER                 PIC S999.
41         77  PREVIOUS-ACCOUNT-NUMBER     PIC X(5).
42         77  PREVIOUS-REGION-NUMBER      PIC X(5).
43         77  PREVIOUS-SELLER-NUMBER      PIC X(5).
44
45         01  DETAIL-LINE.
46             05   CARRIAGE-CONTROL        PIC X.
47             05   REGION-NUMBER-OUT       PIC Z(4)9.
48             05   REGION-TOTAL-OUT        PIC BBB$$$$,$$9.99.
49             05   SELLER-NUMBER-OUT       PIC B(5)Z(4)9.
50             05   SELLER-TOTAL-OUT        PIC BBB$$$$,$$9.99.
51             05   ACCOUNT-NUMBER-OUT      PIC B(5)Z(4)9.
52             05   ACCOUNT-TOTAL-OUT       PIC BBB$$$$,$$9.99.
53             05   FINAL-TOTAL-OUT         PIC B(8)$$$$,$$9.99.
54
```

```
55          01  HEADING-LINE.
56              05  CARRIAGE-CONTROL          PIC X.
57              05  FILLER                    PIC X(40)
58                  VALUE 'REGION      TOTAL      SALESPERSON      TOTAL'.
59              05  FILLER                    PIC X(46)
60                  VALUE '       ACCOUNT     TOTAL            FINAL TOTAL'.
61              05  FILLER                    PIC X(10)
62                  VALUE '        PAGE'.
63              05  PAGE-NUMBER-OUT           PIC Z(6)9.
64
65          01  TOTALS.
66              05  ACCOUNT-TOTAL             PIC S9(6)V99.
67              05  SELLER-TOTAL              PIC S9(6)V99.
68              05  REGION-TOTAL              PIC S9(6)V99.
69              05  FINAL-TOTAL               PIC S9(6)V99.
70
71          PROCEDURE DIVISION.
72          A000-PREPARE-SALES-REPORT.
73              OPEN   INPUT ACCOUNT-FILE
74                     OUTPUT REPORT-FILE.
75              MOVE ZERO                     TO FINAL-TOTAL.
76              MOVE 55                       TO LINE-NUMBER.
77              MOVE 'Y'                      TO MORE-DATA-FLAG.
78              MOVE ZERO                     TO PAGE-NUMBER.
79              READ ACCOUNT-FILE
80                      AT END MOVE 'N' TO MORE-DATA-FLAG.
81              PERFORM B010-PROCESS-REGION-GROUP
82                  UNTIL NO-MORE-DATA.
83              MOVE SPACES TO DETAIL-LINE.
84              MOVE FINAL-TOTAL TO FINAL-TOTAL-OUT.
85              PERFORM X010-LINE-OUT.
86              CLOSE ACCOUNT-FILE
87                      REPORT-FILE.
88              STOP RUN.
89
90          B010-PROCESS-REGION-GROUP.
91              MOVE ZERO TO REGION-TOTAL.
92              MOVE REGION-NUMBER TO PREVIOUS-REGION-NUMBER.
93              PERFORM C010-PROCESS-SELLER-GROUP UNTIL
94                      REGION-NUMBER IS NOT EQUAL TO PREVIOUS-REGION-NUMBER
95                  OR NO-MORE-DATA.
96              MOVE SPACES TO DETAIL-LINE.
97              MOVE PREVIOUS-REGION-NUMBER TO REGION-NUMBER-OUT.
98              MOVE REGION-TOTAL TO REGION-TOTAL-OUT.
99              PERFORM X010-LINE-OUT.
100             ADD REGION-TOTAL TO FINAL-TOTAL.
101
102         C010-PROCESS-SELLER-GROUP.
103             MOVE ZERO TO SELLER-TOTAL.
104             MOVE SELLER-NUMBER TO PREVIOUS-SELLER-NUMBER.
105             PERFORM D010-PROCESS-ACCOUNT-GROUP UNTIL
106                     SELLER-NUMBER IS NOT EQUAL TO PREVIOUS-SELLER-NUMBER
107                 OR REGION-NUMBER IS NOT EQUAL TO PREVIOUS-REGION-NUMBER
108                 OR NO-MORE-DATA.
109             MOVE SPACES TO DETAIL-LINE.
110             MOVE PREVIOUS-SELLER-NUMBER TO SELLER-NUMBER-OUT.
111             MOVE SELLER-TOTAL TO SELLER-TOTAL-OUT.
112             PERFORM X010-LINE-OUT.
113             ADD SELLER-TOTAL TO REGION-TOTAL.
114
```

```
115          D010-PROCESS-ACCOUNT-GROUP.
116              MOVE ZERO TO ACCOUNT-TOTAL.
117              MOVE ACCOUNT-NUMBER TO PREVIOUS-ACCOUNT-NUMBER.
118              PERFORM E010-PROCESS-ACCOUNT-RECORD UNTIL
119                  ACCOUNT-NUMBER IS NOT EQUAL TO PREVIOUS-ACCOUNT-NUMBER
120                  OR SELLER-NUMBER IS NOT EQUAL TO PREVIOUS-SELLER-NUMBER
121                  OR REGION-NUMBER IS NOT EQUAL TO PREVIOUS-REGION-NUMBER
122                  OR NO-MORE-DATA.
123              MOVE SPACES TO DETAIL-LINE.
124              MOVE PREVIOUS-ACCOUNT-NUMBER TO ACCOUNT-NUMBER-OUT.
125              MOVE ACCOUNT-TOTAL TO ACCOUNT-TOTAL-OUT.
126              PERFORM X010-LINE-OUT.
127              ADD ACCOUNT-TOTAL TO SELLER-TOTAL.
128
129          E010-PROCESS-ACCOUNT-RECORD.
130              ADD SALE-AMOUNT TO ACCOUNT-TOTAL.
131              READ ACCOUNT-FILE
132                  AT END MOVE 'N' TO MORE-DATA-FLAG.
133
134          X010-LINE-OUT.
135              ADD 1 TO LINE-NUMBER.
136     *            SEE IF WE ARE AT THE END OF THE PAGE
137     *            IF SO, PRINT A NEW PAGE HEADING
138          IF LINE-NUMBER IS GREATER THAN 55
139              ADD 1 TO PAGE-NUMBER
140              MOVE PAGE-NUMBER TO PAGE-NUMBER-OUT
141              WRITE REPORT-RECORD FROM HEADING-LINE
142                  AFTER ADVANCING PAGE
143              MOVE SPACES TO REPORT-RECORD
144              WRITE REPORT-RECORD
145                  AFTER ADVANCING 2 LINES
146              MOVE 4 TO LINE-NUMBER.
147          WRITE REPORT-RECORD FROM DETAIL-LINE
148              AFTER ADVANCING 1 LINE.
149
150     ********************** END OF PROGRAM **********************
151
```

FIGURE 9.7 A program to produce three-level control totals.

When this program was run, it produced the output shown earlier, in Figure 9.1, page 216.

9.12 A SPECIFICATION CHANGE

Any program that is used for any length of time can be expected to change. Management may request new information; tax laws may change; new computer equipment may require partial reprogramming; long-standing errors in a program may finally surface and have to be corrected. We can't predict when, or where, or how the program will have to be changed, but we can guarantee that *most programs will require change eventually!* The work of installing such changes is called program maintenance and is a major activity in most data processing installations. In fact, it has been estimated that maintenance accounts for two-thirds or more of the typical data processing budget.

For some practice in dealing with maintenance, let us suppose that the "customer," or "user," the person or organization using the sales report, asks us to make the following changes:

1. The customer informs us that we misunderstood the desired arrangement of the printed report: the account and region totals are reversed from their desired positions.
2. The customer has decided that the final total should be printed in the same column as the region total, which is now the rightmost column. Furthermore, the final total should be identified by the words FINAL TOTAL printed to the left of the dollar amount. Finally on this point, the customer is concerned that it could occasionally happen that the final total would be the only line printed after the heading line at the top of a new page. Therefore, the final total should always be printed at the bottom of the last page even if that makes the last page run over 55 lines.
3. Another column is to be added to the report, printed between the account number and the account total, giving the number of sales in that account group.
4. If any individual sale exceeds $1000, an asterisk is to be printed after the count of transactions for that group.
5. The customer indicates that the company is considering a reorganization of the sales division that would make it possible for an account to be serviced by more than one salesperson. We have been asked if this would cause any problems in reporting the sales summary.

9.13 RESPONDING TO THE SPECIFICATION CHANGES

Some of these changes are simple, but the last one is very difficult and raises serious problems.

Reversing the position of the region and account totals is a simple matter of modifying the arrangement of the elementary items in DETAIL-LINE, and changing the heading.

Making sure that the final total prints at the bottom of the last page requires us to sidestep the logic of X010-LINE-OUT, which is a simpler solution than inserting new logic to handle the final total line separately within that routine. Rather than develop new logic, we simply put a WRITE statement in A000-PREPARE-SALES-REPORT instead of performing X010-LINE-OUT.

Counting the transactions is a matter of setting up a data item to hold the count, modifying DETAIL-LINE to provide space for it, adding a statement in E010-PROCESS-ACCOUNT-RECORD to add 1 to this total for each transa for and inserting a statement in D010-PROCESS-ACCOUNT-GROUP to move it position in DETAIL-LINE.

Generating an asterisk for a large transaction means providing space in DETAIL-LINE, inserting an IF statement in E010-PROCESS-ACCO RECORD, and adding another IF in D010-PROCESS-ACCOUNT-GROUP.

The last thing that the customer would like to do really cannot be done, at least not without showing the figures for one account in more than one place. For instance, if sellers 1 and 2 can both service account 17, say, then there will be a total for account 17 under seller 1 and another total for account 17 under seller 2. Nowhere will there be one single number giving the total—by all salespeople—for account 17.

The best we can do for the customer in this case is to point out what the organization of the sales report will be if this change is made and suggest that, if summarizations of sales by account are really needed, it will be necessary to go through another processing stage altogether and to produce a separate document. This would require re-sorting the input file so it is in sequence on region number as the major control, account number as the intermediate, and salesperson as the minor. Now a program like this one but with slightly different logic and output will produce a report giving the total for each account and within that, the amount sold by each person who services the account.

9.14 RUNNING THE REVISED REPORT

The necessary changes were made in the program of Figure 9.7, and the revised program was run with the same data as before. The output is shown in Figure 9.8.

ACCOUNT	TOTAL	NUMBER	SALESPERSON	TOTAL	REGION	TOTAL	PAGE	1
20	$17.00	3						
24	$36.00	4						
27	$184.00	9						
			1	$237.00				
17	$26.00	11						
24	$266.90	14						
			2	$292.90				
10	$87.50	15						
16	$54.75	18						
			12	$142.25				
					1	$672.15		
40	$50.12	20						
41	$105.99	21						
			4	$156.11				
44	$1,594.14	27						
			39	$1,594.14				
					2	$1,750.25		
30	$1,180.94	31						
35	$69.26	34						
3	$157.43	36						
9	$45.00	38						
	$1,234.56	39*						
3	$276.02	51*						
			15	$2,963.21				
					3	$2,963.21		
				FINAL TOTAL		$5,385.61		

FIGURE 9.8 The output of a modified version of the program of Figure 9.7. The modified version contains errors, and the output is not correct.

It seems to be about what we want, except that the figures for the number of transactions are wrong, and there are asterisks in some wrong places. (In fact, since we have not shown the sample data, it is conceivable that these counts could be correct, but, in fact, they are wrong. In any case, even without seeing the data, it seems unlikely that *every* account will have more records than the previous one.) We seem to be having logic trouble again. What happened? The first thing to check is to make sure that the locations for the total named **NO-OF-TRANSACTIONS** is initialized to zero. This was done, but unfortunately in the wrong place. The initialization statement had been placed in **A000-PREPARE-SALES-REPORT**. While this set the field to zero once, it was never reset to zero after printing each account total line. This is a very common type of mistake, which frequently involves data initialized by **VALUE** clauses; this is why we tend to use **VALUE** clause only for "constant" types of data items. The solution to the problem is to move the initialization statement from **A000-PREPARE-SALES-REPORT** to the start of **D010-PROCESS-ACCOUNT-GROUP**.

The problem with the extra asterisks is that once the asterisk flag was set, it was never reset to a blank. The resetting needs to be done as part of the initialization in **D010-PROCESS-ACCOUNT-GROUP**.

A final corrected program is shown in Figure 9.9; it produced the output of Figure 9.10.

```
 1          IDENTIFICATION DIVISION.
 2          PROGRAM-ID.
 3              3LEVEL2.
 4          AUTHOR.
 5              D. GOLDEN.
 6          DATE-WRITTEN.
 7              FEBRUARY 12, 1989.
 8          *
 9          *  THIS PROGRAM PRODUCES A SIMPLE THREE-LEVEL SUMMARY REPORT FOR
10          *  A SALES ACCOUNTING SYSTEM   (CORRECTED VERSION)
11          *
12
13          ENVIRONMENT DIVISION.
14          INPUT-OUTPUT SECTION.
15          FILE-CONTROL.
16              SELECT ACCOUNT-FILE              ASSIGN TO "C09P03.ACC".
17              SELECT REPORT-FILE               ASSIGN TO "C09P03.REP".
18
19          DATA DIVISION.
20          FILE SECTION.
21
22          FD  ACCOUNT-FILE
23              LABEL RECORDS ARE OMITTED.
24          01  ACCOUNT-RECORD.
25              05  REGION-NUMBER           PIC X(5).
26              05  SELLER-NUMBER           PIC X(5).
27              05  ACCOUNT-NUMBER          PIC X(5).
28              05  SALE-AMOUNT             PIC 9(5)V99.
29              05  FILLER                  PIC X(58).
30
```

```
31          FD   REPORT-FILE
32               LABEL RECORDS ARE OMITTED.
33          01   REPORT-RECORD              PIC X(133).
34
35          WORKING-STORAGE SECTION.
36
37          77   ASTERISK-FLAG             PIC X.
38               88  ASTERISK-FLAG-ON                      VALUE 'Y'.
39          77   LINE-NUMBER               PIC S99.
40          77   MORE-DATA-FLAG            PIC X.
41               88  NO-MORE-DATA                          VALUE 'N'.
42          77   PAGE-NUMBER               PIC S999.
43          77   PREVIOUS-ACCOUNT-NUMBER   PIC X(5).
44          77   PREVIOUS-REGION-NUMBER    PIC X(5).
45          77   PREVIOUS-SELLER-NUMBER    PIC X(5).
46
47          01   DETAIL-LINE.
48               05  CARRIAGE-CONTROL      PIC X.
49               05  ACCOUNT-NUMBER-OUT    PIC Z(4)9.
50               05  ACCOUNT-TOTAL-OUT     PIC BBB$$$$,$$9.99.
51               05  NO-OF-TRANSACTIONS-OUT PIC BBZZ9.
52               05  ASTERISK-OUT          PIC X.
53               05  SELLER-NUMBER-OUT     PIC B(5)Z(4)9.
54               05  SELLER-TOTAL-OUT      PIC BBB$$$$,$$9.99.
55               05  REGION-NUMBER-OUT     PIC B(5)Z(4)9.
56               05  REGION-TOTAL-OUT      PIC BBB$$$$,$$9.99.
57
58          01   FINAL-TOTAL-LINE.
59               05  CARRIAGE-CONTROL      PIC X.
60               05  FILLER                PIC X(44) VALUE SPACES.
61               05  FILLER                PIC X(11) VALUE 'FINAL TOTAL'.
62               05  FINAL-TOTAL-OUT       PIC B(7)$$$$,$$9.99.
63
64
65          01   HEADING-LINE.
66               05  CARRIAGE-CONTROL      PIC X.
67               05  FILLER                PIC X(41)
68               VALUE 'ACCOUNT    TOTAL    NUMBER  SALESPERSON  '.
69               05  FILLER                PIC X(39)
70               VALUE 'TOTAL       REGION    TOTAL       PAGE'.
71               05  PAGE-NUMBER-OUT       PIC Z(6)9.
72
73          01   TOTALS.
74               05  ACCOUNT-TOTAL         PIC S9(6)V99.
75               05  SELLER-TOTAL          PIC S9(6)V99.
76               05  REGION-TOTAL          PIC S9(6)V99.
77               05  FINAL-TOTAL           PIC S9(6)V99.
78               05  NO-OF-TRANSACTIONS    PIC S999.
79
80          PROCEDURE DIVISION.
81          A000-PREPARE-SALES-REPORT.
82               OPEN  INPUT ACCOUNT-FILE
83                     OUTPUT REPORT-FILE.
84               MOVE ZERO                 TO FINAL-TOTAL.
85               MOVE 55                   TO LINE-NUMBER.
86               MOVE 'Y'                  TO MORE-DATA-FLAG.
87               MOVE ZERO                 TO PAGE-NUMBER.
88               READ ACCOUNT-FILE
89                   AT END MOVE 'N' TO MORE-DATA-FLAG.
```

```
90          PERFORM B010-PROCESS-REGION-GROUP
91              UNTIL NO-MORE-DATA.
92          MOVE FINAL-TOTAL TO FINAL-TOTAL-OUT.
93          WRITE REPORT-RECORD FROM FINAL-TOTAL-LINE
94              AFTER ADVANCING 3 LINES.
95          CLOSE ACCOUNT-FILE
96              REPORT-FILE.
97          STOP RUN.
98
99      B010-PROCESS-REGION-GROUP.
100         MOVE ZERO TO REGION-TOTAL.
101         MOVE REGION-NUMBER TO PREVIOUS-REGION-NUMBER.
102         PERFORM C010-PROCESS-SELLER-GROUP UNTIL
103             REGION-NUMBER IS NOT EQUAL TO PREVIOUS-REGION-NUMBER
104             OR NO-MORE-DATA.
105         MOVE SPACES TO DETAIL-LINE.
106         MOVE PREVIOUS-REGION-NUMBER TO REGION-NUMBER-OUT.
107         MOVE REGION-TOTAL TO REGION-TOTAL-OUT.
108         PERFORM X010-LINE-OUT.
109         ADD REGION-TOTAL TO FINAL-TOTAL.
110
111     C010-PROCESS-SELLER-GROUP.
112         MOVE ZERO TO SELLER-TOTAL.
113         MOVE SELLER-NUMBER TO PREVIOUS-SELLER-NUMBER.
114         PERFORM D010-PROCESS-ACCOUNT-GROUP UNTIL
115             SELLER-NUMBER IS NOT EQUAL TO PREVIOUS-SELLER-NUMBER
116             OR REGION-NUMBER IS NOT EQUAL TO PREVIOUS-REGION-NUMBER
117             OR NO-MORE-DATA.
118         MOVE SPACES TO DETAIL-LINE.
119         MOVE PREVIOUS-SELLER-NUMBER TO SELLER-NUMBER-OUT.
120         MOVE SELLER-TOTAL TO SELLER-TOTAL-OUT.
121         PERFORM X010-LINE-OUT.
122         ADD SELLER-TOTAL TO REGION-TOTAL.
123
124     D010-PROCESS-ACCOUNT-GROUP.
125         MOVE ZERO TO ACCOUNT-TOTAL.
126         MOVE ZERO TO NO-OF-TRANSACTIONS.
127         MOVE 'N' TO ASTERISK-FLAG.
128         MOVE ACCOUNT-NUMBER TO PREVIOUS-ACCOUNT-NUMBER.
129         PERFORM E010-PROCESS-ACCOUNT-RECORD UNTIL
130             ACCOUNT-NUMBER IS NOT EQUAL TO PREVIOUS-ACCOUNT-NUMBER
131             OR SELLER-NUMBER IS NOT EQUAL TO PREVIOUS-SELLER-NUMBER
132             OR REGION-NUMBER IS NOT EQUAL TO PREVIOUS-REGION-NUMBER
133             OR NO-MORE-DATA.
134         MOVE SPACES TO DETAIL-LINE.
135         MOVE PREVIOUS-ACCOUNT-NUMBER TO ACCOUNT-NUMBER-OUT.
136         MOVE ACCOUNT-TOTAL TO ACCOUNT-TOTAL-OUT.
137         MOVE NO-OF-TRANSACTIONS TO NO-OF-TRANSACTIONS-OUT.
138         IF ASTERISK-FLAG-ON
139             MOVE '*' TO ASTERISK-OUT.
140         PERFORM X010-LINE-OUT.
141         ADD ACCOUNT-TOTAL TO SELLER-TOTAL.
142
143     E010-PROCESS-ACCOUNT-RECORD.
144         ADD SALE-AMOUNT TO ACCOUNT-TOTAL.
145         ADD 1 TO NO-OF-TRANSACTIONS.
146         IF SALE-AMOUNT IS GREATER THAN 1000.00
147             MOVE 'Y' TO ASTERISK-FLAG.
148         READ ACCOUNT-FILE
149             AT END MOVE 'N' TO MORE-DATA-FLAG.
150
```

```
151          X010-LINE-OUT.
152              ADD 1 TO LINE-NUMBER.
153          *           SEE IF WE ARE AT THE END OF THE PAGE
154          *           IF SO, PRINT A NEW PAGE HEADING
155              IF LINE-NUMBER IS GREATER THAN 55
156                  ADD 1 TO PAGE-NUMBER
157                  MOVE PAGE-NUMBER TO PAGE-NUMBER-OUT
158                  WRITE REPORT-RECORD FROM HEADING-LINE
159                      AFTER ADVANCING PAGE
160                  MOVE SPACES TO REPORT-RECORD
161                  WRITE REPORT-RECORD
162                      AFTER ADVANCING 2 LINES
163                  MOVE 4 TO LINE-NUMBER.
164              WRITE REPORT-RECORD FROM DETAIL-LINE
165                  AFTER ADVANCING 1 LINE.
166
167      ********************* END OF PROGRAM *********************
```

FIGURE 9.9   A correctly modified program for producing three-level control totals.

ACCOUNT	TOTAL	NUMBER	SALESPERSON	TOTAL	REGION	TOTAL	PAGE	1
20	$17.00	3						
24	$36.00	1						
27	$184.00	5						
			1	$237.00				
17	$26.00	2						
24	$266.90	3						
			2	$292.90				
10	$87.50	1						
16	$54.75	3						
			12	$142.25				
					1	$672.15		
40	$50.12	2						
41	$105.99	1						
			4	$156.11				
44	$1,594.14	6						
			39	$1,594.14				
					2	$1,750.25		
30	$1,180.94	4						
35	$69.26	3						
38	$157.43	2						
49	$45.00	2						
60	$1,234.56	1*						
78	$276.02	12						
			15	$2,963.21				
					3	$2,963.21		
				FINAL TOTAL		$5,385.61		

FIGURE 9.10   A three-level control total report produced by the program of Figure 9.9.

For one last word about this program, it should be obvious that we can now develop control break programs for any number of levels, from one on up. The pattern of the program is clear, and the general structure applies to any number of levels. Of course, there are many different correct ways of expressing program logic, and the structure shown in this example can be modified as necessary to fit different circumstances.

REVIEW QUESTIONS

1. What would the one-level program produce from the following input (in the sequence given)?

Account Number	Amount
15	$1
15	2
17	3
17	2
17	6
16	5
17	3
16	2
19	7
19	8
19	4

2. Suppose the input file for the one-level program were in descending sequence on account number. What would the program do? Would there be any simple way to present the results with the account numbers in ascending sequence?

3. Suppose the client for the program of this chapter were to request that the region numbers and total for the region be printed on a line *before* the salesperson and account totals for the region, and similarly for the salesperson total. How would you respond?

4. Is the following pseudocode logically equivalent to that of Figure 9.3? That is, would a program based on it produce the same results as does the program of Figure 9.4?

```
PRODUCE-SALES-REPORT:
      open files
      get account record; at end set more-data-flag to 'N'
      IF more data remains THEN
            set final total to zero
            set account total to zero
            move current account number to previous account number
            PERFORM-UNTIL no more data
                  IF current and previous account numbers are different THEN
                        perform account total processing
                  ENDIF
                  add sale amount to account total, final total
                  get account record; at end set more-data-flag to 'N'
            ENDPERFORM
```

perform account total processing
    set up final total line
    print final total line
ENDIF
close files

ACCOUNT-TOTAL-PROCESSING:
    set up account total line
    print account total line
    move current account number to previous account number
    move zero to account total

ANSWERS TO REVIEW QUESTIONS

1. ACCOUNT NUMBER	AMOUNT	FINAL TOTAL
15	$ 3	
17	11	
16	5	
17	3	
16	2	
19	19	
	43	

There would be no error indication, since the program does not check for the sequence of the input. See Exercise 4.

2. The program would produce the same kind of report as shown in the chapter, but with the account total in descending sequence on account number. There would be no simple way to reverse the sequence, since it would not be possible to begin printing the report until the last account group had been computed. One way or another, the results would have to be stored, probably on a temporary file, and then the file would have to be sorted into ascending sequence before printing.

3. You would have to explain that this is impossible without considerable extra effort, since the total for a region is not known until all the salesperson totals within the region have been computed, and the total for a salesperson is not known until all that person's accounts have been added. To do what was asked would require some way to save the subordinate totals in temporary storage. This can be done (although we haven't yet learned the techniques), but it would be costly in time.

4. Yes, with the small difference that if the input file is empty, this version would print no output while the text version would print a final total of zero. This shows that there is seldom just one good way to design a program.

EXERCISES

*1. Modify Exercise 7 of Chapter 7 so that no more than 45 detail lines are written on a page.

*2. Modify the program of Figure 9.7 so that when an account total is printed, the region and seller number of the account are also printed, and when a salesperson total is printed, the region number of the salesperson is also printed.

3. Modify the program of Figure 9.7 so that it prints, to the left of the final total on the bottom line, the sum of the sales amounts for sales over $1000.00, together with the percentage of the total sales that these large sales represent.

*4. Modify the one-level program of Figure 9.4 to check for a sequence error, which consists of any instance in which the account number of a record is less than that of the previous record. If such a sequence error is found, the program should write a brief error message and stop.

5. Modify the three-level program of Figure 9.7 so that it performs a sequence check similar to that described in the previous exercise. *Hint*: Make a group item of region number, seller number, and account number, so that the sequence check can be made with just one IF. Will this falsely signal an error when the account number is less than the previous account number, but the region number is larger than the previous region number?

6. (This exercise is suitable for a small project.)
The Commercial Real Estate Corporation (CREC) manages office buildings in several cities. Rental data for each office is maintained in records with the following format:

Columns 1-5	building number
Columns 6-9	office number
Columns 10-15	office size in square feet
Columns 16-21	annual rent per square foot
Columns 22-27	monthly surcharges
Columns 28	occupied code (Y or N)
Columns 29-30	rental agent number

Monthly rent for an office is computed as 1/12 the annual rent times the office size, plus monthly surcharges if any.

Prepare a report showing rental income for the current month for all properties managed by CREC. The report is to have the following format:

Columns 3-4	rental agent number
Columns 8-20	total rent for all buildings managed by this agent
Columns 25-29	building number
Columns 33-45	total rent for this building
Columns 49-52	office number
Columns 56-65	monthly rent for this office

---

* Answers to starred exercises will be found in Appendix IV at the end of the book.

The report is to show rent for occupied offices only (those with a value of **Y** for the occupied code), and should show total rental for each building, for each rental agent, and for the company. Any field containing a dollar amount should begin with a dollar sign, should have leading zeros suppressed, and should have commas in appropriate places. There should be a heading at the top of each page and there should be no more than 50 detail lines per page.

There may be errors in the data and invalid records should be detected and rejected. To be valid, all fields in a record must be numeric, except for the "occupied code" field that must contain either **Y** or **N**. If you detect an invalid record, print the record on an error report with an appropriate error message. You may choose any format for the error report you wish, but it should be neat and easily understood by a clerk who is reading the report. In other words, simply printing the record image with a message such as "**ERROR FOUND**" is not acceptable. Finally, you must assume that a record may contain more than one error; all errors in a record should be detected and reported.

A sample of the monthly rental report is shown below:

```
                    MONTHLY RENTAL REPORT                    PAGE 001

   AGENT      TOTAL      BUILDING      TOTAL      OFFICE      TOTAL


                                                  1001      $10,000.00
                                                  2500      $    250.00
                             10    $   10,250.00

                                                  100      $ 2,500.00
                                                  200      $ 2,500.00
                                                  300      $25,000.00
                          12345    $   30,000.00
     10   $   40,250.00

                                                  8888      $99,999.99
                                                  9999      $99,999.99
                          99999    $  199,999.98
     99   $  199,999.98

  TOTAL    $  240,249.98
```

CHAPTER 10

DATA REPRESENTATION AND RELATED TOPICS

10.1 INTRODUCTION

In this chapter we shall discuss a number of matters related to the representation of information within a computer: the various forms in which data may be stored, choices available in the assignment of items to computer storage, and how to give the same area of computer storage different names with possibly different attributes. Since some of these topics depend considerably on the computer you are using, we shall also look at the way in which the Microsoft COBOL compiler can make your program be compatible with various other compilers.

10.2 DATA REPRESENTATION

The most basic unit of information in any computer is the *bit*, which is an abbreviation for *binary digit*. "Binary" means "having two values," and a binary digit is one that has only the values zero and one. A binary number is one in which the digits are allowed to take on only the values zero and one, and where the digits are multiplied by successive powers of 2, rather than powers of 10 as in decimal. Thus, where the decimal number 2073 means

$$2 \times 1000 = 2000$$
$$+ 0 \times 100 = 0$$
$$+ 7 \times 10 = 70$$
$$+ 3 \times 1 = 3$$

the binary number 1101 means

$$1 \times 8 = 8$$
$$+ 1 \times 4 = 4$$
$$+ 0 \times 2 = 0$$
$$+ 1 \times 1 = 1$$

Thus the binary number 1101 is the equivalent of the decimal number 13 or, as we might write, $1101_2 = 13_{10}$.

When large binary numbers must be written, it is more convenient to combine the bits into groups of four and write the hexadecimal (base 16) equivalent of each group, according to the following table:

Binary Number	Decimal Equivalent	Hexadecimal Equivalent
0001	1	1
0010	2	2
0011	3	3
0100	4	4
0101	5	5
0110	6	6
0111	7	7
1000	8	8
1001	9	9
1010	10	A
1011	11	B
1100	12	C
1101	13	D
1110	14	E
1111	15	F

For example, the binary number 0010 0010 1101 1000 0001 0000 1111 1011 could be written in hexadecimal as 22D810FB, which is considerably simpler and takes less space.

10.3 BYTES

In the IBM PC and compatible computers, bits are combined into groups of eight bits called *bytes*. A computer capable of compiling a COBOL program, even a microcomputer, typically has over 500,000 bytes of internal storage; at the time of this writing most microcomputers have about 655,000 bytes of internal storage, and the larger computers in IBM's PS/2 series have several million bytes of storage*. Mainframe computers can offer users what appears to the program to be over 16,000,000 bytes of internal storage, although they frequently use a technique called *virtual memory*, which makes other storage devices appear to be part of internal memory; however, the details of virtual memory are irrelevant to our discussion.

Internal storage, which is also called RAM, for *random access memory*, is most commonly made from integrated circuits. A byte of information can be retrieved from internal storage in a fraction of one microsecond (millionth of a second) in any computer, and in a few nanoseconds (billionths of a second) in many computers. Internal storage is distinguished from auxiliary storage, which consists of devices like magnetic disks and tapes, where access times are no faster than milliseconds (thousandths of a second) and can sometimes

---

* Computer memory is frequently measured in terms of kilobytes, or *K bytes*, which is actually 1024 bytes. Thus, 128K bytes of memory is 131,072 bytes in decimal, 640K bytes is 655,360, and so on.

be measured in seconds or even minutes. We shall consider these latter devices in Chapter 15.

Each byte of internal storage has associated with it an *address* by which it is identified. Operations on data items are specified, in the object program, in terms of the contents of addressed locations in internal storage. Where we write

    ADD 1 TO RECORD-COUNT

the object program might have an instruction to obtain the contents of location 12536, which the computer had assigned as the location where **RECORD-COUNT** is to be stored for the particular program; add to this the contents of 13044, where the computer has stored the value 1; and finally place the sum back in 12536.

Bytes may be handled individually or grouped into *fields*. In a microcomputer, a *word* is two consecutive bytes, and a *double word* is a field consisting of two words. (Occasionally we will also refer to half a byte, four bits; this is called a *nibble*.) Fields are not required to consist of just these groupings, however. A field can be of any size from one byte up to some limit whose value depends on the computer. For our purposes, we can assume that fields can be made as large as necessary. When a field consists of more than one byte, the address of the leftmost byte is the address of the entire field.

10.4 FORMS OF DATA REPRESENTATION IN MICROCOMPUTERS

The *byte* is a basic building block. To store character data (PIC A or PIC X) **COBOL** simply reserves a string of bytes long enough to hold the field. To store numeric data, however, **COBOL** has several options whose exact operation depends on the particular computer you are using. We will first discuss how data, particularly numeric data, can be stored in a microcomputer. Later, we will discuss how data can be stored in a mainframe computer, and how this affects the Microsoft **COBOL** compiler.

The basic formats for storing data are:

    DISPLAY
    COMPUTATIONAL
    COMPUTATIONAL-3

We shall discuss each of these formats in detail in the following sections.

10.5 DISPLAY USAGE

The simplest form of representation of information is for one byte to contain one character. Since this is the form in which information must appear when it is to be printed, this is called **DISPLAY** usage.

For alphanumeric information this is the only way that data can be represented; for numeric data, there are other choices, which we discuss below. Each alphanumeric character is assigned an eight-bit code. Figure 10.1 shows some of the most commonly used characters and their EBCDIC and ASCII (see Section 5.8) representations.

Observe that the characters in Figure 10.1 are listed in ascending sequence on the ASCII binary representations, which is also their ascending sequence when characters are compared in a relation condition. In other words, the characters in Figure 10.1 are shown in collating sequence, which in fact is determined by the binary representation of the characters.

All 256 of the possible eight-bit combinations can be stored in the computer. Not all 256 eight-bit combinations have printable graphic symbols associated with them, however. If it is necessary to get such information out of the computer, it has to be converted to some other form (such as hexadecimal digits) that is printable. We shall have no occasion to deal with such information in this book, other than to note that if an attempt is made to print a byte containing a nonprinting combination, a blank is usually produced.

The internal representation of numeric data (**PIC 9**) in **DISPLAY** format places one digit in each byte. The digit is placed in the rightmost four bits, which are called the *numeric bits*. The leftmost four bits, called the *zone bits*, hold bit combinations of no interest to us right now except that the zone bits of one byte, generally the rightmost byte, contain the sign of the entire number. Here is how the seven bytes of +4135729 would appear in **DISPLAY** format:

0011 0100	0011 0001	0011 0011	0011 0101	0011 0111	0011 0010	0011 1001
4	1	3	5	7	2	+ 9

If we wrote this as a negative number (-4135729), it would look exactly the same except that the rightmost byte would be *0111* 1001 to indicate a negative value.

Notice that the full byte—zone bits plus numeric bits—forms the ASCII representation of each digit (see Figure 10.1), except for the rightmost byte if the number is negative. This byte, which contains the sign of the number in the zone bits, forms the ASCII representation of a character other than the digit stored in the byte if the number is negative. For -4135729, for example, the rightmost byte contains the representation of the letter y instead of the digit 9. The rightmost byte of a negative numeric field will always contain the representation of some nonnumeric character; if the field is unsigned or if its value is positive, then all bytes will contain the ASCII representation of the digits contained in them.

It is possible to specify that an item has display format by writing the word **DISPLAY** in its data description entry in the Data Division. This is rarely done, however, since in the absence of any explicit declaration about usage, the compiler assumes as a default that an item is **DISPLAY**.

10.6 COMPUTATIONAL-3 USAGE

In **DISPLAY** format we used one byte to store each digit. However, since the zone bits are the same for each byte (except possibly the sign byte), almost half the space in the field is wasted. To make more efficient use of storage, we can use a second format called *packed decimal*. In this format the decimal digits are packed two to a byte except for the right nibble of the rightmost byte, which

Graphic Symbol	ASCII Binary Code	EDCDIC Binary Code
space	0010 0000	0100 0000
$	0010 0100	0101 1011
&	0010 0110	0101 0000
' (quote)	0010 0111	0111 1101
(	0010 1000	0100 1101
)	0010 1001	0101 1101
*	0010 1010	0101 1100
+	0010 1011	0100 1110
, (comma)	0010 1100	0110 1011
- (minus)	0010 1101	0110 0000
. (period)	0010 1110	0100 1011
0	0011 0000	1111 0000
1	0011 0001	1111 0001
2	0011 0010	1111 0010
3	0011 0011	1111 0011
4	0011 0100	1111 0100
5	0011 0101	1111 0101
6	0011 0110	1111 0110
7	0011 0111	1111 0111
8	0011 1000	1111 1000
9	0011 1001	1111 1001
; (semicolon)	0011 1011	0101 1110
<	0011 1100	0100 1100
=	0011 1101	0111 1101
>	0011 1110	0110 1110
A	0100 0001	1100 0001
B	0100 0010	1100 0010
C	0100 0011	1100 0011
D	0100 0100	1100 0100
E	0100 0101	1100 0101
F	0100 0110	1100 0110
G	0100 0111	1100 0111
H	0100 1000	1100 1000
I	0100 1001	1100 1001
J	0100 1010	1101 0001
K	0100 1011	1101 0010
L	0100 1100	1101 0011
M	0100 1101	1101 0100
N	0100 1110	1101 0101
O	0100 1111	1101 0110
P	0101 0000	1101 0111
Q	0101 0001	1101 1000
R	0101 0010	1101 1001
S	0101 0011	1110 0010
T	0101 0100	1110 0011
U	0101 0101	1110 0100
V	0101 0110	1110 0101
W	0101 0111	1110 0110
X	0101 1000	1110 0111
Y	0101 1001	1110 1000
Z	0101 1010	1110 1001

FIGURE 10.1 The representation of selected characters in ASCII and EBCDIC.

holds the sign for the entire number. Here, for example, is how the number +4135729 would appear in packed decimal format:

0100 0001	0011 0101	0111 0010	1001 1100
4 1	3 5	7 2	9 +

If the number were negative it would look exactly the same except for the rightmost byte, which would contain 1001 *1101* to indicate a negative value.

We see that the number has been represented in four bytes, whereas in DISPLAY format it required seven. A number with eight digits would require eight bytes in DISPLAY format and five in packed decimal; the left nibble of the leftmost byte would be filled with zeros in the packed format. In short, the packed format uses just over half as much storage space as the DISPLAY.

The packed decimal format is specified in a COBOL program by entering the clause COMPUTATIONAL-3 or COMP-3 in the data description entry for an item. Thus, we might have

```
05  ACCOUNT-TOTAL     PIC S9(5)V99 COMPUTATIONAL-3.
```

or, more commonly,

```
05  ACCOUNT-TOTAL     PIC S9(5)V99 COMP-3.
```

It is also possible to write a more complete entry

```
05  ACCOUNT-TOTAL     PIC S9(5)V99 USAGE IS COMPUTATIONAL-3.
```

This form is seldom used.

The COMPUTATIONAL-3 clause (and the COMPUTATIONAL clause considered below) may be written at any level. If a group is described as COMPUTATIONAL-3, then every elementary item in the group is defined to be COMPUTATIONAL-3. However, we recommend that descriptive characteristics such as this be defined at the elementary level.

10.7 COMPUTATIONAL USAGE

Numeric data may also be stored in *pure binary* format, rather than decimal; this usage is specified in the data description entry by the term COMPUTATIONAL or COMP. Although the computer can perform arithmetic involving fields in DISPLAY or COMPUTATIONAL-3 format, it is generally more efficient to use binary fields. Furthermore, COMPUTATIONAL fields are frequently used in connection with indexing and subscripting, which we shall consider in Chapter 14. However, the cost of converting data between DISPLAY format and COMPUTATIONAL format often is higher than the cost of doing arithmetic in DISPLAY or COMPUTATIONAL-3, so the latter tends to be used more frequently.

The terms DISPLAY and COMPUTATIONAL are meant to suggest that data items in DISPLAY format are suitable for entering data into the computer or sending information out from it, whereas items in COMPUTATIONAL format may be used only internally. If we attempt to READ a number from a computer terminal into a COMPUTATIONAL-3 item, for example, or attempt to WRITE a COMPUTATIONAL item, the results will be meaningless. (However, the DISPLAY statement automatically converts `COMPUTATIONAL` or `COMPUTATIONAL-3` items to `DISPLAY` format before printing them.) When we move an item in `DISPLAY` form to an item with one of the `COMPUTATIONAL` forms, the compiler arranges an appropriate conversion of format, as it does when we specify arithmetic on a `DISPLAY` item. There is no conversion, however, if we try to `READ` into or `WRITE` from a `COMPUTATIONAL` item.

Likewise, great confusion results from a group `MOVE` in which the elementary items are not of the same usage. For example, if the elementary items in one group item are all `DISPLAY`, we should not move the group to another group having elementary items that are `COMPUTATIONAL-3`!

COBOL-85

10.8 DATA REPRESENTATION IN COBOL-85

Data representation in `COBOL-85` is essentially the same as in previous versions of `COBOL`, but some of the names have changed. For example, standard `COBOL-85` does not include the name `COMPUTATIONAL-3`. It uses the term `BINARY` to specify binary numeric data, and the term `PACKED-DECIMAL` to specify decimal numeric data that is not in `DISPLAY` format. The term `COMPUTATIONAL` can be used by compiler implementers to specify any type of arithmetic data they choose. For the Microsoft `COBOL` compiler, `BINARY` is exactly equivalent to `COMPUTATIONAL`, and `PACKED-DECIMAL` is equivalent to `COMPUTATIONAL-3`.

END COBOL-85

10.9 MICROCOMPUTERS AND IBM MAINFRAMES

One of the features of the Microsoft `COBOL` compiler which makes it very powerful is its ability to *emulate* (that is, "act like") various other compilers. In particular, the Microsoft compiler can compile programs which are being developed for use on IBM mainframe computers. The basic process is this: first the program is developed and tested on a microcomputer using the Microsoft compiler; then the program is transported to the mainframe; finally it is re-compiled using the IBM compiler and given a final test on the mainframe.

Most `COBOL` statements work the same whether they are executed on a microcomputer or on a mainframe. However, there are some very important differences between the way numeric data is stored on a microcomputer and the way it is stored on an IBM mainframe. To begin with, although a byte on the mainframe is eight bits, a word (or *fullword*) consists of four bytes. Two consecutive bytes are called a *halfword*, while a *double word* consists of eight consecutive bytes. `COMPUTATIONAL` fields can be stored in a halfword, a fullword, or two fullwords, depending on the size of the field.

At the machine language level in the System/360, predecessor to the current IBM mainframe computers, binary fields were required to be *aligned* on appropriate *boundaries*. Thus, a binary halfword number was required to begin at a byte with an address that was a multiple of 2; binary fullword numbers began on bytes with addresses that were multiples of four; and double word data began with addresses that were multiples of eight. In general, to maintain compatibility with older hardware and to improve efficiency, the current IBM **COBOL** compilers still support these alignment standards even though the hardware no longer requires it. The **COBOL** programmer is not required to organize storage so that items have these characteristics, but if they do not, the object program will not be as efficient. This inefficiency can be significant, and can erase the time savings of having the data in binary form.

The Microsoft **COBOL** compiler offers many options about the way a program is compiled. For example, you can select whether or not to print a listing of the program, which of several ways of assigning files should be used (we will discuss this option in Chapter 13), whether or not to generate code to be used by ANIMATOR, and so on. In many cases you will select a set of options, then compile many programs using those options. So that you need not write the same option list over and over each time you compile a program, you can specify your option set once then store it in a file called **COBOL.DIR** ("COBOL directives"). This file is an ASCII text file and can be created using any word processor or editor. The last line of directives in this file must end with a carriage return: any directives on the final line of **COBOL.DIR** are ignored.

Although the compiler has over a hundred different directives, we are only interested in five of them right now. These are the directives that control whether or not the Microsoft compiler is to emulate a mainframe compiler (and if so, which one), and whether to imitate the way in which mainframe compilers store numeric data or simply use the basic byte-oriented microcomputer mode. The directives are:

ANS85	emulate the 1985 ANSI COBOL standard
OSVS	emulate the IBM OS/VS COBOL mainframe compiler
VSC2	emulate the IBM VS COBOL II mainframe compiler
ALIGN	select between byte-oriented alignment and word-oriented alignment for 01-level and 77-level data items
IBMCOMP	select between byte-oriented alignment and word-oriented alignment for **COMPUTATIONAL** data items within a structure

For example, if we want the compiler to use the **COBOL-85** standard and use byte alignment for all data, we create a **COBOL.DIR** file which contains the following line:

```
ANS85 ALIGN"1" NOIBMCOMP
```

This tells the compiler to use the 1985 ANSI **COBOL** standard for program syntax and execution, align 01 and 77-level data items on byte boundaries (i.e., bytes whose addresses are multiples of 1), and do not force **COMPUTATIONAL** data to be consistant with mainframe storage requirements.

On the other hand, if we create a COBOL.DIR file which contains

```
VSC2 ALIGN"8" IBMCOMP
```

the compiler will emulate the IBM VS **COBOL** II compiler, will align **01** and **77**-level items on boundaries which are compatible with mainframe requirements (bytes whose address are multiples of 8, or double words), and will align **COMPUTATIONAL** data on boundaries which are compatible with an IBM mainframe. In other words, a program which is developed using these options can be transferred to a mainframe, recompiled and tested, and will have a very high probability of working with no change whatever.

We conclude this section by pointing out that most of this discussion is of concern only to programmers who want to maintain compatibility with mainframe computers. In most other cases you can ignore the COBOL.DIR file and simply use the compiler's default directives with no problems at all.

10.10 THE SYNCHRONIZED CLAUSE

In the preceding section we discussed the way in which mainframe compilers align COMPUTATIONAL data on hardware boundaries. However, this alignment is not done automatically. To force data to be aligned it is necessary to use the SYNCHRONIZED clause, which may also be written SYNC (pronounced "sink"). When this clause is specified for an item, the compiler assigns storage so that the item begins on a proper boundary. If the item would otherwise not have begun on the boundary, *slack bytes* are inserted between the end of the previous item and this one; these slack bytes have no other function and are never used by the program.

For a COMPUTATIONAL item small enough to fit in a mainframe halfword, which means one having a PICTURE character string with no more than four 9s, a SYNCHRONIZED item is aligned on a halfword boundary. Larger binary items are aligned on fullword boundaries. Level 01 and level 77 items are always aligned on fullword boundaries, whether or not the SYNCHRONIZED clause is used. Although microcomputer hardware does not have these boundary requirements, if you use the IBMCOMP directive and the SYNC clause the compiler will force binary data to the proper boundaries for mainframe compatibility.

The following examples show how slack bytes are inserted:

```
       As written                                Slack marked with FILLER

01  GROUP-A.                            01  GROUP-A.
    05  FLD-1    PIC X.                     05  FLD-1    PIC X.
    05  FLD-2    PIC 9(4) COMP SYNC.        05  FILLER   PIC X.
                                            05  FLD-2    PIC 9(4)
                                                         COMP SYNC.


01  GROUP-B.                            01  GROUP-B.
    05  FLD-3    PIC X.                     05  FLD-3    PIC X.
    05  FLD-4    PIC 9(8) COMP SYNC.        05  FILLER   PIC XXX.
    05  FLD-5    PIC X.                     05  FLD-4    PIC 9(8)
    05  FLD-6    PIC 9(18) COMP SYNC.                    COMP SYNC.
                                            05  FLD-5    PIC X.
                                            05  FILLER   PIC XXX.
                                            05  FLD-6    PIC 9(18)
                                                         COMP SYNC.
```

Notice that as many slack bytes as necessary are inserted ahead of the COMPUTATIONAL fields to force them to start on either a halfword or fullword boundary, depending on the size of the field.

As we mentioned at the end of the previous section, this topic is of concern only to programmers who need to maintain compatibility with mainframe computers. Although the SYNCHRONIZED clause is allowed in programs developed for use on microcomputers, it has no effect since the only boundary used on a microcomputer is the byte.

10.11 THE JUSTIFIED CLAUSE

Very occasionally it is necessary to override the normal positioning of alpha-numeric items that are larger or smaller than the receiving field to which they are being sent. The normal action, we recall, is that if the item is longer than the receiving field, extra characters on the *right* are dropped, and if the item is shorter than the receiving field, the extra positions on the *right* are filled with spaces. When the JUSTIFIED (or simply JUST) clause is written, the action is switched from right to left: extra characters on the *left* are dropped from long items, and extra positions on the *left* are filled with spaces for short items. The JUSTIFIED clause may be used only for elementary items, and may *never* be used for numeric or edited numeric items.

JUSTIFIED and SYNCHRONIZED may seem somewhat similar at first glance, but they are quite different. SYNCHRONIZED has to do with the assignment of storage to an item, and to the possible insertion of slack bytes. The compiler would carry out its function for a SYNCHRONIZED item even if no Procedure Division statement ever sent anything to the item. JUSTIFIED, on the other hand, has no connection with the assignment of storage to an item; its action is completely independent of whether or not the item being sent to a receiving field is SYNCHRONIZED.

In most commercial applications, SYNCHRONIZED will be found useful mostly with COMPUTATIONAL items (Chapter 14). JUSTIFIED is rarely used.

10.12 THE REDEFINES CLAUSE

It is often useful to allow the same computer storage area to be described by different data description entries. This is the function of the REDEFINES clause, which has the general format:

level-number data-name-**1** REDEFINES data-name-2

For a simple example, suppose that a program reads a tax rate figure that may be either dollars per hundred, such as 4.239, or dollars per thousand, such as 42.39. What appears on the input record is just the numeric digits; else-where there is a code that specifies which form the digits represent. It would be convenient to describe this field with two PICTURE clauses, having the character strings **9V999** and **99V99**, so that the arithmetic would be correct for both. This is precisely what the REDEFINES clause permits. We can write

```
05   RATE.
     10   RATE-CODE                        PIC X.
     10   100-RATE                         PIC 9V999.
     10   1000-RATE REDEFINES 100-RATE     PIC 99V99.
```

Here, **1000-RATE** is data-name-1 and **100-RATE** is data-name-2. This entry (including RATE-CODE) consists of only five characters, not nine. **100-RATE** and **1000-RATE** are different descriptions of the same storage area. Now, in the Procedure Division, we may write

MULTIPLY ASSESSMENT BY 100-RATE GIVING TAX

and the compiler will set up the arithmetic operations so that the decimal points are handled properly for a four-digit tax rate having three decimal places. Elsewhere, we may write

```
MULTIPLY ASSESSMENT BY 1000-RATE GIVING TAX
```

and the compiler will set up the object program to handle a four-digit tax rate having two decimal places. We shall explore other ways to use the REDEFINES clause after we consider the rules governing its use.

10.13   RULES FOR THE REDEFINES CLAUSE

Use of the REDEFINES clause is subject to the following rules:

1. When the REDEFINES clause is used it must immediately follow data-name-1. That is, we may *not* write

   ```
   05  A-FIELD              PIC XXX REDEFINES B-FIELD.
   ```

2. The level numbers of data-name-1 and data-name-2 must be identical, but must not be **66** or **88**.

3. The REDEFINES clause must not be used in level **01** entries in the File Section. If multiple descriptions of a File Section record area are given, an automatic redefinition is assumed. In other words, REDEFINES is not needed in this case.

4. No entry having a level number numerically lower than the level number of data-name-2 may occur between the data description entries of data-name-2 and data-name-1. That is, we are *not* permitted to write things like

   ```
   05  NAME-1.
       10  INITIALS       PIC XX.
       10  LAST-NAME-1    PIC X(23).
   05  NAME-2.
       10  INITIAL        PIC X.
       10  LAST-NAME-2 REDEFINES LAST-NAME-1
                          PIC X(24).
   ```

5. Redefinition starts at data-name-1 and ends when a level number less than or equal to that of data-name-1 is encountered. For example, consider this structure:

   ```
   01  INPUT-RECORD.
       05  FIELD-1.
           10  SUB-FIELD-A    PIC XXX.
           10  SUB-FIELD-B    PIC X(4).
       05  FIELD-2 REDEFINES FIELD-1.
           10  SUB-FIELD-C    PIC X.
           10  SUB-FIELD-D    PIC X(6).
       05  FIELD-3            PIC X(20).
   ```

   Redefinition stops before **05 FIELD-3**, since its level number is equal to that of the entry with the REDEFINES.

6. Multiple redefinitions of the same storage area are permitted. The entries giving the new descriptions of the storage area must follow the entries defining the area being redefined, without intervening entries that define new areas. Multiple redefinitions of the same storage area must all use the

data-name of the entry that originally defined the area. Thus the following structure is legal.

```
05   A                      PIC 9(4).
05   B REDEFINES A          PIC 9V999.
05   C REDEFINES A          PIC 99V99.
```

The following structure is an example of a violation of this rule:

```
05   A                      PIC 9(4).
05   B REDEFINES A          PIC 9V999.
05   C REDEFINES B          PIC 99V99.
```

7. When the level number of data-name-1 is other than **01**, it must specify the same number of character positions as the data item referenced by data-name-2 contains. This rule emphasizes that what **REDEFINES** does is to give a different name and (usually) attributes to *one storage area*. The size of the storage area that is redefined does not change.

   The reason this restriction does not apply to **01** level data names is that it may occasionally be useful to do in the Working-Storage Section what is done automatically in the File Section, namely, to obtain a redefinition with different length records. When several records are defined on the same storage area, either through implicit redefinition in the File Section or through an explicit **REDEFINES** in **01** level entries in the Working-Storage Section, the longest record controls the amount of storage allocated; all records are aligned on the leftmost character.

8. The entries giving a new description (the entries under dataname-1) must not contain any **VALUE** clauses other than level **88** condition name entries. The area being redefined is permitted to have **VALUE** clauses.

10.14   EXAMPLES OF THE USEFULNESS OF THE REDEFINES CLAUSE

One common situation where the **REDEFINES** is useful has already been suggested in the example at the beginning of Section 10.12. Whenever data has alternative formats, we need to be able to describe all the possibilities, and then to utilize other characteristics of the input to determine which one applies.

For example, suppose that an employee's name may appear with the first name either before or after the last name, depending on the value of **FORMAT-CODE**. In the Data Division we write

```
05   NAME-2.
     10   FIRST-NAME-2        PIC X(10).
     10   LAST-NAME-2         PIC X(15).
05   NAME-1 REDEFINES NAME-2.
     10   LAST-NAME-1         PIC X(15).
     10   FIRST-NAME-1        PIC X(10).
```

The storage layout for the 25 characters of the name is shown at the top of the next page.

1 2 3 4 5 6 7 8 9 10 11 12 13 14 15 16 17 18 19 20 21 22 23 24 25

FIRST-NAME-2	LAST-NAME-2
LAST-NAME-1	FIRST-NAME-1

Now we can write statements such as this:

```
IF FORMAT-CODE = '1'
    MOVE LAST-NAME-1 TO LAST-NAME-OUT
ELSE
    IF FORMAT-CODE = '2'
        MOVE LAST-NAME-2 TO LAST-NAME-OUT
    ELSE
        PERFORM D055-CODE-ERROR.
```

It is not necessary that the data items in a redefinition have any logical relationship to each other. Consider this example:

```
05  SIZE-INFO.
    10  FRAME-SIZE          PIC X(4).
    10  HORSEPOWER          PIC 99V99.
    10  SHAFT-LENGTH        PIC 99V9.
05  RATINGS REDEFINES SIZE-INFO.
    10  TEMPERATURE-RISE    PIC 999.
    10  OVERLOAD            PIC 9V99.
    10  INSULATION          PIC XX.
    10  KW                  PIC 99V9.
```

Here is the storage layout for these 11 characters:

1 2 3 4 5 6 7 8 9 10 11

FRAME-SIZE	HORSEPOWER	SHAFT-LENGTH
TEMPERATURE-RISE	OVERLOAD	INSULATION	KW

Finally, an item can be redefined simply to assign it different attributes, so that the compiler will treat it differently in different Procedure Division operations. Consider the following situation. An input item contains a price; if the actual input consists of anything but digits, we want to discard the record after printing the bad data so that it can be corrected. This means that the price needs to be defined both as numeric, for normal processing, and as alphanumeric, for handling when it is in error. Here is the solution:

```
10  X-PRICE                     PIC X(7).
10  9-PRICE REDEFINES X-PRICE   PIC 9(5)V99.
```

Now, in any Procedure Division reference to **X-PRICE**, the seven characters will be treated as alphanumeric. In any reference to **9-PRICE** they will be treated as numeric, with two decimal places.

We end this section with a warning: do not use **REDEFINES** in such a way that it obscures the structure of the data, particularly if you use multiple **REDEFINES** in a single structure. For example, the following definition is *legal*, but it is not very readable.

```
01   TRANSACTION-RECORD.
     05   RECORD-TYPE               PIC X.
     05   CUST-NUMBER               PIC X(7).
     05   CODE-FIELD REDEFINES CUST-NUMBER.
          10   INV-CODE             PIC X(6).
          10   FILLER               PIC X.
     05   DATE-AND-CODE.
          10   SALE-DATE            PIC 9(6).
          10   SALE-DATE-X REDEFINES SALE-DATE
                                    PIC X(6).
          10   ITEM-CODE            PIC X(5).
     05   ITEM-DESC REDEFINES DATE-AND-CODE
                                    PIC X(11).
     05   REORDER-QTY               PIC 9(4).
     05   SALE-QTY REDEFINES REORDER-QTY
                                    PIC 9(4).
     05   AMOUNT                    PIC 9(5)V99.
     05   QTY-ON-HAND REDEFINES AMOUNT
                                    PIC 9(7).
```

The programmer was working with a program that processes both sales and inventory transaction records from the same input file. Noticing that several of the fields on these records seemed to overlap, he then created a single transaction record that contained all the fields. A much better approach, both for readability and ease of maintenance, would be to create two separate records, one of which redefines the other.

```
01   SALES-RECORD.
     05   RECORD-TYPE-S             PIC X.
     05   CUST-NUMBER               PIC X(7).
     05   SALE-DATE                 PIC 9(6).
     05   SALE-DATE-X REDEFINES SALE-DATE PIC X(6).
     05   ITEM-CODE                 PIC X(5).
     05   SALE-QTY                  PIC 9(4).
     05   AMOUNT                    PIC 9(5)V99.
01   INVENTORY-RECORD REDEFINES SALES-RECORD.
     05   RECORD-TYPE-I             PIC X.
     05   INV-CODE                  PIC X(6).
     05   ITEM-DESC                 PIC X(10).
     05   REORDER-QTY               PIC 9(4).
     05   QTY-ON-HAND               PIC 9(5).
```

Not only are these structures easier to understand, we can now modify either record as needed without worrying about how the format of the other record might be affected. Furthermore, several fields in **INVENTORY-RECORD** have been shortened or eliminated to reflect the sizes actually needed by the program, rather than what is convenient for redefinition.

10.15   DATA NAME QUALIFICATION

COBOL does not require that all the data names in a program be unique. If a name appears in more than one place, it must be written with enough *qualifiers* to establish which occurrence is meant. This process is called *data name qualification*. The higher-level qualifiers are written after the data name, preceded by **OF** or **IN**, which are interchangeable.

Consider an example. Suppose we have these record descriptions:

```
01  IN-REC.
        05  NAME             PIC X(30).
        05  EMP-NO           PIC X(7).
        05  HOURS-WORKED     PIC 99V99.
01  OUT-REC.
        05  NAME             PIC X(30).
        05  FILLER           PIC XXX.
        05  EMP-NO           PIC X(7).
        05  FILLER           PIC X(4).
        05  HOURS-WORKED     PIC Z9.99.
```

It will clearly not do to write things like

```
MOVE NAME TO NAME.
```

The compiler would report back "**NAME NOT UNIQUE**." We write instead

```
MOVE NAME OF IN-REC TO NAME OF OUT-REC.
```

or

```
MOVE HOURS-WORKED IN IN-REC TO HOURS-WORKED IN OUT-REC.
```

It is permissible to have a hierarchy of levels, with qualification used to whatever extent is necessary to achieve a unique identification. Consider this structure:

```
01  TRANS.
        05  INSURED.
            10  INITIALS        PIC XXX.
            10  LAST-NAME       PIC X(24).
        05  BENEFICIARY.
            10  INITIALS        PIC XXX.
            10  LAST-NAME       PIC X(24).
01  MASTER.
        05  INSURED.
            10  INITIALS        PIC XXX.
            10  LAST-NAME       PIC X(24).
        05  BENEFICIARY.
            10  INITIALS        PIC XXX.
            10  LAST-NAME       PIC X(24).
```

An identifier such as **LAST-NAME** certainly is not unique, since there are four occurrences of it. But **LAST-NAME OF INSURED** is not unique either, since **INSURED** occurs twice. We must write **LAST-NAME OF INSURED OF TRANS**, or **LAST-NAME OF BENEFICIARY OF MASTER**, or whatever is meant. On the other hand, suppose that the record definition for **TRANS** were this:

```
01  TRANS.
        05  INSURED.
            10  INITIALS        PIC XXX.
            10  LAST-NAME       PIC X(24).
```

With the same definition for **MASTER** as before, we have **INITIALS** and **LAST-NAME** appearing three times, but **INSURED** only twice. **LAST-NAME OF**

INSURED would not be unique, but since LAST-NAME appears only once in TRANS, we could get a unique name by writing LAST-NAME OF TRANS. It would not be incorrect to write LAST-NAME OF INSURED OF TRANS, but it is not necessary to give all the possible qualifications. Likewise, LAST-NAME OF BENEFI-CIARY would be unique. LAST-NAME OF INSURED OF MASTER would need the full qualification, since neither LAST-NAME nor INSURED is unique.

Actually, it is uncommon for data name qualification to extend beyond one level, if it is used at all. When the formats of related records are closely similar, such as an old master record and a new master record for the same file, using the same names for all items and then using data name qualification is an attractive alternative to making up completely different names.

10.16 MOVE CORRESPONDING

When data name qualification is used, it sometimes happens that one wants to move all items having the same name from one group item to another. (We assume that the two groups are not *identical*, because then a group MOVE does the job.) Suppose that we have record descriptions like these:

```
01   TRANS.
     05   ACCOUNT          PIC X(9).
     05   AMOUNT           PIC 9(5)V99.
     05   TRANS-CODE       PIC X.
     05   TRANS-DATE       PIC X(5).
01   TRANS-OUT.
     05   ACCOUNT          PIC X(9).
     05   FILLER           PIC XXX.
     05   NAME             PIC X(30).
     05   FILLER           PIC XXX.
     05   TRANS-DATE       PIC X(5).
     05   FILLER           PIC XXX.
     05   AMOUNT           PIC ZZ,ZZ9.99.
```

Observe that ACCOUNT, AMOUNT, and TRANS-DATE appear in both records, although not in the same order; that TRANS-CODE appears in TRANS but not in TRANS-OUT; that NAME appears in TRANS-OUT but not in TRANS. We assume that NAME is to be found in another record named MASTER. To move the four items from the input records to TRANS-OUT it is possible to write four MOVE statements:

```
MOVE ACCOUNT OF TRANS        TO ACCOUNT OF TRANS-OUT.
MOVE NAME OF MASTER          TO NAME OF TRANS-OUT.
MOVE TRANS-DATE OF TRANS     TO TRANS-DATE OF TRANS-OUT.
MOVE AMOUNT OF TRANS         TO AMOUNT OF TRANS-OUT.
```

However, the MOVE CORRESPONDING option provides a simpler way:

```
MOVE NAME OF MASTER          TO NAME OF TRANS-OUT.
MOVE CORRESPONDING TRANS     TO TRANS-OUT.
```

The effect is exactly the same as that of the four MOVE statements shown previously.

The format of the **MOVE CORRESPONDING** is as follows.

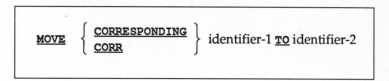

Two rules govern the use of the **MOVE CORRESPONDING** option:

1. Data items are taken to be **CORRESPONDING** when they have the same name and qualification, up to but not including identifier-1 and identifier-2.
2. Any elementary item containing a **REDEFINES** clause is ignored, as is any elementary item containing a **RENAMES**, **OCCURS**, or **USAGE IS INDEX** clause. These latter are considered in Chapters 14 and 20.

MOVE CORRESPONDING is superficially attractive, but it has pitfalls that have caused experienced programmers to minimize its use. The main trouble is that it tends to create problems when a program is changed, as virtually all programs are if they are used for any length of time. One of the things in a program that most generally changes is the format of records, and experience has shown that record format changes frequently cause a **MOVE CORRESPONDING** to give undesired results. The effort of writing out the **MOVE** statements explicitly is a rather minor part of the total cost of developing a program successfully, and doing so has the further advantage of providing easier understanding of how the program works. Ease of understanding, reduced chance of error, and ease of maintenance are far more important than the saving of a bit of typing time.

REVIEW QUESTIONS

Many of the following questions and exercises refer specifically to the ASCII character set and PC-compatible microcomputers. If you are using a different computer or character set you may wish to answer the questions for your computer. However, answers given in this book will be for ASCII characters. Assume that the default directives for microcomputer data storage are in use unless a question specifically states otherwise.

1. Show the ASCII and EBCDIC representations of the following characters:

   A1,$KR7

2. How many bytes are there in the **DISPLAY** and **COMPUTATIONAL-3** representations of these numbers?

   +173
   -42611329
   +109011365

3. Show the **DISPLAY** and **COMPUTATIONAL-3** representations, at the bit level, of these numbers:

   +123
   -67

4. Show the storage layout, in bytes, of the following records, assuming NOIBMCOMP:

a. 01 A-REC.
```
    05  A-1      PIC S999 COMP-3.
    05  A-2      PIC XXX.
    05  A-3      PIC S999.
    05  A-4      PIC S9(4) COMP-3.
```

b. 01 B-REC.
```
    05  B-1      PIC XXX VALUE 'YES'.
    05  B-2      PIC S999 COMP.
    05  B-3      PIC S9(6) COMP.
    05  B-4      PIC S9 COMP-3.
    05  B-5      PIC XXX.
```

c. 01 C-REC.
```
    05  C-1      PIC XXX VALUE 'YES'.
    05  C-2      PIC S999 COMP SYNC.
    05  C-3      PIC S9(6) COMP SYNC.
    05  C-4      PIC S9 COMP-3.
    05  C-5      PIC XXX.
```

d. Assume that the IBMCOMP directive is in use.
```
01  D-REC.
    05  D-1      PIC XXX VALUE 'YES'.
    05  D-2      PIC S999 COMP SYNC.
    05  D-3      PIC S9(6) COMP SYNC.
    05  D-4      PIC S9 COMP-3.
    05  D-5      PIC XXX.
```

5. May **SYNCHRONIZED** be used with **COMPUTATIONAL-3**? With **DISPLAY**?

6. Suppose the IBMCOMP directive is in use. Would this change your answer to question 5?

7. How many characters in storage are described by the following?
```
05  A.
    10  A-1      PIC XX.
    10  A-2      PIC 999.
05  B REDEFINES A.
    10  B-1      PIC 9.
    10  B-2      PIC X.
    10  B-3      PIC XXX.
05  C REDEFINES A    PIC X(5).
```

8. Find errors in the following examples of the use of **REDEFINES**.

a. FD A-FILE
```
        LABEL RECORDS ARE STANDARD.
    01  A.
        05  A1       PIC X(20).
        05  A2       PIC X(60).
    01  B REDEFINES A.
        05  B1       PIC X(40).
```

```
        05   B2          PIC X(40).

b.  05   CAT.
        10   KITTY-CAT    PIC X(10).
        10   PUSSY-CAT    PIC X(8).
        10   TOM-CAT      PIC X(12).
    05   DOG REDEFINES CAT.
        10   PUPPY-DOG    PIC X(8).
        10   FIDO         PIC X(12).
        10   BRANDY       PIC X(12).

c.  05   CARS.
        10   FORD         PIC X(10).
        10   CHEVY        PIC X(10).
        10   DODGE        PIC X(10).
        10   TRUCKS REDEFINES CARS.
            15   FORD     PIC X(10).
            15   CHEVY    PIC X(10).
            15   DODGE    PIC X(10).

d.  05   LITTLE-KIDS.
        10   TOM                      PIC XX.
        10   ALIZA                    PIC XX.
        10   RACHEL                   PIC XX.
    05   OLDER-KIDS.
        10   CHARLIE REDEFINES TOM    PIC XX.
        10   JUDE REDEFINES ALIZA     PIC XX.
        10   CINDY REDEFINES RACHEL   PIC XX.

e.  05   GINIS-FRIENDS.
        10   JOHN                     PIC X(12).
        10   PETE REDEFINES JOHN      PIC X(12).
        10   DOUG REDEFINES PETE      PIC X(12).
```

9. REDEFINES is not permitted at the **01** level in the File Section. What can be done when this facility is needed?

10. Given the following Data Division entries:

```
01   TEMPORARY-RECORD.
    05   COLORS.
        10   RED              PIC X.
        10   BLUE.
            15   SKY          PIC X.
            15   ROBINS-EGG   PIC X.
        10   GREEN.
            15   PEA          PIC X.
            15   GRASS        PIC X.
        10   WHITE            PIC X.

01   PAINT-RECORD.
    05   COLORS.
        10   WHITE            PIC X.
        10   PINK             PIC X.
        10   BLUE.
            15   SKY          PIC X.
            15   NAVY         PIC X.
        10   RED.
            15   FIRE-ENGINE  PIC X.
            15   BARN         PIC X.
```

are the following statements legal?

a. `MOVE RED TO PINK.`

b. `MOVE WHITE TO PINK.`

c. `MOVE ROBINS-EGG TO BARN.`

d. `MOVE SKY OF TEMPORARY-RECORD TO SKY OF PAINT-RECORD.`

e. `MOVE SKY OF BLUE OF COLORS OF TEMPORARY-RECORD TO SKY OF PAINT-RECORD.`

f. `MOVE GRASS TO WHITE OF PAINT-RECORD.`

g. `MOVE BLUE OF TEMPORARY-RECORD TO BLUE OF PAINT-RECORD.`

h. `MOVE COLORS OF TEMPORARY-RECORD TO COLORS OF PAINT-RECORD.`

11. Given the following Data Division entries:

```
01  OFFICE.
    05  DESK          PIC XXX.
    05  CHAIR-1       PIC XXX.
    05  CHAIR-2       PIC XXX.
    05  LAMP          PIC XXX.
    05  BOOKCASE      PIC XXX.

01  LIVING-ROOM.
    05  SOFA          PIC XXX.
    05  LAMP-1        PIC XXX.
    05  LAMP-2        PIC XXX.
    05  CHAIR-1       PIC XXX.
    05  CHAIR-2       PIC XXX.
    05  CHAIR-3       PIC XXX.
```

what would this statement do?

`MOVE CORRESPONDING OFFICE TO LIVING-ROOM.`

ANSWERS TO REVIEW QUESTIONS

1. ASCII:

0100 0001	0011 0001	0010 1100	0010 0100	0100 1011	0101 0010	0011 0111
A	1	,	$	K	R	7

1100 0001	1111 0001	0110 1011	0101 1011	1101 0010	1101 1001	1111 0111
A	1	,	$	K	R	7

EBCDIC:

2. The decimal number +173 takes three bytes in **DISPLAY**; the bit representation is

`0011 0001 0011 0111 0011 0011`

This can also be written in hexadecimal as 31 37 33. In COMPUTATIONAL-3 the same number takes two bytes:

```
0001 0111 0011 1100
```

This is 173C in hexadecimal.

The number -42611329 takes eight bytes in DISPLAY (34 32 36 31 31 33 32 79) and five in COMPUTATIONAL-3 (04 26 11 32 9D). The number +109011365 takes nine bytes in DISPLAY (31 30 39 30 31 31 33 36 35) and five in COMPUTATIONAL-3 (10 90 11 36 5C). If your answers don't agree, review the handling of the sign in each form and also what happens in COMPUTATIO-NAL-3 with an even number of digits.

3.　　COMPUTATIONAL-3:

```
0001 0010 0011 1100
 1    2    3    +

0000 0110 0111 1101
 0    6    7    -
```

DISPLAY:

```
0011 0001 0011 0010 0011 0011
      1         2    +    3

0011 0110 0111 0111
      6    -    7
```

4.

A-1	A-2	A-3	A-4

B-1	B-2	B-3	B-4	B-5

C-1	C-2	C-3	C-4	C-5

D-1		D-2		D-3	D-4	D-5

slack bytes

5. In the computers we are discussing, neither COMPUTATIONAL-3 nor DISPLAY items are required to have any prescribed boundary alignment, so the SYNCHRONIZED clause has no meaning. If present, it is ignored.

6. No. IBM mainframes do not require boundary alignment for COMPUTATIONAL-3 or DISPLAY.

7. Five characters total. The five characters may be referred to in the Procedure Division as a two-character alphanumeric item and a three-character numeric item (group item A); or as a one-character numeric item, a one-character alphanumeric item, and a three-character item (group item B); or as a five-character alphanumeric item (item C).

8. **a.** Redefinition at level **01** in the File Section is not permitted; redefinition is automatic for multiple record descriptions in an **FD**.

   b. **CAT** and **DOG** do not have the same number of characters.

   c. **TRUCKS**, at level **10**, cannot redefine a level **05** entry.

   d. This violates the rule that no entry having a numerically smaller level number may occur between an item and its redefinition.

   e. Redefinitions may not be "chained" in this way. Make the third entry

   ```
   10    DOUG REDEFINES JOHN      PIC X(12).
   ```

9. Redefinition is achieved automatically; nothing need be done to achieve it. That is, if the **FD** for a file is followed by a number of **01** level entries, they are all considered to be alternative definitions of the same storage space.

10. **a.** Illegal; **RED** is not unique.

    b. Illegal; **WHITE** is not unique.

    c. No problem.

    d. No problem. Note that neither name needs to be qualified by **COLORS** or **BLUE**, although it would be legal to do so.

    e. Legal, although the full qualification of the first name is not required.

    f. No problem.

    g. No problem.

    h. No problem.

11. It would move **CHAIR-1** and **CHAIR-2** of **OFFICE** to the elementary items of the same name in **LIVING-ROOM**.

EXERCISES

*1. Give the binary and hexadecimal equivalents of these decimal numbers.

7
8
19
23
34

2. Give the binary and hexadecimal equivalents of these decimal numbers.

4
9
17
32
36

* Answers to starred exercises will be found in Appendix IV at the end of the book.

*3. Give the binary and decimal equivalents of these hexadecimal numbers.

    4
    B
    10
    14

4. Give the binary and decimal equivalents of these hexadecimal numbers.

    1
    F
    20
    2A

*5. Show the **COMPUTATIONAL-3** and **DISPLAY** representations of these decimal numbers. Use as few bytes as will hold the number.

    +123
    +1234
    -90345
    -6

6. Show the **COMPUTATIONAL-3** and **DISPLAY** representations of these decimal numbers. Use as few bytes as will hold the number.

    400
    +1603429
    9876
    +42

*7. Show the binary representations of these characters.

    2
    B
    M
    W
    +
    (

8. Show the binary representations of these characters.

    7
    S
    R
    A
    $
)

*9. Show the storage layout created from the following Data Division entry.

```
01   RECORD-1.
     05   FLD-1          PIC XX.
     05   FLD-2          PIC 9(4).
     05   FLD-3          PIC 9.
     05   FLD-4          PIC XXX.
01   RECORD-2 REDEFINES RECORD-1.
     05   FLD-5          PIC X(5).
     05   FLD-6          PIC 9(5).
```

10. Show the storage layout created from the following Data Division entry.

```
01   SAM.
     04   GEORGE          PIC X.
     04   HARRY           PIC 9(8).
     04   DAVE            PIC X(7).
01   TOM REDEFINES SAM    PIC X(16).
```

CHAPTER 11

COMPOUND CONDITIONALS AND THE SEED CATALOG PROGRAM

11.1 INTRODUCTION

We have reached a point where we need to pull together the concepts we have been learning to see how they can be used in a program. The program we shall study checks one line of a seed catalog order for validity, a more involved task than it might seem at first.*

The program reads sets of data from an input terminal. Each data set represents one line in a catalog order, and contains an order number, a catalog number, a size code, a quantity, an item description, and a price. (We imagine that this program is part of a larger program that handles other aspects of the order, such as the name and address of the customer and the total amount of the order.) We are to perform certain tests on the data to determine whether it has any of several possible errors that would make it impossible to process. If a data set has none of these errors, we are write it in edited form to a processing file. If a data field contains an error, we inform the person using the program that an error exists and require that the data be re-entered correctly.

The validity checks that we are to make are as follows:

1. A catalog number should be entirely numeric.
2. The first digit of the catalog number should not be 0 or 2.
3. If the first digit of the catalog number is 1, 8, or 9, then there should not be a size code.
4. The only permissible size codes are A, D, G, J, K, L, S, T, U, and blank.
5. The quantity must be numeric. Two digits are allowed for the quantity and both of them must be present.

---

* This illustration was inspired by perusal of the W. Atlee Burpee Company seed catalog. The data processing personnel at the Burpee Company have indicated that this example is representative of some of the kinds of things they do, but the details of the program were invented by the authors. Of course, the complete data processing operations of the company are very much more complex than this illustration shows.

6. The price is five digits with two assumed decimal places. Leading zeros must be present.
7. The price must be exactly divisible by the quantity. (If not, the customer has miscopied something or has made an error in multiplication.)
8. The price must not be greater than $125. (Such a price may be legitimate— and certainly welcome—, but since most orders are much smaller than this, it *may* be an error.)

These are by no means the only possible errors. In fact, as we observed before, it is not meaningful to claim to have thought of all possible errors. One obvious possibility is that although the catalog number passes the tests here, there is nevertheless no such number—either because the customer wrote it down incorrectly or because it was keyed incorrectly. Checking this, however, involves access to a master file of all catalog numbers. The techniques involved in matching a transaction file against a master file will concern us in Chapters 13 and 15.

Most of these errors are directed at mistakes the customer might make in writing down the information on the order form. It is difficult to write a program that tries to anticipate the kinds of errors that can be made in keying data into a computer, such as omitting one character. We can only hope that an error of that kind would cause at least one of the validity checks to fail, which is generally true.

11.2 MORE ON COMPOUND CONDITIONALS

It is clear from the specifications of the seed catalog program that it will be necessary to test for a variety of combinations of input data. The most natural way to specify such operations in a **COBOL** program involves the use of compound conditionals in **IF** statements, which we now explore briefly.

In Chapter 5, when the **IF** statement was introduced, it was mentioned that relation conditions can be combined by using the logical operators **AND**, **OR**, and **NOT**. The only examples we have seen thus far have involved only one of these operators in any one relation condition. Actually, they may be combined in any way the programmer pleases, subject to one important rule. Let us summarize the earlier material and then see what happens when the operators are combined.

1. A compound condition consisting of simple conditions connected by **AND**s is satisfied if and only if each one of the simple conditions is satisfied. For example, consider this:

```
IF      AGE IS GREATER THAN 60
    AND LENGTH-OF-SERVICE IS GREATER THAN 20
    AND DEPT-NO = '123'
    PERFORM D010-DEPT-123-RETIREMENT.
```

The routine named will be performed only if all three of the simple conditions are true. For example, if age is greater than 60 and length of service is greater than 20 but the department number is not 123, then the compound condition is not true.

2. A compound condition consisting of simple conditions connected by ORs is satisfied if any one or more of the simple conditions is satisfied. Consider this IF statement:

```
IF      DEPT = '6'
    OR DEPT = '12'
    OR DEPT = '17'
    OR DEPT = '39'
    ADD 1 TO SPECIAL-ORDER.
```

The ADD statement will be executed if any of the simple conditions is true. In this example it is obvious that not more than one condition can be true at any one time. In the following statement, however, zero, one, two, or three of them could be true depending on the values of the variables:

```
IF      DEPT = '43'
    OR PROD-CODE = 'AG'
    OR PRIORITY-CODE = 'C'
    PERFORM E155-RUSH-ORDER.
```

3. When a compound condition contains both AND and OR without parentheses, the *operator precedence rule* says that ANDs are performed before ORs. Consider this example:

```
IF A = 1 OR B = 1 AND C = 1 . . .
```

Without the precedence rule we would not know which of the following correctly describes what is meant by the compound condition:

a. It is true whenever A is one, or B is one and C is one.

b. It is true whenever A is one or B is one, and C is one. (The punctuation in these sentences is crucial.)

The operator precedence rule tells us that the first interpretation is correct.

One way to suggest that the difference is important is to appeal to the analogy in arithmetic, where we know that $1 + (2 \times 3)$ is not the same as $(1 + 2) \times 3$. A more convincing proof is simply to write down all possible true/false combinations of the three variables and compare the results with the two possible interpretations, as follows:

A=1	B=1	C=1	B=1 AND C=1	A=1 OR (B=1 AND C=1)	A=1 OR B=1	(A=1 OR B=1) AND C=1
T	T	T	T	T	T	T
T	T	F	F	T	T	F
T	F	T	F	T	T	T
T	F	F	F	T	T	F
F	T	T	T	T	T	T
F	T	F	F	F	T	F
F	F	T	F	F	F	F
F	F	F	F	F	F	F

The two columns (5 and 7) in which the two results are different prove that they are two different functions.

Here are some additional examples that suggest some of the possibilities in writing compound conditions using AND and OR:

```
IF      HOURS-WORKED = 40 AND SALARY-CODE = 'W'
    OR HOURS-WORKED = 80 AND SALARY-CODE = 'S'
    PERFORM C030-NORMAL-PAY.
```

```
IF      (COL-1 = 'X' OR COL-1 = 'Y' OR COL-1 = 'Z')
    AND COL-2 = '4'
    ADD 1 TO SHEEP.

IF      (COL-1 = 'A' OR COL-1 = 'V')
    AND COL-2 = '3'
    OR  (COL-1 = 'A' OR COL-1 = 'W')
    AND COL-2 = '4'
    ADD 1 TO GOATS.
```

COBOL-85

COBOL-85 has added a feature to the evaluation of compound conditionals that can be quite useful. Consider the following example:*

```
IF A / B  < 1 OR A / B > 10
    MOVE 'Y' TO FLAG.
```

If **B** is equal to zero, this statement will cause an abnormal termination, since division by zero is illegal. We might consider correcting the problem by testing **B** as follows:

```
IF B NOT = 0  AND  (A / B < 1 OR A / B > 10)
    MOVE 'Y' TO FLAG.
```

Unfortunately, on most **COBOL** compilers this still will not work. Although the first condition (**B NOT = 0**) is false if **B** equals zero, compilers prior to COBOL-85 evaluate the entire condition, causing the abend. COBOL-85 produces code that stops evaluating a condition as soon as the truth or falsity of the expression can be determined. In the example above, as soon as the program determines that **B** is equal to zero, the first part of the condition is false which means that the entire condition must be false, regardless of the value of the expression within the parentheses. Therefore, evaluation stops immediately and no abend occurs.

In COBOL-85, evaluation of a compound condition that uses only **ANDs** will stop as soon as one of the subconditions is found to be false; evaluation of a compound condition that uses only **ORs** will stop as soon as one of the subconditions is found to be true. This is called short-circuiting the evaluation of the compound condition. If the compound condition uses both **ANDs** and **ORs**, evaluation continues as far as necessary. This addition to COBOL-85 avoids some common errors and occasionally saves some execution time. However, if necessary you can always test for a critical condition by using a nested **IF** statement, as in the following code:

```
IF B NOT = 0
    IF A / B  10
        MOVE 'Y' TO FLAG.
```

END COBOL-85

It is possible to describe the desired precedence by the use of parentheses, as we have already seen in the illustrations. Parentheses may also be used to

---

* Notice that we have a simple arithmetic expression, **A / B**, as part of each relation condition. We will discuss this a bit more in Chapter 13, but defer a complete explanation till Chapter 20. For now, simply accept it as a valid part of the example.

make a **NOT** apply to a compound condition rather than just the first simple condition in it. For an example of how this might be useful, consider this:

```
IF COL-16 = '7' OR COL-16 = '8'
    NEXT SENTENCE
ELSE
    ADD 1 TO SPECIAL-COUNT.
```

Suppose we wish to reverse the condition so that the statement is written in a more direct form without the **NEXT SENTENCE** phrase. It might be tempting to write

```
IF COL-16 NOT = '7' OR COL-16 NOT = '8'
    ADD 1 TO SPECIAL-COUNT.
```

This is a very common mistake. The problem is that at least one of the simple conditions will always be true; column 16 will always either not contain a 7 or not contain an 8, or not contain either one. Thus the compound condition is always true. If it is desired to write this without parentheses, then the logical operator must be **AND**, not **OR**:

```
IF COL-16 NOT = '7' AND COL-16 NOT = '8'
    ADD 1 TO SPECIAL-COUNT.
```

This formulation may seem artificial and therefore hamper easy understanding. An alternative is to use the **NOT** to reverse the effect of the entire compound condition as originally written.

```
IF NOT (COL-16 = '7' OR COL-16 = '8')
    ADD 1 TO SPECIAL-COUNT.
```

This example demonstrates one of two important rules for compound conditionals. These rules, called *DeMorgan's Laws*, are as follows:

1. **NOT (C1 AND C2)** is equivalent to **NOT C1 OR NOT C2**
2. **NOT (C1 OR C2)** is equivalent to **NOT C1 AND NOT C2**

where **C1** and **C2** are any conditions. The example we showed is an instance of the second law, where **C1** is "**COL-16 = '7'**" and **C2** is "**COL-16 = '8'**".

The review questions at the end of the chapter contain a number of opportunities for practice in interpreting logical expressions using **AND**, **OR**, and **NOT** with parentheses.

11.3 ABBREVIATED COMBINED RELATION CONDITIONS

It is possible to condense combined conditions by omitting elements that are repeated. The omitted elements are then said to be *implied*. In the following discussion recall that we defined a simple condition in terms of a subject, a relation, and an object.

11.4 IMPLIED SUBJECT

When a compound condition has the same subject immediately preceding each relation, then only the first occurrence of the subject need be written, with the omitted subjects being implied.

Thus, instead of

```
IF SERVICE IS GREATER THAN 10 AND SERVICE IS LESS THAN 21
    ADD 1 TO GROUP-3-COUNT.
```

we could write

```
IF SERVICE IS GREATER THAN 10 AND LESS THAN 21
    ADD 1 TO GROUP-3-COUNT.
```

Similarly, instead of

```
IF    CATALOG-FIRST-DIGIT OF ORDER-RECORD = '0'
   OR CATALOG-FIRST-DIGIT OF ORDER-RECORD = '2'
   MOVE 'X' TO FIRST-DIGIT-INVALID.
```

we could write

```
IF CATALOG-FIRST-DIGIT OF ORDER-RECORD = '0' OR = '2'
   MOVE 'X' TO FIRST-DIGIT-INVALID.
```

11.5 IMPLIED SUBJECT AND RELATIONAL OPERATOR

When the simple conditions in a compound condition have the same subject and the same relational operator, then only the first occurrence of the subject and relational operator need be written. Thus the example just stated could also be written

```
IF CATALOG-FIRST-DIGIT OF ORDER-RECORD = '0' OR '2'
   MOVE 'X' TO FIRST-DIGIT-INVALID.
```

This form of abbreviation applies whether or not all logical operators are the same. Thus

```
IF A = B OR A = C AND A = D . . .
```

could be written as

```
IF A = B OR C AND D
```

Note that a complete condition (subject, relational operator, and object) must be expressed first, before anything else is added. Thus the statement

```
IF A > B OR = B . . .
```

cannot be abbreviated

```
IF A > OR = B . . .
```

COBOL-85

Of course, in **COBOL-85** it could be written as

```
IF A >= B . . .
```

or as

```
IF A GREATER THAN OR EQUAL TO B . . .
```

END COBOL-85

Great care should be exercised to be sure that conditions involving **AND**, **OR**, and **NOT** really express what is meant, and that the meaning be *clear* as well as accurate. For example, does

```
IF A NOT = B AND C . . .
```

mean

```
IF A NOT = B AND A NOT = C . . .
```

or does it mean

```
IF A NOT = B AND A = C . . .
```

In fact, the second meaning is the one the compiler would use, although it is not likely that this is what the programmer wanted. Many programmers follow the maxim, "When in doubt, spell it out." A few extra parentheses or a bit more writing are much preferable to the possibility of mistake or misunderstanding.

Very complex and condensed logical expressions can be built up by using the three logical operators in conjunction with implied subjects and relational operators. Care must be exercised, however, that conciseness is not gained at the expense of accuracy or clarity. In fact, these condensed forms should be used only when their usage *improves* understandability.

11.6 DESIGN OF THE SEED CATALOG PROGRAM

Now that we have studied conditional expressions in more depth, we can proceed to the design of the seed catalog program. The basic program structure is relatively simple. However, we show the hierarchy chart for this program because it contains one interesting feature. See Figure 11.1.

The basic logic of the program is the following. In order to validate orders we must validate one line, repeatedly. To validate a line, we get each of the appropriate data fields, make sure that the price is a multiple of the quantity, then write the completed line. Two of the fields, the order number and the item description, require no validation. For each of the remaining fields, however, we must edit the field and, if necessary, ask the user to re-enter the data until it is correct. What is unusual is that when we validate the quantity and price together, we may need to ask the user to re-enter either the price or the quantity (or both) once again. As a result, we need to call the "get valid quantity" and "get valid price" modules from different levels of the program. To avoid having a module call another module which is at a higher level in the hierarchy chart, we place each of these modules at the lowest level at which it is called, even though this means having a module at level three call a module at level five or six.

The logic of the individual modules is straightforward enough that it can be read from the program. The omission of a complete program design in this case should not be taken as a minimization of the importance of the subject. It is just that in this case, the program is nearly as easy to read as the pseudocode would be. It is always desirable that a program should be, as much as possible, its own documentation, because then we can be sure that the "documentation" is always up to date. This is a problem, because when programs are changed

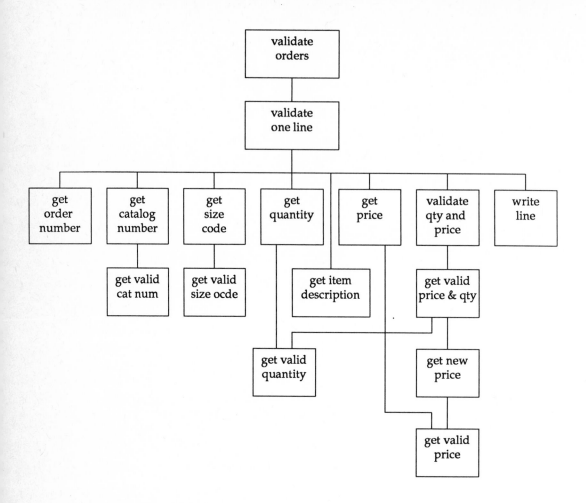

FIGURE 11.1 Hierarchy chart for the seed catalog program.

sometimes the associated pseudocode is not changed, and a program design document that is out of date is worse than useless. However, even though you may not wish to keep hierarchy charts and pseudocode *after* a program is written, they should always be used to *plan* the program.

11.7   THE SEED CATALOG ORDER PROGRAM

Looking at the Environment Division of the program shown in Figure 11.2 we see that the only **SELECT** statement is for the processing file, the file that will contain the formatted image of order lines for further processing. The definition of the file in the **FILE SECTION** is very simple since the program will do most of its work using fields in Working-Storage. Since we get input data from **ACCEPT** statements, no other files are needed.

```
1          IDENTIFICATION DIVISION.
2          PROGRAM-ID.
3              SEEDS.
4          DATE-WRITTEN.
5              MARCH 21, 1989.
6
7          ENVIRONMENT DIVISION.
8          INPUT-OUTPUT SECTION.
9          FILE-CONTROL.
10             SELECT PROCESSING-FILE          ASSIGN TO 'C11P01.PRO'.
11
12         DATA DIVISION.
13
14         FILE SECTION.
15         FD  PROCESSING-FILE
16             LABEL RECORDS ARE STANDARD.
17         01  PROCESSING-LINE                 PIC X(132).
18
19         WORKING-STORAGE SECTION.
20         77  BLANK-LINE                      PIC X(80) VALUE SPACES.
21         77  CHOICE-CODE                     PIC X.
22         77  PRICE-LIMIT                     PIC  999V99 VALUE 125.00.
23         77  PRICE-LIMIT-EDIT                PIC  $ZZ9.99.
24         77  TEST-REMAINDER                  PIC S999V99 COMP-3.
25         77  UNIT-PRICE                      PIC S999V99 COMP-3.
26
27         01  CURSOR-LOCATION.
28             05  ROW-LOC                     PIC 99.
29             05  COL-LOC                     PIC 99.
30
31         01  ERROR-FLAGS.
32             05  VALID-CATALOG-NUMBER        PIC X.
33             05  VALID-SIZE-CODE             PIC X.
34             05  VALID-PRICE                 PIC X.
35             05  VALID-PRICE-AND-QTY         PIC X.
36
37         01  ORDER-DATA.
38             05  ORDER-NUMBER                PIC X(6).
39                 88  LAST-ORDER-LINE             VALUE '000000', SPACES.
40             05  RECORD-TYPE                 PIC X.
41             05  CATALOG-NUMBER.
42                 10  CATALOG-FIRST-DIGIT     PIC X.
43                 10  CATALOG-REMAINING       PIC X(4).
44             05  SIZE-CODE                   PIC X.
45             05  QUANTITY                    PIC 99.
46             05  ITEM-DESCRIPTION            PIC X(40).
47             05  PRICE                       PIC 999V99.
48
49         01  OUTPUT-LINE.
50             05  ORDER-NUMBER                PIC Z(5)9.
51             05  CATALOG-NUMBER.
52                 10  CATALOG-FIRST-DIGIT     PIC BBX.
53                 10  CATALOG-REMAINING       PIC BX(4).
54             05  SIZE-CODE                   PIC BX.
55             05  QUANTITY                    PIC BBZ9.
56             05  PRICE                       PIC BB$$$9.99.
57             05  ITEM-DESCRIPTION            PIC BBX(40).
58             05  FILLER                      PIC X(59) VALUE SPACES.
59
```

```
60          PROCEDURE DIVISION.
61          A000-VALIDATE-ORDERS.
62              OPEN OUTPUT PROCESSING-FILE.
63              MOVE PRICE-LIMIT TO PRICE-LIMIT-EDIT.
64              MOVE LOW-VALUES TO ORDER-NUMBER OF ORDER-DATA.
65              PERFORM B010-VALIDATE-ONE-LINE
66                  UNTIL LAST-ORDER-LINE.
67              CLOSE PROCESSING-FILE.
68              STOP RUN.
69
70          B010-VALIDATE-ONE-LINE.
71              PERFORM C010-GET-ORDER-NUMBER.
72              IF NOT LAST-ORDER-LINE
73                  MOVE SPACES TO ERROR-FLAGS
74                  PERFORM C020-GET-CATALOG-NUMBER
75                  PERFORM C030-GET-SIZE-CODE
76                  PERFORM C040-GET-QUANTITY
77                  PERFORM C050-GET-ITEM-DESCRIPTION
78                  PERFORM C060-GET-PRICE
79                  PERFORM C070-VALIDATE-QTY-AND-PRICE
80                  PERFORM C080-WRITE-PROCESSING-LINE.
81
82          C010-GET-ORDER-NUMBER.
83              DISPLAY 'Enter order number:'          AT 0101
84                  WITH BLANK SCREEN.
85              ACCEPT ORDER-NUMBER OF ORDER-DATA      AT 0125.
86
87          C020-GET-CATALOG-NUMBER.
88              MOVE 'N' TO VALID-CATALOG-NUMBER.
89              PERFORM D010-GET-VALID-CATALOG-NUMBER
90                  UNTIL VALID-CATALOG-NUMBER = 'Y'.
91
92          C030-GET-SIZE-CODE.
93              MOVE 'N' TO VALID-SIZE-CODE.
94              PERFORM D020-GET-VALID-SIZE-CODE
95                  UNTIL VALID-SIZE-CODE = 'Y'.
96
97          C040-GET-QUANTITY.
98              MOVE 04 TO ROW-LOC.
99              MOVE 01 TO COL-LOC.
100             PERFORM E010-GET-VALID-QUANTITY.
101
102         C050-GET-ITEM-DESCRIPTION.
103             DISPLAY 'Enter item description:'      AT 0501
104             ACCEPT ITEM-DESCRIPTION OF ORDER-DATA AT 0525.
105
106         C060-GET-PRICE.
107             MOVE 'N' TO VALID-PRICE.
108             MOVE 06 TO ROW-LOC.
109             MOVE 01 TO COL-LOC.
110             PERFORM F010-GET-VALID-PRICE
111                 UNTIL VALID-PRICE = 'Y'.
112
113         C070-VALIDATE-QTY-AND-PRICE.
114             MOVE 'N' TO VALID-PRICE-AND-QTY.
115             PERFORM D030-GET-VALID-PRICE-AND-QTY
116                 UNTIL VALID-PRICE-AND-QTY = 'Y'.
117
```

```
118        C080-WRITE-PROCESSING-LINE.
119            MOVE CORRESPONDING ORDER-DATA TO OUTPUT-LINE.
120            WRITE PROCESSING-LINE FROM OUTPUT-LINE
121                    AFTER ADVANCING 2 LINES.
122
123        D010-GET-VALID-CATALOG-NUMBER.
124            DISPLAY 'Enter catalog number:'                AT 0201.
125            ACCEPT CATALOG-NUMBER OF ORDER-DATA            AT 0225.
126            IF CATALOG-NUMBER OF ORDER-DATA IS NOT NUMERIC
127                DISPLAY 'CATALOG NUMBER CONTAINS '          AT 0325
128                DISPLAY 'A NON-NUMERIC CHARACTER'           AT 0349
129                DISPLAY 'PLEASE RE-ENTER THE CATALOG NUMBER' AT 0425
130            ELSE
131                IF CATALOG-FIRST-DIGIT OF ORDER-DATA = '0' OR '2'
132                    DISPLAY 'FIRST DIGIT OF CATALOG '       AT 0325
133                    DISPLAY 'NUMBER IS INVALID        '     AT 0348
134                    DISPLAY 'PLEASE RE-ENTER THE CATALOG NUMBER'
135                                                            AT 0425
136                ELSE
137                    DISPLAY '                         '     AT 0325
138                    DISPLAY '                         '     AT 0349
139                    DISPLAY '                         '
140                                                            AT 0425
141                    MOVE 'Y' TO VALID-CATALOG-NUMBER.
142
143        D020-GET-VALID-SIZE-CODE.
144            DISPLAY 'Enter size code:'                      AT 0301.
145            ACCEPT SIZE-CODE OF ORDER-DATA                 AT 0325.
146            IF SIZE-CODE OF ORDER-DATA = 'A' OR 'D' OR 'G' OR 'J'
147                OR 'K' OR 'L' OR 'S' OR 'T' OR 'U' OR ' '
148                MOVE 'Y' TO VALID-SIZE-CODE
149                DISPLAY '                         '         AT 0425
150                DISPLAY '                         '         AT 0525
151            ELSE
152                DISPLAY 'THERE IS NO SUCH SIZE CODE'        AT 0425
153                DISPLAY 'PLEASE RE-ENTER THE SIZE CODE'     AT 0525.
154            IF VALID-SIZE-CODE = 'Y'
155                IF (CATALOG-FIRST-DIGIT OF ORDER-DATA =
156                        '1' OR '8' OR '9')   AND
157                    SIZE-CODE OF ORDER-DATA IS NOT EQUAL TO SPACES
158                    DISPLAY 'THIS ITEM DOES NOT TAKE A SIZE CODE'
159                                                            AT 0425
160                    DISPLAY 'PLEASE RE-ENTER THE SIZE CODE' AT 0525
161                    MOVE 'N' TO VALID-SIZE-CODE
162                ELSE
163                    DISPLAY '                         '
164                                                            AT 0425
165                    DISPLAY '                         '     AT 0525
166                    MOVE 'Y' TO VALID-SIZE-CODE.
167
168        D030-GET-VALID-PRICE-AND-QTY.
169            MOVE 'Y' TO VALID-PRICE-AND-QTY.
170            DIVIDE PRICE OF ORDER-DATA BY QUANTITY OF ORDER-DATA
171                    GIVING UNIT-PRICE REMAINDER TEST-REMAINDER
172                ON SIZE ERROR MOVE 'N' TO VALID-PRICE-AND-QTY.
173            IF TEST-REMAINDER NOT EQUAL TO ZERO
174                MOVE 'N' TO VALID-PRICE-AND-QTY.
175            IF VALID-PRICE-AND-QTY = 'N'
176                DISPLAY 'EITHER PRICE OR QUANTITY IS WRONG.' AT 0801
```

```
177                         DISPLAY 'DO YOU WISH TO RE-ENTER THE PRICE, ' AT 0901
178                         DISPLAY 'THE QUANTITY, OR BOTH (P/Q/B)?'      AT 0936
179                         ACCEPT CHOICE-CODE                            AT 0968
180                         IF CHOICE-CODE = 'P'
181                             MOVE 11 TO ROW-LOC
182                             MOVE 01 TO COL-LOC
183                             PERFORM E020-GET-NEW-PRICE
184                         ELSE
185                             IF CHOICE-CODE = 'Q'
186                                 MOVE 11 TO ROW-LOC
187                                 MOVE 01 TO COL-LOC
188                                 PERFORM E010-GET-VALID-QUANTITY
189                             ELSE
190                                 MOVE 11 TO ROW-LOC
191                                 MOVE 01 TO COL-LOC
192                                 PERFORM E020-GET-NEW-PRICE
193                                 MOVE 12 TO ROW-LOC
194                                 MOVE 01 TO COL-LOC
195                                 PERFORM E010-GET-VALID-QUANTITY
196                     ELSE
197                         DISPLAY BLANK-LINE                            AT 0801
198                         DISPLAY BLANK-LINE                            AT 0901
199                         DISPLAY BLANK-LINE                            AT 1001
200                         DISPLAY BLANK-LINE                            AT 1101
201                         DISPLAY BLANK-LINE                            AT 1201.
202
203             E010-GET-VALID-QUANTITY.
204                 DISPLAY 'Enter quantity:'           AT CURSOR-LOCATION.
205                 MOVE 25 TO COL-LOC.
206                 ACCEPT QUANTITY OF ORDER-DATA       AT CURSOR-LOCATION.
207
208             E020-GET-NEW-PRICE.
209                 MOVE 'N' TO VALID-PRICE.
210                 PERFORM F010-GET-VALID-PRICE
211                     UNTIL VALID-PRICE = 'Y'.
212
213             F010-GET-VALID-PRICE.
214                 DISPLAY 'Enter price:'              AT CURSOR-LOCATION.
215                 MOVE 25 TO COL-LOC.
216                 ACCEPT PRICE OF ORDER-DATA          AT CURSOR-LOCATION.
217                 IF PRICE OF ORDER-DATA IS GREATER THAN PRICE-LIMIT
218                     ADD 1 TO ROW-LOC
219                     DISPLAY 'PRICE MUST NOT EXCEED '  AT CURSOR-LOCATION
220                     MOVE 47 TO COL-LOC
221                     DISPLAY PRICE-LIMIT-EDIT        AT CURSOR-LOCATION
222                     ADD   1 TO ROW-LOC
223                     MOVE 25 TO COL-LOC
224                     DISPLAY 'PLEASE RE-ENTER THE PRICE'
225                                                     AT CURSOR-LOCATION
226                     SUBTRACT 2 FROM ROW-LOC
227                     MOVE 01 TO COL-LOC
228                 ELSE
229                     ADD 1 TO ROW-LOC
230                     DISPLAY '                                       '
231                                                     AT CURSOR-LOCATION
232                     ADD 1 TO ROW-LOC
233                     DISPLAY '                        '
234                                                     AT CURSOR-LOCATION
235                     SUBTRACT 2 FROM ROW-LOC
```

```
236                 MOVE 01 TO COL-LOC
237                 MOVE 'Y' TO VALID-PRICE.
238
239      **************** END OF PROGRAM *******************************
```

FIGURE 11.2 An interactive program to get valid data for lines in an order from a seed catalog.

The major structures in Working-Storage are ORDER-DATA, which contains the fields needed to store one data set; and OUTPUT-LINE, which will contain the formatted data line. We really don't need to combine the fields for a data set into a structure since we will be getting them one at a time from the terminal. However, by defining ORDER-DATA we emphasize that these are not unrelated fields, but rather are all associated with one line of an order. Similarly, we have defined all error flags in the structure ERROR-FLAGS to emphasize the relationship between them. As for OUTPUT-LINE, we have defined this structure in Working-Storage rather than in the FILE SECTION so that we can initialize blank fields with a VALUE clause.

As in previous programs where we read data from the terminal, we define one input field, ORDER-NUMBER in this case, to be used as an end of data flag. Notice that we have defined two values for LAST-ORDER-LINE; users may enter an order number of zero or blank, as they prefer, to terminate the data.

The first few paragraphs of the program contain nothing new. In the main paragraph, we do some initialization, validate order lines until we run out of data, then stop the run. B010-VALIDATE-ONE-LINE performs a series of paragraphs to get the data for an order line, checks to be sure that the price is a multiple of the quantity, then writes the edited data to the processing file; of course, if the value of the order number indicates an end of file flag, none of the remaining steps are performed.

The C-level paragraphs are fairly familiar, but they do contain some features worth noting. To begin with, except for verifying that certain fields were numeric, previous programs have assumed that data values were entered correctly. Here we do not. For example, we use C020-GET-CATALOG-NUMBER to control the process of getting a valid catalog number rather than just accepting the value the user enters. The paragraph sets a flag, then performs D010-GET-VALID-CATALOG-NUMBER until the user provides an acceptable value. Similar procedures are used in several other C-level paragraphs.

We demonstrate another new feature in C040-GET-QUANTITY. Since we may be asking for the quantity from two different places in the input process (once when we get the initial quantity, and possibly a second time when we compare quantity and price), we cannot use constant values for the cursor position in the ACCEPT and DISPLAY statements. Therefore, we define CURSOR-POSITION (lines 27-29) and use this variable to specify the cursor position in paragraph E010-GET-VALID-QUANTITY. A similar process is used when we ask for the price. Notice that since ROW-LOC and COL-LOC are both numeric fields, we can use arithmetic operations to define their values if we wish.

The actual data editing begins in D010-GET-VALID-CATALOG-NUMBER. To begin with, notice that since CATALOG-NUMBER appears in both ORDER-DATA and OUTPUT-LINE, we must use qualification on lines 125 and 126 to establish which one we mean; similar qualification is needed for the other input variables.

The process used to get a valid catalog number demonstrates the basic editing procedure. Following the prompt on line 124 the user enters a catalog number. If the catalog number is not numeric, or if the first digit is invalid, an error message is displayed and the user is asked to re-enter the data. (Notice the use of the implied subject on line 131.) Since the value of **VALID-CATALOG-NUMBER** has not been changed, the **PERFORM** statement on line 89 will cause **D010-GET-VALID-CATALOG-NUMBER** to be executed again and execution returns to line 124. However, if the data is valid, the statments on lines 137-141 erase any previous error messages and set **VALID-CATALOG-NUMBER** to 'Y', thus terminating the loop. Two display statements are used to show the messages for display line 3 simply because the text for these message is too long to fit on one program line.

Although **D020-GET-VALID-SIZE-CODE** follows the same basic pattern there are a few differences. There are two validity tests for the size code and we have carried out each test as a separate set of statements. While it might be possible to perform both tests at once, there is no advantage in doing so and it would complicate the code. Since there is no point in performing the second test (lines 155-157) unless the size code has passed the first test, we test **VALID-SIZE-CODE** on line 154. This also eliminates the need for displaying more than one error message at a time.

The **IF** statement on lines 155-157 illustrates the use of the implied subject and implied relational operator together with parentheses to alter what would otherwise be the normal precedence of the logical operators. Without the parentheses the meaning would be that the record is invalid if the first digit of the catalog number is 1 or 8, or if it is 9 and there is a size code. In other words, since **AND** takes precedence over **OR**, the testing of the size code would be combined only with a catalog first digit of 9. The result of this would be that a line in which the first digit of the catalog number is 1 or 8 would be considered erroneous regardless of the value of the size code, which is not what is desired.

Skipping down to **F010-GET-VALID-PRICE** for a moment, let us look at the price editing process. The only validity test needed is to make sure that the price is less than or equal to **PRICE-LIMIT**, which has been initialized to $125 (line 22). Since we are using **CURSOR-LOCATION** to set the position for **ACCEPT** and **DISPLAY** statement, we adjust the values of **COL-LOC** and **ROW-LOC** as needed to get the proper positioning. Because the paragraph is executed in a loop (lines 110 and 210), we subtract 2 from the **ROW-LOC** and move 1 to **COL-LOC** after all messages have been displayed. This brings the cursor back to the proper position for the **DISPLAY** statement on line 214 if the paragraph is executed again. Also, we use **PRICE-LIMIT-EDIT** instead of **PRICE-LIMIT** to show the limit so that the value appears in edited form; **PRICE-LIMIT-EDIT** is initialized in the main paragraph on line 63.

When execution finally reaches **D030-GET-VALID-PRICE-AND-QTY**, we know that both price and quantity have passed the basic tests. That is, both fields are numeric and the price is within the proper range. When we perform the division on line 170 there are two possible errors. First, we can get a size error; this probably means that although the quantity is numeric, it is equal to zero. Second, we might have a valid result, but the remainder might be non-zero indicating that the price is not an exact multiple of the quantity. Since we don't know whether the error was cause by the price or the quantity or both, we give the user the option of re-entering either or both of these values. Although the code needed to get new data values is slightly more complicated than before, the process basically is the same as in previous paragraphs.

The rest of the program contains no special features. Printing headings on the output file has been omitted here partly to save space by not repeating familiar material, but also partly on the grounds that in a realistic application the results might very well go onto preprinted forms that do not require the program to produce the headings.

Before concluding this section we should mention one last point. If you compare the program code to the validity requirements at the beginning of the chapter, you will notice that we have not tested quantity or price for being numeric. Since these fields are defined as PIC 9's, the **ACCEPT** statement will not accept anything but valid numbers so the test is made automatically. On the other hand, since **CATALOG-NUMBER** is defined with **X**'s, we must make the edit test explicitly.

11.8   THE RESULTS OF RUNNING THE PROGRAM

This program was run with a small sample of representative data. Figure 11.3 shows the output that was written to the processing file when the program was run with this data. The headings at the top of the report were not printed by the program, but were added for readability.

Several entries were typed initially with invalid values. The edit routines caught these errors and correct values were used instead. Figure 11.4 shows a screen image for a typical error message. The program had accepted both quantity and price as being numeric, and had verified that price was within the allowed range. Obviously, however, dividing price by quantity produced a size error. The program displayed the error message and the user indicated that quantity was the value to be re-entered. Figure 11.4 shows the screen just

Order Number	Catalog Number	SZ CD	Qty	Price	Description
123456	5 1656	A	1	$0.45	ALASKA PEAS
123456	9 4342		1	$20.95	GARDEN AND TREE SPRAYER
123456	6 2638	U	2	$7.00	HONEYCROSS CORN - 1 LB
222233	9 3188		1	$17.95	EARTHWORMS - PKG OF 2000
222340	9 3526		1	$2.75	PRAYING MANTIS EGG CASES
222235	3 3183	L	2	$4.00	NASTURTIUM - MIXED COLORS - 1 OZ
222236	4 1939	J	1	$1.05	PHLOX - GRANIFLORA - 1/8 OZ
222237	3 3761	D	2	$3.90	HIBISCUS
222238	6 9088	U	1	$8.80	GARLIC SETS - 2 LBS
222390	7 2577	U	1	$1.20	LITTLE MARVEL PEAS - 1/2 LB
222240	5 2829	L	2	$5.50	HOT PEPPER - LONG RED CAYENNE - 1 OZ
123456	3 2241	S	1	$2.75	CUCUMBER - WEST INDIAN GHERKIN - 1/4 LB
122345	1 3466		1	$18.65	ABUNDANCE PEAR

FIGURE 11.3   The contents of **PROCESSING-FILE** when the program of Figure 11.2 was run with sample data.

before the correct value was typed. In testing a program such as this be sure that you test each error routine, both alone and in combination with other errors.

11.9   A BATCH VERSION OF THE SEED CATALOG PROGRAM

If the seed catalog program were written to run in batch mode, as is frequently done on mainframe computers, its structure would be substantially different even though the functions it performed are basically unchanged. We will not show a complete version of the batch program, but it is worth discussing some of the major changes.

The structure of the program is shaped by two basic factors:

1. Input data cannot be obtained from the terminal but must be read from a file.
2. Errors cannot be corrected as the program runs; instead, the program must write error messages which allow the user to correct data after the run is finished.

One result is that we need three files: one for input data, one for valid output lines, and one for error messages.

Although the input record is similar to **ORDER-DATA** in Figure 11.1, the data editing is not done on a field by field basis, but rather is performed for an

```
Enter order number:      222236
Enter catalog number:    41939
Enter size code:         J
Enter quantity:          00
Enter item description:  PHLOX - GRANIFLORA - 1/8 OZ
Enter price:             00105

Either price or quantity is wrong.
Do you wish to re-enter the price, the quantity, or both (P/Q/B)?   Q

Enter quantity:          00
```

FIGURE 11.4   A sample editing screen from the seed catalog program.

entire record at a time. Since we can't correct any errors until execution is done, we want to catch as many errors as possible at one time so that we don't have to make repeated runs if a record has more than one error. Furthermore, to make it easier for users to relate errors to records in the input file, we should print all error messages for a given record together in a readable manner. Although we could print each message as an error is detected, it is easier and more effective to set flags when each error is detected; when we have edited all fields for the record we can either write the data to the processing file (if there are no flags set), or print the record on the error message file followed by any appropriate messages.

Editing the individual fields is similar to the process used in the interactive program, except for price and quantity. In most cases we simply make the edit test, then set an error flag if the test fails. (There should be a separate flag for each type of error so that we can tell what messages to print when we are finished with the record.) The problem with price and quantity is that if they contain invalid, non-numeric data we may want to treat them as alphanumeric fields, in printing error messages for example. On the other hand, if the data is valid we want to treat the fields as numeric.

The solution to this problem is to define the fields as both numeric and alphanumeric, using the REDEFINES clause as shown below.

```
01    ORDER-RECORD.
      05    ORDER-NUMBER                  PIC X(6).
      05    RECORD-TYPE                   PIC X.
      05    CATALOG-NUMBER.
            10    CATALOG-FIRST-DIGIT     PIC X.
            10    CATALOG-REMAINING       PIC X(4).
      05    SIZE-CODE                     PIC X.
      05    X-QTY                         PIC XX.
      05    9-QTY REDEFINES X-QTY         PIC 99.
      05    ITEM-DESCRIPTION              PIC X(40).
      05    X-PRICE                       PIC X(5).
      05    9-PRICE REDEFINES X-PRICE     PIC 999V99.
```

With this data structure we can, for example, test to see if the price is numeric by writing

```
IF X-PRICE IS NOT NUMERIC
   MOVE 'X' TO PRICE-ERROR-FLAG.
```

and we can test to see if a numeric price is within the proper range by writing

```
IF X-PRICE IS NUMERIC AND 9-PRICE GREATER THAN PRICE-LIMIT
   MOVE 'X' TO LARGE-PRICE-FLAG.
```

Similarly, when we are writing the data to an output file, we can use either a field's alphanumeric definition or its numeric definition, depending on the requirements of the output record.

Although this discussion does not, of course, give a full definition of the batch version of the seed catalog program it does present the key points. Exercise 9 requires you to complete the program.

REVIEW QUESTIONS

1. Shown below are five pairs of skeleton IF statements. Do the two statements in each pair have the same effect?

   a. `IF A = 1 AND B = 2 OR C = 2 AND D = 2 . . .`

   `IF (A = 1 AND B = 2) OR (C = 2 AND D = 2) . . .`

   b. `IF      TRANSFER-CODE NOT = '1'`
   `   OR TRANSACTION-AMOUNT IS NOT NUMERIC . . .`

   `IF  NOT (TRANSFER-CODE = '1'`
   `    OR    TRANSACTION-AMOUNT IS NUMERIC) . . .`

   c. `IF SAM < 30 AND GEORGE > 40 OR RUTH = 50 . . .`

   `IF (SAM < 30 AND GEORGE > 40) OR RUTH = 50 . . .`

   d. `IF (WEATHER = CLOUDY AND TEMP > 60) AND TEMP < 85`
   `   OR WEATHER = CLEAR AND TEMP < 75 . . .`

   `IF WEATHER = CLOUDY AND (TEMP > 60 AND TEMP < 85)`
   `   OR WEATHER = CLEAR AND TEMP < 75 . . .`

   e. `IF A = 1 OR A NOT = 1 . . .`

   `IF NOT (A = 1 AND A = 2) . . .`

2. Shown below are three groups of skeleton IF statements. Do the statements in each group have the same effect?

   a. `IF A = 1 OR A = 2 OR A = 4 . . .`

   `IF A = 1 OR 2 OR 4 . . .`

   b. `IF (A = 1 OR A = 2) AND (B = 6 OR 8) . . .`

   `IF (A = 1 OR 2) AND (B = 6 OR 8) . . .`

   `IF A = 1 OR 2 AND B = 6 OR 8 . . .`

   c. `IF A = 1 OR 2 OR 9 AND B = SPACES . . .`

   `IF (A = 1 OR 2 OR 9) AND B = SPACES . . .`

3. In discussing a batch version of the seed catalog program, we said it would be easier to set flags and write the messages later than to write each error message as the corresponding error is detected. Why do you think this is so?

4. In Section 11.9 we used the statement

   ```
   IF X-PRICE IS NUMERIC AND 9-PRICE GREATER THAN PRICE-LIMIT
       MOVE 'X' TO LARGE-PRICE.
   ```

   to test whether the price is within the proper range.
   What would be the effect if we had written this instead?

   ```
   IF X-PRICE IS NUMERIC AND X-PRICE GREATER THAN PRICE-LIMIT
       MOVE 'X' TO LARGE-PRICE.
   ```
   How about this?

```
IF X-PRICE IS NUMERIC AND X-PRICE IS GREATER THAN '12500'
    MOVE 'X' TO LARGE-PRICE.
```

How about this?

```
IF 9-PRICE IS GREATER THAN PRICE-LIMIT
    MOVE 'X' TO LARGE-PRICE.
```

ANSWERS TO REVIEW QUESTIONS

1. a. No difference. The parentheses express the effect of the precedence rule.

b. Not the same at all; it is not permissible to "factor out" **NOT** in this way. Change the **OR** in the second statement to **AND**, however, and the two statements are the same. (Work it out with examples.) This is an instance of DeMorgan's Laws.

c. No difference. Again, the parentheses simply express the precedence rule.

d. No difference. The two uses of the parentheses express the idea that the three elements joined by **AND**s may be grouped either way in reducing the evaluation to operations on pairs of values. This is similar to the *associative rule* in arithmetic, which says, for instance, that $(A \times B) \times C = A \times (B \times C)$.

e. Oddly enough, these two *are* equivalent, in the sense that both of them are always true regardless of the value of **A**. **A** must always either equal 1 or not equal 1, so that the first statement is always true. Likewise, **A** can never be equal to both 1 and 2 at the same time, so the expression in parentheses is always false and its negation is always true.

2. a. The two are equivalent.

b. The first two are equivalent to each other, but the third is quite different. In the third form, without the parentheses, the **AND** is a higher ranking operator than the **OR**—the implied subjects have nothing to do with it. The effect of the third form is as if we had written

```
IF A = 1 OR (A = 2 AND B = 6) OR B = 8 . . .
```

c. The two are not equivalent, as discussed in the chapter in connection with the seed catalog order program.

3. There are two problems. First, until you check price and quantity you don't know how to print the order line. That is, if the fields are not numeric they must be printed in an alphanumeric (PIC X) format; but if they are numeric they should be printed in edited numeric format. More important, you don't know until detecting the first error whether to write the order line to the processing file or the error message file. If you write the order line as soon as you find the first error, then you have to set a flag to tell the program not to write it again if another error is found. The way described is simpler, on balance.

4. The first alternative would fail in comparing an alphanumeric quantity (**X-PRICE**) with a numeric quantity (**PRICE-LIMIT**). The second version would give correct results, but the meaning is less obvious. The third version would apply the test even if the price had been found to be nonnumeric, making the test meaningless; that is, certain nonnumeric values would be "less" than the value of **PRICE-LIMIT**, but the comparison would be meaningless.

EXERCISES

*1. Write an **IF** statement to place an **X** in **INVALID-CODE-FLAG** if **COLUMN-23-CODE** contains anything except 1, 2, or 3.

 2. Write an **IF** statement to do the following: If **COL-29** contains any digit, add 1 to **CLASS-A**; if **COL-29** contains A, B, or R, add 1 to **CLASS-B**; if **COL-29** contains C, F, G, H, S, or W, add 1 to **CLASS-C**; if none of these is true, add 1 to **CLASS-ERROR** and move X to **CLASS-ERROR-FLAG**. Use implied subjects and relational operators to shorten the statement.

*3. Write an **IF** statement that will add 1 to **REGULAR-COUNT** if **SIZE-A** is in the range of 14 to 36 inclusive and **SIZE-B** is less than 50, and add 1 to **SPECIAL-COUNT** otherwise.

 4. Write an **IF** statement to place an **X** in **NORMAL-CASE** if **VOLUME** is in any of the ranges 12-19, 27-46, or 83-91 (all ranges inclusive), and place an **X** in **ERROR-CASE** otherwise. If you are using **COBOL-85**, write this once using the >= and <= operators, and once without using them.

*5. Modify the program of Figure 11.2 to produce an appropriate error message if the order number is not numeric.

 6. Modify the program in Figure 11.2 so that it produces column headings for the processing file as shown in Figure 11.3. You may use the routine **X010-LINE-OUT** in Figure 9.7.

 7. The actual program on which the seed catalog program is based does not automatically reject prices which exceed $125 but simply flags them as possible errors. Modify the program in Figure 11.2 so that when the price exceeds **PRICE-LIMIT** the user has the choice of entering a new price or telling the program to accept the given price as valid.

 8. Modify the program of Figure 11.2 so that if the catalog number is 14100, 78667, 74005, 53512, 15537, or 92528, then a message is displayed warning of a possible error. The message should be **"CHECK THAT DESCRIPTION MATCHES CATALOG NUMBER"** and the user should have the option of accepting the catalog number or entering a new one.

The problem here is that these six catalog numbers are used in the sample order form shown in the seed catalog; people fairly frequently miscopy these numbers in writing their orders. In a related situation, manufacturers frequently place an identification card in wallets with a sample Social Security number. People surprisingly often copy these numbers as their own Social Security number. This phenomenon of "pocketbook numbers" is one reason why Social Security numbers are not always unique.

*9. Write a batch version of the seed catalog program.

---

* Answers to starred exercises will be found in Appendix IV at the end of the book.

CHAPTER 12

ENHANCED INTERACTIVE PROCESSING

12.1 INTRODUCTION

When computerized data processing began in the late 1950's and early 1960's, programs were run in batch mode and it frequently would take several hours, if not a full day, for results to become available. Even today, it can take from several minutes to many hours to get the results of a batch program. Furthermore, no matter how fast the results of batch programs can be made available, there is no way of interacting with the program until it completes execution. As a result, one common reason for wanting to run data processing applications on microcomputers is the ability to use interactive processing.

There are advantages and disadvantages to both batch and interactive processing, and each mode is suited to certain types of applications. However, because of the increasing use of interactive processing and the role that screen displays play in this type of program, it is appropriate to consider some of the screen processing capabilities of Microsoft **COBOL** beyond the relatively simple **ACCEPT** and **DISPLAY** that we have used so far.

Using the seed catalog program from Chapter 11, we introduce the Screen Section, which allows us to define the layout of a computer screen in the Data Division rather than depending on Procedure Division statements. We will begin with a very basic program, then show a more complete one. We will also introduce some of the more sophisticated screen options such as colors, reverse video, blinking displays, and so on. Following this we will show a program that demonstrates how menus can be used to guide the program user through execution of the program. Finally, we will discuss some of the highlights of ADIS, the Microsoft **COBOL ACCEPT/DISPLAY** control module.

12.2 A SCREEN-ORIENTED VERSION OF THE SEED CATALOG PROGRAM

The first revision of the seed catalog program, shown in Figure 12.1, presents a basic introduction to the Screen Section, a new section of the Data Division. The Screen Section allows us to define the format of data shown on a CRT screen in an entry called a *screen description*. The basic concept of the screen description is that it allows us to define the format and use of a CRT screen layout in the Data Division rather than having to use procedural statements to control every **ACCEPT** and **DISPLAY** operation. When the Screen Section is used in a program it must be the *last* section in the Data Division.

The definition of the screen description **ORDER-SCREEN** begins on line 47 of Figure 12.1. We will look at this definition in more detail shortly, but for now we only want to observe the main features. The entries in **ORDER-SCREEN** are divided into two types. The first type displays text on the screen. For example, lines 55-56 will print "Enter catalog number:" beginning in column one. The second type of entry accepts data typed by the user. The code in lines 57-60, for example, will accept a five-digit numeric item and store it in **CATALOG-NUMBER OF ORDER-DATA**. Notice that except for the 01-level entry none of the entries has a data name. In this example we don't refer to any of the fields individually, so we are not required to give any of them names.

```
1        IDENTIFICATION DIVISION.
2        PROGRAM-ID.
3            SEEDS-2.
4        DATE-WRITTEN.
5            APRIL 6, 1989.
6        *
7        *    SEED CATALOG PROGRAM USING BASIC SCREEN DEFINITION.
8        *
9
10       ENVIRONMENT DIVISION.
11       INPUT-OUTPUT SECTION.
12       FILE-CONTROL.
13           SELECT PROCESSING-FILE          ASSIGN TO 'CH12P01.PRO'.
14
15
16       DATA DIVISION.
17       FILE SECTION.
18       FD  PROCESSING-FILE
19           LABEL RECORDS ARE STANDARD.
20       01  PROCESSING-LINE                 PIC X(132).
21
22       WORKING-STORAGE SECTION.
23       01  ORDER-DATA.
24           05   ORDER-NUMBER               PIC X(6).
25                88  LAST-ORDER-LINE            VALUE '000000', SPACES.
26           05   RECORD-TYPE                PIC X.
27           05   CATALOG-NUMBER.
28                10   CATALOG-FIRST-DIGIT   PIC X.
29                10   CATALOG-REMAINING     PIC X(4).
30           05   SIZE-CODE                  PIC X.
31           05   QUANTITY                   PIC 99.
32           05   ITEM-DESCRIPTION           PIC X(40).
33           05   PRICE                      PIC 999V99.
34
35       01  OUTPUT-LINE.
36           05   ORDER-NUMBER               PIC Z(5)9.
```

```
37          05  CATALOG-NUMBER.
38              10  CATALOG-FIRST-DIGIT    PIC BBX.
39              10  CATALOG-REMAINING      PIC BX(4).
40          05  SIZE-CODE                  PIC BX.
41          05  QUANTITY                   PIC BBZ9.
42          05  PRICE                      PIC BB$$$$9.99.
43          05  ITEM-DESCRIPTION           PIC BBX(40).
44          05  FILLER                     PIC X(59) VALUE SPACES.
45
46      SCREEN SECTION.
47      01  ORDER-SCREEN.
48          05  BEEP  VALUE 'Enter order number:'
49              BLANK SCREEN
50              LINE 1  COLUMN 1.
51          05                             PIC X(6)
52              TO ORDER-NUMBER OF ORDER-DATA
53              REVERSE-VIDEO
54              COLUMN + 6.
55          05  VALUE 'Enter catalog number:'
56              LINE + 1 COLUMN 1.
57          05                             PIC 9(5)
58              TO CATALOG-NUMBER OF ORDER-DATA
59              REVERSE-VIDEO
60              COLUMN 25.
61          05  VALUE 'Enter size code:'
62              LINE + 1 COLUMN 1.
63          05                             PIC X
64              TO SIZE-CODE OF ORDER-DATA
65              REVERSE-VIDEO
66              COLUMN 25.
67          05  VALUE 'Enter quantity:'
68              LINE + 1 COLUMN 1.
69          05                             PIC Z9
70              TO QUANTITY OF ORDER-DATA
71              REVERSE-VIDEO
72              COLUMN 25.
73          05  VALUE 'Enter description:'
74              LINE + 1 COLUMN 1.
75          05                             PIC X(40)
76              TO ITEM-DESCRIPTION OF ORDER-DATA
77              REVERSE-VIDEO
78              COLUMN 25.
79          05  VALUE 'Enter price:'
80              LINE + 1 COLUMN 1.
81          05                             PIC ZZ9.99
82              TO PRICE OF ORDER-DATA
83              REVERSE-VIDEO
84              COLUMN 25.
85
86
87      PROCEDURE DIVISION.
88      A000-VALIDATE-ORDERS.
89          OPEN OUTPUT PROCESSING-FILE.
90          MOVE LOW-VALUES TO ORDER-NUMBER OF ORDER-DATA.
91          PERFORM B010-VALIDATE-ONE-LINE
92              UNTIL LAST-ORDER-LINE.
93          CLOSE PROCESSING-FILE.
94          STOP RUN.
95
```

```
96          B010-VALIDATE-ONE-LINE.
97              DISPLAY ORDER-SCREEN AT 0510.
98              ACCEPT  ORDER-SCREEN AT 0510.
99              IF NOT LAST-ORDER-LINE
100                 MOVE CORRESPONDING ORDER-DATA TO OUTPUT-LINE
101                 WRITE PROCESSING-LINE FROM OUTPUT-LINE
102                     AFTER ADVANCING 2 LINES.
103
104         **************** END OF PROGRAM *****************************
```

FIGURE 12.1 A basic screen processing version of the seed catalog program.

To use this screen definition we need only refer to the **01**-level identifier in an **ACCEPT** or **DISPLAY** statement. As a result, the code in the Procedure Division becomes very simple. For each order line, we **DISPLAY ORDER-SCREEN** beginning at column 10 of line 5, then **ACCEPT ORDER-SCREEN** at the same position. The **DISPLAY** statement causes all prompt fields to be written to the screen, but does not process any input. When we execute the **ACCEPT** statement on line 98, the cursor moves to the first input field and waits for us to enter a data value. As each input field is filled, we use the tab key to move to the next input field. After all fields have been filled, we press the enter key to terminate input for that set of data, and execution continues with the IF statement on line 99. The last statements of the paragraph write the data to the output file, and the loop repeats. Notice that all input processing is triggered by the one **ACCEPT** statement on line 98. The **DISPLAY** statement automatically causes all output fields of **ORDER-SCREEN** to be processed with no processing of any input, and the **ACCEPT** statement automatically causes all input fields to be processed while the output fields are ignored.

12.3 THE SCREEN DEFINITION

Now that we see the general structure of the program, let us take a closer look at the details of **ORDER-SCREEN**. To begin with, notice that each entry in **ORDER-SCREEN** defines one field on the screen, either input or output. The location of a field is defined by using **LINE** and **COLUMN** clauses; the formats of these clauses are:

$$\underline{\text{LINE}} \quad \left[\text{NUMBER IS} \left[\left\{ \begin{array}{c} \underline{\text{PLUS}} \\ + \\ - \end{array} \right\} \right] \left\{ \begin{array}{c} \text{identifier-1} \\ \text{integer-1} \end{array} \right\} \right]$$

$$\left\{ \begin{array}{c} \underline{\text{COLUMN}} \\ \underline{\text{COL}} \end{array} \right\} \left[\text{NUMBER IS} \left[\left\{ \begin{array}{c} \underline{\text{PLUS}} \\ + \\ - \end{array} \right\} \right] \left\{ \begin{array}{c} \text{identifier-2} \\ \text{integer-2} \end{array} \right\} \right]$$

For example, on line 50 we specify that the first field begins at line 1, column 1. However, we can see from the screen shown in Figure 12.2 that when the program runs, the text begins in the center of the screen, several lines from the top. The reason for this is that line and column numbers are relative to the starting position of the screen definition on the physical CRT screen. Since the **ACCEPT** and **DISPLAY** statements on lines 97 and 98 begin the screen definition at line 5, column 10, all field positions within the definition are relative to this starting point.

```
Enter order number:      123456
Enter catalog number:    51656
Enter size code:         A
Enter quantity:           1
Enter description:       ALASKA PEAS
Enter price:             __0.45
```

FIGURE 12.2 A sample screen from the program in Figure 12.1.

As we look at successive entries in **ORDER-SCREEN** we see other forms of the **LINE** and **COLUMN** clauses. On line 54, for example, there is no **LINE** clause, and the **COLUMN** clause specifies a relative column position. When the **LINE** clause is omitted the compiler assumes that the current field will be on the same line as the previous field. In the **COLUMN** clause, using "+" starts the field a given number of columns past the last character of the previous field. In the example, the field will begin six columns past the end of the preceding prompt. We can use the word **PLUS** instead of "+", or we can use "-" if we want the current field to start before the end of the previous field. Note that either "+" or "-" must be preceded and followed by at least one blank.

We must emphasize that the screen definition only defines the format of an area on the CRT screen; it does not define any data, either input or output, associated with that screen area. This is the reason we need not provide names for fields that we do not refer to individually. This also means that we do not always need to provide a **PICTURE** clause for a screen field, and that when we do provide a **PICTURE** it need not follow quite the same rules as in other Data Division entries. For example, the prompt field defined on lines 55 and 56 has no **PICTURE** clause. The reason is that the text of the prompt provides all the field definition required. We use the **VALUE** clause to define the text, then use the **LINE** and **COLUMN** clauses to tell where the field is located; no additional definition is required.

When the field only contains text, the **VALUE** clause is sufficient to tell **COBOL** what should be displayed on the screen. However, if we wish to display data from elsewhere in the Data Division or to accept data for input, we must specify which data item is to provide the output or receive the input. To specify where input data is to be stored, we use the **TO** clause, as shown on line 82. Thus, the field defined on lines 81-84 is a six-character field, beginning on the same line as the previous field but starting in column 25, which will accept numeric input and store the value entered in **PRICE OF ORDER-DATA**. Notice that the picture for this field is **ZZ9.99**. Normally a numeric field used in an **ACCEPT** statement may not include editing characters if the data is to be used in later numeric calculations. However, the picture for **PRICE** is **999V99**, which is pure numeric. The screen definition picture only defines the way in which the data is to appear on the screen, not the way it is to be stored in memory.

There are a few other clauses used in **ORDER-SCREEN** which allow us to make the screen handling a bit more sophisticated than we have done in previous examples. The word **BEEP** (line 48) causes the computer to sound a tone when the field is displayed; in this example we are signalling the user that a new set of order data is to be entered. **BLANK SCREEN** causes the entire screen to be erased and places the cursor at line 1, column 1. This happens to be exactly where we want the cursor, but if we wanted it elsewhere we could use **LINE** and **COLUMN** clauses as appropriate. We can also write **BLANK LINE**, which erases the current line from the cursor position to the end of the line. Finally, the **REVERSE-VIDEO** clause causes a field to be displayed with the foreground and background colors reversed. For example, if the screen is a monochrome screen that normally displays white letters on a black background, a **REVERSE-VIDEO** field would display black letters on a white background. This feature can be used to make fields where data is to be entered stand out from text or prompt fields.

The screen definition shown in Figure 12.1 is fairly simple and has no intermediate group fields. This is not true in general, however. Certain clauses in the Screen Section may be used at any level, either elementary or group. Others must be used only at the elementary level. In particular, of the clauses we have used in this example, only **REVERSE-VIDEO** may be used at the group level. **BEEP**, **BLANK SCREEN** (or **BLANK LINE**), **COLUMN**, **LINE**, **PIC**, and **VALUE** may only be used in elementary descriptions. Indeed, the **COBOL** compiler *requires* that at least one of these clauses appear in every elementary field definition.

We have tried to describe what the various screen definition clauses in Figure 12.1 actually do and how they affect the program. However, screen handling is, quite obviously, a visual process, and in this case a picture is definitely worth a thousand words. We strongly recommend that you run the example program, or one of your own choosing, and see how the screen actually appears. Be sure that you can relate each visual characteristic to its corresponding screen description clause.

12.4 AN IMPROVED VERSION OF THE SEED CATALOG PROGRAM

You have probably noticed that the program in Figure 12.1 has one very serious defect: it does not include the data editing that was actually the major objective of the program in the first place. The problem is that we defined all fields on the screen in *one* screen definition. This is no problem when we display the screen; it simply means that all prompts appear at once. However, it also means that when we accept the screen, we cannot interrupt the input process to edit what has been typed; we can move from one input field to another by pressing the tab key, or we can terminate input for the screen by pressing Enter, but those are our only options. Of course, we could modify the program to accept an entire set of data, then edit each field in the set one by one. This is not really a very good solution, however, since it means that the user won't see any error message until all the data for an order has been entered. Furthermore, if *any* field were in error, then *all* fields would have to be retyped.

A better solution to the problem is shown in Figure 12.3. We still define ORDER-SCREEN as a single screen definition, but we also provide screen names for each of the input fields; for example, the field that accepts the order number (lines 65-69) is called SCREEN-ORDER-NUMBER. With a few exceptions, the resulting program is very similar to the first version of the seed catalog program shown in Figure 11.1.

```
1          IDENTIFICATION DIVISION.
2          PROGRAM-ID.
3              SEEDS-3.
4          DATE-WRITTEN.
5              APRIL 13, 1989.
6       *
7       *    THE SEED CATALOG PROGRAM USING BASIC SCREEN DEFINITION.
8       *    DATA EDITING INCLUDED.
9       *
10
11
12         ENVIRONMENT DIVISION.
13         INPUT-OUTPUT SECTION.
14         FILE-CONTROL.
15             SELECT PROCESSING-FILE            ASSIGN TO 'CH12P02.PRO'.
16
17
18         DATA DIVISION.
19         FILE SECTION.
20         FD  PROCESSING-FILE
21             LABEL RECORDS ARE STANDARD.
22         01  PROCESSING-LINE                   PIC X(132).
23
24         WORKING-STORAGE SECTION.
25         77  CHOICE-CODE                       PIC X.
26         77  PRICE-LIMIT                       PIC  999V99 VALUE 125.00.
27         77  PRICE-LIMIT-EDIT                  PIC  $ZZ9.99.
28         77  TEST-REMAINDER                    PIC S999V99 COMP-3.
29         77  UNIT-PRICE                        PIC S999V99 COMP-3.
30
```

```
31          01   ERROR-FLAGS.
32               05   VALID-CATALOG-NUMBER          PIC X.
33               05   VALID-SIZE-CODE               PIC X.
34               05   VALID-PRICE                   PIC X.
35               05   VALID-PRICE-AND-QTY           PIC X.
36
37          01   ORDER-DATA.
38               05   ORDER-NUMBER                  PIC X(6).
39                    88   LAST-ORDER-LINE             VALUE '000000', SPACES.
40               05   RECORD-TYPE                   PIC X.
41               05   CATALOG-NUMBER.
42                    10   CATALOG-FIRST-DIGIT      PIC X.
43                    10   CATALOG-REMAINING        PIC X(4).
44               05   SIZE-CODE                     PIC X.
45               05   QUANTITY                      PIC 99.
46               05   ITEM-DESCRIPTION              PIC X(40).
47               05   PRICE                         PIC 999V99.
48
49          01   OUTPUT-LINE.
50               05   ORDER-NUMBER                  PIC Z(5)9.
51               05   CATALOG-NUMBER.
52                    10   CATALOG-FIRST-DIGIT      PIC BBX.
53                    10   CATALOG-REMAINING        PIC BX(4).
54               05   SIZE-CODE                     PIC BX.
55               05   QUANTITY                      PIC BBZ9.
56               05   PRICE                         PIC BB$$$9.99.
57               05   ITEM-DESCRIPTION              PIC BBX(40).
58               05   FILLER                        PIC X(59) VALUE SPACES.
59
60          SCREEN SECTION.
61          01   ORDER-SCREEN.
62               05   VALUE 'Enter order number:'
63                    BLANK SCREEN
64                    LINE 5  COLUMN 10.
65               05   SCREEN-ORDER-NUMBER           PIC X(6)
66                    TO ORDER-NUMBER OF ORDER-DATA
67                    REVERSE-VIDEO
68                    COLUMN + 6.
69               05   VALUE 'Enter catalog number:'
70                    LINE + 1 COLUMN 10.
71               05   SCREEN-CATALOG-NUMBER         PIC 9(5)
72                    TO CATALOG-NUMBER OF ORDER-DATA
73                    REVERSE-VIDEO
74                    COLUMN 34.
75               05   VALUE 'Enter size code:'
76                    LINE + 1 COLUMN 10.
77               05   SCREEN-SIZE-CODE              PIC X
78                    TO SIZE-CODE OF ORDER-DATA
79                    REVERSE-VIDEO
80                    COLUMN 34.
81               05   VALUE 'Enter quantity:'
82                    LINE + 1 COLUMN 10.
83               05   SCREEN-QUANTITY               PIC Z9
84                    TO QUANTITY OF ORDER-DATA
85                    REVERSE-VIDEO
86                    COLUMN 34.
87               05   VALUE 'Enter description:'
88                    LINE + 1 COLUMN 10.
```

```
89          05   SCREEN-DESCRIPTION              PIC X(40)
90               TO ITEM-DESCRIPTION OF ORDER-DATA
91               REVERSE-VIDEO
92               COLUMN 34.
93          05   VALUE 'Enter price:'
94               LINE + 1 COLUMN 10.
95          05   SCREEN-PRICE                    PIC ZZ9.99
96               TO PRICE OF ORDER-DATA
97               REVERSE-VIDEO
98               COLUMN 34.
99
100
101     PROCEDURE DIVISION.
102     A000-VALIDATE-ORDERS.
103         OPEN OUTPUT PROCESSING-FILE.
104         MOVE PRICE-LIMIT TO PRICE-LIMIT-EDIT.
105         MOVE LOW-VALUES TO ORDER-NUMBER OF ORDER-DATA.
106         PERFORM B010-VALIDATE-ONE-LINE
107             UNTIL LAST-ORDER-LINE.
108         CLOSE PROCESSING-FILE.
109         STOP RUN.
110
111     B010-VALIDATE-ONE-LINE.
112         DISPLAY ORDER-SCREEN.
113         PERFORM C010-GET-ORDER-NUMBER.
114         IF NOT LAST-ORDER-LINE
115             MOVE SPACES TO ERROR-FLAGS
116             PERFORM C020-GET-CATALOG-NUMBER
117             PERFORM C030-GET-SIZE-CODE
118             PERFORM C040-GET-QUANTITY
119             PERFORM C050-GET-ITEM-DESCRIPTION
120             PERFORM C060-GET-PRICE
121             PERFORM C070-VALIDATE-QTY-AND-PRICE
122             PERFORM C080-WRITE-PROCESSING-LINE.
123
124     C010-GET-ORDER-NUMBER.
125         ACCEPT SCREEN-ORDER-NUMBER.
126
127     C020-GET-CATALOG-NUMBER.
128         MOVE 'N' TO VALID-CATALOG-NUMBER.
129         PERFORM D010-GET-VALID-CATALOG-NUMBER
130             UNTIL VALID-CATALOG-NUMBER = 'Y'.
131
132     C030-GET-SIZE-CODE.
133         MOVE 'N' TO VALID-SIZE-CODE.
134         PERFORM D020-GET-VALID-SIZE-CODE
135             UNTIL VALID-SIZE-CODE = 'Y'.
136
137     C040-GET-QUANTITY.
138         ACCEPT SCREEN-QUANTITY.
139
140     C050-GET-ITEM-DESCRIPTION.
141         ACCEPT SCREEN-DESCRIPTION.
142
143     C060-GET-PRICE.
144         MOVE 'N' TO VALID-PRICE.
145         PERFORM E010-GET-VALID-PRICE
146             UNTIL VALID-PRICE = 'Y'.
147
```

```
148        C070-VALIDATE-QTY-AND-PRICE.
149            MOVE 'N' TO VALID-PRICE-AND-QTY.
150            PERFORM D030-GET-VALID-PRICE-AND-QTY
151                UNTIL VALID-PRICE-AND-QTY = 'Y'.
152
153        C080-WRITE-PROCESSING-LINE.
154            MOVE CORRESPONDING ORDER-DATA TO OUTPUT-LINE.
155            WRITE PROCESSING-LINE FROM OUTPUT-LINE
156                    AFTER ADVANCING 2 LINES.
157
158        D010-GET-VALID-CATALOG-NUMBER.
159            ACCEPT SCREEN-CATALOG-NUMBER.
160            IF CATALOG-NUMBER OF ORDER-DATA IS NOT NUMERIC
161                DISPLAY 'Catalog number contains '          AT 1325
162                        WITH BEEP
163                DISPLAY 'a non-numeric character.'           AT 1349
164                DISPLAY 'Please re-enter the catalog number.' AT 1425
165            ELSE
166                IF CATALOG-FIRST-DIGIT OF ORDER-DATA = '0' OR '2'
167                    DISPLAY 'First digit of catalog '        AT 1325
168                            WITH BEEP
169                    DISPLAY 'number is invalid.        '      AT 1348
170                    DISPLAY 'Please re-enter the catalog number.'
171                                                             AT 1425
172                ELSE
173                    DISPLAY SPACE WITH BLANK LINE            AT 1301
174                    DISPLAY SPACE WITH BLANK LINE            AT 1401
175                    MOVE 'Y' TO VALID-CATALOG-NUMBER.
176
177        D020-GET-VALID-SIZE-CODE.
178            ACCEPT SCREEN-SIZE-CODE.
179            IF SIZE-CODE OF ORDER-DATA = 'A' OR 'D' OR 'G' OR 'J'
180                OR 'K' OR 'L' OR 'S' OR 'T' OR 'U' OR ' '
181                MOVE 'Y' TO VALID-SIZE-CODE
182                DISPLAY SPACE WITH BLANK LINE                AT 1301
183                DISPLAY SPACE WITH BLANK LINE                AT 1501
184            ELSE
185                DISPLAY 'There is no such size code.'        AT 1425
186                        WITH BEEP
187                DISPLAY 'Please re-enter the size code.'      AT 1525.
188            IF VALID-SIZE-CODE = 'Y'
189                IF (CATALOG-FIRST-DIGIT OF ORDER-DATA =
190                        '1' OR '8' OR '9')   AND
191                    SIZE-CODE OF ORDER-DATA IS NOT EQUAL TO SPACES
192                    DISPLAY 'This item does not take a size code.'
193                            WITH BEEP                        AT 1425
194                    DISPLAY 'Please re-enter the size code.' AT 1525
195                    MOVE 'N' TO VALID-SIZE-CODE
196                ELSE
197                    DISPLAY SPACE WITH BLANK LINE            AT 1401
198                    DISPLAY SPACE WITH BLANK LINE            AT 1501
199                    MOVE 'Y' TO VALID-SIZE-CODE.
200
201        D030-GET-VALID-PRICE-AND-QTY.
202            MOVE 'Y' TO VALID-PRICE-AND-QTY.
203            DIVIDE PRICE OF ORDER-DATA BY QUANTITY OF ORDER-DATA
204                    GIVING UNIT-PRICE REMAINDER TEST-REMAINDER
205                ON SIZE ERROR MOVE 'N' TO VALID-PRICE-AND-QTY.
```

```
206        IF TEST-REMAINDER NOT EQUAL TO ZERO
207            MOVE 'N' TO VALID-PRICE-AND-QTY.
208        IF VALID-PRICE-AND-QTY = 'N'
209            DISPLAY 'Either price or quantity is wrong.' AT 1405
210                WITH BEEP
211            DISPLAY 'Do you wish to re-enter the price, ' AT 1505
212            DISPLAY 'the quantity, or both (P/Q/B)?'      AT 1540
213            ACCEPT CHOICE-CODE                            AT 1572
214            IF CHOICE-CODE = 'P' OR 'p'
215                MOVE 'N' TO VALID-PRICE
216                PERFORM E010-GET-VALID-PRICE
217                    UNTIL VALID-PRICE = 'Y'
218            ELSE
219                IF CHOICE-CODE = 'Q' OR 'q'
220                    ACCEPT SCREEN-QUANTITY
221                ELSE
222                    ACCEPT SCREEN-QUANTITY
223                    MOVE 'N' TO VALID-PRICE
224                    PERFORM E010-GET-VALID-PRICE
225                        UNTIL VALID-PRICE = 'Y'
226        ELSE
227            DISPLAY SPACE WITH BLANK LINE                 AT 1401
228            DISPLAY SPACE WITH BLANK LINE                 AT 1501.
229
230    E010-GET-VALID-PRICE.
231        ACCEPT SCREEN-PRICE.
232        IF PRICE OF ORDER-DATA IS GREATER THAN PRICE-LIMIT
233            DISPLAY 'Price must not exceed '              AT 1425
234                WITH BEEP
235            DISPLAY PRICE-LIMIT-EDIT                      AT 1447
236            DISPLAY 'Please re-enter the price.'          AT 1525
237        ELSE
238            DISPLAY SPACE WITH BLANK LINE                 AT 1401
239            DISPLAY SPACE WITH BLANK LINE                 AT 1501
240            MOVE 'Y' TO VALID-PRICE.
241
242    **************** END OF PROGRAM ********************************
```

FIGURE 12.3   The seed catalog program with editing.

Since the text for all the basic prompts—those that do not involve errors—has been defined in ORDER-SCREEN, we only need to DISPLAY ORDER-SCREEN (line 112) to write these prompts on the screen. When we want to get a particular input value, we accept the elementary-level screen definition for that item. For example, on line 125 we have the statement

ACCEPT SCREEN-ORDER-NUMBER.

The TO clause in the definition of this field automatically transfers data to ORDER-NUMBER OF ORDER-DATA, so we do not need to refer to ORDER-NUMBER explicitly in the ACCEPT statement.

When an error is detected in a data item—for example, if the catalog number is not numeric—we use DISPLAY statements as before to print error messages. However, we have added some new features. Most of the screen formatting options that can be specified in a screen definition can also be specified on individual **DISPLAY** statements by using the **WITH** clause. For example, when an error message is **DISPLAY**ed we use **WITH BEEP** to alert the user. If errors have been detected we need to erase the error messages after a correct value has been entered, so we use **WITH BLANK LINE**. Notice that although the only purpose of **DISPLAY** statements such as the ones on lines 173 and 174 is to blank the lines on the screen, **DISPLAY** still requires that something actually be written to the screen. That is, we could not simply write

```
DISPLAY WITH BLANK LINE AT 1301.
```

Therefore, we simply **DISPLAY** a single space.

The remainder of this program, especially the editing logic, is very similar to the original seed catalog program in Chapter 11 and needs no further comment. You should compare Figure 12.3 to Figure 11.1 to see what differences there are between the two versions.

12.5 IMPROVING THE SCREEN

When we first introduced the **DISPLAY** statement at the start of this book, we used a very simple version. There was very little formatting and output lines were simply written to the screen one after another. When the screen became full everything on the screen moved up one line to make room for a new line, and the top line simply rolled off and was lost. The type of output is called *scrolling* output; the lines *scroll* up the screen. As we progressed, we added a few more features to enhance **DISPLAY**ed output. In particular, the **AT** clause on the **DISPLAY** statement allows us to use *non-scrolling* output, output that always appears at a fixed location on the screen. Finally, the Screen Section and the **WITH** clause on the **DISPLAY** statement allow us to add a number of new features to enhance the way that data is displayed and accepted through the CRT. However, in spite of these improvements the basic design of our screen output is still closely related to the style required by the original scrolling version of **DISPLAY**. It is time to move beyond that design.

To begin with, we will reorganize the fields on the screen. We will put a highlighted title at the top of the screen telling what function the screen performs, and will write the data fields left to right across the screen instead of in a vertical column. Since we assume that the user generally is familiar with the screen and its operation, we will omit the word "Enter" from each prompt, leaving only a field identifier. Finally, under the assumption that the user has a color monitor, we will add color to the screen.* A sample screen for this new format is shown in Figure 12.4.

The program is shown in Figure 12.5. Although the line and column numbers have changed, most of the definition of **ORDER-SCREEN** is the same as Figure 12.3. However, there are a few changes. First, we have defined colors for the screen with the **BACKGROUND-COLOR** and **FOREGROUND-COLOR** clauses on lines 57 and 58. The color selection in Microsoft **COBOL** is designed for use on any color monitor, regardless of whether enhanced graphic capabilities are available. Therefore, there are only eight colors, numbered 0 - 7. They are:

---

* Unfortunately, since this book is not printed in color all screens show in black and white. If you have a color monitor, try a few examples to see how color looks.

```
                        SEED CATALOG ORDER ENTRY


order number:  123456      catalog number:  51656
size code:  A              quantity:   1        price:    0.45
description:  Alaska Peas_____
```

FIGURE 12.4 A sample of the enhanced seed catalog screen.

0 black
1 blue
2 green
3 cyan
4 red
5 magenta
6 brown
7 white

The foreground and background color selections can be specified at any level in the screen definition. If they are specified at the group level they apply to all fields in that group, unless overridden by other selections for individual fields. If no colors are selected explicitly, the default colors are black for background and white for foreground.

We must offer a word of caution. Careful use of colors can enhance a **DISPLAY** screen, call attention to items of special interest, and generally make the screen easier to work with. However, many color combinations make text hard to read and can strain the eyes. Experiment with various colors, and be wary of using color for no good purpose.

```
1          IDENTIFICATION DIVISION.
2          PROGRAM-ID.
3              SEEDS-4.
4          DATE-WRITTEN.
5              APRIL 25, 1989.
6
```

```
7           ENVIRONMENT DIVISION.
8           INPUT-OUTPUT SECTION.
9           FILE-CONTROL.
10              SELECT PROCESSING-FILE          ASSIGN TO 'CH12P03.PRO'.
11
12          DATA DIVISION.
13
14          FILE SECTION.
15          FD  PROCESSING-FILE
16              LABEL RECORDS ARE STANDARD.
17          01  PROCESSING-LINE                 PIC X(132).
18
19          WORKING-STORAGE SECTION.
20          77  CHOICE-CODE                     PIC X.
21          77  PRICE-LIMIT                     PIC  999V99 VALUE 125.00.
22          77  PRICE-LIMIT-EDIT                PIC  $ZZ9.99.
23          77  TEST-REMAINDER                  PIC S999V99 COMP-3.
24          77  UNIT-PRICE                      PIC S999V99 COMP-3.
25
26          01  ERROR-FLAGS.
27              05  VALID-CATALOG-NUMBER        PIC X.
28              05  VALID-SIZE-CODE             PIC X.
29              05  VALID-PRICE                 PIC X.
30              05  VALID-PRICE-AND-QTY         PIC X.
31
32          01  ORDER-DATA.
33              05  ORDER-NUMBER                PIC X(6).
34                  88  LAST-ORDER-LINE            VALUE '000000', SPACES.
35              05  RECORD-TYPE                 PIC X.
36              05  CATALOG-NUMBER.
37                  10  CATALOG-FIRST-DIGIT     PIC X.
38                  10  CATALOG-REMAINING       PIC X(4).
39              05  SIZE-CODE                   PIC X.
40              05  QUANTITY                    PIC 99.
41              05  ITEM-DESCRIPTION            PIC X(40).
42              05  PRICE                       PIC 999V99.
43
44          01  OUTPUT-LINE.
45              05  ORDER-NUMBER                PIC Z(5)9.
46              05  CATALOG-NUMBER.
47                  10  CATALOG-FIRST-DIGIT     PIC BBX.
48                  10  CATALOG-REMAINING       PIC BX(4).
49              05  SIZE-CODE                   PIC BX.
50              05  QUANTITY                    PIC BBZ9.
51              05  PRICE                       PIC BB$$$$9.99.
52              05  ITEM-DESCRIPTION            PIC BBX(40).
53              05  FILLER                      PIC X(59) VALUE SPACES.
54
55          SCREEN SECTION.
56          01  ORDER-SCREEN
57                  BACKGROUND-COLOR IS 1
58                  FOREGROUND-COLOR IS 7.
59              05  VALUE 'SEED CATALOG ORDER ENTRY'
60                  BLANK SCREEN                HIGHLIGHT
61                  LINE 6  COLUMN 29.
62              05  VALUE 'order number:'
63                  LINE 9  COLUMN 5.
```

```
64              05    SCREEN-ORDER-NUMBER              PIC X(6)
65                    TO ORDER-NUMBER OF ORDER-DATA
66                    REVERSE-VIDEO
67                    COLUMN + 3.
68              05    VALUE 'catalog number:'
69                    COLUMN 31.
70              05    SCREEN-CATALOG-NUMBER           PIC X(5)
71                    TO CATALOG-NUMBER OF ORDER-DATA
72                    REVERSE-VIDEO
73                    COLUMN + 3.
74              05    VALUE 'size code:'
75                    LINE + 1  COLUMN 5.
76              05    SCREEN-SIZE-CODE               PIC X
77                    TO SIZE-CODE OF ORDER-DATA
78                    REVERSE-VIDEO
79                    COLUMN + 3.
80              05    VALUE 'quantity:'
81                    COLUMN 31.
82              05    SCREEN-QUANTITY                PIC Z9
83                    TO QUANTITY OF ORDER-DATA
84                    REVERSE-VIDEO
85                    COLUMN + 3.
86              05    VALUE 'price:'
87                    COLUMN 51.
88              05    SCREEN-PRICE                   PIC ZZ9.99
89                    TO PRICE OF ORDER-DATA
90                    REVERSE-VIDEO
91                    COLUMN + 3.
92              05    VALUE 'description:'
93                    LINE + 1  COLUMN 5.
94              05    SCREEN-DESCRIPTION             PIC X(40)
95                    TO ITEM-DESCRIPTION OF ORDER-DATA
96                    COLUMN + 3.
97
98        01    PRICE-ERR-SCREEN.
99              05    FROM QUANTITY OF ORDER-DATA  PIC Z9
100                   REVERSE-VIDEO
101                   LINE 10  COLUMN 42.
102              05 FROM PRICE OF ORDER-DATA       PIC ZZ9.99
103                   REVERSE-VIDEO HIGHLIGHT
104                   LINE 10   COLUMN 59.
105
106       01    QTY-ERR-SCREEN.
107              05    FROM QUANTITY OF ORDER-DATA  PIC Z9
108                   REVERSE-VIDEO HIGHLIGHT
109                   LINE 10   COLUMN 42.
110              05    FROM PRICE OF ORDER-DATA     PIC ZZ9.99
111                   REVERSE-VIDEO
112                   LINE 10   COLUMN 59.
113
114       01    QTY-PRICE-ERR-SCREEN1.
115              05    FROM QUANTITY OF ORDER-DATA  PIC Z9
116                   REVERSE-VIDEO BLINK
117                   LINE 10   COLUMN 42.
118              05    FROM PRICE OF ORDER-DATA     PIC ZZ9.99
119                   REVERSE-VIDEO BLINK
120                   LINE 10   COLUMN 59.
121              05    VALUE 'Either price or quantity is wrong.'
122                   LINE 13   COLUMN 5.
```

```
123                  05   VALUE 'Do you wish to re-enter the price, '
124                       LINE 14   COLUMN 5.
125                  05   VALUE 'the quantity, or both (P/Q/B)?' COLUMN.
126                  05   SCREEN-CHOICE-CODE           PIC X
127                       TO CHOICE-CODE
128                       COLUMN + 3.
129
130          01   QTY-PRICE-ERR-SCREEN2.
131                  05   FROM QUANTITY OF ORDER-DATA  PIC Z9
132                       REVERSE-VIDEO HIGHLIGHT
133                       LINE 10   COLUMN 42.
134                  05   FROM PRICE OF ORDER-DATA     PIC ZZ9.99
135                       REVERSE-VIDEO HIGHLIGHT
136                       LINE 10   COLUMN 59.
137
138
139          PROCEDURE DIVISION.
140          A000-VALIDATE-ORDERS.
141              OPEN OUTPUT PROCESSING-FILE.
142              MOVE PRICE-LIMIT TO PRICE-LIMIT-EDIT.
143              MOVE LOW-VALUES TO ORDER-NUMBER OF ORDER-DATA.
144              PERFORM B010-VALIDATE-ONE-LINE
145                  UNTIL LAST-ORDER-LINE.
146              CLOSE PROCESSING-FILE.
147              STOP RUN.
148
149          B010-VALIDATE-ONE-LINE.
150              DISPLAY ORDER-SCREEN.
151              PERFORM C010-GET-ORDER-NUMBER.
152              IF NOT LAST-ORDER-LINE
153                  MOVE SPACES TO ERROR-FLAGS
154                  PERFORM C020-GET-CATALOG-NUMBER
155                  PERFORM C030-GET-SIZE-CODE
156                  PERFORM C040-GET-QUANTITY
157                  PERFORM C050-GET-PRICE
158                  PERFORM C060-VALIDATE-QTY-AND-PRICE
159                  PERFORM C070-GET-ITEM-DESCRIPTION
160                  PERFORM C080-WRITE-PROCESSING-LINE.
161
162          C010-GET-ORDER-NUMBER.
163              ACCEPT SCREEN-ORDER-NUMBER.
164
165          C020-GET-CATALOG-NUMBER.
166              MOVE 'N' TO VALID-CATALOG-NUMBER.
167              PERFORM D010-GET-VALID-CATALOG-NUMBER
168                  UNTIL VALID-CATALOG-NUMBER = 'Y'.
169
170          C030-GET-SIZE-CODE.
171              MOVE 'N' TO VALID-SIZE-CODE.
172              PERFORM D020-GET-VALID-SIZE-CODE
173                  UNTIL VALID-SIZE-CODE = 'Y'.
174
175          C040-GET-QUANTITY.
176              ACCEPT SCREEN-QUANTITY.
177
178          C050-GET-PRICE.
179              MOVE 'N' TO VALID-PRICE.
180              PERFORM E010-GET-VALID-PRICE
181                  UNTIL VALID-PRICE = 'Y'.
182
```

```
183          C060-VALIDATE-QTY-AND-PRICE.
184              MOVE 'N' TO VALID-PRICE-AND-QTY.
185              PERFORM D030-GET-VALID-PRICE-AND-QTY
186                  UNTIL VALID-PRICE-AND-QTY = 'Y'.
187
188          C070-GET-ITEM-DESCRIPTION.
189              ACCEPT SCREEN-DESCRIPTION.
190
191          C080-WRITE-PROCESSING-LINE.
192              MOVE CORRESPONDING ORDER-DATA TO OUTPUT-LINE.
193              WRITE PROCESSING-LINE FROM OUTPUT-LINE
194                      AFTER ADVANCING 2 LINES.
195
196          D010-GET-VALID-CATALOG-NUMBER.
197              ACCEPT SCREEN-CATALOG-NUMBER.
198              IF CATALOG-NUMBER OF ORDER-DATA IS NOT NUMERIC
199                  DISPLAY 'Catalog number contains '          AT 1416
200                          WITH BEEP BLANK LINE
201                  DISPLAY 'a non-numeric character.'           AT 1440
202                  DISPLAY 'Please re-enter the catalog number.' AT 1516
203              ELSE
204                  IF CATALOG-FIRST-DIGIT OF ORDER-DATA = '0' OR '2'
205                      DISPLAY 'First digit of catalog '        AT 1416
206                              WITH BEEP BLANK LINE
207                      DISPLAY 'number is invalid.'             AT 1439
208                      DISPLAY 'Please re-enter the catalog number.'
209                                                              AT 1516
210                  ELSE
211                      DISPLAY SPACE WITH BLANK LINE            AT 1401
212                      DISPLAY SPACE WITH BLANK LINE            AT 1501
213                      MOVE 'Y' TO VALID-CATALOG-NUMBER.
214
215          D020-GET-VALID-SIZE-CODE.
216              ACCEPT SCREEN-SIZE-CODE.
217              IF SIZE-CODE OF ORDER-DATA = 'A' OR 'D' OR 'G' OR 'J'
218                  OR 'K' OR 'L' OR 'S' OR 'T' OR 'U' OR ' '
219                  MOVE 'Y' TO VALID-SIZE-CODE
220                  DISPLAY SPACE WITH BLANK LINE               AT 1401
221                  DISPLAY SPACE WITH BLANK LINE               AT 1501
222              ELSE
223                  DISPLAY 'There is no such size code.'       AT 1416
224                          WITH BEEP BLANK LINE
225                  DISPLAY 'Please re-enter the size code.'    AT 1516.
226              IF VALID-SIZE-CODE = 'Y'
227                  IF (CATALOG-FIRST-DIGIT OF ORDER-DATA =
228                          '1' OR '8' OR '9')  AND
229                      SIZE-CODE OF ORDER-DATA IS NOT EQUAL TO SPACES
230                      DISPLAY 'This item does not take a size code.'
231                              WITH BEEP BLANK LINE            AT 1416
232                      DISPLAY 'Please re-enter the size code.' AT 1516
233                      MOVE 'N' TO VALID-SIZE-CODE
234                  ELSE
235                      DISPLAY SPACE WITH BLANK LINE           AT 1401
236                      DISPLAY SPACE WITH BLANK LINE           AT 1501
237                      MOVE 'Y' TO VALID-SIZE-CODE.
238
```

```
239          D030-GET-VALID-PRICE-AND-QTY.
240              MOVE 'Y' TO VALID-PRICE-AND-QTY.
241              DIVIDE PRICE OF ORDER-DATA BY QUANTITY OF ORDER-DATA
242                      GIVING UNIT-PRICE REMAINDER TEST-REMAINDER
243                  ON SIZE ERROR MOVE 'N' TO VALID-PRICE-AND-QTY.
244              IF TEST-REMAINDER NOT EQUAL TO ZERO
245                  MOVE 'N' TO VALID-PRICE-AND-QTY.
246              IF VALID-PRICE-AND-QTY = 'N'
247                  DISPLAY QTY-PRICE-ERR-SCREEN1
248                  ACCEPT SCREEN-CHOICE-CODE
249                  IF CHOICE-CODE = 'P' OR 'p'
250                      DISPLAY PRICE-ERR-SCREEN
251                      MOVE 'N' TO VALID-PRICE
252                      PERFORM E010-GET-VALID-PRICE
253                          UNTIL VALID-PRICE = 'Y'
254                  ELSE
255                      IF CHOICE-CODE = 'Q' OR 'q'
256                          DISPLAY QTY-ERR-SCREEN
257                          ACCEPT SCREEN-QUANTITY
258                      ELSE
259                          DISPLAY QTY-PRICE-ERR-SCREEN2
260                          ACCEPT SCREEN-QUANTITY
261                          MOVE 'N' TO VALID-PRICE
262                          PERFORM E010-GET-VALID-PRICE
263                              UNTIL VALID-PRICE = 'Y'
264              ELSE
265                  DISPLAY SPACE WITH BLANK LINE            AT 1301
266                  DISPLAY SPACE WITH BLANK LINE            AT 1401.
267
268          E010-GET-VALID-PRICE.
269              ACCEPT SCREEN-PRICE.
270              IF PRICE OF ORDER-DATA IS GREATER THAN PRICE-LIMIT
271                  DISPLAY 'Price must not exceed '  AT 1716
272                          WITH BEEP
273                  DISPLAY PRICE-LIMIT-EDIT           AT 1738
274                  DISPLAY '.'                        AT 1745
275                  DISPLAY 'Please re-enter the price.'
276                                                     AT 1816
277              ELSE
278                  DISPLAY SPACE WITH BLANK LINE      AT 1701
279                  DISPLAY SPACE WITH BLANK LINE      AT 1801
280                  MOVE 'Y' TO VALID-PRICE.
281
282          **************** END OF PROGRAM *****************************
```

FIGURE 12.5 An improved version of the seed catalog program, with enhanced screen handling.

Most of the Procedure Division in Figure 12.5 is the same as before, except that we have rearranged the order of some of the C-level paragraphs to reflect the format of the screen. The only significant difference is in D030-GET-VALID-PRICE-AND-QTY. Rather than using DISPLAY statements to show error messages, we use additional screen definitions. For example, on line 247 we DISPLAY QTY-PRICE-ERR-SCREEN1. This screen, defined on lines 114-128, re-writes the price and quantity on the screen. Notice the use of the FROM clause on lines 115 and 118 to DISPLAY the current values of price and quantity. Just as the TO clause takes the contents of a screen field and moves it to a data item, the FROM clause takes the contents of a data item and moves it to the screen.

We have used another new clause, **BLINK**, to call attention to the two fields that may be in error. The effect of this screen from the user's viewpoint is that the price and quantity values start blinking, while the error message appears under the data portion of the screen.

After the user indicates which of the fields is to be corrected (P, Q, or B), we **DISPLAY** one of three screen definitions—**PRICE-ERR-SCREEN**, **QTY-ERR-SCREEN**, or **QTY-PRICE-ERR-SCREEN2**—to stop the blinking. The field that is correct is **DISPLAY**ed normally, while the field to be corrected is **DISPLAY**ed in a non-blinking, highlighted format. Observe how we can use combinations of blinking, highlighting, reverse video, and color to call the user's attention to particular parts of the screen.

Although the output of this program has a much more professional look and feel to it than does the output from the previous programs, there is still room for improvement. For example, there should probably be a way of rejecting an entire data set rather than requiring that all errors be corrected immediately. We leave this and other possible improvements as an exercise for the student.

12.6 MENU-DRIVEN PROGRAMS

The programs presented in the preceding sections all perform one simple task: edit seven data fields and write a valid output record. Clearly, a clerk using this program would not need much instruction to be able to use the program correctly. One of the advantages of interactive processing, however, is that it can use *menus* to provide guidance to users when the task to be performed is more complex, or when the program is capable of performing several tasks.

Consider, for example, a more complete version of the seed catalog program. In addition to simply accepting order data, we might use a file of products sold by the seed company to be certain that the catalog number in the order actually represents a valid product. (In fact, we will show how this is done in Chapter 15.) Furthermore, besides the data needed for individual lines in an order, we would probably want to enter header data giving the customer's name and address, and trailer data giving the total amount of the order, plus any special shipping or handling charges or sales tax. If we have the customer's name and address available, we might wish to add them to a mailing file used for advertising the company's products. We might also wish to change records on the product file, or correct questionable data that had been stored temporarily on a special handling file for further clarification. Finally, we would need to process the records written as output from the program so that the warehouse gets instructions to fill the order and the accounting department gets data needed for billing or other financial records. In other words, when we extend the seed catalog program to include realistic requirements, we have an order entry system that would need to perform tasks such as the following:

- add, change, or delete records on a product file
- add the names of new customers to a mailing file
- modify data already on the mailing file
- correct questionable data and move it to a valid data file for processing

- produce shipping and accounting files from records on the valid data file
- produce sales and other management reports
- validate order data

In batch systems it is likely that each of these tasks would be performed by a separate program, and, indeed, this might be the case with interactive systems as well. However, it is possible, and in some cases desirable, to perform all these tasks in a single program. If we do so, it is necessary to provide the user with a menu to guide him or her through the steps needed to perform any specific activity.

The following hierarchy chart shows part of a program to perform these functions.

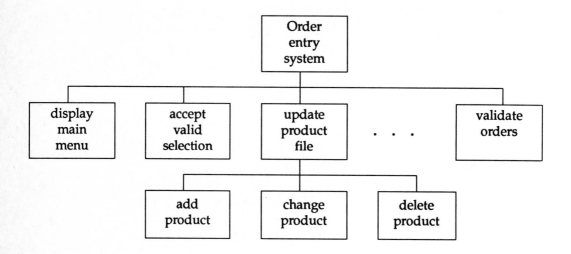

FIGURE 12.6 A partial hierarchy chart for an interactive program for an order entry system.

This basic operation of this system is as follows. When the program begins, the main menu is displayed on the screen. The user is asked to select one of six options from the menu, each of which corresponds to a major task performed by the program. (To save space, not all of these tasks are shown on the hierarchy chart.) The program then executes a sub-section to perform the requested task. If, for example, the user selects task number 6 (validate orders), the program executes code that looks very much like the Procedure Division of the program in Figure 12.5. The only major difference is that when the user elects to terminate the task, control returns to the main menu so that other tasks can be requested.

Depending on the complexity of the task selected, second level menus may be necessary. For example, if the user is updating the product file, different displays are used depending on whether a record is being added, changed, or removed. Figure 12.7 shows what the required program might look like. Since we are only interested in how the menus are used, lower level modules only **DISPLAY** a message showing that the module has been reached instead of performing the complete task. Although the complete program would require the use of several files, this skeleton version uses only **ACCEPT** and **DISPLAY** statements for I/O so the Environment Division is empty and the File Section has been omitted.

```
1        IDENTIFICATION DIVISION.
2        PROGRAM-ID.
3            ORDER-ENTRY.
4        DATE-WRITTEN.
5            MAY 9, 1989.
6
7
8        ENVIRONMENT DIVISION.
9        *        FILE SPECIFICATIONS HAVE BEEN OMITTED TO SIMPLIFY
10       *        THE PROGRAM.
11
12
13       DATA DIVISION.
14
15       WORKING-STORAGE SECTION.
16
17       01  CONTINUE-FLAG              PIC X.
18       01  END-PRODUCT-UPDATE-FLAG    PIC X.
19       01  ID-NUMBER                  PIC X(6).
20       01  MAIN-SELECTION-ERROR       PIC X(26)
21           VALUE 'SELECTION MUST BE 1-6 OR Q'.
22       01  PASS-SYSTEM                        PIC X(6) VALUE 'TESTXX'.
23       01  PASS-USER                          PIC X(6) VALUE LOW-VALUES.
24       01  SELECTION                  PIC X.
25       01  TERMINATE-FLAG             PIC X.
26       01  UPDATE-PRODUCT-SELECTION-ERROR
27                                      PIC X(26)
28           VALUE 'SELECTION MUST BE 1-3 OR Q'.
29       01  VALID-SELECTION-FLAG       PIC X.
30           88  VALID-SELECTION                     VALUE 'Y'.
31
32       SCREEN SECTION.
33       01  MAIN-MENU
34               BACKGROUND-COLOR IS 5
35               FOREGROUND-COLOR IS 7.
36           05  VALUE 'ABC CORPORATION'          BLANK SCREEN HIGHLIGHT
37                                                LINE 02  COLUMN 33.
38           05  VALUE 'ORDER ENTRY SYSTEM'       LINE 04  COLUMN 32.
39           05  VALUE '+--------------------------+' LINE 08  COLUMN 28.
40           05  VALUE '| ORDER ENTRY MAIN MENU   |' LINE 09  COLUMN 28.
41           05  VALUE '+--------------------------+' LINE 10  COLUMN 28.
42           05  VALUE '| 1   UPDATE PRODUCT FILE |' LINE 11  COLUMN 28.
43           05  VALUE '| 2   UPDATE MAILING FILE |' LINE 12  COLUMN 28.
44           05  VALUE '| 3   SPECIAL HANDLING    |' LINE 13  COLUMN 28.
45           05  VALUE '| 4   SHIP ORDERS         |' LINE 14  COLUMN 28.
46           05  VALUE '| 5   PRODUCE REPORTS     |' LINE 15  COLUMN 28.
47           05  VALUE '| 6   VALIDATE ORDERS     |' LINE 16  COLUMN 28.
48           05  VALUE '| Q   QUIT ORDER ENTRY    |' LINE 17  COLUMN 28.
49           05  VALUE '+--------------------------+' LINE 18  COLUMN 28.
50           05  VALUE 'SELECT ONE OPTION:  '       LINE 20  COLUMN 28.
```

```
51          01   UPDATE-PRODUCT-MENU.
52               05   VALUE 'ABC CORPORATION'                BLANK SCREEN HIGHLIGHT
53                                                           LINE 02   COLUMN 33.
54               05   VALUE 'ORDER ENTRY SYSTEM'             LINE 04   COLUMN 32.
55               05   VALUE '+------------------------+' LINE 08   COLUMN 28.
56               05   VALUE '|   UPDATE PRODUCT MENU   |' LINE 09   COLUMN 28.
57               05   VALUE '+------------------------+' LINE 10   COLUMN 28.
58               05   VALUE '| 1   ADD     RECORD      |' LINE 11   COLUMN 28.
59               05   VALUE '| 2   CHANGE RECORD       |' LINE 12   COLUMN 28.
60               05   VALUE '| 3   DELETE RECORD       |' LINE 13   COLUMN 28.
61               05   VALUE '| Q   RETURN TO MAIN MENU |' LINE 14   COLUMN 28.
62               05   VALUE '+------------------------+' LINE 15   COLUMN 28.
63               05   VALUE 'SELECT ONE OPTION:  '        LINE 17   COLUMN 28.
64          01   ID-MENU.
65               05   VALUE 'PLEASE ENTERY YOUR ID NUMBER:  ' BLANK SCREEN.
66               05   SCREEN-ID                            PIC X(6)
67                    PROMPT CHARACTER '.'                 TO ID-NUMBER.
68          01   PASSWORD-MENU.
69               05   VALUE 'PLEASE ENTER YOUR PASSWORD' LINE 02   COLUMN 01.
70               05   VALUE ' (IT WILL NOT BE DISPLAYED):  '.
71               05   SCREEN-PASSWORD                      PIC X(6)
72                    SECURE                               TO PASS-USER.
73
74
75          PROCEDURE DIVISION.
76          A000-ORDER-ENTRY-CONTROL.
77              MOVE 'N' TO TERMINATE-FLAG.
78              DISPLAY ID-MENU.
79              ACCEPT SCREEN-ID.
80              DISPLAY PASSWORD-MENU.
81              ACCEPT SCREEN-PASSWORD.
82              IF PASS-USER = PASS-SYSTEM
83                  PERFORM B010-MAIN-MENU-DRIVER
84                      UNTIL TERMINATE-FLAG = 'Y'
85                  DISPLAY ' '                  WITH BLANK SCREEN
86              ELSE
87                  DISPLAY 'INVALID PASSWORD.  RUN TERMINATED.'
88                                              AT 0301.
89              STOP RUN.
90
91          B010-MAIN-MENU-DRIVER.
92      *        DISPLAY THE MAIN MENU SCREEN
93              DISPLAY MAIN-MENU.
94      *        GET THE SELECTION VARIABLE
95              MOVE 'N' TO VALID-SELECTION-FLAG.
96              PERFORM UNTIL VALID-SELECTION
97                  ACCEPT SELECTION          AT 2048
98                                              WITH REVERSE-VIDEO
99                  IF SELECTION = '1' OR '2' OR '3' OR '4' OR '5' OR '6' OR
100                            'Q' OR 'q' THEN
101                      MOVE 'Y' TO VALID-SELECTION-FLAG
102                  ELSE
103                      DISPLAY MAIN-SELECTION-ERROR
104                                      AT 2228
105                                      WITH BACKGROUND-COLOR 5
106                                          FOREGROUND-COLOR 7
107                  END-IF
108              END-PERFORM.
109      *        EXECUTE THE SELECTED TASK
```

```
110                 EVALUATE SELECTION
111                     WHEN '1'
112                         MOVE 'N' TO END-PRODUCT-UPDATE-FLAG
113                         PERFORM C010-UPDATE-PRODUCT-FILE
114                             UNTIL END-PRODUCT-UPDATE-FLAG = 'Y'
115                     WHEN '2'
116                         PERFORM C020-UPDATE-MAILING-FILE
117                     WHEN '3'
118                         PERFORM C030-SPECIAL-HANDLING
119                     WHEN '4'
120                         PERFORM C040-SHIP-ORDERS
121                     WHEN '5'
122                         PERFORM C050-PRODUCE-REPORTS
123                     WHEN '6'
124                         PERFORM C060-VALIDATE-ORDERS
125                     WHEN OTHER
126                         MOVE 'Y' TO TERMINATE-FLAG
127                 END-EVALUATE.
128
129         C010-UPDATE-PRODUCT-FILE.
130             DISPLAY UPDATE-PRODUCT-MENU.
131             MOVE 'N' TO VALID-SELECTION-FLAG.
132             PERFORM UNTIL VALID-SELECTION
133                 ACCEPT SELECTION          AT 1748
134                                             WITH REVERSE-VIDEO
135                 IF SELECTION = '1' OR '2' OR '3' OR 'Q' OR 'q' THEN
136                     MOVE 'Y' TO VALID-SELECTION-FLAG
137                 ELSE
138                     DISPLAY UPDATE-PRODUCT-SELECTION-ERROR
139                                     AT 1928
140                                         WITH BACKGROUND-COLOR 5
141                                             FOREGROUND-COLOR 7
142                 END-IF
143             END-PERFORM.
144             EVALUATE SELECTION
145                 WHEN '1'
146                     PERFORM D010-ADD-PRODUCT-RECORD
147                 WHEN '2'
148                     PERFORM D020-CHANGE-PRODUCT-RECORD
149                 WHEN '3'
150                     PERFORM D030-DELETE-PRODUCT-RECORD
151                 WHEN OTHER
152                     MOVE 'Y' TO END-PRODUCT-UPDATE-FLAG
153             END-EVALUATE.
154
155         C020-UPDATE-MAILING-FILE.
156             DISPLAY 'UPDATE-MAILING-FILE MODULE REACHED'
157                     WITH BLANK SCREEN AT 0101.
158             DISPLAY 'PRESS RETURN TO CONTINUE' AT 0201.
159             ACCEPT CONTINUE-FLAG.
160
161         C030-SPECIAL-HANDLING.
162             DISPLAY 'SPECIAL-HANDLING MODULE REACHED'
163                     WITH BLANK SCREEN AT 0101.
164             DISPLAY 'PRESS RETURN TO CONTINUE' AT 0201.
165             ACCEPT CONTINUE-FLAG.
166
167         C040-SHIP-ORDERS.
168             DISPLAY 'SHIP-ORDERS MODULE REACHED'
169                     WITH BLANK SCREEN AT 0101.
```

```
170                    DISPLAY 'PRESS RETURN TO CONTINUE' AT 0201.
171                    ACCEPT CONTINUE-FLAG.
172
173               C050-PRODUCE-REPORTS.
174                    DISPLAY 'PRODUCE-REPORTS MODULE REACHED'
175                         WITH BLANK SCREEN AT 0101.
176                    DISPLAY 'PRESS RETURN TO CONTINUE' AT 0201.
177                    ACCEPT CONTINUE-FLAG.
178
179               C060-VALIDATE-ORDERS.
180                    DISPLAY 'VALIDATE-ORDERS MODULE REACHED'
181                         WITH BLANK SCREEN AT 0101.
182                    DISPLAY 'PRESS RETURN TO CONTINUE' AT 0201.
183                    ACCEPT CONTINUE-FLAG.
184
185               D010-ADD-PRODUCT-RECORD.
186                    DISPLAY 'ADD-PRODUCT-RECORD MODULE REACHED'
187                         WITH BLANK SCREEN AT 0101.
188                    DISPLAY 'PRESS RETURN TO CONTINUE' AT 0201.
189                    ACCEPT CONTINUE-FLAG.
190
191               D020-CHANGE-PRODUCT-RECORD.
192                    DISPLAY 'CHANGE-PRODUCT-RECORD MODULE REACHED'
193                         WITH BLANK SCREEN AT 0101.
194                    DISPLAY 'PRESS RETURN TO CONTINUE' AT 0201.
195                    ACCEPT CONTINUE-FLAG.
196
197               D030-DELETE-PRODUCT-RECORD.
198                    DISPLAY 'DELETE-PRODUCT-RECORD MODULE REACHED'
199                         WITH BLANK SCREEN AT 0101.
200                    DISPLAY 'PRESS RETURN TO CONTINUE' AT 0201.
201                    ACCEPT CONTINUE-FLAG.
```

FIGURE 12.7 An interactive program demonstrating the use of menus in the seed catalog order entry system.

The Working-Storage Section contains flags that are used in various parts of the program, a few sample error messages, and variables used to accept a user's identification number and password. We shall discuss the use of these variables as we go through the program.

The bulk of the program's Data Division lies in the Screen Section. We have two main screen definitions, plus two smaller ones used to get an identification number and password from the user. This example indicates the true function of screen definitions. That is, the main definitions define the format and function of two distinctly different screens, not just different messages on the same screen. By defining the format of a screen for menu selection or data entery in the Data Division, we can concentrate on processing data in the Procedure Division without being distracted by the need to format screen text.

The main paragraph of the Procedure Division begins by asking the user to enter an identification number. The purpose of the identification number is to verify that the person using the order entry system is, in fact, authorized to do so. In a complete version of the program there would be a list of valid numbers that we could use to verify the one entered by the user; in this example we will accept any number entered. Notice the **PROMPT** clause on line

67. When we accept **SCREEN-PASSWORD**, a row of dots is displayed on the screen to show the user how many characters should be entered. We can use **PROMPT** with any input field, but in many cases there is no need to do so since **COBOL** usually will supply a prompt of underscore characters automatically. If we wish to override the default prompt character, or wish to supply a prompt where none is provided automatically, the **PROMPT** clause allows us to specify a character to use as the prompt character.

After the user has entered the identification number we **DISPLAY PASSWORD-MENU**, which asks for a password. Passwords provide a double measure of security, since the user must enter both the identification number and a correct password before he or she will be given access to the program. Again, in a real program a list of valid passwords is provided rather than simply checking against a test password as is done here.

Since the purpose of the password is to provide an extra measure of security for the program, we don't want the password to be displayed on the screen where anyone walking past could see it. Therefore, we use the **SECURE** clause. When this clause is used in an input field, the characters typed by the user are not echoed on the screen. Of course, this means that the user can't detect any typing mistakes, but it does provide the security needed in special cases. The phrase **NO-ECHO** may be used instead of **SECURE**, and has exactly the same effect. In the example, once the user has entered a password it is checked against a test password and the program only continues if the two passwords match.

In **B010-MAIN-MENU-DRIVER** we display the main menu on the screen, then allow the user to select an entry from this menu. We use a **PERFORM** loop and a compound **IF** statement to make sure that the selection is a valid one. (The **PERFORM** statement, as well as several other statement in this program, is written in **COBOL-85**. This was done simply to demonstrate the use of **COBOL-85** and the code can easily be converted to older versions of **COBOL** if you wish.) If the selection is not valid, we display an error message and ask the user to make another selection. Notice that we must specify the background and foreground colors when we display the error message on lines 103-106. Since **MAIN-SELECTION-ERROR** is not part of **MAIN-MENU**, it will be displayed in white on black unless we specify other colors.

Once a valid selection code has been entered, it is used to perform one of the function paragraphs, or to set **TERMINATE-FLAG**. Most of the function paragraphs **DISPLAY** a simple message, then return to the calling routine. The function paragraph to update the product file, however, displays a second-level menu using much the same technique as was used to control the main menu. Although these functions modules are simple **DISPLAY** paragraphs in this example, in a real program they would each control an order entry function and would consist of major blocks of code, with still more menus displayed in each subsystem. The menus produced by the program are shown in Figures 12.8 and 12.9.

12.7 CONTROLLING ACCEPT AND DISPLAY FUNCTIONS

To give you maximum flexibility and control over the way in which **ACCEPT** and **DISPLAY** statements work, Microsoft **COBOL** uses a special system called

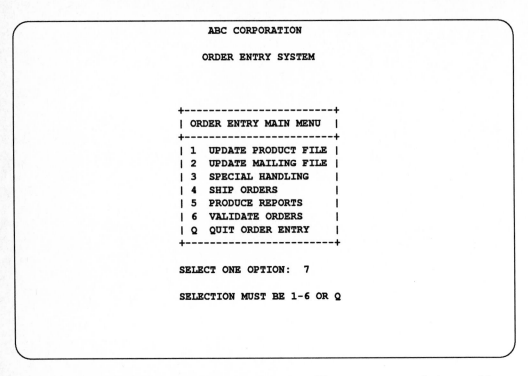

```
                  ABC CORPORATION

                 ORDER ENTRY SYSTEM



         +-----------------------+
         | ORDER ENTRY MAIN MENU  |
         +-----------------------+
         | 1   UPDATE PRODUCT FILE |
         | 2   UPDATE MAILING FILE |
         | 3   SPECIAL HANDLING    |
         | 4   SHIP ORDERS         |
         | 5   PRODUCE REPORTS     |
         | 6   VALIDATE ORDERS     |
         | Q   QUIT ORDER ENTRY    |
         +-----------------------+

         SELECT ONE OPTION:   7

         SELECTION MUST BE 1-6 OR Q
```

FIGURE 12.8 The main menu produced by the order entry program. The error message at the bottom of the screen image was triggered when the user entered an invalid selection.

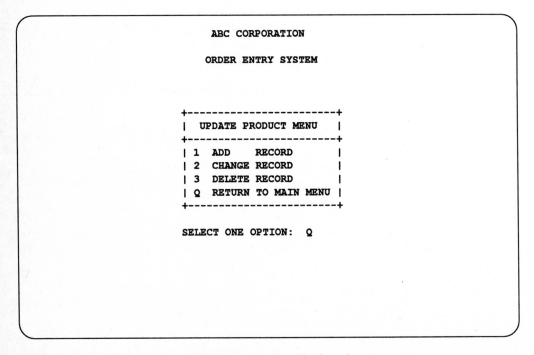

```
                  ABC CORPORATION

                 ORDER ENTRY SYSTEM



         +-----------------------+
         |   UPDATE PRODUCT MENU   |
         +-----------------------+
         | 1   ADD      RECORD     |
         | 2   CHANGE RECORD       |
         | 3   DELETE RECORD       |
         | Q   RETURN TO MAIN MENU |
         +-----------------------+

         SELECT ONE OPTION:   Q
```

FIGURE 12.9 The "update product" subordinate menu produced by the order entry program.

ADIS (`ACCEPT` and `DISPLAY`) to control operation of these statements. For example, if you do not use a `PROMPT` clause on an input field, `COBOL` automatically uses underscore (_) as the prompt character. However, you can modify ADIS to use any character you wish as the default prompt. You can also use ADIS to control things like

- whether or not an `ACCEPT` statement displays the current value of an input field before accepting a new value
- how the program responds if you try to type too many characters into an input field
- what default colors should be used in a Screen Section item for which no color is specified
- the exact text to be used for `ACCEPT`/`DISPLAY` error messages
- the position of `ACCEPT`/`DISPLAY` error messages on the screen.

The ADIS system consists of three parts:

- a data base (ADISCTRL) which defines the default values for the various ADIS functions;
- a program (ADISCF.EXE) which allows you to alter default values in ADISCTRL;
- three program modules in the `COBOL` library (ADIS.OBJ, ADISINIT.OBJ, and ADISKEY.OBJ) which are used during your program's execution to control `ACCEPT` and `DISPLAY` functions.

We will not discuss ADIS in detail since a full discussion of the system is beyond the scope of this book. However, we do wish to summarize the basic operation of ADIS.

If your program uses the Screen Section, or any `ACCEPT` or `DISPLAY` functions except the basic scrolling modes, `COBOL` uses the three library modules listed above to control the operation of screen I/O. When your program runs, these routines use the current values in the ADISCTRL data base to determine how `ACCEPT` and `DISPLAY` should work. This means that the library routines and the data base must be available to your program during execution. You can accomplish this in either of two ways. Perhaps the simplest approach begins by linking ADIS.OBJ, ADISINIT.OBJ, and ADISKEY.OBJ to create ADIS.EXE.* For example, you can execute:

```
LINK ADIS.OBJ+ADISINIT.OBJ+ADISKEY.OBJ,ADIS.EXE;
```

Then, when you execute your program, make certain that the current path includes the directory containing ADIS.EXE and ADISCTRL.

If you prefer to make your program independent of the ADIS run-time library, you need to link the library modules to your program after compilation. For example, if your program is called MYPROG, compile the program as

---

* We assume that you are familiar with the basic function of the LINK program and of paths. If not, Chapter 4 of the *Microsoft COBOL Optimizing Compiler Operating Guide* tells how to use LINK and how to create ADIS.EXE, and several of the introductory chapters in the manual describe the use of paths. Alternatively, refer to any book about the MS-DOS operating system for a discussion of LINK and paths.

described at the start of this book, then link it using a command such as the following:

```
LINK MYPROG+ADIS.OBJ+ADISINIT.OBJ+ADISKEY.OBJ;
```

You should be aware, however, that this approach will increase the size of your object program (MYPROG.EXE in this example), by about 80,000 bytes. Furthermore, you must still use the default ADIS options unless ADISCTRL is available to your program during execution.

As you can see from this brief description, the data base in ADISCTRL plays an important roll in determining how **ACCEPT** and **DISPLAY** statements operate. ADISCTRL actually contains up to 16 different control configurations, each of which defines the status of over two dozen **ACCEPT/DISPLAY** options as well as specifying the text of ADIS error message. You can use the program ADISCF to load a configuration from ADISCTRL, modify any of its options, then save the modified configuration in the data base. You can create completely new configurations, or simply save variations of existing configurations. Finally, ADISCF can be used to select which of your different configurations should be used when you run your **COBOL** programs.

One of the advantages of the ADIS system is that you can change options without recompiling or relinking your program. For example, suppose you want to try various combinations of default screen colors to see which combination looks best. You can run ADISCF to change the defaults, then run your program. If you want to try different defaults, use ADISCF again to change the data base in ADISCTRL, then rerun your program. You can make as many tests as you wish, and at no time do you need to change your program.

A more detailed discussion of how ADISCF works is beyond our present scope, and in most cases the default ADIS configuration is quite satisfactory. If you are interested in a further explanation of ADIS, see the Microsoft COBOL *Operating Guide*.

REVIEW QUESTIONS

1. What is the function of the Screen Section?
2. Can the Screen Section go anywhere in the Data Division?
3. In some of the example programs we used the Tab key to move from one field to the next, and in others we used the Enter key. When do we use one key or the other?
4. Which clauses may only be used in elementary items in the Screen Section?
5. Can a field on the screen be used for both input and output in the same screen definition?
6. What is the function of each of the following:
   - ADISCTRL
   - ADISCF.EXE
   - ADIS.OBJ, ADISINIT.OBJ, ADISKEY.OBJ
7. Why do we use menus in a program?

8. Suppose we have two **01**-level screen definitions, **SCREEN1** and **SCREEN2**. If we specify foreground and background colors for **SCREEN1**, **DISPLAY SCREEN1**, then **DISPLAY SCREEN2**, will the same colors be used for **SCREEN2**?

9. Why can we give a screen definition input field an edited-numeric picture such as $$$$,$$$,$$9.99 even if the data entered will eventually be used in an arithmetic operation?

ANSWERS TO REVIEW QUESTIONS

1. The Screen Section defines the way in which screen images—data, prompts, and text—will appear on the CRT screen.

2. No. The Screen Section must be the last section in the Data Division.

3. If the **ACCEPT** statement refers to a 01-level screen definition then we get all input data with a single **ACCEPT**, and we must use the Tab key to move from field to field within the screen; if we press the Enter key the **ACCEPT** terminates. If we specify an elementary-level field in the **ACCEPT** statement, then we are only accepting a single data value and the Enter key is used to terminate the input. Another **ACCEPT** statement must then be used to get then next field.

4. **BEEP**, **BLANK** (**LINE** or **SCREEN**), **COLUMN**, **LINE**, **PICTURE**, and **VALUE** may only be used in elementary field definitions.

5. Certainly. You might wish to display the current value of a variable, then have the user enter a new value. The code might look something like the following:

```
05   SCREEN-PRICE      PIC $ZZ,ZZ9.99
     REVERSE-VIDEO
     FROM UNIT-PRICE
     TO UNIT-PRICE.
```

Alternatively, you could define the field as follows:

```
05   SCREEN-PRICE      PIC $ZZ,ZZ9.99
     REVERSE-VIDEO
     USING UNIT-PRICE.
```

The **USING** clause is exactly equivalent to having both **FROM** and **TO** clauses for the same field.

6. ADISCTRL is the data base that defines the default values for ADIS screen handling. ADISCF.EXE is the control program that allows you to change values in ADISCTRL. ADIS.OBJ, ADISINIT.OBJ, and ADISKEY.OBJ are library modules which control execution of **ACCEPT** and **DISPLAY** operations at run time.

7. We use menus to guide a user through execution of a program and to indicate the various alternative functions that the program can perform.

8. No. The colors specified for a screen definition apply only to that screen definition and do not affect other screens or **ACCEPT** and **DISPLAY** statements that do not reference a screen definition. If you wish to use the same colors for several screens you might use ADIS to change the

default colors. Most commonly, however, you would simply use FOREGROUND-COLOR and BACKGROUND-COLOR clauses on each of the screen definitions.

9. The picture specified in the screen definition only determines how the data will look on the screen. The picture of the variable used in the TO clause determines how the data will be stored in memory. As long as this picture conforms to the normal requirements for arithmetic fields, we have no problem.

EXERCISES

*1. Revise the program in Figure 12.7 so that it does not use COBOL-85 statements.

2. Modify the program in Figure 12.5 so that the user can reject the entire data set instead of being required to enter all fields correctly. The simplest approach is to require the user either to accept or reject the data after all fields have been entered. However, you may wish to try more sophisticated techniques that would allow a user to reject a data set without entering all fields.

*3. Revise the payroll program in Figure 7.4 to check for overflow in calculating the gross pay (see Figure 8.5). If an overflow error is detected, give the user the option of accepting the data, rejecting all data, or correcting hours-worked or pay-rate fields. Use screen definitions to format your screens, and make the screen processing as professional looking as you can. Do not simply copy the input format shown in Chapter 7.

* Answers to selected exercises will be found in Appendix IV at the end of the book.

CHAPTER 13

UPDATING SEQUENTIAL FILES

13.1 INTRODUCTION

This chapter develops one of the most fundamental techniques of data processing: updating a sequential file. The program for this operation is developed in seven stages, in a sequence that is important in its own right. We concentrate first on the highest level control logic and bring in additional details of the required processing only after we have assured ourselves that the high level logic is correct. This process, which is called *top-down development*, will be described as we go along.

The process of updating a sequential file generally requires that the data involved comes from files that are sorted in a specific sequence. Therefore, until we learn how to sort data in Chapter 18 we will assume that all data comes from files that have somehow been sorted as needed. This requirement means that we will not be doing much with interactive processing in this chapter. We will, however, begin the chapter by discussing some additional techniques for assigning disk files.

13.2 ASSIGNING FILES

Up to now, whenever we have used files in a program we have assigned the **COBOL** file to the corresponding disk file by coding the disk file's name in a **SELECT** statement. For example, the statement

```
SELECT DATA-FILE      ASSIGN TO 'MYFILE.DAT'.
```

assigns the **COBOL** file **DATA-FILE**, a file in your program, to MYFILE.DAT, a physical file on a disk. This assignment technique, called *fixed file assignment*, has the advantage that it is simple to use and puts all the assignment information right in front of you. However, it has the disadvantage that if you want to run the program using a different disk file, say YOURFILE.DAT, you have to recompile the program. In most business applications a **COBOL** program is run using many different disk files, and it is neither practical nor desirable to modify the program for each different run. What we need is a different technique for making file assignments.

Microsoft **COBOL** has two additional techniques for assigning files. The first method, called *external file assignment*, is best suited for use in a batch mode and is identical to the technique used by IBM mainframes. The second method, *dynamic file assignment*, is designed for use in an interactive environment, and allows you to enter the name of the disk file through the keyboard.

13.3 EXTERNAL FILE ASSIGNMENT

The external file assignment technique, so called because the assignment is made outside the **COBOL** program, uses the SET command of MS-DOS to determine which disk file will be used. Using external assignment is a two-step process. First, in your program, write a **SELECT** statement such as the following:

```
SELECT DATA-FILE    ASSIGN TO EXTERNAL INPUT.
```

Then, before you run the program, execute a statement from DOS such as this:

```
SET INPUT=A:MYFILE.DAT
```

The SET statement creates what may be thought of as a character variable belonging to the operating system, **INPUT** in this example, and assigns a character string as its value.* Then, when you run the **COBOL** program, the value of this string is taken to be the name of the disk file. In the example above, the **COBOL** file **DATA-FILE** will be assigned to the disk file A:MYFILE.DAT.

Notice the sequence of steps you need to perform. First, assign the **COBOL** file to an *external file reference*. In the example, **DATA-FILE** is the **COBOL** file and **INPUT** is the external file reference. This external file reference must not be defined in your program; any attempt to do so will cause an error. Second, before you run your program use the MS-DOS SET statement to create an MS-DOS variable whose name is the same as the name of the external file reference in your program. The value that you assign to this MS-DOS variable then becomes the name of the disk file used by your program. If you wish to change the disk file, simply execute another SET statement. You do not need to make any changes to your program.

IBM uses a similar technique to assign disk files to **COBOL** files in its mainframe version of **COBOL**, although of course the statement used in the mainframe operating system is different from that used in MS-DOS. However, IBM does not use the word **EXTERNAL** in its **SELECT** statement. If you wish, you may write the **SELECT** statement in Microsoft **COBOL** without using **EXTERNAL**, providing you use the external assignment option in COBOL.DIR. (See Section 10.9 if you do not recall the function of COBOL.DIR.) The external assignment option is selected by adding ASSIGN"EXTERNAL" to your COBOL.DIR file.

---

* This type of variable is called an *environment* variable.

Some older version of IBM COBOL use prefixes as part of the external file reference. For example, the SELECT statement shown above might be written as

```
SELECT DATA-FILE     ASSIGN TO UT-S-INPUT.
```

To allow compatibility with this format, the Microsoft compiler ignores everything before the right-most hyphen. Thus, the example above would be exactly equivalent to the example at the start of this section.

13.4 DYNAMIC FILE ASSIGNMENT

One of the advantages of using an interactive program is that you can provide the names of disk files to the program while the program is running. For example, consider the program in Figure 13.1. This is a slightly simplified version of the program that was used to provide line numbers for all program listings in this book. After programs were executed to make certain they worked properly, the source code files were run through NUMBER-TEXT to produce listings with line numbers.

```
1        IDENTIFICATION DIVISICN.
2        PROGRAM-ID.
3            NUMBER-TEXT.
4        AUTHOR.
5            D. GOLDEN.
6        DATE-WRITTEN.
7            MAY 28, 1989.
8
9        ENVIRONMENT DIVISION.
10       INPUT-OUTPUT SECTION.
11       FILE-CONTROL.
12           SELECT TEXT-FILE              ASSIGN TO TEXTIN.
13           SELECT NUMBERED-FILE          ASSIGN TO TEXTOUT.
14
15       DATA DIVISION.
16       FILE SECTION.
17       FD   TEXT-FILE
18            LABEL RECORDS STANDARD.
19       01   TEXT-RECORD.
20            05   SOURCE-TEXT              PIC X(72).
21            05   FILLER                   PIC X(8).
22
23       FD   NUMBERED-FILE
24            LABEL RECORDS STANDARD.
25       01   NUMBERED-RECORD              PIC X(77).
26
27       WORKING-STORAGE SECTION.
28       01   TEXTIN                       PIC X(25).
29       01   TEXTOUT                      PIC X(25).
30
31       01   WORK-RECORD.
32            05   LINE-NUMBER              PIC ZZ9BB.
33            05   OUTPUT-TEXT              PIC X(72).
34
```

```
35          01  LINE-COUNT                      PIC 9(5) COMP VALUE 0.
36
37          01  MORE-LINES-REMAIN-FLAG          PIC X VALUE 'Y'.
38              88  NO-MORE-LINES-REMAIN            VALUE 'N'.
39
40
41          PROCEDURE DIVISION.
42          A000-NUMBER-LINES.
43              DISPLAY 'Enter name of source code file:  '
44                  WITH NO ADVANCING.
45              ACCEPT TEXTIN.
46              DISPLAY 'Enter name of numbered file:  '
47                  WITH NO ADVANCING.
48              ACCEPT TEXTOUT.
49              OPEN INPUT TEXT-FILE
50                  OUTPUT NUMBERED-FILE.
51              READ TEXT-FILE
52                  AT END MOVE 'N' TO MORE-LINES-REMAIN-FLAG.
53              PERFORM B010-NUMBER-A-LINE
54                  UNTIL NO-MORE-LINES-REMAIN.
55              CLOSE TEXT-FILE
56                  NUMBERED-FILE.
57              STOP RUN.
58
59          B010-NUMBER-A-LINE.
60              ADD 1 TO LINE-COUNT.
61              MOVE LINE-COUNT TO LINE-NUMBER.
62              MOVE SOURCE-TEXT TO OUTPUT-TEXT.
63              WRITE NUMBERED-RECORD FROM WORK-RECORD.
64              READ TEXT-FILE
65                  AT END MOVE 'N' TO MORE-LINES-REMAIN-FLAG.
```

FIGURE 13.1 An example of dynamic file assignment.

The basic logic of this program is very simple. The input file contains the source code of a COBOL program, while the output file will contain the same lines of text prefixed by line numbers. The program files TEXT-FILE and NUMBERED-FILE are assigned to file identifiers called TEXTIN and TEXTOUT, respectively. However, rather than representing actual file names or operating system variables, TEXTIN and TEXTOUT are variables defined in Working-Storage (lines 28-29). In the Procedure Division the program begins by asking the user to enter the names of the two disk files, then accepts these names into TEXTIN and TEXTOUT. Figure 13.2 shows a typical screen image for the program execution. The file produced as "cobnbr.nbr" is the one shown in Figure 13.1.

Although we have declared TEXTIN and TEXTOUT in Working-Storage as PIC X(25) variables it is not necessary to do so. If you do not declare the file identifiers, COBOL assumes a definition of PIC X(65); this field length is sufficient to contain a complete path, including subdirectories.* This method of assigning files dynamically as the program executes is the default assignment mode for Microsoft COBOL, so you don't really need to do anything to COBOL.DIR. However, if you wish to emphasize that you are using dynamic

---

* If you aren't familiar with subdirectories don't worry about it; you probably aren't using them.

```
C>cobnbr.exe
Enter name of source code file:   cobnbr.cbl
Enter name of numbered file:   cobnbr.nbr
```

FIGURE 13.2   Typical execution of the program shown in Figure 13.1.

assignment for documentation, add the phrase ASSIGN"DYNAMIC" to your COBOL.DIR file.

The choice between the three techniques for file assignment—fixed file assignment, external file assignment, and dynamic file assignment—depends on the application. Fixed file assignment is useful if you are *always* going to use the same file(s) when you run the program. External file assignment is best if you are trying to maintain mainframe compatibility, or if the program will be run as part of an MS-DOS batch job where you want to be able to use different files but don't want to have to be present during program execution. Finally, dynamic assignment is best suited to interactive execution where you want to be able to specify files while the program executes.

We should point out that it is not necessary to use only one technique in a program. For example, suppose you have the following **SELECT** statements in a program:

```
SELECT FILE-A        ASSIGN TO 'STANDARD.DAT'.
SELECT FILE-B        ASSIGN TO EXTERNAL MAINFILE.
SELECT FILE-C        ASSIGN TO FILE-IDENT.
```

FILE-A will be assigned using fixed assignment; **FILE-B** will be assigned using external assignment, requiring a SET statement to give a value to **MAINFILE**; and **FILE-C** will be assigned using dynamic assignment, with the program assigning a value to **FILE-IDENT** during execution.

13.5   FILE UPDATING

Now that we know how to assign files, we can discuss how to use file updating to modify files. *File updating* refers to any situation in which we have a master file of information about a group of related people or objects that must periodically be modified as a result of changes in the status of the people or things that are described by the file. There are literally thousands of different kinds of file updating applications. For concreteness, we shall talk about one of the most common, that of inventory control. In this example, we assume that some company maintains a record for each item in its warehouse. Each record, at an absolute minimum, must contain some kind of identification of the item, such as a stock number or part number, and a quantity that says how many of that item are in the warehouse. In fact, there would be a good deal of additional information, some of which we shall sketch later after the basic processing logic is clear. For our initial purposes we shall call these two elements of information about each stock item the *key* and the *quantity*.

The master file, consisting of a record for each item in the inventory, is assumed to be in ascending sequence on the keys of the items. That is, the first record in the file is the one that has the lowest key in the entire file, in terms of the machine's collating sequence (see Section 5.8). The second record is the one having the next higher key, and so on. This sequential nature of the file organization is fundamental to the processing logic that we shall develop.

Besides this master file we have a *transaction file* that gives information about changes in the status of inventory items. The most common changes are *receipts* of new stock from suppliers and *shipments* of stock to customers. It is also necessary, however, to be able to enter *adjustments* to any of the information in the master file. An example would be when a physical inventory count shows that the actual quantity on hand is different from that shown in the master file, perhaps because of various kinds of errors in the past or because of some kind of fraud. It is also necessary to be able to handle *additions* to the master file, when the company begins to stock new items, and *deletions*, when it drops them from inventory altogether.

The master and transaction files are the two input files to the program. The most important output file is an updated version of the master, which reflects all the changes dictated by the transaction file. There is also a much smaller file listing all of the deletions of items from the inventory, which can be combined with a listing of various kinds of errors. In the final version of the program at the end of this chapter, we shall produce a file of order recommendations for items for which the stock is getting low. The overall relationships of these five files is shown in Figure 13.3. The dotted line connecting the new master to the old master is based on the fact that this kind of program is run periodically, perhaps every week. Each time the program is run, what we are calling the old master is the file that was called the new master the previous time the program was run.

There is more to the story, in terms of the processing that is required and the kinds of errors that must be detected. We shall postpone the discussion of these matters, however, until we have worked out the logic of a program that will handle this much.

13.6 A SIMPLE MERGE PROGRAM

We begin with an operation that is the simplest one possible, while still related to the one that we eventually want to produce. We begin with two files named **IN-FILE-1** and **IN-FILE-2**, both in ascending sequence on the keys in their records. The operation of merging consists of producing one output file, here called **OUT-FILE**, that is also in ascending sequence on the keys of its records. A generalized merge permits either file to have records with the same key and permits *matches*, that is, a condition where a record in one file has the same key as a record in the other file. In the file update program these duplicate keys and matched keys have special significance that must be taken into consideration. In a merge, however, we take no account of such situations and simply produce an output file that is in ascending sequence on the keys of its records.

You will notice in the following material that we show no design specifications. Hierarchy charts and pseudocode specifications were written in the development of all of the programs. However, since the emphasis in the programs is specifically on the logic of the programs, there is remarkably little difference between the pseudocode and the programs. This is hardly surpris-

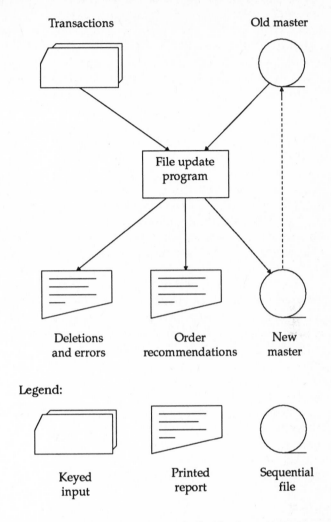

Transactions   Old master

File update
program

Deletions   Order   New
and errors   recommendations   master

Legend:

Keyed   Printed   Sequential
input   report   file

FIGURE 13.3 Run diagram of a file updating application that is used in the illustrative programs

ing because the function of the pseudocode is precisely to encourage a close
focus on the program logic rather than on the details of processing. All this
being true, and since space in a textbook is at a premium, is seems best to omit
the pseudocode. We cannot emphasize too strongly, however, that while the
pseudocode may not be needed as documentation *after* the program has been
written, it is a vital part of the *design* process.

A program for the merge process is shown in Figure 13.4. After reading
one record from each input file we enter a PERFORM...UNTIL loop that is
repeated until both keys are equal to HIGH-VALUES.* HIGH-VALUES is moved to
the keys by the AT END phrase of the READ statements. The logic of selecting a
record from either IN-FILE-1 or IN-FILE-2 is based on a comparison of the

* HIGH-VALUES is a figurative constant; in its place the compiler supplies the largest
data value in the computer's collating sequence. LOW-VALUES, in like manner, represents the smallest values in the computer's collating sequence.

keys of the two records. If **KEY-1**, the key of the record from **IN-FILE-1**, is less than **KEY-2**, the key of the record from **IN-FILE-2**, then we write the record from **IN-FILE-1** to the output file and read another record from **IN-FILE-1**. If **KEY-1** is not less than **KEY-2**, that is, if they are equal or if **KEY-1** is greater, then we write the record from **IN-FILE-2** to the output file and read another record from **IN-FILE-2**. Assuming only that both input files are in ascending sequence, this logic guarantees that the records on the output file will also be in ascending sequence.

The **ASSIGN** clauses in lines 11-13 assign the files to **INFILE1**, **INFILE2**, and **OUTFILE**. Unless stated otherwise in this chapter we will assume that COBOL.DIR has specified ASSIGN"EXTERNAL", and that the names in **AS-SIGN** clauses are the names of external identifiers. We do not want to use internal assignment because the kinds of programs we will be looking at for the remainder of the chapter typically are used with many different files. We could use dynamic assignment, but the code needed to get file names simply distracts from the main object of the program. Therefore, we default to external assignment and assume that disk file names are assigned by SET statements.

The only other aspect of the program that is perhaps not entirely familiar is the use of the **READ...INTO** option. The problem is that we want to have access to the key of a record after we have reached the end of the file. In some versions of **COBOL** the record area is not available after the end of file is reached. Therefore, we define a record in the File Section and use the **READ...INTO** to get the information into the Working-Storage Section record area where all processing is done on it.

In Microsoft **COBOL** the problem is not quite so serious. When the end of file is reached an empty record is "read" into the record area, destroying any previous data. However, if the **AT END** clause moves data into the record area, that data remains in the record and can be used by the program. None the less, we still prefer to use the File Section only for I/O, and do all the program's work in the Working-Storage Section.

```
1       IDENTIFICATION DIVISION.
2       PROGRAM-ID.
3           MERGE1.
4       DATE-WRITTEN.
5           JUNE 7, 1989.
6       *      SIMPLE MERGE
7
8       ENVIRONMENT DIVISION.
9       INPUT-OUTPUT SECTION.
10      FILE-CONTROL.
11          SELECT IN-FILE-1              ASSIGN TO INFILE1.
12          SELECT IN-FILE-2              ASSIGN TO INFILE2.
13          SELECT OUT-FILE               ASSIGN TO OUTFILE.
14
15      DATA DIVISION.
16      FILE SECTION.
17
```

```
18          FD   IN-FILE-1
19               LABEL RECORDS ARE STANDARD.
20          01   IN-RECORD-1-BUFFER            PIC X(80).
21
22          FD   IN-FILE-2
23               LABEL RECORDS ARE STANDARD.
24          01   IN-RECORD-2-BUFFER            PIC X(80).
25          FD   OUT-FILE
26               LABEL RECORDS ARE STANDARD.
27          01   OUT-RECORD.
28               05   OUT-KEY                  PIC X(5).
29               05   REST-OF-RECORD           PIC X(75).
30
31          WORKING-STORAGE SECTION.
32
33          01   IN-RECORD-1.
34               05   KEY-1                    PIC X(5).
35               05   REST-OF-RECORD-1         PIC X(75).
36
37          01   IN-RECORD-2.
38               05   KEY-2                    PIC X(5).
39               05   REST-OF-RECORD-2         PIC X(75).
40
41
42          PROCEDURE DIVISION.
43          A000-MERGE-TWO-FILES.
44               OPEN INPUT IN-FILE-1
45                          IN-FILE-2
46                  OUTPUT OUT-FILE.
47               PERFORM B020-READ-1.
48               PERFORM B030-READ-2.
49               PERFORM B010-MERGE-LOGIC
50                  UNTIL KEY-1 = HIGH-VALUES  AND  KEY-2 = HIGH-VALUES.
51               CLOSE IN-FILE-1
52                     IN-FILE-2
53                        OUT-FILE.
54               STOP RUN.
55
56          B010-MERGE-LOGIC.
57               IF KEY-1 IS LESS THAN KEY-2
58                   WRITE OUT-RECORD FROM IN-RECORD-1
59                   PERFORM B020-READ-1
60               ELSE
61                   WRITE OUT-RECORD FROM IN-RECORD-2
62                   PERFORM B030-READ-2.
63
64          B020-READ-1.
65               READ IN-FILE-1 INTO IN-RECORD-1
66                   AT END MOVE HIGH-VALUES TO KEY-1.
67
68          B030-READ-2.
69               READ IN-FILE-2 INTO IN-RECORD-2
70                   AT END MOVE HIGH-VALUES TO KEY-2.
71
72      ********************* END OF PROGRAM *************************
```

FIGURE 13.4   A program to merge two files.

Here are two sample input files and the resulting output file produced by the execution of this program. Since we are interested primarily in the keys, the main body of the records has been reduced to the letter **A** for **IN-FILE-1** and to the letter **B** for **IN-FILE-2**.

File 1	File 2	Merged File
00001A	00002B	00001A
00003A	00004B	00002B
00007A	00005B	00003A
00010A	00005B	00004B
00010A	00007B	00005B
00012A	00012B	00005B
00015A	00015B	00007B
	00015B	00007A
	00020B	00010A
		00010A
		00012B
		00012A
		00015B
		00015B
		00015A
		00020B

There is no need to try to demonstrate that this program works for all the kinds of special cases that one can think of, but here is a sample showing that the program correctly handles a one-record file and that it operates correctly no matter which file runs out first.

File 1	File 2	Merged File
00019C	00001D	00001D
	00008D	00008D
	00016D	00016D
	00017D	00017D
		00019C

13.7 THE MERGE PROGRAM WITH SEQUENCE CHECKING

Any program written to process files that are supposed to be in ascending sequence will rapidly get into deep trouble if the files are, in fact, *not* in sequence. It is therefore advisable to check the sequence of the incoming records, especially since doing so is quite simple. A modified program is shown in Figure 13.5. The major changes are the introduction of three new items at the end of the Working-Storage Section and changes in the paragraphs named **B020-READ-1** and **B030-READ-2**. Since we are always going to be comparing a record with a previous record, we must have somewhere to save the keys of the previous records, for both files. To prevent the possibility of a false error indication on the very first record of each file, we initialize both of these *save items* to **LOW-VALUES**. A sequence error flag is used to signal the mainline logic if an error occurs. In the mainline paragraph the **UNTIL** phrase of the **PERFORM** is modified to make the loop stop if a sequence error is detected.

```
1           IDENTIFICATION DIVISION.
2           PROGRAM-ID.
3               MERGE2.
4           DATE-WRITTEN.
5               JUNE 7, 1989.
6         *          MERGE WITH SEQUENCE CHECKING
7
8           ENVIRONMENT DIVISION.
9           INPUT-OUTPUT SECTION.
10          FILE-CONTROL.
11              SELECT IN-FILE-1               ASSIGN TO INFILE1.
12              SELECT IN-FILE-2               ASSIGN TO INFILE2.
13              SELECT OUT-FILE               ASSIGN TO OUTFILE.
14
15          DATA DIVISION.
16          FILE SECTION.
17
18          FD  IN-FILE-1
19              LABEL RECORDS ARE STANDARD.
20          01  IN-RECORD-1-BUFFER            PIC X(80).
21
22          FD  IN-FILE-2
23              LABEL RECORDS ARE STANDARD.
24          01  IN-RECORD-2-BUFFER            PIC X(80).
25          FD  OUT-FILE
26              LABEL RECORDS ARE STANDARD.
27          01  OUT-RECORD.
28              05  OUT-KEY                    PIC X(5).
29              05  REST-OF-RECORD            PIC X(75).
30
31          WORKING-STORAGE SECTION.
32
33          01  IN-RECORD-1.
34              05  KEY-1                      PIC X(5).
35              05  REST-OF-RECORD-1          PIC X(75).
36
37          01  IN-RECORD-2.
38              05  KEY-2                      PIC X(5).
39              05  REST-OF-RECORD-2          PIC X(75).
40
41          01  PREVIOUS-KEY-1                PIC X(5) VALUE LOW-VALUES.
42          01  PREVIOUS-KEY-2                PIC X(5) VALUE LOW-VALUES.
43
44          01  SEQUENCE-ERROR-FLAG          PIC X    VALUE 'N'.
45              88  SEQUENCE-ERROR                    VALUE 'Y'.
46
47
48          PROCEDURE DIVISION.
49          A000-MERGE-TWO-FILES.
50              OPEN INPUT IN-FILE-1
51                         IN-FILE-2
52                   OUTPUT OUT-FILE.
53              PERFORM B020-READ-1.
54              PERFORM B030-READ-2.
55              PERFORM B010-MERGE-LOGIC
56                  UNTIL (KEY-1 = HIGH-VALUES  AND  KEY-2 = HIGH-VALUES)
57                        OR SEQUENCE-ERROR.
58              IF SEQUENCE-ERROR
59                  DISPLAY 'SEQUENCE ERROR - JOB ABORTED'.
```

```
60                  CLOSE IN-FILE-1
61                        IN-FILE-2
62                        OUT-FILE.
63                  STOP RUN.
64
65             B010-MERGE-LOGIC.
66                  IF KEY-1 IS LESS THAN KEY-2
67                        WRITE OUT-RECORD FROM IN-RECORD-1
68                        PERFORM B020-READ-1
69                  ELSE
70                        WRITE OUT-RECORD FROM IN-RECORD-2
71                        PERFORM B030-READ-2.
72
73             B020-READ-1.
74                  READ IN-FILE-1 INTO IN-RECORD-1
75                        AT END MOVE HIGH-VALUES TO KEY-1.
76                  IF KEY-1 IS LESS THAN PREVIOUS-KEY-1
77                        MOVE 'Y' TO SEQUENCE-ERROR-FLAG
78                  ELSE
79                        MOVE KEY-1 TO PREVIOUS-KEY-1.
80
81             B030-READ-2.
82                  READ IN-FILE-2 INTO IN-RECORD-2
83                        AT END MOVE HIGH-VALUES TO KEY-2.
84                  IF KEY-2 IS LESS THAN PREVIOUS-KEY-2
85                        MOVE 'Y' TO SEQUENCE-ERROR-FLAG
86                  ELSE
87                        MOVE KEY-2 TO PREVIOUS-KEY-2.
88
89             ********************** END OF PROGRAM *************************
```

FIGURE 13.5 A program to merge two files and stop with an error message if a sequence error is detected.

This program is written on the assumption that if any sequence error is found, the situation is unrecoverable and the job should be stopped. It is hardly acceptable, however, to stop a job in midstream and give no warning that processing was not completed. The approach to this problem taken here is to use the DISPLAY statement to print a notification of the situation, which is acceptable for this simple example. Normally, however, this is *not* a satisfactory way of dealing with the problem. In a more complete program we would write an error message, either on an output file or on the screen, not only telling what had happened but giving the user enough information to be able to track down the cause of the error. In fact, we might not even want to stop the program after detecting a single sequence error. For example, if the input files were prepared by clerks keying the data into a terminal, errors are not unlikely and, if they are not too damaging, we might wish to continue processing. We would generally keep count of the number of errors and give up only if that number exceeded some reasonable maximum. (This approach is shown later in this chapter.) On the other hand, if both input files were the output of computer programs such that sequence errors ought to be virtually impossible, then we might indeed stop after detecting one error, since such an error would be indicative of some kind of very serious processing problem.

13.8 THE SIMPLEST POSSIBLE UPDATE LOGIC

Recall that our strategy in developing a complete update program is to concentrate first on the top-level logic and to worry about the details of processing later. As we begin, we shall also call on a tactic we have used before, that of starting with a simpler problem.

To be specific, we shall simplify the program by ignoring additions and deletions. Any transaction that matches a master is assumed to contain information to be used in updating the master information. The second simplification is that we shall not do the updating. When a match is discovered, we invoke a paragraph that contains nothing but a DISPLAY statement, which will prove that we reached it and will show the keys of the records. The final simplification—a major one—is to ignore the possibility of errors in the files.

The basic logic of this most elementary version has a close resemblance to the logic of the simple merge, but with important differences. Similarities exist in that whenever the key of the master record is less than the key of the transaction record, we write the old master to the new master (output) file and read another old master record. Two kinds of differences can be noted. First, since we are assuming no errors, it can never happen that the transaction key is less than the old master key; this could occur only because of an unmatched transaction, which is an error, or because of an addition record, which we are not considering here. Second, when the old master and the transaction have equal keys, we carry out the updating operation and read another transaction, but *we do not write anything*. It is entirely permissible to have a number of transactions for the same master record, the transactions to be applied in sequence. For instance, there may have been several receipts of stock from suppliers and many shipments of stock to customers since the last updating of the file. As long as transactions come in having the same key as the old master, we simply continue to update that one old master record. Eventually, we get a transaction with a higher key, which will force the writing of the old master record.

13.9 TOP-DOWN PROGRAM DEVELOPMENT AND PROGRAM STUBS

The program is shown in Figure 13.6. With the logic clearly understood, and drawing on the similarity of the merge program, there is almost nothing to explain except one matter of terminology. The paragraph that is named B040-UPDATE-MASTER, which does not do any processing but simply signals that it was reached, is called a *stub*. Stubs are used during program development by the top-down approach while we are concentrating on the top-level logic. During this stage all we really want to know is that the program sections represented by the stubs have been reached.

This method of program development is called *top-down development*, since it concentrates first on the high-level logic and postpones the details until later. The approach is followed deliberately, as a matter of policy. The theory is that the top-level logic is the most crucial and the most likely to be wrong; therefore, it should receive the most testing. Writing the first version of the program with almost total concentration on the top logic and almost no concentration on the details of processing has this result.

```
1            IDENTIFICATION DIVISION.
2            PROGRAM-ID.
3               UPDATE1.
4            DATE-WRITTEN.
5               JUNE 7, 1989.
6
7            ENVIRONMENT DIVISION.
8            INPUT-OUTPUT SECTION.
9            FILE-CONTROL.
10               SELECT TRANSACTION-FILE        ASSIGN TO TRANS.
11               SELECT OLD-MASTER-FILE         ASSIGN TO OLDMAST.
12               SELECT NEW-MASTER-FILE         ASSIGN TO NEWMAST.
13
14           DATA DIVISION.
15
16           FILE SECTION.
17
18           FD  TRANSACTION-FILE
19               LABEL RECORDS ARE STANDARD.
20           01  TRANSACTION-BUFFER            PIC X(80).
21
22           FD  OLD-MASTER-FILE
23               LABEL RECORDS ARE STANDARD.
24           01  OLD-MASTER-BUFFER            PIC X(80).
25
26           FD  NEW-MASTER-FILE
27               LABEL RECORDS ARE STANDARD.
28           01  NEW-MASTER.
29               05  NM-KEY                   PIC X(5).
30               05  NM-QUANTITY              PIC 9(5).
31               05  FILLER                   PIC X(70).
32
33           WORKING-STORAGE SECTION.
34
35           01  OLD-MASTER.
36               05  OM-KEY                   PIC X(5).
37               05  OM-QUANTITY              PIC 9(5).
38               05  FILLER                   PIC X(70).
39
40           01  TRANSACTION.
41               05  TR-KEY                   PIC X(5).
42               05  TR-QUANTITY              PIC 9(5).
43               05  FILLER                   PIC X(70).
44
45
46           PROCEDURE DIVISION.
47           A000-UPDATE-FILE.
48               OPEN INPUT TRANSACTION-FILE
49                          OLD-MASTER-FILE
50                    OUTPUT NEW-MASTER-FILE.
51               PERFORM B020-READ-TRANSACTION.
52               PERFORM B030-READ-MASTER.
53               PERFORM B010-UPDATE-LOGIC
54                   UNTIL OM-KEY = HIGH-VALUES  AND  TR-KEY = HIGH-VALUES.
55               CLOSE TRANSACTION-FILE
56                     OLD-MASTER-FILE
57                     NEW-MASTER-FILE.
58               STOP RUN.
59
```

```
60              B010-UPDATE-LOGIC.
61                  IF OM-KEY IS LESS THAN TR-KEY
62                      WRITE NEW-MASTER FROM OLD-MASTER
63                      PERFORM B030-READ-MASTER
64                  ELSE
65                      PERFORM B040-UPDATE-MASTER
66                      PERFORM B020-READ-TRANSACTION.
67
68              B020-READ-TRANSACTION.
69                  READ TRANSACTION-FILE INTO TRANSACTION
70                      AT END MOVE HIGH-VALUES TO TR-KEY.
71
72              B030-READ-MASTER.
73                  READ OLD-MASTER-FILE INTO OLD-MASTER
74                      AT END MOVE HIGH-VALUES TO OM-KEY.
75
76              B040-UPDATE-MASTER.
77                  DISPLAY ' OM ', OM-KEY, ' TR ', TR-KEY.
78
79              ******************* END OF PROGRAM ***************************
```

FIGURE 13.6 A program for the simplest possible file update.

The alternative approach, called bottom-up development, would have us first write the program sections that do the detailed processing. To test them independently of the complete program, we would have to write small programs called *drivers*. The first testing of the top-level logic would not be possible until all of the lower-level program sections had been developed. While bottom-up development is not used to any great extent, it is occasionally productive to combine top-down and bottom-up development. That is, although the major emphasis is on top-down development, critical bottom level modules may be developed concurrently to be sure they will work. However, we shall generally use only top-down development.

13.10 THE OUTPUT OF THE PROGRAM

This program was run with small sample files, shown here together with the output produced as a result of the DISPLAY statement and the new master file.

Old Master		Transaction		Displayed Output				New Master	
Key	Qty	Key	Qty					Key	Qty
00002	00111	00008	00050	OM	00008	TR	00008	00002	00111
00008	00123	00021	00100	OM	00021	TR	00021	00008	00123
00011	00200	00024	01000	OM	00024	TR	00024	00011	00200
00021	00210	00037	12300	OM	00037	TR	00037	00021	00210
00024	00099	00051	00000	OM	00051	TR	00051	00024	00099
00036	01234							00036	01234
00037	12345							00037	12345
00051	54321							00051	54321
00059	43210							00059	43210
00061	32109							00061	32109

We see that the paragraph named **B040-UPDATE-MASTER** was reached for each of the transactions, since each transaction matches a master. We also see that the new master is an exact copy of the old master; this is as it should be because we have not yet provided for additions, deletions, or actual updating.

13.11 PROCESSING ADDITIONS AND DELETIONS

Now we consider the two important transaction types of additions and deletions. An addition, we recall, is a record describing some inventory item not previously stocked by the company. An addition record comes in from the transaction file and is to be inserted in the proper place in the new master. Such a transaction should, of course, not match any record in the old master; if it does, either someone was unaware of the existence of that stock number or perhaps the stock number was entered incorrectly. In this version of the program, however, we are still ignoring the possibility of errors.

The other new transaction deals with the deletion process, in which a record in the old master is not to be written to the new master, since the company is no longer stocking that inventory item. A deletion transaction obviously *should* match an old master record, but again we are ignoring the possibility of error. When a deletion match occurs, we are required simply to write the deleted old master record onto a deletion report and carry on.

The program to implement these new features is shown in Figure 13.7. We observe that the record description for the transaction now includes a field to identify which of five different types of transactions is being processed, and that there are level **88** entries associated with each transaction code to make the Procedure Division logic easier to read. We assume that the records for any one transaction key are in sequence on the basis of transaction code. This guarantees, for instance, that receipts are processed before shipments; if this were not true, the processing of shipments first could give a false indication of an out-of-stock condition. Arranging a file so that it is in sequence on two different fields this way is a normal part of sorting operations, one approach to which is considered in Chapter 18.

```
1      IDENTIFICATION DIVISION.
2      PROGRAM-ID.
3          UPDATE2.
4      DATE-WRITTEN.
5          JUNE 7, 1989.
6
7      ENVIRONMENT DIVISION.
8      INPUT-OUTPUT SECTION.
9      FILE-CONTROL.
10         SELECT TRANSACTION-FILE        ASSIGN TO TRANS.
11         SELECT OLD-MASTER-FILE         ASSIGN TO OLDMAST.
12         SELECT NEW-MASTER-FILE         ASSIGN TO NEWMAST.
13         SELECT DELETION-FILE           ASSIGN TO DELETION.
14
15     DATA DIVISION.
16
17     FILE SECTION.
18
```

```
19        FD   TRANSACTION-FILE
20             LABEL RECORDS ARE STANDARD.
21        01   TRANSACTION-BUFFER                    PIC X(80).
22
23        FD   OLD-MASTER-FILE
24             LABEL RECORDS ARE STANDARD.
25        01   OLD-MASTER-BUFFER                     PIC X(80).
26
27        FD   NEW-MASTER-FILE
28             LABEL RECORDS ARE STANDARD.
29        01   NEW-MASTER.
30             05  NM-KEY                            PIC X(5).
31             05  NM-QUANTITY                       PIC 9(5).
32             05  FILLER                            PIC X(70).
33
34        FD   DELETION-FILE
35             LABEL RECORDS ARE STANDARD.
36        01   DELETION-REPORT.
37             05  CARRIAGE-CONTROL                  PIC X.
38             05  DELETION-LINE                     PIC X(132).
39
40     WORKING-STORAGE SECTION.
41
42        01   OLD-MASTER.
43             05  OM-KEY                            PIC X(5).
44             05  OM-QUANTITY                       PIC 9(5).
45             05  FILLER                            PIC X(70).
46
47        01   TRANSACTION.
48             05  TR-KEY                            PIC X(5).
49             05  TR-QUANTITY                       PIC 9(5).
50             05  TR-TRANSACTION-CODE               PIC X.
51                 88  ADDITION                          VALUE '1'.
52                 88  ADJUSTMENT                        VALUE '2'.
53                 88  RECEIPT                           VALUE '3'.
54                 88  SHIPMENT                          VALUE '4'.
55                 88  DELETION                          VALUE '5'.
56             05  FILLER                            PIC X(69).
57
58
59     PROCEDURE DIVISION.
60     A000-UPDATE-FILE.
61         OPEN INPUT TRANSACTION-FILE
62                    OLD-MASTER-FILE
63              OUTPUT NEW-MASTER-FILE
64                    DELETION-FILE.
65         PERFORM C010-READ-TRANSACTION.
66         PERFORM C020-READ-MASTER.
67         PERFORM B010-UPDATE-LOGIC
68              UNTIL OM-KEY = HIGH-VALUES  AND  TR-KEY = HIGH-VALUES.
69         CLOSE TRANSACTION-FILE
70               OLD-MASTER-FILE
71               NEW-MASTER-FILE
72               DELETION-FILE.
73         STOP RUN.
74
75     B010-UPDATE-LOGIC.
76         IF OM-KEY IS LESS THAN TR-KEY
77             WRITE NEW-MASTER FROM OLD-MASTER
78             PERFORM C020-READ-MASTER
```

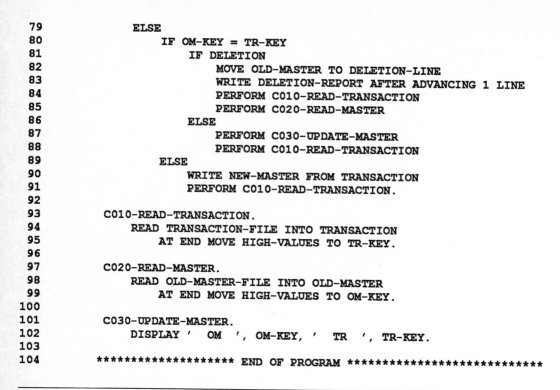

```
79                     ELSE
80                        IF OM-KEY = TR-KEY
81                            IF DELETION
82                                MOVE OLD-MASTER TO DELETION-LINE
83                                WRITE DELETION-REPORT AFTER ADVANCING 1 LINE
84                                PERFORM C010-READ-TRANSACTION
85                                PERFORM C020-READ-MASTER
86                            ELSE
87                                PERFORM C030-UPDATE-MASTER
88                                PERFORM C010-READ-TRANSACTION
89                        ELSE
90                            WRITE NEW-MASTER FROM TRANSACTION
91                            PERFORM C010-READ-TRANSACTION.
92
93          C010-READ-TRANSACTION.
94              READ TRANSACTION-FILE INTO TRANSACTION
95                  AT END MOVE HIGH-VALUES TO TR-KEY.
96
97          C020-READ-MASTER.
98              READ OLD-MASTER-FILE INTO OLD-MASTER
99                  AT END MOVE HIGH-VALUES TO OM-KEY.
100
101         C030-UPDATE-MASTER.
102             DISPLAY ' OM ', OM-KEY, ' TR ', TR-KEY.
103
104         ******************* END OF PROGRAM ***************************
```

FIGURE 13.7 A program for file updating with addition and deletion records but no error checking.

There are two changes in the Procedure Division. First, we have revised the hierarchy slightly, moving the read and update paragraphs down a level to reflect the second change, the increased complexity of **B010-UPDATE-LOGIC**. The fundamental logic of this paragraph is based on the fact that the old master key and the transaction key can have three relative values:

1. The old master key can be less than the transaction key; this means that there are no more transactions for this master;
2. The old master key can be equal to the transaction key; this means that the transaction should be applied to the master;
3. The old master key can be greater than the transaction key; this means that the transaction represents a new inventory item that should be added to the master file.

When the program decides that there are no further transactions for the old master record (indeed, there may have been none at all) the processing is exactly the same as it was in the previous version of the program. When we find a match, however, we must now check to see whether it is a deletion. If so, it is handled in the manner shown. If not, the transaction must be (assuming no errors) either an adjustment, a receipt, or a shipment; therefore, we perform **C030-UPDATE-MASTER** and read another transaction. Finally, if the old master key is neither less than the transaction key nor equal to it, then the old master key must be greater than the transaction key, and (again assuming no errors) this can only represent an addition. In this case we write the new master record from the transaction and get another transaction.

There is one aspect of the file processing in this program that is not immediately obvious. Notice that when we write DELETION-REPORT we use the ADVANCING clause, but when we write NEW-MASTER we do not. Furthermore, although we have allowed for a carriage control character in DELETION-REPORT there is no such provision in NEW-MASTER. The difference between the two files is that DELETION-FILE is a *print* file and is going to a printer, while NEW-MASTER-FILE is a *data* file and is going to some other output medium, probably a disk. The carriage control character is necessary only when you use the ADVANCING clause, and even then only when you are trying to maintain compatibility with IBM's mainframe version of COBOL. The ADVANCING clause is used only for print files, so if a file is used for data the ADVANCING clause should not be used, and all characters in the file records, including the first character, contain data.

We have allowed for carriage control characters in this program to demonstrate the procedure to be used if you need mainframe compatibility. Remember, however, that Microsoft COBOL does not need the carriage control character and does not use it even if you include it in your records. In the following examples we will not bother using a carriage control character.

The program was run with the same old master file used to test the first version and a transaction file that included all five types of transactions. They are presented in Figure 13.8, together with the output produced.

Old Master		Transaction		
Key	Qty	Key	Qty	Code
00002	00111	00008	00050	4
00008	00123	00015	00999	1
00011	00200	00021	00100	3
00021	00210	00024	01000	3
00024	00099	00024	00050	4
00036	01234	00024	00040	4
00037	12345	00036	00000	5
00051	54321	00037	12300	2
00059	43210	00051	00000	5
00061	32109	00059	01000	3
		00061	01234	4

Displayed Output				Deletions		New Master	
				Key	Qty	Key	Qty
OM	00008	TR	00008	00036	01234	00002	00111
OM	00021	TR	00021	00051	54321	00008	00123
OM	00024	TR	00024			00011	00200
OM	00024	TR	00024			00015	09991
OM	00024	TR	00024			00021	00210
OM	00037	TR	00037			00024	00099
OM	00059	TR	00059			00037	12345
OM	00061	TR	00061			00059	43210
						00061	32109

FIGURE 13.8 Data and output for the program in Figure 13.7.

We see that C030-UPDATE-MASTER was reached for all of the transactions representing adjustments, receipts, or shipments. The two transactions representing deletions are seen to have been handled correctly and the new master file is correct, in that it contains the records in the old master file, plus the addition, minus the deletions. The fact that the transaction code of the addition is included in the new master is a minor detail that will be corrected later.

13.12 PROVISION FOR HANDLING ERRORS

It would be foolish and irresponsible to write a program of this type assuming that all the data is correct. It is essential to build the program so that it checks for various kinds of errors. In the next version of the program we shall check for four possibilities: an addition where there is already an existing master, a transaction other than an addition for which there is no master, a transaction file sequence error, and a master file sequence error. Since unmatched transactions in particular must be expected occasionally, and since they are not disabling, we shall keep an error count and not stop the job unless the number of errors exceeds 10. (If there are a great many errors, it probably indicates some kind of completely disabling mistake, such as using the wrong files for input.)

The revised program is shown in Figure 13.9; it contains a number of changes from the previous version. As we add code to implement the new features we have discussed, the structure of the program becomes more complicated, particularly the nested IF statement in B010-UPDATE-LOGIC. We have broken out some of the functions into separate paragraphs for clarity, and modified some of the existing code to make the program more realistic (but still rather skeletal) and less like a textbook example.

```
1          IDENTIFICATION DIVISION.
2          PROGRAM-ID.
3              UPDATE3.
4          DATE-WRITTEN.
5              JUNE 7, 1989.
6
7          ENVIRONMENT DIVISION.
8          INPUT-OUTPUT SECTION.
9          FILE-CONTROL.
10             SELECT LOG-FILE              ASSIGN TO LOGFILE.
11             SELECT NEW-MASTER-FILE       ASSIGN TO NEWMAST.
12             SELECT OLD-MASTER-FILE       ASSIGN TO OLDMAST.
13             SELECT TRANSACTION-FILE      ASSIGN TO TRANS.
14
15         DATA DIVISION.
16
17         FILE SECTION.
18
19         FD  LOG-FILE
20             LABEL RECORDS ARE STANDARD.
21         01  LOG-RECORD.
22             05  LOG-KEY                  PIC X(5).
23             05  LOG-QUANTITY             PIC 9(5).
24             05  LOG-TRANSACTION-CODE     PIC X.
25             05  LOG-MESSAGE              PIC X(121).
26
```

```
27          FD   NEW-MASTER-FILE
28               LABEL RECORDS ARE STANDARD.
29          01   NEW-MASTER.
30               05   NM-KEY                      PIC X(5).
31               05   NM-QUANTITY                 PIC 9(5).
32               05   FILLER                      PIC X(70).
33
34          FD   OLD-MASTER-FILE
35               LABEL RECORDS ARE STANDARD.
36          01   OLD-MASTER-BUFFER               PIC X(80).
37
38          FD   TRANSACTION-FILE
39               LABEL RECORDS ARE STANDARD.
40          01   TRANSACTION-BUFFER              PIC X(80).
41
42          WORKING-STORAGE SECTION.
43
44          77   ERROR-COUNT                     PIC S999.
45          77   OM-KEY-PREVIOUS                 PIC X(5).
46          77   SEQUENCE-ERROR-FLAG             PIC X.
47          77   TR-KEY-PREVIOUS                 PIC X(5).
48
49          01   ERROR-MESSAGES.
50               05   BAD-ADDITION-MSG           PIC X(50) VALUE
51                    '   THIS ADDITION MATCHES AN EXISTING MASTER'.
52               05   DELETE-MSG                 PIC X(50) VALUE
53                    '   THIS MASTER RECORD HAS BEEN DELETED'.
54               05   MASTER-SEQUENCE-ERROR-MSG  PIC X(50) VALUE
55                    '   THIS MASTER IS OUT OF SEQUENCE'.
56               05   TERMINATION-MSG            PIC X(50) VALUE
57                    'MORE THAN 10 ERRORS - JOB TERMINATED'.
58               05   TRANS-SEQUENCE-ERROR-MSG   PIC X(50) VALUE
59                    '   THIS TRANSACTION IS OUT OF SEQUENCE'.
60               05   UNMATCHED-TRANS-MSG        PIC X(50) VALUE
61                    '   THERE IS NO MASTER FOR THIS TRANSACTION'.
62
63          01   OLD-MASTER.
64               05   OM-KEY                      PIC X(5).
65               05   OM-QUANTITY                 PIC 9(5).
66               05   FILLER                      PIC X(70).
67
68          01   TRANSACTION.
69               05   TR-KEY                      PIC X(5).
70               05   TR-QUANTITY                 PIC 9(5).
71               05   TR-TRANSACTION-CODE         PIC X.
72                    88   ADDITION                          VALUE '1'.
73                    88   ADJUSTMENT                        VALUE '2'.
74                    88   RECEIPT                           VALUE '3'.
75                    88   SHIPMENT                          VALUE '4'.
76                    88   DELETION                          VALUE '5'.
77               05   FILLER                      PIC X(69).
78
79
80          PROCEDURE DIVISION.
81          A000-UPDATE-FILE.
82          *         INITIALIZE WORK AREAS
83               MOVE ZERO                       TO ERROR-COUNT.
84               MOVE LOW-VALUES                 TO OM-KEY-PREVIOUS.
85               MOVE LOW-VALUES                 TO TR-KEY-PREVIOUS.
86               OPEN INPUT TRANSACTION-FILE
87                          OLD-MASTER-FILE
```

```
 88                         OUTPUT NEW-MASTER-FILE
 89                                LOG-FILE.
 90          *          GET PRIMING RECORDS
 91              PERFORM X010-GET-VALID-TRANSACTION.
 92              PERFORM X020-GET-VALID-MASTER.
 93          *          PROCESS THE FILES
 94              PERFORM B010-UPDATE-LOGIC
 95                  UNTIL (OM-KEY = HIGH-VALUES   AND   TR-KEY = HIGH-VALUES)
 96                          OR ERROR-COUNT IS GREATER THAN 10.
 97              IF ERROR-COUNT IS GREATER THAN 10
 98                  WRITE LOG-RECORD FROM TERMINATION-MSG
 99                          AFTER ADVANCING 1 LINE.
100              CLOSE TRANSACTION-FILE
101                    OLD-MASTER-FILE
102                    NEW-MASTER-FILE
103                    LOG-FILE.
104              STOP RUN.
105
106          B010-UPDATE-LOGIC.
107              IF OM-KEY IS LESS THAN TR-KEY
108                  WRITE NEW-MASTER FROM OLD-MASTER
109                  PERFORM X020-GET-VALID-MASTER
110              ELSE
111                  IF OM-KEY = TR-KEY
112                      PERFORM C010-APPLY-TRANSACTION
113                      PERFORM X010-GET-VALID-TRANSACTION
114                  ELSE
115                      IF ADDITION
116                          PERFORM C020-ADD-MASTER
117                          PERFORM X010-GET-VALID-TRANSACTION
118                      ELSE
119                          PERFORM C030-INVALID-TRANSACTION
120                          PERFORM X010-GET-VALID-TRANSACTION.
121
122          C010-APPLY-TRANSACTION.
123              IF DELETION
124                  PERFORM D010-DELETE-MASTER
125                  PERFORM X020-GET-VALID-MASTER
126              ELSE
127                  IF ADDITION
128                      PERFORM D030-INVALID-ADDITION
129                  ELSE
130                      PERFORM D020-UPDATE-MASTER.
131
132          C020-ADD-MASTER.
133              WRITE NEW-MASTER FROM TRANSACTION.
134
135          C030-INVALID-TRANSACTION.
136              MOVE TRANSACTION TO LOG-RECORD.
137              MOVE UNMATCHED-TRANS-MSG TO LOG-MESSAGE.
138              WRITE LOG-RECORD AFTER ADVANCING 1 LINE.
139              ADD 1 TO ERROR-COUNT.
140
141          D010-DELETE-MASTER.
142              MOVE OLD-MASTER TO LOG-RECORD.
143              MOVE DELETE-MSG TO LOG-MESSAGE.
144              WRITE LOG-RECORD AFTER ADVANCING 1 LINE.
145
```

```
146        D020-UPDATE-MASTER.
147            DISPLAY ' OM ', OM-KEY, ' TR ', TR-KEY.
148
149        D030-INVALID-ADDITION.
150            MOVE TRANSACTION TO LOG-RECORD.
151            MOVE BAD-ADDITION-MSG TO LOG-MESSAGE.
152            WRITE LOG-RECORD AFTER ADVANCING 1 LINE.
153            ADD 1 TO ERROR-COUNT.
154
155        X010-GET-VALID-TRANSACTION.
156            MOVE '?' TO SEQUENCE-ERROR-FLAG.
157            PERFORM Y010-READ-TRANSACTION
158                UNTIL      SEQUENCE-ERROR-FLAG = 'N'
159                    OR ERROR-COUNT IS GREATER THAN 10.
160
161        X020-GET-VALID-MASTER.
162            MOVE '?' TO SEQUENCE-ERROR-FLAG.
163            PERFORM Y020-READ-MASTER
164                UNTIL      SEQUENCE-ERROR-FLAG = 'N'
165                    OR ERROR-COUNT IS GREATER THAN 10.
166
167        Y010-READ-TRANSACTION.
168            READ TRANSACTION-FILE INTO TRANSACTION
169                AT END MOVE HIGH-VALUES TO TR-KEY.
170            IF TR-KEY IS LESS THAN TR-KEY-PREVIOUS
171                MOVE TRANSACTION TO LOG-RECORD
172                MOVE TRANS-SEQUENCE-ERROR-MSG TO LOG-MESSAGE
173                WRITE LOG-RECORD AFTER ADVANCING 1 LINE
174                ADD 1 TO ERROR-COUNT
175            ELSE
176                MOVE 'N' TO SEQUENCE-ERROR-FLAG.
177            MOVE TR-KEY TO TR-KEY-PREVIOUS.
178
179        Y020-READ-MASTER.
180            READ OLD-MASTER-FILE INTO OLD-MASTER
181                AT END MOVE HIGH-VALUES TO OM-KEY.
182            IF OM-KEY IS LESS THAN OM-KEY-PREVIOUS
183                MOVE OLD-MASTER TO LOG-RECORD
184                MOVE MASTER-SEQUENCE-ERROR-MSG TO LOG-MESSAGE
185                WRITE LOG-RECORD AFTER ADVANCING 1 LINE
186                ADD 1 TO ERROR-COUNT
187            ELSE
188                MOVE 'N' TO SEQUENCE-ERROR-FLAG.
189            MOVE OM-KEY TO OM-KEY-PREVIOUS.
190
191        ******************** END OF PROGRAM ***************************
```

FIGURE 13.9   A fairly complete file update program, with additions, deletions, and basic error checking.

The first changes simply involve the order in which files are defined. Both in the SELECT statements in the FILE-CONTROL paragraph and in the FDs in the FILE SECTION we have placed the files in alphabetical order. Although this is certainly not mandatory, it frequently makes it easier to locate a definition when you need to refer to it during program maintenance. We have also changed the name of the print file from DELETION-FILE to LOG-FILE because this name more accurately reflects the usage of the file. That is, it will not only be used to list deleted records, it will be used to log all changes and errors found during processing. The output from the log file would enable the program user to determine what major activity had occurred during a run. In a real program, of course, the output from the log file would be formatted more extensively and would include column headings, page numbers, and so on; again we have omitted these familiar details to save space and to allow a focus on other matters.

In the Working-Storage Section we have added several level **77** items to count errors, track file keys, and report sequence errors. We have also included several error and diagnostic messages in the structure **ERROR-MESSAGES**. The remainder of Working-Storage is as in the previous program.

The main paragraph of the Procedure Division begins by initializing various Working-Storage items. Although this initialization could have been done in the Working-Storage Section using **VALUE**, we will generally reserve the **VALUE** clause for data that is not changed during execution, such as constants, headings, messages, and so on. Initializing changeable data in the Procedure Division emphasizes which of these variables must be given initial values. We have also changed the **PERFORM** statement so that it will terminate if we find too many errors, in which case the program will also print an appropriate error message.

Paragraph **B010-UPDATE-LOGIC** has been changed considerably from the version in Figure 13.7. Because the paragraph is controlling much more activity than in the previous example, we have moved almost all the detail to lower level paragraphs and left only the control structure and several **PERFORM** statements. The basic control structure is much the same as in the previous example: if the old master key is less than the transaction key, we are done with the master record so we write a new master record and get the next old master; if the master key is equal to the transaction key we apply the transaction to the master and get the next transaction. If the master key is greater than the transaction key, however, we have a new situation. In the previous version of the program we assumed that this case means that we are adding a new master record. In this current program, we may indeed be adding a new record, but we might also have an erroneous transaction key, one that does not correspond to any master record. If we have an addition, we add the new master record and get the next transaction; if we have any other type of transaction we process the error and get the next transaction. By using **PER-FORM** statements to take care of the processing details, we leave a relatively clear and simple structure in **B010-UPDATE-LOGIC**.

The structure of the lower levels of the program has changed completely from the version in Figure 13.7. To begin with, we now have paragraphs to perform the functions of applying a transaction to the master record, adding a new master record, and reporting a transaction with an invalid key.

Paragraph **C010-APPLY-TRANSACTION** is itself a control paragraph and performs no detailed work; as in the previous paragraph, this allows us to concentrate on the structure of the function while leaving the details for lower level paragraphs. At this point in the program a transaction falls into one of three classes: it can be a deletion, causing a record to be removed from the master file; it can be an addition, which is an error since we would be trying to add a master record with the same key as an existing master record; or it can be any other type of transaction, which is used to update the current master record. Although the details of *how* each of these activities is carried out fall to still lower level paragraphs, the logic of *when* the tasks are performed is clear. Notice that applying a transaction does not involve getting the next transaction; that function is performed in **B010-UPDATE-LOGIC**.

The work required to add a new master record is simple and is unchanged from the previous program: we merely write the new master from the transaction. We have placed this in a separate paragraph primarily to keep the structure of **C010-APPLY-TRANSACTION** simple, but also to prepare for future enhancements in which the activity becomes more complex.

Processing an invalid transaction is also quite easy. We simply write an appropriate error message and increment the error count.

The next three paragraphs, at the **D** level of hierarchy, are also clear and should require no explanation. Where these activities match the previous version of the program, they are unchanged.

The remaining paragraphs, which involve getting records from the input files, have changed considerably. To begin with, we have renumbered the paragraphs as "utility" paragraphs at the **X** and **Y** levels. The reason is that they are now called from several levels of hierarchy; **X020-GET-VALID-MASTER**, for instance, is used at levels **A**, **B**, and **C**. Furthermore, the names have been revised to reflect the fact that we are no longer simply reading a record: we are getting the next valid record from a file. The higher levels of the program should not be concerned with how these valid records are obtained, only that they are made available.

The checking procedure for sequence errors is more complex than it was in the second version of the program. This is because we do not wish to stop when we find a sequence error, unless we have found a total of more than 10 errors. Paragraph **X010-GET-VALID-TRANSACTION** begins by giving a value of "**?**" to an error flag, because we don't know yet if we have a sequence error or not. Then it says to perform another paragraph until the flag equals "**N**" (no sequence error was found) or the maximum error limit is exceeded. The performed paragraph does the actual reading, checks for a sequence error and handles it if one is found, and moves the transaction key to the previous transaction key. Getting a valid master record is handled in the same way.

The old master and transaction files used to demonstrate the operation of this program have been expanded to include various kinds of errors, as may be seen on the following page.

We see that these conditions have been handled in the way the program specifies, although other ways of treating them could be defended. The second transaction, for instance, is not processed even though it has a matching master record. At the expense of considerable extra complication, the program could be written to try to process out-of-sequence transactions, but there do have to be limits on how many abnormal conditions one tries to cope with. Also, note that an out-of-sequence old master is not written to the new master. Likewise, an out-of-sequence deletion record does not result in the deletion of the record when the new master is written. Considering that file sequence errors are ordinarily rather serious matters that usually have to be handled by resequencing the files and running the job again, it is probably reasonable not to try to deal with all these situations, beyond simply detecting them.

Old Master			Transaction		
Key	Qty		Key	Qty	Code
00002	00111		00003	00100	4
00008	00123		00002	00010	2
00011	00200		00008	00050	4
00021	00210		00011	98765	1
00024	00099		00015	00999	1
00036	01234		00021	00100	3
00037	12345		00024	01000	3
00051	54321		00024	00050	4
00059	43210		00024	00040	4
00061	32109		00037	12300	2
00070	22222		00036	00000	5
00068	33333		00051	00000	5
00080	44444		00052	00000	5
			00059	01000	3
			00061	01234	4

			Displayed Output			New Master	

Displayed Output				New Master	
				Key	Qty
OM	00008	TR	00008	00002	00111
OM	00021	TR	00021	00008	00123
OM	00024	TR	00024	00011	00200
OM	00024	TR	00024	00015	00999
OM	00024	TR	00024	00021	00210
OM	00037	TR	00037	00024	00099
OM	00059	TR	00059	00036	01234
OM	00061	TR	00061	00037	12345
				00059	43210
				00061	32109
				00070	22222
				00080	44444

Log File

Transaction

Key	Qty	Code	
00003	00100	4	THERE IS NO MASTER FOR THIS TRANSACTION
00002	00010	2	THIS TRANSACTION IS OUT OF SEQUENCE
00011	98765	1	THIS ADDITION MATCHES AN EXISTING MASTER
00036	00000	5	THIS TRANSACTION IS OUT OF SEQUENCE
00051	54321		THIS MASTER RECORD HAS BEEN DELETED
00052	00000	5	THERE IS NO MASTER FOR THIS TRANSACTION
00068	33333		THIS MASTER IS OUT OF SEQUENCE

13.13 UPDATING THE MASTER ON A MATCH

Now it is time to consider the processing to be done when there is a normal match between the transaction and the master; that is, an adjustment, a receipt, or a shipment. This is, of course, the heart of the whole application, in one sense, but since it is subordinate to the top-level file processing logic of the program we have postponed our consideration of it until this point.

Actually, with the rudimentary record contents that we have specified thus far, the processing is not very difficult. The only possible adjustment is to update the old master quantity with the transaction quantity. For a receipt, we add the transaction quantity to the old master quantity. For a shipment, we basically want to subtract the transaction quantity from the old master quantity, but we must do so only if there is sufficient stock on hand. If there is not, we need to signal this fact, which can be done in the log file report. (In real life one would ordinarily ship as much as there is on hand and back-order the rest, but we shall not concern ourselves with this complication.)

While we are processing the transaction we have an easy opportunity to check that the transaction is valid (in the range 1 through 5); if not, we can print an error message on the log file. We will get to the updating operation if the transaction is anything other than 1 or 5. It would be possible to assume in the updating section that if the transaction code is not 2 or 3 it must be 4, but we would be ill-advised to place this much faith in the correctness of input.

Figure 13.10 shows the program modified to update the master record. The only change required in the Data Division is the addition of two new error messages, one for an invalid transaction code and one for an insufficient-stock condition. In the Procedure Division, we have modified the paragraph named **D020-UPDATE-MASTER** and added three paragraphs at level **E** to carry out the different update operations. The simple operations to be carried out in these three paragraphs could, of course, have been written in **D020-UPDATE-MASTER** as one nested **IF** statement, but the method used results in clearer code and easier maintenance.

```
 1          IDENTIFICATION DIVISION.
 2          PROGRAM-ID.
 3              UPDATE4.
 4          DATE-WRITTEN.
 5              JUNE 7, 1989.
 6
 7          ENVIRONMENT DIVISION.
 8          INPUT-OUTPUT SECTION.
 9          FILE-CONTROL.
10              SELECT LOG-FILE                ASSIGN TO LOGFILE.
11              SELECT NEW-MASTER-FILE         ASSIGN TO NEWMAST.
12              SELECT OLD-MASTER-FILE         ASSIGN TO OLDMAST.
13              SELECT TRANSACTION-FILE        ASSIGN TO TRANS.
14
15          DATA DIVISION.
16
17          FILE SECTION.
18
19          FD  LOG-FILE
20              LABEL RECORDS ARE STANDARD.
21          01  LOG-RECORD.
22              05  LOG-KEY                    PIC X(5).
23              05  LOG-QUANTITY               PIC 9(5).
24              05  LOG-TRANSACTION-CODE       PIC X.
25              05  LOG-MESSAGE                PIC X(121).
26
27          FD  NEW-MASTER-FILE
28              LABEL RECORDS ARE STANDARD.
```

```
29          01  NEW-MASTER.
30              05  NM-KEY                         PIC X(5).
31              05  NM-QUANTITY                    PIC 9(5).
32              05  FILLER                         PIC X(70).
33
34          FD  OLD-MASTER-FILE
35              LABEL RECORDS ARE STANDARD.
36          01  OLD-MASTER-BUFFER                  PIC X(80).
37
38          FD  TRANSACTION-FILE
39              LABEL RECORDS ARE STANDARD.
40          01  TRANSACTION-BUFFER                 PIC X(80).
41
42      WORKING-STORAGE SECTION.
43
44          77  ERROR-COUNT                        PIC S999.
45          77  OM-KEY-PREVIOUS                    PIC X(5).
46          77  SEQUENCE-ERROR-FLAG                PIC X.
47          77  TR-KEY-PREVIOUS                    PIC X(5).
48
49          01  ERROR-MESSAGES.
50              05  BAD-ADDITION-MSG               PIC X(50) VALUE
51                  '   THIS ADDITION MATCHES AN EXISTING MASTER'.
52              05  BAD-TRANS-CODE-MSG             PIC X(50) VALUE
53                  '   TRANSACTION CODE ILLEGAL'.
54              05  DELETE-MSG                     PIC X(50) VALUE
55                  '   THIS MASTER RECORD HAS BEEN DELETED'.
56              05  MASTER-SEQUENCE-ERROR-MSG      PIC X(50) VALUE
57                  '   THIS MASTER IS OUT OF SEQUENCE'.
58              05  OUT-OF-STOCK-MSG               PIC X(50) VALUE
59                  '   INSUFFICIENT STOCK TO SHIP AMOUNT SPECIFIED'.
60              05  TERMINATION-MSG                PIC X(50) VALUE
61                  'MORE THAN 10 ERRORS - JOB TERMINATED'.
62              05  TRANS-SEQUENCE-ERROR-MSG       PIC X(50) VALUE
63                  '   THIS TRANSACTION IS OUT OF SEQUENCE'.
64              05  UNMATCHED-TRANS-MSG            PIC X(50) VALUE
65                  '   THERE IS NO MASTER FOR THIS TRANSACTION'.
66
67          01  OLD-MASTER.
68              05  OM-KEY                         PIC X(5).
69              05  OM-QUANTITY                    PIC 9(5).
70              05  FILLER                         PIC X(70).
71
72          01  TRANSACTION.
73              05  TR-KEY                         PIC X(5).
74              05  TR-QUANTITY                    PIC 9(5).
75              05  TR-TRANSACTION-CODE            PIC X.
76                  88  ADDITION                            VALUE '1'.
77                  88  ADJUSTMENT                          VALUE '2'.
78                  88  RECEIPT                             VALUE '3'.
79                  88  SHIPMENT                            VALUE '4'.
80                  88  DELETION                            VALUE '5'.
81              05  FILLER                         PIC X(69).
82
83
84      PROCEDURE DIVISION.
85      A000-UPDATE-FILE.
86  *           INITIALIZE WORK AREAS
87          MOVE ZERO                          TO ERROR-COUNT.
88          MOVE LOW-VALUES                    TO OM-KEY-PREVIOUS.
89          MOVE LOW-VALUES                    TO TR-KEY-PREVIOUS.
```

```
90                    OPEN INPUT TRANSACTION-FILE
91                              OLD-MASTER-FILE
92                         OUTPUT NEW-MASTER-FILE
93                                LOG-FILE.
94         *         GET PRIMING RECORDS
95                    PERFORM X010-GET-VALID-TRANSACTION.
96                    PERFORM X020-GET-VALID-MASTER.
97         *         PROCESS THE FILES
98                    PERFORM B010-UPDATE-LOGIC
99                        UNTIL (OM-KEY = HIGH-VALUES  AND  TR-KEY = HIGH-VALUES)
100                            OR ERROR-COUNT IS GREATER THAN 10.
101                   IF ERROR-COUNT IS GREATER THAN 10
102                       WRITE LOG-RECORD FROM TERMINATION-MSG
103                               AFTER ADVANCING 1 LINE.
104                   CLOSE TRANSACTION-FILE
105                         OLD-MASTER-FILE
106                         NEW-MASTER-FILE
107                         LOG-FILE.
108                   STOP RUN.
109
110       B010-UPDATE-LOGIC.
111           IF OM-KEY IS LESS THAN TR-KEY
112               WRITE NEW-MASTER FROM OLD-MASTER
113               PERFORM X020-GET-VALID-MASTER
114           ELSE
115               IF OM-KEY = TR-KEY
116                   PERFORM C010-APPLY-TRANSACTION
117                   PERFORM X010-GET-VALID-TRANSACTION
118               ELSE
119                   IF ADDITION
120                       PERFORM C020-ADD-MASTER
121                       PERFORM X010-GET-VALID-TRANSACTION
122                   ELSE
123                       PERFORM C030-INVALID-TRANSACTION
124                       PERFORM X010-GET-VALID-TRANSACTION.
125
126       C010-APPLY-TRANSACTION.
127           IF DELETION
128               PERFORM D010-DELETE-MASTER
129               PERFORM X020-GET-VALID-MASTER
130           ELSE
131               IF ADDITION
132                   PERFORM D030-INVALID-ADDITION
133               ELSE
134                   PERFORM D020-UPDATE-MASTER.
135
136       C020-ADD-MASTER.
137           WRITE NEW-MASTER FROM TRANSACTION.
138
139       C030-INVALID-TRANSACTION.
140           MOVE TRANSACTION TO LOG-RECORD.
141           MOVE UNMATCHED-TRANS-MSG TO LOG-MESSAGE.
142           WRITE LOG-RECORD AFTER ADVANCING 1 LINE.
143           ADD 1 TO ERROR-COUNT.
144
145       D010-DELETE-MASTER.
146           MOVE OLD-MASTER TO LOG-RECORD.
147           MOVE DELETE-MSG TO LOG-MESSAGE.
148           WRITE LOG-RECORD AFTER ADVANCING 1 LINE.
149
```

```
150          D020-UPDATE-MASTER.
151              IF        SHIPMENT
152                  PERFORM E010-PROCESS-SHIPMENT
153              ELSE IF RECEIPT
154                  PERFORM E020-PROCESS-RECEIPT
155              ELSE IF ADJUSTMENT
156                  PERFORM E030-PROCESS-ADJUSTMENT
157              ELSE
158                  MOVE TRANSACTION TO LOG-RECORD
159                  MOVE BAD-TRANS-CODE-MSG TO LOG-MESSAGE
160                  WRITE LOG-RECORD AFTER ADVANCING 1 LINE
161                  ADD 1 TO ERROR-COUNT.
162
163          D030-INVALID-ADDITION.
164              MOVE TRANSACTION TO LOG-RECORD.
165              MOVE BAD-ADDITION-MSG TO LOG-MESSAGE.
166              WRITE LOG-RECORD AFTER ADVANCING 1 LINE.
167              ADD 1 TO ERROR-COUNT.
168
169          E010-PROCESS-SHIPMENT.
170              IF OM-QUANTITY IS NOT LESS THAN TR-QUANTITY
171                  SUBTRACT TR-QUANTITY FROM OM-QUANTITY
172              ELSE
173                  MOVE TRANSACTION TO LOG-RECORD
174                  MOVE OUT-OF-STOCK-MSG TO LOG-MESSAGE
175                  WRITE LOG-RECORD AFTER ADVANCING 1 LINE
176                  ADD 1 TO ERROR-COUNT.
177
178          E020-PROCESS-RECEIPT.
179              ADD TR-QUANTITY TO OM-QUANTITY.
180
181          E030-PROCESS-ADJUSTMENT.
182              MOVE TR-QUANTITY TO OM-QUANTITY.
183
184          X010-GET-VALID-TRANSACTION.
185              MOVE '?' TO SEQUENCE-ERROR-FLAG.
186              PERFORM Y010-READ-TRANSACTION
187                  UNTIL      SEQUENCE-ERROR-FLAG = 'N'
188                         OR ERROR-COUNT IS GREATER THAN 10.
189
190          X020-GET-VALID-MASTER.
191              MOVE '?' TO SEQUENCE-ERROR-FLAG.
192              PERFORM Y020-READ-MASTER
193                  UNTIL      SEQUENCE-ERROR-FLAG = 'N'
194                         OR ERROR-COUNT IS GREATER THAN 10.
195
196          Y010-READ-TRANSACTION.
197              READ TRANSACTION-FILE INTO TRANSACTION
198                  AT END MOVE HIGH-VALUES TO TR-KEY.
199              IF TR-KEY IS LESS THAN TR-KEY-PREVIOUS
200                  MOVE TRANSACTION TO LOG-RECORD
201                  MOVE TRANS-SEQUENCE-ERROR-MSG TO LOG-MESSAGE
202                  WRITE LOG-RECORD AFTER ADVANCING 1 LINE
203                  ADD 1 TO ERROR-COUNT
204              ELSE
205                  MOVE 'N' TO SEQUENCE-ERROR-FLAG.
206              MOVE TR-KEY TO TR-KEY-PREVIOUS.
207
208          Y020-READ-MASTER.
209              READ OLD-MASTER-FILE INTO OLD-MASTER
210                  AT END MOVE HIGH-VALUES TO OM-KEY.
```

```
211                IF OM-KEY IS LESS THAN OM-KEY-PREVIOUS
212                    MOVE OLD-MASTER TO LOG-RECORD
213                    MOVE MASTER-SEQUENCE-ERROR-MSG TO LOG-MESSAGE
214                    WRITE LOG-RECORD AFTER ADVANCING 1 LINE
215                    ADD 1 TO ERROR-COUNT
216                ELSE
217                    MOVE 'N' TO SEQUENCE-ERROR-FLAG.
218                MOVE OM-KEY TO OM-KEY-PREVIOUS.
219
220       ******************* END OF PROGRAM **************************
```

FIGURE 13.10 A file update program containing code that updates the master file.

The program was tested with the data used with the program UPDATE3. The old master and transaction files again, together with the new master and log files produced by this program, are shown below.

Old Master Key Qty	Transaction Key Qty Code	New Master Key Qty
0000200111	00003001004	0000200111
0000800123	00002000102	0000800073
0001100200	00008000504	0001100200
0002100210	00011987651	00015009991
0002400099	00015009991	0002100310
0003601234	00021001003	0002401009
0003712345	00024010003	0003601234
0005154321	00024000504	0003712300
0005943210	00024000404	0005944210
0006132109	00037123002	0006130875
0007022222	00036000005	0007022222
0006833333	00051000005	0008044444
0008044444	00052000005	
	00059010003	
	00061012344	

Log File

```
Transaction
Key    Qty  Code

00003001004   THERE IS NO MASTER FOR THIS TRANSACTION
00002000102   THIS TRANSACTION IS OUT OF SEQUENCE
00011987651   THIS ADDITION MATCHES AN EXISTING MASTER
00036000005   THIS TRANSACTION IS OUT OF SEQUENCE
0005154321    THIS MASTER RECORD HAS BEEN DELETED
00052000005   THERE IS NO MASTER FOR THIS TRANSACTION
0006833333    THIS MASTER IS OUT OF SEQUENCE
```

Observe that the log messages are the same as those for UPDATE3, which is reasonable since UPDATE3 contained the same error checking features as this program does. The new master, however, is different since now we are actually updating the master. Let us see how the program operated.

The first transaction produced an unmatched-transaction error message. The second produced an out-of-sequence message even though it matches the first master; the master was not updated. The third transaction, the one with the key of 00008, had a quantity of 50 and a transaction code of 4, which is a shipment. We see that where the old master for this item had a quantity of 123, the new master has a quantity of 73. The next transaction (key=00011) was an erroneous addition. The next one was a legitimate addition. For item 0021, we received a shipment of 100; the old master quantity was increased from 210 to 310. The next three transactions are all for item 0024, for which we have a receipt of 1000 and two shipments totaling 90; we see that the old master quantity has been increased by 910. The transaction for item 0037 is an adjustment of the quantity that was done correctly. Item 0052 is an unmatched transaction. The receipt for 0059 was handled correctly, as was the shipment for 0061. The items in the old master for which there were no transactions were copied correctly to the new master.

13.14 THE COMPLETE PROGRAM

With all of the important logic apparently working correctly, we may now take the final step of incorporating all the processing that is actually required of the program.

The most important extension from the simplified version that we have considered thus far is the inclusion of more information from the master records. Besides a quantity, which we now rename as quantity on hand, we need a *quantity on order* to show how much stock is on its way from suppliers. We also need a *reorder point*; whenever the amount of stock on hand plus the amount on order falls below this number we will issue an instruction to order more stock. When this is done, it is necessary to have in the master record a reorder quantity. Finally, there must be provision for an alphanumeric description of the stock item.

Here is the record description for the master, as it will appear in the program.

```
01  OLD-MASTER.
    05  OM-KEY                      PIC X(5).
    05  OM-QUAN-ON-HAND             PIC 9(5).
    05  OM-QUAN-ON-ORDER            PIC 9(5).
    05  OM-REORDER-POINT            PIC 9(5).
    05  OM-REORDER-QUAN             PIC 9(5).
    05  OM-DESCRIPTION              PIC X(20).
```

In earlier versions of the program we arbitrarily defined the master record to be 80 characters long, the length of one line on the CRT. Now that we have defined the fields in the record precisely we will use the record's actual length, 45 characters.

A realistic inventory control file would contain much additional information. It would provide for handling back orders. It might have some information about how long stock has been on order, and would probably have some information about vendors from whom stock can be ordered. It would have information about physical locations of the stock in the warehouse. A complete inventory system can be a very elaborate affair, which we can no more than sketch in a program that is primarily intended to teach other things.

The transaction records in our final version must be expanded to contain everything that is in the old master, since a transaction may be an addition to the master file. Furthermore, there needs to be an adjustment code so that we can specify which of the items in a master record is to be changed. This means, in summary, that a transaction record has everything that a master record has plus a transaction code and an adjustment code that tells which item in the master record is to be adjusted. The complete record description for the transaction can be seen in the program in Figure 13.11. As with the master records, we now have enough detail that we can show the length of the transaction record precisely, both in Working-Storage and in the File Section.

```
1        IDENTIFICATION DIVISION.
2        PROGRAM-ID.
3            UPDATE5.
4        DATE-WRITTEN.
5            JUNE 7, 1989.
6
7        ENVIRONMENT DIVISION.
8        INPUT-OUTPUT SECTION.
9        FILE-CONTROL.
10           SELECT LOG-FILE              ASSIGN TO LOGFILE.
11           SELECT NEW-MASTER-FILE       ASSIGN TO NEWMAST.
12           SELECT OLD-MASTER-FILE       ASSIGN TO OLDMAST.
13           SELECT ORDER-FILE            ASSIGN TO ORDERS.
14           SELECT TRANSACTION-FILE      ASSIGN TO TRANS.
15
16       DATA DIVISION.
17
18       FILE SECTION.
19
20       FD  LOG-FILE
21           LABEL RECORDS ARE STANDARD.
22       01  LOG-RECORD.
23           05  FILLER                   PIC X(45).
24           05  LOG-MESSAGE              PIC X(50).
25
26       FD  NEW-MASTER-FILE
27           LABEL RECORDS ARE STANDARD.
28       01  NEW-MASTER.
29           05  NM-KEY                   PIC X(5).
30           05  NM-QUANTITY              PIC 9(5).
31           05  NM-QUAN-ON-ORDER         PIC 9(5).
32           05  NM-REORDER-POINT         PIC 9(5).
33           05  NM-REORDER-QUAN          PIC 9(5).
34           05  NM-DESCRIPTION           PIC X(20).
35
36       FD  OLD-MASTER-FILE
37           LABEL RECORDS ARE STANDARD.
38       01  OLD-MASTER-BUFFER            PIC X(45).
39
40       FD  ORDER-FILE
41           LABEL RECORDS ARE STANDARD.
42       01  ORDER-RECORD.
43           05  OR-KEY                   PIC X(5).
44           05  FILLER                   PIC XXX.
45           05  OR-QUANTITY              PIC Z(5)9.
46           05  FILLER                   PIC XXX.
47           05  OR-DESCRIPTION           PIC X(20).
48
```

```
49      FD   TRANSACTION-FILE
50           LABEL RECORDS ARE STANDARD.
51      01   TRANSACTION-BUFFER                PIC X(47).
52
53      WORKING-STORAGE SECTION.
54
55      77   ERROR-COUNT                       PIC S999.
56      77   OM-KEY-PREVIOUS                   PIC X(5).
57      77   SEQUENCE-ERROR-FLAG               PIC X.
58      77   TR-KEY-PREVIOUS                   PIC X(5).
59
60      01   ERROR-MESSAGES.
61          05   BAD-ADDITION-MSG             PIC X(50) VALUE
62               '   THIS ADDITION MATCHES AN EXISTING MASTER'.
63          05   BAD-ADJ-CODE-MSG             PIC X(50) VALUE
64               '  BAD ADJUSTMENT CODE'.
65          05   BAD-TRANS-CODE-MSG           PIC X(50) VALUE
66               '   TRANSACTION CODE ILLEGAL'.
67          05   DELETE-MSG                   PIC X(50) VALUE
68               '  THIS MASTER RECORD HAS BEEN DELETED'.
69          05   MASTER-SEQUENCE-ERROR-MSG    PIC X(50) VALUE
70               '  THIS MASTER IS OUT OF SEQUENCE'.
71          05   OUT-OF-STOCK-MSG             PIC X(50) VALUE
72               '  INSUFFICIENT STOCK TO SHIP AMOUNT SPECIFIED'.
73          05   TERMINATION-MSG              PIC X(50) VALUE
74               'MORE THAN 10 ERRORS - JOB TERMINATED'.
75          05   TRANS-SEQUENCE-ERROR-MSG     PIC X(50) VALUE
76               '  THIS TRANSACTION IS OUT OF SEQUENCE'.
77          05   UNMATCHED-TRANS-MSG          PIC X(50) VALUE
78               '  THERE IS NO MASTER FOR THIS TRANSACTION'.
79
80      01   OLD-MASTER.
81          05   OM-KEY                       PIC X(5).
82          05   OM-QUAN-ON-HAND              PIC 9(5).
83          05   OM-QUAN-ON-ORDER             PIC 9(5).
84          05   OM-REORDER-POINT             PIC 9(5).
85          05   OM-REORDER-QUAN              PIC 9(5).
86          05   OM-DESCRIPTION               PIC X(20).
87
88      01   TRANSACTION.
89          05   TR-KEY                       PIC X(5).
90          05   TR-QUANTITY                  PIC 9(5).
91          05   TR-TRANSACTION-CODE          PIC X.
92              88   ADDITION                           VALUE '1'.
93              88   ADJUSTMENT                         VALUE '2'.
94              88   RECEIPT                            VALUE '3'.
95              88   SHIPMENT                           VALUE '4'.
96              88   DELETION                           VALUE '5'.
97          05   TR-ADJUSTMENT-CODE           PIC 9.
98          05   TR-QUAN-ON-ORDER             PIC 9(5).
99          05   TR-REORDER-POINT             PIC 9(5).
100         05   TR-REORDER-QUAN              PIC 9(5).
101         05   TR-DESCRIPTION               PIC X(20).
102
103
104     PROCEDURE DIVISION.
105     A000-UPDATE-FILE.
106     *        INITIALIZE WORK AREAS
107         MOVE ZERO                         TO ERROR-COUNT.
108         MOVE LOW-VALUES                   TO OM-KEY-PREVIOUS.
109         MOVE LOW-VALUES                   TO TR-KEY-PREVIOUS.
```

```
110              OPEN INPUT TRANSACTION-FILE
111                         OLD-MASTER-FILE
112                  OUTPUT NEW-MASTER-FILE
113                         LOG-FILE
114                         ORDER-FILE.
115       *         GET PRIMING RECORDS
116              PERFORM X010-GET-VALID-TRANSACTION.
117              PERFORM X020-GET-VALID-MASTER.
118       *         PROCESS THE FILES
119              PERFORM B010-UPDATE-LOGIC
120                  UNTIL (OM-KEY = HIGH-VALUES  AND  TR-KEY = HIGH-VALUES)
121                         OR ERROR-COUNT IS GREATER THAN 10.
122              IF ERROR-COUNT IS GREATER THAN 10
123                  WRITE LOG-RECORD FROM TERMINATION-MSG
124                         AFTER ADVANCING 1 LINE.
125              CLOSE TRANSACTION-FILE
126                    OLD-MASTER-FILE
127                    NEW-MASTER-FILE
128                    LOG-FILE
129                    ORDER-FILE.
130              STOP RUN.
131
132       B010-UPDATE-LOGIC.
133              IF OM-KEY IS LESS THAN TR-KEY
134                  PERFORM C040-CHECK-QUANTITY
135                  WRITE NEW-MASTER FROM OLD-MASTER
136                  PERFORM X020-GET-VALID-MASTER
137              ELSE
138                  IF OM-KEY = TR-KEY
139                      PERFORM C010-APPLY-TRANSACTION
140                      PERFORM X010-GET-VALID-TRANSACTION
141                  ELSE
142                      IF ADDITION
143                          PERFORM C020-ADD-MASTER
144                          PERFORM X010-GET-VALID-TRANSACTION
145                      ELSE
146                          PERFORM C030-INVALID-TRANSACTION
147                          PERFORM X010-GET-VALID-TRANSACTION.
148
149       C010-APPLY-TRANSACTION.
150              IF DELETION
151                  PERFORM D010-DELETE-MASTER
152                  PERFORM X020-GET-VALID-MASTER
153              ELSE
154                  IF ADDITION
155                      PERFORM D030-INVALID-ADDITION
156                  ELSE
157                      PERFORM D020-UPDATE-MASTER.
158
159       C020-ADD-MASTER.
160              MOVE TR-KEY                      TO NM-KEY.
161              MOVE TR-QUANTITY                 TO NM-QUANTITY.
162              MOVE TR-QUAN-ON-ORDER            TO NM-QUAN-ON-ORDER.
163              MOVE TR-REORDER-POINT            TO NM-REORDER-POINT.
164              MOVE TR-REORDER-QUAN             TO NM-REORDER-QUAN.
165              MOVE TR-DESCRIPTION              TO NM-DESCRIPTION.
166              WRITE NEW-MASTER.
167
```

```
168          C030-INVALID-TRANSACTION.
169              MOVE TRANSACTION TO LOG-RECORD.
170              MOVE UNMATCHED-TRANS-MSG TO LOG-MESSAGE.
171              WRITE LOG-RECORD AFTER ADVANCING 1 LINE.
172              ADD 1 TO ERROR-COUNT.
173
174          C040-CHECK-QUANTITY.
175              IF OM-QUAN-ON-ORDER + OM-QUAN-ON-HAND < OM-REORDER-POINT
176                  MOVE SPACES                 TO ORDER-RECORD
177                  MOVE OM-KEY                 TO OR-KEY
178                  MOVE OM-DESCRIPTION         TO OR-DESCRIPTION
179                  MOVE OM-REORDER-QUAN        TO OR-QUANTITY
180                  WRITE ORDER-RECORD AFTER ADVANCING 1 LINE
181                  ADD OM-REORDER-QUAN TO OM-QUAN-ON-ORDER.
182
183          D010-DELETE-MASTER.
184              MOVE OLD-MASTER TO LOG-RECORD.
185              MOVE DELETE-MSG TO LOG-MESSAGE.
186              WRITE LOG-RECORD AFTER ADVANCING 1 LINE.
187
188          D020-UPDATE-MASTER.
189              IF      SHIPMENT
190                  PERFORM E010-PROCESS-SHIPMENT
191              ELSE IF RECEIPT
192                  PERFORM E020-PROCESS-RECEIPT
193              ELSE IF ADJUSTMENT
194                  PERFORM E030-PROCESS-ADJUSTMENT
195              ELSE
196                  MOVE TRANSACTION TO LOG-RECORD
197                  MOVE BAD-TRANS-CODE-MSG TO LOG-MESSAGE
198                  WRITE LOG-RECORD AFTER ADVANCING 1 LINE
199                  ADD 1 TO ERROR-COUNT.
200
201          D030-INVALID-ADDITION.
202              MOVE TRANSACTION TO LOG-RECORD.
203              MOVE BAD-ADDITION-MSG TO LOG-MESSAGE.
204              WRITE LOG-RECORD AFTER ADVANCING 1 LINE.
205              ADD 1 TO ERROR-COUNT.
206
207          E010-PROCESS-SHIPMENT.
208              IF OM-QUAN-ON-HAND IS NOT LESS THAN TR-QUANTITY
209                  SUBTRACT TR-QUANTITY FROM OM-QUAN-ON-HAND
210              ELSE
211                  MOVE TRANSACTION TO LOG-RECORD
212                  MOVE OUT-OF-STOCK-MSG TO LOG-MESSAGE
213                  WRITE LOG-RECORD AFTER ADVANCING 1 LINE
214                  ADD 1 TO ERROR-COUNT.
215
216          E020-PROCESS-RECEIPT.
217              ADD TR-QUANTITY TO OM-QUAN-ON-HAND.
218              SUBTRACT TR-QUANTITY FROM OM-QUAN-ON-ORDER.
219
220          E030-PROCESS-ADJUSTMENT.
221              IF      TR-ADJUSTMENT-CODE = 1
222                  MOVE TR-QUANTITY TO OM-QUAN-ON-HAND
223              ELSE IF TR-ADJUSTMENT-CODE = 2
224                  MOVE TR-QUANTITY TO OM-QUAN-ON-ORDER
225              ELSE IF TR-ADJUSTMENT-CODE = 3
226                  MOVE TR-QUANTITY TO OM-REORDER-POINT
227              ELSE IF TR-ADJUSTMENT-CODE = 4
228                  MOVE TR-QUANTITY TO OM-REORDER-QUAN
```

```
229                    ELSE IF TR-ADJUSTMENT-CODE = 5
230                        MOVE TR-DESCRIPTION TO OM-DESCRIPTION
231                    ELSE
232                        MOVE TRANSACTION TO LOG-RECORD
233                        MOVE BAD-ADJ-CODE-MSG TO LOG-MESSAGE
234                        WRITE LOG-RECORD AFTER ADVANCING 1 LINE
235                        ADD 1 TO ERROR-COUNT.
236
237        X010-GET-VALID-TRANSACTION.
238            MOVE '?' TO SEQUENCE-ERROR-FLAG.
239            PERFORM Y010-READ-TRANSACTION
240                UNTIL     SEQUENCE-ERROR-FLAG = 'N'
241                        OR ERROR-COUNT IS GREATER THAN 10.
242
243        X020-GET-VALID-MASTER.
244            MOVE '?' TO SEQUENCE-ERROR-FLAG.
245            PERFORM Y020-READ-MASTER
246                UNTIL     SEQUENCE-ERROR-FLAG = 'N'
247                        OR ERROR-COUNT IS GREATER THAN 10.
248
249        Y010-READ-TRANSACTION.
250            READ TRANSACTION-FILE INTO TRANSACTION
251                AT END MOVE HIGH-VALUES TO TR-KEY.
252            IF TR-KEY IS LESS THAN TR-KEY-PREVIOUS
253                MOVE TRANSACTION TO LOG-RECORD
254                MOVE TRANS-SEQUENCE-ERROR-MSG TO LOG-MESSAGE
255                WRITE LOG-RECORD AFTER ADVANCING 1 LINE
256                ADD 1 TO ERROR-COUNT
257            ELSE
258                MOVE 'N' TO SEQUENCE-ERROR-FLAG.
259            MOVE TR-KEY TO TR-KEY-PREVIOUS.
260
261        Y020-READ-MASTER.
262            READ OLD-MASTER-FILE INTO OLD-MASTER
263                AT END MOVE HIGH-VALUES TO OM-KEY.
264            IF OM-KEY IS LESS THAN OM-KEY-PREVIOUS
265                MOVE OLD-MASTER TO LOG-RECORD
266                MOVE MASTER-SEQUENCE-ERROR-MSG TO LOG-MESSAGE
267                WRITE LOG-RECORD AFTER ADVANCING 1 LINE
268                ADD 1 TO ERROR-COUNT
269            ELSE
270                MOVE 'N' TO SEQUENCE-ERROR-FLAG.
271            MOVE OM-KEY TO OM-KEY-PREVIOUS.
272
273        ******************** END OF PROGRAM *************************
```

FIGURE 13.11 The complete file update program, including more complete files and adjustments for all record fields.

This version of the program contains a number of changes from previous versions. To begin with, we have added a new file, ORDER-FILE, which requires a SELECT statement in the Environment Division and an FD in the Data Division. This file will be used for order recommendations when stock is found to be low. The record description for ORDER-FILE provides for a bit of editing, but in the interests of simplicity and space the program does not show the printing of headings or counting of pages and lines that would normally be provided.

The records **LOG-RECORD** and **NEW-MASTER** have both been modified. The change to **LOG-RECORD** is simple, made primarily to emphasize the more general usage of the record in this version of the program. We have also reduced the legnth of **LOG-MESSAGE** to 50 characters since that is all that is needed to hold the actual messages. The revised format of **NEW-MASTER** reflects the more detailed file definition that we are using.

In the Working-Storage Section we have added a message to report an invalid adjustment code on a transaction, and the formats of **OLD-MASTER** and **TRANSACTION** have been revised to fit our new requirements.

In the Procedure Division, the only change in **B010-UPDATE-LOGIC** is a statement to perform **C040-CHECK-QUANTITY** before a master record is written to **NEW-MASTER-FILE**. It is important to understand why this code, which determines whether or not we need to order more merchandise, is placed at this point in the program. It will, of course, be done any time an old master has no activity, that is, no matching transaction. In this case, the execution of the reordering decision will ordinarily not result in the placement of another order. But then again, it may, so it is not wrong to check even in this case. When an old master does have activity, whether that consists of adjustments, receipts, or shipments—or any combination of the three—we do not want to make the reordering decision until all the transactions have been processed. As the program has been written, the old master is modified in its Working-Storage location and is not written until a new transaction is found that has a different key. When this occurs, the modified old master is forced out to the new master file, and it is at precisely this point that we want to make the reordering decision.

The paragraph that makes this decision, **C040-CHECK-QUANTITY**, contains one new feature that we may note in passing and then shall defer until Chapter 20 for a complete explanation. We see that within a relation condition it is permissible to write an arithmetic expression, using a plus sign. What we want to know is whether the sum of the quantity on order and the quantity on hand is less than the reorder point. The statement shown expresses exactly that. If you wish to use simple arithmetic expressions of this sort without looking ahead to the full story in Chapter 20, just keep the arithmetic *very simple* and always write a space before and a space after the arithmetic operators.

The last thing to be done when it has been determined that more stock is needed is to add the reorder quantity to the quantity on order. This is necessary because otherwise the next time the inventory control program is run it would again order some more stock. This is the main function of the quantity-on-order field.

Aside from the changes needed to build the new master record in **C020-ADD-MASTER**, the only remaining changes involve modification of the three level **E** paragraphs. We see now why we did not simply include these paragraphs as in-line code in the nested **IF** of **D020-UPDATE-MASTER**, in the previous version of the program. We are able to modify the three update paragraphs as needed, with no change to the code that controls their execution. Of these three paragraphs, the most significant change has to do with the processing of adjustments, since we how have an adjustment code that indicates which of five fields is being changed. The nested **IF** statement that we have used is the code that we developed in Section 5.14 for the case structure. If you are using **COBOL-85**, you may replace this code with an equivalent

EVALUATE statement. Basically, we are executing one of five different actions depending on the value of **TR-ADJUSTMENT-CODE**, with a sixth action to take care of the error case if **TR-ADJUSTMENT-CODE** has an illegal value.

We note one final feature of this program from an inventory control standpoint. When a receipt is processed, it represents the completion of a cycle that was begun when the stock item was ordered in a previous execution of the program. When the material was ordered, that quantity was added to the quantity on order. Now, when it is received, the quantity must be subtracted from the quantity on order and added to the quantity on hand. Naturally, in real life there would have to be provision for handling partial shipments, incorrect quantities, and various other considerations.

The program was run with sample files. Here is the sample old master.

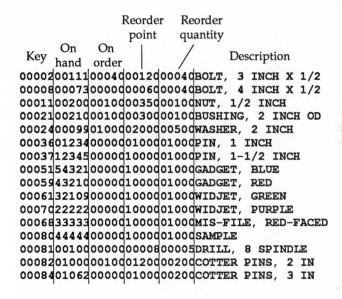

Key	On hand	On order	Reorder point	Reorder quantity	Description
00002	00111	00040	00120	00040	BOLT, 3 INCH X 1/2
00008	00073	00000	00060	00040	BOLT, 4 INCH X 1/2
00011	00200	00100	00350	00100	NUT, 1/2 INCH
00021	00210	00100	00300	00100	BUSHING, 2 INCH OD
00024	00099	01000	02000	00500	WASHER, 2 INCH
00036	01234	00000	01000	01000	PIN, 1 INCH
00037	12345	00000	10000	01000	PIN, 1-1/2 INCH
00051	54321	00000	10000	01000	GADGET, BLUE
00059	43210	00000	10000	01000	GADGET, RED
00061	32109	00000	10000	01000	WIDJET, GREEN
00070	22222	00000	10000	01000	WIDJET, PURPLE
00068	33333	00000	10000	01000	MIS-FILE, RED-FACED
00080	44444	00000	10000	01000	SAMPLE
00081	00100	00000	00008	00005	DRILL, 8 SPINDLE
00082	01000	00100	01200	00200	COTTER PINS, 2 IN
00084	01062	00000	01000	00200	COTTER PINS, 3 IN

The transaction file that was used appears at the top of the next page.

When the program was run the log file report contained the following:

```
000010001021                                   THIS TRANSACTION IS OUT OF SEQUENCE
00011987651 111112222233333ERROR ENTRY         THIS ADDITION MATCHES AN EXISTING MASTER
00024012004                                     INSUFFICIENT STOCK TO SHIP AMOUNT SPECIFIED
00036000005                                     THIS TRANSACTION IS OUT OF SEQUENCE
00051543210000010000001000GADGET, BLUE          THIS MASTER RECORD HAS BEEN DELETED
00052000005                                     THERE IS NO MASTER FOR THIS TRANSACTION
00059001230                                     TRANSACTION CODE ILLEGAL
00068333330000010000001000MIS-FILE, RED-FACED   THIS MASTER IS OUT OF SEQUENCE
000810000029                                    BAD ADJUSTMENT CODE
```

This is the order report:

```
00008      40    BOLT, 4 INCH X 1/2
00011     100    NUT, 1/2 INCH
00024     500    WASHER, 2 INCH
00080      30    SAMPLE
00082     200    COTTER PINS, 2 IN
00084     200    COTTER PINS, 3 IN
```

```
                              ┌ Transaction code
                            ┌ Adjustment code
         Key   Qty        │ │
         0000200010|4|
         0000100010|2|1
         0000800050|4|
         0001198765|1|  111112222233333ERROR ENTRY
         0001500999|1|  008880077700666A CORRECT ADDITION
         0002100100|3|
         0002400500|3|
         0002400050|4|
         0002400040|4|
         0002401200|4|
         000371230021|
         00036000005|
         00051000005|
         00052000005|
         0005901000|4|
         0005900123|0|
         0006101234|4|
         0008000010|2|1
         0008000022|2|
         0008000050|2|3
```

Here is the new master that was produced.

```
                    Reorder    Reorder
                     point    quantity
       On    On                              Description
Key   hand  order     │          /
00002|00101|00040|00120|00040|BOLT, 3 INCH X 1/2
00008|00023|00040|00060|00040|BOLT, 4 INCH X 1/2
00011|00200|00200|00350|00100|NUT, 1/2 INCH
00015|00999|00888|00777|00666|A CORRECT ADDITION
00021|00310|00000|00300|00100|BUSHING, 2 INCH OD
00024|00509|01000|02000|00500|WASHER, 2 INCH
00036|01234|00000|01000|01000|PIN, 1 INCH
00037|12300|00000|01000|01000|PIN, 1-1/2 INCH
00059|42210|00000|01000|01000|GADGET, RED
00061|30875|00000|01000|01000|WIDJET, GREEN
00070|22222|00000|01000|01000|WIDJET, PURPLE
00080|00010|00052|00050|00030|SAMPLE
00081|00100|00000|00008|00005|DRILL, 6 SPINDLE
00082|01000|00300|01200|00200|COTTER PINS, 2 IN
00084|00862|00200|00100|00200|COTTER PINS, 3 IN
```

A careful study of these sample files will be rewarded with a thorough understanding of the logic of this program. The best way to do this is to take the transactions in sequence and satisfy yourself that the outputs are correct for the conditions represented. As one example, consider stock item 24. The old master began with 99 on hand and 1000 on order. The first transaction for this stock item represented a receipt of 500. The next two transactions represented shipments of 50 and 40 giving a quantity on hand of 509. The last transaction attempted to ship 1200. The impossibility of doing this was noted in the log report. With 509 on hand and 500 still on order after subtracting the shipment of 500, the quantity on hand plus the quantity on order was less than the reorder point of 2000, so another order was placed. This left the quantity on order at 1000 again, as we note in the new master.

Inspection of the other transactions will show that all of the various kinds of transactions and the variations of adjustments were handled correctly and that all of the erroneous transactions were reported properly. This is not an exhaustive test to really satisfy ourselves that the program will handle all eventualities for which it was designed, but at least it indicates that there are no glaring errors.

REVIEW QUESTIONS

1. Here is a pseudocode representation of the logic of the merge program without sequence checking. Does it represent the same logic as the program of Figure 13.4? Could the program be written in this fashion without separate paragraphs for the READ statements?

   ```
   Open files
   Read a file-1 record; at end move HIGH-VALUES to KEY-1
   Read a file-2 record; at end move HIGH-VALUES to KEY-2
   PERFORM-UNTIL KEY-1 = HIGH-VALUES and KEY-2 = HIGH-VALUES
      IF KEY-1 is less than KEY-2 THEN
         Write output record from file-1 record
         Read a file-1 record; at end move HIGH-VALUES to KEY-1
      ELSE
         Write output record from file-2 record
         Read a file-2 record; at end move HIGH-VALUES to KEY-2
      ENDIF
   ENDPERFORM
   Close files
   Stop
   ```

2. Suppose that in a file updating application, the master file is in ascending sequence but the transaction file is in descending sequence. Could program logic be devised to do the updating? If not, what would have to be done before the transaction could be processed?

3. Suppose that a master file in a file updating application were lost or destroyed. What would have to be done to reconstruct it?

4. Suppose that in the sample old master file shown following UPDATE1, the first two records were reversed. What would UPDATE1 produce, given the same transaction file? What would the program do if the master file were correct but the first two records of the transaction file were reversed?

5. Suppose that the transactions for one stock item consisted of a number of shipments followed by a deletion. Would the logic of the program of Figure 13.7 (UPDATE2) handle this situation correctly?

6. What would happen with the program of Figure 13.7 if a deletion record were followed by shipments or receipts for the same stock item?

7. It is generally believed that the use of level 88 entries improves readability. For instance, an **IF** statement that begins

   ```
   IF ADDITION . . .
   ```

   is easier to understand without looking at the Data Division than the equivalent statement

   ```
   IF TR-TRANSACTION-CODE = '1' . . .
   ```

   Can you think of a circumstance where readability considerations might argue for writing the tests in the second form?

8. The versions of the file update program from Figure 13.9 (**UPDATE3**) on all sequence check the transaction file and the old master file but they do not sequence check the new master file. Can you think of reasons why it might be advisable to include such a sequence check of the output?

ANSWERS TO REVIEW QUESTIONS

1. The logic is identical. The program could be written this way, but using separate paragraphs for input usually makes the code easier to read and modify.

2. Program logic cannot be set up to handle sequential file updating unless the two files are in the same sequence on the same key. Under certain limited circumstances it might be possible to find a way to process the transactions, but the real solution would be to sort the transaction file into the same sequence as the master.

3. The file updating program would have to be run using the previous copies of the master file and the transaction file that was processed against it. It is customary to retain copies of old master and transaction files for just this purpose.

4. The program would process the erroneous master file correctly. It would detect equality of the first master and first transaction, update the master, and get another transaction. This new transaction would force out the first three master records, even though not in correct sequence, and everything else would proceed normally.

   With the first two transaction records reversed, the program would read master records until it found the one with the key 00021, which would be updated correctly. On reading another transaction, the update logic would compare an old master key of 00021 with a transaction key of 00008; since the old master key is not less than the transaction key, it would do the updating and thus create a garbled master record. Subsequent records would be processed correctly.

5. Yes.

6. This should not happen because it was specified that the transactions for any one key will be in sequence on the transaction code. Since this error is possible, however, the sequence checking of the transaction file really ought to include an appropriate test for this error possibility.

To answer the question as posed, however, the first transaction after the deletion would be treated as an addition, and the new master would be thoroughly garbled. The rudimentary checking of the program in Figure 13.9 would catch this error.

7. During program testing or debugging, whether of the original program or of the program as changed during maintenance, it is necessary to determine that the program acts correctly in response to specific data. At this stage it is, of course, necessary to know the actual values of the data items rather than the more descriptive condition names. It can be argued that since the programmer has to know the actual codes anyway, it is preferable to write the IF statements to use the codes and possibly use a comment to indicate what they stand for. The alternative argument, however, is that this type of testing is generally a short-term activity, and that the more common requirement is to be able to determine what *function* the program is supposed to be performing. This requirement is met better by condition names, and one can use the Data Division to prepare test data if necessary.

8. It might seem that there would be no point to sequence checking the output, since the only ways the output could be out of sequence are rather unlikely. One way this could happen would be for the input to be out of sequence but for the program not to catch the error. Another would be undetected computer malfunction. Another would be an error in program logic. It could be argued that undetected computer malfunction is extremely unlikely and that the other two types of errors are very unlikely once the program has been tested thoroughly.

   However, since a sequence error in the new master is indicative of very serious errors that will disable the next cycle of processing completely, it is sometimes felt desirable to make a check of this kind even though the error is very unlikely to occur. This is especially true since sequence checking does not appreciably complicate the program and since it takes very little machine time. Such a check is especially useful during program testing, before it is known with assurance that the logic is correct. (Admittedly, however, this is not done very often in actual programs once testing is finished.)

EXERCISES

*1. There are occasions when files to be merged should not have any matching records. Prepare pseudocode for a merge program that makes two error tests:

   a. It sequence checks both files and stops on finding any error.

   b. It stops if the keys of the records from the two files are the same.

2. Prepare pseudocode and write a program to check for sequence errors in an input file and also check for duplicate records. The program should print an appropriate message and stop if either condition is detected.

---

* Answers to starred exercises will be found in Appendix IV at the end of the book.

*3. Write a program to merge three input files, each of which is in ascending sequence on a key. Include sequence checking.

4. The program in Figure 13.11 (**UPDATE5**) checks the key, the transaction code, and the adjustment code of the transaction file but assumes that the quantity, quantity on order, reorder point, and reorder quantity are all valid. Modify the program so that it will validate these four fields as being numeric before it accepts the transaction as valid. The program should test all fields, not just stop when the first error is found. That is, if more than one field is in error, the transaction record should be printed *once*, but error messages should be printed for *all* fields in error. You should move the editing of the transaction code and the adjustment code to this point in the program so that all editing except sequence checking is done as part of the input process. In other words, once a transaction record is accepted as valid, it should contain no data errors except (possibly) not matching a master record. (No matter how many errors you find in one transaction record, only add 1 to **ERROR–COUNT** for the entire record.)

*5. The program of Figure 13.7 (**UPDATE2**) and the programs following it will not operate correctly if an addition record is followed by other transactions for the same key. Modify the program so that this type of transaction file can be processed correctly. This is much harder than it might sound. Try it first on the relatively simple program in Figure 13.7, then when you have the technique developed, apply it to the program in Figure 13.11 (**UPDATE5**).

*6. Modify the program of Figure 13.11 so that it distinguishes between file sequence errors and errors in the transaction data. Errors in the transaction file other than sequence errors should be allowed up to a maximum of 100; since they are to be expected and do not affect other transactions, they are not too serious. However, since sequence errors are usually disabling and indicative of serious trouble, especially on the master file, report all sequence errors and allow only *ten* sequence errors on the transaction file or *one* sequence error on the old master file before processing is halted.

7. Modify the program of Figure 13.11 so that when there is insufficient stock on hand to process a shipment, as many as are on hand are shipped and the difference is added to the quantity back-ordered, a new field in the master record. Create appropriate test data and test the program.

8. (This exercise is suitable for a project.)
Assume that a company's employee payroll records have the following format:

Columns 1-5	employee pay number	9(5)
Columns 6-30	employee name	X(25)
Columns 31-39	social security number	9(9)
Columns 40-47	year-to-date gross pay	9(6)V99
Columns 48-55	year-to-date federal tax	9(6)V99
Columns 56-62	year-to-date state tax	9(5)V99
Columns 63-69	year-to-date city tax	9(5)V99

Columns 70-77	year-to-date net pay	9(6)V99
Column 78	pay type; **H** for hourly, **S** for salaried	X
Columns 79-85	weekly salary or hourly pay rate	9(5)V99 BBB99V99
Columns 86-87	municipality code	99

This file may be updated by three types of transactions. The functions and formats of these transactions are:

1. add a new employee

Column 1	record type (**A**)
Columns 2-6	employee pay number
Columns 7-31	employee name
Columns 32-40	social security number
Columns 41	pay type; **H** or **S**
Columns 42-48	for salaried employees, weekly salary; for hourly employees, hourly pay rate
Columns 49-50	municipality code

2. delete an employee

Column 1	record type (**B**)
Columns 2-6	employee pay number
Columns 7-50	not used

3. weekly pay record (for hourly employees only)

Columns 1	record type (**C**)
Columns 2-6	employee pay number
Columns 8-12	department number
Columns 13-16	hours worked; numeric, 2 decimals
Columns 17-50	not used

The weekly payroll transaction file is sorted on employee pay number, and on record type within employee. Two reports are produced by the payroll program. The first is the Weekly Payroll Report. For each employee paid during the week, the report shows the following:

Columns 1-5	employee pay number	PIC 9(5)
Columns 8-32	employee name	PIC X(25)
Columns 35-43	gross pay	PIC ZZ,ZZ9.99
Columns 46-54	total deductions	PIC ZZ,ZZ9.99
Columns 57-65	net pay	PIC ZZ,ZZ9.99

At the bottom of the report is a line showing total gross pay, total deductions, and total net pay for the company. At the top of each page is a line containing column headings.

All salaried employees are paid each week. Hourly employees are paid in any given week only if there is a pay record for them. Because an hourly employee can work in more than one department in a week, an hourly employee may have more than one pay record. The employee's pay is based on total hours, regardless of the department(s) in which these hours are accrued. Hourly employees are paid at base rate for the first 37.5 hours worked and at 1.5 times base for hours in excess of 37.5.

Deductions consist of federal tax (25% of gross pay), state tax (5% of gross pay), and city tax. City tax varies depending on where the employee lives; this is coded in the municipality code field. Using the municipality code, city tax is calculated as follows:

Municipality	Tax
03	1.50% of gross pay
07	2.00%
15	5.25%
23	3.75%
77	2.50%

The employee's net pay is the gross pay minus the sum of all deductions.

After an employee has been paid, the various year-to-date total fields in his or her master payroll record are updated by adding the current values of gross pay, federal tax, state tax, city tax, and net pay to the old year-to-date totals. The updated record is then written to a new master payroll file. Of course, for hourly employees the payroll record must be written to the new master file regardless of whether or not the employee was actually paid during the week.

The second report produced by the payroll program is the Payroll Activity Log. If an employee is added to the master payroll file, all year-to-date fields in the new record are initialized to zero and a message is written to the Activity Log indicating the employee's pay number, name, social security number, pay type (hourly or salaried), weekly salary or hourly pay rate, and municipality code.

If an employee is deleted from the master payroll file, a message is written to the Activity Log showing all data in the payroll record. (In a real payroll system employee records are not actually removed from the system when an employee leaves the company since for tax purposes records must be maintained at least until the end of the year. However, these records may be transferred to an *inactive* file for the sake of efficiency.)

Design of the actual format of the Payroll Activity Log is left as part of the exercise. However, remember that all reports should be designed to be used by people who are not programmers and who do not have the time or interest to guess what the information on the report means. Design reports to be as useful as possible, not just to minimize the amount of code you have to write.

Optional added feature: Assume that payroll transaction records may contain errors. To be valid, the record type must be A, B, or C. In a type A record the pay number, social security number, salary or hourly pay rate, and municipality code must be numeric. The pay type must be H or S, and for hourly employees the pay rate must not exceed $99.99. For type B records, the pay number must be numeric and the remainder of the record must be blank. For type C records, the pay number, department number, and hours worked must be numeric; hours worked must not exceed 80.00; and the remainder of the record must be blank. For type A records, there must not be a record already on the master file with the same pay number; and for type B and C records there must be a match with a record on the master file.

CHAPTER 14

TABLE HANDLING

14.1   INTRODUCTION

In this chapter we shall study the COBOL facilities for handling groups of related items with *subscripting* and *indexing*. These features permit us to refer to a large number of related items by one name, selecting—by using appropriate subscripts or indices—the one part of the large group that is desired.

14.2   THE BASICS OF SUBSCRIPTING

Suppose that we need to be able to refer to a list of 100 accounts in Working-Storage, each six digits long. It would certainly be possible to give them 100 different names, such as ACCOUNT-1, ACCOUNT-2, etc., up to ACCOUNT-100. The Data Division would have to include an entry for each of the different data names, which may be sketched as follows:

```
01   ACCOUNT-GROUP.
     05   ACCOUNT-1          PIC 9(6).
     05   ACCOUNT-2          PIC 9(6).
     .
     .
     .
     05   ACCOUNT-99         PIC 9(6).
     05   ACCOUNT-100        PIC 9(6).
```

This would be time-consuming both for the programmer and for the compiler, would be highly error prone, and in many cases would lead to hopelessly complicated Procedure Division code.

By using subscripts we can, instead, give the entire list a single name such as ACCOUNT. We inform the compiler that the name ACCOUNT stands for 100 different items—not just one—by writing the clause OCCURS 100 TIMES in the Data Division entry for ACCOUNT. This might be done as follows:

```
01   TABLE-OF-ACCOUNTS.
     05   ACCOUNT           PIC 9(6) OCCURS 100 TIMES.
```

This indicates to the compiler that **ACCOUNT** is the name of a subscripted data item having 100 elements, each element being six digits in length. **ACCOUNT** has been shown as a 05 level name because the **OCCURS** clause may not be written at the **01** or **77** levels. The **01** level name shown in this entry refers to the group containing the table and has no necessary relationship to the name of the subscripted data item. However, as the **01** level name implies, **ACCOUNT** is now generally referred to as a *table* in **COBOL**.

In the Procedure Division, when we want to refer to a particular item out of the 100 items that are described by the general name **ACCOUNT**, we follow the name with parentheses enclosing an integer in the range of 1 to 100. Thus if we want to refer to the first item in the table, we can write

    ACCOUNT (1)

If we want the fourteenth item in the table, we can write

    ACCOUNT (14)

We will commonly leave a space between the data name and the left parenthesis, although this is not required.

If the only way to refer to a particular element of a subscripted data item were to use literals, subscripting would be of limited use. This is not all we can do, however; it is possible to use a variable as a subscript. We might, for instance, write

    ACCOUNT (ACCOUNT-NUMBER)

ACCOUNT-NUMBER must be an integer data item that has been given a value by previous statements. Whatever value **ACCOUNT-NUMBER** has would be used to select the corresponding element from the table named **ACCOUNT**. It is the programmer's responsibility to be sure that the value of a subscript is never less than 1 nor greater than the number of elements in the table. If a subscript outside these limits is used, the result depends on the compiler options being used. If you use the default options for the Microsoft compiler, you will get an error message at run time when the subscript goes outside the valid range, and your program will terminate.

Some compilers, such as the IBM mainframe **COBOL** compiler, do not check subscripts. If a subscript goes outside the bounds defined for the array, no error message is produced. If you are reading from the array, you will read whatever data happens to be adjacent to the array in memory. If you are storing data into the array, you will write on top of the data adjacent to your array. In some cases no serious error will occur, although your results will almost certainly be wrong. In other cases, however, you may alter vital information, or even attempt to write outside the memory limits of your computer. In these cases you will certainly have serious problems during execution.

We recommend that you check subscripts very carefully to be sure they are within proper bounds, either with code in your program or with the builtin subscript checking of the Microsoft **COBOL** compiler. However, if you wish to maintain compatibility with a compiler that does not use subscript checking, include the NOBOUND directive in your COBOL.DIR file. For maximum efficiency, if you use NOBOUND you should also use NOBOUNDOPT. If you use these directives, remember that the responsibility for checking subscripts will lie with your program.

In the example above, ACCOUNT-NUMBER is used as a subscript. It is permitted to be either binary (COMPUTATIONAL usage) or decimal (DISPLAY or COMPUTATIONAL-3 usage). However, unless there is good reason not to do so, we prefer subscripts to be binary items since this is the most efficient form. This is achieved by writing COMPUTATIONAL SYNC in the Data Division entry for a subscript item. For our example, we could write

```
01  ACCOUNT-NUMBER          PIC 999 COMP SYNC.
```

(Even though the SYNC clause may not be necessary, it is better to make the intention clear by writing the clauses as shown.)

14.3 A SIMPLE PROGRAM ILLUSTRATING SUBSCRIPTING

In Figure 14.1 we have the Data and Procedure Divisions for a program that employs subscripting to develop a frequency table describing input data. We are given a file whose records each contain a four-digit number identifying a year, together with other data that we will not process. The year identification should be 1988, 1989, 1990, or 1991. The function of the program is to produce a line showing the number of records for each year and a count of the total number of records outside this range.

```
13         DATA DIVISION.
14
15         FILE SECTION.
16
17         FD   IN-FILE
18              LABEL RECORDS ARE STANDARD.
19         01   IN-RECORD.
20              05   ACCOUNT-NUMBER          PIC X(6).
21              05   YEAR                    PIC 9(4).
22              05   FILLER                  PIC X(70).
23
24         FD   REPORT-FILE
25              LABEL RECORDS ARE STANDARD.
26         01   REPORT-RECORD.
27              05   YEAR-COUNT-OUT          PIC Z(6)9 OCCURS 4 TIMES.
28              05   BAD-DATA-COUNT-OUT      PIC Z(6)9.
29
30         WORKING-STORAGE SECTION.
31
32         01   YEAR-TABLE.
33              05   YEAR-COUNT              PIC S9(4) COMP SYNC
34                                           OCCURS 4 TIMES.
35         01   BAD-DATA-COUNT              PIC S9(4) COMP SYNC.
36
37         01   MORE-DATA-REMAINS-FLAG      PIC X VALUE 'Y'.
38              88   MORE-DATA-REMAINS            VALUE 'Y'.
39              88   NO-MORE-DATA-REMAINS         VALUE 'N'.
40
41         01   YEAR-SUBSCRIPT              PIC S9 COMP SYNC.
42
```

```
43        PROCEDURE DIVISION.
44        A000-COUNT-DATA.
45            MOVE 0 TO YEAR-COUNT (1).
46            MOVE 0 TO YEAR-COUNT (2).
47            MOVE 0 TO YEAR-COUNT (3).
48            MOVE 0 TO YEAR-COUNT (4).
49            MOVE 0 TO BAD-DATA-COUNT.
50            OPEN INPUT IN-FILE
51                 OUTPUT REPORT-FILE.
52            PERFORM B010-COUNT-YEARS
53                 UNTIL NO-MORE-DATA-REMAINS.
54            PERFORM B020-WRITE-TABLE.
55            CLOSE IN-FILE
56                  REPORT-FILE.
57            STOP RUN.
58
59        B010-COUNT-YEARS.
60            READ IN-FILE
61                AT END MOVE 'N' TO MORE-DATA-REMAINS-FLAG.
62            IF MORE-DATA-REMAINS
63                IF YEAR IS LESS THAN 1988 OR IS GREATER THAN 1991
64                    ADD 1 TO BAD-DATA-COUNT
65                ELSE
66                    SUBTRACT 1987 FROM YEAR GIVING YEAR-SUBSCRIPT
67                    ADD 1 TO YEAR-COUNT (YEAR-SUBSCRIPT).
68
69        B020-WRITE-TABLE.
70            MOVE YEAR-COUNT (1) TO YEAR-COUNT-OUT (1).
71            MOVE YEAR-COUNT (2) TO YEAR-COUNT-OUT (2).
72            MOVE YEAR-COUNT (3) TO YEAR-COUNT-OUT (3).
73            MOVE YEAR-COUNT (4) TO YEAR-COUNT-OUT (4).
74            MOVE BAD-DATA-COUNT TO BAD-DATA-COUNT-OUT.
75            WRITE REPORT-RECORD AFTER ADVANCING 1 LINE.
```

FIGURE 14.1 The Data and Procedure Divisions of a program using subscripting to produce a frequency table.

The program operates with a table (YEAR-TABLE) having four locations for recording the four counts. This table is shown in the Working-Storage Section with an OCCURS clause specifying that YEAR-COUNT has four elements. Since we never do anything with these locations other than use them in arithmetic and as source items in MOVE statements, it makes the program slightly more efficient to designate them as COMPUTATIONAL. The data item named YEAR-SUB-SCRIPT is also COMPUTATIONAL and SYNCHRONIZED.

The Procedure Division begins by moving zeros to all elements of the table, and to BAD-DATA-COUNT. It is necessary to do something of this sort, since an item that has an OCCURS clause is not allowed to have a VALUE clause. Although there are other ways of initializing a table (which we will discuss in the following sections), all but one of them are variations on this approach. COBOL does not have a statement that says "Move this constant to every element of the table," and trying to move an initial value to the group item YEAR-TABLE will frequently give incorrect results.

After we initialize the table, the following code is very similar to previous programs. In the processing paragraph named B010-COUNT-YEARS we get the information from a record and then inspect the year to see if it is in the range

1988 to 1991, inclusive. If it is not, we add one to the count of bad data. If the year is valid, we now need to add one to the appropriate element of **YEAR-COUNT**. We must somehow make the correspondence between year 1988 and subscript 1, between year 1989 and subscript 2, etc. An easy way to do this is to subtract 1987 from the year number, giving a result in the range 1 to 4. This value is then used as the subscript.

When all the records have been processed, we need to move the values to the output line and print them. This is done using subscripted variables as well, taking advantage of the fact that the item named **REPORT-RECORD** in the File Section has an **OCCURS** clause on its 05 level entry for **YEAR-COUNT-OUT**.

14.4 ENTERING VALUES INTO A TABLE USING REDEFINES

Even in the previous example, which primarily involved producing table values by execution of a program, it was necessary to give initial values to the elements of the table. If we wish to do the reverse, namely, to select entries from values already in a table, initialization becomes even more important. For an example, suppose that records in an input file contain, among other things, a transaction date represented as a six-digit number. For example, July 4, 1990 might be represented as 900704. We wish to convert the representation of the month, 07 in the example, into its English equivalent and print the text as part of a report. The question is how to arrange the Data Division so that a subscripted value—which must have an **OCCURS** clause and must not have a **VALUE** clause—can be associated with 12 **VALUE** clauses giving the names of the months. Figure 14.2 shows how the **REDEFINES** clause provides the answer.

```
WORKING-STORAGE SECTION.

01    MONTH-NAME-VALUES.
      05    FILLER                PIC X(9) VALUE 'JANUARY  '.
      05    FILLER                PIC X(9) VALUE 'FEBRUARY '.
      05    FILLER                PIC X(9) VALUE 'MARCH    '.
      05    FILLER                PIC X(9) VALUE 'APRIL    '.
      05    FILLER                PIC X(9) VALUE 'MAY      '.
      05    FILLER                PIC X(9) VALUE 'JUNE     '.
      05    FILLER                PIC X(9) VALUE 'JULY     '.
      05    FILLER                PIC X(9) VALUE 'AUGUST   '.
      05    FILLER                PIC X(9) VALUE 'SEPTEMBER'.
      05    FILLER                PIC X(9) VALUE 'OCTOBER  '.
      05    FILLER                PIC X(9) VALUE 'NOVEMBER '.
      05    FILLER                PIC X(9) VALUE 'DECEMBER '.

01    MONTH-NAME-TABLE REDEFINES MONTH-NAME-VALUES.
      05    MONTH-NAME             PIC X(9) OCCURS 12 TIMES.

01    MONTH-NUMBER                 PIC S99 COMP SYNC.

01    MONTH-TEXT                   PIC X(9).
```

FIGURE 14.2 An illustration of the use of **REDEFINES** to enter values into a table in Working-Storage.

Given this table, we could then write code such as

```
MOVE MONTH-NAME (MONTH-NUMBER) TO MONTH-TEXT.
```

We see that the `01` level entry named `MONTH-NAME-VALUES` has 12 filler entries at the `05` level, each containing the name of a month. Each entry is 9 characters long, corresponding to the longest month's name (September); all entries in a table must be of the same length. After the group item consisting of these 12 fillers, another `01` level entry with a `REDEFINES` clause follows. Subordinate to it at the `05` level is an entry with the clause `OCCURS 12 TIMES`. It is this last data name, the one that has an `OCCURS` clause, that is written with a subscript in the Procedure Division.

It is worth pausing to consider the way in which the correspondence between a month name and and a month number is established. `MONTH-NAME-VALUES` and `MONTH-NAME-TABLE` are both group items, and the number of characters in each of them must accordingly be established by counting the number of characters of the elementary items of which they are composed. The compiler determines that `MONTH-NAME-VALUES` consists of 12 entries of nine characters each, which is 108 characters. The compiler then determines that the group item named `MONTH-NAME-TABLE` consists of an elementary item having nine characters, which occurs 12 times, and which also totals 108 characters. The correspondence between a code of 01 and the name January is established by the fact that the name January occurs first in the list of elementary items in `MONTH-NAME-VALUES`. Likewise, July is associated with the code 07 only because that name is the seventh one in the list. If the lines in the source program were to be mixed up so that July appeared as the first `05` level entry under `MONTH-NAME-VALUES` and January as the seventh, the program would, of course, produce results that would be correct in terms of the information supplied to it; and "900704" would become January 04, 1990.

This type of Data Division structure will frequently be seen in programs involving subscripting and indexing and should be understood thoroughly. This structure can be shown in skeleton form as follows:

```
01   NAME-1.
     05   FILLER      ...          PIC ... VALUE ...
     .
     .
     .
01   NAME-2 REDEFINES NAME-1.
     05   SUBSCRIPTED-NAME         PIC ... OCCURS ...
```

`SUBSCRIPTED-NAME` is the only one that will appear in the Procedure Division; this is the name that is written with a subscript. `NAME-1` and `NAME-2` are required simply to make the `REDEFINES` work. It is good programming style to make these names correspond to the subscripted name that will be used in the Procedure Division, but no information is taken from such correspondence by the compiler. Also, the `PIC` clauses for `NAME-1` and `SUBSCRIPTED-NAME` should be identical.

14.5 ENTERING VALUES INTO A TABLE FROM A FILE

Using **REDEFINES** to initialize a table is a technique that is useful only if the initial table values never change, as was the case in the previous example. In many cases, however, the initial values of the table entries may change from run to run, which would require changing the source code and recompiling the program every time the program was run—which is not an acceptable procedure. In these situations, we generally load the table data from an input file.

For example, consider the seed catalog program introduced in Chapter 11. Suppose that in addition to the data validation already in the program, we want to be certain that every catalog number in an order matches a number in a master file. One way to do this is to load all catalog numbers from a master inventory file into a table, then search the table for every order record to be certain that the catalog number in the order record is in the table. We will discuss ways of searching the table shortly; for now, we want to consider how the table might be loaded.

The program segment in Figure 14.3 shows the code that could be used to initialize the table of catalog numbers. To save space we have not shown the complete program, only the parts that would be added to load the table.

The first addition needed is, of course, the definition of a new file, **CATA-LOG-FILE**, which contains the valid catalog numbers. Presumably the file contains data about each catalog item, but we have defined only the one field needed for this program.

In the Working-Storage Section we define the table itself, as well as two additional variables we will need. The table has been defined to have 1000 entries; we will assume for simplicity that **CATALOG-FILE** contains no more than 1000 records, although in a real program we would check to make sure that we do not accidentally try to load more records than the table has room for. Notice that **VALID-NUMBER-MAX** has an initial value of 1000, the maximum table size. This variable serves two functions. First, during the loading process it tells us how large the table actually is if we wish to test for possible overflow (loading too many records into the table). Second, after the table has been loaded **VALID-NUMBER-MAX** tells how many records have *actually* been loaded into the table; we will need this information later when we try to search for specific records in the table.

X-CATALOG is the variable we will use as a subscript for table entries. We will tend to use the prefix **X** in a variable name to indicate that it is being used as an index or subscript for a table.

In the Procedure Division, paragraph **A000-VALIDATE-ORDERS** is exactly the same as it was in Figure 11.1, except that we have added the statement

```
PERFORM B020-LOAD-VALID-NUMBER.
```

as the first statement of the paragraph. This statement controls all activity required to load the table, including opening and closing **CATALOG-FILE**, initializing the subscript and end of file flag, and setting the updated value for **VALID-NUMBER-MAX**. These activities are all part of the task of loading the table, and do not belong in the main paragraph.

```
       SELECT CATALOG-FILE            ASSIGN TO CATALOG.
           .
           .
           .
   FD  CATALOG-FILE
       LABEL RECORDS ARE STANDARD.
   01  CATALOG-RECORD.
       05  MASTER-CATALOG-NUMBER     PIC X(5).
       05  REST-OF-RECORD            PIC X(65).
           .
           .
           .

   WORKING-STORAGE SECTION.
   77  VALID-NUMBER-MAX              PIC S9(4)   COMP SYNC
                                                 VALUE +1000.
   77  X-CATALOG                     PIC S9(4)   COMP SYNC.

   01  CATALOG-NUMBER-TABLE.
       05  VALID-NUMBER              PIC X(5) OCCURS 1000 TIMES.
           .
           .
           .

   PROCEDURE DIVISION.
   A000-VALIDATE-ORDERS.
       PERFORM B020-LOAD-VALID-NUMBERS.
       OPEN OUTPUT PROCESSING-FILE.
       MOVE PRICE-LIMIT TO PRICE-LIMIT-EDIT.
       MOVE LOW-VALUES TO ORDER-NUMBER OF ORDER-DATA.
       PERFORM B010-VALIDATE-ONE-LINE
           UNTIL LAST-ORDER-LINE.
       CLOSE PROCESSING-FILE.
       STOP RUN.
           .
           .
           .

   B020-LOAD-VALID-NUMBERS.
       OPEN INPUT CATALOG-FILE.
       MOVE 'Y' TO MORE-DATA-REMAINS-FLAG.
       MOVE ZERO TO X-CATALOG.
       READ CATALOG-FILE
           AT END MOVE 'N' TO MORE-DATA-REMAINS-FLAG.
       PERFORM C030-LOAD-CATALOG-RECORD
           UNTIL NO-MORE-DATA-REMAINS.
       CLOSE CATALOG-FILE.
       MOVE X-CATALOG TO VALID-NUMBER-MAX.
           .
           .
           .

   C030-LOAD-CATALOG-RECORD.
       ADD 1 TO X-CATALOG.
       MOVE MASTER-CATALOG-NUMBER TO VALID-NUMBER (X-CATALOG).
       READ CATALOG-FILE
           AT END MOVE 'N' TO MORE-DATA-REMAINS-FLAG.
```

FIGURE 14.3 COBOL code to load a table of valid catalog numbers from a master file.

B020-LOAD-VALID-NUMBER is very much like the driver paragraphs we have seen in examples up to now. It begins by opening the data file, initializing variables, and reading the priming record. It performs a work paragraph (which in this case loads entries in the table) until the data file is empty, then closes the data file and sets the new value for **VALID-NUMBER-MAX**. At this point, the table has been loaded and **VALID-NUMBER-MAX** tells how many entries are actually in use in the table.

C030-LOAD-CATALOG-RECORD is very simple and requires little discussion. The only point of interest is to note that at all times **X-CATALOG** tells how many records are actually contained in the table. An alternative, for example, is to initialize the subscript to one, then add one to it after a record has been loaded so that it points to the next available space. The problem with this approach is that when we reach the end of the input file, the subscript contains a value one *greater* than the number of records in the file, and we have to subtract one from **X-CATALOG** to get the correct value for **VALID-NUMBER-MAX**.

COBOL-85

14.6 INITIALIZING A TABLE WITH A VALUE CLAUSE

In **COBOL-85** we are permitted to place a **VALUE** clause on elements of a table. In this case, every element in the table is initialized to the specified value. For example, we could initialize the table in Figure 14.1 as follows instead of using code in the Procedure Division.

```
01  YEAR-TABLE.
    05  YEAR-COUNT              PIC S9(4) COMP SYNC
                                OCCURS 4 TIMES VALUE ZERO.
```

In the following example, each entry in the table contains a structure, and each occurrence of the structure contains an occurrence of **X-FIELD** and **9-FIELD**. Each occurrence of **X-FIELD** is initialized to spaces, and each occurrence of **9-FIELD** is initialized to zero.

```
01  TABLE-AREA.
    05  WORK-TABLE   OCCURS 100 TIMES.
        10  X-FIELD             PIC X(5)     VALUE SPACES.
        10  9-FIELD             PIC 9(5)V99 VALUE ZERO.
```

END COBOL-85

14.7 SUBSCRIPTED VARIABLES WITH TWO OR MORE SUBSCRIPTS

A subscripted variable in **COBOL** is not restricted to just one subscript, but may have two or three. (In **COBOL-85** a subscripted variable may have up to seven subscripts, which is far more than is likely to be needed in the kinds of problems **COBOL** deals with.) For an example of how this works, suppose that we must process a two-way table showing the enrollment in a school system classified by grade and year. We assume that the school system has grades 1 to

12 and that we are dealing with the years 1988 to 1991. This means that the table will have 48 entries, showing the enrollment for each grade for each year. Written in the form in which it might be displayed in a school system report, the table would be as follows:

	1988	1989	1990	1991
1	240	239	229	205
2	299	280	277	260
3	257	255	238	220
4	230	230	220	215
5	225	220	210	200
6	220	215	218	208
7	210	209	195	205
8	105	200	204	190
9	260	266	270	289
10	270	270	274	270
11	300	301	290	309
12	310	320	315	337

A subscripted variable is established as having two subscripts by writing a group item name having two subordinate OCCURS clauses. For this application the Data Division entry could be

```
01  SIZE-TABLE.
    05  SIZE-BY-GRADE                 OCCURS 12 TIMES.
        10  SIZE-BY-GRADE-AND-YEAR    PIC 999 OCCURS 4 TIMES.
```

SIZE-TABLE is an 01 level entry made necessary by the fact that an OCCURS clause is not permitted at the 01 level. SIZE-BY-GRADE has an OCCURS clause establishing that the number of occurrences of this level is 12 and that the corresponding subscript can therefore range from 1 to 12. This entry does not have a PICTURE clause. SIZE-BY-GRADE-AND-YEAR is subordinate to SIZE-BY-GRADE and has an OCCURS clause establishing that there are four occurrences of this level and that the corresponding subscript ranges from 1 to 4. It also has a PICTURE clause showing the nature of the elementary items of which the table is composed.

This structure of the Data Division entry for SIZE-TABLE establishes that when we write

```
SIZE-BY-GRADE-AND-YEAR (1, 2)
```

in the Procedure Division we mean the first grade and the second year. If the Data Division entry had been

```
01  SIZE-TABLE.
    05  SIZE-BY-YEAR                  OCCURS 4 TIMES.
        10  SIZE-BY-GRADE-AND-YEAR    PIC 999 OCCURS 12 TIMES.
```

then the reference

```
SIZE-BY-GRADE-AND-YEAR (1, 2)
```

would be to the first year and the second grade. What is important is not the names used, which the compiler obviously cannot interpret, but the order of the OCCURS clauses.

Looking at paragraph B020-LOAD-TABLE in Figure 14.4, we see that it is similar to B010-COUNT-YEARS in Figure 14.1 except that here we have two subscripts. Observe in the last line in the paragraph that GRADE is a DISPLAY item, since it is part of the input record, whereas YEAR-SUBSCRIPT has been defined as COMPUTATIONAL. This means trivial extra work for the compiler but no real difficulty in keeping such matters straight. If the program involved a good deal of manipulation of these table elements, the constant internal conversion from DISPLAY to COMPUTATIONAL could cause some inefficiencies. The solution would be to do the conversion once by moving GRADE to a COMPUTATIONAL item and always using the latter as a subscript.

```
1       IDENTIFICATION DIVISION.
2       PROGRAM-ID.
3           ENROLLMENT-REPORT.
4       DATE-WRITTEN.
5           JUNE 16, 1989.
6
7       ENVIRONMENT DIVISION.
8       INPUT-OUTPUT SECTION.
9       FILE-CONTROL.
10          SELECT ENROLLMENT-FILE          ASSIGN TO ENROLL.
11
12      DATA DIVISION.
13
14      FILE SECTION.
15
16      FD  ENROLLMENT-FILE
17          LABEL RECORDS ARE STANDARD.
18      01  ENROLLMENT-RECORD.
19          05   GRADE                      PIC 99.
20          05   YEAR                       PIC 9(4).
21          05   ENROLLMENT                 PIC 999.
22
23      WORKING-STORAGE SECTION.
24
25      77  ERROR-COUNT                      PIC S9(4) COMP SYNC.
26      77  GRADE-SUBSCRIPT                  PIC 99    COMP SYNC.
27      77  MORE-DATA-REMAINS-FLAG           PIC X.
28          88   MORE-DATA-REMAINS                      VALUE 'Y'.
29          88   NO-MORE-DATA-REMAINS                   VALUE 'N'.
30      77  YEAR-SUBSCRIPT                   PIC 9     COMP SYNC.
31
32      01  SIZE-TABLE.
33          05   SIZE-BY-GRADE              OCCURS 12 TIMES.
34              10   SIZE-BY-GRADE-AND-YEAR PIC 999 OCCURS 4 TIMES.
35
36      PROCEDURE DIVISION.
37      A000-CREATE-ENROLLMENT-TABLE.
38          MOVE ZERO TO ERROR-COUNT.
39          MOVE 'Y'  TO MORE-DATA-REMAINS-FLAG.
40          MOVE 1 TO GRADE-SUBSCRIPT.
41          PERFORM B010-INITIALIZE-TABLE
42              UNTIL GRADE-SUBSCRIPT > 12.
43          OPEN INPUT ENROLLMENT-FILE.
44          PERFORM B020-LOAD-TABLE
45              UNTIL NO-MORE-DATA-REMAINS.
```

```
46              DISPLAY SIZE-BY-GRADE-AND-YEAR (1, 1).
47              DISPLAY SIZE-BY-GRADE-AND-YEAR (1, 2).
48              DISPLAY SIZE-BY-GRADE-AND-YEAR (1, 3).
49              DISPLAY SIZE-BY-GRADE-AND-YEAR (1, 4).
50              DISPLAY SIZE-BY-GRADE (1).
51              DISPLAY SIZE-BY-GRADE-AND-YEAR (2, 3).
52              CLOSE ENROLLMENT-FILE.
53              STOP RUN.
54
55          B010-INITIALIZE-TABLE.
56              MOVE ZERO TO SIZE-BY-GRADE-AND-YEAR (GRADE-SUBSCRIPT, 1).
57              MOVE ZERO TO SIZE-BY-GRADE-AND-YEAR (GRADE-SUBSCRIPT, 2).
58              MOVE ZERO TO SIZE-BY-GRADE-AND-YEAR (GRADE-SUBSCRIPT, 3).
59              MOVE ZERO TO SIZE-BY-GRADE-AND-YEAR (GRADE-SUBSCRIPT, 4).
60              ADD 1 TO GRADE-SUBSCRIPT.
61
62          B020-LOAD-TABLE.
63              READ ENROLLMENT-FILE
64                  AT END MOVE 'N' TO MORE-DATA-REMAINS-FLAG.
65              IF MORE-DATA-REMAINS
66                  IF      YEAR < 1988 OR > 1991
67                      OR   GRADE < 1 OR > 12
68                      ADD 1 TO ERROR-COUNT
69                  ELSE
70                      SUBTRACT 1987 FROM YEAR GIVING YEAR-SUBSCRIPT
71                      MOVE ENROLLMENT TO
72                          SIZE-BY-GRADE-AND-YEAR (GRADE, YEAR-SUBSCRIPT).
```

FIGURE 14.4 A program illustrating operations on a table with two subscripts.

In the main-line routine for this program DISPLAY statements are used to show a few values from this table. The first four DISPLAY statements print the enrollments for grade 1 in all four years. The next DISPLAY statement demonstrates another capability of COBOL subscripting. If we write only one subscript for a variable that is defined as having two, using the name on the highest-level OCCURS clause, then we obtain all of the elements corresponding to that one subscript. In this case we obtain the entries for all four years at grade 1. Another way of looking at this is to say that SIZE-BY-GRADE is a one-subscript table, each of whose elements contains 12 characters.

Here are the results that were printed when this program was run with sample data.

```
240
239
229
205
240239229205
277
```

We see in the fifth line what was produced when we called for SIZE-BY-GRADE (1). This shows the enrollments for all four years in the first grade, as may be seen by comparing the fifth line with the first four lines.

Tables with three subscripts are handled in an entirely equivalent manner. That is, the Data Division definition of the table has three OCCURS clauses. The Procedure Division references to individual elements of the table are written with three subscripts separated by commas. It is unusual, however, to find commercial application programs that involve more than two subscripts.

14.8 THE PERFORM ... VARYING OPTION

Thus far we have been dealing with the mechanics of subscripting and have not seen an illustration of its real power. The true value of subscripting is found in arranging the program to change subscript values rather than simply writing literals or subscript data items that are given one value. We have seen some simple examples of this type of subscript modification in the code to initialize tables in some of the sample programs, but now we go a step further.

Consider, for instance, an extension of the school enrollment application. Suppose that when the program is given the number of a year, it is to print the total enrollment for that year in all 12 grades, together with the sum of all the entries in the table. (The latter value has no direct meaning in itself, but could be used, for instance, to find the average enrollment for the four years.)

We assume that some part of the program, not shown, has obtained the year number and stored it in a variable called **YEAR-NUMBER**. To get the total, we need to initialize a variable (which we may as well call **TOTAL**) to zero, then add all the enrollment figures for that year to **TOTAL**. This in turn means that we need a way to have a subscript variable take on the values from 1 to 12 in succession. Although we showed one way to do this in Figure 14.4 when we initialized the table, it is done much more easily by using the **VARYING** form of the **PERFORM** verb, which is shown in the following general format:

$$
\begin{array}{l}
\underline{\text{PERFORM}} \text{ procedure-name-1 } [\underline{\text{THRU}} \text{ procedure-name-2}] \\[1em]
\underline{\text{VARYING}} \left\{ \begin{array}{l} \text{index-name-1} \\ \text{identifier-1} \end{array} \right\} \quad \underline{\text{FROM}} \quad \left\{ \begin{array}{l} \text{index-name-2} \\ \text{identifier-2} \\ \text{literal-1} \end{array} \right\} \\[2em]
\underline{\text{BY}} \left\{ \begin{array}{l} \text{literal-2} \\ \text{identifier-3} \end{array} \right\} \quad \underline{\text{UNTIL}} \text{ condition-1}
\end{array}
$$

Figure 14.5 shows how easily the **PERFORM** verb carries out the needed operations. The variable name written after the **VARYING** in the first **PERFORM** statement is given a succession of values. The starting value is established by the **FROM** phrase, and the amount by which the subscript variable is to be changed between repetitions is given in the **BY** phrase. Finally, we indicate the termination condition with an **UNTIL** phrase. This means that the paragraph named **D010-TOTALLER** will be executed first with **GRADE-SUBSCRIPT** equal to 1. **GRADE-SUBSCRIPT** will then be increased by one and **D010-TOTALLER** will be executed again. Eventually **D010-TOTALLER** will have been executed with **GRADE-SUBSCRIPT** equal to 12. Now when **GRADE-SUBSCRIPT** is increased by one, the **UNTIL** condition will be satisfied and the repetitions stop.

```
C010-SUM-EXAMPLES.
    SUBTRACT 1988 FROM YEAR-NUMBER GIVING YEAR-SUBSCRIPT.
    MOVE ZERO TO TOTAL.
    PERFORM D010-TOTALLER
        VARYING GRADE-SUBSCRIPT FROM 1 BY 1
                UNTIL GRADE-SUBSCRIPT > 12.
    DISPLAY YEAR-NUMBER '   ' TOTAL.

    MOVE ZERO TO TOTAL.
    PERFORM D010-TOTALLER
        VARYING GRADE-SUBSCRIPT FROM 1 BY 1
                UNTIL GRADE-SUBSCRIPT > 12
        AFTER YEAR-SUBSCRIPT FROM 1 BY 1
                UNTIL YEAR-SUBSCRIPT > 4.
    DISPLAY TOTAL.

D010-TOTALLER.
    ADD SIZE-BY-GRADE-AND-YEAR (GRADE-SUBSCRIPT, YEAR-SUBSCRIPT)
            TO TOTAL.
```

FIGURE 14.5 An illustration of the use of the PERFORM . . . VARYING statement with

This portion of the program could be represented by the following pseudocode:

```
set grade-subscript to 1
PERFORM-UNTIL grade-subscript > 12
    execute the totaller function
    add 1 to grade-subscript
ENDPERFORM
```

More generally, the PERFORM . . . VARYING is equivalent to this pseudocode:

```
set identifier-1 to the FROM value
PERFORM-UNTIL the condition is true
    execute procedure-1 through procedure-2
    add the BY value to identifier-1
ENDPERFORM
```

There are two points to observe about this structure. First, the PERFORM statement allows you to execute a sequence of paragraphs, rather than just a single paragraph; we shall *never* use this option. Second, remember that PERFORM-UNTIL (and the COBOL PERFORM statement) tests the UNTIL condition *before* the loop is executed, and that identifier-1 is changed *inside* the loop *after* the paragraph is executed. These factors determine the value that identifier-1 will have at the end of the loop.

The first PERFORM. . .VARYING in Figure 14.5 is about the simplest possible form of that verb. In general, the FROM and BY phrases are both permitted to be either literals or identifiers, and we may write any condition whatever in the UNTIL phrase. The condition can be compound and in some circumstances will not involve the subscripted variable at all. Suggestions of some of these possibilities may be found in the Review Questions at the end of the chapter.

The **PERFORM ... VARYING** option may be written to run through two or more subscripts in succession, as shown in the following general format:

<u>PERFORM</u> procedure-name-1 [<u>THRU</u> procedure-name-2]

<u>VARYING</u> $\left\{ \begin{array}{l} \text{index-name-1} \\ \text{identifier-1} \end{array} \right\}$ <u>FROM</u> $\left\{ \begin{array}{l} \text{index-name-2} \\ \text{identifier-2} \\ \text{literal-1} \end{array} \right\}$

<u>BY</u> $\left\{ \begin{array}{l} \text{literal-2} \\ \text{identifier-3} \end{array} \right\}$ <u>UNTIL</u> condition-1

$\left[\begin{array}{l} \end{array} \right.$ <u>AFTER</u> $\left\{ \begin{array}{l} \text{index-name-3} \\ \text{identifier-4} \end{array} \right\}$ <u>FROM</u> $\left\{ \begin{array}{l} \text{index-name-4} \\ \text{identifier-5} \\ \text{literal-3} \end{array} \right\}$

<u>BY</u> $\left\{ \begin{array}{l} \text{literal-4} \\ \text{identifier-6} \end{array} \right\}$ <u>UNTIL</u> condition-2 $\left. \begin{array}{l} \end{array} \right]$

$\left[\begin{array}{l} \end{array} \right.$ <u>AFTER</u> $\left\{ \begin{array}{l} \text{index-name-5} \\ \text{identifier-7} \end{array} \right\}$ <u>FROM</u> $\left\{ \begin{array}{l} \text{index-name-6} \\ \text{identifier-8} \\ \text{literal-5} \end{array} \right\}$

<u>BY</u> $\left\{ \begin{array}{l} \text{literal-6} \\ \text{identifier-9} \end{array} \right\}$ <u>UNTIL</u> condition-3 $\left. \begin{array}{l} \end{array} \right]$

The second **PERFORM** in Figure 14.5 says to set **GRADE-SUBSCRIPT** to 1 and then run **YEAR-SUBSCRIPT** through all the values from 1 to 4. Then **GRADE-SUBSCRIPT** is increased to 2 and **YEAR-SUBSCRIPT** is again run through all the values from 1 to 4. This process continues until **D010-TOTALLER** has been performed for all 48 combinations of the values of the two subscripts.

The pseudocode for this version of the **PERFORM ... VARYING** is

```
set grade-subscript to 1
set year-subscript to 1
PERFORM-UNTIL grade-subscript > 12
   PERFORM-UNTIL year-subscript > 4
      execute the totaller function
      add 1 to year-subscript
   ENDPERFORM
   set year-subscript to 1
   add 1 to grade-subscript
ENDPERFORM
```

The general **PERFORM . . . VARYING** is equivalent to:

```
set identifier-1 to its FROM value
set identifier-4 to its FROM value
set identifier-7 to its FROM value
PERFORM-UNTIL condition-1 is true
    PERFORM-UNTIL condition-2 is true
        PERFORM-UNTIL condition-3 is true
            execute procedure-1 through procedure-2
            increment identifier-7 by its BY value
        END-PERFORM
        set identifier-7 to its FROM value
        increment identifier-4 by its BY value
    ENDPERFORM
    set identifier-4 to its FROM value
    increment identifier-1 by its BY value
ENDPERFORM
```

The **PERFORM...VARYING** form is used heavily in table handling programs, and it is important to be very clear about exactly how it works. Study the pseudocode until you are certain you understand how and when the basic functions of the **PERFORM** loop are executed:

1. Initializing the subscript or index variable (which is generally called the *loop variable*);
2. Testing for the end of the loop;
3. Executing the performed paragraph;
4. Incrementing the loop variable.

It is not required that the loop variable be a subscript or an index. It could be a variable to which we are giving a succession of values for some other purpose, or it could be a simple counter that tells how many times the performed paragraph was executed before the **UNTIL** clause stopped execution.

COBOL-85

Just as **COBOL-85** permits the use of **END-PERFORM** with the **PERFORM . . . UNTIL** statement, it permits **END-PERFORM** with **PERFORM . . . VARYING**. The complete form of the **PERFORM . . . VARYING** statement in **COBOL-85** is as shown at the op of the next page.

This usage is as you would expect. That is, you may omit the procedure name(s) and use an in-line imperative statement instead, followed by the **END-PERFORM**. Note also that since **COBOL-85** allows up to seven levels of subscripting, there may be up to six **AFTER** clauses.

END COBOL-85

14.9 INDEXING

In addition to subscripting, **COBOL** provides a second way of referring to tables of data, called *indexing*. Indexing and subscripting are very similar in some respects and quite different in others. From an application programmer's

$$\underline{\text{PERFORM}} \left[\text{procedure-name-1} \left[\begin{Bmatrix} \underline{\text{THROUGH}} \\ \underline{\text{THRU}} \end{Bmatrix} \text{procedure-name-2} \right] \right]$$

$$\underline{\text{VARYING}} \begin{Bmatrix} \text{index-name-1} \\ \text{identifier-1} \end{Bmatrix} \underline{\text{FROM}} \begin{Bmatrix} \text{index-name-2} \\ \text{identifier-2} \\ \text{literal-1} \end{Bmatrix}$$

$$\underline{\text{BY}} \begin{Bmatrix} \text{literal-2} \\ \text{identifier-3} \end{Bmatrix} \underline{\text{UNTIL}} \text{ condition-1}$$

$$\left[\underline{\text{AFTER}} \begin{Bmatrix} \text{index-name-3} \\ \text{identifier-4} \end{Bmatrix} \underline{\text{FROM}} \begin{Bmatrix} \text{index-name-4} \\ \text{identifier-5} \\ \text{literal-3} \end{Bmatrix} \right.$$

$$\left. \underline{\text{BY}} \begin{Bmatrix} \text{literal-4} \\ \text{identifier-6} \end{Bmatrix} \underline{\text{UNTIL}} \text{ condition-2} \right] \ldots$$

[imperative-statement-1 $\underline{\text{END-PERFORM}}$]

point of view, the main differences are that the object program in many cases can deal with indexed variables more efficiently than it can with subscripted variables, and with indexing we have a powerful new verb, SEARCH. Along with these advantages, there are a few new matters of mechanics that we must consider.

We inform the compiler that a table will be referenced with indexing by setting up its description in the Data Division, just as we would when using subscripts, and by adding the clause INDEXED BY. This clause specifies that indexing is desired and establishes the name of the index. For example, a table having one index could be established with this Data Division entry:

```
01   TABLE-OF-ACCOUNTS.
     05   ACCOUNT             PIC 9(6) OCCURS 100 TIMES
                              INDEXED BY ACCOUNT-INDEX.
```

(The INDEXED BY clause is written on a separate line only for reasons of clarity and space.) The OCCURS clause specifies that the table contains 100 entries. By looking at this, the compiler knows that the variable is either subscripted or indexed; the INDEXED BY clause tells it that the variable is indexed and identifies the index variable. As a result, we can write in the Procedure Division statements similar to the following.

```
MOVE ACCOUNT (ACCOUNT-INDEX) TO ACCOUNT-OUT.
```

When we write the name of a variable in an INDEXED BY clause, we establish that variable as an index name. No other definition of the index is required; indeed, no other is permitted. Furthermore, the index is associated with the table whose definition contains the INDEXED BY clause, and it should not be used with any other table. **COBOL** also requires that any particular reference to a table use indices only or subscripts only; a mixture of the two is not permitted. For example, if we have the following data

```
01  TABLE-AREA.
    05  TABLE-1            OCCURS 10 TIMES INDEXED BY X-1.
        10  TABLE-2        PIC X(5)
                           OCCURS 20 TIMES INDEXED BY X-2.
01  SUB-1                  PIC 99 COMP SYNC.
01  SUB-2                  PIC 99 COMP SYNC.
```

we can write

```
TABLE-2 (X1, X2)   or   TABLE-2 (SUB-1, SUB-2)
```

but not

```
TABLE-2 (X1, SUB-2)   or   TABLE-2 (SUB-1, X2)
```

However, **COBOL-85** *does* permit mixing subscripts and indices in this manner.

An index name is also special in that it may not be used in any sort of arithmetic operation (**ADD**, **SUBTRACT**, etc.), in a **MOVE** statement, or in **ACCEPT** or **DISPLAY** statements. To carry out arithmetic or **MOVE** operations on index names, we have the **SET** statement, which is shown in the general formats below.

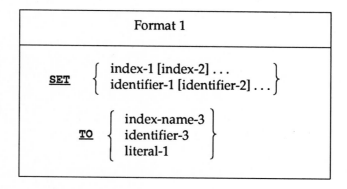

Format 1
SET { index-1 [index-2] . . . / identifier-1 [identifier-2] . . . }
TO { index-name-3 / identifier-3 / literal-1 }

Format 2
SET index-name-1 [index-name-2] . . .
{ **UP BY** / **DOWN BY** } { identifier-1 / literal-1 }

This is most commonly used to give an initial value to an index name, as in statements like these:

```
SET ACCOUNT-INDEX TO 1.
SET ACCOUNT-INDEX TO RECORD-FIELD-6.
```

Statements of this type have the same function as a MOVE, including carrying out any necessary conversions of data representation. In the SET statement the sending item is on the right and the receiving item is on the left; this reversal of the pattern of the MOVE statement may not be obvious at first glance. The arithmetic permitted on index names is restricted to addition and subtraction using the UP BY and DOWN BY variations of SET as shown in these examples:

```
SET LIST-INDEX UP BY 8.
SET INDEX-OF-FIELDS UP BY FIELD-2.
SET INDEX-A DOWN BY 1.
SET POINTER-A DOWN BY FIELD-LENGTH.
```

Index names cannot be used in ACCEPT or DISPLAY statements. However, you can use a SET statement, for example, to store the value of an index name in a numeric variable, then DISPLAY the numeric variable. Likewise, you can ACCEPT a value into a numeric variable, then use SET to assign that value to an index name.

It is permitted to use index names in relation conditions, but doing so involves slightly complex rules since it is necessary to be clear about exactly what an index represents internally. Since we shall have no reason to utilize this feature, the reader should refer to the Microsoft COBOL manual for details.

It is occasionally necessary to be able to store a value of an index name for later retrieval. This can be done using a SET statement together with a temporary storage location that is defined with a USAGE IS INDEX (or simply USAGE INDEX) clause. This feature would be used only in fairly sophisticated programs, and we shall make no further use of it in this book.

COBOL-85

14.10 THE SET STATEMENT AND CONDITION NAMES

In COBOL-85 there is a use of the SET statement that has nothing to do with index variables. Recall that condition names (level 88 items) allow us to test the value of a variable without actually knowing the specific values that the variable may take. For example, we might have

```
01  COLOR                          PIC X.
    88  RED                        VALUE 'A'.
    88  BLUE                       VALUE 'B'.
    88  YELLOW                     VALUE 'C'.
    88  GREEN                      VALUE 'D'.
    88  PURPLE                     VALUE 'E'.
```

and we could write

```
IF GREEN
     MOVE 'GREEN' TO COLOR-TEXT.
```

However, in order to set the color to green, we would have to know the proper code value and write

```
MOVE 'D' TO COLOR.
```

In COBOL-85 we can use the SET statement to write

```
SET GREEN TO TRUE.
```

The result of this statement is exactly the same as the previous MOVE statement (that is, we move 'D' to COLOR), but the Procedure Division code does not depend on the specific values used by COLOR. This presents two advantages. First, using the SET statement provides better documentation of the function being performed than simply moving a code to COLOR. Secondly (and more importantly), the exact value used for each color code is completely defined in the Data Division; if we wish to change these values we do so in the Data Division and do not need to modify any Procedure Division code.

END COBOL-85

14.11 THE SEARCH VERB

One of the primary motivations for using indexing, in addition to increased speed in some cases, is that it makes possible the use of the SEARCH verb. To understand how this verb functions and what its usefulness is, let us look once more at the seed catalog program. In Section 14.5 we showed how a table of valid catalog numbers might be loaded into the program. We will now consider how this table might be used.

The catalog number is a five-digit number, which means that potentially there are 100,000 catalog numbers. However, we have assumed that less than 1000 of these numbers correspond to actual products, and, to determine if the catalog number on an order record is valid, we need to be able to find the record's catalog number in the table.

We could, of course, allow a one-character entry for each possible catalog number and mark this entry as either 'Y' or 'N', depending on whether the corresponding catalog number is valid or not. This would allow us simply to use the catalog number on the order record as a subscript into the table and test the value of the table entry. However, this would require 100,000 bytes of memory, as opposed to the 5000 bytes required by the method we are using; even on large computers this savings in memory is not to be ignored.

The program in Figure 14.6 shows how this can be accomplished.

```
1        IDENTIFICATION DIVISION.
2        PROGRAM-ID.
3             SEEDS-5.
4        DATE-WRITTEN.
5             JUNE 16, 1989.
6
```

```
 7          ENVIRONMENT DIVISION.
 8          INPUT-OUTPUT SECTION.
 9          FILE-CONTROL.
10              SELECT CATALOG-FILE                  ASSIGN TO CATALOG.
11              SELECT PROCESSING-FILE               ASSIGN TO PROCESS.
12
13          DATA DIVISION.
14
15          FILE SECTION.
16          FD  CATALOG-FILE
17              LABEL RECORDS ARE STANDARD.
18          01  CATALOG-RECORD.
19              05  MASTER-CATALOG-NUMBER            PIC X(5).
20              05  REST-OF-RECORD                   PIC X(65).
21
22          FD  PROCESSING-FILE
23              LABEL RECORDS ARE STANDARD.
24          01  PROCESSING-LINE                      PIC X(72).
25
26          WORKING-STORAGE SECTION.
27          77  CHOICE-CODE                          PIC X.
28          77  MORE-DATA-REMAINS-FLAG               PIC X.
29              88  NO-MORE-DATA-REMAINS                 VALUE 'N'.
30          77  PRICE-LIMIT                          PIC  999V99 VALUE 125.00.
31          77  PRICE-LIMIT-EDIT                     PIC  $ZZ9.99.
32          77  TEST-REMAINDER                       PIC S999V99 COMP-3.
33          77  UNIT-PRICE                           PIC S999V99 COMP-3.
34          77  VALID-NUMBER-MAX                     PIC S9(4)    COMP SYNC
35                                                        VALUE +1000.
36
37          01  CATALOG-NUMBER-TABLE.
38              05  VALID-NUMBER                     PIC X(5) OCCURS 1000 TIMES
39                                                       INDEXED BY X-CATALOG.
40
41          01  ERROR-FLAGS.
42              05  VALID-CATALOG-NUMBER             PIC X.
43              05  VALID-SIZE-CODE                  PIC X.
44              05  VALID-PRICE                      PIC X.
45              05  VALID-PRICE-AND-QTY              PIC X.
46
47          01  ORDER-DATA.
48              05  ORDER-NUMBER                     PIC X(6).
49                  88  LAST-ORDER-LINE                  VALUE '000000', SPACES.
50              05  RECORD-TYPE                      PIC X.
51              05  CATALOG-NUMBER.
52                  10  CATALOG-FIRST-DIGIT          PIC X.
53                  10  CATALOG-REMAINING            PIC X(4).
54              05  SIZE-CODE                        PIC X.
55              05  QUANTITY                         PIC 99.
56              05  ITEM-DESCRIPTION                 PIC X(40).
57              05  PRICE                            PIC 999V99.
58
59          01  OUTPUT-LINE.
60              05  ORDER-NUMBER                     PIC Z(5)9.
61              05  CATALOG-NUMBER.
62                  10  CATALOG-FIRST-DIGIT          PIC BBX.
63                  10  CATALOG-REMAINING            PIC BX(4).
64              05  SIZE-CODE                        PIC BX.
```

```
65              05   QUANTITY                        PIC BBZ9.
66              05   PRICE                           PIC BB$$$9.99.
67              05   ITEM-DESCRIPTION                PIC BBX(40).
68
69         SCREEN SECTION.
70         01  ORDER-SCREEN
71                 BACKGROUND-COLOR IS 1
72                 FOREGROUND-COLOR IS 7.
73              05   VALUE 'SEED CATALOG ORDER ENTRY'
74                 BLANK SCREEN                      HIGHLIGHT
75                 LINE 6   COLUMN 29.
76              05   VALUE 'order number:'
77                 LINE 9   COLUMN 5.
78              05   SCREEN-ORDER-NUMBER             PIC X(6)
79                 TO ORDER-NUMBER OF ORDER-DATA
80                 REVERSE-VIDEO
81                 COLUMN + 3.
82              05   VALUE 'catalog number:'
83                 COLUMN 31.
84              05   SCREEN-CATALOG-NUMBER           PIC X(5)
85                 TO CATALOG-NUMBER OF ORDER-DATA
86                 REVERSE-VIDEO
87                 COLUMN + 3.
88              05   VALUE 'size code:'
89                 LINE + 1   COLUMN 5.
90              05   SCREEN-SIZE-CODE                PIC X
91                 TO SIZE-CODE OF ORDER-DATA
92                 REVERSE-VIDEO
93                 COLUMN + 3.
94              05   VALUE 'quantity:'
95                 COLUMN 31.
96              05   SCREEN-QUANTITY                 PIC Z9
97                 TO QUANTITY OF ORDER-DATA
98                 REVERSE-VIDEO
99                 COLUMN + 3.
100             05   VALUE 'price:'
101                COLUMN 51.
102             05   SCREEN-PRICE                    PIC ZZ9.99
103                TO PRICE OF ORDER-DATA
104                REVERSE-VIDEO
105                COLUMN + 3.
106             05   VALUE 'description:'
107                LINE + 1   COLUMN 5.
108             05   SCREEN-DESCRIPTION              PIC X(40)
109                TO ITEM-DESCRIPTION OF ORDER-DATA
110                COLUMN + 3.
111
112        01  PRICE-ERR-SCREEN.
113             05   FROM QUANTITY OF ORDER-DATA  PIC Z9
114                REVERSE-VIDEO
115                LINE 10   COLUMN 42.
116              05 FROM PRICE OF ORDER-DATA       PIC ZZ9.99
117                REVERSE-VIDEO HIGHLIGHT
118                LINE 10   COLUMN 59.
119
120        01  QTY-ERR-SCREEN.
121             05   FROM QUANTITY OF ORDER-DATA  PIC Z9
122                REVERSE-VIDEO HIGHLIGHT
123                LINE 10   COLUMN 42.
```

```
124              05  FROM PRICE OF ORDER-DATA      PIC ZZ9.99
125                  REVERSE-VIDEO
126                  LINE 10   COLUMN 59.
127
128        01  QTY-PRICE-ERR-SCREEN1.
129              05  FROM QUANTITY OF ORDER-DATA  PIC Z9
130                  REVERSE-VIDEO BLINK
131                  LINE 10   COLUMN 42.
132              05  FROM PRICE OF ORDER-DATA      PIC ZZ9.99
133                  REVERSE-VIDEO BLINK
134                  LINE 10   COLUMN 59.
135              05  VALUE 'Either price or quantity is wrong.'
136                  LINE 13   COLUMN 5.
137              05  VALUE 'Do you wish to re-enter the price, '
138                  LINE 14   COLUMN 5.
139              05  VALUE 'the quantity, or both (P/Q/B)?' COLUMN.
140              05  SCREEN-CHOICE-CODE            PIC X
141                  TO CHOICE-CODE
142                  COLUMN + 3.
143
144        01  QTY-PRICE-ERR-SCREEN2.
145              05  FROM QUANTITY OF ORDER-DATA  PIC Z9
146                  REVERSE-VIDEO HIGHLIGHT
147                  LINE 10   COLUMN 42.
148              05  FROM PRICE OF ORDER-DATA      PIC ZZ9.99
149                  REVERSE-VIDEO HIGHLIGHT
150                  LINE 10   COLUMN 59.
151
152
153        PROCEDURE DIVISION.
154        A000-VALIDATE-ORDERS.
155            PERFORM B020-LOAD-VALID-NUMBERS.
156            OPEN OUTPUT PROCESSING-FILE.
157            MOVE PRICE-LIMIT TO PRICE-LIMIT-EDIT.
158            MOVE LOW-VALUES TO ORDER-NUMBER OF ORDER-DATA.
159            PERFORM B010-VALIDATE-ONE-LINE
160                UNTIL LAST-ORDER-LINE.
161            CLOSE PROCESSING-FILE.
162            STOP RUN.
163
164        B010-VALIDATE-ONE-LINE.
165            DISPLAY ORDER-SCREEN.
166            PERFORM C010-GET-ORDER-NUMBER.
167            IF NOT LAST-ORDER-LINE
168                MOVE SPACES TO ERROR-FLAGS
169                PERFORM C020-GET-CATALOG-NUMBER
170                PERFORM C030-GET-SIZE-CODE
171                PERFORM C040-GET-QUANTITY
172                PERFORM C050-GET-PRICE
173                PERFORM C060-VALIDATE-QTY-AND-PRICE
174                PERFORM C070-GET-ITEM-DESCRIPTION
175                PERFORM C080-WRITE-PROCESSING-LINE.
176
177        B020-LOAD-VALID-NUMBERS.
178            OPEN INPUT CATALOG-FILE.
179            MOVE 'Y' TO MORE-DATA-REMAINS-FLAG.
180            READ CATALOG-FILE
181                AT END MOVE 'N' TO MORE-DATA-REMAINS-FLAG.
```

```
182                   PERFORM C090-LOAD-CATALOG-RECORD
183                       VARYING X-CATALOG FROM 1 BY 1
184                       UNTIL NO-MORE-DATA-REMAINS.
185                   CLOSE CATALOG-FILE.
186                   SET X-CATALOG DOWN BY 1.
187                   SET VALID-NUMBER-MAX TO X-CATALOG.
188
189               C010-GET-ORDER-NUMBER.
190                   ACCEPT SCREEN-ORDER-NUMBER.
191
192               C020-GET-CATALOG-NUMBER.
193                   MOVE 'N' TO VALID-CATALOG-NUMBER.
194                   PERFORM D010-GET-VALID-CATALOG-NUMBER
195                       UNTIL VALID-CATALOG-NUMBER = 'Y'.
196
197               C030-GET-SIZE-CODE.
198                   MOVE 'N' TO VALID-SIZE-CODE.
199                   PERFORM D020-GET-VALID-SIZE-CODE
200                       UNTIL VALID-SIZE-CODE = 'Y'.
201
202               C040-GET-QUANTITY.
203                   ACCEPT SCREEN-QUANTITY.
204
205               C050-GET-PRICE.
206                   MOVE 'N' TO VALID-PRICE.
207                   PERFORM E010-GET-VALID-PRICE
208                       UNTIL VALID-PRICE = 'Y'.
209
210               C060-VALIDATE-QTY-AND-PRICE.
211                   MOVE 'N' TO VALID-PRICE-AND-QTY.
212                   PERFORM D030-GET-VALID-PRICE-AND-QTY
213                       UNTIL VALID-PRICE-AND-QTY = 'Y'.
214
215               C070-GET-ITEM-DESCRIPTION.
216                   ACCEPT SCREEN-DESCRIPTION.
217
218               C080-WRITE-PROCESSING-LINE.
219                   MOVE CORRESPONDING ORDER-DATA TO OUTPUT-LINE.
220                   WRITE PROCESSING-LINE FROM OUTPUT-LINE
221                           AFTER ADVANCING 2 LINES.
222
223               C090-LOAD-CATALOG-RECORD.
224                   MOVE MASTER-CATALOG-NUMBER TO VALID-NUMBER (X-CATALOG).
225                   READ CATALOG-FILE
226                       AT END MOVE 'N' TO MORE-DATA-REMAINS-FLAG.
227
228               D010-GET-VALID-CATALOG-NUMBER.
229                   ACCEPT SCREEN-CATALOG-NUMBER.
230                   IF CATALOG-NUMBER OF ORDER-DATA IS NOT NUMERIC
231                       DISPLAY 'Catalog number contains '        AT 1416
232                               WITH BEEP BLANK LINE
233                       DISPLAY 'a non-numeric character.'         AT 1440
234                       DISPLAY 'Please re-enter the catalog number.' AT 1516
235                   ELSE
236                       IF CATALOG-FIRST-DIGIT OF ORDER-DATA = '0' OR '2'
237                           DISPLAY 'First digit of catalog '       AT 1416
238                                   WITH BEEP BLANK LINE
239                           DISPLAY 'number is invalid.'            AT 1439
240                           DISPLAY 'Please re-enter the catalog number.'
241                                                                  AT 1516
```

```
242                    ELSE
243                        SET X-CATALOG TO 1
244                        SEARCH VALID-NUMBER
245                            AT END
246                                DISPLAY 'Catalog number is not ' AT 1416
247                                    WITH BEEP BLANK LINE
248                                DISPLAY 'in the master file.'     AT 1438
249                                DISPLAY 'Please re-enter the catalog number.'
250                                                          AT 1516
251                            WHEN VALID-NUMBER (X-CATALOG) =
252                                    CATALOG-NUMBER OF ORDER-DATA
253                                DISPLAY SPACE WITH BLANK LINE      AT 1401
254                                DISPLAY SPACE WITH BLANK LINE      AT 1501
255                                MOVE 'Y' TO VALID-CATALOG-NUMBER.
256
257        D020-GET-VALID-SIZE-CODE.
258            ACCEPT SCREEN-SIZE-CODE.
259            IF SIZE-CODE OF ORDER-DATA = 'A' OR 'D' OR 'G' OR 'J'
260                OR 'K' OR 'L' OR 'S' OR 'T' OR 'U' OR ' '
261                MOVE 'Y' TO VALID-SIZE-CODE
262                DISPLAY SPACE WITH BLANK LINE                   AT 1401
263                DISPLAY SPACE WITH BLANK LINE                   AT 1501
264            ELSE
265                DISPLAY 'There is no such size code.'          AT 1416
266                        WITH BEEP BLANK LINE
267                DISPLAY 'Please re-enter the size code.'    AT 1516.
268            IF VALID-SIZE-CODE = 'Y'
269                IF (CATALOG-FIRST-DIGIT OF ORDER-DATA =
270                        '1' OR '8' OR '9')    AND
271                    SIZE-CODE OF ORDER-DATA IS NOT EQUAL TO SPACES
272                    DISPLAY 'This item does not take a size code.'
273                            WITH BEEP BLANK LINE              AT 1416
274                    DISPLAY 'Please re-enter the size code.' AT 1516
275                    MOVE 'N' TO VALID-SIZE-CODE
276                ELSE
277                    DISPLAY SPACE WITH BLANK LINE            AT 1401
278                    DISPLAY SPACE WITH BLANK LINE            AT 1501
279                    MOVE 'Y' TO VALID-SIZE-CODE.
280
281        D030-GET-VALID-PRICE-AND-QTY.
282            MOVE 'Y' TO VALID-PRICE-AND-QTY.
283            DIVIDE PRICE OF ORDER-DATA BY QUANTITY OF ORDER-DATA
284                    GIVING UNIT-PRICE REMAINDER TEST-REMAINDER
285            ON SIZE ERROR MOVE 'N' TO VALID-PRICE-AND-QTY.
286            IF TEST-REMAINDER NOT EQUAL TO ZERO
287                MOVE 'N' TO VALID-PRICE-AND-QTY.
288            IF VALID-PRICE-AND-QTY = 'N'
289                DISPLAY QTY-PRICE-ERR-SCREEN1
290                ACCEPT SCREEN-CHOICE-CODE
291                IF CHOICE-CODE = 'P' OR 'p'
292                    DISPLAY PRICE-ERR-SCREEN
293                    MOVE 'N' TO VALID-PRICE
294                    PERFORM E010-GET-VALID-PRICE
295                        UNTIL VALID-PRICE = 'Y'
296                ELSE
297                    IF CHOICE-CODE = 'Q' OR 'q'
298                        DISPLAY QTY-ERR-SCREEN
299                        ACCEPT SCREEN-QUANTITY
```

```
300                       ELSE
301                           DISPLAY QTY-PRICE-ERR-SCREEN2
302                           ACCEPT SCREEN-QUANTITY
303                           MOVE 'N' TO VALID-PRICE
304                           PERFORM E010-GET-VALID-PRICE
305                               UNTIL VALID-PRICE = 'Y'
306               ELSE
307                   DISPLAY SPACE WITH BLANK LINE          AT 1301
308                   DISPLAY SPACE WITH BLANK LINE          AT 1401.
309
310       E010-GET-VALID-PRICE.
311           ACCEPT SCREEN-PRICE.
312           IF PRICE OF ORDER-DATA IS GREATER THAN PRICE-LIMIT
313               DISPLAY 'Price must not exceed '           AT 1716
314                   WITH BEEP
315               DISPLAY PRICE-LIMIT-EDIT                   AT 1738
316               DISPLAY '.'                                AT 1745
317               DISPLAY 'Please re-enter the price.'
318                                                          AT 1816
319           ELSE
320               DISPLAY SPACE WITH BLANK LINE              AT 1701
321               DISPLAY SPACE WITH BLANK LINE              AT 1801
322               MOVE 'Y' TO VALID-PRICE.
323
324       **************** END OF PROGRAM ******************************
```

FIGURE 14.6 A revised version of the seed catalog program, showing the use of index variables and the **SEARCH** verb.

This program, based on Figure 12.5, contains several changes from Figure 14.3. To begin with, we have changed the definitions in Working-Storage so that **X-CATALOG** is now an index associated with the table **VALID-NUMBER**. We have also changed the way in which the table loading paragraph (renamed **C090-LOAD-CATALOG-RECORD**) is executed, using a **PERFORM . . . VARYING** instead of a simple **PERFORM . . . UNTIL**. There are two reasons for this change. First, use of the **PERFORM . . . VARYING** eliminates the need to initialize and increment **X-CATALOG**. Second, it avoids a problem in initializing **X-CATALOG**. Since the lowest valid index value for the table is 1, statements such as

```
SET X-CATALOG TO ZERO.
SET X-CATALOG TO 0.
```

are illegal. We would have to change the program so that **X-CATALOG** could be initialized to 1, which complicates the table loading process slightly.

Notice that we must decrement **X-CATALOG** by 1 before we store it in **VALID-NUMBER-MAX**. Remember that the **PERFORM. . .VARYING** statement increments the loop variable *after* the paragraph has been performed. This means that even after the end of file is detected and **MORE-DATA-REMAINS-FLAG** is set to **'N'**, **X-CATALOG** is still incremented once more before it is tested by the condition in the **UNTIL** clause.

The **SEARCH** verb is shown in `D010-GET-VALID-CATALOG-NUMBER` (line 244). If the catalog number is numeric, we go on to test whether its first digit is valid. If this digit is valid, we test the entire number to see if it is valid. If the number is not numeric, or if the first digit is invalid, it cannot possibly be valid so we needn't bother with the table search. (Alternatively, we might perform *only* the table search on the grounds that if the number contains any error it certainly won't be in the table. In any case, we should point out that this paragraph is nested about as deeply as any **IF** statement ever should be!)

We begin by initializing **X-CATALOG** to one, then execute the **SEARCH** verb, which has the following general format:

$$
\textbf{SEARCH}\ \text{identifier-1}\ \left[\ \underline{\textbf{VARYING}}\ \left\{ \begin{array}{l} \text{index-name-1} \\ \text{identifier-2} \end{array} \right\} \right]
$$

$$
[\textbf{AT}\ \underline{\textbf{END}}\ \text{imperative-statement-1}]
$$

$$
\underline{\textbf{WHEN}}\ \text{condition-1}\ \left\{ \begin{array}{l} \text{imperative-statement-2} \\ \underline{\textbf{NEXT}}\ \underline{\textbf{SENTENCE}} \end{array} \right\}
$$

$$
\left[\ \underline{\textbf{WHEN}}\ \text{condition-2}\ \left\{ \begin{array}{l} \text{imperative-statement-3} \\ \underline{\textbf{NEXT}}\ \underline{\textbf{SENTENCE}} \end{array} \right\} \right]\ \ldots
$$

Immediately following the word **SEARCH** we write the name of the item that contains the **INDEXED BY** clause; this is the table that will be searched. Next is an optional **AT END** phrase in which we specify what is to be done (other than proceeding to the next statement) if the program goes all the way through the table without ever satisfying the condition in the **WHEN** phrase. In the **WHEN** phrase, we write a condition followed by an imperative statement or **NEXT SENTENCE**. For the **SEARCH** verb to make any sense, the condition in the **WHEN** phrase must involve the indexed variable. Here we have specified that when the input catalog number is equal to a catalog number in the table, we want to clear lines 14 and 15, then set the flag to stop the loop; executing the **WHEN** phrase automatically stops the search. It is permissible to have any number of **WHEN** phrases specifying differing circumstances and differing actions; the search stops when any one of them is satisfied.

After completing the search, either **X-CATALOG** will point to the entry in **VALID-NUMBER** that matches the input catalog number, or **VALID-CATALOG-NUMBER** will still be set to 'N'. Although this program simply looks to see if the catalog number is in the table, it is quite common that a program will use other fields in the table entry containing the target key.

The program was run using the data from Chapter 11 and a sample catalog file. As before, several entries were intentionally keyed with data errors and produced the expected error messages. In addition, some entries were keyed with invalid catalog numbers. These produced error messages such as the one shown on the next page.

```
                        SEED CATALOG ORDER ENTRY


order number:   222237      catalog number:   33761
size code:                  quantity:   0       price:    0.00
description:



            Catalog number is not in the master file.
            Please re-enter the catalog number.
```

14.12 THE SEARCH ALL OPTION

In carrying out the search of a table using the **SEARCH** verb (without the **ALL**), the program simply inspects the table entries one by one, starting wherever the index variable currently points (which is why we were careful to reset **X-CATALOG** to 1 in line 243) and proceeding one entry at a time until a **WHEN** condition is satisfied or the end of the table is reached. If a match is not found until the last entry of the table, the program must have tested all of the previous entries. Assuming a random distribution of the items to be searched for, we expect that the average search will go halfway through the table before finding a match. For a long table this becomes wastefully time consuming. The **SEARCH ALL** form is a much faster alternative, providing that one condition about the table can be met.

If the table entries to be searched can be placed either in ascending or descending sequence, the use of the **SEARCH ALL** form in the program can proceed as follows. The program first compares the item being searched for with the item in the middle of the table. If by lucky chance they match, the search is completed. If not, it has been established whether the item being searched for is in the first half of the table or the second half. Either way, half of the table has been completely eliminated from further consideration. The program next inspects the item at the midway point of the half of the table where the item could be. This process is continued, each time narrowing down the range of possibilities by half, until the match is found or it is established that there is no match. Because of this factor of 2, the process is called a *binary* *search*; this has no relation to binary representation, and the table being searched certainly does not have to be in binary form. The speed advantage of **SEARCH ALL** becomes greater and greater as the size of the table increases. For example, in a table with 100 entries, **SEARCH** requires an average of 50 comparisons while **SEARCH ALL** requires only 7. This is good but not spectacular. However, if the table contains 1000 entries, **SEARCH** requires 500 comparisons while **SEARCH ALL** requires only 10, a dramatic saving.

The format of the **SEARCH ALL** verb is as follows.

$$\underline{\text{SEARCH ALL}}\ \text{identifier-1}\ [\underline{\text{AT END}}\ \text{imperative-statement-1}]$$

$$\underline{\text{WHEN}}\ \text{condition-1}\ \left\{ \begin{array}{l} \text{imperative-statement-2} \\ \underline{\text{NEXT SENTENCE}} \end{array} \right\}$$

To use the **SEARCH ALL** form, we must specify in the Data Division which item in the table is to be used for the search and whether the table is in ascending or descending sequence on this item. For example, the Data Division entry for the table in Figure 14.6 would become

```
01   CATALOG-NUMBER-TABLE.
     05 VALID-NUMBER              PIC X(5) OCCURS 1000 TIMES
                                  ASCENDING KEY IS VALID-NUMBER
                                  INDEXED BY X-CATALOG.
```

Inserting the **ASCENDING KEY** clause here and changing the **SEARCH** to **SEARCH ALL** are the only changes required in the program. Since the **SEARCH ALL** handles all operations with the index, the **SET** statement before the **SEARCH** can be deleted. If it is left in the program, it has no effect, since **SEARCH ALL** ignores the initial value of the index.

The **SEARCH ALL** permits only one **WHEN** phrase, but the condition in that **WHEN** phrase may be compound. This is useful when the search is to be made on several items simultaneously. For example, suppose that only certain size codes are valid with each catalog number. That is, the valid size codes for 33183 might be A, G, and L, the valid size codes for 62638 might be D and U, and so on. We can modify the table in the seed catalog program as follows:

```
01   CATALOG-NUMBER-TABLE.
     05   VALID-ENTRY             OCCURS 1000 TIMES
                                  ASCENDING KEY IS VALID-NUMBER
                                  ASCENDING KEY IS VALID-SIZE
                                  INDEXED BY X-CATALOG.
          10   VALID-NUMBER       PIC X(5).
          10   VALID-SIZE         PIC X.
```

We assume that the catalog file contains one record for each valid combination of catalog number and size, and the table is loaded accordingly. The match we seek now would be on both catalog number and size. To carry out this search we change the **SEARCH ALL** statement to

```
          SEARCH ALL VALID-ENTRY
             AT END
                   DISPLAY 'Catalog number or size' AT 1416
                       WITH BEEP BLANK LINE
                   DISPLAY ' code is invalid.'        AT 1438
                   DISPLAY 'Please re-enter the data.'
                                                      AT 1516
             WHEN VALID-NUMBER (X-CATALOG) =
                       CATALOG-NUMBER OF ORDER-DATA   AND
                   VALID-SIZE (X-CATALOG) =
                       SIZE-CODE OF ORDER-DATA
                   DISPLAY SPACE WITH BLANK LINE      AT 1401
                   DISPLAY SPACE WITH BLANK LINE      AT 1501
                   MOVE 'Y' TO VALID-CATALOG-NUMBER.
```

Of course, it would also be necessary to modify the program to permit the user to re-enter the catalog number or size code.

It is important to remember that the order of the **ASCENDING KEY** phrases must be from major to minor. That is, because the phrase for **VALID-NUMBER** comes first, the program knows that **VALID-NUMBER** is the major key and **VALID-SIZE** is the minor key.

14.13 TABLE INITIALIZATION AND THE SEARCH STATEMENTS

It should be clear by now that initialization of data is always important, but when you use either **SEARCH** or **SEARCH ALL**, it is particularly important that *all* entries of the table be initialized correctly, even if they do not contain valid data. For instance, consider the following table definition:

```
01  ACCOUNT-TABLE-AREA.
    05  ACCOUNT-TABLE-MAX    PIC S999 COMP SYNC VALUE 500.
    05  ACCOUNT-TABLE        OCCURS 500 TIMES
                             ASCENDING KEY IS ACCOUNT-NUMBER
                             INDEXED BY ACCOUNT-INDEX.
        10  ACCOUNT-NUMBER   PIC 9(5) COMP-3.
        10  ACCOUNT-NAME     PIC X(25).

01  CURRENT-ACCOUNT          PIC 9(5) COMP-3.
01  ACCOUNT-FLAG             PIC X.
```

Suppose that we have loaded **ACCOUNT-TABLE** from an input file and stored the number of records loaded, 425 for example, in **ACCOUNT-TABLE-MAX**. We want to search the account table until we find an entry that matches the current value of **CURRENT-ACCOUNT**. We can do this with the following statements:

```
SET ACCOUNT-INDEX TO 1.
SEARCH ACCOUNT-TABLE
    AT END MOVE 'N' TO ACCOUNT-FLAG
    WHEN CURRENT-ACCOUNT = ACCOUNT-NUMBER (ACCOUNT-INDEX)
        MOVE 'Y' TO ACCOUNT-FLAG.
```

There are two problems with this approach. First, since we are searching even those entries that do not have valid data in them, we will require an average of 250 accesses per search instead of the 213 average that would be required if we looked only at valid entries. Much more important, however, is the fact that since we have not initialized entries 426 through 500, we do not know what they contain. In most cases they will not contain valid packed decimal data, but even if they do the results of testing this data will be meaningless.

There are several possible solutions to the problem. In most cases, the simplest is to make use of the fact that `ACCOUNT-TABLE-MAX` contains the number of valid entries in the table. We can modify the search code to make use of this information as follows:

```
SET ACCOUNT-INDEX TO 1.
SEARCH ACCOUNT-TABLE
    AT END MOVE 'N' TO ACCOUNT-FLAG
    WHEN ACCOUNT-INDEX > ACCOUNT-TABLE-MAX
        MOVE 'N' TO ACCOUNT-FLAG
    WHEN CURRENT-ACCOUNT = ACCOUNT-NUMBER (ACCOUNT-INDEX)
        MOVE 'Y' TO ACCOUNT-FLAG.
```

The order of the two **WHEN** clauses is important. If the value of **CURRENT-ACCOUNT** is not in the table, the statement will eventually set **ACCOUNT-INDEX** to 426. The first **WHEN** clause will then be true and the statement will terminate (after moving '**N**' to **ACCOUNT-FLAG**) before it tries to compare **CURRENT-AC-COUNT** to **ACCOUNT-NUMBER (426)**.

An alternative solution is to initialize **ACCOUNT-TABLE** so that all entries contain a value for **ACCOUNT-NUMBER** that is a valid packed decimal value but which is not the value of any actual account, such as 00000 or 99999.

If we are using the **SEARCH ALL** option, we *must* initialize the table, since we cannot limit the value of **ACCOUNT-INDEX** to the range defined by **ACCOUNT-TABLE-MAX**. Further, since all values of **ACCOUNT-NUMBER** must be in increasing order (although duplicates are allowed), the only value we could assign for an initial value is something greater than any actual account number, such as 99999. If the key field is nonnumeric, you may wish to use **HIGH-VALUES** as the initial value. Do not use this with numeric data, however, since **HIGH-VALUES** is generally not a valid numeric value.

14.14   A PROGRAM TO PROCESS A TWO-LEVEL TABLE WITH INDEXING

To show how a program might use several tables at once and tables with more than one level, we shall consider the following application. An input file contains one record for each employee of a company. Among other information, an employee record contains one character showing the employee's sex (M for male and F for female), the employee's length of service with the company in years, the employee's age, and a code showing whether the employee is a member of management or not (1 for management, 2 for nonmanagement). We want to produce a tabulation showing the distribution of employees by age and length of service, within each of the four combinations of male/female, and management/nonmanagement. (A glance at Figure 14.7 will make this clearer than any verbal description could.)

The program must be designed to produce the numbers of employees in each of the various categories and then to print these numbers in an easily readable form. Both of these parts of the work of the program can usefully employ indexing. The determination of what age and length of service brackets an employee falls into is most easily done by using the **SEARCH** verb, and appropriate tables must be established for this purpose.

MANAGEMENT PERSONNEL REPORT

MANAGEMENT

	MALE								FEMALE							
SERVICE->	1-4	5-9	10-14	15-19	20-23	24-31	32-39	40-48	1-4	5-9	10-14	15-19	20-23	24-31	32-39	40-48
AGE																
17-20	1	0	0	0	0	0	0	0	0	0	0	0	0	0	0	0
21-27	5	3	0	0	0	0	0	0	1	2	0	0	0	0	0	0
28-32	1	4	7	0	0	0	0	0	0	1	2	0	0	0	0	0
33-39	3	2	3	4	1	0	0	0	2	4	2	1	0	0	0	0
40-44	3	5	4	4	1	1	0	0	0	2	4	6	0	4	0	0
45-51	2	9	5	5	3	3	0	0	0	4	2	6	3	0	0	0
52-57	4	3	2	3	5	5	8	0	3	6	3	3	4	1	2	0
58-62	1	2	0	10	4	5	9	3	1	2	2	3	3	6	3	2
63-65	1	1	0	6	1	3	2	1	0	0	0	4	1	1	1	0

NON-MANAGEMENT

AGE	1-4	5-9	10-14	15-19	20-23	24-31	32-39	40-48	1-4	5-9	10-14	15-19	20-23	24-31	32-39	40-48
17-20	3	0	0	0	0	0	0	0	3	0	0	0	0	0	0	0
21-27	1	6	0	0	0	0	0	0	3	1	0	0	0	0	0	0
28-32	2	5	1	0	0	0	0	0	0	4	2	0	0	0	0	0
33-39	6	2	5	3	0	0	0	0	4	7	8	4	1	0	0	0
40-44	5	1	7	2	6	4	0	0	3	2	3	2	4	1	0	0
45-51	3	1	3	3	6	12	2	0	2	6	5	4	5	9	0	0
52-57	3	7	4	6	2	6	7	0	4	2	5	7	2	6	2	0
58-62	3	3	4	4	5	7	6	2	3	6	2	2	2	5	7	4
63-65	1	1	3	1	5	4	2	2	2	1	2	4	3	3	0	4

FIGURE 14.7 A report showing the distribution of employees by four categories. This is the output of the program of Figure 14.9.

The basic structure of the program involves two major functions: building the table, and printing the results. In addition, because we cannot use a VALUE clause or simple MOVE statement to initialize the table so that all entries contain zero, we will consider this to be a separate function. A complete hierarchy chart for this program is shown in Figure 14.8.

The program based on this hierarchy chart is shown in Figure 14.9. There is nothing remarkable about the first two divisions of the program or the File Section of the Data Division. The data name LOS stands for "length of service." Looking at the Working-Storage Section, we see a table that is established for use by the SEARCH verb in determining which age bracket the employee falls into. We shall consider how the values were chosen when we look at the SEARCH verb. A similar table defines the values for use in searching for the proper length of service bracket. The table named STATISTICS-TABLE holds the tabulations of the numbers of employees in the various categories. The names of the 05 and 10 levels of this table are meant to suggest rows and columns. (We have used the prefix T in front of ROW and COLUMN because COLUMN is a reserved word.)

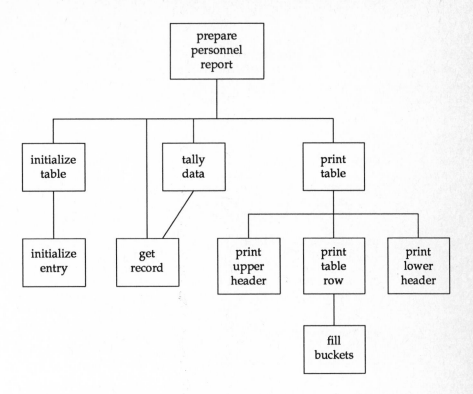

FIGURE 14.8 Hierarchy chart for program to produce report in Figure 14.7.

```
1              IDENTIFICATION DIVISION.
2              PROGRAM-ID.
3                  NEWSTATS.
4              DATE-WRITTEN.
5                  JUNE 16, 1989.
6
7              ENVIRONMENT DIVISION.
8              INPUT-OUTPUT SECTION.
9              FILE-CONTROL.
10                 SELECT EMPLOYEE-MASTER-IN        ASSIGN TO MASTER.
11                 SELECT REPORT-FILE               ASSIGN TO REPORT.
12
13             DATA DIVISION.
14             FILE SECTION.
15
16             FD  EMPLOYEE-MASTER-IN
17                 LABEL RECORDS ARE STANDARD.
18             01  EMPLOYEE-MASTER-REC.
19                 05   EMPLOYEE-NUMBER        PIC 9(4).
20                 05   FILLER                 PIC X.
21                 05   SEX                    PIC X.
22                      88   MALE                   VALUE 'M'.
23                      88   FEMALE                 VALUE 'F'.
24                 05   FILLER                 PIC XXX.
25                 05   LOS                    PIC 99.
26                 05   FILLER                 PIC XXX.
```

```
27                05  AGE                    PIC 99.
28                05  FILLER                 PIC XXX.
29                05  MANAGEMENT-CODE        PIC X.
30                    88  MANAGEMENT             VALUE '1'.
31                    88  NON-MANAGEMENT         VALUE '2'.
32                05  FILLER                 PIC X(60).
33
34        FD  REPORT-FILE
35            LABEL RECORDS ARE STANDARD.
36        01  REPORT-RECORD              PIC X(132).
37
38        WORKING-STORAGE SECTION.
39
40        77  MORE-DATA-REMAINS-FLAG     PIC X.
41            88  MORE-DATA-REMAINS          VALUE 'Y'.
42            88  NO-MORE-DATA-REMAINS       VALUE 'N'.
43
44        01  AGE-TABLE-VALUES.
45            05  FILLER                 PIC X(18)
46                                       VALUE '212833404552586366'.
47        01  AGE-TABLE-X REDEFINES AGE-TABLE-VALUES.
48            05  AGE-TABLE              PIC 99 OCCURS 9 TIMES
49                                       INDEXED BY AGE-INDEX.
50
51        01  LOS-TABLE-VALUES           PIC X(16)
52                                       VALUE '0510152024324049'.
53        01  LOS-TABLE-X REDEFINES LOS-TABLE-VALUES.
54            05  LOS-TABLE              PIC 99 OCCURS 9 TIMES
55                                       INDEXED BY LOS-INDEX.
56
57        01  STATISTICS-TABLE.
58            05  T-ROW OCCURS 18 TIMES INDEXED BY ROW-INDEX.
59                10  T-COLUMN OCCURS 16 TIMES INDEXED BY COL-INDEX.
60                    15  STATISTICS     PIC S9(4) COMP SYNC.
61
62        01  ROW-IDENT-VALUES.
63            05  FILLER                     PIC X(25)
64                            VALUE '17-2021-2728-3233-3940-44'.
65            05  FILLER                     PIC X(20)
66                            VALUE '45-5152-5758-6263-65'.
67            05  FILLER                     PIC X(25)
68                            VALUE '17-2021-2728-3233-3940-44'.
69            05  FILLER                     PIC X(20)
70                            VALUE '45-5152-5758-6263-65'.
71        01  ROW-IDENT-X REDEFINES ROW-IDENT-VALUES.
72            05  ROW-IDENT              PIC X(5) OCCURS 18 TIMES
73                                       INDEXED BY ROW-IDENT-INDEX.
74
75        01  REPORT-LINE-DETAIL.
76            05  ROW-IDENT-OUT          PIC X(8).
77            05  BUCKET                 PIC BBZZZ9 OCCURS 16 TIMES
78                                       INDEXED BY BUCKET-INDEX.
79            05  FILLER                 PIC X(28) VALUE SPACES.
80
81        01  HEADER-1.
82            05  FILLER                     PIC X(45) VALUE SPACES.
83            05  FILLER                     PIC X(87)
84                            VALUE 'MANAGEMENT PERSONNEL REPORT'.
85
```

```
86          01   HEADER-2.
87               05   FILLER                    PIC X(52) VALUE SPACES.
88               05   FILLER                    PIC X(80) VALUE 'MANAGEMENT'.
89
90          01   HEADER-3.
91               05   FILLER                    PIC X(31) VALUE SPACES.
92               05   FILLER                    PIC X(49) VALUE 'MALE'.
93               05   FILLER                    PIC X(52) VALUE 'FEMALE'.
94
95          01   HEADER-4.
96               05   FILLER                    PIC X(9) VALUE 'SERVICE->'.
97               05   FILLER                    PIC X(48) VALUE
98                    '  1-4    5-9 10-14 15-19 20-23 24-31 32-39 40-48 '.
99               05   FILLER                    PIC X(75) VALUE
100                   '  1-4    5-9 10-14 15-19 20-23 24-31 32-39 40-48 '.
101
102         01   HEADER-5.
103              05   FILLER                    PIC X(50) VALUE SPACES.
104              05   FILLER                    PIC X(82) VALUE 'NON-MANAGEMENT'.
105
106         PROCEDURE DIVISION.
107         A000-EMPLOYEE-STATISTICS.
108              PERFORM B010-INIT-STAT-TABLE.
109              MOVE 'Y' TO MORE-DATA-REMAINS-FLAG.
110              OPEN INPUT EMPLOYEE-MASTER-IN
111                   OUTPUT REPORT-FILE.
112              PERFORM X010-GET-EMPLOYEE-REC.
113              PERFORM B020-TALLY-DATA
114                   UNTIL NO-MORE-DATA-REMAINS.
115              PERFORM B030-PRINT-TABLE.
116              CLOSE EMPLOYEE-MASTER-IN
117                   REPORT-FILE.
118              STOP RUN.
119
120         B010-INIT-STAT-TABLE.
121              PERFORM C010-INIT-STAT-CELL
122                   VARYING ROW-INDEX FROM 1 BY 1 UNTIL ROW-INDEX > 18
123                   AFTER   COL-INDEX FROM 1 BY 1 UNTIL COL-INDEX > 16.
124
125         B020-TALLY-DATA.
126              SET AGE-INDEX ROW-INDEX TO 1.
127              SEARCH AGE-TABLE VARYING ROW-INDEX
128                   WHEN AGE < AGE-TABLE (AGE-INDEX) NEXT SENTENCE.
129              SET LOS-INDEX COL-INDEX TO 1.
130              SEARCH LOS-TABLE VARYING COL-INDEX
131                   WHEN LOS < LOS-TABLE (LOS-INDEX) NEXT SENTENCE.
132              IF FEMALE
133                   SET COL-INDEX UP BY 8.
134              IF NON-MANAGEMENT
135                   SET ROW-INDEX UP BY 9.
136              ADD 1 TO STATISTICS (ROW-INDEX, COL-INDEX).
137              PERFORM X010-GET-EMPLOYEE-REC.
138
139         B030-PRINT-TABLE.
140              PERFORM C020-PRINT-UPPER-HEADER.
141              PERFORM C030-PRINT-TABLE-ROW
142                   VARYING ROW-INDEX FROM 1 BY 1
143                   UNTIL ROW-INDEX > 9.
144              PERFORM C040-PRINT-LOWER-HEADER.
```

```
145                      PERFORM C030-PRINT-TABLE-ROW
146                          VARYING ROW-INDEX FROM 10 BY 1
147                          UNTIL ROW-INDEX > 18.
148
149             C010-INIT-STAT-CELL.
150                 MOVE ZERO TO STATISTICS (ROW-INDEX, COL-INDEX).
151
152             C020-PRINT-UPPER-HEADER.
153                 WRITE REPORT-RECORD FROM HEADER-1 AFTER ADVANCING PAGE.
154                 WRITE REPORT-RECORD FROM HEADER-2 AFTER ADVANCING 2 LINES.
155                 WRITE REPORT-RECORD FROM HEADER-3 AFTER ADVANCING 2 LINES.
156                 WRITE REPORT-RECORD FROM HEADER-4 AFTER ADVANCING 2 LINES.
157                 MOVE 'AGE' TO REPORT-RECORD.
158                 WRITE REPORT-RECORD AFTER ADVANCING 2 LINES.
159                 MOVE SPACES TO REPORT-RECORD.
160                 WRITE REPORT-RECORD AFTER ADVANCING 1 LINE.
161
162             C030-PRINT-TABLE-ROW.
163                 PERFORM D010-FILL-BUCKETS
164                     VARYING COL-INDEX FROM 1 BY 1
165                     UNTIL COL-INDEX > 16.
166                 SET ROW-IDENT-INDEX TO ROW-INDEX.
167                 MOVE ROW-IDENT (ROW-IDENT-INDEX) TO ROW-IDENT-OUT.
168                 WRITE REPORT-RECORD FROM REPORT-LINE-DETAIL
169                         AFTER ADVANCING 1 LINE.
170
171             C040-PRINT-LOWER-HEADER.
172                 WRITE REPORT-RECORD FROM HEADER-5 AFTER ADVANCING 2 LINES.
173                 MOVE SPACES TO REPORT-RECORD.
174                 WRITE REPORT-RECORD AFTER ADVANCING 1 LINE.
175
176             D010-FILL-BUCKETS.
177                 SET BUCKET-INDEX TO COL-INDEX.
178                 MOVE STATISTICS (ROW-INDEX, COL-INDEX)
179                         TO BUCKET (BUCKET-INDEX).
180
181             X010-GET-EMPLOYEE-REC.
182                 READ EMPLOYEE-MASTER-IN
183                     AT END MOVE 'N' TO MORE-DATA-REMAINS-FLAG.
184
185             ************ END OF PROGRAM ************
```

FIGURE 14.9   A program to produce an employee distribution table like that shown in Figure 14.7.

Next we have a table setting up the row identifications that will be printed on the output report. This is also accomplished with indexing. Then comes a work area that will be used in printing the body of the table; we shall discuss this more in connection with the Procedure Division. Finally, there are values for the five header lines that are printed on the report.

The structure of the Procedure Division clearly reflects the hierarchy chart. After the table is initialized to zeros, the program performs two major functions: tally the data and print the table. Notice the two UNTIL conditions in B010-INIT-STAT-TABLE. The table contains 18 rows and 16 columns, and we continue the loop until ROW-INDEX is *greater than* 18 and COL-INDEX is *greater than* 16. If we had tested for equality instead, the program would not have initialized the last row and column of the table, since the **PERFORM** loop terminates as soon as the **UNTIL** condition becomes true. This type of code is used commonly in processing tables and its use should be understood thoroughly.

The next paragraph, **B020-TALLY-DATA**, begins by setting **AGE-INDEX** and **ROW-INDEX** to 1; it is possible to set any number of index data names using one **SET** statement in this way, just as any number of ordinary data names can be set to the same value with one **MOVE**. The **SEARCH** statement is different in two ways from the examples we studied earlier. First, it has a **VARYING** phrase, which means simply that as we step through **AGE-TABLE** with its **AGE-INDEX**, the index named **ROW-INDEX** will automatically be incremented at the same time. Accordingly, when we have found our place in **AGE-TABLE** we shall also know in which row of **STATISTICS-TABLE** we want to add a 1. Second, this **SEARCH** statement does not have an **AT END** phrase. We assume that since the data is coming from a master file and has presumably been subject to extensive editing, it is very likely to be correct. If it is felt that this assumption is not justified, modifying the program accordingly would involve no new concepts.

The condition in this **SEARCH** tests **AGE**, which is the employee's age from the input record, against successive entries in **AGE-TABLE**. Consider how this works. Observe on the report in Figure 14.7 that the first age category is 17 through 20. That means that if the employee is less than 21, he or she is in the first age bracket. That is why the first entry in the age table is 21, not 20. If this comparison does not stop the search, then the employee is evidently older than 20 and is not in the first age bracket. The next test is whether the employee's age is less than 28. If the age was not less than 21 but is less than 28, then the employee's age must be in the range of 21 to 27, which is the second bracket. These comparisons continue until the condition is finally satisfied, at which time we get out of the search. A similar set of search combinations finds the appropriate bracket for length of service.

Now we come to the handling of the male/female and management/non-management factors. Looking at the output in Figure 14.7, we see that the left half of the table is for men and the right half is for women. Since there are eight columns in each half of the table, this means that if the employee is a woman, the column index that has just been determined by the second **SEARCH** must be increased by 8. A similar analysis shows that if the employee is not a member of management, the row index should be increased by 9. At this stage we have row and column indices pointing to one element in the table of statistics. The **ADD** statement with its doubly indexed data name increments the proper element.

When all of the input has been processed by the paragraphs we have just studied, it is time to print the report. Looking at **B030-PRINT-TABLE**, we see that it begins by performing **C020-PRINT-UPPER-HEADER**, which consists of a number of **WRITE** statements involving no new concepts. We then have a **PERFORM** that carries out **C030-PRINT-TABLE-ROW** with **ROW-INDEX** running through the values from 1 to 9 in succession; again notice that we test for **ROW-INDEX** *greater than* 9. With **ROW-INDEX** having been given a value, **C030-PRINT-TABLE-ROW**, as its name suggests, prints all of the 16 elements in that row together with the row identification. To do this, it is necessary to move the row identification and the 16 values to temporary locations, both so that they may be edited and so that the values can be gotten into one consecutive string of characters for printing. This moving of elements from the doubly indexed table to the singly indexed work area is accomplished with another **PERFORM**. This **PERFORM** runs **COL-INDEX** through all the values from 1 to 16. For each, it **PERFORMS D010-FILL-BUCKETS**. **D010-FILL-BUCKETS** first gives **BUCKET-INDEX** the same value as **COL-INDEX**, then moves the proper element of the statistics table to the proper element of **BUCKET**. After the 16 values have been moved, the index **ROW-IDENT-INDEX** is given the same value as **ROW-INDEX** with a **SET**, and the row identification is moved to the output area for printing.

Finally, referring again to **B030-PRINT-TABLE**, we see that it carries out the paragraph **C040-PRINT-LOWER-HEADER** and then prints all the rows of the statistics table from 10 to 18.

You may perhaps wonder whether it is necessary to have a distinct index name for every table. For example, **COL-INDEX** and **BUCKET-INDEX** both run through the values from 1 to 18 and both always have the same value at the time they are used. It might therefore appear that **BUCKET** could just as well be indexed with **COL-INDEX** as with **BUCKET-INDEX**. It turns out, however, because of the way indices relate to the assignment of tables to storage, that this is true only in special circumstances. It is entirely possible to learn what those circumstances are, since they are described in the Microsoft **COBOL** manual. On the other hand, there is very little advantage in doing so and there can be some loss of understandability. As a general rule, it is good practice simply to give every table its own distinct index name(s).

14.15 SYNCHRONIZED DATA IN TABLES

In Chapter 10 we discussed the relationship between **COMPUTATIONAL** data, the **SYNCHRONIZED** phrase, and slack bytes in programs that have been compiled with the IBMCOMP directive. The same considerations apply if the **COMPUTATIONAL** fields are contained in a table, but with one additional factor. For example, consider the following table, based on an example in Section 10.10:

```
01   TABLE-AREA.
     05   TABLE-B                OCCURS 100 TIMES.
          10   FLD-3             PIC X.
          10   FLD-4             PIC 9(8)   COMP SYNC.
          10   FLD-5             PIC X.
          10   FLD-6             PIC 9(18) COMP SYNC.
          10   FLD-7             PIC X.
```

From the example in Chapter Ten, we know that there are three bytes of slack inserted between **FLD-3** and **FLD-4**, and three bytes of slack between **FLD-5** and **FLD-6**. We don't need to worry about the alignment of **FLD-7** since character data can be aligned on any byte. However, notice the storage layout shown in the diagram at the top of the next page.

The first entry of **TABLE-B** begins in the first byte of word 1 and continues through the first byte of word 6. Because of the slack bytes (fields **SLACK1** and **SLACK2**), **FLD-4** and **FLD-6** begin on word boundaries for this entry, as they are required to do by the **SYNC** clauses. However, the second entry of **TABLE-B** begins in the *second* byte of word 6. Since **FLD-3** is followed by three bytes of slack, this means that **FLD-4** also begins in the second byte of a word (word 7) and is not aligned properly. **FLD-6** also begins in the second byte of a word and is misaligned. In other words, when a structure containing binary data is

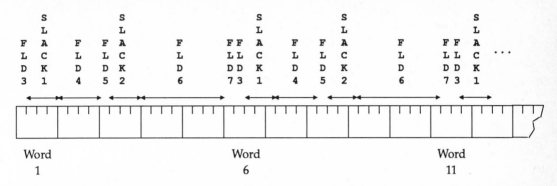

contained in a table, it is not sufficient to align the first entry of the table; slack must be included so that *all* entries of the table are aligned.

The compiler accomplishes this by inserting additional slack at the end of each record so that following records align properly. Thus, the example given above is equivalent to the following.

```
01  TABLE-AREA.
    05  TABLE-B             OCCURS 100 TIMES.
        10  FLD-3           PIC X.
        10  SLACK-1         PIC XXX.
        10  FLD-4           PIC 9(8)   COMP SYNC.
        10  FLD-5           PIC X.
        10  SLACK-2         PIC XXX.
        10  FLD-6           PIC 9(18) COMP SYNC.
        10  FLD-7           PIC X.
        10  SLACK-3         PIC XXX.
```

This gives the alignment shown in the following diagram, which keeps all synchronized binary fields on the proper boundaries.

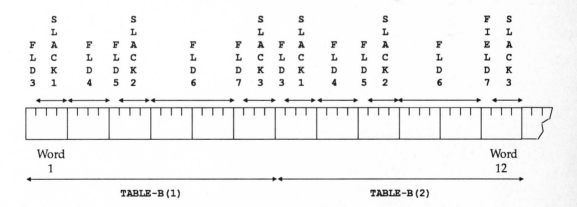

The exact mechanism for determining where the compiler will insert slack bytes for alignment can become somewhat complicated. Remember, however, that these considerations only apply if you use the IBMCOMP directive so that the program will be compatible with IBM mainframe requirements. In this case, we recommend that the serious programmer study the Microsoft or IBM manuals.

14.16 SUMMARY

Subscripting and indexing are powerful features of COBOL. Mastery of their use sufficient for most applications requires only a modest investment of study and practice. To become completely familiar with all of the implications of these features is a serious undertaking, but one that is not required of all programmers. Since this is an elementary text, those who desire to know the full story must refer to other sources, such as the Microsoft COBOL manuals.

REVIEW QUESTIONS

1. Which of the following is *not* an advantage of subscripting (or indexing)?
   a. Saves time and effort in writing the Data Division.
   b. Makes possible shortcuts in writing the Procedure Division.
   c. Simplifies the compilation of the source program.
2. Which of the following best summarizes the subscripting concept?
   a. Subscripting is a way to improve object program efficiency by reducing the number of different data names in a program.
   b. Subscripting is a way to let one data name refer to a whole table of data items, with a particular one (or group) being specified by the value(s) of the subscript(s) written after the data name.
   c. Subscripting is a way to simplify writing of the Data Division, which at the same time makes the Procedure Division easier to write.
   d. Subscripting is a way to write a more compact Procedure Division.
3. What is the difference between subscripting and indexing?
4. Identify three errors in the following subscripting example. (If you are using COBOL-85 there are only two errors.)

   ```
   MOVE ZERO TO AMOUNT IN TRANS (2) OF TAPEX(0,1,RATE+1).
   ```

5. What will the following do?
   In the Data Division:

   ```
   01   SUM-TABLE-AREA COMPUTATIONAL.
        05   SUM-TABLE            PIC 9(5) OCCURS 100 TIMES.
   ```

   In the Procedure Division:

   ```
   ADD DOLLARS TO SUM-TABLE (X-ACCOUNT).
   ```

6. Assuming the Data Division entry of Question 5, what will this do?

   ```
   MOVE ZERO TO TOTAL-A.
   MOVE 1 TO SUBSCRIPT.
   PERFORM PARAGRAPH-A
       UNTIL SUBSCRIPT > 100.
           .
           .
           .
   PARAGRAPH-A.
       ADD SUM-TABLE (SUBSCRIPT) TO TOTAL-A.
       ADD 1 TO SUBSCRIPT.
   ```

7. What will the following put into object program storage when the object program is loaded? (There are 50 fillers.)

```
01   NAME-RECORD.
     05   FILLER              PIC X(10) VALUE 'JONES'.
     05   FILLER              PIC X(10) VALUE 'SMITH'.
     05   FILLER              PIC X(10) VALUE 'ANDERSON'.
         .
         .
         .
     05   FILLER              PIC X(10) VALUE 'THOMPSON'.
01   NAME TABLE REDEFINES NAME-RECORD.
     05   NAME-A              PIC X(10) OCCURS 50 TIMES.
```

8. In the program of Figure 14.1 why not change the entries for REPORT-RECORD and YEAR-TABLE as follows:

```
01   YEAR-TABLE.
     03   YEAR-GROUP.
          05   YEAR-COUNT      PIC S9(4) COMP OCCURS 4 TIMES.

01   REPORT-RECORD.
     03   REPORT-GROUP-OUT.
          05 YEAR-COUNT-OUT    PIC Z(6)9 OCCURS 4 TIMES.
     03   BAD-DATA-COUNT-OUT   PIC X(6)9.
```

and then in the Procedure Division in place of the four MOVE statements in the paragraph named B020-WRITE-TABLE insert

```
MOVE YEAR-GROUP TO REPORT-GROUP-OUT.
```

9. Why could COBOL not have been designed so that the compiler would deduce that a variable is subscripted from the fact that it is written with a subscript in the Procedure Division and thus avoid the need for the OCCURS clause in the Data Division?

10. What would happen in the VARYING data-name option of the PERFORM if the procedure called by the PERFORM changed the value of the data-name? Would the original or the changed value determine the number of repetitions?

11. What would be the difference between the results of these two examples?

a.
```
     MOVE ZERO TO TOTAL-A.
     MOVE 1 TO SUBSCRIPT.
     PERFORM ROUTINE-A
          UNTIL SUBSCRIPT > 10.
         .
         .
         .
   ROUTINE-A.
       ADD DATA-B (SUBSCRIPT) TO TOTAL-A.
       ADD 1 TO SUBSCRIPT.
```

b.
```
      MOVE ZERO TO TOTAL-A.
      PERFORM ROUTINE-B
          VARYING SUBSCRIPT FROM 1 BY 1
          UNTIL SUBSCRIPT > 10.
      .
      .
      .
  ROUTINE-B.
      ADD DATA-B (SUBSCRIPT) TO TOTAL-A.
```

12. How many times will the procedure named **ROUTINE-X** be executed by these **PERFORM** statements?

   a.
   ```
   PERFORM ROUTINE-X
       VARYING X FROM 1 BY 1 UNTIL X = 10.
   ```

   b.
   ```
   PERFORM ROUTINE-X
       VARYING X FROM 1 BY 1 UNTIL X > 10.
   ```

   c.
   ```
   PERFORM ROUTINE-X
       VARYING X FROM 1 BY 1 UNTIL X < 10.
   ```

   d.
   ```
   PERFORM ROUTINE-X
       VARYING X FROM 5 BY 1 UNTIL X > 10.
   ```

   e.
   ```
   PERFORM ROUTINE-X
       VARYING X FROM 1 BY 1 UNTIL X = NUMBER-A.
   ```

13. Consider the following example:

   ```
   PERFORM ROUTINE-C
       VARYING A FROM 1 BY 1 UNTIL A > 2
       AFTER   B FROM 1 BY 1 UNTIL B > 3.
   ```

   Write out the six pairs of values that would be taken on by **A** and **B** in the order in which they would appear.

14. Given the following Data Division entry:

   ```
   01  TABLE-AREA.
       05  SUB-1        PIC 999 COMP SYNC.
       05  TABLE-A      PIC X(50) OCCURS 100 TIMES
                        INDEXED BY X-1.
   ```

   and an appropriate definition for **INPUT-FILE** and **INPUT-RECORD**, what value would be displayed in each of the following cases if **INPUT-FILE** contained exactly 50 records in each case?

   a.
   ```
       MOVE 'Y' TO MORE-DATA-FLAG.
       PERFORM LOAD-TABLE
           VARYING X-1 FROM 1 BY 1
           UNTIL MORE-DATA-FLAG = 'N'.
       SET SUB-1 TO X-1.
       DISPLAY SUB-1.
       .
       .
       .
   LOAD-TABLE.
       READ INPUT-FILE
           AT END MOVE 'N' TO MORE-DATA-FLAG.
       IF MORE-DATA-FLAG = 'Y'
           MOVE INPUT-RECORD TO TABLE-A (X-1).
   ```

b.
```
        MOVE 'Y' TO MORE-DATA-FLAG.
        READ INPUT-FILE
            AT END MOVE 'N' TO MORE-DATA-FLAG.
        PERFORM LOAD-TABLE
            VARYING X-1 FROM 1 BY 1
            UNTIL MORE-DATA-FLAG = 'N'.
        SET SUB-1 TO X-1.
        DISPLAY SUB-1.
            .
            .
            .

    LOAD-TABLE.
        MOVE INPUT-RECORD TO TABLE-A (X-1).
        READ INPUT-FILE
            AT END MOVE 'N' TO MORE-DATA-FLAG.
```

c.
```
        MOVE 'Y' TO MORE-DATA-FLAG.
        MOVE ZERO TO SUB-1.
        READ INPUT-FILE
            AT END MOVE 'N' TO MORE-DATA-FLAG.
        PERFORM LOAD-TABLE
            UNTIL MORE-DATA-FLAG = 'N'.
        DISPLAY SUB-1.
            .
            .
            .

    LOAD-TABLE.
        ADD 1 TO SUB-1.
        MOVE INPUT-RECORD TO TABLE-A (SUB-1).
        READ INPUT-FILE
            AT END MOVE 'N' TO MORE-DATA-FLAG.
```

15. Given the following Data Division entries

```
    FILE SECTION.
        .
        .
        .

    01  OUTPUT-LINE.
        05  SAMPLE-ITEM-OUT      PIC Z(4)9 OCCURS 12 TIMES.
        .
        .
        .

    WORKING-STORAGE SECTION.
    01  SAMPLE-TABLE.
        05  SAMPLE-ITEM          PIC 9(5) OCCURS 12 TIMES.
```

what would the following Procedure Division statements do?

```
        MOVE SPACES TO OUTPUT-LINE.
        PERFORM PARAGRAPH-1
            VARYING N FROM 1 BY 1 UNTIL N > 12.
        WRITE OUTPUT-LINE.
            .
            .
            .

    PARAGRAPH-1.
        MOVE SAMPLE-ITEM (N) TO SAMPLE-ITEM-OUT (N).
```

16. Given the same Data Division entries as in Question 15, what would the following Procedure Division statements do?

```
MOVE SPACES TO OUTPUT-LINE.
PERFORM PARAGRAPH-2
    VARYING N FROM 1 BY 1 UNTIL N > 12.
    .
    .
    .

PARAGRAPH-2.
    MOVE SAMPLE-ITEM (N) TO SAMPLE-ITEM-OUT (1).
    WRITE OUTPUT-LINE.
```

ANSWERS TO REVIEW QUESTIONS

1. Part (c) might be true in isolated instances but certainly not in general.

2. Part (a) is not true at all in general; (b) is completely true; (c) is true to a certain extent, but the meaning of "easier" is subject to argument; (d) is true in most cases, but not always, and it is not the main point.

3. The major differences have to do with the way tables are stored and accessed in the object program, which can have a bearing on the speed of execution of that program. Since we did not discuss these matters—which are fairly complex—subscripting and indexing will, no doubt, have seemed to be very similar. From a source program standpoint, the differences are that with indexing we use the INDEXED BY clause in the Data Division and in the Procedure Division we are able to use the SET, SEARCH, and SEARCH ALL verbs.

4. **a.** A qualifier must not be subscripted.

   b. A subscript must be greater than zero.

   c. In versions of COBOL prior to COBOL-85, subscripts cannot be arithmetic expressions; only literals and data names are permitted as subscripts. Indices, however, may be followed by a + or a - and an integer, and in COBOL-85 a subscript may also be followed by a + or a - and an integer.
   Although not required, there should generally be a space between a data name and a left parenthesis, and following the comma between subscripts; absence of such spaces was an error in earlier versions of COBOL.

5. Add the dollar amount (defined elsewhere) to the element of SUM-TABLE identified by the current value of X-ACCOUNT (defined elsewhere).

6. Form the sum of the 100 dollar amounts in SUM-TABLE. (This assumes, of course, that TOTAL-A and SUBSCRIPT have been defined elsewhere.)

7. Establish a table of 50 names available to the program without reading any data records.

8. This would work nicely except that editing can be performed only on elementary items. If the number of items were larger than four, we would use the PERFORM ... VARYING in a loop rather than writing many MOVE statements.

9. Without the OCCURS clause, the compiler would not know how much storage to allocate to the data item.

10. The changed value would probably be used. However, this may vary between compilers and the results are not always easily predicted. In any case, code that alters the data-name tends to make the execution of the loop harder to understand and should be avoided.

11. There would be no difference in the results but there might be some difference in the object code produced by the compiler.

12. **a.** 9.

   b. 10.

   c. None.

   d. 6.

   e. One time less than the value of **NUMBER-A**, if **NUMBER-A** is greater than or equal to 1. If **NUMBER-A** is less than 1 the loop will be performed endlessly, since **X** will never be equal to **NUMBER-A**.

13. **A** = 1, **B** = 1; 1, 2; 1, 3; 2, 1; 2, 2; 2, 3.

14. **a.** 52

   b. 51

   c. 50

15. The 12 items in **SAMPLE-TABLE** would be edited and printed on one line.

16. The 12 items in **SAMPLE-TABLE** would be edited and printed on 12 lines.

EXERCISES

*1. Two tables of 50 entries each have already been established in the Data Division; they are named **SET-UP** and **UNIT-TIME**. **JOB-TIME** is a non-subscripted variable. Write a statement to compute **JOB-TIME** as the sum of the thirteenth entries of the two tables.

2. Continuing with Exercise 1, there is a third table of 50 entries named **NUMBER-OF-UNITS**. Write a statement to compute **JOB-TIME** for the thirteenth entry of these tables, where **JOB-TIME** is the sum of **SET-UP** plus the product of **UNIT-TIME** multiplied by the **NUMBER-OF-UNITS**.

*3. A table named **SALES** has 50 entries corresponding to 50 salespeople whose numbers run from 1 to 50. Write statements to do the following: after reading a record from a file named **SALES-DATA**, values will be available for **SELLER-NUMBER** and **AMOUNT**. Using **SELLER-NUMBER** as a subscript, add **AMOUNT** to the appropriate entry in **SALES**.

4. An electric utility billing operation requires that **KWH** be multiplied by a value from a table named **RATE**, where the appropriate entry in the rate table is given by the value of **SERVICE-TYPE**. Write a statement using subscripting to perform the multiplication and make the result the new value of an item named **BILLING-AMOUNT**.

*5. A table named **A-TIME** contains five entries corresponding to the five working days of a week. Using a **PERFORM** with the **VARYING** option, write a program segment to get the sum of these five items and then divide by 5 to produce **AVERAGE-TIME**.

* Answers to starred exercises will be found in Appendix IV at the end of the book.

6. Data is the same as in Exercise 5, except **B-TIME** has seven entries. Write a program segment using a **PERFORM ... VARYING** statement to form the sum of the seven entries and also to produce in **B-COUNT** the number of those entries that are nonzero. Divide the total by **B-COUNT** to get average time; place this division in an **IF** statement that first checks that **B-COUNT** is nonzero and places zero in **AVERAGE-TIME** if it is.

*7. The table named **SALES** has 50 entries corresponding to 50 salespeople whose numbers run from 1 to 50. Write a program segment that will display the number and the sales amount for the salesperson having the largest sales in the table.

8. Given the same information as in Exercise 7, write a program segment to display the seller number and amount for the salesperson having the smallest sales. Any sales amounts that are zero should be excluded, however, so that the problem statement actually requests the smallest *nonzero* sales amount.

*9. Suppose that the 40 students in a **COBOL** programming class have been given numbers from 1 to 40. Write the Data Division entries necessary to establish a table of the 40 names corresponding to the 40 numbers.

10. Using the table in Exercise 9, write a program to produce a listing of the names and numbers of all students in the class.

*11. Using the enrollment table in the program of Figure 14.4, write a program to produce a listing of the enrollments for all 12 grades in 1990. The enrollments should be printed on 12 lines and each line should be identified with its grade.

12. Using the enrollment table in the program of Figure 14.4, write a program to produce a table like that shown at the start of Section 14.7.

*13. Using the enrollment table in the program of Figure 14.4, write a program to compute and print, for all 12 grades, the average enrollment over four years. The averages should be rounded to the nearest whole number and should be identified by grade.

14. Using the enrollment table in the program of Figure 14.4, write a program to compute and print the total enrollment for each of the four years. These totals should be identified with the years.

*15. Using the enrollment table in the program of Figure 14.4, write a program that will read a record specifying a year, then locate and print the largest enrollment for that year. The line of output should contain the year, the grade, and the enrollment.

16. Using the enrollment table in the program of Figure 14.4, write a program that will read a record specifying a year, then compute and print the total enrollment for that year.

*17. Modify the table loading procedure of Figure 14.3 to detect overflow (attempting to load more records into the table than there is room for). The program should not terminate immediately but should continue until the end of the input file is reached. However, do not attempt to insert records beyond the actual size of the table; overflow records should simply be discarded. After the end of the input file is reached, print an error message telling how many records were in the input file and how large the table actually is, then terminate the run.

18. Modify the program of Figure 14.9 in the following ways.

   a. The word **MANAGEMENT** in the second line of the heading is actually misplaced and should be on the same line as the word **AGE**.

   b. Validate the data by determining that the codes for male/female, management/nonmanagement are correct, that the age is not less than 17 nor greater than 65, and that the length of service is nonzero and less than 49.

   c. Insert a count of the number of input records. If the count exceeds 9999, display a message and terminate execution without printing the table.

19. (This exercise is suitable for a project.)

   Modify Exercise 14 of Chapter 5 according to the following specifications.

   Instead of coding the municipality codes and tax rates directly into the program, the program should read a municipality tax file, load the data into a table, and search the table to find the entry that matches the municipality code in an employee pay record.

   The records in the municipality tax file have the following format:

Columns 1-2	municipality code	PIC 99
Columns 3-6	tax rate	PIC 99V99

   Design an appropriate table to hold this data. If the table overflows while it is being loaded, count the total number of records in the municipality file, print a message telling the user what happened and how large the table needs to be to hold the entire file, and stop the run. When you are processing the payroll data, if a municipality code is specified that is not in the table, produce an appropriate error message. You may either process payroll data interactively or from a file. If the data comes from a file in batch mode, print the error message on a log file and go on to the next payroll record. The log file should contain appropriate column headings and data fields should be edited. If you are typing the payroll data interactively, display an error message on the CRT and allow the user to re-enter the municipality code. In either case, the error message should contain enough information in a readable format so that a clerk using the program would be able to locate and correct the invalid data.

CHAPTER 15

FILE STORAGE DEVICES AND PROGRAMMING

15.1   INTRODUCTION

Most business applications of computers involve processing large files of more or less permanent information. For example, a payroll application requires a payroll file that contains information about each employee; a purchasing application requires a file of data about vendors from whom supplies can be obtained; and an order fulfillment application requires a file of information about the company's own products with which to verify data in customers' orders.

In each of these examples the data has one or more of the following characteristics:

1. It is relatively constant; although some items may change from time to time the file as a whole shows little change from run to run.
2. It may be used by several programs; for example, a vendor file may be used by an accounts payable program was well as a purchasing program.
3. It usually must be in a particular sequence for processing.

For this type of data it is usually easiest to enter the data once, edit it to remove errors, then leave the data on a file for future use. You will find, therefore, that interactive processing is usually limited to controlling the execution of programs and the initial entry of data for editing, while files are used to provide data for most other types of processing.

Files differ in characteristics such as the number of records, the amount of data in each record, whether or not the records are in order on some key, and the sequence in which records may be accessed. File storage media differ in characteristics such as cost, the maximum and average time with which a record can be located, and the speed with which a record can be read once it has been located. File processing applications differ in characteristics such as the fraction of the records in a file that are processed in a typical run, whether the records are retrieved sequentially or randomly, whether new records are added to the file, and whether or not existing records are modified.

All of these considerations, and others, interact to determine how files should be stored and how programs to process them are written. Although a thorough discussion of files is beyond the scope of this book, this chapter presents the highlights of file storage devices and illustrates some of the more important concepts related to file processing.

15.2 STORAGE DEVICES

In general, files are stored on two types of devices, magnetic tapes and magnetic disks. On microcomputers, disks are further divided into hard disks and floppy disks.

Magnetic tape, which operates on a principle essentially the same as that used to operate audio or video recorders in the home, can store large quantities of information more cheaply than any other storage medium now available, and it can be written and read very rapidly. Furthermore, more than one file can be stored on a single tape. However, data stored on a magnetic tape must be processed sequentially. That is, in order to read a record stored at the end of a file it is necessary to read all preceding records on the file. Even worse, if you want to use a file which is stored at the end of a tape, you must read past all preceding files! Finally, tape drives for microcomputers are relatively expensive. At the time of this writing, a typical tape drive designed for use as a data storage device costs more than a high-quality 80286-based computer. For these reasons, magnetic tape is seldom used with microcomputers except for small drives designed only to store backup copies of disk files. However, tapes are used fairly commonly on mainframe computers; if you are developing software intended for use on a mainframe you should probably study the use of magnetic tapes in an appropriate manual or textbook.

For microcomputers, the most common medium for storing data files is the *floppy disk*. Indeed, it is unlikely that you have gotten this far in this book without having used a floppy disk. Although all disks are alike in principle, they vary greatly in detail. A complete discussion of disk principles and formats is beyond the scope of this book, but we do wish to discuss some of the basic concepts.

The principle by which a disk operates is the same as that used for a magnetic tape. That is, the surface of the disk is covered with a metal oxide which can be magnetized to store information. The disk rotates continuously, which moves the data past read/write heads that perform the I/O operations. To locate data on a disk, the disk is divided into concentric *tracks*, typically 40 tracks per side (see Figure 15.1). The tracks are further subdivided into *sectors*, typically 9 sectors per track with 512 bytes per sector. This means that a typical floppy disk can hold 512 x 9 x 40 x 2 = 368,640 (or 360K) bytes of data. Of course, these numbers vary somewhat depending on the exact nature of the disk. Floppy disks come in several sizes, most commonly 5-1/4" and 3-1/2", and with varying numbers of tracks per side. The result is that although many floppy disks do in fact store only 360K bytes of data, they can also be designed to store well over a million bytes.

Floppy disks have the advantage that they are relatively portable. If you have data files stored on a floppy disk you can remove the disk when you are not using it, put it in storage or make copies to be certain that files will not be

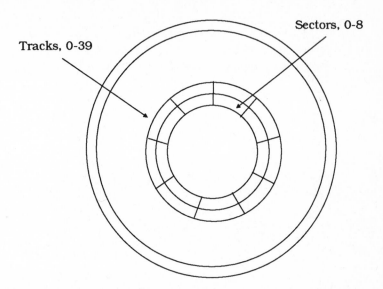

FIGURE 15.1 Schematic representation of a floppy disk.

lost, move the files from one computer to another, and keep libraries of disks storing as many files as you wish. However, floppy disks have two serious disadvantages. First, even the largest floppy disks are relatively small. For example, the Microsoft COBOL compiler comes on 14 360K floppy disks. Second, floppy disks are relatively slow. That is, the time required to find data on a floppy disk, then transfer the data into the computer, can take anywhere from several milliseconds (thousandths of a second) to several seconds. When you consider that the central processor of the computer operates at speeds on the order of millionths or even billionths of a second, you realize that this is slow indeed.

One way to improve this situation is to use a *hard disk*. Conceptually, a hard disk looks like two or more floppy disks stacked one above the other. (You should realize that this is a conceptual description only. Physically, there is a considerable difference in appearance between hard disks and floppy disks.) A typical hard disk consists of two *disk platters* with two surfaces each, giving a total of four recording surfaces. Each surface contains 611 tracks, each track contains 17 sectors, and each sector contains 512 bytes. Therefore, the disk has 512 x 17 x 611 x 4 = 21,272,576 bytes, or about 21 megabytes (Mbytes) of storage. This is the equivalent of almost 58 floppy disks. (As with floppy disks, these figures vary considerably between different hard disks. Hard disks are available that store hundreds of Mbytes.)

As important as the increased size of a hard disk is, even more important in many cases is the fact that hard disks operate much faster than floppy disks. Because hard disks rotate over 10 times as fast as floppy disks, information on a hard disk can be located much faster than on a floppy disk. Furthermore, once this information has been located it can be transferred into the computer much faster from a hard disk than from a floppy disk. The result is that if speed of data access is a prime consideration in an application, you are much better off using a hard disk than a floppy disk.

Hard disks have several disadvantages, however. First, their capacity is limited. Software such as spread sheet programs, database processors, word processors, project management systems, and compilers and linkers, typically require several megabytes of storage each, plus the space required for the data files used by this software. Although 20 Mbytes sounds like quite a bit of storage it can disappear very rapidly! Even though an individual floppy disk only holds a fraction of the data that a hard disk does, the number of floppy disks that you can keep for data storage is virtually unlimited.

A second disadvantage of hard disks is that their size tends to make them hard to organize. On a large hard disk, you may have hundred or even thousands of files stored on the disk. Finding the one you want for a particular job can sometimes be quite a problem. Even worse, if anything happens to damage the disk, *all* your information can be lost, not just a few files. Finally, hard disks are not portable. If you have a file stored on a hard disk on one computer and want to use that file on a different computer, you must copy the file to a floppy disk, then reload it onto the second computer.

We are not trying to argue in favor of any one type of storage medium. Each one has its use, and the experience programmer should learn the advantages and disadvantages of each. In any case, the precise nature of a disk is generally irrelevant to the COBOL program. What is of concern is the nature of the file or files stored on the disk. With this in mind, let us now look at the various types of COBOL files in more detail.

15.3   THE COBOL FILE DESCRIPTION

The COBOL programmer is not required to know how the various actions of file storage and accessing are carried out, but it is necessary to know how to specify to the compiler what the characteristics of the files are. That is the function of the file description (FD) entry of the File Section of the Data Division. Looking now at the program code shown in Figure 15.2, the FD entries for the files show some of the alternatives available.

The entry for TRANSACTION-FILE contains all the commonly used clauses, even though they are all optional in this case. The order shown is typical although most compilers accept the FD clauses in any order.

The first clause specifies the *blocking factor* for the file. On mainframe computers, the efficiency of tape or disk access is improved tremendously by reading or writing more than one record at a time. To facilitate this type of access, records are stored in groups called *blocks*, and rather than accessing one record at a time the hardware accesses one block at a time. The blocking factor is the number of records stored in one block. TRANSACTION-FILE has only one record per block so we write

        BLOCK CONTAINS 1 RECORDS

which specifies a blocking factor of one. (Notice that we must write RECORDS even though there is only one record per block.) On the other hand, the BLOCK CONTAINS clause for OLD-MASTER-FILE indicates that this file has a blocking factor of 25.

```
IDENTIFICATION DIVISION.
PROGRAM-ID.
    FILE-UPDATE.
DATE-WRITTEN.
    JULY 5, 1989.

ENVIRONMENT DIVISION.
INPUT-OUTPUT SECTION.
FILE-CONTROL.
    SELECT TRANSACTION-FILE   ASSIGN TO TRANS.
    SELECT OLD-MASTER-FILE    ASSIGN TO OLDMAST.
    SELECT NEW-MASTER-FILE    ASSIGN TO NEWMAST.
    SELECT MESSAGE-FILE       ASSIGN TO MESSAGES.

DATA DIVISION.

FILE SECTION.

FD  TRANSACTION-FILE
    BLOCK CONTAINS 1 RECORDS
    RECORD CONTAINS 62 CHARACTERS
    LABEL RECORDS ARE STANDARD
    DATA RECORD IS TRANSACTION-REC.
01  TRANSACTION-REC            PIC X(62).

FD  OLD-MASTER-FILE
    BLOCK CONTAINS 25 RECORDS
    LABEL RECORDS STANDARD.
01  OLD-MASTER-REC             PIC X(135).

FD  NEW-MASTER-FILE
    BLOCK CONTAINS 25 RECORDS
    LABEL RECORDS STANDARD.
01  NEW-MASTER-REC             PIC X(135).

FD  MESSAGE-FILE
    LABEL RECORDS OMITTED.
01  MESSAGE-REC                PIC X(80).
```

FIGURE 15.2 Representative **FD** entries.

For microcomputers, the concept of blocking is ignored. The effect of blocking is achieved by using sectors, and MS-DOS does not require that a sector be an exact multiple of the record size. Therefore, the **BLOCK CONTAINS** clause is ignored in Microsoft **COBOL**. It may be used for documentation if you intend to transfer the program to a mainframe computer, but it has no effect otherwise.

We should mention that if you look at **COBOL** programs written for IBM mainframe computers, you will frequently see a clause such as this:

BLOCK CONTAINS 0 RECORDS

This does not literally mean that the block contains no records. Rather, it is an instruction to the computer to get the blocking factor from the physical file or from the file assignment statement in the Job Control Language.

COBOL-85

In **COBOL-85**, you omit the **BLOCK CONTAINS** clause to tell the compiler to obtain the block size from the file, rather than writing

    BLOCK CONTAINS 0 RECORDS

In older versions of **COBOL**, omitting the **BLOCK CONTAINS** clause is equivalent to writing

    BLOCK CONTAINS 1 RECORDS

so you must be careful which version of **COBOL** you are using. Of course, these considerations apply only if you intend to transfer the program to a mainframe computer; the **BLOCK CONTAINS** clause is always treated as documentation in Microsoft **COBOL**.

END COBOL-85

The **RECORD CONTAINS** clause tells how many characters are contained in records in the file. This clause is optional since the compiler can determine that information by inspecting the record definition. Similarly, the **DATA RECORD** clause is optional. This clause specifies the name(s) of the data record(s) in the file. However, this information can also be determined by inspecting the data record definitions following the **FD**. If the file has several different record descriptions, then it is possible to write a **DATA RECORDS ARE** clause, but this is also optional.

The **LABEL RECORDS** clause is always required on mainframe computers even if the file has no labels. Labels are special records at the beginning and/or end of a file that contain information about the file. The most common usage of a label is to provide an identification to the program to establish that the proper reel of tape has been mounted on a tape drive. In an installation with a library containing thousands of reels of tape even the most careful operators will make occasional mistakes, picking up the wrong tape, mounting a tape on the wrong tape drive, or getting reels of a multireel file out of sequence. Information in a label record at the beginning of a tape makes it possible for the program to check that it is processing the reel of tape that it expects. For Microsoft **COBOL**, the **LABEL RECORDS** clause is always treated as documentation and ignored otherwise. However, because it is used so commonly with other compilers we will generally include it in our examples. The most common use of the **LABEL RECORDS** clause simply specifies **LABEL RECORDS ARE STANDARD**, which tells the compiler to use whatever labelling conventions have been defined as standard for the computer being used. An alternative that can be used for files that are going to a printer or are coming from a CRT or terminal is to specify that **LABEL RECORDS ARE OMITTED**. Since files associated with these simple input/output devices have no labels, the **OMITTED** option may be used, as is shown in the **FD** for **MESSAGE-FILE**.

The **FD** entries for **OLD-MASTER-FILE** and **NEW-MASTER-FILE** are typical for disk files. The **RECORD CONTAINS** and **DATA RECORD** clauses have been omitted since they are optional, even for mainframe computers. The **LABEL RECORDS** clause indicates that standard labels are being used. For purposes of documentation, the **BLOCK CONTAINS** clause indicates that if this program were run on a mainframe instead of a microcomputer, there should be 25 records per block in each file. Any time a nonzero blocking factor is used, be certain to include the word **RECORDS** in the clause. If we write only

    BLOCK CONTAINS 25

this states that we want blocks to contain 25 *characters*, which is certainly not what is intended.

15.4   A PROGRAM USING DISK STORAGE SEQUENTIALLY

Our first example file program uses a disk for temporary storage of groups of records from an input file. It uses the disk as a sequential storage medium and involves a technique, which we have not discussed previously, in which a file is opened and closed many times in the course of executing one program.

The application can be thought of as an extension of the seed company order processing program that was considered in previous chapters. Since we are concentrating on files in this chapter, we get data from an input file rather than using **ACCEPT** and **DISPLAY** statements. The input file consists of records representing lines from customers' orders. Each line is shown in skeleton form for this example program so that we can concentrate on the new disk storage concepts and techniques; a record consists only of an order number and 74 characters of unspecified transaction data. For our purposes here we assume that the transaction data is entirely numeric; this can be thought of as an indication of all of the kinds of data validation that were done in Chapter 11.

A complete customer order may consist of any number of order lines, from one to dozens. Our task is to inspect all the lines of any one customer order and to determine whether any of the lines contain an error. If any one or more lines of the order does contain an error, we are to write the entire order to a special handling file. If the order is completely error-free, we are to write the entire order to a normal handling file. This requirement makes it impossible to print the lines as they are read from the input, since we do not know until we have read all the lines from an order where the output should go. We must accordingly store the entire order temporarily until we know where it goes, and then must read it back and direct it to the appropriate output file.

This will be the first program in which we have a file that is used as both input and output in the same program. We will open it for output before writing the order lines onto it. When the program logic detects the end of the order group, the file will be closed and immediately opened as input so that we can get the records back into the computer and write them to the appropriate output file. The disk is being used here as a sequential storage medium, in that we write the records to it in the sequence in which they appear and read them back in the same sequence, and we emphasize this by specifying **ACCESS IS SEQUENTIAL** on the **SELECT** statement for **WORK-FILE**. Actually, the clause is redundant since sequential access is the default mode (which is why we have never had to specify it before), but adding the clause documents the file's intended usage.

The design of the program contains no surprises. In the Working-Storage Section, we have one flag to indicate the end of the input file of order records that we are processing, and a separate one to indicate the end of the temporary disk file. Another flag indicates whether any errors were found in an order, and a save area contains the order number of the current record.

The program, shown in figure 15.3, begins with code that should be quite familiar by now. In **B010-VALIDATE-ONE-ORDER** we save the current order number, make sure that the error flag is off, then open the temporary disk file for output. **C010-EDIT-LINE** writes all of the records for one order onto that file, checking each one to determine if it contains an error and setting the error flag if so. When a control break is detected, the temporary disk file is closed and then immediately reopened as input. Then, depending on the setting of the error flag, all of the records in the temporary disk storage are written either to the special handling file or the normal handling file.

```
1          IDENTIFICATION DIVISION.
2          PROGRAM-ID.
3              SEED3.
4          DATE-WRITTEN.
5              JULY 5, 1989.
6
7          ENVIRONMENT DIVISION.
8          INPUT-OUTPUT SECTION.
9          FILE-CONTROL.
10             SELECT WORK-FILE                  ASSIGN TO WORK
11                     ACCESS IS SEQUENTIAL.
12             SELECT ORDER-FILE                 ASSIGN TO ORDERS.
13             SELECT NORMAL-HANDLING-FILE       ASSIGN TO NORMAL.
14             SELECT SPECIAL-HANDLING-FILE      ASSIGN TO SPECIAL.
15
16         DATA DIVISION.
17
18         FILE SECTION.
19
20         FD  WORK-FILE
21             LABEL RECORDS ARE STANDARD.
22         01  WORK-RECORD                       PIC X(80).
23
24         FD  ORDER-FILE
25             LABEL RECORDS ARE OMITTED.
26         01  ORDER-RECORD.
27             05  ORDER-NUMBER                  PIC X(6).
28             05  ORDER-DATA                    PIC X(74).
29
30         FD  NORMAL-HANDLING-FILE
31             LABEL RECORDS ARE OMITTED.
32         01  NORMAL-LINE                       PIC X(80).
33
34         FD  SPECIAL-HANDLING-FILE
35             LABEL RECORDS ARE OMITTED.
36         01  SPECIAL-LINE                      PIC X(80).
37
```

```
38          WORKING-STORAGE SECTION.
39
40          01   MORE-DATA-REMAINS-FLAG              PIC X.
41               88   MORE-DATA-REMAINS                   VALUE 'Y'.
42               88   NO-MORE-DATA-REMAINS                VALUE 'N'.
43
44          01   MORE-WORK-REMAINS-FLAG              PIC X.
45               88   MORE-WORK-REMAINS                   VALUE 'Y'.
46               88   NO-MORE-WORK-REMAINS               VALUE 'N'.
47
48          01   ERRORS-FOUND-FLAG                  PIC X.
49               88   ERRORS-FOUND                       VALUE 'Y'.
50
51          01   PREVIOUS-ORDER-NUMBER              PIC X(6).
52
53
54          PROCEDURE DIVISION.
55          A000-VALIDATE-ORDERS.
56              OPEN INPUT ORDER-FILE
57                   OUTPUT NORMAL-HANDLING-FILE
58                          SPECIAL-HANDLING-FILE.
59              MOVE 'Y' TO MORE-DATA-REMAINS-FLAG.
60              READ ORDER-FILE
61                  AT END MOVE 'N' TO MORE-DATA-REMAINS-FLAG.
62              PERFORM B010-VALIDATE-ONE-ORDER
63                  UNTIL NO-MORE-DATA-REMAINS.
64              CLOSE ORDER-FILE
65                    NORMAL-HANDLING-FILE
66                    SPECIAL-HANDLING-FILE.
67              STOP RUN.
68
69          B010-VALIDATE-ONE-ORDER.
70              MOVE ORDER-NUMBER TO PREVIOUS-ORDER-NUMBER.
71              MOVE 'N' TO ERRORS-FOUND-FLAG.
72              OPEN OUTPUT WORK-FILE.
73              PERFORM C010-EDIT-LINE
74                  UNTIL ORDER-NUMBER IS NOT EQUAL TO PREVIOUS-ORDER-NUMBER
75                        OR NO-MORE-DATA-REMAINS.
76              CLOSE WORK-FILE.
77
78              OPEN INPUT WORK-FILE.
79              MOVE 'Y' TO MORE-WORK-REMAINS-FLAG.
80              IF ERRORS-FOUND
81                  PERFORM C020-WRITE-TO-SPECIAL-HANDLING
82                      UNTIL NO-MORE-WORK-REMAINS
83              ELSE
84                  PERFORM C030-WRITE-TO-NORMAL-HANDLING
85                      UNTIL NO-MORE-WORK-REMAINS.
86              CLOSE WORK-FILE.
87
88          C010-EDIT-LINE.
89              IF ORDER-DATA IS NOT NUMERIC
90                  MOVE 'Y' TO ERRORS-FOUND-FLAG.
91              WRITE WORK-RECORD FROM ORDER-RECORD.
92              READ ORDER-FILE
93                  AT END MOVE 'N' TO MORE-DATA-REMAINS-FLAG.
94
```

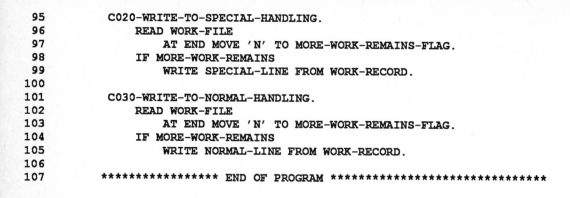

```
95            C020-WRITE-TO-SPECIAL-HANDLING.
96                READ WORK-FILE
97                    AT END MOVE 'N' TO MORE-WORK-REMAINS-FLAG.
98                IF MORE-WORK-REMAINS
99                    WRITE SPECIAL-LINE FROM WORK-RECORD.
100
101           C030-WRITE-TO-NORMAL-HANDLING.
102               READ WORK-FILE
103                   AT END MOVE 'N' TO MORE-WORK-REMAINS-FLAG.
104               IF MORE-WORK-REMAINS
105                   WRITE NORMAL-LINE FROM WORK-RECORD.
106
107           **************** END OF PROGRAM ******************************
```

FIGURE 15.3 A program using temporary disk storage.

15.5 LINE SEQUENTIAL FILES

Sequential COBOL files are normally written on the disk as a long string of characters. For example, if WORK-FILE in the preceding program contained 10 records, it would simply be stored on the disk as 800 bytes, with nothing to tell where one record ends and the next one begins. The only way that the program knows how many bytes of data to read or write for one record is by the size of the record defined in the FD entry for WORK-FILE. If we should write another program containing a file with 40-byte records, that program could read WORK-FILE as a file of 20 records, each of which was 40 bytes long, and there would be no confusion at all. (Of course, whether or not the data means anything when it is divided into 40-byte records is another question entirely.)

As long as we only write files to be read by other COBOL programs, or read files that were written by other COBOL programs, there is no problem. COBOL programs can read or write files with fixed length records, called *record sequential* files, with no difficulty as long as we specify the correct record lengths in the FD entries. However, if we are writing files to be printed, or if we are reading files that were created by a word processor or text editor, we have a different situation.

To save space on the disk, text editors and similar programs remove any trailing spaces at the end of a line. Of course, this means that it is not possible to tell where a line ends just by counting the bytes. Therefore, every line is terminated with the two-byte hexadecimal sequence 0D0A (carriage return, line feed). This type of file, where lines are of varying lengths and each line is terminated with the 0D0A sequence, is called *line sequential*. When COBOL reads a record from a line sequential file, it reads up to the 0D0A terminator, then pads the rest of the record with as many blanks as are necessary to bring it up to the specified length for that file. On output, any trailing blanks are removed and a 0D0A sequence is added to the record before it is written to the file. Furthermore, if the file is being written as a print file (using the ADVANCING clause), page eject characters and other line spacing characters are inserted as needed to get the proper line spacing.

The default file type for Microsoft COBOL is record sequential. If you wish to have sequential files treated as line sequential, you must specify the directive SEQUENTIAL"LINE" at compile-time. Generally, this means that you should include SEQUENTIAL"LINE" in the COBOL.DIR file. If you neglect to specify the SEQUENTIAL"LINE" directive for line sequential files, the 0D0A terminator is read as two bytes of ordinary data and is otherwise ignored! The record sequential and line sequential options only apply to sequential files; the files discussed in the remainder of this chapter (indexed and relative record) have their own formats.

15.6 INDEXED FILES

Disk storage, as we have seen, can be used sequentially and is commonly used in this way. However, more importantly, it can also be used as random access storage, which means that we can retrieve records in any sequence we wish without any unbearable penalty for "skipping around" in the file. If the nature of the application makes random access an essential part of the approach, then we turn to the file organization and programming techniques that use random processing. There are several such methods of accessing disk storage, the most common being *indexed* and *relative record*. We will discuss the indexed method first. Indexed files are frequently called *indexed sequential* files, since they can be used both sequentially and randomly.

Although an indexed file appears to the COBOL programmer to be a single file, it actually consists of two parts: a *data storage* area, which contains the data records stored in the file; and an *index* area, which contains an index used to find records in the data area.* When you specify a name for the physical disk file (such as PRODUCT.IND) Microsoft COBOL uses this name for the data storage area, then creates a second file with the extension IDX (e.g., PRODUCT.IDX) for the index area.

When an indexed file is created it frequently is created sequentially, with all records sorted on a key field.** As the file is built, the record keys are used to build an index that can be used to find individual records very rapidly. When we wish to access records in the file, we can do so in two different ways. First, we can use the indexed file as an ordinary sequential file. If we use this method, the file is used exactly like any other sequential file. The second approach, however, allows us to access selected records randomly, in any order we wish. If we use this method, we specify the key of the record we wish to use, and the index uses this key to find the desired record and retrieve it without passing over intervening records in the file.

An indexed file is different from an ordinary sequential file in another regard: it is possible to insert new records into the file after it has been created and delete records from the file without rewriting the entire file.

This is a highly condensed version of how indexed files actually work. One of the topics in the further study of programming is a more thorough consideration of how some of these operations are carried out and their various implications for programming and for data management. What has been presented here is adequate for an introductory study of the subject, but it should be understood that this is hardly a complete explanation.

* In some implementations there are actually three parts, the third area being used to store records that do not fit into the data area. However, we will not be concerned with these implementation details.

** It is also possible to create the file randomly. In this case, the ACCESS clause should be writeen ACCESS IS RANDOM. In either case, the resulting file looks the same.

15.7   A PROGRAM TO CREATE AN INDEXED FILE

Continuing with our use of the seed catalog order system for illustrative purposes, we now consider how an indexed file of the company's products could be created. As before, this will be a skeleton version with regard to the actual record contents so that we can concentrate on the new file processing techniques. Specifically, we assume that we are given a file consisting of one record for each product that the company sells. Each record contains a five-character catalog number, three size codes and corresponding prices, and a forty-character description. The entire file is to be written onto an indexed sequential file, with a certain amount of compression of the data to save disk space.

The program shown in Figure 15.4 demonstrates the **SELECT** statement required to create an indexed file. This statement contains four new clauses: **ORGANIZATION, ACCESS, RECORD KEY**, and **FILE STATUS**. The **ORGANIZATION** clause tells the compiler that the file will be an indexed file. Since an indexed file can be accessed either sequentially or randomly, the **COBOL** compiler must know which is to be used for this particular file. Therefore we specify that **ACCESS IS SEQUENTIAL**. As in the previous example, sequential access is the default and the **ACCESS** clause could have been omitted from the statement. However, with random access files in particular it is a good idea to specify the access method for documentation purposes, even if the compiler does not require it. With the **RECORD KEY** clause, we specify what field in the output record should be used to index the file as it is created on disk; this clause is always required when an indexed file is used, and always specifies a field in the record of the indexed file. The fact that data name qualification is used here is entirely unrelated to indexed file considerations.

The **FILE STATUS** clause deserves particular mention because it can be very useful and is not limited to random access files. The variable named in the **FILE STATUS** clause is defined in the Working-Storage Section and must have either **PIC 99** or **PIC XX**. Whenever any I-O operation is performed on the file being selected, **IS-PRODUCT-FILE** in this example, a two-digit code indicating the result of that operation is stored in the file status variable. The first digit of the status variable, called *status key* 1, indicates the basic result of the operation. The values returned are:

0 - successful completion
1 - AT END
2 - invalid key
3 - hardware error
4 - logic error
9 - other error

The value of the second digit of the status variable, *status key* 2, depends on the exact nature of the result and the value of status key 1. For example, a file status value of 10 indicates a normal end of file, while 46 indicates an attempt to read past the end-of-file mark on a file. Although we will only use it in connection with random access files, the **FILE STATUS** clause may be used with any **COBOL** file and can be very useful in determining the exact nature of a file-related error.

```
1          IDENTIFICATION DIVISION.
2          PROGRAM-ID.
3              BUILD-ISAM.
4          DATE-WRITTEN.
5              JULY 5, 1989.
6
7          ENVIRONMENT DIVISION.
8          INPUT-OUTPUT SECTION.
9          FILE-CONTROL.
10             SELECT PRODUCT-FILE              ASSIGN TO PRODUCTS.
11             SELECT IS-PRODUCT-FILE           ASSIGN TO ISPROD
12                     ORGANIZATION IS INDEXED
13                     ACCESS IS SEQUENTIAL
14                     RECORD KEY IS CATALOG-NUMBER OF IS-PRODUCT-RECORD
15                     FILE STATUS IS IS-STATUS.
16
17         DATA DIVISION.
18
19         FILE SECTION.
20
21         FD   PRODUCT-FILE
22              LABEL RECORDS ARE STANDARD.
23         01   PRODUCT-RECORD.
24              05   CATALOG-NUMBER            PIC X(5).
25              05   SIZE-1                    PIC X.
26              05   PRICE-1                   PIC 99V99.
27              05   SIZE-2                    PIC X.
28              05   PRICE-2                   PIC 99V99.
29              05   SIZE-3                    PIC X.
30              05   PRICE-3                   PIC 99V99.
31              05   DESCRIPTION               PIC X(40).
32
33         FD   IS-PRODUCT-FILE
34              LABEL RECORDS ARE STANDARD.
35         01   IS-PRODUCT-RECORD.
36              05   CATALOG-NUMBER            PIC X(5).
37              05   SIZE-1                    PIC X.
38              05   PRICE-1                   PIC S99V99   COMP-3.
39              05   SIZE-2                    PIC X.
40              05   PRICE-2                   PIC S99V99   COMP-3.
41              05   SIZE-3                    PIC X.
42              05   PRICE-3                   PIC S99V99   COMP-3.
43              05   DESCRIPTION               PIC X(40).
44
45         WORKING-STORAGE SECTION.
46
47         01   INVALID-KEY-FLAG              PIC X VALUE 'N'.
48              88   INVALID-KEY-FOUND              VALUE 'Y'.
49
50         01   IS-STATUS                     PIC 99 VALUE 00.
51
52         01   MORE-DATA-REMAINS-FLAG        PIC X.
53              88   MORE-DATA-REMAINS             VALUE 'Y'.
54              88   NO-MORE-DATA-REMAINS          VALUE 'N'.
55
56
```

```
57          PROCEDURE DIVISION.
58          A000-CREATE-INDEXED-PROD-FILE.
59              OPEN INPUT  PRODUCT-FILE
60                    OUTPUT IS-PRODUCT-FILE.
61              MOVE 'Y' TO MORE-DATA-REMAINS-FLAG.
62              PERFORM B010-TRANSFER-ONE-RECORD
63                  UNTIL NO-MORE-DATA-REMAINS  OR  INVALID-KEY-FOUND.
64              IF INVALID-KEY-FOUND
65                  DISPLAY 'DUPLICATE OR SEQ ERROR - JOB ABORTED'
66                  DISPLAY 'FILE STATUS IS ' IS-STATUS.
67              CLOSE PRODUCT-FILE
68                    IS-PRODUCT-FILE.
69              STOP RUN.
70
71          B010-TRANSFER-ONE-RECORD.
72              READ PRODUCT-FILE
73                      AT END MOVE 'N' TO MORE-DATA-REMAINS-FLAG.
74              IF MORE-DATA-REMAINS
75                  MOVE CORRESPONDING PRODUCT-RECORD TO IS-PRODUCT-RECORD
76                  WRITE IS-PRODUCT-RECORD
77                      INVALID KEY MOVE 'Y' TO INVALID-KEY-FLAG.
78
79          ********************** END OF PROGRAM ************************
```

FIGURE 15.4 A program for creating an indexed sequential file.

In previous chapters we emphasized the idea that information coming into or going out of the computer must be in DISPLAY format. Actually that statement is too strong, since it applies only to information coming from input or going to output that must be read by people, such as CRT input and printed output. Information that is going to file storage, whether tape or disk, may be in any format that is convenient. The binary format (COMPUTATIONAL) is not generally used for data that involves dollars and cents, but the packed format (COMPUTATIONAL-3) frequently is. For purposes of illustration, we have shown the four-byte prices being compressed into three bytes by placing them in COMPUTATIONAL-3 fields.

The Procedure Division involves just one new feature. The basic idea is simply to read each record and immediately write it to the indexed file. However, two kinds of errors could be encountered in the input: there could be two or more records with the same key, or the records could be out of sequence. When a COBOL program is creating a new indexed file, it requires that every record in the file have a unique key and that the records be sorted in strictly ascending sequence on that key. If an attempt is made to write to the indexed file a record whose key is not strictly greater than the key of the preceding record, an error condition is raised. To detect that error condition and allow the program to respond to it, we have added the INVALID KEY clause to the WRITE statement for the indexed file. Just as the AT END clause is executed only when a special condition (end of file) is encountered during a read, so the INVALID KEY clause is executed only when a special condition (duplicate or out of sequence key) is encountered during a write.

Here is a listing of a ten-record file that was used to test this program:

Catalog number	Size Price	Size Price	Size Price	Description
33597	A0050	G0250	0000	STOCKS - TRYSOMIC 7 WEEKS MIXED COLORS
36574	A0050	G0150	0000	STOCKS - GIANT COLUMN MIXED COLORS
37515	A0035	H0100	0000	SWEET WILLIAM PINK BEAUTY
39156	A0035	H0100	0000	SWEET WILLIAM PURE WHITE
43125	A0035	H0105	K0325	ZINNIAS - GIANTS OF CALIFORNIA MIXED
50013	A0045	K0100	L0185	CABBAGE, BURPEES DANISH ROUNDHEAD
51904	A0075	J0450	0000	CRENSHAH MELON, BURPEES EARLY HYBRID
62471	A0075	T0185	U0250	HYBRID CORN, HONEY AND CREAM
62547	A0050	L0110	S0275	CUCUMBER, BURPEE PICKLER
96461	1595	0000	0000	COMPOST KIT

Observe that there are no size codes for the last item because it is one that does not require a size code. Further, several of the items have only two size codes. Items that have fewer than three prices have zeros for the missing prices, since if these fields are left blank the attempt to convert the blanks to packed decimal may produce invalid results.

15.8   A PROGRAM TO PRINT AN INDEXED FILE

It is not possible to use MS-DOS commands such as PRINT or TYPE to list the indexed file that was produced by the previous program because it can be accessed meaningfully only by programs using indexed sequential software. Also, since the records contain packed decimal data, human beings would not be able to read that information without appropriate format conversions anyway. Although the program shown in Figure 15.5 only prints the indexed file, it is shown because it demonstrates how indexed files can be accessed sequentially after they have been created.

```
1        IDENTIFICATION DIVISION.
2        PROGRAM-ID.
3            PRINT-PRODUCT.
4        DATE-WRITTEN.
5            JULY 5, 1989.
6
7        ENVIRONMENT DIVISION.
8        INPUT-OUTPUT SECTION.
9        FILE-CONTROL.
10           SELECT IS-PRODUCT-FILE          ASSIGN TO ISPROD
11                   ORGANIZATION IS INDEXED
12                   ACCESS IS SEQUENTIAL
13                   RECORD KEY IS CATALOG-NUMBER OF IS-PRODUCT-RECORD.
14           SELECT REPORT-FILE              ASSIGN TO REPORT.
15
16       DATA DIVISION.
17
```

```
18              FILE SECTION.
19
20          FD  IS-PRODUCT-FILE
21              LABEL RECORDS ARE STANDARD.
22          01  IS-PRODUCT-RECORD.
23              05  CATALOG-NUMBER              PIC X(5).
24              05  SIZE-1                      PIC X.
25              05  PRICE-1                     PIC S99V99   COMP-3.
26              05  SIZE-2                      PIC X.
27              05  PRICE-2                     PIC S99V99   COMP-3.
28              05  SIZE-3                      PIC X.
29              05  PRICE-3                     PIC S99V99   COMP-3.
30              05  DESCRIPTION                 PIC X(40).
31
32          FD  REPORT-FILE
33              LABEL RECORDS ARE OMITTED.
34          01  REPORT-LINE.
35              05  CATALOG-NUMBER              PIC X(5).
36              05  SIZE-1                      PIC BBX.
37              05  PRICE-1                     PIC ZZ9.99.
38              05  SIZE-2                      PIC BBX.
39              05  PRICE-2                     PIC ZZ9.99.
40              05  SIZE-3                      PIC BBX.
41              05  PRICE-3                     PIC ZZ9.99.
42              05  DESCRIPTION                 PIC BBX(40).
43
44          WORKING-STORAGE SECTION.
45
46          01  MORE-DATA-REMAINS-FLAG          PIC X.
47              88  MORE-DATA-REMAINS               VALUE 'Y'.
48              88  NO-MORE-DATA-REMAINS            VALUE 'N'.
49
50          PROCEDURE DIVISION.
51          A000-PRINT-PRODUCTS.
52              OPEN  INPUT IS-PRODUCT-FILE
53                    OUTPUT REPORT-FILE.
54              MOVE 'Y' TO MORE-DATA-REMAINS-FLAG.
55              PERFORM B010-PRINT-RECORD
56                      UNTIL NO-MORE-DATA-REMAINS.
57              CLOSE IS-PRODUCT-FILE
58                    REPORT-FILE.
59              STOP RUN.
60
61          B010-PRINT-RECORD.
62              READ IS-PRODUCT-FILE
63                      AT END MOVE 'N' TO MORE-DATA-REMAINS-FLAG.
64              IF MORE-DATA-REMAINS
65                  MOVE SPACES TO REPORT-LINE
66                  MOVE CORRESPONDING IS-PRODUCT-RECORD TO REPORT-LINE
67                  WRITE REPORT-LINE AFTER ADVANCING 1 LINE.
68
69          *********************** END OF PROGRAM ***********************
```

FIGURE 15.5 A program to print the contents of an indexed file.

The program is similar to that of Figure 15.4, since both programs access the indexed file sequentially. Again we include the `ACCESS IS SEQUENTIAL` clause for documentation in the `SELECT` statement even though it could have been omitted (since sequential access is the default). However, we omitted the `FILE STATUS` clause since the use of `IS-PRODUCT-FILE` is quite straightforward. Although the `SELECT` statement identifies `IS-PRODUCT-FILE` as an indexed file, the remainder of the program looks just like any other program reading an ordinary sequential file.

Here is the output produced when this program was run, taking as its input the file produced by the program in Figure 15.5.

```
33597  A  0.50  G  2.50       0.00  STOCKS - TRYSOMIC 7 WEEKS MIXED COLORS
36574  A  0.50  G  1.50       0.00  STOCKS - GIANT COLUMN MIXED COLORS
37515  A  0.35  H  1.00       0.00  SWEET WILLIAM  PINK BEAUTY
39156  A  0.35  H  1.00       0.00  SWEET WILLIAM  PURE WHITE
43125  A  0.35  H  1.05  K  3.25  ZINNIAS - GIANTS OF CALIFORNIA MIXED
50013  A  0.45  K  1.00  L  1.85  CABBAGE, BURPEES DANISH ROUNDHEAD
51904  A  0.75  J  4.50       0.00  CRENSHAH MELON, BURPEES EARLY HYBRID
62471  A  0.75  T  1.85  U  2.50  HYBRID CORN, HONEY AND CREAM
62547  A  0.50  L  1.10  S  2.75  CUCUMBER, BURPEE PICKLER
96461     15.95       0.00       0.00  COMPOST KIT
```

15.9 AN ORDER VALIDATION PROGRAM

We will now see how an indexed file can be accessed in the random mode. To do this we will consider a program that is a modification of the program in Figure 15.3, which printed messages on one of two files depending on whether or not an order contained any errors. The idea now is that a complete customer order consists of a header record that gives the customer's name and address, as many body records as there are separate items in the customer's order, and a trailer record giving the order total, handling charge, and tax as computed by the customer. Every record, of whatever type, contains an order number in the first six characters. Every record type has as its next character either a 1, 2, or 3 that identifies it as a header, body, or trailer record, respectively. The program is required not only to validate each line of the customer order, as we did in Figure 15.3, but also to determine that the complete order group does consist of one header record followed by one or more body records followed by one trailer record. No validation of the header record is required other than to establish that exactly one is present, but for the trailer record it would ordinarily be necessary to check that the customer's computation of the total matches the sum of all the prices on the body records. We shall not actually do the validation of either the body records or the trailer records, but shall leave these operations as stubs that may be completed by the student as exercises. The program is shown in Figure 15.6.

```
1            IDENTIFICATION DIVISION.
2            PROGRAM-ID.
3                VALIDATE-ORDERS.
4            DATE-WRITTEN.
5                JULY 5, 1989.
6
7            ENVIRONMENT DIVISION.
8            INPUT-OUTPUT SECTION.
9            FILE-CONTROL.
10               SELECT ORDER-FILE                ASSIGN TO ORDERS.
11               SELECT IS-PRODUCT-FILE           ASSIGN TO ISPROD
12                       ORGANIZATION IS INDEXED
13                       ACCESS IS RANDOM
14                       RECORD KEY IS CATALOG-NUMBER OF IS-PRODUCT-RECORD
15                       FILE STATUS IS IS-STATUS.
16               SELECT TEMP-DISK-FILE            ASSIGN TO TEMPDISK.
17               SELECT NORMAL-HANDLING-FILE      ASSIGN TO NORMAL.
18               SELECT SPECIAL-HANDLING-FILE     ASSIGN TO SPECIAL.
19
20           DATA DIVISION.
21
22           FILE SECTION.
23
24           FD  ORDER-FILE
25               LABEL RECORDS ARE OMITTED.
26           01  ORDER-RECORD.
27               05   ORDER-NUMBER                PIC X(6).
28               05   RECORD-TYPE                 PIC X.
29                    88   HEADER                           VALUE '1'.
30                    88   BODY                             VALUE '2'.
31                    88   TRAILER                          VALUE '3'.
32               05   FILLER                      PIC X(73).
33
34           01  HEADER-RECORD.
35               05   ORDER-NUMBER                PIC X(6).
36               05   RECORD-TYPE                 PIC X.
37               05   NAME-AND-ADDRESS            PIC X(73).
38
39           01  BODY-RECORD.
40               05   ORDER-NUMBER                PIC X(6).
41               05   RECORD-TYPE                 PIC X.
42               05   CATALOG-NUMBER.
43                    10   CATALOG-FIRST-DIGIT    PIC X.
44                    10   CATALOG-REMAINING      PIC X(4).
45               05   SIZE-CODE                   PIC X.
46               05   QUANTITY                    PIC 99.
47               05   ITEM-DESCRIPTION            PIC X(40).
48               05   X-PRICE                     PIC X(5).
49               05   9-PRICE REDEFINES X-PRICE   PIC 9(3)V99.
50               05   FILLER                      PIC X(20).
51
52           01  TRAILER-RECORD.
53               05   ORDER-NUMBER                PIC X(6).
54               05   RECORD-TYPE                 PIC X.
55               05   SUB-TOTAL                   PIC 9(3)V99.
56               05   HANDLING-CHARGE             PIC 9V99.
57               05   TAX                         PIC 99V99.
58               05   GRAND-TOTAL                 PIC 9(3)V99.
59               05   FILLER                      PIC X(56).
```

```
60
61          FD  IS-PRODUCT-FILE
62              LABEL RECORDS ARE STANDARD.
63          01  IS-PRODUCT-RECORD.
64              05  CATALOG-NUMBER          PIC X(5).
65              05  SIZE-1                  PIC X.
66              05  PRICE-1                 PIC S99V99  COMP-3.
67              05  SIZE-2                  PIC X.
68              05  PRICE-2                 PIC S99V99  COMP-3.
69              05  SIZE-3                  PIC X.
70              05  PRICE-3                 PIC S99V99  COMP-3.
71              05  DESCRIPTION             PIC X(40).
72
73          FD  TEMP-DISK-FILE
74              LABEL RECORDS ARE STANDARD.
75          01  TEMP-DISK-RECORD.
76              05  ORDER-NUMBER            PIC X(6).
77              05  FILLER                  PIC X(74).
78
79          FD  NORMAL-HANDLING-FILE
80              LABEL RECORDS ARE OMITTED.
81          01  NORMAL-HANDLING-RECORD      PIC X(132).
82
83
84          FD  SPECIAL-HANDLING-FILE
85              LABEL RECORDS ARE OMITTED.
86          01  SPECIAL-HANDLING-RECORD     PIC X(132).
87
88          WORKING-STORAGE SECTION.
89
90          01  CURRENT-ORDER-NUMBER        PIC X(6).
91
92          01  ERROR-FLAGS.
93              88  RECORD-OK                          VALUE SPACES.
94              05  CAT-NO-NOT-NUMERIC      PIC X.
95              05  FIRST-DIGIT-INVALID     PIC X.
96              05  INVALID-SIZE-CODE       PIC X.
97              05  NO-SUCH-SIZE-CODE       PIC X.
98              05  QTY-NOT-NUMERIC         PIC X.
99              05  PRICE-NOT-NUMERIC       PIC X.
100             05  INVALID-PRICE-OR-QTY    PIC X.
101             05  LARGE-PRICE             PIC X.
102             05  MISSING-HEADER          PIC X.
103             05  MISSING-TRAILER         PIC X.
104             05  INVALID-CATALOG-NUMBER  PIC X.
105             05  INVALID-RECORD-TYPE     PIC X.
106
107         01  ERRORS-FOUND-FLAG           PIC X.
108             88  ERRORS-FOUND                       VALUE 'Y'.
109
110         01  IS-STATUS                   PIC 99 VALUE 00.
111
112         01  MORE-ORDERS-FLAG            PIC X.
113             88  MORE-ORDERS                        VALUE 'Y'.
114             88  NO-MORE-ORDERS                     VALUE 'N'.
115
116         01  MORE-TEMP-RECORDS-FLAG      PIC X.
117             88  MORE-TEMP-RECORDS                  VALUE 'Y'.
118             88  NO-MORE-TEMP-RECORDS               VALUE 'N'.
```

```
119
120
121            PROCEDURE DIVISION.
122            A000-VALIDATE-CATALOG-ORDERS.
123               OPEN   INPUT ORDER-FILE
124                             IS-PRODUCT-FILE
125                     OUTPUT NORMAL-HANDLING-FILE
126                             SPECIAL-HANDLING-FILE.
127                 MOVE 'Y' TO MORE-ORDERS-FLAG.
128                 READ ORDER-FILE
129                      AT END MOVE 'N' TO MORE-ORDERS-FLAG.
130                 PERFORM B010-PROCESS-ONE-ORDER
131                      UNTIL NO-MORE-ORDERS  OR  IS-STATUS > 29.
132                 IF IS-STATUS > 29
133                     DISPLAY 'INDEXED FILE STATUS IS ', IS-STATUS.
134                 CLOSE ORDER-FILE
135                       IS-PRODUCT-FILE
136                       NORMAL-HANDLING-FILE
137                       SPECIAL-HANDLING-FILE.
138                 STOP RUN.
139
140            B010-PROCESS-ONE-ORDER.
141                 MOVE 'N' TO ERRORS-FOUND-FLAG.
142                 MOVE SPACES TO ERROR-FLAGS.
143                 MOVE ORDER-NUMBER OF ORDER-RECORD TO CURRENT-ORDER-NUMBER.
144                 OPEN OUTPUT TEMP-DISK-FILE.
145                 IF HEADER
146                     PERFORM C010-VALIDATE-HEADER-RECORD;
147                     WRITE TEMP-DISK-RECORD FROM ORDER-RECORD;
148                     READ ORDER-FILE
149                          AT END MOVE 'N' TO MORE-ORDERS-FLAG
150                 ELSE
151                     MOVE 'Y' TO ERRORS-FOUND-FLAG
152                     MOVE 'X' TO MISSING-HEADER.
153                 PERFORM C020-PROCESS-BODY-RECORD
154                        UNTIL ORDER-NUMBER OF ORDER-RECORD
155                             IS NOT EQUAL TO CURRENT-ORDER-NUMBER  OR
156                             NO-MORE-ORDERS  OR
157                             NOT BODY.
158                 IF ORDER-NUMBER OF ORDER-RECORD = CURRENT-ORDER-NUMBER  AND
159                         TRAILER  AND  MORE-ORDERS
160                     PERFORM C030-VALIDATE-TRAILER-RECORD;
161                     WRITE TEMP-DISK-RECORD FROM ORDER-RECORD;
162                     READ ORDER-FILE
163                          AT END MOVE 'N' TO MORE-ORDERS-FLAG
164                 ELSE
165                     MOVE 'Y' TO ERRORS-FOUND-FLAG
166                     MOVE 'X' TO MISSING-TRAILER.
167                 IF NOT HEADER  AND  NOT BODY  AND  NOT TRAILER  AND
168                         MORE-ORDERS
169                     MOVE 'Y' TO ERRORS-FOUND-FLAG;
170                     MOVE 'X' TO INVALID-RECORD-TYPE;
171                     WRITE TEMP-DISK-RECORD FROM ORDER-RECORD;
172                     READ ORDER-FILE
173                          AT END MOVE 'N' TO MORE-ORDERS-FLAG.
174                 CLOSE TEMP-DISK-FILE.
175                 OPEN INPUT TEMP-DISK-FILE.
176                 MOVE 'Y' TO MORE-TEMP-RECORDS-FLAG.
```

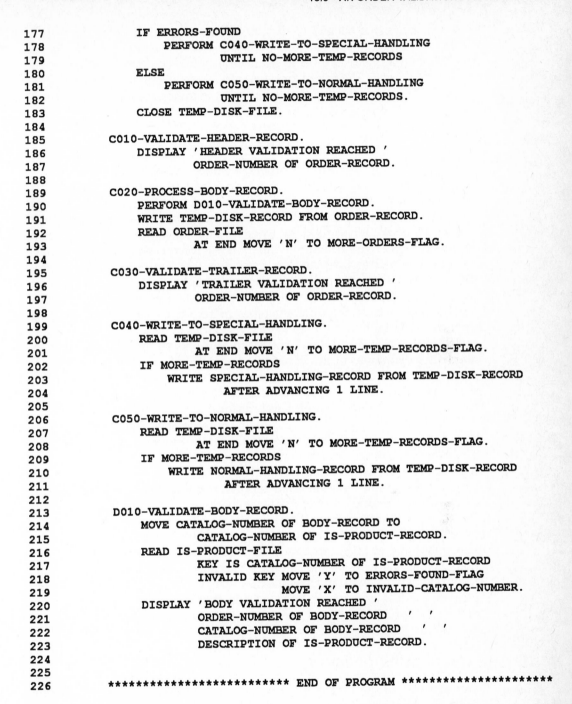

```
177             IF ERRORS-FOUND
178                 PERFORM C040-WRITE-TO-SPECIAL-HANDLING
179                     UNTIL NO-MORE-TEMP-RECORDS
180             ELSE
181                 PERFORM C050-WRITE-TO-NORMAL-HANDLING
182                     UNTIL NO-MORE-TEMP-RECORDS.
183             CLOSE TEMP-DISK-FILE.
184
185         C010-VALIDATE-HEADER-RECORD.
186             DISPLAY 'HEADER VALIDATION REACHED '
187                     ORDER-NUMBER OF ORDER-RECORD.
188
189         C020-PROCESS-BODY-RECORD.
190             PERFORM D010-VALIDATE-BODY-RECORD.
191             WRITE TEMP-DISK-RECORD FROM ORDER-RECORD.
192             READ ORDER-FILE
193                     AT END MOVE 'N' TO MORE-ORDERS-FLAG.
194
195         C030-VALIDATE-TRAILER-RECORD.
196             DISPLAY 'TRAILER VALIDATION REACHED '
197                     ORDER-NUMBER OF ORDER-RECORD.
198
199         C040-WRITE-TO-SPECIAL-HANDLING.
200             READ TEMP-DISK-FILE
201                     AT END MOVE 'N' TO MORE-TEMP-RECORDS-FLAG.
202             IF MORE-TEMP-RECORDS
203                 WRITE SPECIAL-HANDLING-RECORD FROM TEMP-DISK-RECORD
204                     AFTER ADVANCING 1 LINE.
205
206         C050-WRITE-TO-NORMAL-HANDLING.
207             READ TEMP-DISK-FILE
208                     AT END MOVE 'N' TO MORE-TEMP-RECORDS-FLAG.
209             IF MORE-TEMP-RECORDS
210                 WRITE NORMAL-HANDLING-RECORD FROM TEMP-DISK-RECORD
211                     AFTER ADVANCING 1 LINE.
212
213         D010-VALIDATE-BODY-RECORD.
214             MOVE CATALOG-NUMBER OF BODY-RECORD TO
215                     CATALOG-NUMBER OF IS-PRODUCT-RECORD.
216             READ IS-PRODUCT-FILE
217                     KEY IS CATALOG-NUMBER OF IS-PRODUCT-RECORD
218                     INVALID KEY MOVE 'Y' TO ERRORS-FOUND-FLAG
219                         MOVE 'X' TO INVALID-CATALOG-NUMBER.
220             DISPLAY 'BODY VALIDATION REACHED '
221                     ORDER-NUMBER OF BODY-RECORD    ' '
222                     CATALOG-NUMBER OF BODY-RECORD    ' '
223                     DESCRIPTION OF IS-PRODUCT-RECORD.
224
225
226         *********************** END OF PROGRAM *********************
```

FIGURE 15.6 A program to validate orders from a seed catalog, using an indexed file to obtain product information and a sequential file for intermediate storage.

The program shown in Figure 15.6 contains some new features in the SELECT statement for IS-PRODUCT-FILE. As before, the ORGANIZATION clause specifies that the organization of the file is indexed. However, the ACCESS clause specifies that **ACCESS IS RANDOM,** which allows us to access records in the file randomly. To perform a random access we must specify where the key can be found in the record being searched for; this requirement is met by the **RECORD KEY** clause. The record key always refers to a field in the records of the indexed file; it tells where to find the key that uniquely identifies each record.

15.10   THE DEFINITION OF MULTIPLE RECORD TYPES

As we read the file of customer orders, we don't know until after we have a record in the computer whether it is a header, a body, or a trailer record. That can be determined only by reading the record and then inspecting the record type field in it. The record-type field must always be in the same place in all records of the file for us to know where to look for it, but the three types of records can otherwise be entirely different. As it happens here, they all have an order number as their first six bytes and they are otherwise altogether different. In a different application they might not even have the order number in the same place in each record. We are able to specify in the File Section what the formats of the different types of record codes are, by using the implicit redefinition that applies to **01** level entries in the File Section. This, we recall, means that all **01** level entries in any one **FD** are considered to be alternative definitions of the same record area. What we have done here is to set up a first record definition that is used only to define the three values of the record type code that always appears as the seventh byte of every record, then follow this with definitions of the records for the header, body, and trailer.

The rest of the Data Division contains nothing new. The definition of the records in the indexed file is identical to that of the program that created them. The Working-Storage Section contains the definition of several end-of-file flags and numerous error flags. Even though most of these error flags are not used in this example, they are listed here as a reminder that a complete version of the program would do all of this error checking.

We should note, perhaps, that some of the file descriptions specify **LABEL RECORDS ARE STANDARD** while others specify **LABEL RECORDS ARE OMITTED.** Remember that in Microsoft **COBOL** the **LABEL RECORDS** clause is actually optional. None the less, we indicate files that are used as disk data files with **LABEL RECORDS ARE STANDARD,** while files that are basically data input or print files are marked with **LABEL RECORDS ARE OMITTED.** This is done partly for documentation and partly to be consistent with other compilers.

15.11   THE PROCEDURE DIVISION

The structure of the Procedure Division reflects the logical structure of the order file. The order file contains a series of one or more orders. Each order consists of one header record, one or more body records, and one trailer record, assuming there are no errors. The main line logic in the first paragraph reads the first record on the order file to start things off, then executes **B010-PROCESS-ONE-ORDER** repeatedly until the program runs out of data.

As its name implies, paragraph **B010-PROCESS-ONE-ORDER** has the job of processing one complete order. It begins by resetting all error flags to indicate that no errors have been found yet, saving the order number of the current order record as the current order number, and opening the temporary disk file for output so that we can save the records for this order. Since an order is supposed to begin with a header record, the program checks to make sure that we have, in fact, read a header. If the record is a header record, we validate the header, write it to the temporary storage file, and read the next order record. If the record is not a header, we mark the appropriate error flags and continue until we find a match on record type.

At this point in the program, we are ready to start processing body records for the current order. The program continues to do so until one of three conditions occurs:

1. An order record is read whose order number is not the same as the current order;
2. The program runs out of order records;
3. A record other than a body record is read.

If the order number of the order record is the same as the current order number and if the record is a trailer, then we have read the trailer for the current order. In this case the program validates the trailer record, writes it to the temporary disk file, and reads the first record of the next order. If the record is not a trailer for the current order or if we have run out of order records, then the program simply marks error flags and continues.

We have now finished processing the data for an order and have written all records for that order to the temporary disk file. The remainder of this paragraph is essentially the same as the corresponding code in Figure 15.3.

C010-VALIDATE-HEADER-RECORD and C030-VALIDATE-TRAILER-RECORD use DISPLAY statements; in a complete program these stubs would perform appropriate error checking for the header and trailer records, respectively. C020-PROCESS-BODY-RECORD validates a body record, then reads the next order record.

The paragraph named D010-VALIDATE-BODY-RECORD is the one that involves reading the indexed file. The basic idea is that we want to determine whether there is such a catalog number as the one the customer has written and, if there is, to determine whether the customer's information is consistent with the nature of the product as it is described in the product file. We begin by moving the catalog number from the body record to the location in the indexed record that has been defined in the SELECT statement to be the record key for the product file. The READ statement that follows looks for the record specified by the key and executes the INVALID KEY clause only if the record is not on the file; in that case, the appropriate error flags are set. Notice the KEY IS clause. Since COBOL actually allows you to define more than one key for an indexed file, this clause tells the READ statement which key you are using for this particular READ. Our example, however, will use only one key. Normally the READ statement would be followed by code that would do a thorough job of validating a body record, including various tests based on information available in the product record. For this stub paragraph we simply DISPLAY the order number of the body record and other useful information.

The assumption in organizing the program this way is that when errors are detected in a seed order, they must be corrected manually after output from the program has been inspected by a human being. Naturally, if there are errors that can be corrected by the program—incorrect totals might be one such error—this should be done to reduce the amount of human effort required. We might also use interactive processing at this point to correct some errors immediately rather than waiting until the entire run is finished.

Notice in the first paragraph that the **PERFORM** statement on lines 130-131 will accept any value of **IS-STATUS** less than 30 as being valid. The reason is that a status value of 23, indicating record not found during a **READ**, may very well occur and is not a serious error. It simply means that the **READ** statement in **D010-VALIDATE-BODY-RECORD** failed to find a record on the product file. We expect that this will occur in some cases, so we simply mark the appropriate error flags and continue the run. A more precise approach to testing the file status flag would be to test the flag for specific errors after each I-O operation, then set a file error flag when appropriate. The approach shown is much simpler, however, and was used only to suggest the basic technique.

Here is an illustrative file used to test this program and to demonstrate its operation. It contains three order groups that pass all the validation tests, those with the order numbers of 111111, 444444, and 666666. All of the other groups contain errors of one type or another that cause the validation routines here to reject the order. Many of them contain other errors, some of which would be caught by a full-scale validation program and others of which are simple data input errors that would go through the system.

```
1111111J H GRIESMER  INNINGWOOD ROAD  OSSINING, NY 10562
111111250013A01CABBAGE                                    00045
11111262471T01CORN, HYBRID                                00185
11111237515H02WHITE SWEET WILLIAM                         00200
1111113003200500001600386
222222296461 01COMPOST KIT                                01495
2222223014950500120016015
3333331S I GOODMAN  4 ICHTHYIC LANE STATEN ISLAND, NY 10312
333333239156A01PINK BEAUTY SWEET WILLIAM                  00035
333333237515A01PURE WHITE SWEET WILLIAM                   00035
4444441JAMES SCALZO  2 DONALD LANE OSSINING, NY 10562
444444262471U02CORN                                       00370
444444262547L01PICKLES                                    00110
4444443004800500002400554
5555551M P BARNHARD  43 DONALD LANE  OSSINING, NY 10562
555555243125K05GIANT ZINNIAS                              01625
555555233597G02TRYSOMIC STOCKS                            00500
555555239156A01PLAIN WHITE SWEET WILLIAM                  00035
5555553021700100011302373
5555554
666666250013K01CABBAGE                                    00100
6666661S J GOODMAN  4 RUE POISSON  BROOKLYN, NY 10452
6666663001000050000000150
7777773000450500000000095
777777250031A01CABBAGE                                    00045
7777771S K GOODMAN  4 FISCHLICHE STRASSE  BRONX, NY 11220
8888881S L GOODMAN  4 DAGISH AVE.  FLUSHING, NY 11361
888888252159L01COLLARDS                                   00080
888888250211K01CHICKORY, WITLOOF                          00095
8888883001750050000000225
999999251904J01CRENSHAH MELNO                             00450
```

When the program was executed with this input, it produced the following output on the **DISPLAY** file.

```
HEADER VALIDATION REACHED 111111
BODY VALIDATION REACHED 111111   50013   CABBAGE, BURPEES DANISH ROUNDHEAD
BODY VALIDATION REACHED 111111   62471   HYBRID CORN, HONEY AND CREAM
BODY VALIDATION REACHED 111111   37515   SWEET WILLIAM  PINK BEAUTY
TRAILER VALIDATION REACHED 111111
BODY VALIDATION REACHED 222222   96461   COMPOST KIT
TRAILER VALIDATION REACHED 222222
HEADER VALIDATION REACHED 333333
BODY VALIDATION REACHED 333333   39156   SWEET WILLIAM  PURE WHITE
BODY VALIDATION REACHED 333333   37515   SWEET WILLIAM  PINK BEAUTY
HEADER VALIDATION REACHED 444444
BODY VALIDATION REACHED 444444   62471   HYBRID CORN, HONEY AND CREAM
BODY VALIDATION REACHED 444444   62547   CUCUMBER, BURPEE PICKLER
TRAILER VALIDATION REACHED 444444
HEADER VALIDATION REACHED 555555
BODY VALIDATION REACHED 555555   43125   ZINNIAS - GIANTS OF CALIFORNIA MIXED
BODY VALIDATION REACHED 555555   33597   STOCKS - TRYSOMIC 7 WEEKS MIXED COLORS
BODY VALIDATION REACHED 555555   39156   SWEET WILLIAM  PURE WHITE
TRAILER VALIDATION REACHED 555555
BODY VALIDATION REACHED 666666   50013   CABBAGE, BURPEES DANISH ROUNDHEAD
HEADER VALIDATION REACHED 666666
TRAILER VALIDATION REACHED 666666
TRAILER VALIDATION REACHED 777777
BODY VALIDATION REACHED 777777   50031   CABBAGE, BURPEES DANISH ROUNDHEAD
HEADER VALIDATION REACHED 777777
HEADER VALIDATION REACHED 888888
BODY VALIDATION REACHED 888888   52159   CABBAGE, BURPEES DANISH ROUNDHEAD
BODY VALIDATION REACHED 888888   50211   CABBAGE, BURPEES DANISH ROUNDHEAD
TRAILER VALIDATION REACHED 888888
BODY VALIDATION REACHED 999999   51904   CRENSHAH MELON, BURPEES EARLY HYBRID
```

This listing demonstrates that the appropriate routines were reached for validation of body and trailer records, but it also reveals some ways in which the program output is not as helpful as it might be. Look, for instance, at the three successive entries for cabbage near the end of the listing. Actually, all three of these entries represent catalog numbers for which there was no master record, and the description is simply a carryover from the last valid catalog number of the previous order.

Here is the content of the normal handling file with its three good orders.

```
1111111J H GRIESMER  INNINGWOOD ROAD  OSSINING, NY 10562
11111125 0013A01CABBAGE                                 00045
111111262471T01CORN, HYBRID                             00185
111111237515H02WHITE SWEET WILLIAM                      00200
1111113003200500016 00386
4444441JAMES SCALZO  2 DONALD LANE OSSINING, NY 10562
444444262471U02CORN                                     00370
444444262547L01PICKLES                                  00110
4444443004800500024 00554
6666661S J GOODMAN  4 RUE POISSON  BROOKLYN, NY 10452
666666300100005000000 0150
```

The special handling file is as follows.

```
222222296461 01COMPOST KIT                              01495
222222301495 0500120016015
3333331S I GOODMAN  4 ICHTHYIC LANE STATEN ISLAND, NY 10312
333333239156A01PINK BEAUTY SWEET WILLIAM                00035
```

```
333333237515A01PURE WHITE SWEET WILLIAM                    00035
5555551M P BARNHARD  43 DONALD LANE  OSSINING, NY 10562
555555243125K05GIANT ZINNIAS                               01625
555555233597G02TRYSOMIC STOCKS                             00500
555555239156A01PLAIN WHITE SWEET WILLIAM                   00035
55555530217001000113O2373
5555554
666666250013K01CABBAGE                                     00100
7777773000450500000000095
777777250031A01CABBAGE                                     00045
7777771S K GOODMAN  4 FISCHLICHE STRASSE  BRONX, NY 11220
8888881S L GOODMAN  4 DAGISH AVE.  FLUSHING, NY 11361
888888252159L01COLLARDS                                    00080
888888250211K01CHICKORY, WITLOOF                           00095
8888883001750050000000225
999999251904J01CRENSHAH MELNO                              00450
```

We said before that the group with order number 666666 is a valid group and, indeed, it does appear on the normal handling file. Notice, however, that one record from this group also appears on the special handling file. What happened was that the first record of the group, a body record, was treated as a group with no header and marked for special handling. However, the next record, a header for order 666666, was treated as the start of a new group, one that had a header and a trailer but no body records. Since the program does not check for this condition, the group was accepted as valid. We leave it to the reader to study each of the remaining order groups and note the various kinds of errors that cause these orders to be rejected.

15.12 A PROGRAM TO UPDATE AN INDEXED FILE

An indexed sequential file, like any other, ordinarily must be updated from time to time. New records must be added to the file, old records must be deleted, and changes must be made to existing records. These operations are especially easy with an indexed file since the access method handles all the problems associated with finding space for the addition records, and also maintains the index so that records can still be accessed either randomly or sequentially.

A program that updates the seed company product file is shown in Figure 15.7. Observe the **ACCESS IS RANDOM** clause. Notice also that the transaction record for this application has been modified to include an update code that designates the type of update that is to be performed.

```
1     IDENTIFICATION DIVISION.
2     PROGRAM-ID.
3         UPDATE-PRODUCT.
4     DATE-WRITTEN.
5         JULY 5, 1989.
6
7     ENVIRONMENT DIVISION.
8     INPUT-OUTPUT SECTION.
9     FILE-CONTROL.
10        SELECT UPDATE-FILE           ASSIGN TO UPDATES.
```

```
11              SELECT IS-PRODUCT-FILE          ASSIGN TO ISPROD
12                  ORGANIZATION IS INDEXED
13                  ACCESS IS RANDOM
14                  RECORD KEY IS CATALOG-NUMBER OF IS-PRODUCT-RECORD
15                  FILE STATUS IS IS-STATUS.
16
17          DATA DIVISION.
18
19          FILE SECTION.
20
21          FD  UPDATE-FILE
22              LABEL RECORDS ARE OMITTED.
23          01  UPDATE-RECORD.
24              05  CATALOG-NUMBER              PIC X(5).
25              05  SIZE-1                      PIC X.
26              05  PRICE-1                     PIC 99V99.
27              05  SIZE-2                      PIC X.
28              05  PRICE-2                     PIC 99V99.
29              05  SIZE-3                      PIC X.
30              05  PRICE-3                     PIC 99V99.
31              05  DESCRIPTION                 PIC X(40).
32              05  UPDATE-CODE                 PIC X.
33                  88  ADDITION                        VALUE '1'.
34                  88  DELETION                        VALUE '2'.
35                  88  CORRECTION                      VALUE '3'.
36
37          FD  IS-PRODUCT-FILE
38              LABEL RECORDS ARE STANDARD.
39          01  IS-PRODUCT-RECORD.
40              05  CATALOG-NUMBER              PIC X(5).
41              05  SIZE-1                      PIC X.
42              05  PRICE-1                     PIC 99V99  COMP-3.
43              05  SIZE-2                      PIC X.
44              05  PRICE-2                     PIC 99V99  COMP-3.
45              05  SIZE-3                      PIC X.
46              05  PRICE-3                     PIC 99V99  COMP-3.
47              05  DESCRIPTION                 PIC X(40).
48
49          WORKING-STORAGE SECTION.
50
51          01  INVALID-KEY-FLAG               PIC X.
52              88  INVALID-KEY                         VALUE 'Y'.
53
54          01  IS-STATUS                       PIC 99 VALUE 00.
55
56          01  MORE-DATA-REMAINS-FLAG          PIC X.
57              88  MORE-DATA-REMAINS                   VALUE 'Y'.
58              88  NO-MORE-DATA-REMAINS                VALUE 'N'.
59
60          PROCEDURE DIVISION.
61          A000-UPDATE-PRODUCT-FILE.
62              OPEN INPUT UPDATE-FILE
63                   I-O   IS-PRODUCT-FILE.
64              MOVE 'Y' TO MORE-DATA-REMAINS-FLAG.
65              PERFORM B010-PROCESS-ONE-UPDATE
66                   UNTIL NO-MORE-DATA-REMAINS.
67              CLOSE UPDATE-FILE
68                   IS-PRODUCT-FILE.
```

```
69                   STOP RUN.
70
71           B010-PROCESS-ONE-UPDATE.
72               READ UPDATE-FILE
73                       AT END MOVE 'N' TO MORE-DATA-REMAINS-FLAG.
74               IF MORE-DATA-REMAINS
75                   IF      ADDITION
76                       PERFORM C010-ADDITION
77                   ELSE IF DELETION
78                       PERFORM C020-DELETION
79                   ELSE IF CORRECTION
80                       PERFORM C030-CORRECTION
81                   ELSE
82                       PERFORM C040-INVALID-TYPE.
83
84           C010-ADDITION.
85               MOVE CATALOG-NUMBER OF UPDATE-RECORD TO
86                       CATALOG-NUMBER OF IS-PRODUCT-RECORD.
87               MOVE CORRESPONDING UPDATE-RECORD TO IS-PRODUCT-RECORD.
88               WRITE IS-PRODUCT-RECORD
89                       INVALID KEY
90                               DISPLAY 'BAD ADDITION; RECORD ALREADY '
91                                       'EXISTS FOR '
92                                       CATALOG-NUMBER OF IS-PRODUCT-RECORD.
93
94           C020-DELETION.
95               MOVE CATALOG-NUMBER OF UPDATE-RECORD TO
96                       CATALOG-NUMBER OF IS-PRODUCT-RECORD.
97               MOVE 'N' TO INVALID-KEY-FLAG.
98               READ IS-PRODUCT-FILE
99                       KEY IS CATALOG-NUMBER OF IS-PRODUCT-RECORD
100                      INVALID KEY MOVE 'Y' TO INVALID-KEY-FLAG.
101              IF INVALID-KEY
102                  DISPLAY 'BAD DELETION; NO RECORD IN FILE FOR '
103                          CATALOG-NUMBER OF IS-PRODUCT-RECORD
104              ELSE
105                  DELETE IS-PRODUCT-FILE
106                          INVALID KEY
107                                  DISPLAY 'BIG TROUBLES AT '
108                                      CATALOG-NUMBER OF IS-PRODUCT-RECORD
109                                  DISPLAY 'FILE STATUS IS ' IS-STATUS.
110
111          C030-CORRECTION.
112              MOVE CATALOG-NUMBER OF UPDATE-RECORD TO
113                      CATALOG-NUMBER OF IS-PRODUCT-RECORD.
114              MOVE 'N' TO INVALID-KEY-FLAG.
115              READ IS-PRODUCT-FILE
116                      KEY IS CATALOG-NUMBER OF IS-PRODUCT-RECORD
117                      INVALID KEY MOVE 'Y' TO INVALID-KEY-FLAG.
118              IF INVALID-KEY
119                  DISPLAY 'BAD CORRECTION; NO RECORD IN FILE FOR '
120                          CATALOG-NUMBER OF IS-PRODUCT-RECORD
121              ELSE
122                  MOVE CORRESPONDING UPDATE-RECORD TO IS-PRODUCT-RECORD
123                  REWRITE IS-PRODUCT-RECORD
124                          INVALID KEY
```

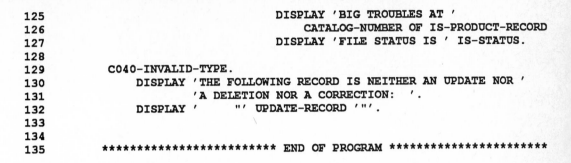

```
125                                    DISPLAY 'BIG TROUBLES AT '
126                                       CATALOG-NUMBER OF IS-PRODUCT-RECORD
127                                    DISPLAY 'FILE STATUS IS ' IS-STATUS.
128
129           C040-INVALID-TYPE.
130               DISPLAY 'THE FOLLOWING RECORD IS NEITHER AN UPDATE NOR '
131                   'A DELETION NOR A CORRECTION:   '.
132               DISPLAY '       "' UPDATE-RECORD '"'.
133
134
135           *********************** END OF PROGRAM ***********************
```

FIGURE 15.7 A program to update an indexed sequential file.

In the **OPEN** statement for the indexed file we find a new feature: the file is opened for both input and output. Since we must read the records to be sure that they exist before we make deletions and corrections, the file is input; since records must be written for all three types of transactions, the file is also output.

Paragraph **B010-PROCESS-ONE-UPDATE** is executed once for each update until the input file of updates is exhausted. So long as data remains, it simply determines what type of update is involved and performs an appropriate routine.

For additions, we must set the record key equal to the key of the update record to permit checking for the possibility that a record with this key already exists in the file. In the operation of adding a record where there should not be a matching record in the file, the **INVALID KEY** clause is activated if a matching record is found. That is, the program will not write a new record if its key matches the key of a record already on the file; an attempt to do so raises the invalid key condition.

To delete a record from the file, we first get the record, thus guaranteeing that a record with the specified key does exist in the file. The **INVALID KEY** clause on this **READ** is activated if there is no such record; in this case we **DISPLAY** an appropriate message. If the record does exist in the file, we delete the record from the file with a new verb that exists for this purpose, **DELETE**. Observe that **DELETE** specifies the file name, not the record name; the value of the record key determines which record will be deleted.

Since we have already checked to make certain that the record exists, there is no way to get an invalid key without a serious failure of either the hardware or the access routines. In this example, we simply display a message indicating that something is very seriously wrong if the invalid key condition is raised. Actually, one would ordinarily terminate program execution if this happened. If we wished, we could omit the **READ** step and simply **DELETE** the record, using the **INVALID KEY** clause to notify us if the record is not actually on the file. The choice between the two approaches is mostly a matter of style.

To carry out a correction, we obtain the existing record, which in this example is needed primarily to establish that the record does indeed exist on the file. The record is modified to contain the new data, then we use another new verb, **REWRITE**, to replace the record on the file. Notice the difference between **WRITE** and **REWRITE**. **WRITE** is used to insert a new record on the file;

an invalid key condition exists if the new record duplicates an existing record. REWRITE is used to modify an existing record, and an invalid key condition indicates that the record does not exist, which is generally a serious error.

The following data shows a file of updates to be applied to the master file that was shown in previous examples.

```
31658A0100P0400 0000SNAPDRAGON, BRIGHT BUTTERFLIES, MIXED    1
36160A0050K0150L0175ROYAL SWEET PEAS, MIXED                  1
50013                                                        2
15131 0550 0000 0000APPLE TREE, JONATHAN                     1
43125A0035H0105K0325ZINNIAS, GIANTS OF CALIFORNIA, MIXED     3
36574A0050G0150 0000STOCKS - GIANT COLUMN MIXED COLORS       1
62471A0075T0185U0350HYBRID CORN, HONEY AND CREAM             3
61218A0035L0060S0125TURNIPS, PURPLE-TOP WHITE GLOBE      1
62547                                                        2
51094A0075J0450 0000CRENSHAW MELON, BURPEES EARLY HYBRID     3
50260A0075J0450 0000EGGPLANT, EARLY BEAUTY HYBRID            1
51367A0050T0145U0275DECORATIVE CORN, RAINBOW                 1
12345                                                        2
31773A0075G0225 0000VERBENA, RUFFLED WHITE                   1
```

When the program was executed, the following DISPLAY messages were produced.

```
BAD ADDITION; RECORD ALREADY EXISTS FOR 36574
THE FOLLOWING RECORD IS NEITHER AN UPDATE NOR A DELETION NOR A CORRECTION:
    "61218A0035L0060S0125TURNIPS, PURPLE-TOP WHITE GLOBE      1  "
BAD CORRECTION; NO RECORD IN FILE FOR 51094
BAD DELETION; NO RECORD IN FILE FOR 12345
```

We can now use the program in Figure 15.5 to print the updated file, giving the following output.

```
15131      5.50      0.00      0.00  APPLE TREE, JONATHAN
31658  A  1.00  P  4.00      0.00  SNAPDRAGON, BRIGHT BUTTERFLIES, MIXED
31773  A  0.75  G  2.25      0.00  VERBENA, RUFFLED WHITE
33597  A  0.50  G  2.50      0.00  STOCKS - TRYSOMIC 7 WEEKS MIXED COLORS
36160  A  0.50  K  1.50  L  1.75  ROYAL SWEET PEAS, MIXED
36574  A  0.50  G  1.50      0.00  STOCKS - GIANT COLUMN MIXED COLORS
37515  A  0.35  H  1.00      0.00  SWEET WILLIAM  PINK BEAUTY
39156  A  0.35  H  1.00      0.00  SWEET WILLIAM  PURE WHITE
43125  A  0.35  H  1.05  K  3.25  ZINNIAS, GIANTS OF CALIFORNIA, MIXED
50260  A  0.75  J  4.50      0.00  EGGPLANT, EARLY BEAUTY HYBRID
51367  A  0.50  T  1.45  U  2.75  DECORATIVE CORN, RAINBOW
51904  A  0.75  J  4.50      0.00  CRENSHAW MELON, BURPEES EARLY HYBRID
62471  A  0.75  T  1.85  U  3.50  HYBRID CORN, HONEY AND CREAM
96461     15.95      0.00      0.00  COMPOST KIT
```

Notice that the various updates have been carried out correctly. The addition records are all present, other than the one that was a duplication. The two valid deletion updates have resulted in the removal of records from the file. The two valid corrections have modified the corresponding records properly. The most important thing to notice about this output is that the records are in sequence on the key even though the updating inserted new records at various places in the file, including three records before the first record in the file as originally created. This ability to access and update a file randomly and still to retrieve records sequentially when convenient is the essence of indexed file processing.

We must emphasize that the examples we have shown, while presenting some of the most common uses of indexed files, do not begin to cover the full range of this topic. We strongly urge the serious COBOL programmer to study the use of indexed files more fully in an advanced text or in a COBOL manual.

15.13   RELATIVE RECORD FILES

Although indexed files are useful in many applications, they are not the only random access technique available to the COBOL programmer. One of the basic requirements of an indexed file is that the file must be sorted on a key field, and that this field be unique for every record.*

However, there are applications in which a record may have no obvious key, or may have more than one key, or in which the key may not be unique. In any of these cases, the indexed sequential method cannot be used. In cases such as these, relative files are commonly used.

A relative file is one in which records are retrieved by specifying their relative record number, that is, how far they are from the start of the file. This is analogous to the way in which records are accessed in a table, where you simply provide the subscript number of a particular record to be able to refer to it. In many ways, a relative file may be thought of as a very large table stored on a disk. You should be careful not to carry this analogy too far, however! There are very important differences between tables stored in memory and relative files stored on a disk. The details of how you refer to a record in a file look nothing like the details of how you refer to a record in a table. However, just as in a table, records in a relative file are referred to by record number, not by key. Furthermore, once the file has been created, it is not possible to insert new records between existing records. However, just as we do with a table, it is possible to move existing records around to make room for new data, or to write new records into "empty" entries, called *dummy* records.

15.14   A PROGRAM TO CREATE A RELATIVE RECORD FILE

We now will use the seed catalog product file to demonstrate how a relative record file might be built. The following example (Figure 15.8) is analogous to the program in Figure 15.4 that showed the construction of an indexed file. Again, this will be a skeleton program so that we can concentrate on the file processing techniques.

---

* Although indexed files may have additional keys (called *secondary keys*) which permit duplicate values, the major key (called the *prime key*) must be unique for each record. We shall not discuss secondary keys in this book.

```
1              IDENTIFICATION DIVISION.
2              PROGRAM-ID.
3                  BUILD-RELATIVE.
4              DATE-WRITTEN.
5                  JULY 5, 1989.
6
7              ENVIRONMENT DIVISION.
8              INPUT-OUTPUT SECTION.
9              FILE-CONTROL.
10                 SELECT PRODUCT-FILE               ASSIGN TO PRODUCTS.
11                 SELECT REL-PRODUCT-FILE           ASSIGN TO RELPROD
12                         ORGANIZATION IS RELATIVE
13                         ACCESS IS SEQUENTIAL
14                         RELATIVE KEY IS PRODUCT-KEY
15                         FILE STATUS IS REL-STATUS.
16
17             DATA DIVISION.
18
19             FILE SECTION.
20
21             FD  PRODUCT-FILE
22                 LABEL RECORDS ARE STANDARD.
23             01  PRODUCT-RECORD.
24                 05   CATALOG-NUMBER         PIC X(5).
25                 05   SIZE-1                 PIC X.
26                 05   PRICE-1                PIC 99V99.
27                 05   SIZE-2                 PIC X.
28                 05   PRICE-2                PIC 99V99.
29                 05   SIZE-3                 PIC X.
30                 05   PRICE-3                PIC 99V99.
31                 05   DESCRIPTION            PIC X(40).
32
33             FD  REL-PRODUCT-FILE
34                 LABEL RECORDS ARE STANDARD.
35             01  REL-PRODUCT-RECORD.
36                 05   CATALOG-NUMBER         PIC X(5).
37                 05   SIZE-1                 PIC X.
38                 05   PRICE-1                PIC 99V99  COMP-3.
39                 05   SIZE-2                 PIC X.
40                 05   PRICE-2                PIC 99V99  COMP-3.
41                 05   SIZE-3                 PIC X.
42                 05   PRICE-3                PIC 99V99  COMP-3.
43                 05   DESCRIPTION            PIC X(40).
44
45             WORKING-STORAGE SECTION.
46
47             01  MORE-DATA-REMAINS-FLAG      PIC X.
48                 88   MORE-DATA-REMAINS              VALUE 'Y'.
49                 88   NO-MORE-DATA-REMAINS           VALUE 'N'.
50
51             01  PRODUCT-KEY                 PIC 9(8) COMP SYNC.
52
53             01  REL-STATUS                  PIC 99 VALUE 00.
54
55
56             PROCEDURE DIVISION.
57             A000-CREATE-RELATIVE-PROD-FILE.
58                 OPEN  INPUT PRODUCT-FILE
```

```
59                      OUTPUT REL-PRODUCT-FILE.
60               MOVE 'Y' TO MORE-DATA-REMAINS-FLAG.
61               MOVE 1 TO PRODUCT-KEY.
62               PERFORM B010-TRANSFER-ONE-RECORD
63                      UNTIL NO-MORE-DATA-REMAINS.
64               DISPLAY 'FILE STATUS IS ' REL-STATUS.
65               CLOSE PRODUCT-FILE
66                     REL-PRODUCT-FILE.
67               STOP RUN.
68
69        B010-TRANSFER-ONE-RECORD.
70               READ PRODUCT-FILE
71                      AT END MOVE 'N' TO MORE-DATA-REMAINS-FLAG.
72               IF MORE-DATA-REMAINS
73                  MOVE CORRESPONDING PRODUCT-RECORD TO REL-PRODUCT-RECORD
74                  WRITE REL-PRODUCT-RECORD
75                      INVALID KEY
76                          DISPLAY 'FILE CAPACITY EXCEEDED; '
77                                  'CANNOT WRITE '
78                              CATALOG-NUMBER OF REL-PRODUCT-RECORD
79                          DISPLAY 'FILE STATUS IS ' REL-STATUS.
80
81
82        ************************ END OF PROGRAM ************************
```

FIGURE 15.8 A program for creating a relative record file.

There are several points to notice about the **SELECT** statement for the relative file. First, the **ORGANIZATION** clause tells that this is a relative record file by specifying **ORGANIZATION IS RELATIVE**. Second, as we did with the indexed files, we have specified that **ACCESS IS SEQUENTIAL** even though this is the default and not really required. Finally, we have included a **RELATIVE KEY** clause instead of a **RECORD KEY** clause. In relative record files a record is identified by its position in the file (its relative record number), just as an entry in a table is identified by its position in the table (its subscript number). Instead of a subscript we use the relative key to specify the relative record number. Since the key for a relative record file specifies a record number, it may be any integer field whose value does not exceed the physical size of the file. We have shown **PRODUCT-KEY** to be a fullword binary field, but this is not required. We have also specified a **FILE STATUS** clause again, although in this program we will not make much use of the status flag.

The Procedure Division in Figure 15.8 is very much like the one in Figure 15.4, although there are a few differences. We have initialized **PRODUCT-KEY** to one, and from then on the value of **PRODUCT-KEY** is automatically incremented by one every time a record is written to **REL-PRODUCT-FILE**. Actually, this initialization is shown more for documentation than anything else, to emphasize that the first record in the file has a record key of one. When creating a relative file we can omit the **RELATIVE KEY** clause entirely and the program will do just as it does in our example.

As with indexed files, the **WRITE** statement for a relative file has an **INVALID KEY** clause. However, with relative files the only situation that can cause an invalid key condition is if the value of the relative key exceeds the physical capacity of the file. If this happens, we simply display an error message and continue, although a more complete program would have more sophisticated error handling code.

15.15 A PROGRAM TO UPDATE A RELATIVE RECORD FILE

The program to print a relative record file is almost identical to that shown in Figure 15.5 to print an indexed file, and we leave the actual construction of such a program to the student; the output should look much like that for the corresponding indexed file, although you might wish to include the relative record number as part of the output. Instead, let us focus on the problems involved in updating a relative record file. The first problem we have is finding the record we wish to update. When we were working with indexed files we simply used the catalog number as the record key and proceeded from there. With relative files this won't work. In the first place, one of the reasons that one wishes to use relative files is often that there is no field that can be used as a record key. Even if there is such a field, it is not always numeric and so cannot be used as the relative key, and even if it is numeric, it is not always suitable for use as the relative key. For example, the catalog number in the seed catalog example is a five-digit number, which means that we can have 100,000 different catalog numbers. However, it is highly unlikely that the seed company actually has anywhere near this many products. If we try to use the catalog number directly as the relative key, we will have a huge file that is 95 percent empty. We will defer the solution to this problem for a bit, and for now we will simply assume that the relative key is somehow known to us and is presented to the program as part of **UPDATE-RECORD**, shown in Figure 15.9.

```
1           IDENTIFICATION DIVISION.
2           PROGRAM-ID.
3               UPDATE-RELATIVE.
4           DATE-WRITTEN.
5               JULY 6, 1987.
6
7           ENVIRONMENT DIVISION.
8           INPUT-OUTPUT SECTION.
9           FILE-CONTROL.
10              SELECT UPDATE-FILE              ASSIGN TO RELUPDATE.
11              SELECT REL-PRODUCT-FILE        ASSIGN TO RELPROD
12                  ORGANIZATION IS RELATIVE
13                  ACCESS IS RANDOM
14                  RELATIVE KEY IS PRODUCT-NUMBER
15                  FILE STATUS IS REL-STATUS.
16
17          DATA DIVISION.
18
19          FILE SECTION.
20          FD  UPDATE-FILE
21              LABEL RECORDS ARE OMITTED.
22          01  UPDATE-RECORD.
23              05  CATALOG-NUMBER             PIC X(5).
24              05  PRODUCT-NUMBER             PIC 9(5).
25              05  SIZE-1                     PIC X.
26              05  PRICE-1                    PIC 99V99.
```

```
27                   05   SIZE-2                    PIC X.
28                   05   PRICE-2                   PIC 99V99.
29                   05   SIZE-3                    PIC X.
30                   05   PRICE-3                   PIC 99V99.
31                   05   DESCRIPTION               PIC X(40).
32                   05   UPDATE-CODE               PIC X.
33                        88   ADDITION                       VALUE '1'.
34                        88   DELETION                       VALUE '2'.
35                        88   CORRECTION                     VALUE '3'.
36
37          FD   REL-PRODUCT-FILE
38               LABEL RECORDS ARE STANDARD.
39          01   REL-PRODUCT-RECORD.
40                   05   CATALOG-NUMBER            PIC X(5).
41                   05   SIZE-1                    PIC X.
42                   05   PRICE-1                   PIC 99V99   COMP-3.
43                   05   SIZE-2                    PIC X.
44                   05   PRICE-2                   PIC 99V99   COMP-3.
45                   05   SIZE-3                    PIC X.
46                   05   PRICE-3                   PIC 99V99   COMP-3.
47                   05   DESCRIPTION               PIC X(40).
48
49          WORKING-STORAGE SECTION.
50
51          01   MORE-DATA-REMAINS-FLAG            PIC X.
52               88   MORE-DATA-REMAINS                        VALUE 'Y'.
53               88   NO-MORE-DATA-REMAINS                     VALUE 'N'.
54
55          01   REC-FOUND-FLAG                   PIC X.
56               88   REC-FOUND                                VALUE 'Y'.
57               88   REC-NOT-FOUND                            VALUE 'N'.
58
59          01   REL-STATUS                       PIC 99 VALUE 00.
60
61          PROCEDURE DIVISION.
62
63          A000-UPDATE-PRODUCT-FILE.
64               OPEN INPUT UPDATE-FILE
65                    I-O    REL-PRODUCT-FILE.
66               MOVE 'Y' TO MORE-DATA-REMAINS-FLAG.
67               PERFORM B010-PROCESS-ONE-UPDATE
68                       UNTIL NO-MORE-DATA-REMAINS   OR   REL-STATUS > 29.
69               IF REL-STATUS > 29
70                   DISPLAY 'FILE STATUS IS ' REL-STATUS.
71               CLOSE UPDATE-FILE
72                     REL-PRODUCT-FILE.
73               STOP RUN.
74
75          B010-PROCESS-ONE-UPDATE.
76               READ UPDATE-FILE
77                       AT END MOVE 'N' TO MORE-DATA-REMAINS-FLAG.
78               IF MORE-DATA-REMAINS
79                   IF       ADDITION
80                       PERFORM C010-ADDITION
81                   ELSE IF DELETION
82                       PERFORM C020-DELETION
```

```
83                       ELSE IF CORRECTION
84                           PERFORM C030-CORRECTION
85                       ELSE
86                           PERFORM C040-INVALID-TYPE.
87
88        C010-ADDITION.
89            MOVE CORRESPONDING UPDATE-RECORD TO REL-PRODUCT-RECORD
90            WRITE REL-PRODUCT-RECORD
91                    INVALID KEY
92                            DISPLAY 'BAD ADDITION FOR '
93                                    CATALOG-NUMBER OF UPDATE-RECORD
94                                    '; RECORD ALREADY EXISTS AT '
95                                    PRODUCT-NUMBER.
96
97        C020-DELETION.
98            DELETE REL-PRODUCT-FILE
99                    INVALID KEY
100                           DISPLAY 'BAD DELETION FOR '
101                                   CATALOG-NUMBER OF UPDATE-RECORD
102                                   '; NO RECORD IN FILE AT '
103                                   PRODUCT-NUMBER.
104
105       C030-CORRECTION.
106           MOVE 'Y' TO REC-FOUND-FLAG.
107           READ REL-PRODUCT-FILE
108                   INVALID KEY MOVE 'N' TO REC-FOUND-FLAG.
109           IF REC-NOT-FOUND
110               DISPLAY 'BAD CORRECTION FOR '
111                       CATALOG-NUMBER OF UPDATE-RECORD
112                       '; NO RECORD IN FILE AT ' PRODUCT-NUMBER
113           ELSE
114               MOVE CORRESPONDING UPDATE-RECORD TO REL-PRODUCT-RECORD
115               REWRITE REL-PRODUCT-RECORD
116                       INVALID KEY
117                               DISPLAY 'BIG TROUBLES AT ' PRODUCT-NUMBER
118                               DISPLAY 'FILE STATUS IS ' REL-STATUS.
119
120       C040-INVALID-TYPE.
121           DISPLAY 'THE FOLLOWING RECORD IS NEITHER AN UPDATE NOR '
122                   'A DELETION NOR A CORRECTION:  '.
123           DISPLAY '      "' UPDATE-RECORD '"'.
124
125       *********************** END OF PROGRAM **********************
```

FIGURE 15.9 A program to update a relative record file.

The Procedure Division of the program in Figure 15.9 very similar to that of the indexed file update program in Figure 15.7. The major difference is that we do not need to move any value to a key field since we have declared PRODUCT-NUMBER, located in UPDATE-RECORD, to be the relative key. The relative key may be located anywhere in the Data Division *except* in a record that is part of the FD entry for the relative file. Compare the remainder of the code in the two programs of Figures 15.7 and 15.9. Although there are differences between the programs, they are primarily differences of style intended to demonstrate alternative approaches to performing various tasks.

If we print the updated file, using the same test data as we used to build and update an indexed file in Sections 15.7 - 15.12, we get this output.

```
33597   A   0.50   G   2.50        0.00   STOCKS - TRYSOMIC 7 WEEKS MIXED COLORS
36574   A   0.50   G   1.50        0.00   STOCKS - GIANT COLUMN MIXED COLORS
37515   A   0.35   H   1.00        0.00   SWEET WILLIAM   PINK BEAUTY
39156   A   0.35   H   1.00        0.00   SWEET WILLIAM   PURE WHITE
43125   A   0.35   H   1.05   K   3.25   ZINNIAS, GIANTS OF CALIFORNIA, MIXED
51904   A   0.75   J   4.50        0.00   CRENSHAH MELON, BURPEES EARLY HYBRID
62471   A   0.75   T   1.85   U   3.50   HYBRID CORN, HONEY AND CREAM
96461      15.95        0.00        0.00   COMPOST KIT
31658   A   1.00   P   4.00        0.00   SNAPDRAGON, BRIGHT BUTTERFLIES, MIXED
36160   A   0.50   K   1.50   L   1.75   ROYAL SWEET PEAS, MIXED
15131       5.50        0.00        0.00   APPLE TREE, JONATHAN
50260   A   0.75   J   4.50        0.00   EGGPLANT, EARLY BEAUTY HYBRID
51367   A   0.50   T   1.45   U   2.75   DECORATIVE CORN, RAINBOW
31773   A   0.75   G   2.25        0.00   VERBENA, RUFFLED WHITE
```

Notice that although all the records are the same as we had in the indexed file, these records are not in numeric order. The reason is that new records are simply inserted wherever we specify in the update record, and there is no attempt made by the file access software to keep records in any order.

15.16   A TECHNIQUE FOR COMPUTING RELATIVE RECORD NUMBERS

In most cases the records in a relative record file do not contain fields that can be used directly as record keys. There are numerous techniques for converting data fields into values that can be used as records keys, and a thorough discussion of these techniques is beyond the scope of this text. However, we will present a brief discussion of a common technique called *hash coding* and will show some simple examples of its use.

Hash coding involves performing a simple calculation on a numeric field and using the result of this calculation as the key for the record being processed. For example, if our record contains a telephone number and we wish to use this as the basis for our key, we can extract selected digits from the number to form the relative key. Specifically, suppose that we have the telephone number 555-1234, and we wish to use the second, third, fourth, and fifth digits as the key. We could simply define the following fields in Working-Storage:

```
01   PHONE-NUMBER              PIC X(7).
01   KEY-FIELDS   REDEFINES PHONE-NUMBER.
     02   FILLER               PIC X.
     02   PHONE-KEY            PIC 9(4).
     02   FILLER               PIC XX.
```

then use PHONE-KEY as the relative key to access the record. In this example, the relative key would contain 5512.

A common technique for hashing a number to produce a key is used when we wish to produce keys in a specific range; this is what is required if we wish to allow for a specific number of records on a file. For example, if we want to allow for 3000 records on a relative record file, we need to have a key in the range 1-3000. We can produce this by dividing the numeric field by 3000 (which gives a remainder in the range of 0-2999), adding 1 to the remainder, and using the result as the key. Other calculations are possible, but this division-remainder technique is very common.

One problem that occurs in hash coding is that two or more records may hash to the same value. For example, using the division-remainder example described above, both 3100 and 6100 produce a key value of 101. This condition is called a *collision*, since we are trying to assign two records to the same file location. The solution is to assign the first record to location 101, then assign any colliding records to other locations in the file. We will demonstrate how this technique works in the following examples.

15.17 USING A HASH KEY TO CREATE A RELATIVE FILE

The following program (Figure 15.10) is similar to the one shown in Figure 15.8, except that we will use a simple division-remainder hash coding algorithm to determine where records are located in the file. Since the catalog number is numeric, we will use this as the basis of our hashing process. We assume that the seed company has about 4000 products. To allow for future growth, we would normally allow for 5000 records on the file, and the keys we calculate would be in the range 1-5000. However, to save file space during testing we will use a file size of 50.

```
1          IDENTIFICATION DIVISION.
2          PROGRAM-ID.
3              BUILD-HASHED.
4          DATE-WRITTEN.
5              JULY 6, 1989.
6
7          ENVIRONMENT DIVISION.
8          INPUT-OUTPUT SECTION.
9          FILE-CONTROL.
10             SELECT PRODUCT-FILE            ASSIGN TO PRODUCTS.
11             SELECT REL-PRODUCT-FILE        ASSIGN TO RELPROD
12                   ORGANIZATION IS RELATIVE
13                   ACCESS IS RANDOM
14                   RELATIVE KEY IS PRODUCT-KEY
15                   FILE STATUS IS REL-STATUS.
16
17         DATA DIVISION.
18
19         FILE SECTION.
20
21         FD  PRODUCT-FILE
22             LABEL RECORDS ARE STANDARD.
23         01  PRODUCT-RECORD.
24             05  CATALOG-NUMBER            PIC 9(5).
25             05  SIZE-1                    PIC X.
26             05  PRICE-1                   PIC 99V99.
27             05  SIZE-2                    PIC X.
28             05  PRICE-2                   PIC 99V99.
29             05  SIZE-3                    PIC X.
```

```
30                 05  PRICE-3                    PIC 99V99.
31                 05  DESCRIPTION                PIC X(40).
32
33          FD  REL-PRODUCT-FILE
34              LABEL RECORDS ARE STANDARD.
35          01  REL-PRODUCT-RECORD.
36                 05  CATALOG-NUMBER             PIC 9(5).
37                 05  SIZE-1                     PIC X.
38                 05  PRICE-1                    PIC 99V99   COMP-3.
39                 05  SIZE-2                     PIC X.
40                 05  PRICE-2                    PIC 99V99   COMP-3.
41                 05  SIZE-3                     PIC X.
42                 05  PRICE-3                    PIC 99V99   COMP-3.
43                 05  DESCRIPTION                PIC X(40).
44
45          WORKING-STORAGE SECTION.
46
47          01  FILE-FULL-FLAG                 PIC X.
48              88  FILE-FULL                          VALUE 'Y'.
49
50          01  FILE-SIZE                      PIC 9(5) COMP SYNC VALUE 50.
51
52          01  KEY-QUOTIENT                   PIC 9(5) COMP SYNC.
53
54          01  MORE-DATA-REMAINS-FLAG         PIC X.
55              88  MORE-DATA-REMAINS                  VALUE 'Y'.
56              88  NO-MORE-DATA-REMAINS               VALUE 'N'.
57
58          01  PRODUCT-KEY                    PIC 9(5) COMP SYNC.
59
60          01  RECORD-INSERTED-FLAG           PIC X.
61              88  RECORD-INSERTED                    VALUE 'Y'.
62
63          01  REL-STATUS                     PIC 99 VALUE 00.
64
65          01  START-KEY                      PIC S9(5) COMP SYNC.
66
67
68          PROCEDURE DIVISION.
69          A000-CREATE-RELATIVE-PROD-FILE.
70              OPEN INPUT PRODUCT-FILE
71                   OUTPUT REL-PRODUCT-FILE.
72              MOVE 'Y' TO MORE-DATA-REMAINS-FLAG.
73              PERFORM B010-TRANSFER-ONE-RECORD
74                     UNTIL NO-MORE-DATA-REMAINS.
75              DISPLAY 'FILE STATUS IS ' REL-STATUS.
76              CLOSE PRODUCT-FILE
77                    REL-PRODUCT-FILE.
78              STOP RUN.
79
80          B010-TRANSFER-ONE-RECORD.
81              READ PRODUCT-FILE
82                     AT END MOVE 'N' TO MORE-DATA-REMAINS-FLAG.
83              IF MORE-DATA-REMAINS
84                  MOVE CORRESPONDING PRODUCT-RECORD TO
85                       REL-PRODUCT-RECORD
86                  PERFORM C010-INSERT-REL-RECORD
87                  IF FILE-FULL
88                      DISPLAY 'FILE CAPACITY EXCEEDED; CANNOT WRITE '
89                          CATALOG-NUMBER OF PRODUCT-RECORD.
```

```
90
91          C010-INSERT-REL-RECORD.
92              DIVIDE CATALOG-NUMBER OF PRODUCT-RECORD BY FILE-SIZE
93                      GIVING KEY-QUOTIENT
94                      REMAINDER PRODUCT-KEY.
95              ADD 1 TO PRODUCT-KEY.
96              MOVE 'N' TO FILE-FULL-FLAG.
97              MOVE 'N' TO RECORD-INSERTED-FLAG.
98              MOVE PRODUCT-KEY TO START-KEY.
99              PERFORM D010-PROBE
100                     UNTIL RECORD-INSERTED  OR  FILE-FULL.
101
102         D010-PROBE.
103             MOVE 'Y' TO RECORD-INSERTED-FLAG.
104             WRITE REL-PRODUCT-RECORD
105                     INVALID KEY MOVE 'N' TO RECORD-INSERTED-FLAG.
106             IF NOT RECORD-INSERTED
107                 PERFORM E100-INCREMENT-KEY
108                 IF PRODUCT-KEY = START-KEY
109                     MOVE 'Y' TO FILE-FULL-FLAG.
110
111         E100-INCREMENT-KEY.
112             ADD 1 TO PRODUCT-KEY.
113             IF PRODUCT-KEY > FILE-SIZE
114                 MOVE 1 TO PRODUCT-KEY.
115
116         *********************** END OF PROGRAM ***********************
```

FIGURE 15.10 A program to create a relative file using hashing.

The first change is in the **SELECT** statement for **REL-PRODUCT-FILE**. Notice that the access is random, since records will be inserted according to the results of the hashing algorithm, not in sequential order.

The first paragraph in the Procedure Division is standard. The next paragraph, **B010-TRANSFER-ONE-RECORD**, is also straightforward. We read a record from **PRODUCT-FILE**, move the update data to the file record, then use **C010-INSERT-REL-RECORD** to insert the new record in the file. If the file is full and there is no room to insert the new record, we display a simple error message.

The algorithm for computing the relative key begins by dividing the catalog number of the input product record by the file size, adding 1 to the remainder, and storing the sum as the relative key. However, we may have a collision condition in which two or more records generate the same initial key value. Therefore, we may have to try several locations on the file before we find one available for the new record. This testing is done in **D010-PROBE**. Here we begin the probing by trying to write the record at the location initially calculated for the relative key. We assume that the insertion will work, then use the **INVALID KEY** clause to tell if we failed; the invalid key condition occurs if we attempt to write a record into a location that already contains a record. In this case we must increment the key and try again. If incrementing the key has brought us back to the starting point, the file is full and we set **FILE-FULL-FLAG**. Notice that we cannot simply add 1 to **PRODUCT-KEY** when it is incremented; we must test to see if we have reached the end of the file. If so, then

PRODUCT-KEY is reset to one and the search continues beginning at the start of the file.

The result of this key calculation algorithm is that the division-remainder step is used merely to find the starting point for record insertion. In case of a collision, successive records are simply placed in the first empty space in the file, treating the file as a large circular list of records. Although there are more sophisticated and efficient ways of dealing with the collision problem, this technique has the advantage of being simple to implement and understand.

We used the program of Figure 15.10 and the data used to build the previous files, then printed the resulting file. The print program was modified to show the relative record number as well as the record, and produced the following results. Notice that the file records are not in any particular sequence, nor is every location in the file in use. This is the result of the hashing algorithm, which scatters the records throughout the file.

```
(00005)  51904  A  0.75  J  4.50      0.00  CRENSHAH MELON, BURPEES EARLY HYBRID
(00007)  39156  A  0.35  H  1.00      0.00  SWEET WILLIAM  PURE WHITE
(00012)  96461     15.95       0.00   0.00  COMPOST KIT
(00014)  50013  A  0.45  K  1.00  L  1.85  CABBAGE, BURPEES DANISH ROUNDHEAD
(00016)  37515  A  0.35  H  1.00      0.00  SWEET WILLIAM  PINK BEAUTY
(00022)  62471  A  0.75  T  1.85  U  2.50  HYBRID CORN, HONEY AND CREAM
(00025)  36574  A  0.50  G  1.50      0.00  STOCKS - GIANT COLUMN MIXED COLORS
(00026)  43125  A  0.35  H  1.05  K  3.25  ZINNIAS - GIANTS OF CALIFORNIA MIXED
(00048)  33597  A  0.50  G  2.50      0.00  STOCKS - TRYSOMIC 7 WEEKS MIXED COLORS
(00049)  62547  A  0.50  L  1.10  S  2.75  CUCUMBER, BURPEE PICKLER
```

15.18   USING A HASH KEY TO UPDATE A RELATIVE FILE

Let us now examine a program (Figure 15.11) to update the hashed file created by the program in Figure 15.10.

```
1         IDENTIFICATION DIVISION.
2         PROGRAM-ID.
3             UPDATE-HASHED.
4         DATE-WRITTEN.
5             JULY 6, 1989.
6
7         ENVIRONMENT DIVISION.
8         INPUT-OUTPUT SECTION.
9         FILE-CONTROL.
10            SELECT UPDATE-FILE            ASSIGN TO UPDATES.
11            SELECT REL-PRODUCT-FILE       ASSIGN TO RELPROD
12                    ORGANIZATION IS RELATIVE
13                    ACCESS IS RANDOM
14                    RELATIVE KEY IS PRODUCT-KEY
15                    FILE STATUS IS REL-STATUS.
16
17        DATA DIVISION.
18
19        FILE SECTION.
20
21        FD  UPDATE-FILE
22            LABEL RECORDS ARE OMITTED.
23        01  UPDATE-RECORD.
24            05  CATALOG-NUMBER            PIC 9(5).
```

```
25                05   SIZE-1                      PIC X.
26                05   PRICE-1                     PIC 99V99.
27                05   SIZE-2                      PIC X.
28                05   PRICE-2                     PIC 99V99.
29                05   SIZE-3                      PIC X.
30                05   PRICE-3                     PIC 99V99.
31                05   DESCRIPTION                 PIC X(40).
32                05   UPDATE-CODE                 PIC X.
33                     88   ADDITION                    VALUE '1'.
34                     88   DELETION                    VALUE '2'.
35                     88   CORRECTION                  VALUE '3'.
36
37        FD   REL-PRODUCT-FILE
38             LABEL RECORDS ARE STANDARD.
39        01   REL-PRODUCT-RECORD.
40                05   CATALOG-NUMBER              PIC X(5).
41                05   SIZE-1                      PIC X.
42                05   PRICE-1                     PIC 99V99   COMP-3.
43                05   SIZE-2                      PIC X.
44                05   PRICE-2                     PIC 99V99   COMP-3.
45                05   SIZE-3                      PIC X.
46                05   PRICE-3                     PIC 99V99   COMP-3.
47                05   DESCRIPTION                 PIC X(40).
48
49        WORKING-STORAGE SECTION.
50
51        01   FILE-FULL-FLAG              PIC X VALUE 'N'.
52             88   FILE-FULL                       VALUE 'Y'.
53
54        01   FILE-SIZE                   PIC 9(5) COMP SYNC VALUE 50.
55
56        01   KEY-QUOTIENT               PIC 9(5) COMP SYNC.
57
58        01   MORE-DATA-REMAINS-FLAG      PIC X.
59             88   MORE-DATA-REMAINS               VALUE 'Y'.
60             88   NO-MORE-DATA-REMAINS            VALUE 'N'.
61
62        01   PRODUCT-KEY                 PIC 9(5) COMP SYNC.
63
64        01   RECORD-FOUND-FLAG           PIC X.
65             88   RECORD-FOUND                    VALUE 'Y'.
66             88   RECORD-NOT-FOUND                VALUE 'N'.
67
68        01   REL-STATUS                  PIC 99 VALUE 00.
69
70        01   START-KEY                   PIC S9(5) COMP SYNC.
71
72
73        PROCEDURE DIVISION.
74        A000-UPDATE-PRODUCT-FILE.
75             OPEN INPUT UPDATE-FILE
76                   I-O   REL-PRODUCT-FILE.
77             MOVE 'Y' TO MORE-DATA-REMAINS-FLAG.
78             PERFORM B010-PROCESS-ONE-UPDATE
79                    UNTIL NO-MORE-DATA-REMAINS   OR   REL-STATUS > 29.
80             IF REL-STATUS > 29
81                 DISPLAY 'FILE STATUS IS ' REL-STATUS.
82             CLOSE UPDATE-FILE
83                    REL-PRODUCT-FILE.
84             STOP RUN.
```

```
85
86            B010-PROCESS-ONE-UPDATE.
87                READ UPDATE-FILE
88                        AT END MOVE 'N' TO MORE-DATA-REMAINS-FLAG.
89                IF MORE-DATA-REMAINS
90                    IF      ADDITION
91                        PERFORM C010-ADDITION
92                    ELSE IF DELETION
93                        PERFORM C020-DELETION
94                    ELSE IF CORRECTION
95                        PERFORM C030-CORRECTION
96                    ELSE
97                        PERFORM C040-INVALID-TYPE.
98
99        C010-ADDITION.
100           PERFORM X010-COMPUTE-KEY.
101           IF FILE-FULL
102               DISPLAY 'BAD ADDITION; FILE IS FULL; CANNOT ADD '
103                       CATALOG-NUMBER OF UPDATE-RECORD
104           ELSE
105               IF RECORD-FOUND
106                   DISPLAY 'BAD ADDITION; RECORD ALREADY EXISTS FOR '
107                           CATALOG-NUMBER OF UPDATE-RECORD
108               ELSE
109                   MOVE CORRESPONDING UPDATE-RECORD TO
110                           REL-PRODUCT-RECORD
111                   WRITE REL-PRODUCT-RECORD
112                           INVALID KEY
113                               DISPLAY 'BIG TROUBLES AT ' PRODUCT-KEY
114                               DISPLAY 'FILE STATUS IS ' REL-STATUS.
115
116       C020-DELETION.
117           PERFORM X010-COMPUTE-KEY.
118           IF NOT RECORD-FOUND
119               DISPLAY 'BAD DELETION; NO RECORD IN FILE FOR '
120                       CATALOG-NUMBER OF UPDATE-RECORD
121           ELSE
122               DELETE REL-PRODUCT-FILE
123                       INVALID KEY
124                           DISPLAY 'BIG TROUBLES AT ' PRODUCT-KEY
125                           DISPLAY 'FILE STATUS IS ' REL-STATUS.
126
127       C030-CORRECTION.
128           PERFORM X010-COMPUTE-KEY.
129           IF RECORD-NOT-FOUND
130               DISPLAY 'BAD CORRECTION; NO RECORD IN FILE FOR '
131                       CATALOG-NUMBER OF UPDATE-RECORD
132           ELSE
133               MOVE CORRESPONDING UPDATE-RECORD TO REL-PRODUCT-RECORD
134               REWRITE REL-PRODUCT-RECORD
135                       INVALID KEY
136                           DISPLAY 'BIG TROUBLES AT ' PRODUCT-KEY
137                           DISPLAY 'FILE STATUS IS ' REL-STATUS.
138
139       C040-INVALID-TYPE.
140           DISPLAY 'THE FOLLOWING RECORD IS NEITHER AN UPDATE NOR '
141                   'A DELETION NOR A CORRECTION:  '.
142           DISPLAY '     "' UPDATE-RECORD '"'.
143
```

```
144          X010-COMPUTE-KEY.
145              DIVIDE CATALOG-NUMBER OF UPDATE-RECORD BY FILE-SIZE
146                      GIVING KEY-QUOTIENT
147                      REMAINDER PRODUCT-KEY.
148              ADD 1 TO PRODUCT-KEY.
149              MOVE 'X' TO RECORD-FOUND-FLAG.
150              MOVE PRODUCT-KEY TO START-KEY.
151              PERFORM X020-PROBE
152                      UNTIL RECORD-FOUND  OR  RECORD-NOT-FOUND  OR
153                          FILE-FULL.
154
155          X020-PROBE.
156              READ REL-PRODUCT-FILE
157                      INVALID KEY MOVE 'N' TO RECORD-FOUND-FLAG.
158              IF RECORD-FOUND-FLAG = 'X'
159                  IF CATALOG-NUMBER OF REL-PRODUCT-RECORD =
160                      CATALOG-NUMBER OF UPDATE-RECORD
161                      MOVE 'Y' TO RECORD-FOUND-FLAG
162                  ELSE
163                      PERFORM X030-INCREMENT-KEY
164                      IF PRODUCT-KEY = START-KEY
165                          MOVE 'Y' TO FILE-FULL-FLAG.
166
167          X030-INCREMENT-KEY.
168              ADD 1 TO PRODUCT-KEY.
169              IF PRODUCT-KEY > FILE-SIZE
170                  MOVE 1 TO PRODUCT-KEY.
171
172          *********************** END OF PROGRAM ***********************
```

FIGURE 15.11   A program to update a hash-coded relative record file.

The general organization of this program is very similar to that of previous update examples. The **SELECT** statement for **REL-PRODUCT-FILE** and the **FD** for the file should be familiar by now, and paragraphs preceding **X010-COMPUTE-KEY** in the Procedure Division are similar to those in Figure 15.9.

The work required to locate the proper record in the file is contained in the three paragraphs beginning with **X010-COMPUTE-KEY**. While the code in these paragraphs is similar to that used in the program that created the hash-coded version of **REL-PRODUCT-FILE**, there are a few important differences. First, notice that we initialize **RECORD-FOUND-FLAG** to **X**, which is neither **RECORD-FOUND** nor **RECORD-NOT-FOUND**. The reason for this is indicated by the **UNTIL** condition in the following **PERFORM** statement. Since this program is going to be modifying records that already exist on the relative file we want to search the file until one of three conditions is satisfied:

1. The record we want to update has been found;
2. A dummy record has been found, which indicates that the record we are looking for is not in the file;
3. We have gone all the way through the file and have arrived back at our starting point, which indicates that the file is full.

Since we don't know which of these conditions will terminate the **PERFORM**, **RECORD-FOUND-FLAG** is initialized to a neutral value. Paragraph **X020-PROBE** sets the flag to **N** if a dummy record is found or to **Y** if a record is found whose catalog number matches the catalog number of the update record. If the file is full, **FILE-FULL-FLAG** is set to **Y**.

The resulting file, using the updates from previous examples, is shown below. Again notice that although the updates have been made correctly, the new records are scattered randomly through the file by the hashing algorithm.

```
(00005)  51904  A  0.75  J  4.50        0.00  CRENSHAH MELON, BURPEES EARLY HYBRID
(00007)  39156  A  0.35  H  1.00        0.00  SWEET WILLIAM  PURE WHITE
(00009)  31658  A  1.00  P  4.00        0.00  SNAPDRAGON, BRIGHT BUTTERFLIES, MIXED
(00011)  36160  A  0.50  K  1.50  L  1.75  ROYAL SWEET PEAS, MIXED
(00012)  96461     15.95        0.00        0.00  COMPOST KIT
(00013)  50260  A  0.75  J  4.50        0.00  EGGPLANT, EARLY BEAUTY HYBRID
(00016)  37515  A  0.35  H  1.00        0.00  SWEET WILLIAM  PINK BEAUTY
(00018)  51367  A  0.50  T  1.45  U  2.75  DECORATIVE CORN, RAINBOW
(00022)  62471  A  0.75  T  1.85  U  3.50  HYBRID CORN, HONEY AND CREAM
(00024)  31773  A  0.75  G  2.25        0.00  VERBENA, RUFFLED WHITE
(00025)  36574  A  0.50  G  1.50        0.00  STOCKS - GIANT COLUMN MIXED COLORS
(00026)  43125  A  0.35  H  1.05  K  3.25  ZINNIAS, GIANTS OF CALIFORNIA, MIXED
(00032)  15131      5.50        0.00        0.00  APPLE TREE, JONATHAN
(00048)  33597  A  0.50  G  2.50        0.00  STOCKS - TRYSOMIC 7 WEEKS MIXED COLORS
```

The examples and discussion that we have presented to demonstrate the use of hash coding and relative files should give you a general idea of what these files look like and how they can be used. However, the power and flexibility of direct access files goes far beyond what we can cover in this book. A more complete study of these topics is strongly recommended.

REVIEW QUESTIONS

1. In the program of Figure 15.3, how many times will the paragraph names **B010-VALIDATE-ONE-ORDER** be executed? The question actually has to do with the **PERFORM ... UNTIL** in the main paragraph, which is of the same form as that in programs that have carried out a performed paragraph once for each record in a file.

2. What would the program in Figure 15.3 do with a jumbled input file, where the records for any one order were not properly grouped together?

3. In the program of Figure 15.4 what would the occurrence of an invalid key indicate?

4. In the program of Figure 15.4 there is no priming **READ** in the main paragraph. Instead, the performed paragraph begins with a **READ** and if that **READ** does not detect the end of the file, there is a **WRITE**. Would it have been possible to use the program skeleton that has appeared in most of the other programs in the book, where there is a priming **READ** and where the performed paragraph begins with a **WRITE** followed by a **READ**?

5. Can you suggest a situation where it might be advantageous to sort the transactions in an indexed file updating applications even though the index file will have **ACCESS MODE IS RANDOM**?

6. In the program of Figure 15.6, what will happen if an order has two header records? How about two trailer records?

7. In the program of Figure 15.8, suppose we initialized **PRODUCT-KEY** to 100 instead of 1. Would we then start writing at record 100 instead of record 1?

8. Compare the program of Figure 15.8 to the program of Figure 15.4. How does the invalid key condition differ in the two programs?

9. We discussed the use of hash coding to locate a record in a relative file if there was no field that could be used directly as the relative key. Can you suggest other methods of locating records in a relative file besides hash coding?

ANSWERS TO REVIEW QUESTIONS

1. The paragraph will be carried out as many times as there are *orders* in the file. In the extreme case of a file consisting of one order having many records, the paragraph would be carried out once. The point is that control stays in the paragraph until the **PERFORM** logic in the main paragraph determines either that the beginning of a new group has been detected or that the end of the file has been reached.

2. The results would essentially be meaningless, but the program would run without error indication, processing whatever groups it might find. The answer to this unacceptable state of affairs is to include sequence checking in the program.

3. In the creation of an indexed file, the records are required to be in ascending sequence and there must be no duplicate keys. The **INVALID KEY** phrase checks for the occurrence of either of these errors in the input.

4. Certainly. The program was written as it was partly to demonstrate that we usually do have this choice, but mostly because this way fits in better with the requirements of the program of Figure 15.4

5. Transactions can be processed against an indexed file somewhat more rapidly if they are in sequence than if they are not. However, it would be unusual for the time savings to be large enough to justify the time required to sort the transactions.

6. If the order has two headers, the first header is treated as an order without a trailer record and is reported accordingly, while the second header is treated as the start of a new order. If there are two trailer records, the second trailer is treated as an order without a header record.

7. No. In Microsoft **COBOL** (and most other current versions of **COBOL**), if the file is defined with **ACCESS IS SEQUENTIAL** and is opened for output, the relative key is ignored in determining where records are to be written. If present, the relative key is assigned the record number as the record is written but that is its only use. In earlier versions of **COBOL**, prior to **COBOL-74**, the relative key could be used to set the location of the record being written.

8. In a relative file (Figure 15.8), the invalid key condition indicated that you are trying to write a record beyond the physical bounds of the file. In

an indexed file (Figure 15.4), the invalid key condition indicates a duplicate key or a record out of sequence, both related to errors in the input.

9. There are several other ways of locating records in a relative record file. One of the most common is to use a secondary file, such as an indexed file, as a *key* file. Records in the indexed file would use some key field as the record key of the. file, then would contain the relative key of the actual data record as data in the indexed records. To find a record in the relative file, you would use its key to find a record in the indexed file, then use the data in the indexed record as the relative key to find the record in the relative file.

EXERCISES

1. Modify the program in Figure 15.3 so that it sequence checks the transaction file.

2. Write a program to print the product file from Figure 15.10. The output should look like that shown in Figure 15.12 on page 455.

3. Revise the program of figure 15.4 to create the indexed file randomly, by changing the **ACCESS** clause to **ACCESS IS RANDOM**. Scramble the records in **PRODUCT-FILE** so that they are no longer in sequence. Print the resulting indexed file and compare your listing with the one on page 427.

4. Modify the program in Figure 15.6 to include sequence checking.

5. Modify the program in Figure 15.6 to include validation of the trailer record. This will require totaling the amounts on the body records.

6. Add checking to the program of Figure 15.6 so that it labels as erroneous any order that does not contain exactly one header record, at least one body record, and exactly one trailer record, in that order.

7. Modify the program of Figure 15.6 so that the catalog file is a relative record file instead of an indexed file. Use hash coding to find records.

8. Combine the program of Figure 15.6 with an appropriately modified version of the program in Figure 11.1 to produce a complete validation program for the seed catalog orders.

9. (This exercise is suitable for a project.)

    The product file for the National Widget Corporation has the following format:

Columns 1-5	product code	PIC AA999
Columns 6-30	product description	PIC X(25)
Columns 31-35	sales for three weeks ago	PIC 9(5)
Columns 36-40	sales for two weeks ago	PIC 9(5)
Columns 41-45	sales for last week	PIC 9(5)
Columns 46-50	inventory level	PIC 9(5)
Columns 51-57	selling price in dollars and cents	PIC 9(5)V99

When merchandise is received from a supplier, a record with the following format is prepared:

Column 1	record type ("A")	PIC X
Columns 2-6	product code	PIC AA999
Columns 7-12	quantity received	PIC 9(6)
Columns 13-19	supplier code	PIC 99A9(4)
Columns 20-25	purchase order number	PIC 9(6)
Columns 26-31	date received (YYMMDD)	PIC 9(6)
Columns 32-47	not used	

When merchandise is sold, a sales record is prepared, in the following format:

Column 1	record type ("B")	PIC X
Columns 2-6	product code	PIC AA999
Columns 7-14	transaction number	PIC 9(8)
Columns 15-21	customer number	PIC 9(7)
Columns 22-25	quantity sold	PIC 9(4)
Columns 26-33	amount of sale	PIC 9(6)V99
Columns 34-39	date of sale (YYMMDD)	PIC 9(6)
Columns 40-47	not used	

If merchandise is returned by a customer, a record describing the return is prepared with the following format:

Column 1	record type ("C")	PIC X
Columns 2-6	product code	PIC AA999
Columns 7-14	reference number	PIC 9(8)
Columns 15-22	credit number	PIC 9(8)
Columns 23-29	customer number	PIC 9(7)
Columns 30-33	quantity returned	PIC 9(4)
Columns 34-41	credit amount	PIC 9(6)V99
Columns 42-47	date of return (YYMMDD)	PIC 9(6)

An inventory maintenance program uses the transaction records (receipt, sales, and return) to maintain the current inventory level of all products. At the end of each working day, all transactions for the day are processed against the master file. The records are not sorted; they are simply in chronological order, i.e., the order in which the various activities occurred. When a merchandise receipt is processed, the quantity received is added to the current inventory level. For sales records the quantity sold is subtracted from the current inventory level, and for returns the quantity returned is added to the inventory level.

To prevent data entry errors from causing errors in the inventory processing, the transactions are edited before they are processed. The record type must be A, B, or C. The product code must correspond to a record in the product file, and the merchandise quantity must be numeric. Dates must be valid. That is, the month must be in the range 1-12, the day must be valid for the month (February 30, for example, is not valid), and the date must be less than or equal to the date on which the data is being processed. Finally, if the inventory level ever goes below zero this should be reported as an error.

The product file is maintained as a relative file, keyed to product code. Keys are computed using a hashing algorithm based on product code, with linear probing being used to resolve collisions. The hashing algorithm is the following:

1. Convert the first letter of the product code to its numeric equivalent; that is, A = 1, B = 2, ..., Z = 26;
2. Multiply the result of step 1 by 1000;
3. Add the numeric portion of the product code to the result of step 2;
4. Divide the result of step 3 by 7500 and add 1 to the remainder;
5. The result of step 4 is the relative key.

For example, suppose we have a product code of KB152. The numeric equivalent of K is 11. Multiplying this by 1000 gives 11000. To this we add 152, giving 11152. Dividing 11152 by 7500 gives a quotient of 1 (which we ignore) and a remainder of 3652. Adding 1 to the remainder gives the relative key of 3653.

Assume you have a sequential product master file, sorted on product key. Write a program to convert this to a relative file using a technique similar to that shown in Figure 15.11. Write a second program to print the relative file. Finally, write a program that takes a file of transaction records in the formats given above and applies these transactions to the master file to update the inventory level. Be sure that your update program makes the edit tests required, reports any errors detected, and rejects invalid transaction records. Print the relative file both before and after the update program is run.

10. The same as Exercise 9, except create an indexed file for the product file instead of a relative file.

CHAPTER 16

CHARACTER MANIPULATION

16.1 INTRODUCTION

A considerable amount of the work that is performed in a typical COBOL program involves manipulating character data. We have seen examples of this when we move numeric data into a numeric edited field, or simply MOVE one character field to another. However, these examples all involve moving one complete field to another, and there are times when we need to perform manipulation of the characters within a single field. We may need to count the number of times a particular character occurs in a field, we may need to replace all occurrences of one character with another (such as replacing blanks by zeros or zeros by blanks), or we may need to extract selected portions of a field (such as separating house number and street name in a field keyed simply as "address"). COBOL has three statements for character manipulation: INSPECT, STRING, and UNSTRING. We shall discuss each of these statements and show how each might be used. In the following discussion, the term "string" will be used to represent a sequence of characters, generally a single field.

16.2 THE INSPECT STATEMENT

Consider the following record:

```
01   PAY-RECORD.
     05   EMPLOYEE-ID        PIC X(6).
     05   DEPARTMENT         PIC XX.
     05   ACCOUNT-NUMBER     PIC X(5).
     05   REGULAR-HOURS      PIC 99V99.
     05   OVERTIME-HOURS     PIC 99V99.
```

Suppose we discover that leading zeros in **REGULAR-HOURS** and **OVER-TIME-HOURS** have been entered as spaces. Further, we find that if the value of either field is zero, it has been left entirely blank. This creates several serious processing problems. If we try to perform arithmetic on a field containing all blanks we will probably get an error, possibly even an abend. Furthermore, if we test these fields to see if they are numeric, leading blanks will not be numeric. Up to now we have no good way of dealing with this problem. Although we could test to see if a field is equal to spaces, this complicates the program and still does not deal with the problem of *leading* spaces in a field that is not entirely blank. Some computers may treat leading spaces as zero, but we should not count on all computer hardware conveniently giving the right result. We could require that the data be rekeyed in the input file, but for large files this would not be practical, and there is a much better solution in any case.

A simple solution to the problem lies with the **INSPECT** statement. Before we process the data in the record, we execute the following statements:

```
INSPECT REGULAR-HOURS  REPLACING LEADING SPACES BY ZERO.
INSPECT OVERTIME-HOURS REPLACING LEADING SPACES BY ZERO.
```

These statements scan **REGULAR-HOURS** and **OVERTIME-HOURS** and substitute a zero for each leading space. We could also write

```
INSPECT REGULAR-HOURS  REPLACING ALL SPACES BY ZERO.
INSPECT OVERTIME-HOURS REPLACING ALL SPACES BY ZERO.
```

However, this would change *all* blanks to zeros, including spaces that were erroneously keyed in the middle of a field or at the right end of the field, which we do not want.

The basic functions of the **INSPECT** statement are the following:

1. Count the number of times a specified sequence of characters occurs in a string;
2. Replace specified characters with other characters;
3. Do both counting and replacing.

The actual format of the **INSPECT** statement is quite complex and we will not attempt to show it here or discuss all its possible uses. We will, however, show a few examples of what can be done with the **INSPECT**.

The first option is to count occurrences of characters in any of several possible contexts:

1. All occurrences of a character in a string;
2. All *leading* occurrences of a character; that is, before any other character occurs in the string;
3. All occurrences of a character *before* the *first* occurrence of some other specified character;
4. All occurrences of a character *after* the *first* occurrence of some other specified character;
5. All characters occurring *before* some *specified* character;
6. All characters occurring *after* some *specified* character.

For example, we might have statements such as the following:

INSPECT Statement	Sample	Resulting value of COUNTER
INSPECT SAMPLE TALLYING COUNTER FOR ALL '0'.	102030	3
INSPECT SAMPLE TALLYING COUNTER FOR ALL LEADING '0'.	102030	0
INSPECT SAMPLE TALLYING COUNTER FOR ALL LEADING '0'.	002030	2
INSPECT SAMPLE TALLYING COUNTER FOR ALL '0' BEFORE '3'.	002030	3
INSPECT SAMPLE TALLYING COUNTER FOR ALL '0' AFTER '3'.	003030	2
INSPECT SAMPLE TALLYING COUNTER FOR CHARACTERS BEFORE 'C'.	AABACA	4
INSPECT SAMPLE TALLYING COUNTER FOR CHARACTERS AFTER 'B'.	AABABA	3

For this version of the INSPECT statement we specify the identifier to be examined, then specify the variable used to tally the number of character occurrences found, and finally define the characters to be counted and the context in which they occur. It is important to note that the TALLYING option does not *store* the character count in the tallying variable (COUNTER in the examples), it *adds* the count to the current value of the variable. Thus in the preceding examples, we assume that COUNTER has a value of zero prior to the execution of each INSPECT statement.

We have already seen one example of the second INSPECT option, replacing leading blanks with zeros. Just as tallying can be done in several different contexts, so can replacing. In fact, the replacing option can also be limited to replacing just the first occurrence of a character. The following examples will demonstrate some of the replacing options. We will use the underscore character (_) to denote blanks.

INSPECT Statement	SAMPLE Before	SAMPLE After
INSPECT SAMPLE REPLACING ALL SPACES BY ZERO.	__2_3_	002030
INSPECT SAMPLE REPLACING LEADING SPACES BY ZERO.	__2_3_	002_3_
INSPECT SAMPLE REPLACING ALL 'A' BY 'B' BEFORE 'X'.	AABXAA	BBBXAA
INSPECT SAMPLE REPLACING CHARACTERS BY 'Z' AFTER 'X'.	AAXXBC	AAXZZZ
INSPECT SAMPLE REPLACING ALL 'A' BY 'X', 'B' BY 'Y', 'C' BY 'Z' AFTER SPACE.	ABC_ABC	XYC_XYZ
INSPECT SAMPLE REPLACING ALL 'ABC' BY 'XYZ' AFTER SPACE.	ABC_ABC	ABC_XYZ
INSPECT SAMPLE REPLACING FIRST 'X' AFTER 'Y' BY 'Z'.	XYXYXX	XYZYXX

Finally, we can perform both tallying and replacing in the same operation. As with the previous examples of the TALLYING option, we assume that COUNTER is set to zero prior to the execution of each INSPECT statement.

INSPECT Statement	SAMPLE Before	After	COUNTER

INSPECT SAMPLE TALLYING COUNTER
   FOR ALL '0'
   REPLACING '0' BY SPACE.
	0016047	__16_47	3

INSPECT SAMPLE TALLYING COUNTER
   FOR LEADING '0'
   REPLACING FIRST '0' BY 'X'.
	0016047	X016047	2

INSPECT SAMPLE TALLYING COUNTER
   FOR LEADING '*'
   REPLACING ALL '.' BY ',',
   FIRST '*' BY '$'.
	****.123.456	$***,123,456	4

As we indicated at the start of this section, these examples merely scratch the surface of what can be done with the **INSPECT** statement. For instance, the **INSPECT** statement can be used in combination with the **UNSTRING** statement (see Section 16.4) to extract data from strings. The serious **COBOL** programmer should study the Microsoft **COBOL** manual for further details.

16.3 THE STRING STATEMENT

The **STRING** statement permits us to assemble fields from various locations into one combined string. In its simplest form it is no different from a series of **MOVE**s, but features are available to do things that can be accomplished only with much greater effort otherwise.

For example, suppose that we have these entries in the Working-Storage Section of a program.

```
WORKING-STORAGE SECTION.

01   CREDIT-MASTER-RECORD.
     05   CUSTOMER-NUMBER        PIC X(5).
     05   CUSTOMER-NAME          PIC X(20).
     05   CUSTOMER-ADDRESS       PIC X(60).
     05   OLD-BALANCE            PIC $$,$$9.99.

01   MONTHLY-SUMMARY-RECORD.
     05   CURRENT-PURCHASES      PIC $$,$$9.99.
     05   CREDIT-AVAILABLE       PIC $$,$$9.99.
     05   BALANCE-DUE            PIC $$,$$9.99.

01   INITIAL-POSITION           PIC 99.
```

We wish to prepare a line containing, in sequence, **CUSTOMER-NAME**, **CUSTOMER-NUMBER**, **OLD-BALANCE**, **CURRENT-PURCHASES**, **BALANCE-DUE**, and **CREDIT-AVAILABLE**. For simplicity, we shall assume that only a single space is required between fields, although providing any number of spaces would not be difficult. All of the items except **CREDIT-AVAILABLE** are to be moved to the combined output line in their entirety. **CREDIT-AVAILABLE**, however, is to have its decimal point and the cents position deleted. Finally, we want to be able to make the starting position of the first field in the line variable. We can imagine that certain classes of accounts might need to be indented differently from others, for instance.

All of this can be done with the statements shown on the next page.

```
MOVE SPACES TO BILLING-RECORD.
MOVE 14 TO INITIAL-POSITION.

STRING
    CUSTOMER-NAME DELIMITED BY SIZE
    SPACE
    CUSTOMER-NUMBER DELIMITED BY SIZE
    SPACE
    OLD-BALANCE DELIMITED BY SIZE
    SPACE
    CURRENT-PURCHASES DELIMITED BY SIZE
    SPACE
    BALANCE-DUE DELIMITED BY SIZE
    SPACE
    CREDIT-AVAILABLE DELIMITED BY '.'
        INTO BILLING-RECORD
        WITH POINTER INITIAL-POSITION.

WRITE BILLING-RECORD.
```

We begin by moving spaces to the output line, which is called **BILLING-RECORD**, to remove any contents that might be in positions of the record in which we shall place no data. We then place 14 in the item that will be used as a pointer to determine where the first field is placed in the line. Now comes the **STRING** statement. In this we list all of the items that are to be combined into one string. For each, we indicate whether it is delimited by size, which means simply that the entire item is to be moved, or whether it is delimited by some character in the field. For **CREDIT-AVAILABLE** we indicate that it is delimited by a period, which means that only the characters before the decimal point will be moved. We then indicate the name of the item (**BILLING-RECORD**) that will hold the combined string and designate the pointer.

When the **WITH POINTER** clause is used, the **STRING** statement automatically updates the value of the pointer so that after the statement has been executed, the pointer points to the first byte following the end of the string. For example, if the pointer initially contains the value 1 and we insert strings with a total of 15 bytes, the pointer will contain the value 16 after execution of the **STRING** statement.

Here is a line produced when these statements were executed with illustrative data in the records:

```
J. B. HUGHES        12609 $1,058.40    $126.27 $1,184.67    $815
```

The general format for the **STRING** statement is as follows:

$$\text{STRING} \quad \left\{ \left\{ \begin{array}{l} \text{identifier-1} \\ \text{literal-1} \end{array} \right\} \cdots \text{DELIMITED BY} \left\{ \begin{array}{l} \text{identifier-2} \\ \text{literal-2} \\ \textbf{SIZE} \end{array} \right\} \right\} \cdots$$

INTO identifier-3

[**WITH POINTER** identifier-4]

[**ON OVERFLOW** imperative-statement]

COBOL-85

In **COBOL-85**, the **STRING** statement may be terminated with an optional **END-STRING** phrase.

END COBOL-85

Observe that we are able to intermix data items and literals at will. Providing more than one space between fields in the example above would be a simple matter of using nonnumeric literals. Delimiters can also be identifiers, which means that we can use the value of some other problem data to terminate transmission of fields. An **ON OVERFLOW** option is available to specify what should be done if there is insufficient space in the receiving item for all the items being sent to it. Although we have shown only a simple example, it should be obvious that the **STRING** statement can be used to perform tasks like removing blanks from the ends of fields in name and address lines, producing customized form letters, and so on.

16.4   THE UNSTRING STATEMENT

The **UNSTRING** statement is the opposite of the **STRING** statement in that it permits us to distribute fields within one combined item into any number of separate elementary items. The sending field must contain delimiters that can be used to determine the lengths of the fields that are to be distributed. We shall consider one simple but useful example and then shall sketch the other features that are available.

We are given a file of records each consisting of a person's name and address. A legitimate address in this application is allowed to have from two to five lines. The information for the lines of an address is keyed in a record with equal signs for delimiters. For example, here are the sample input records to be used with the program that we shall study shortly:

```
D G GOLDEN=CLEVELAND STATE UNIVERSITY=CLEVELAND, OHIO 44115=
MR. ASHLEY H. WOODSON=223 MAPLE PLACE=APT. 3D=ANYTOWN, USA 12345=
MS. J. D. APPLETON=ENGINEERING DEPT.=ACME MFG. CO.=1200 YORK=ARKVILLE, GA 36000=
MR. T.H.JONES=MAIL DROP 23K=BLDG. 239=GENERAL ELECTRONICS=ROSETOWN, PA 18900=
JAMES B. THOMPSON, ESQ.=SMALLTOWN, NY 14200=
JAMES B. THOMPSON, ESQ.==SMALLTOWN, NY 14200=
ROGER MILLS=
MR. ROGER B. SHILLITO 23 ELM STREET GEORGETOWN, PA 15200
J C CLARK=DATA PROC=MAIL CODE 45=NORTH PLANT BLDG. 6=ACME CO.=ACKLEY, NJ 03800=
```

We wish to produce mailing labels for each address. Each label is to consist of six lines, the sixth line always being blank. We will assume that each line can be up to 40 characters long, since this is the length of typical mailing labels. If the input record contains only one line, it is assumed to be mistyped and we shall replace it with an error message. (In real life other measures would probably need to be taken, but this is sufficient to indicate the possibilities.) Likewise, if an address contains more than five lines, it will be considered to be erroneous.

A program to read such records and print the labels is shown in Figure 16.1. Everything is familiar until we come to the paragraph that is named **B010-PRODUCE-ONE-LABEL**. We begin by clearing the storage space for all six lines and resetting the flag that will tell us if there are more than five lines. We then move zero to the item that will count the number of fields filled, with which we can determine if there was only one line. The **UNSTRING** statement is fairly straightforward. We indicate what the delimiter is; name the items that are to receive the fields separated by this delimiter; specify the item that is to receive the tally of fields filled; and specify what to do if information remains in the sending item after all receiving items have been filled. The rest of the program is routine.

There is one subtle point to be careful of, however. **UNSTRING** scans the sending item to the end of the item, not just to the last delimiter. Any spaces to the right of the last delimiter are treated as a blank field and the end of the sending item is treated as an implied delimiter. Thus, for example, the first record produces *four* lines, the last of which consists of 20 blanks.

```
 1          IDENTIFICATION DIVISION.
 2          PROGRAM-ID.
 3              UNSTRING-DEMO.
 4          DATE-WRITTEN.
 5              JUNE 22, 1989.
 6
 7          ENVIRONMENT DIVISION.
 8          INPUT-OUTPUT SECTION.
 9          FILE-CONTROL.
10              SELECT ADDRESS-FILE          ASSIGN TO ADDRESS.
11              SELECT LABEL-FILE            ASSIGN TO LABELS.
12
13          DATA DIVISION.
14
15          FILE SECTION.
16
17          FD  ADDRESS-FILE
18              LABEL RECORDS ARE STANDARD.
19          01  ADDRESS-RECORD               PIC X(80).
20
21          FD  LABEL-FILE
22              LABEL RECORDS ARE STANDARD.
23          01  LABEL-RECORD                 PIC X(40).
24
25          WORKING-STORAGE SECTION.
26
27          01  ADDRESS-WORK-AREA.
28              05  ADDRESS-LINE-1           PIC X(40).
29              05  ADDRESS-LINE-2           PIC X(40).
30              05  ADDRESS-LINE-3           PIC X(40).
31              05  ADDRESS-LINE-4           PIC X(40).
32              05  ADDRESS-LINE-5           PIC X(40).
33              05  ADDRESS-LINE-6           PIC X(40).
34
35          01  FIELDS-FILLED                PIC 99.
36
37          01  FIELD-OVERFLOW-FLAG          PIC X.
38              88  FIELD-OVERFLOW                   VALUE 'Y'.
39
```

```
40          01  MORE-DATA-REMAINS-FLAG      PIC X.
41              88  NO-MORE-DATA-REMAINS            VALUE 'N'.
42
43
44      PROCEDURE DIVISION.
45      A000-PRODUCE-LABELS.
46          OPEN INPUT ADDRESS-FILE
47              OUTPUT LABEL-FILE.
48          MOVE 'Y' TO MORE-DATA-REMAINS-FLAG.
49          READ ADDRESS-FILE
50              AT END MOVE 'N' TO MORE-DATA-REMAINS-FLAG.
51          PERFORM B010-PRODUCE-ONE-LABEL
52              UNTIL NO-MORE-DATA-REMAINS.
53          CLOSE ADDRESS-FILE
54                LABEL-FILE.
55          STOP RUN.
56
57      B010-PRODUCE-ONE-LABEL.
58          MOVE SPACES TO              ADDRESS-WORK-AREA.
59          MOVE 'N' TO                 FIELD-OVERFLOW-FLAG.
60          MOVE ZERO TO                FIELDS-FILLED.
61          UNSTRING ADDRESS-RECORD DELIMITED BY '='
62              INTO ADDRESS-LINE-1
63                   ADDRESS-LINE-2
64                   ADDRESS-LINE-3
65                   ADDRESS-LINE-4
66                   ADDRESS-LINE-5
67                   ADDRESS-LINE-6
68              TALLYING IN FIELDS-FILLED
69              ON OVERFLOW MOVE 'Y' TO FIELD-OVERFLOW-FLAG.
70          IF FIELDS-FILLED IS LESS THAN 3  OR  FIELD-OVERFLOW
71              MOVE 'BAD ADDRESS' TO ADDRESS-WORK-AREA.
72          WRITE LABEL-RECORD FROM ADDRESS-LINE-1.
73          WRITE LABEL-RECORD FROM ADDRESS-LINE-2.
74          WRITE LABEL-RECORD FROM ADDRESS-LINE-3.
75          WRITE LABEL-RECORD FROM ADDRESS-LINE-4.
76          WRITE LABEL-RECORD FROM ADDRESS-LINE-5.
77          WRITE LABEL-RECORD FROM ADDRESS-LINE-6.
78          READ ADDRESS-FILE
79              AT END MOVE 'N' TO MORE-DATA-REMAINS-FLAG.
80
81      ********************* END OF PROGRAM *************************
```

FIGURE 16.1 A program using the **UNSTRING** statement to distribute variable length fields of an input record to separate lines for printing.

Here is the output produced when the input records shown earlier were processed by this program.

```
D G GOLDEN
CLEVELAND STATE UNIVERSITY
CLEVELAND, OHIO 44115



MR. ASHLEY H. WOODSON
223 MAPLE PLACE
APT. 3D
ANYTOWN, USA 12345
```

```
MS. J. D. APPLETON
ENGINEERING DEPT.
ACME MFG. CO.
1200 YORK
ARKVILLE, GA 36000


MR. T.H.JONES
MAIL DROP 23K
BLDG. 239
GENERAL ELECTRONICS
ROSETOWN, PA 18900


JAMES B. THOMPSON, ESQ.
SMALLTOWN, NY 14200



JAMES B. THOMPSON, ESQ.

SMALLTOWN, NY 14200



BAD ADDRESS



BAD ADDRESS



BAD ADDRESS
```

The **UNSTRING** statement provides a number of other capabilities that are not illustrated in this program, as we see by considering the following general format:

UNSTRING identifier-1

$\left[\text{\underline{DELIMITED} BY [\underline{ALL}]} \left\{ \begin{array}{l} \text{identifier-2} \\ \text{literal-1} \end{array} \right\} \left[\text{OR [\underline{ALL}]} \left\{ \begin{array}{l} \text{identifier-3} \\ \text{literal-2} \end{array} \right\} \right] \dots \right]$

[**INTO** identifier-4 [**DELIMITER** IN identifier-5] [**COUNT** IN identifier-6] . . .

[WITH **POINTER** identifier-7] [**TALLYING** IN identifier-8]

[ON **OVERFLOW** imperative-statement]

COBOL-85

In **COBOL-85**, the **UNSTRING** statement may be terminated with an optional **END-UNSTRING** phrase.

END COBOL-85

We see that delimiters may be either identifiers or literals and that there may be any number of them. We could, for instance, have an **UNSTRING** statement with this phrase in it

UNSTRING RECORD-A DELIMITED BY ALL SPACES OR '/' OR FIELD-A

This would mean that any one or more blanks is a delimiter, or that a slash is a delimiter, or that the contents of **FIELD-A** is a delimiter. In all cases, delimiters may be one or more characters.

It is possible to specify, for any field moved, that a count of the number of characters in the field should be placed in a specified location. The pointer option allows us to begin unstringing the sending item at other than the first character in it.

The **STRING** and **UNSTRING** statements are very powerful features of the **COBOL** language. They permit us to do in a simple way things that in some instances would otherwise be extremely difficult to do and much less easy to understand, and in some installations they are used quite frequently.

16.5 ASSIGNING FILES THROUGH THE COMMAND LINE

We will conclude this chapter with a slightly more extensive version of the line numbering program introduced in Chapter 13. Recall that this program reads a **COBOL** source file and produces a numbered version of the file. In Chapter 13, we used the **ACCEPT** statement to get the names of the input and output files. Now we will use some of the chateracter processing techniques we have seen in this chapter to get the file names in a more sophisticated way.

The *command line* is that part of an MS-DOS statement line following the program name. For example, when you compile a **COBOL** program you type a statement such as the following:

COBOL MYPROG ANIM, NUL;

The command line consists of "MYPROG ANIM,NUL;". We can read the command line into a program by adding **FROM COMMAND-LINE** to an **ACCEPT** statement. Thus,

ACCEPT COMMAND-TEXT FROM COMMAND-LINE

will copy the command line text into the **COBOL** variable **COMMAND-TEXT**. Figure 16.2 shows how we can use the command line to get file names.

To use this program, we write the name of the input file and (optionally) the output file in the command line. If the name of the output file is omitted, the program will automatically use the same name as the input file, with the extension change to "NBR". Thus, the following examples are equivalent:

```
COBNBR MYPROG.CBL MYPROG.NBR
COBNBR MYPROG.CBL
```

The program begins by using **ACCEPT ... FROM COMMAND-LINE** to copy the file name(s) into the variable **FILE-IDS**. We can see that each file name in the command line is terminated by a space, so we use the **UNSTRING** statement on lines 50-53 to copy the input and output file names into **TEXTIN** and **TEXTOUT**, respectively. Of course, if there is no output name in the command line then **TEXTOUT** is blank, so we test **TEXTOUT** and, if necessary, compute the output file name in **B020-BUILD-OUTPUT-NAME**.

We don't know whether or not the file name in **TEXTIN** contains an extension (that is, the name could either have the format MYPROG or MYPROG.CBL), so we look for the first dot in **TEXTIN**. If there is a dot, then we set the scan delimiter to "."; otherwise we leave it as a space. Finally, the **STRING** statement gets the first part of the input file name and appends ".NBR" to complete the name of the output file. Note that we could have combined lines 80 and 81 into the single phrase

```
'.NBR'      DELIMITED BY SIZE
```

The approach shown was used to emphase the three parts of an MS-DOS file name: name, dot, and extension. Although this program is fairly simple, it demonstrates the general concept of what we need to do to get data from the command line into the program.

```
1          IDENTIFICATION DIVISION.
2          PROGRAM-ID.
3              NUMBER-TEXT.
4          AUTHOR.
5              D. GOLDEN.
6          DATE-WRITTEN.
7              OCTOBER 7, 1988.
8
9          ENVIRONMENT DIVISION.
10         INPUT-OUTPUT SECTION.
11         FILE-CONTROL.
12             SELECT TEXT-FILE                ASSIGN TO TEXTIN.
13             SELECT NUMBERED-FILE            ASSIGN TO TEXTOUT.
14
15         DATA DIVISION.
16
17         FILE SECTION.
18
19         FD  TEXT-FILE
20             LABEL RECORDS STANDARD.
21         01  TEXT-RECORD.
22             05  SOURCE-TEXT                 PIC X(72).
23             05  FILLER                      PIC X(8).
24
25         FD  NUMBERED-FILE
26             LABEL RECORDS STANDARD.
27         01  NUMBERED-RECORD                 PIC X(77).
28
```

```
29              WORKING-STORAGE SECTION.
30
31              01   DOT-COUNT                    PIC 99        VALUE ZERO.
32              01   FILE-IDS                     PIC X(80).
33              01   SCAN-DELIMITER               PIC X         VALUE SPACE.
34              01   TEXTIN                       PIC X(25).
35              01   TEXTOUT                      PIC X(25).
36
37              01   WORK-RECORD.
38                   05   LINE-NUMBER             PIC ZZ9BB.
39                   05   OUTPUT-TEXT             PIC X(72).
40
41              01   LINE-COUNT                   PIC 9(5) COMP VALUE 0.
42
43              01   MORE-LINES-REMAIN-FLAG       PIC X VALUE 'Y'.
44                   88   NO-MORE-LINES-REMAIN          VALUE 'N'.
45
46
47              PROCEDURE DIVISION.
48              A000-NUMBER-LINES.
49                  ACCEPT FILE-IDS FROM COMMAND-LINE.
50                  UNSTRING FILE-IDS
51                          DELIMITED BY SPACE
52                          INTO TEXTIN
53                              TEXTOUT.
54                  IF TEXTOUT = SPACES
55                      PERFORM B020-BUILD-OUTPUT-NAME.
56                  OPEN INPUT TEXT-FILE
57                      OUTPUT NUMBERED-FILE.
58                  READ TEXT-FILE
59                      AT END MOVE 'N' TO MORE-LINES-REMAIN-FLAG.
60                  PERFORM B010-NUMBER-A-LINE
61                      UNTIL NO-MORE-LINES-REMAIN.
62                  CLOSE TEXT-FILE
63                      NUMBERED-FILE.
64                  STOP RUN.
65
66              B010-NUMBER-A-LINE.
67                  ADD 1 TO LINE-COUNT.
68                  MOVE LINE-COUNT TO LINE-NUMBER.
69                  MOVE SOURCE-TEXT TO OUTPUT-TEXT.
70                  WRITE NUMBERED-RECORD FROM WORK-RECORD.
71                  READ TEXT-FILE
72                      AT END MOVE 'N' TO MORE-LINES-REMAIN-FLAG.
73
74              B020-BUILD-OUTPUT-NAME.
75                  INSPECT TEXTIN
76                      TALLYING DOT-COUNT FOR ALL '.'.
77                  IF DOT-COUNT  ZERO
78                      MOVE '.' TO SCAN-DELIMITER.
79                  STRING TEXTIN DELIMITED BY SCAN-DELIMITER
80                          '.'       DELIMITED BY SIZE
81                          'NBR'     DELIMITED BY SIZE
82                          INTO TEXTOUT.
```

FIGURE 16.2 The complete file numbering program.

REVIEW QUESTIONS

1. Show what the contents of **SAMPLE** and **COUNTER** would be after the execution of each of the following **INSPECT** statements with the initial values of the eleven-character **SAMPLE** that are shown, and an initial value of zero for **COUNTER**.

	SAMPLE
| ```
INSPECT SAMPLE TALLYING COUNTER
    FOR CHARACTERS BEFORE ','.
``` | $128,064.32 |
| ```
INSPECT SAMPLE REPLACING
    ALL '*' BY SPACE.
``` | $*****12.69 |
| ```
INSPECT SAMPLE TALLYING COUNTER
    FOR ALL '-' REPLACING ALL '-' BY SPACE.
``` | 535-22-1583 |
| ```
INSPECT SAMPLE REPLACING
    FIRST '.' BY 'X'.
``` | 9A6.77X.,XX |
| ```
INSPECT SAMPLE TALLYING COUNTER
    FOR ALL SPACES.
``` | JOHN   SMITH |
| ```
INSPECT SAMPLE TALLYING COUNTER
    FOR ALL '.' REPLACING ALL '.' BY SPACE.
``` | T.F.X.JONES |
| ```
INSPECT SAMPLE TALLYING COUNTER
    FOR ALL LEADING SPACES.
``` | 1.23 |

2. What is the difference between the **STRING** and **UNSTRING** statements?
3. What is the function of the **DELIMITED** clause in the **STRING** statement? The **POINTER** clause?
4. What happens in the **UNSTRING** statement if there are too many substrings in the sending field to fit into the receiving fields? What if there are too few substrings to fill the receiving fields?

ANSWERS TO REVIEW QUESTIONS

1.

SAMPLE	COUNTER
No Change	4
$ 12.69	No Change
535 22 1583	2
9A6X77X.,XX	No Change
No Change	2
T F X JONES	3
No Change	7
```

2. The **STRING** statement takes strings from several elementary fields and connects them together to form one long string in a new field. The **UNSTRING** statement extracts strings from one elementary field and distributes them into several separate elementary fields.

3. The **DELIMITED** clause tells the program how to detect the end of a string in a sending field. The string might consist of the entire sending field, or just the portion terminated by a specified character. The **POINTER** clause tells the program where to start building the new string in the receiving field.

4. If there is not sufficient space in the receiving fields in an **UNSTRING** statement, the overflow condition is raised and the action specified in the **ON OVERFLOW** clause is executed. Any space in the receiving fields not filled by substrings from the sending field is left unchanged.

EXERCISES

*1. Write **INSPECT** statements to do the following.
   a. Change all the blank characters in **ITEM-A** to zeros.
   b. Change the first A in **ITEM-B** to 2.
   c. Place in **STRING-TALLY** a count of the number of leading asterisks in **ITEM-C**.
   d. Convert all leading asterisks in **ITEM-D** to zeros and place in **COUNTER** a count of the number of leading asterisks.
   e. Change all characters in **ITEM-E** that precede the first X to 9s.

2. Write **INSPECT** statements to do the following.
   a. Count the number of commas in **GRAND-TOTAL** and place that number in **COMMAS**.
   b. Replace the first blank in **LAST-NAME** with a period.
   c. Change all the characters in **ERROR-FIELD** up to the first hyphen to blanks, and place a count of the number of characters replaced in **COUNTER**.

*3. Assume that a customer record has the following format:

```
01  CUSTOMER-RECORD.
    05  CUSTOMER-NAME.
        10  LAST-NAME           PIC X(15).
        10  FIRST-NAME          PIC X(15).
        10  TITLE               PIC X(5).
    05  CUSTOMER-ADDRESS.
        10  HOUSE-NUMBER        PIC X(5).
        10  STREET-NAME         PIC X(15).
        10  CITY                PIC X(15).
        10  STATE               PIC X(15).
        10  ZIP                 PIC X(5).
    05  REST-OF-RECORD          PIC X(110).
```

---

* Answers to starred exercises will be found in Appendix IV at the end of the book.

TITLE contains the customer's title such as Mr., Mrs., Ms., Dr., etc. Using the customer record as input, write a program segment that will produce the heading and salutation for a form letter. There should be no extra blanks anywhere in the text. The output should resemble the following:

Ms. Mary Smith
123 Main St.
Anytown, Ohio 44999

Dear Ms. Smith:

4. Suppose you are given a file of records containing heading lines like the example shown in Exercise 3. The records have the format **PIC X(50)**, and there are three records for each customer; assume there are no errors in the data. Write a program that will read this file as input and create a file of customer records having the format shown at the start of Exercise 3; set **REST-OF-RECORD** to spaces.

CHAPTER 17

THE REPORT WRITER

17.1 INTRODUCTION

All the programs we have examined so far have required some form of printed output. Although we tended to make this output as simple as possible to save space and avoid complication, in actual programs preparing the formatted output for reports can require as much work as calculating the results to be reported. This is particularly true if the report involves control breaks, as we saw in Chapter 9; you may wish to review Chapter 9 before proceeding.

In this chapter we will present some features of COBOL that can simplify the work of producing reports. We will begin with some options available for sequential print files, then go on to discuss the COBOL Report Writer.

17.2 PRINT FILE ENHANCEMENTS

A task common to most reports is producing a heading at the top of each page. Using only the material we have presented so far, this requires defining a variable to be used as a line counter. The counter is initialized at the start of the program, incremented each time a line is printed or skipped over, tested to see if we are at the bottom of the page, then reset at the start of the next page. However, we can let COBOL do most of this work by using the LINAGE clause. To demonstrate how this works we have modified the payroll program of Figure 8.5 to allow the program to print the report on more than one page, with column headings at the top of each page. We have omitted those parts of the program that do not relate to producing the report, as seen in Figure 17.1.

```
1          IDENTIFICATION DIVISION.
2          PROGRAM-ID.
3             PAYROLL5.
4          DATE-WRITTEN.
5             JUNE 25, 1989.
6
```

```
 7              ENVIRONMENT DIVISION.
 8              INPUT-OUTPUT SECTION.
 9              FILE-CONTROL.
10                  SELECT PAYROLL-FILE        ASSIGN TO PAYROLL.
11                  SELECT REPORT-FILE         ASSIGN TO REPORT.
12
13              DATA DIVISION.
14              FILE SECTION.
15              FD  PAYROLL-FILE
16                  LABEL RECORDS ARE STANDARD.
17              01  PAYROLL-RECORD.
18                  05  I-PAYROLL-NUMBER      PIC X(5).
19                  05  I-NAME                PIC X(20).
20                  05  I-HOURS-WORKED        PIC 99V9.
21                  05  FILLER                PIC X(3).
22                  05  I-PAYRATE             PIC 99V999.
23                  05  I-DEPENDENTS          PIC 99.
24                  05  FILLER                PIC X(42).
25
26              FD  REPORT-FILE
27                  LABEL RECORDS ARE OMITTED
28                  LINAGE IS 15 LINES
29                      WITH FOOTING AT 15
30                      LINES AT TOP 3
31                      LINES AT BOTTOM 3.
32              01  REPORT-RECORD             PIC X(75).
33
34              WORKING-STORAGE SECTION.
                    .
                    .
                    .
40              77  W-OUT-OF-RECORDS-FLAG     PIC X.
41                  88  OUT-OF-RECORDS                        VALUE 'Y'.
                    .
                    .
                    .
51              01  HEADING-LINE-1.
52                  05  FILLER                PIC X(26)
53                      VALUE 'PAYROLL CALCULATION REPORT'.
54                  05  FILLER                PIC X(41)     VALUE SPACES.
55                  05  REPORT-DATE.
56                      10  MM                PIC Z9/.
57                      10  DD                PIC 99/.
58                      10  YY                PIC 99.
59
60              01  HEADING-LINE-2.
61                  05  FILLER                PIC X(42)
62                      VALUE 'NUMBER             NAME             HOURS  RATE '.
63                  05  FILLER                PIC X(29)
64                      VALUE ' DEP  GROSS      TAX      NET'.
65
66              01 NORMAL-OUTPUT-LINE.
67                  05  O-PAYROLL-NUMBER      PIC X(5).
68                  05  O-NAME                PIC BBX(20).
69                  05  O-HOURS-WORKED        PIC BBZ9.9.
70                  05  O-PAYRATE             PIC BBZ9.999.
71                  05  O-DEPENDENTS          PIC BBZ9.
72                  05  O-GROSS-PAY           PIC BB$$$9.99.
73                  05  O-TAX                 PIC BB$$$9.99.
74                  05  O-NET-PAY             PIC BB$$$9.99.
75
```

```
76          01   ERROR-RECORD.
77               05   BAD-DATA               PIC X(38).
78               05   FILLER                 PIC X(4)         VALUE SPACES.
79               05   ERROR-MESSAGE          PIC X(30).
80
81          01   MESSAGE-1                   PIC X(30)
82               VALUE 'INVALID DATA IN THIS RECORD'.
83          01   MESSAGE-2                   PIC X(30)
84               VALUE 'GROSS PAY SUSPICIOUSLY LARGE'.
85
86          01   W-TODAYS-DATE.
87               05   YY                     PIC 99.
88               05   MM                     PIC 99.
89               05   DD                     PIC 99.
90
91
92          PROCEDURE DIVISION.
93          A000-PRODUCE-PAYROLL-CALC.
94               OPEN INPUT  PAYROLL-FILE
95                    OUTPUT REPORT-FILE.
96               ACCEPT W-TODAYS-DATE FROM DATE.
97               MOVE CORRESPONDING W-TODAYS-DATE TO REPORT-DATE.
98               PERFORM X010-PRINT-COLUMN-HEADINGS.
99               PERFORM C010-GET-VALID-PAY-REC.
100              PERFORM B010-CALC-EMP-PAYROLL
101                  UNTIL OUT-OF-RECORDS.
102              CLOSE PAYROLL-FILE
103                    REPORT-FILE.
104              STOP RUN.
105
106         B010-CALC-EMP-PAYROLL.
107              PERFORM C020-COMPUTE-GROSS-PAY.
108              IF NO-SIZE-ERROR
109                  PERFORM C030-COMPUTE-EXEMPTIONS
110                  PERFORM C040-COMPUTE-TAX
111                  PERFORM C050-COMPUTE-NET-PAY
112                  PERFORM C060-PRINT-OUTPUT
113              ELSE
114                  PERFORM C070-PRINT-ERROR-OUTPUT.
115              PERFORM C010-GET-VALID-PAY-REC.
            .
            .
            .
153         C060-PRINT-OUTPUT.
154              MOVE I-PAYROLL-NUMBER      TO O-PAYROLL-NUMBER.
155              MOVE I-NAME                TO O-NAME.
156              MOVE I-HOURS-WORKED        TO O-HOURS-WORKED.
157              MOVE I-PAYRATE             TO O-PAYRATE.
158              MOVE I-DEPENDENTS          TO O-DEPENDENTS.
159              MOVE W-TAX                 TO O-TAX.
160              MOVE W-GROSS-PAY           TO O-GROSS-PAY.
161              MOVE W-NET-PAY             TO O-NET-PAY.
162              WRITE REPORT-RECORD FROM NORMAL-OUTPUT-LINE
163                        AFTER ADVANCING 1 LINE
164                       AT END-OF-PAGE
165                          PERFORM X010-PRINT-COLUMN-HEADINGS.
166
167         C070-PRINT-ERROR-OUTPUT.
168              MOVE PAYROLL-RECORD TO BAD-DATA.
169              MOVE MESSAGE-2 TO ERROR-MESSAGE.
```

```
170          WRITE REPORT-RECORD FROM ERROR-RECORD
171                    AFTER ADVANCING 1 LINE
172                    AT EOP PERFORM X010-PRINT-COLUMN-HEADINGS.
          .
          .
          .
183      E020-EDIT-PAYROLL-RECORD.
184          IF     I-PAYROLL-NUMBER IS NOT NUMERIC
185             OR I-HOURS-WORKED   IS NOT NUMERIC
186             OR I-PAYRATE        IS NOT NUMERIC
187             OR I-DEPENDENTS     IS NOT NUMERIC
188             MOVE PAYROLL-RECORD TO BAD-DATA
189             MOVE MESSAGE-1 TO ERROR-MESSAGE
190             WRITE REPORT-RECORD FROM ERROR-RECORD
191                    AFTER ADVANCING 1 LINE
192                    AT EOP PERFORM X010-PRINT-COLUMN-HEADINGS
193          ELSE
194             MOVE 'Y' TO W-VALID-RECORD-FLAG.
195
196      X010-PRINT-COLUMN-HEADINGS.
197          WRITE REPORT-RECORD FROM HEADING-LINE-1
198                    AFTER ADVANCING PAGE.
199          WRITE REPORT-RECORD FROM HEADING-LINE-2
200                    AFTER ADVANCING 2 LINES.
201          MOVE SPACES TO REPORT-RECORD.
202          WRITE REPORT-RECORD AFTER ADVANCING 2 LINES.
```

FIGURE 17.1 A report program using the **LINAGE** clause and **WRITE** statement enhancements.

The **SELECT** statements and the **FD** entry for **PAYROLL-FILE** are the same as they were in Figure 8.5, but the **FD** for **REPORT-FILE** has a new clause, the **LINAGE** clause. The **LINAGE** clause divides the report page into three sections: blank space at the top of the page (**LINES AT TOP**), blank space at the bottom of the page (**LINES AT BOTTOM**), and the body of the report (**LINAGE**) which contains *all* text printed by the **COBOL** program, including column headings. In the program above, for example, there will be 3 blank lines at the top of each page, 3 blank lines at the bottom of each page, and 15 lines in the report body, including the 5 lines used by the column headings; this gives a total page length of 21 lines. Normally a page is much longer than this, typically 66 lines, and we have used a shorter page only for this example. If we were printing the report on standard paper, the **LINAGE** clause might look like the following:

```
LINAGE IS 60 LINES
    WITH FOOTING AT 60
    LINES AT TOP 3
    LINES AT BOTTOM 3.
```

The **FOOTING** clause is used in connection with the **WRITE** statement, and we will discuss this shortly.

In the Procedure Division, the first paragraph is much as it was in Figure 8.5, with a few minor changes. First, we have moved the code that initializes the date field in the heading into the main paragraph. The heading will now be printed repeatedly, but we want to carry out the initialization only once. We also use **MOVE CORRESPONDING** to rearrange the fields in **REPORT-DATE** to a more familiar sequence. The second change in this paragraph simply involves renumbering the **CALC-EMP-PAYROLL** paragraph, since there is now only one paragraph at the **B** level.

In **B010-CALC-EMP-PAYROLL** the only change is that we have taken the code that prints erroneous data and moved it to a separate paragraph.

Paragraphs **C010-GET-VALID-PAY-REC** through **C050-COMPUTE-NET-PAY** are unchanged, which brings us to **C060-PRINT-NORMAL-OUTPUT** and the **END-OF-PAGE** clause in the **WRITE** statement. This new clause makes use of the **LINAGE** information in the **FD** entry to tell when it is time to skip to a new page. Whenever you specify a **LINAGE** clause for a file, **COBOL** automatically creates a special reserved variable for that file called **LINAGE-COUNTER**. When you open the file for output or when you start a new page, **LINAGE-COUNTER** is automatically set to one. Whenever you write to the file, **LINAGE-COUNTER** is incremented by the number of lines specified in the **ADVANCING** clause, so that it always points to the line being written on the page. When a **WRITE** statement causes **LINAGE-COUNTER** to become greater than or equal to the value in the **FOOTING** clause, the **END-OF-PAGE** condition becomes true and the statement in the **AT END-OF-PAGE** clause is executed.

The order in which some of these actions takes place is critical. When **LINAGE-COUNTER** becomes greater than or equal to the **FOOTING** value, the **WRITE** statement prints the current line, and only then is the **END-OF-PAGE** action executed. Consider what this means in the current example. We begin the program by printing a heading at the top of a page, which takes five lines including the two blanks printed after the second line of text. **LINAGE-COUNTER** is now set to 5. When we print the first line of output, the **ADVANCING** clause specifies

```
AFTER ADVANCING 1 LINE
```

so **LINAGE-COUNTER** is now set to 6. This continues for the next eight records. When we are ready to print the tenth record (on line 15), the following actions occur:

1. **LINAGE-COUNTER** is incremented to 15;
2. The program detects that **LINAGE-COUNTER** is equal to the **FOOTING** value and prepares the **END-OF-PAGE** condition;
3. The **WRITE** statement prints the current line;
4. The **END-OF-PAGE** action is executed;
5. Because the **END-OF-PAGE** action causes the printer to skip to the top of a new page, **LINAGE-COUNTER** is reset to 1.

The **WRITE** statement in **C070-PRINT-ERROR-OUTPUT** is almost identical to that of the previous paragraph, except that we use **EOP** instead of **END-OF-PAGE**. **EOP** is an acceptable abbreviation for **END-OF-PAGE** and the meanings are identical. We have used both formats only to demonstrate the alternatives.

We can now show the complete **WRITE** statement for sequential files; see the top of the next page.

The output from the program is shown in Figure 17.2 and is much the same as in Chapter 8. There are three blank lines at the top of each page and three at the bottom. Dashed lines show where the page margins would be.

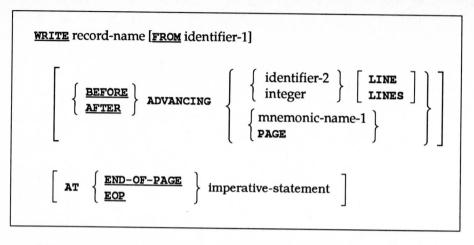

We conclude this section by mentioning that the LINAGE-COUNTER can be referred to (but not changed) in the Procedure Division. For example, if we wanted to allow several lines at the bottom of the page so that certain text was not split over two pages, we might write

```
IF LINAGE-COUNTER IS GREATER THAN 55
    PERFORM X010-PRINT-COLUMN-HEADINGS.
```

If more than one file has a LINAGE clause, its use can be qualified by the file name. For example,

```
IF LINAGE-COUNTER OF ERROR-REPORT-FILE > 55 . . .
```

17.3 REPORT WRITER CONCEPTS

Although the LINAGE and END-OF-PAGE clauses simplify some of the work of producing reports, a considerable amount still remains for the programmer to do. However, many of the tasks needed to produce a report are repeated from report to report and follow much the same pattern in many types of reports. The function of the Report Writer is to let the computer do the routine work for you. In particular, the Report Writer performs the following activities:

1. Detects control breaks;
2. Computes subtotals for control groups, as well as a grand total for the entire report;
3. Prints headings and footings before and after control groups;
4. Controls the page format, including producing headings and footings on each page.

The statements used to control the Report Writer are found in three places in the program. First, in the File Section we put a clause in the FD entry for the report file that tells the program that this report will be generated by the Report Writer. Second, in a new section of the Data Division called the *Report Section* we define what the report is to look like. This includes describing the format of the report pages, telling what headings and footings look like, defining control groups and control variables, and generally specifying what various lines on a page will look like and where report data will come from. Finally, in the Procedure Division we have a few simple statements that start a

```
----------------------------------------------------------------


PAYROLL CALCULATION REPORT                                4/22/87

NUMBER        NAME            HOURS  RATE   DEP  GROSS     TAX      NET


12345  THOS H. KELLY          20.0   5.350   0  $107.00  $22.47  $84.53
12401  HENRY JENSEN           40.0   7.500   1  $300.00  $52.50 $247.50
12511  NANCY KAHN             40.0   7.500   3  $300.00  $31.50 $268.50
UILKMB. R. BROOKS        400   0575002   INVALID DATA IN THIS RECORD
26017  JANE MILANO            10.0   6.875   3   $68.75   $0.00  $68.75
12  4KAY DELUCCIA          400   0600004   INVALID DATA IN THIS RECORD
26109  PETER W. SHERWOOD      40.0  10.000   5  $400.00  $31.50 $368.50
26222  GEORGE M. MULVANEY     41.0  10.000   5  $415.00  $34.65 $380.35
26500A. W. ENWRIGHT        40   0545001   INVALID DATA IN THIS RECORD
27511  RUTH GARRISON          50.0  10.000   4  $550.00  $73.50 $476.50


----------------------------------------------------------------


PAYROLL CALCULATION REPORT                                4/22/87

NUMBER        NAME            HOURS  RATE   DEP  GROSS     TAX      NET


28819  LEO X. BUTLER          40.1  10.000   2  $401.50  $63.32 $338.18
28820D. X. IANNUZZI      450   4.50003   INVALID DATA IN THIS RECORD
28821K. L. NG, JR.       350    450003   INVALID DATA IN THIS RECORD
28822DANIEL REINER       350   045000C   INVALID DATA IN THIS RECORD
28822L. E. SIMON         388   06000 3   INVALID DATA IN THIS RECORD
28839QA. REAL BAD-ONE    3 8   4.5KJXX   INVALID DATA IN THIS RECORD
7HGV6GARBAGE-CASE-1      ..M.,M.,M.,M.   INVALID DATA IN THIS RECORD
 NJI9GARBAGE-CASE-2      GV 6 46  8  H   INVALID DATA IN THIS RECORD
     GARBAGE-CASE-3 ----------++++++,M   INVALID DATA IN THIS RECORD
29000  ANNE HENDERSON         40.2  10.000   3  $403.00  $53.13 $349.87


----------------------------------------------------------------


PAYROLL CALCULATION REPORT                                4/22/87

NUMBER        NAME            HOURS  RATE   DEP  GROSS     TAX      NET


29001  JULIA KIPP             40.3  10.000   1  $404.50  $74.45 $330.05
99999IMA TESTCASE        999   9999999   GROSS PAY SUSPICIOUSLY LARGE


----------------------------------------------------------------
```

FIGURE 17.2 Output from the program in Figure 17.1.

report, tell what data will be used in producing the report, and terminate the report. The bulk of these specifications will fall in the Report Section of the Data Division. In most cases, if you can define the format of the report you have done the hardest part of using the Report Writer.

To demonstrate how the Report Writer works, we will revise the three-level control program presented in Figure 9.7.

17.4   THE THREE-LEVEL CONTROL PROGRAM

Recall that the three-level control program is based on a simple sales accounting system. A company has divided its sales territory into several regions, each of which is identified by a five-character code. In addition, each salesperson and each customer account is identified by other five-character codes. As input to the program we are given a file of account records, each of which specifies a sales region, a salesperson, an account, and the amount of the sale. The file is sorted by region, salesperson, and account, in that order. The purpose of the program is to produce a report that shows the total sales for each region, the total sales for each salesperson within the region, and the total sales for each of the salesperson's customers.

This report is unusual in that the individual sales records—the detail records that contain the basic data—do not appear in the report. The report is actually a summary, showing only totals for each of the control variables. To demonstrate a more typical use of the Report Writer, we shall produce a slight variation of this report to show the sales records as well as the totals. The program is shown in Figure 17.3, and a sample of the report is in Figure 17.4.

```
1        IDENTIFICATION DIVISION.
2        PROGRAM-ID.
3             3LEVEL3A.
4        AUTHOR.
5             D. GOLDEN.
6        DATE-WRITTEN.
7             JUNE 25, 1989.
8        *
9        *    THIS PROGRAM PRODUCES A SIMPLE THREE-LEVEL REPORT FOR A
10       *    SALES ACCOUNTING SYSTEM, USING THE COBOL REPORT WRITER
11       *
12
13       ENVIRONMENT DIVISION.
14       INPUT-OUTPUT SECTION.
15       FILE-CONTROL.
16           SELECT ACCOUNT-FILE        ASSIGN TO ACCOUNT.
17           SELECT REPORT-FILE         ASSIGN TO REPORT.
18
19       DATA DIVISION.
20       FILE SECTION.
21
22       FD  ACCOUNT-FILE
23           LABEL RECORDS ARE STANDARD.
24       01  ACCOUNT-RECORD.
```

```
25          05   REGION-NUMBER               PIC X(5).
26          05   SELLER-NUMBER               PIC X(5).
27          05   ACCOUNT-NUMBER              PIC X(5).
28          05   SALE-AMOUNT                 PIC 9(5)V99.
29          05   FILLER                      PIC X(58).
30
31    FD   REPORT-FILE
32         REPORT IS SALES-REPORT
33         RECORD CONTAINS 85 CHARACTERS
34         LABEL RECORDS ARE OMITTED.
35
36   WORKING-STORAGE SECTION.
37
38    77   MORE-DATA-FLAG              PIC X.
39         88   NO-MORE-DATA               VALUE 'N'.
40
41   REPORT SECTION.
42    RD   SALES-REPORT
43         CONTROLS ARE FINAL
44                         REGION-NUMBER
45                         SELLER-NUMBER
46                         ACCOUNT-NUMBER
47         PAGE LIMIT IS 63 LINES
48              HEADING       3
49              FIRST DETAIL 7
50              LAST DETAIL  59
51              FOOTING       63.
52    01   TYPE IS PAGE HEADING.
53         05   LINE IS 3.
54              10   COLUMN 72               PIC X(5)   VALUE 'PAGE '.
55              10   COLUMN 77               PIC ZZ9
56                      SOURCE IS PAGE-COUNTER.
57         05   LINE IS 5.
58              10   COLUMN 1                PIC X(35)
59                      VALUE 'REGION     TOTAL   SELLER     TOTAL'.
60              10   COLUMN 39               PIC X(27)
61                      VALUE 'ACCOUNT   AMOUNT      TOTAL'.
62              10   COLUMN 69               PIC X(11)
63                      VALUE 'FINAL TOTAL'.
64    01   CUSTOMER-SALE TYPE DETAIL LINE PLUS 1.
65         05   COLUMN 39                    PIC Z(4)9
66                      SOURCE IS ACCOUNT-NUMBER.
67         05   COLUMN 45   PIC $$$,$$9.99 SOURCE IS SALE-AMOUNT.
68    01   TYPE CONTROL FOOTING ACCOUNT-NUMBER LINE PLUS 1.
69         05   COLUMN 39
70                   PIC Z(4)9 SOURCE IS ACCOUNT-NUMBER.
71         05   ACCOUNT-TOTAL-OUT   COLUMN 56
72                   PIC $$$,$$9.99 SUM SALE-AMOUNT.
73    01   TYPE CONTROL FOOTING SELLER-NUMBER LINE PLUS 1.
74         05   COLUMN 20
75                   PIC Z(4)9 SOURCE IS SELLER-NUMBER.
76         05   SELLER-TOTAL-OUT COLUMN 26
77                   PIC $$$,$$9.99 SUM ACCOUNT-TOTAL-OUT.
78    01   TYPE CONTROL FOOTING REGION-NUMBER LINE PLUS 1.
79         05   COLUMN 1
80                   PIC Z(4)9       SOURCE IS REGION-NUMBER.
81         05   REGION-TOTAL-OUT COLUMN 7
82                   PIC $$$,$$9.99 SUM SELLER-TOTAL-OUT.
```

```
83          01   TYPE CONTROL FOOTING FINAL LINE PLUS 1.
84               05   COLUMN 69
85                           PIC $$$$,$$9.99 SUM REGION-TOTAL-OUT.
86
87
88          PROCEDURE DIVISION.
89          A000-PREPARE-SALES-REPORT.
90               OPEN   INPUT ACCOUNT-FILE
91                      OUTPUT REPORT-FILE.
92               MOVE 'Y' TO MORE-DATA-FLAG.
93               INITIATE SALES-REPORT.
94               READ ACCOUNT-FILE
95                      AT END MOVE 'N' TO MORE-DATA-FLAG.
96               PERFORM B010-PROCESS-SALES-REPORT
97                  UNTIL NO-MORE-DATA.
98               TERMINATE SALES-REPORT.
99               CLOSE ACCOUNT-FILE
100                      REPORT-FILE.
101              STOP RUN.
102
103         B010-PROCESS-SALES-REPORT.
104              GENERATE CUSTOMER-SALE.
105              READ ACCOUNT-FILE
106                     AT END MOVE 'N' TO MORE-DATA-FLAG.
107
108         *********************** END OF PROGRAM ***********************
```

FIGURE 17.3 A program that produces a three-level control break report using the **COBOL** Report Writer.

The first change from the program used in Chapter 9 occurs in the **FD** entry for **REPORT-FILE**. We have two new clauses, **REPORT IS** and **RECORD CONTAINS**, but more unusual is the fact that there is no record description for this file! The clause

REPORT IS SALES-REPORT

tells the **COBOL** compiler that all output to **REPORT-FILE** will be produced by a report named **SALES-REPORT** that will be defined in a later part of the Data Division. Therefore, we do not define any file records in the **FD** entry. However, we do want to tell the compiler how long each record is to be, and this is accomplished by the clause

REPORT CONTAINS 85 CHARACTERS

which specifies enough space for an 85-character line of text.

The next change is in the Working-Storage Section, and it is a striking one. All Working-Storage data but the end-of-file flag has been deleted. None of this data is needed any longer since all the work that it performed in the original program is now performed in the Report Section.

The Report Section comes after the Working-Storage Section (and before the Screen Section, if one is used) and specifies the format of all headings and report lines, as well as telling how the report is to be computed. We shall skip over this section for the moment and look at the remainder of the program, returning to the Report Section after we have seen the output from the program.

The main paragraph of the Procedure Division looks fairly familiar in format, although there are some new statements. The most obvious change from Chapter 9 is that the paragraph is much shorter than in the original program. We begin by opening the two files that the program uses, including **REPORT-FILE**. Even though the output to this file is controlled by the Report Writer, we must still open and close it just as we would any other file.

After initializing the end-of-file flag for the input file, we execute a new statement, **INITIATE SALES-REPORT**. **SALES-REPORT** is the name of the report defined in the Report Section, and the **INITIATE** statement prepares this report for execution. Various counters, totals, and flags, including a line counter and a page counter, all internal to the Report Writer and mostly invisible to the programmer, are given their initial values. At this point the Report Writer is ready to produce the first line of output, but nothing has been written yet.

The next two statements of the driver paragraph read the first input record and perform the paragraph that controls the report output. Both of these statements are much as they were in previous programs.

After the program has read all the data in **ACCOUNT-FILE**, we exit from the **PERFORM** statement and go on to another new statement, **TERMINATE SALES-REPORT**. As you might guess, this statement ends the report. Any outstanding totals are printed, including the grand total for company sales, and the report is concluded. Any attempt to write additional data to **SALES-REPORT** will produce an error.

The work paragraph, **B010-PRODUCE-SALES-REPORT**, consists of only two statements, a **GENERATE** statement and a **READ** statement. The **GENERATE** statement tells the Report Writer to produce one more line of detail on the report. In this example, the Report Writer takes the data in the current **ACCOUNT-RECORD** and prepares to write it to **SALES-REPORT**. However, it first checks to see if a control break has occurred. If so, any appropriate subtotals are printed and internal variables are reset before the detail record is printed.

It is clear that the Report Writer saves you a considerable amount of work. The Procedure Division in Figure 9.7 requires six paragraphs and about 70 lines of code, while the one in Figure 17.3 requires only two paragraphs and fewer than 20 lines of code. You should understand, however, that we have not reduced the amount of work that the *computer* has to do during execution. The amount of code in the object program is at least as great when you use the Report Writer as when you write the code yourself.

The report produced by this program is shown in Figure 17.4. The dashed line at the top of the report represents the page margin, and was inserted to emphasize the fact that there are three blank lines at the top of the page preceding the page heading. Although we have provided several detail records for each of the first three accounts, to save space the remaining accounts have only one record each. In a real program, of course, there would likely be many sales records for each account.

17.5   THE REPORT SECTION

Now that we have a sample report to look at, we will return to the Report Section of the program in Figure 17.3. Just as the File Section defines files with an **FD** entry, the Report Section defines reports with **RD** entries, each of which

REGION	TOTAL	SELLER	TOTAL	ACCOUNT	AMOUNT	TOTAL	FINAL TOTAL
				20	$11.50		
				20	$5.50		
				20		$17.00	
				24	$10.25		
				24	$10.00		
				24	$15.75		
				24		$36.00	
				27	$9.00		
				27	$101.00		
				27	$22.00		
				27	$42.60		
				27	$9.40		
				27		$184.00	
		1	$237.00				
				17	$26.00		
				17		$26.00	
				24	$266.90		
				24		$266.90	
		2	$292.90				
				10	$87.50		
				10		$87.50	
				16	$54.75		
				16		$54.75	
		12	$142.25				
1	$672.15						
				40	$50.12		
				40		$50.12	
				41	$105.99		
				41		$105.99	
		4	$156.11				
				44	$1,594.14		
				44		$1,594.14	
		39	$1,594.14				
2	$1,750.25						
				30	$1,180.94		
				30		$1,180.94	
				35	$69.26		
				35		$69.26	
				38	$157.43		
				38		$157.43	
				49	$45.00		
				49		$45.00	
				60	$1,234.56		
				60		$1,234.56	
				78	$276.02		
				78		$276.02	
		15	$2,963.21				
3	$2,963.21						
							$5,385.61

FIGURE 17.4 Example of a report using three-level control totals that was produced using the Report Writer. This output was produced by the program in Figure 17.3.

defines one report. Although our examples will use only one report, we can have as many reports as we wish, each defined by a separate **RD** entry.

The **RD** entry itself performs two functions: it defines the data names to be used as control variables in the report, and it defines the page format. The control variables are defined in the **CONTROLS ARE** clause; in this example the control variables are **FINAL**, **REGION-NUMBER**, **SELLER-NUMBER**, and **ACCOUNT-NUMBER**. **FINAL** is a reserved word that represents the highest level of control. In this program, for instance, it represents a grand total for the entire company. The use of **FINAL** is optional, but if we omit it we cannot produce a total for the company. In any case, control variables must always be listed in order from major to minor. They are usually fields of the input record and may not contain any editing characters in their PICTURE clauses.

The PAGE clause describes the overall format of the report page. It begins with PAGE LIMIT IS, which tells how many lines there are on one page of the report, from the first line of heading (including any blank lines) to the last line at the bottom. In our example we have specified a total of 63 lines.

The HEADING phrase indicates where the first line of heading will begin. We have specified that headings will begin on line 3, so lines 1 and 2 of each page will be blank.

The heading on our report consists of four lines, two of which contain text and two that are blank. Therefore, we want the first line of data to be printed on line 7. This is specified by the FIRST DETAIL phrase. In addition, this phrase controls the location of any subtotals, so that if the report requires more than one page no total line will be printed before line 7.

To determine where the last line of detail on a page will be printed (the sales amounts in this example) we use the LAST DETAIL phrase. Thus, no sales record will be printed after line 59. This leaves us lines 60-63 to print the subtotals for a group. The FOOTING phrase specifies that the last line of footing is line 63, which in this example is also the last line on the page. This means that we will allow subtotals to run to the bottom of the page. In other reports we might wish to allow some space at the bottom of the page for *page footings* just as we have *page headings* at the top of the page. In this case, the FOOTING clause would contain a value that is less than the value in the PAGE LIMIT phrase; later we will show an example of how page footings are used.

The remainder of the RD entry consists of a number of 01 level entries, each of which defines a *report group*. Basically, a report group is a series of one or more lines on a report that print as a group. Report groups fall into one of seven categories:

REPORT HEADING--the report heading appears once, at the start of a report; there may be at most one report heading per report.

PAGE HEADING—the page heading appears at the top of each page; there may be at most one page heading per report, which means that all pages in the report will have the same heading.

CONTROL HEADING—there may be one control heading given for each control variable listed in the CONTROLS ARE clause; the control heading is printed whenever a control break is detected for its associated variable, *before* the detail line containing the new value of the variable is printed.

DETAIL—a detail group is printed whenever a GENERATE statement is executed; there may be as many different detail groups as you wish, and the name specified in the GENERATE statement determines which detail group is to be printed.

CONTROL FOOTING—there may be one control footing associated with each control variable; the control footing is printed whenever a control break is detected for its associated variable, *after* the last detail line containing the old value of the variable has been printed.

PAGE FOOTING—the page footing appears at the bottom of each page; just as with the page heading, there may be at most one page footing per report.

REPORT FOOTING—the report footing appears once, at the end of the report; there may be at most one report footing per report.

We will discuss each of these types of report groups in more detail, including where they appear on the report, as we go through various examples.

The first report group definition for **SALES-REPORT** is a page heading group, and many of the features of this definition are typical of all report group definitions. To begin with, notice that neither the **01** level entry nor any of its subordinate entries has a data name. This is quite common in the Report Section. Although data names may be used (as you can see by the following definition), they are not required except for fields that you wish to refer to elsewhere in the program. Since page headings are produced automatically by the Report Writer, you need never refer to them explicitly so we don't bother with data names.

The first clause in the definition of the page heading group is the **TYPE** clause, which tells the compiler which of the seven report group types we are defining. This is followed by two 05-level subgroups that define the two lines of text in the heading. Each of these subgroups begins with a **LINE** clause that specifies the line on which the subgroup will be printed. In the page heading group, the first subgroup is on line 3 and the second subgroup is on line 5. As we will see in other group definitions, the **LINE** clause has several options; its complete format is:

$$\boxed{\text{LINE NUMBER IS} \quad \left\{ \begin{array}{l} \text{integer-1} \\ \underline{\text{PLUS}} \text{ integer-2} \\ \underline{\text{NEXT}} \text{ PAGE} \end{array} \right\}}$$

If we specify an integer, as in the current definition, the line is printed on the line specified; this is called an *absolute line number*. If we specify the **PLUS** option, the indicated number of lines is added to the current line position to determine where the output will be printed; this type of line number is called a *relative line number*. The **NEXT PAGE** option causes the printer to skip to the top of the next page before printing the line.

COBOL-85

The format for the **LINE** clause shown above is for **COBOL-74**. The format for **COBOL-85** is slightly different.

$$\boxed{\underline{\text{LINE}} \text{ NUMBER IS} \quad \left\{ \begin{array}{l} \text{integer-1} \quad [\text{ON } \underline{\text{NEXT PAGE}}] \\ \underline{\text{PLUS}} \text{ integer-2} \end{array} \right\}}$$

The only real difference that this format makes is that you can specify that the line should print on the next page starting on a line other than the first line of the page.

END COBOL-85

The **10**-level entries in the subgroups of the page heading group each represent one field on a line, and each begins with a **COLUMN** clause. This tells in which column of the line the field begins. The column numbers must always be integer constants, and must appear in ascending order for all fields on a line. Notice that we need not specify fillers for blank fields between fields; any unspecified column positions are automatically filled with blanks. Furthermore, even if you include a carriage control character at the start of the output record in the **FD** entry, this character is not considered part of the report line and may be ignored.

With one exception, the rest of this group definition is quite familiar. The **PICTURE** clause in a report group definition is used in exactly the same way as in any other part of the Data Division, as is the **VALUE** clause. The last new feature of this group definition is, of course, the **SOURCE** clause on line 56. This clause is analogous to a **MOVE** statement in the Procedure Division. It specifies that the value of the identifier named in the clause is to be moved into the current field whenever the report group is printed. In this case we have said that the identifier to be used as the source in the field is a **COBOL**-defined variable called **PAGE-COUNTER**. **PAGE-COUNTER** is used by the Report Writer to keep track of the current page number. It is set to 1 by the **INITIATE** statement, and is incremented by 1 every time the top of a new page is reached. In addition to **PAGE-COUNTER**, the identifier used in a **SOURCE** clause may be any data name defined outside the Report Section, or a special type of Report Section variable called a **SUM** counter; we shall discuss **SUM** counters shortly.

The next report group is a detail group (specified by the **TYPE DETAIL** clause), and has been given a data name, **CUSTOMER-SALE**, so that it can be referred to in the **GENERATE** statement in the Procedure Division. The **LINE** clause of this group has been included as part of the **01**-level entry because the group only defines one line. This **LINE** clause uses the **PLUS** option, which is equivalent to using **AFTER ADVANCING 1 LINE** in a **WRITE** statement.

The third report group is a control footing group. Control footings are always associated with specific control variables, and the variable name must follow immediately after the **TYPE** clause; in this case we are defining the control footing associated with **ACCOUNT-NUMBER**. When a control break occurs for **ACCOUNT-NUMBER** or any control variable higher than **ACCOUNT-NUMBER** in the control hierarchy, the control footing for **ACCOUNT-NUMBER** is printed. The footing is printed after any control footings for subordinate control variables, and before any control footings for higher level control variables. All control footings being printed are printed before the detail line that triggered the control break is printed.

The control footing group introduces a new clause, the **SUM** clause, shown on line 72. Unlike most other clauses, the **SUM** clause may be used *only* in a control footing group. Whenever a **SUM** clause is written the Report Writer creates a **SUM** counter. This counter is used to keep a total for a specified variable, **SALE-AMOUNT** in this case. Notice that **SALE-AMOUNT** is the same variable that was used in the **SOURCE** clause in the preceding detail group. The **SUM** counter is set to zero by the **INITIATE** statement, and is incremented by the current value of **SALE-AMOUNT** each time a **GENERATE** statement is executed for **CUSTOMER-SALE**. After the control footing has been printed, the **SUM** counter is reset to zero and the process repeats. It is important to remember that if the variable being summed is not defined within the Report Section, it must be used as a **SOURCE** variable in a detail group. This is the only way that the Report Writer knows when to update the value of the **SUM** counter.

The next report group is also a control footing group, this time for **SELLER-NUMBER**. The format of this group is much the same as for the previous group, except for one difference in the **SUM** clause. The identifier named in the **SUM** clause on line 77 is the data name associated with the **SUM** clause in the control footing for **ACCOUNT-NUMBER**. Every time the control footing for **AC-COUNT-NUMBER** is printed, the value of its **SUM** counter is added to the **SUM** counter on line 77. In other words, instead of using a variable named in a **SOURCE** clause as the object of a summation, you can also use the **SUM** counter of any lower level control footing. Thus the reason we gave a data name to the entry defined on lines 71-72 is so that the **SUM** counter could be referenced on line 77.

The remaining control groups are also control footings and are much the same as the footing for **SELLER-NUMBER**. For the final control footing we have used a subordinate entry (**05**-level) even though we are only defining one field on one line. Alternatively, we could define the report group in a single entry as follows:

```
01   TYPE CONTROL FOOTING FINAL
         LINE PLUS 1
         COLUMN 69  PIC $$$$,$$9.99 SUM REGION-TOTAL-OUT.
```

Either approach may be used and the choice is largely a matter of personal taste.

17.6 ADDITIONAL REPORT WRITER FEATURES

Suppose we decide that we want to make a few simple changes to the report we just produced. To begin with, we would like to start the output for each region at the top of a new page. In addition, we want to put two blank lines between the last region total and the final total. Both of these changes are accomplished quite easily.

To start each region at the top of a new page, we modify the control footing group for **REGION-NUMBER** as follows:

```
01   TYPE CONTROL FOOTING REGION-NUMBER LINE PLUS 1
                 NEXT GROUP NEXT PAGE.
     05  ...
```

In other words, we simply add the clause

```
NEXT GROUP NEXT PAGE
```

The **NEXT GROUP** clause acts very much like the **LINE** clause, but instead of affecting the printing of the *current* report group, it affects the printing of the *next* report group to be printed. The options for this clause are the same as for the **LINE** clause; we could print the next group on an absolute line number, on a relative line number, or at the top of the next page. The **NEXT GROUP** option does not actually override the **LINE** clause of the following group. Rather, it specifies what line spacing is to take place after the current group has been printed. For example, if we had specified

NEXT GROUP PLUS 2

the program would print two blank lines following the control footing for **REGION-NUMBER**, then print whatever group came next using that group's standard line spacing.

To insert blank lines before the final line, we simply change the **LINE** clause in the control footing group for **FINAL** to **LINE PLUS 3**. The resulting output is shown in Figure 17.5. As in previous examples, the dashed lines represent page margins. To save space, we do not show the blank space at the bottom of each page.

17.7   A COMPREHENSIVE EXAMPLE

To conclude this chapter we present a version of the sales accounting program that uses all the features of the Report Writer that we have presented. The Report Section for this example is shown in Figure 17.6, and the output is shown in Figure 17.7. So that the line spacing produced by the report is very clear, we have added markers and line numbers to the left of each line. These markers are *not* part of the output; they were added to emphasize the page format.

We have set the **PAGE LIMIT** to 35 lines, with **LAST DETAIL** and **FOOTING** modified accordingly, to demonstrate some of the line spacing that will occur. Following the **RD** entry we have the first new report group, a report heading group. This group simply prints the company name at the start of the report. You can see in Figure 17.7 that the report heading appears at the top of the first page but not on any of the other pages. However, in order to allow room for the report heading on line 4 of page 1 we must start the page heading on line 6, which is where it prints on all pages regardless of whether or not the report heading is also printed. Notice that the first line of the page heading has been modified to print a title (SALES REPORT) instead of a page number. The page number will be printed in the page footing, which we will discuss shortly.

After the page heading we have a control heading for **REGION-NUMBER**. The control heading is similar to the control footing in that we must specify the control variable with which the heading is associated. However, control headings do not contain **SUM** clauses since headings are printed at the start of a control group, before any summation for the group has been done. In this example we simply print the number of the region about to be processed.

Notice the control break at the start of region 2 on page 2 of the output. The control break is generated when the Report Writer realizes that the region number on the sales record for account 40 is not the same as the region number on the previous sales record for account 16. At this point a control break is generated for **REGION-NUMBER** and all subordinate control variables, **SELLER-NUMBER** and **ACCOUNT-NUMBER** in this case. It would make no difference whether either **SELLER-NUMBER** or **ACCOUNT-NUMBER** had changed value, although both did in this example. Whenever a control break is generated for a control variable it is also generated for all lower level control variables. The control footings are then printed in order from lowest level to highest, followed by the control headings for the new control groups. If we had defined more than one control heading they would print from highest to lowest.

```
--------------------------------------------------------------------------------
                                                             PAGE    1
REGION    TOTAL    SELLER    TOTAL    ACCOUNT   AMOUNT       TOTAL    FINAL TOTAL
                                        20      $11.50
                                        20       $5.50
                                        20                  $17.00
                                        24      $10.25
                                        24      $10.00
                                        24      $15.75
                                        24                  $36.00
                                        27       $9.00
                                        27     $101.00
                                        27      $22.00
                                        27      $42.60
                                        27       $9.40
                                        27                 $184.00
                      1     $237.00
                                        17      $26.00
                                        17                  $26.00
                                        24     $266.90
                                        24                 $266.90
                      2     $292.90
                                        10      $87.50
                                        10                  $87.50
                                        16      $54.75
                                        16                  $54.75
                     12     $142.25
            1    $672.15
            .
            .
            .
--------------------------------------------------------------------------------
                                                             PAGE    2
REGION    TOTAL    SELLER    TOTAL    ACCOUNT   AMOUNT       TOTAL    FINAL TOTAL
                                        40      $50.12
                                        40                  $50.12
                                        41     $105.99
                                        41                 $105.99
                      4     $156.11
                                        44   $1,594.14
                                        44               $1,594.14
                     39  $1,594.14
            2  $1,750.25
            .
            .
            .
--------------------------------------------------------------------------------
                                                             PAGE    3
REGION    TOTAL    SELLER    TOTAL    ACCOUNT   AMOUNT       TOTAL    FINAL TOTAL
                                        30   $1,180.94
                                        30               $1,180.94
                                        35      $69.26
                                        35                  $69.26
                                        38     $157.43
                                        38                 $157.43
                                        49      $45.00
                                        49                  $45.00
                                        60   $1,234.56
                                        60               $1,234.56
                                        78     $276.02
                                        78                 $276.02
                     15  $2,963.21
            3  $2,963.21
                                                                     $5,385.61
--------------------------------------------------------------------------------
```

FIGURE 17.5 Output demonstrating the use of the NEXT GROUP clause.

```
43          REPORT SECTION.
44          RD  SALES-REPORT
45              CONTROLS ARE FINAL
46                          REGION-NUMBER
47                          SELLER-NUMBER
48                          ACCOUNT-NUMBER
49              PAGE LIMIT IS 35 LINES
50                  HEADING        4
51                  FIRST DETAIL 10
52                  LAST DETAIL   29
53                  FOOTING       33.
54          01  TYPE IS REPORT HEADING LINE 4
55                  COLUMN 39                PIC X(15)
56                      VALUE 'ABC CORPORATION'.
57          01  TYPE IS PAGE HEADING.
58              05  LINE IS 6.
59                  10  COLUMN 40            PIC X(12)
60                          VALUE 'SALES REPORT'.
61              05  LINE IS 7.
62                  10  COLUMN 1             PIC X(35)
63                          VALUE 'REGION     TOTAL    SELLER     TOTAL'.
64                  10  COLUMN 39            PIC X(27)
65                          VALUE 'ACCOUNT   AMOUNT       TOTAL'.
66                  10  COLUMN 69            PIC X(11)
67                          VALUE 'FINAL TOTAL'.
68          01  TYPE CONTROL HEADING REGION-NUMBER LINE PLUS 2.
69              05  COLUMN 1
70                      PIC X(20) VALUE '-----  BEGIN REGION '.
71              05  COLUMN 21
72                      PIC Z(4)9 SOURCE REGION-NUMBER.
73          01  CUSTOMER-SALE TYPE DETAIL LINE PLUS 1.
74              05  COLUMN 39                PIC Z(4)9
75                      SOURCE IS ACCOUNT-NUMBER
76                      GROUP INDICATE.
77              05  COLUMN 45  PIC $$$,$$9.99 SOURCE IS SALE-AMOUNT.
78          01  TYPE CONTROL FOOTING ACCOUNT-NUMBER LINE PLUS 1.
79              05  COLUMN 39
80                      PIC Z(4)9 SOURCE IS ACCOUNT-NUMBER.
81              05  ACCOUNT-TOTAL-OUT  COLUMN 56
82                      PIC $$$,$$9.99 SUM SALE-AMOUNT.
83          01  TYPE CONTROL FOOTING SELLER-NUMBER LINE PLUS 1.
84              05  COLUMN 20
85                      PIC Z(4)9 SOURCE IS SELLER-NUMBER.
86              05  SELLER-TOTAL-OUT COLUMN 26
87                      PIC $$$,$$9.99 SUM ACCOUNT-TOTAL-OUT.
88          01  TYPE CONTROL FOOTING REGION-NUMBER LINE PLUS 1
89                      NEXT GROUP PLUS 5.
90              05  COLUMN 1
91                      PIC Z(4)9      SOURCE IS REGION-NUMBER.
92              05  REGION-TOTAL-OUT COLUMN 7
93                      PIC $$$,$$9.99 SUM SELLER-TOTAL-OUT.
94          01  TYPE CONTROL FOOTING FINAL LINE PLUS 3.
95              05  COLUMN 69
96                      PIC $$$$,$$9.99 SUM REGION-TOTAL-OUT.
97          01  TYPE PAGE FOOTING LINE 34.
98              05  COLUMN 40                PIC X(4) VALUE 'PAGE'.
99              05  COLUMN 45                PIC ZZ9  SOURCE IS PAGE-COUNTER.
100         01  TYPE REPORT FOOTING LINE PLUS 5
101             COLUMN 35
102                     PIC X(27) VALUE '-----  END OF REPORT  -----'.
```

FIGURE 17.6 The Report Section for a comprehensive Report Writer example.

Observe also that the Report Writer prints the region number of the *old* control group on the control footing, and prints the region number of the *new* group on the control heading.

The next report group definition is for the detail group CUSTOMER-SALE. This group is basically unchanged, with one exception. When we print the individual sale amounts, the account number is printed for each sale, which makes it difficult to see where one account number stops and the next one begins. To make it easier to spot the start of a new account, we wish to print the account number only for the first record of an account and leave the field blank for all following records of the account. We accomplish this with the GROUP INDICATE clause. The GROUP INDICATE clause may only be used in an elementary item of a TYPE DETAIL report group. It tells the Report Writer that the field is to be printed only the first time the group is printed after a control or page break.

The next four report groups are the control footings that we have seen in previous examples. The only change here is that we have modified the NEXT GROUP clause of the REGION-NUMBER footing to advance 5 lines instead of skipping to a new page. This was done simply to make it easier to observe the line spacing action of the NEXT GROUP clause. In Figure 17.7 we see that the footing group for region 1 is printed on line 15 of page 2, and that the heading group for region 2 is printed on line 22. This comes about because of the combination of the NEXT GROUP clause in the footing group and the LINE clause of the heading group. The NEXT GROUP clause increments the line counter by 5 after the footing group has been printed, bringing the counter to 20. The LINE clause of the heading group then increments the counter by 2, so the next output is printed on line 22. However, observe the line spacing following the footing group for region 3 on page 3. The output for this group appears on line 24, while the output for the next group, the FINAL control footing, appears on line 27. The reason for this is that the NEXT GROUP clause takes effect only if the next group is for a control variable at the same level or lower than the variable controlling the NEXT GROUP. In other words, when the next group to be printed is at the same level as or lower than REGION-NUMBER, the NEXT GROUP clause affects the spacing; but when the control variable for the next group is FINAL, which is higher than REGION-NUMBER, the NEXT GROUP clause is ignored.

Following the control footings is a page footing. We have simply taken the page number and moved it from the page heading to a page footing so that it prints at the bottom of the page. Notice that the footing prints on line 34, and that the FOOTING phrase of the PAGE LIMIT clause specifies FOOTING 33. The FOOTING phrase tells where the last line of *control* footing can be printed; *page* footings are printed in the space between the FOOTING limit and the end of the page. In this example, that means that page footings can be printed on lines 34 and 35.

The last control group is for the report footing. Observe that the report footing happens to print on a page by itself, at the top of the page, and that there is no page number on that page. The last line of output (other than the page footing) is the grand total on line 27 of page 3. If we simply add 5 to the line counter at this point, as indicated by the LINE clause of the report footing, the report footing would print on line 32 and would be followed by the page footing on line 34. However, a report footing is *always* the last text printed on a report (which is why there is no page footing on page 4), so this spacing is not

```
---------------------------------------------------------------------------------
.
.
.                                    ABC CORPORATION
v
.                                    SALES REPORT
.REGION     TOTAL    SELLER    TOTAL   ACCOUNT   AMOUNT      TOTAL    FINAL TOTAL
.
.
1-----  BEGIN REGION    1
.                                        20      $11.50
.                                                 $5.50
.                                        20                 $17.00
.                                        24      $10.25
v                                                $10.00
.                                                $15.75
.                                        24                 $36.00
.                                        27       $9.00
.                                                $101.00
2                                                $22.00
.                                                $42.60
.                                                 $9.40
.                                        27                $184.00
.                        1    $237.00
v                                        17      $26.00
.                                        17                 $26.00
.                                        24     $266.90
.                                        24                $266.90
.                        2    $292.90
3
.
.
.
.                                    PAGE    1
v
---------------------------------------------------------------------------------
.
.
.
v
.                                    SALES REPORT
.REGION     TOTAL    SELLER    TOTAL   ACCOUNT   AMOUNT      TOTAL    FINAL TOTAL
.
.
1                                        10      $87.50
.                                        10                 $87.50
.                                        16      $54.75
.                                        16                 $54.75
.                       12    $142.25
v    1    $672.15
.
.
.
.
2
.
.-----  BEGIN REGION    2
.                                        40      $50.12
.                                        40                 $50.12
v                                        41     $105.99
.                                        41                $105.99
.                        4    $156.11
.                                        44   $1,594.14
.                                        44               $1,594.14
3                       39  $1,594.14
.    2  $1,750.25
.
.
.
.                                    PAGE    2
v
---------------------------------------------------------------------------------
.
.
```

```
 .
 .
 v
 .                                        SALES REPORT
REGION       TOTAL     SELLER     TOTAL  ACCOUNT   AMOUNT        TOTAL      FINAL TOTAL
 .
 .
1-----   BEGIN REGION        3
 .                                          30    $1,180.94
 .                                          30                 $1,180.94
 .                                          35       $69.26
 .                                          35                   $69.26
 v                                          38      $157.43
 .                                          38                  $157.43
 .                                          49       $45.00
 .                                          49                   $45.00
 .                                          60    $1,234.56
2                                           60                 $1,234.56
 .                                          78      $276.02
 .                                          78                  $276.02
 .                            15  $2,963.21
 .       3  $2,963.21
 v
 .                                                                          $5,385.61
 .
 .
3
 .
 .
 .
 .                                      PAGE    3
 .
------------------------------------------------------------------------------
 .
 .
 .                                -----  END OF REPORT  -----
 v
 .
   .
   .
   .
------------------------------------------------------------------------------
```

FIGURE 17.7 Output from the program in Figure 17.6. This output is comprehensive in that it shows an example of every type of report group.

allowed. To avoid this conflict, the Report Writer ejects a page if the report footing would precede the page footing, sets the line counter to the start of the heading area (line 4), then prints the report footing on this line.

17.8 SUMMARY

The Report Writer features shown in this chapter are sufficient to produce most of the reports shown in this book, and to print much more detail than has been used in many of them. However, there are several features of the Report Writer that are beyond the scope of this book and that should be studied by the more experienced COBOL programmer in a COBOL manual or an advanced textbook. In any case, while the Report Writer is a powerful tool and can save you considerable work, there are times when the only way to produce exactly the output format you want is to use standard Procedure Division code.

REVIEW QUESTIONS

1. What is the general function of the **LINAGE** clause? What are the components of the clause and what is the function of each component?

2. What event in a program creates an end-of-page condition?

3. When an end-of-page condition occurs, what actions are performed by the **EOP** clause?

4. How does the **COBOL** compiler know to which file the output of a report should be directed?

5. What are the Report Writer statements that appear in the Procedure Division? What is the function of each?

6. List the seven report groups; what is the function of each group?

7. Suppose you have the following report groups:

   a. ``01  TYPE CONTROL FOOTING FINAL LINE PLUS 3``
   ``        PIC Z(5)9.99 SUM DETAIL-AMOUNT.``

   b. ``01  TYPE REPORT FOOTING LINE PLUS 3``
   ``        PIC Z(5)9.99 SUM DETAIL-AMOUNT.``

   What would be the difference between using one group or the other?

8. Give the format of the **PAGE** clause of the Report Writer, and tell the function of each part of the clause.

9. Suppose that a report contains several control heading groups and several control footing groups. In what order will the output be printed when a control break occurs?

10. What is the difference in function between the **LINE** clause and the **NEXT GROUP** clause?

11. Assume that the following code is part of a report program.

```
FD  INPUT-FILE
    LABEL RECORDS ARE STANDARD.
01  INPUT-RECORD.
    05  ACCOUNT-NUMBER      PIC X(5).
    05  JAN-SALES           PIC 9(5)V99.
    05  FEB-SALES           PIC 9(5)V99.
    05  MAR-SALES           PIC 9(5)V99.
    .
    .
    .

REPORT SECTION.
RD  SALES-REPORT
    CONTROL IS FINAL
    .
    .
    .
01  SALES-LINE TYPE DETAIL LINE PLUS 1.
    05  COLUMN 11           PIC X(5)       SOURCE ACCOUNT-NUMBER.
    05  COLUMN 19           PIC ZZ,ZZ9.99 SOURCE JAN-SALES.
    05  COLUMN 34           PIC ZZ,ZZ9.99 SOURCE FEB-SALES.
    05  COLUMN 49           PIC ZZ,ZZ9.99 SOURCE MAR-SALES.
```

```
01  TYPE CONTROL FOOTING FINAL LINE PLUS 3
    05  COLUMN 1            PIC X(14) VALUE '1ST QTR TOTALS'.
    05  JAN-TOTAL COLUMN 16 PIC Z,ZZZ,ZZ9.99 SUM JAN-SALES.
    05  FEB-TOTAL COLUMN 31 PIC Z,ZZZ,ZZ9.99 SUM FEB-SALES.
    05  MAR-TOTAL COLUMN 46 PIC Z,ZZZ,ZZ9.99 SUM MAR-SALES.
    05  QTR-TOTAL COLUMN 61 PIC Z,ZZZ,ZZ9.99
                            SUM JAN-TOTAL FEB-TOTAL MAR-TOTAL.
```

What do you think will be printed for the **FINAL** control footing group?

ANSWERS TO REVIEW QUESTIONS

1. The **LINAGE** clause is used in the **FD** entry of a sequential file that is going to a printer, and it controls the general format of a page of output. The **LINAGE** phrase tells how many lines of text, including any headings, can be written on a page. The **FOOTING** phrase specifies where the last line of nonfooting output can be printed; any lines between the line given in the **FOOTING** phrase and the end of the page are reserved for footing text. The **LINES AT TOP** phrase tells how many blank lines will appear at the top of the page; it is not possible to write in this area, and the lines are not part of the **LINAGE** value. Finally, the **LINES AT BOTTOM** phrase tells how many blank lines will appear at the bottom of the page; it is not possible to write in this area, and the lines are not part of the **LINAGE** value.

2. An end-of-page condition occurs when the **ADVANCING** clause of a **WRITE** statement increments **LINAGE-COUNTER** so that its value is greater than or equal to the value in the **FOOTING** phrase. For example, suppose we are writing to a file with the following **LINAGE** clause:

```
LINAGE IS 54 LINES
    WITH FOOTING AT 50
    LINES AT TOP 6
    LINES AT BOTTOM 6
```

As soon as the **ADVANCING** clause increments **LINAGE-COUNTER** so that it has a value greater than or equal to 50, the end-of-page condition occurs.

3. The **WRITE** statement prints the current output record; the statements in the **EOP** clause are executed; if any of the **EOP** statements cause the printer to eject to a new page, **LINAGE-COUNTER** is reset to 1.

4. The **REPORT IS** clause in the **FD** entry tells the compiler that output for the current file comes from a particular report defined in the Report Section.

5. There are three Report Writer statements in the Procedure Division.

   INITIATE—This statement prepares the report for execution. It sets all summation counters to zero and resets all internal data, including the page and line counters. Also, the report heading group, if present, is printed.

   GENERATE—The **GENERATE** statement instructs the Report Writer to print one detail group. If a control break is detected, appropriate control footings and control headings are automatically generated. If a page break is detected, page footings and headings are printed if they have been defined.

   TERMINATE—This statement ends the report. The **FINAL** control break is triggered and any **FINAL** control footings are printed. If a report footing has been defined it is also printed. It is not possible to write any more output to the report without reinitiating the report.

None of these statements opens or closes the report file. This must be done explicitly with **OPEN** and **CLOSE** statements.

6. **REPORT HEADING**—prints a heading at the start of the report.

    PAGE HEADING—prints a heading at the top of each page.

    CONTROL HEADING—there can be one control heading for each control variable; when a control break occurs for a variable, its control heading is printed before the new control group begins.

    DETAIL—prints detail information when a **GENERATE** statement is executed.

    CONTROL FOOTING—there can be one control footing for each control variable; when a control break occurs for a variable, its control footing is printed at the end of the old control group; control footings frequently contain **SUM** clauses to sum data within the control group.

    PAGE FOOTING—prints a footing at the bottom of each page.

    REPORT FOOTING—prints a footing at the end of the report.

7. If you tried using option (b), you would get a compilation error. The **SUM** clause can only be used in a *control footing* group. This is why we need to use **FINAL** as a control variable.

8. The general format of the **PAGE** clause is

    ```
    PAGE LIMIT IS integer-1 LINES
         HEADING        integer-2
         FIRST DETAIL   integer-3
         LAST DETAIL    integer-4
         FOOTING        integer-5
    ```

    The **PAGE LIMIT** phrase tells how many lines there are on a page, including any blank lines at the top or bottom of the page. The **HEADING** phrase tells where the first line of heading may be printed. The **FIRST DETAIL** phrase tells where the first line of detail may be printed, while **LAST DETAIL** tells where the last line of detail may be printed. The **FOOTING** phrase tells where the last line of control footing may be printed. Report headings and footings may be printed anywhere between integer-2 and integer-1. Page headings may be printed anywhere between integer-2 and integer-3. Detail and control heading groups may be printed between integer-3 and integer-4. Control footings may be printed anywhere between integer-3 and integer-5, and page footings may be printed between integer-5 and integer-1.

9. Control footings will be printed in order from minor control variable to major, followed by control headings in order from major to minor, followed by the detail line.

10. The **LINE** clause affects the spacing of the current line, while the **NEXT GROUP** clause affects the spacing of the next report group to be printed, providing that the next group is at the same or lower level of hierarchy than the current group.

11. **JAN-TOTAL** will contain the total January sales for all input records, **FEB-TOTAL** will contain the total February sales for all input records, and **MAR-TOTAL** will contain the total March sales for all input records. **QTR-TOTAL** will contain the total of **JAN-TOTAL**, **FEB-TOTAL**, and **MAR-TOTAL**, the total sales for the first quarter of the year. This is an example of *cross-footing*, in which the total of several columns is added across the line to produce a new total for all columns.

EXERCISES

1. Using the Report Writer, revise the payroll program in Figure 8.5 to print headings at the top of each page of output. Assume that a page is 66 lines from top to bottom, that there are 6 blank lines at the top and 6 blank lines at the bottom, and that there are 54 lines in the body of the page.

*2. Modify the one-level control break program in Figure 9.4 to use the Report Writer for output. Make the following changes to the report format shown in Chapter 9:

    a. Add a column that shows the amount of the sale.
    b. After printing the total for an account, double space before starting the next account.
    c. Triple space before printing the final total.

3. Revise the seed catalog program in Figure 11.1 to use the **LINAGE** and **END-OF-PAGE** clauses. Print headings for the output as shown in Figure 11.2. Assume that a page is 66 lines from top to bottom, that there are 3 blank lines at the top and 3 blank lines at the bottom, and that there are 60 lines in the body of the page. The headings consist of two lines of text followed by two blank lines.

4. Assume that the input to the payroll program in Figure 8.5 has been revised to include a project number and department, as shown below.

```
FD   PAYROLL-FILE
     LABEL RECORDS ARE STANDARD.
01   PAYROLL-RECORD.
     05   I-PAYROLL-NUMBER      PIC X(5).
     05   I-NAME                PIC X(20).
     05   I-HOURS-WORKED        PIC 99V9.
     05   FILLER                PIC X(3).
     05   I-PAYRATE             PIC 99V999.
     05   I-DEPENDENTS          PIC 99.
     05   I-PROJECT             PIC X(5).
     05   I-DEPARTMENT          PIC 999.
     05   FILLER                PIC X(34).
```

The records in this file have been sorted by department, project number, and payroll number. Modify the program as follows:

    a. Create two output files, one for valid data and one for data with errors;
    b. Start the output for each department on a new page; print the department number at the top of the page, after the page heading;
    c. Show the total pay charged to each project;
    d. Leave two blank lines between projects;
    e. For each department, show the total gross pay for all employees in the department, the total tax for the department, and the total net pay for the department;
    f. For the company, show the total gross pay, the total tax, and the total net pay; skip 5 lines before printing the company total.

    Use the Report Writer to produce the modified report.

---

* Answers to starred exercises will be found in Appendix IV at the end of the book.

CHAPTER 18

THE COBOL SORT

18.1 INTRODUCTION

We have referred several times in this book to the necessity for sorting files, that is, placing records into ascending or descending sequence on a key in the records. COBOL provides a way to specify this sorting operation using the SORT verb. The SORT verb has several levels of complexity, although in principle all variations perform the same three steps:

1. Read all records from an input file into a sort work area;
2. Sort the records in the work area;
3. Pass the sorted records from the work area to an output file.

We will begin by examining a very simple sort, then move on to look at the more sophisticated sort options. In the following examples, notice that the programs must all provide the same basic information:

1. Define the formats of the records to be sorted;
2. Define the sort keys;
3. Produce the records that are input to the sort;
4. Sort these records;
5. Process the sorted output records.

18.2 A BASIC SORT EXAMPLE

For our first example, we will assume that the data needed for the three-level control break program studied in Chapters 9 and 17 initially is not sorted. We will sort the records on the first three fields (REGION-NUMBER, SELLER-NUMBER, and ACCOUNT-NUMBER) and write the sorted data to a new file which could be used as input to the control break program. The program needed to perform the sort is shown in Figure 18.1.

```
1              IDENTIFICATION DIVISION.
2              PROGRAM-ID.
3                  SORT1.
4              AUTHOR.
5                  D. GOLDEN.
6              DATE-WRITTEN.
7                  JULY 12, 1989.
8          *
9          *   THIS PROGRAM SORTS DATA RECORDS FROM AN INPUT FILE AND
10         *   WRITES THE SORTED RECORDS TO AN OUTPUT FILE
11         *
12
13             ENVIRONMENT DIVISION.
14             INPUT-OUTPUT SECTION.
15             FILE-CONTROL.
16                 SELECT ACCOUNT-FILE         ASSIGN TO ACCOUNT.
17                 SELECT SORTED-ACCOUNTS      ASSIGN TO SORTED.
18                 SELECT SORT-FILE            ASSIGN TO SORTWORK.
19
20             DATA DIVISION.
21             FILE SECTION.
22
23             FD  ACCOUNT-FILE
24                 LABEL RECORDS ARE STANDARD.
25             01  ACCOUNT-RECORD.
26                 05  REGION-NUMBER           PIC X(5).
27                 05  SELLER-NUMBER           PIC X(5).
28                 05  ACCOUNT-NUMBER          PIC X(5).
29                 05  SALE-AMOUNT             PIC 9(5)V99.
30                 05  FILLER                  PIC X(58).
31
32             FD  SORTED-ACCOUNTS
33                 LABEL RECORDS ARE STANDARD.
34             01  SORTED-ACCOUNT-REC          PIC X(80).
35
36             SD  SORT-FILE.
37             01  SORT-REC.
38                 05  SORT-KEY                PIC X(15).
39                 05  FILLER                  PIC X(65).
40
41
42             PROCEDURE DIVISION.
43             A000-PREPARE-SALES-REPORT.
44                 SORT SORT-FILE
45                     ON ASCENDING KEY SORT-KEY
46                     USING ACCOUNT-FILE
47                     GIVING SORTED-ACCOUNTS.
48                 STOP RUN.
49
50         *********************** END OF PROGRAM ***********************
```

FIGURE 18.1 A simple sort program. Records from **ACCOUNT-FILE** are sorted on the first 15 characters and written to SORTED-ACCOUNTS.

We begin our study of this program by looking at the FILE-CONTROL paragraph. In addition to having SELECT statements for ACCOUNT-FILE and SORTED-ACCOUNTS, the input and output files, we have a SELECT statement for a file called SORT-FILE. SORT-FILE is a work file used in sorting the data. The exact mechanism by which the sort is executed is irrelevant. However, from the point of view of the application programmer, the sort work file is the file which is sorted and which defines the format of the records being sorted; the input and output files exist only to provide the data for the sort and to take up the sorted results. You don't need to create space for the sort file on the disk; the COBOL sort processor does this for you. However, you do need to provide a name for the disk file to be used as the sort work file. For example, if we assume external file assignment, then you would have three environment variables, ACCOUNT, SORTED, and SORTWORK, and each would need to have a file name assigned to it with an MS-DOS SET statement. If you do not assign a file for the sort work file, you may get an error message at run time.

In the File Section we have a new type of entry to define SORT-FILE. Just as a normal file has a file description (FD) to define its structure, a sort file has a sort description (SD) to define it. In the SD clause itself, we have only specified the file name; there are no other clauses. Not only are other clauses not required, they are either illegal or ignored, and should not be used.

In SORT-RECORD we have only defined the fifteen characters that will be used as the sort key and then padded the remainder of the record with filler. We determined that the sort key is the first fifteen characters of the record by looking at ACCOUNT-RECORD. We wish to sort these records by REGION-NUMBER, SELLER-NUMBER, and ACCOUNT-NUMBER, which appear as the first fifteen characters of the record. In a more complex example we could make the format of SORT-RECORD as detailed as we wished.

The Procedure Division is quite simple, consisting only of a SORT statement and STOP RUN. The SORT statement says that we want to sort the file SORT-FILE, that we will use SORT-KEY as the field on which to sort the records, and that the records will be sorted in ascending sequence. If we wished, we could choose a *descending* sort, in which case the output would have the records arranged from largest key to smallest. The USING clause tells us that the input to the sort is coming from ACCOUNT-FILE, and the GIVING clause tells us that the sorted data will be written to SORTED-ACCOUNTS. Notice that we do not open or close any of the files used by the sort. Not only is it not required, it is not permitted to use OPEN or CLOSE statements for any file controlled directly by the sort. This includes the USING and GIVING files, and the sort file itself.

The input to the sort is shown in Figure 18.2, and the sorted output in Figure 18.3.

18.3 THE OUTPUT PROCEDURE

The example in the previous section demonstrates the simplest possible version of the SORT statement. There is only one sort key, the input comes directly from a file, and the output goes directly to another file. If this were the only version of the sort it would be of little value, since sort utility programs can accomplish the same result with much less coding than is needed for a COBOL

```
0000100012000100008750
0000100001000200000550
0000100001000240001000
0000300015000300118094
0000100001000240001575
0000100001000270000900
0000100001000240001025
0000100001000270010100
0000100001000270002200
0000300015000780027602
0000100001000270000940
0000100002000170002600
0000100002000240026690
0000300015000490004500
0000100012000160005475
0000200004000400005012
0000100001000270004260
0000200004000410010599
0000100001000200001150
0000200039000440159414
0000300015000380015743
0000300015000350006926
0000300015000600123456
```

FIGURE 18.2 Input to the sort program in Figure 18.1.

```
0000100001000200000550
0000100001000200001150
0000100001000240001000
0000100001000240001575
0000100001000240001025
0000100001000270000900
0000100001000270010100
0000100001000270002200
0000100001000270000940
0000100001000270004260
0000100002000170002600
0000100002000240026690
0000100012000100008750
0000100012000160005475
0000200004000400005012
0000200004000410010599
0000200039000440159414
0000300015000300118094
0000300015000350006926
0000300015000380015743
0000300015000490004500
0000300015000600123456
0000300015000780027602
```

FIGURE 18.3 Output from the sort.

program. The main advantage of using the **SORT** verb is that it allows you to sort data within a program, then immediately use the sorted output for additional processing. As an example of how this is done we will again use the three-level control break program and will assume that the input data is not sorted, a fairly common situation. We will use the **SORT** verb to sort the input data, then, instead of writing it to a file, we will pass the sorted data to code much like the three-level control break program of Chapter 9. The program to accomplish this is shown in Figure 18.4.

```
1          IDENTIFICATION DIVISION.
2          PROGRAM-ID.
3              SORT2.
4          AUTHOR.
5              D. GOLDEN.
6          DATE-WRITTEN.
7              JULY 12, 1989.
8      *
9      *    THIS PROGRAM SORTS DATA FROM AN INPUT FILE, THEN USES THE
10     *    SORTED DATA TO PRODUCE A SIMPLE THREE-LEVEL SUMMARY REPORT
11     *    FOR A SALES ACCOUNTING SYSTEM
12     *
13
14         ENVIRONMENT DIVISION.
15         INPUT-OUTPUT SECTION.
16         FILE-CONTROL.
17             SELECT ACCOUNT-FILE        ASSIGN TO ACCOUNT.
18             SELECT REPORT-FILE         ASSIGN TO REPORT.
19             SELECT SORT-FILE           ASSIGN TO SORTWORK.
20
21         DATA DIVISION.
22         FILE SECTION.
23
24         FD  ACCOUNT-FILE
25             LABEL RECORDS ARE STANDARD.
26         01  ACCOUNT-RECORD             PIC X(80).
27
28         FD  REPORT-FILE
29             LABEL RECORDS ARE OMITTED.
30         01  REPORT-RECORD              PIC X(132).
31
32         SD  SORT-FILE.
33         01  SORT-REC.
34             05   REGION-NUMBER         PIC X(5).
35             05   SELLER-NUMBER         PIC X(5).
36             05   ACCOUNT-NUMBER        PIC X(5).
37             05   SALE-AMOUNT           PIC 9(5)V99.
38             05   FILLER                PIC X(58).
39
40
41         WORKING-STORAGE SECTION.
42
43         77  ASTERISK-FLAG             PIC X.
44             88   ASTERISK-FLAG-ON                     VALUE 'Y'.
45         77  LINE-NUMBER               PIC S99.
46         77  MORE-DATA-FLAG            PIC X.
47             88   NO-MORE-DATA                         VALUE 'N'.
```

```
48    77   PAGE-NUMBER                        PIC S999.
49    77   PREVIOUS-ACCOUNT-NUMBER            PIC X(5).
50    77   PREVIOUS-REGION-NUMBER             PIC X(5).
51    77   PREVIOUS-SELLER-NUMBER             PIC X(5).
52
53    01   DETAIL-LINE.
54         05   ACCOUNT-NUMBER-OUT            PIC Z(4)9.
55         05   ACCOUNT-TOTAL-OUT             PIC BB$$$$,$$9.99.
56         05   NO-OF-TRANSACTIONS-OUT        PIC BBZZ9.
57         05   ASTERISK-OUT                  PIC X.
58         05   SELLER-NUMBER-OUT             PIC B(5)Z(4)9.
59         05   SELLER-TOTAL-OUT              PIC BBB$$$$,$$9.99.
60         05   REGION-NUMBER-OUT             PIC B(5)Z(5)9.
61         05   REGION-TOTAL-OUT              PIC BBB$$$$,$$9.99.
62
63    01   FINAL-TOTAL-LINE.
64         05   FILLER                        PIC X(44) VALUE SPACES.
65         05   FILLER                        PIC X(11) VALUE 'FINAL TOTAL'.
66         05   FINAL-TOTAL-OUT               PIC B(7)$$$$,$$9.99.
67
68    01   HEADING-LINE.
69         05   FILLER                        PIC X(41)
70              VALUE 'ACCOUNT      TOTAL     NUMBER   SALESPERSON '.
71         05   FILLER                        PIC X(39)
72              VALUE 'TOTAL          REGION      TOTAL       PAGE'.
73         05   PAGE-NUMBER-OUT               PIC Z(6)9.
74
75    01   TOTALS.
76         05   ACCOUNT-TOTAL                 PIC S9(6)V99.
77         05   SELLER-TOTAL                  PIC S9(6)V99.
78         05   REGION-TOTAL                  PIC S9(6)V99.
79         05   FINAL-TOTAL                   PIC S9(6)V99.
80         05   NO-OF-TRANSACTIONS            PIC S999.
81
82
83    PROCEDURE DIVISION.
84    A000-PREPARE-SALES-REPORT.
85         SORT SORT-FILE
86              ON ASCENDING KEY REGION-NUMBER
87                               SELLER-NUMBER
88                               ACCOUNT-NUMBER
89              USING ACCOUNT-FILE
90              OUTPUT PROCEDURE IS B001-GENERATE-REPORT.
91         STOP RUN.
92
93    B001-GENERATE-REPORT SECTION.
94         OPEN OUTPUT REPORT-FILE.
95         MOVE ZERO                     TO FINAL-TOTAL.
96         MOVE 'Y'                      TO MORE-DATA-FLAG.
97         MOVE 55                       TO LINE-NUMBER.
98         MOVE ZERO                     TO PAGE-NUMBER.
99         RETURN SORT-FILE
100             AT END MOVE 'N' TO MORE-DATA-FLAG.
101        PERFORM B010-PROCESS-REGION-GROUP
102             UNTIL NO-MORE-DATA.
103        MOVE FINAL-TOTAL TO FINAL-TOTAL-OUT.
104        WRITE REPORT-RECORD FROM FINAL-TOTAL-LINE
105             AFTER ADVANCING 3 LINES.
106        CLOSE REPORT-FILE.
107
```

```
108              B009-PERFORMED-PROCEDURES SECTION.
109              B010-PROCESS-REGION-GROUP.
110                  MOVE ZERO TO REGION-TOTAL.
111                  MOVE REGION-NUMBER TO PREVIOUS-REGION-NUMBER.
112                  PERFORM C010-PROCESS-SELLER-GROUP UNTIL
113                      REGION-NUMBER IS NOT EQUAL TO PREVIOUS-REGION-NUMBER
114                      OR NO-MORE-DATA.
115                  MOVE SPACES TO DETAIL-LINE.
116                  MOVE PREVIOUS-REGION-NUMBER TO REGION-NUMBER-OUT.
117                  MOVE REGION-TOTAL TO REGION-TOTAL-OUT.
118                  PERFORM X010-LINE-OUT.
119                  ADD REGION-TOTAL TO FINAL-TOTAL.
120
121              C010-PROCESS-SELLER-GROUP.
122                  MOVE ZERO TO SELLER-TOTAL.
123                  MOVE SELLER-NUMBER TO PREVIOUS-SELLER-NUMBER
124                  PERFORM D010-PROCESS-ACCOUNT-GROUP UNTIL
125                      SELLER-NUMBER IS NOT EQUAL TO PREVIOUS-SELLER-NUMBER
126                      OR REGION-NUMBER IS NOT EQUAL TO PREVIOUS-REGION-NUMBER
127                      OR NO-MORE-DATA.
128                  MOVE SPACES TO DETAIL-LINE.
129                  MOVE PREVIOUS-SELLER-NUMBER TO SELLER-NUMBER-OUT.
130                  MOVE SELLER-TOTAL TO SELLER-TOTAL-OUT.
131                  PERFORM X010-LINE-OUT.
132                  ADD SELLER-TOTAL TO REGION-TOTAL.
133
134              D010-PROCESS-ACCOUNT-GROUP.
135                  MOVE ZERO TO ACCOUNT-TOTAL.
136                  MOVE ZERO TO NO-OF-TRANSACTIONS.
137                  MOVE 'N' TO ASTERISK-FLAG.
138                  MOVE ACCOUNT-NUMBER TO PREVIOUS-ACCOUNT-NUMBER.
139                  PERFORM E010-PROCESS-ACCOUNT-RECORD UNTIL
140                      ACCOUNT-NUMBER IS NOT EQUAL TO PREVIOUS-ACCOUNT-NUMBER
141                      OR SELLER-NUMBER  IS NOT EQUAL TO PREVIOUS-SELLER-NUMBER
142                      OR REGION-NUMBER IS NOT EQUAL TO PREVIOUS-REGION-NUMBER
143                      OR NO-MORE-DATA.
144                  MOVE SPACES TO DETAIL-LINE.
145                  MOVE PREVIOUS-ACCOUNT-NUMBER TO ACCOUNT-NUMBER-OUT.
146                  MOVE ACCOUNT-TOTAL TO ACCOUNT-TOTAL-OUT.
147                  MOVE NO-OF-TRANSACTIONS TO NO-OF-TRANSACTIONS-OUT.
148                  IF ASTERISK-FLAG-ON
149                      MOVE '*' TO ASTERISK-OUT.
150                  PERFORM X010-LINE-OUT.
151                  ADD ACCOUNT-TOTAL TO SELLER-TOTAL.
152
153              E010-PROCESS-ACCOUNT-RECORD.
154                  ADD SALE-AMOUNT TO ACCOUNT-TOTAL.
155                  ADD 1 TO NO-OF-TRANSACTIONS.
156                  IF SALE-AMOUNT IS GREATER THAN 1000.00
157                      MOVE 'Y' TO ASTERISK-FLAG.
158                  RETURN SORT-FILE
159                      AT END MOVE 'N' TO MORE-DATA-FLAG.
160
161              X010-LINE-OUT.
162                  ADD 1 TO LINE-NUMBER.
163                  IF LINE-NUMBER IS GREATER THAN 55
164                      ADD 1 TO PAGE-NUMBER
165                      MOVE PAGE-NUMBER TO PAGE-NUMBER-OUT
166                      WRITE REPORT-RECORD FROM HEADING-LINE
167                          AFTER ADVANCING PAGE
```

```
168                    MOVE SPACES TO REPORT-RECORD
169                    WRITE REPORT-RECORD
170                         AFTER ADVANCING 2 LINES
171                    MOVE 4 TO LINE-NUMBER.
172               WRITE REPORT-RECORD FROM DETAIL-LINE
173                    AFTER ADVANCING 1 LINE.
174
175      *********************** END OF PROGRAM ***********************
```

FIGURE 18.4 A program that sorts data from an input file, then uses the sorted data to produce a report.

The program in Figure 18.4 looks like a cross between the sort program in Figure 18.1 and the three-level control break program of Figure 9.9. We have created an **SD** entry for **SORT-FILE**, and, in contrast to the previous example, **ACCOUNT-RECORD** only has a **PICTURE** of **X(80)** while **SORT-RECORD** contains the complete definition of an account record. We have made this change because we do not really use any of the data in **ACCOUNT-FILE** except to feed it into the sort process. However, we will need to refer to the data fields of the sorted data in order to use them in the output procedure. The remainder of the Data Division is as it was in Chapter 9. In the current program, of course, we now refer to fields in the sort file instead of the input file.

The main paragraph of the Procedure Division still contains only a **SORT** statement and a **STOP RUN** statement, but the **SORT** statement is a bit more complicated than before. For one thing, we are now using three sort keys instead of just one. We have declared **REGION-NUMBER** to be the major key, **SELLER-NUMBER** to be the intermediate key, and **ACCOUNT-NUMBER** to be the minor key. Also, rather than sending the sorted output to **SORTED-ACCOUNTS** we wil process it in an *output procedure* called **B001-GENERATE-REPORT**.

The first thing to observe about **B001-GENERATE-REPORT** is that it is a *section*, not an ordinary paragraph. The output procedure of a **SORT** statement must be a section.

COBOL-85

In **COBOL-85** the output procedure may be an ordinary paragraph. However, this flexibility is not valid for all compiler options; you may wish to check the Microsoft manual for the COBOL.DIR options you are using.

END COBOL-85

Just as a paragraph consists of one or more statements, a section consists of one or more paragraphs. It begins with a section header consisting of the section name (just like a paragraph name) followed by the word **SECTION**, and continues until the start of the next section or until the end of the program. Although the first paragraph in a section may have a paragraph name it is not required; notice the difference between sections **B001-GENERATE-REPORT** and **B009-PERFORMED-PROCEDURES**. We also emphasize the reason that **B009-PER-FORMED-PROCEDURES** has been included at all, which is to terminate section **B001-GENERATE-REPORT**. If we did not precede **B010-PROCESS-REGION-GROUP** with a section, after the program had executed the **CLOSE** statement in **B001-GENERATE-REPORT** it would continue on to **B010-PROCESS-REGION-GROUP** and try to execute the paragraph again, causing an error.

B001-GENERATE-REPORT looks much like the driver paragraph in the program of Figure 9.9, except that we do not open or close the input file. Since this section is the output procedure of the **SORT** statement, the input file for the report is **SORT-FILE**; since this has been defined as a sort file (**SD**), it may never be opened or closed explicitly.

The only other new feature in this paragraph is that the **READ** statement has been replaced by a *RETURN* statement. The **RETURN** statement is almost identical to a sequential **READ** statement, except that the file must be a sort file. We **RETURN** from a file, just as we **READ** from a file; we could include an optional **INTO** clause, just as we do in a **READ** statement; and we have an **AT END** clause to indicate when we have reached the end of the sort data. The only restriction on the use of a **RETURN** statement is that it must be used under control of a **SORT** verb. Notice that in **E010-PROCESS-ACCOUNT-RECORD** the **READ** statement has also been replaced by a **RETURN** statement.

The program was run with the sample data shown in Chapter 9 and produced the same output.

18.4   THE INPUT PROCEDURE

Just as we use the output procedure to process output from a sort, we can use the *input procedure* to process input before it reaches the sort. To demonstrate the use of an input procedure, we shall revise the previous example to edit the account records for nonnumeric fields before passing them to the sort. If a record contains any nonnumeric data, it will be rejected and printed with a simple error message; otherwise, it will be passed to **SORT-FILE** for sorting. The program to accomplish this is shown in Figure 18.5.

```
1          IDENTIFICATION DIVISION.
2          PROGRAM-ID.
3             SORT3.
4          AUTHOR.
5             D. GOLDEN.
6          DATE-WRITTEN.
7             JULY 12, 1989.
8       *
9       *    THIS PROGRAM SORTS EDITED DATA FROM AN INPUT FILE, THEN USES
10      *    THE SORTED DATA TO PRODUCE A SIMPLE THREE-LEVEL SUMMARY
11      *    REPORT FOR A SALES ACCOUNTING SYSTEM
12
13         ENVIRONMENT DIVISION.
14         INPUT-OUTPUT SECTION.
15         FILE-CONTROL.
16            SELECT ACCOUNT-FILE          ASSIGN TO ACCOUNT.
17            SELECT LOG-FILE              ASSIGN TO LOGFILE.
18            SELECT REPORT-FILE           ASSIGN TO REPORT.
19            SELECT SORT-FILE             ASSIGN TO SORTWORK.
20
```

```
21          DATA DIVISION.
22          FILE SECTION.
23
24          FD  ACCOUNT-FILE
25              LABEL RECORDS ARE STANDARD.
26          01  ACCOUNT-RECORD.
27              05  REGION-NUMBER-IN        PIC X(5).
28              05  SELLER-NUMBER-IN        PIC X(5).
29              05  ACCOUNT-NUMBER-IN       PIC X(5).
30              05  SALE-AMOUNT-IN          PIC X(7).
31              05  FILLER                  PIC X(58).
32
33          FD  LOG-FILE
34              LABEL RECORDS ARE OMITTED.
35          01  LOG-RECORD.
36              05  LOG-MESSAGE             PIC X(32).
37              05  BAD-RECORD              PIC X(80).
38              05  FILLER                  PIC X(20).
39
40          FD  REPORT-FILE
41              LABEL RECORDS ARE OMITTED.
42          01  REPORT-RECORD               PIC X(132).
43
44          SD  SORT-FILE.
45          01  SORT-RECORD.
46              05  REGION-NUMBER           PIC X(5).
47              05  SELLER-NUMBER           PIC X(5).
48              05  ACCOUNT-NUMBER          PIC X(5).
49              05  SALE-AMOUNT             PIC 9(5)V99.
50              05  FILLER                  PIC X(58).
51
52
53          WORKING-STORAGE SECTION.
54
55          77  ASTERISK-FLAG               PIC X.
56              88  ASTERISK-FLAG-ON                        VALUE 'Y'.
57          77  LINE-NUMBER                 PIC S99.
58          77  MORE-DATA-FLAG              PIC X.
59              88  NO-MORE-DATA                            VALUE 'N'.
60          77  PAGE-NUMBER                 PIC S999.
61          77  PREVIOUS-ACCOUNT-NUMBER     PIC X(5).
62          77  PREVIOUS-REGION-NUMBER      PIC X(5).
63          77  PREVIOUS-SELLER-NUMBER      PIC X(5).
64
65          01  DETAIL-LINE.
66              05  ACCOUNT-NUMBER-OUT      PIC Z(4)9.
67              05  ACCOUNT-TOTAL-OUT       PIC BB$$$$,$$9.99.
68              05  NO-OF-TRANSACTIONS-OUT  PIC BBZZ9.
69              05  ASTERISK-OUT            PIC X.
70              05  SELLER-NUMBER-OUT       PIC B(5)Z(4)9.
71              05  SELLER-TOTAL-OUT        PIC BBB$$$$,$$9.99.
72              05  REGION-NUMBER-OUT       PIC B(5)Z(5)9.
73              05  REGION-TOTAL-OUT        PIC BBB$$$$,$$9.99.
74
75          01  FINAL-TOTAL-LINE.
76              05  FILLER                  PIC X(44) VALUE SPACES.
77              05  FILLER                  PIC X(11) VALUE 'FINAL TOTAL'.
78              05  FINAL-TOTAL-OUT         PIC B(7)$$$$,$$9.99.
79
```

```
80          01   HEADING-LINE.
81               05   FILLER                     PIC X(41)
82                    VALUE 'ACCOUNT     TOTAL     NUMBER   SALESPERSON '.
83               05   FILLER                     PIC X(39)
84                    VALUE 'TOTAL       REGION     TOTAL       PAGE'.
85               05   PAGE-NUMBER-OUT            PIC Z(6)9.
86
87          01   TOTALS.
88               05   ACCOUNT-TOTAL             PIC S9(6)V99.
89               05   SELLER-TOTAL              PIC S9(6)V99.
90               05   REGION-TOTAL              PIC S9(6)V99.
91               05   FINAL-TOTAL               PIC S9(6)V99.
92               05   NO-OF-TRANSACTIONS        PIC S999.
93
94
95          PROCEDURE DIVISION.
96          A000-PREPARE-SALES-REPORT.
97               SORT SORT-FILE
98                   ON ASCENDING KEY REGION-NUMBER
99                                    SELLER-NUMBER
100                                   ACCOUNT-NUMBER
101                  INPUT  PROCEDURE IS B001-EDIT-INPUT
102                  OUTPUT PROCEDURE IS B002-GENERATE-REPORT.
103              STOP RUN.
104
105         B001-EDIT-INPUT SECTION.
106              OPEN INPUT ACCOUNT-FILE
107                  OUTPUT LOG-FILE.
108              MOVE 'Y' TO MORE-DATA-FLAG.
109              READ ACCOUNT-FILE
110                      AT END MOVE 'N' TO MORE-DATA-FLAG.
111              PERFORM B010-EDIT-ACCOUNTS
112                      UNTIL NO-MORE-DATA.
113              CLOSE ACCOUNT-FILE
114                  LOG-FILE.
115
116         B002-GENERATE-REPORT SECTION.
117              OPEN OUTPUT REPORT-FILE.
118              MOVE ZERO                      TO FINAL-TOTAL.
119              MOVE 'Y'                       TO MORE-DATA-FLAG.
120              MOVE 55                        TO LINE-NUMBER.
121              MOVE ZERO                      TO PAGE-NUMBER.
122              RETURN SORT-FILE
123                      AT END MOVE 'N' TO MORE-DATA-FLAG.
124              PERFORM B020-PROCESS-REGION-GROUP
125                      UNTIL NO-MORE-DATA.
126              MOVE FINAL-TOTAL TO FINAL-TOTAL-OUT.
127              WRITE REPORT-RECORD FROM FINAL-TOTAL-LINE
128                      AFTER ADVANCING 3 LINES.
129              CLOSE REPORT-FILE.
130
131         B009-PERFORMED-PROCEDURES SECTION.
132         B010-EDIT-ACCOUNTS.
133              IF    REGION-NUMBER-IN IS NOT NUMERIC
134                 OR SELLER-NUMBER-IN IS NOT NUMERIC
135                 OR ACCOUNT-NUMBER-IN IS NOT NUMERIC
136                 OR SALE-AMOUNT-IN IS NOT NUMERIC
137                   MOVE SPACES TO LOG-RECORD
138                   MOVE 'A FIELD CONTAINS INVALID DATA:  ' TO LOG-MESSAGE
```

```
139                          MOVE ACCOUNT-RECORD TO BAD-RECORD
140                          WRITE LOG-RECORD AFTER ADVANCING 1 LINE
141                      ELSE
142                          RELEASE SORT-RECORD FROM ACCOUNT-RECORD.
143                      READ ACCOUNT-FILE
144                          AT END MOVE 'N' TO MORE-DATA-FLAG.
145
146          B020-PROCESS-REGION-GROUP.
147              MOVE ZERO TO REGION-TOTAL.
148              MOVE REGION-NUMBER TO PREVIOUS-REGION-NUMBER.
149              PERFORM C010-PROCESS-SELLER-GROUP UNTIL
150                      REGION-NUMBER IS NOT EQUAL TO PREVIOUS-REGION-NUMBER
151                  OR NO-MORE-DATA.
152              MOVE SPACES TO DETAIL-LINE.
153              MOVE PREVIOUS-REGION-NUMBER TO REGION-NUMBER-OUT.
154              MOVE REGION-TOTAL TO REGION-TOTAL-OUT.
155              PERFORM X010-LINE-OUT.
156              ADD REGION-TOTAL TO FINAL-TOTAL.
157
158          C010-PROCESS-SELLER-GROUP.
159              MOVE ZERO TO SELLER-TOTAL.
160              MOVE SELLER-NUMBER TO PREVIOUS-SELLER-NUMBER
161              PERFORM D010-PROCESS-ACCOUNT-GROUP UNTIL
162                      SELLER-NUMBER IS NOT EQUAL TO PREVIOUS-SELLER-NUMBER
163                  OR REGION-NUMBER IS NOT EQUAL TO PREVIOUS-REGION-NUMBER
164                  OR NO-MORE-DATA.
165              MOVE SPACES TO DETAIL-LINE.
166              MOVE PREVIOUS-SELLER-NUMBER TO SELLER-NUMBER-OUT.
167              MOVE SELLER-TOTAL TO SELLER-TOTAL-OUT.
168              PERFORM X010-LINE-OUT.
169              ADD SELLER-TOTAL TO REGION-TOTAL.
170
171          D010-PROCESS-ACCOUNT-GROUP.
172              MOVE ZERO TO ACCOUNT-TOTAL.
173              MOVE ZERO TO NO-OF-TRANSACTIONS.
174              MOVE 'N' TO ASTERISK-FLAG.
175              MOVE ACCOUNT-NUMBER TO PREVIOUS-ACCOUNT-NUMBER.
176              PERFORM E010-PROCESS-ACCOUNT-RECORD UNTIL
177                  ACCOUNT-NUMBER IS NOT EQUAL TO PREVIOUS-ACCOUNT-NUMBER
178                  OR SELLER-NUMBER  IS NOT EQUAL TO PREVIOUS-SELLER-NUMBER
179                  OR REGION-NUMBER  IS NOT EQUAL TO PREVIOUS-REGION-NUMBER
180                  OR NO-MORE-DATA.
181              MOVE SPACES TO DETAIL-LINE.
182              MOVE PREVIOUS-ACCOUNT-NUMBER TO ACCOUNT-NUMBER-OUT.
183              MOVE ACCOUNT-TOTAL TO ACCOUNT-TOTAL-OUT.
184              MOVE NO-OF-TRANSACTIONS TO NO-OF-TRANSACTIONS-OUT.
185              IF ASTERISK-FLAG-ON
186                  MOVE '*' TO ASTERISK-OUT.
187              PERFORM X010-LINE-OUT.
188              ADD ACCOUNT-TOTAL TO SELLER-TOTAL.
189
190          E010-PROCESS-ACCOUNT-RECORD.
191              ADD SALE-AMOUNT TO ACCOUNT-TOTAL.
192              ADD 1 TO NO-OF-TRANSACTIONS.
193              IF SALE-AMOUNT IS GREATER THAN 1000.00
194                  MOVE 'Y' TO ASTERISK-FLAG.
195              RETURN SORT-FILE
196                      AT END MOVE 'N' TO MORE-DATA-FLAG.
197
```

```
198          X010-LINE-OUT.
199              ADD 1 TO LINE-NUMBER.
200              IF LINE-NUMBER IS GREATER THAN 55
201                  ADD 1 TO PAGE-NUMBER
202                  MOVE PAGE-NUMBER TO PAGE-NUMBER-OUT
203                  WRITE REPORT-RECORD FROM HEADING-LINE
204                      AFTER ADVANCING PAGE
205                  MOVE SPACES TO REPORT-RECORD
206                  WRITE REPORT-RECORD
207                      AFTER ADVANCING 2 LINES
208                  MOVE 4 TO LINE-NUMBER.
209              WRITE REPORT-RECORD FROM DETAIL-LINE
210                  AFTER ADVANCING 1 LINE.
211
212      ********************** END OF PROGRAM **********************
```

FIGURE 18.5   A sort program using both input and output procedures.

We have added a file called **LOG-FILE** to the program. This file will be used to write error messages for invalid input records. Other than the code needed to declare **LOG-FILE**, the Environment and Data Divisions are the same as in the previous example.

In the driver paragraph of the Procedure Division the **SORT** statement has been changed to take the input to the sort from the input procedure **B001-EDIT-INPUT** instead of directly from **ACCOUNT-FILE**. We have also modified the prefix of **GENERATE-REPORT** to keep the paragraphs and sections in prefix sequence. Given this example, we can now show the complete format of the **SORT** statement.

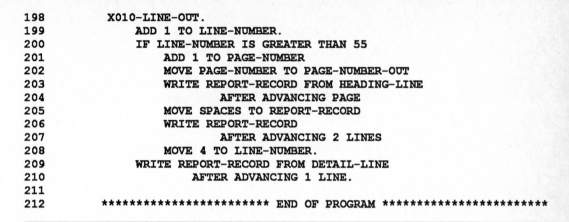

When the **SORT** statement is executed the program first executes **B001-EDIT-INPUT**, which generates the records that are written onto **SORT-FILE**.

When we get to the end of **B001-EDIT-INPUT** the records on **SORT-FILE** are sorted on the specified keys, after which **B002-GENERATE-REPORT** is executed. This section takes the sorted records from **SORT-FILE** and uses them to produce the report.

B001-EDIT-INPUT looks much like the driver paragraph of a program whose function is to produce an edited data file, and **B010-EDIT-ACCOUNTS** is similar to edit paragraphs we have seen in previous chapters. It takes the current input record and tests to see if any of its fields are nonnumeric. If so, an error message is written to **LOG-FILE**. If all fields are numeric, the record is sent to the sort file. However, instead of using **WRITE** we use **RELEASE** to put the records in the file. Just as **RETURN** is analogous to the sequential **READ**, so **RELEASE** is analogous to the sequential **WRITE**. Since **RELEASE** always writes to a file, not a printer, it must not have an **ADVANCING** clause; and, like the **RETURN** statement, it must always be executed under control of a **SORT** statement.

Notice that it makes no difference that both **B001-EDIT-INPUT** and **B002-GENERATE-REPORT** perform paragraphs that are located in **B009-PERFORMED-PROCEDURES**. There is no problem in performing paragraphs across section boundaries. In early versions of **COBOL**, where memory management was more of a problem than it is today, sections played a more important roll in **COBOL** programs. Today, however, they are a relatively minor feature of **COBOL**.

The program in Figure 18.5 was tested using the data file of previous examples, with a few erroneous records added. It produced correct results.

REVIEW QUESTIONS

1. Describe the function of each of the following:
    a. the **SELECT** statement for the sort file
    b. the **SD** entry
    c. the **KEY** clause in the **SORT** statement
    d. the input procedure
    e. the output procedure

2. Write a **SORT** statement for the sales report program that will read the records from **ACCOUNT-FILE**, write them to **SORTED-ACCOUNTS**, and sort the records in the following order:

    ascending on region;
    descending on seller number;
    descending on account number;
    ascending on sale amount

3. Assume that **SORT-FILE** is defined in an **SD** entry, **SORT-RECORD** is a record of **SORT-FILE**, and **SORT-KEY** is a field in **SORT-RECORD**. What is wrong with the following code?

```
PROCEDURE DIVISION.
A000-MAIN.
    SORT SORT-FILE ON ASCENDING KEY SORT-KEY
        INPUT PROCEDURE B001-INPUT
        OUTPUT PROCEDURE B002-OUTPUT.
    STOP RUN.
```

```
B001-INPUT.
    OPEN INPUT IN-FILE
        OUTPUT SORT-FILE.
    MOVE 'Y' TO MORE-RECORDS-FLAG.
    READ IN-FILE AT END MOVE 'N' TO MORE-RECORDS-FLAG.
    PERFORM C010-COPY-TO-SORT UNTIL NO-MORE-RECORDS.
    CLOSE IN-FILE SORT-FILE.

B002-OUTPUT.
    OPEN INPUT SORT-FILE
        OUTPUT OUT-FILE.
    MOVE 'Y' TO MORE-RECORDS-FLAG.
    READ SORT-FILE AT END MOVE 'N' TO MORE-RECORDS-FLAG.
    PERFORM C020-COPY-FROM-SORT UNTIL NO-MORE-RECORDS.
    CLOSE OUT-FILE SORT-FILE.

C010-COPY-TO-SORT.
    WRITE SORT-RECORD FROM IN-RECORD.
    READ IN-FILE AT END MOVE 'N' TO MORE-RECORDS-FLAG.

C020-COPY-FROM-SORT.
    WRITE OUT-RECORD FROM SORT-RECORD.
    READ SORT-FILE AT END MOVE 'N' TO MORE-RECORDS-FLAG.
```

4. Assuming the same conditions as in Question 3, what is wrong with the following code?

```
PROCEDURE DIVISION.
A000-MAIN.
    OPEN INPUT IN-FILE
        OUTPUT OUT-FILE.
    SORT SORT-FILE ON DESCENDING KEY SORT-KEY
        USING IN-FILE
        GIVING OUT-FILE.
    CLOSE IN-FILE OUT-FILE.
    STOP RUN.
```

ANSWERS TO REVIEW QUESTIONS

1. **a.** The SELECT statement for the sort file tells the program which file is to be used as a work area for the data during the sort.

   b. The SD entry defines the sort file and the format(s) of the records to be sorted.

   c. The KEY clause tells which fields are to be used as sort keys, the hierarchy of the keys from major to minor, and whether a particular key field is to be sorted in ascending or descending sequence.

   d. The input procedure produces the records to be sorted. These records may be the result of selecting certain records from an input file, or may be generated as the result of a calculation, or both.

   e. The output procedure processes the sorted records on the sort file.

2.
```
SORT SORT-FILE
    ON ASCENDING KEY REGION-NUMBER
    ON DESCENDING KEY SELLER-NUMBER
                    ACCOUNT-NUMBER
    ON ASCENDING KEY SALE-AMOUNT.
```

3. There are several errors in the code:

    a. neither **BO01-INPUT** nor **BO02-OUTPUT** has been defined to be a section (this is acceptable, however, for **COBOL-85**);

    b. the sort file may not be opened or closed explicitly by the program;

    c. you may not use a sort file in a **READ** or **WRITE** statement; you must use **RETURN** or **RELEASE**.

4. You may not open files used in **USING** or **GIVING** clauses before executing a **SORT** statement, and after the **SORT** has executed the files are already closed. However, *after* the **SORT** statement has been executed you may use **IN-FILE** and **OUT-FILE** as ordinary files, opening and closing them as necessary.

EXERCISES

1. Consider the payroll program in Figure 7.4. Write a program which will read records from **PAYROLL-FILE**, sort them in ascending order on **I-PAYROLL-NUMBER**, and write the sorted records to **SORTED-PAYROLL-FILE**.

2. Same as Exercise 1, except that instead of writing the sorted records to **SORTED-PAYROLL-FILE** you should perform the payroll calculations shown in Figure 7.4 as output procedure of the sort.

3. Using the version of the seed catalog program shown in Figure 11.1, assume that the records in **ORDER-FILE** are in random sequence. Perform the edits shown in Figure 11.1 as the input procedure to a sort. After the records have been entered, sort them into ascending order on **ORDER-NUMBER** before writing them to **PROCESSING-FILE**.

4. If you have studied the Report Writer in Chapter 17, revise the program in Figure 18.5 to use the Report Writer for output. You should see that it is possible to use both the sort and the Report Writer in the same program.

5. (This exercise is suitable for a project.)

   Write a program to produce the payroll reports described in Exercise 8 of Chapter 13. Transaction records are unsorted and must be sorted on employee pay number as the major key and record type as the minor key. Assume that there are errors in the transaction records and that all records must be edited as described in the optional part of Exercise 13.8. Use an Input Procedure to edit the transactions and reject any transaction containing an error. In other words, only valid transactions are to be sorted. After sorting the transactions, use an Output Procedure to produce the main payroll report and the payroll activity log.

CHAPTER 19

SUBPROGRAMS

19.1 INTRODUCTION

Throughout this book we have emphasized the concept of functional modularity, dividing the task that a program must perform into smaller, more manageable tasks, each of which is treated as a module. To build the program, we simply write code that executes the modules in the appropriate sequence. The advantage of this approach, of course, is that modularity allows us to break a problem that is too large to deal with easily into several smaller problems, each of which can be solved without being distracted by the others.

Up to now, we have used paragraphs of the program to implement modules and, in the relatively small problems we have been dealing with so far, this presents little problem. However, as programs become larger and larger they become more and more difficult to deal with even using modular design. One of the problems is simply that the sheer volume of code in a program with 10,000 or 100,000 lines or more strains the capacity of most system software. Many source code editors cannot deal with files this size easily, the work space required by a compiler to compile a large program becomes very large, and the time required to compile 100,000 lines of code in order to change the one or two characters necessary to fix a bug becomes exorbitant.

The solution to these problems is to use *subprograms* to implement modules. A subprogram is a COBOL program, compiled separately from the main program or other subprograms, which is executed under control of the main program or another subprogram. The complete program consists of the main program, plus all subprograms. The subprogram being executed is designated the *called* program, and the one that controls its execution is designated the *calling* program. The calling program may be either the main program or another subprogram.

Using subprograms to implement modules has several advantages over using only paragraphs. We have implied one advantage already; it is frequently much more efficient to implement a program as a set of subprograms, each of which is only a few thousand lines, than to implement it as a single program consisting of many tens of thousands of lines. If the change required for a program only involves a few lines of code, one need only recompile the affected subprogram, then relink all subprograms to create the complete program. Another advantage is that subprograms can be stored in special files called *libraries*, then reused in other programs. This can reduce significantly the amount of work needed to write new programs. Last but not least, subprograms give much better control over the way in which data is passed between modules than paragraphs do. This is very important in program design, but is more properly part of a book on program design techniques.

19.2 USING SUBPROGRAMS

A **COBOL** subprogram has all the characteristics of a **COBOL** program as we have learned them, including all four divisions and all the sections of the Environment and Data Divisions that have been presented to date. For the idea of a subprogram to make any sense, however, it is almost always necessary that there be some way for the calling program and the subprogram to communicate with each other. The calling program needs to be able to specify what data is to be operated on and the names of the variables that the subprogram is to use in sending information back to the calling program. The answer to this need is as follows.

When we are ready to bring a subprogram into action under control of a calling program, we write the verb **CALL**, follow it with the name of the subprogram written in quotes, then the word **USING**, and finally the names of the variables that the calling program is communicating to the subprogram. Within the subprogram, the Procedure Division header is modified to include the word **USING** and the names of the items being communicated. Within the Data Division of the subprogram there must be a new section, called the *Linkage Section*, in which the items named in the subprogram's Procedure Division header are described; the Linkage Section generally follows the Working-Storage Section in the Data Division.

For example, suppose that in a calling program we wrote

```
CALL 'SUBPROG' USING DATA-REC.
```

The subprogram should have **SUBPROG** as its **PROGRAM-ID**. In its Procedure Division header there should be a **USING** phrase, and its Data Division should have a Linkage Section. It is entirely permissible for the subprogram to use the same name for the information being communicated as the calling program used. In this case its Procedure Division header would be

```
PROCEDURE DIVISION USING DATA-REC.
```

In the Linkage Section there would be an entry for **DATA-REC** describing it.

However, it is not necessary for the information named in the two **USING** phrases to have the same names. They must be of the same length and the same structure, but they can certainly have different names. We mentioned before that one of the motives for using subprograms is that they can be used by many different calling programs. This is because the data names used in the **USING** phrase in the subprogram (called *parameters*) need not be the same as the names of the parameters used in the calling program. For example, we could call a subprogram with the heading shown above with any of these statements:

```
CALL 'SUBPROG' USING NEW-REC.
CALL 'SUBPROG' USING MASTER-REC.
CALL 'SUBPROG' USING WORK-DATA.
```

The only requirement is that the length and structure of all the records be the same. In this case, the subprogram will work correctly with no changes to it whatever.

In the example above, the list of parameters in the USING clauses contains only one data name. However, there is really no practical limit to the number of parameters in a parameter list, other than the fact that a list that is too long may be difficult to understand or to use accurately. In the example we shall be using shortly, the parameter list will contain three parameters. There are only two restrictions that apply to parameters. First, they must always be data names; they can be defined anywhere in the Data Division except the Report Section or Screen Section, but they cannot be file names, paragraph names, or literals. Second, they should always be defined at the 77 or 01 levels.

19.3 THE SEQUENTIAL FILE UPDATE PROGRAM WITH SUBPROGRAMS

To demonstrate the use of subprograms, we will use the sequential file update program from Chapter 13. Specifically, we will take the program UPDATE5 in Figure 13.11 and modify it to invoke a subprogram that processes transactions other than additions and deletions. The revised program, UPDATE6, is shown in Figure 19.1. You may wish to review the program in Chapter 13 before continuing.

```
1          IDENTIFICATION DIVISION.
2          PROGRAM-ID.
3              UPDATE6.
4          DATE-WRITTEN.
5              JULY 16, 1989.
6
7          ENVIRONMENT DIVISION.
8          INPUT-OUTPUT SECTION.
9          FILE-CONTROL.
10             SELECT LOG-FILE                 ASSIGN TO LOGFILE.
11             SELECT NEW-MASTER-FILE          ASSIGN TO NEWMAST.
12             SELECT OLD-MASTER-FILE          ASSIGN TO OLDMAST.
13             SELECT ORDER-FILE               ASSIGN TO ORDERS.
14             SELECT TRANSACTION-FILE         ASSIGN TO TRANS.
15
16         DATA DIVISION.
17
18         FILE SECTION.
19
20         FD  LOG-FILE
21             LABEL RECORDS ARE OMITTED.
22         01  LOG-RECORD.
23             05  FILLER                      PIC X(45).
24             05  LOG-MESSAGE                 PIC X(50).
25
26         FD  NEW-MASTER-FILE
27             LABEL RECORDS ARE STANDARD.
```

```
28          01   NEW-MASTER.
29               05   NM-KEY                      PIC X(5).
30               05   NM-QUANTITY                 PIC 9(5).
31               05   NM-QUAN-ON-ORDER            PIC 9(5).
32               05   NM-REORDER-POINT            PIC 9(5).
33               05   NM-REORDER-QUAN             PIC 9(5).
34               05   NM-DESCRIPTION              PIC X(20).
35
36          FD   OLD-MASTER-FILE
37               LABEL RECORDS ARE STANDARD.
38          01   OLD-MASTER-BUFFER               PIC X(45).
39
40          FD   ORDER-FILE
41               LABEL RECORDS ARE OMITTED.
42          01   ORDER-RECORD.
43               05   OR-KEY                      PIC X(5).
44               05   FILLER                      PIC XXX.
45               05   OR-QUANTITY                 PIC Z(5)9.
46               05   FILLER                      PIC XXX.
47               05   OR-DESCRIPTION              PIC X(20).
48
49          FD   TRANSACTION-FILE
50               LABEL RECORDS ARE OMITTED.
51          01   TRANSACTION-BUFFER              PIC X(47).
52
53          WORKING-STORAGE SECTION.
54
55          77   ERROR-COUNT                     PIC S999.
56          77   OM-KEY-PREVIOUS                 PIC X(5).
57          77   SEQUENCE-ERROR-FLAG             PIC X.
58          77   TR-KEY-PREVIOUS                 PIC X(5).
59
60          01   ERROR-MESSAGES.
61               05   BAD-ADDITION-MSG            PIC X(50) VALUE
62                    '   THIS ADDITION MATCHES AN EXISTING MASTER'.
63               05   BAD-ADJ-CODE-MSG            PIC X(50) VALUE
64                    '   BAD ADJUSTMENT CODE'.
65               05   BAD-TRANS-CODE-MSG          PIC X(50) VALUE
66                    '   TRANSACTION CODE ILLEGAL'.
67               05   DELETE-MSG                  PIC X(50) VALUE
68                    '   THIS MASTER RECORD HAS BEEN DELETED'.
69               05   MASTER-SEQUENCE-ERROR-MSG   PIC X(50) VALUE
70                    '   THIS MASTER IS OUT OF SEQUENCE'.
71               05   OUT-OF-STOCK-MSG            PIC X(50) VALUE
72                    '   INSUFFICIENT STOCK TO SHIP AMOUNT SPECIFIED'.
73               05   TERMINATION-MSG             PIC X(50) VALUE
74                    'MORE THAN 10 ERRORS - JOB TERMINATED'.
75               05   TRANS-SEQUENCE-ERROR-MSG    PIC X(50) VALUE
76                    '   THIS TRANSACTION IS OUT OF SEQUENCE'.
77               05   UNMATCHED-TRANS-MSG         PIC X(50) VALUE
78                    '   THERE IS NO MASTER FOR THIS TRANSACTION'.
79
80          01   OLD-MASTER.
81               05   OM-KEY                      PIC X(5).
82               05   OM-QUAN-ON-HAND             PIC 9(5).
83               05   OM-QUAN-ON-ORDER            PIC 9(5).
84               05   OM-REORDER-POINT            PIC 9(5).
85               05   OM-REORDER-QUAN             PIC 9(5).
86               05   OM-DESCRIPTION              PIC X(20).
87
```

```
88         01   TRANSACTION.
89              05   TR-KEY                        PIC X(5).
90              05   TR-QUANTITY                   PIC 9(5).
91              05   TR-TRANSACTION-CODE           PIC X.
92                   88   ADDITION                           VALUE '1'.
93                   88   ADJUSTMENT                         VALUE '2'.
94                   88   RECEIPT                            VALUE '3'.
95                   88   SHIPMENT                           VALUE '4'.
96                   88   DELETION                           VALUE '5'.
97              05   TR-ADJUSTMENT-CODE            PIC 9.
98              05   TR-QUAN-ON-ORDER              PIC 9(5).
99              05   TR-REORDER-POINT              PIC 9(5).
100             05   TR-REORDER-QUAN               PIC 9(5).
101             05   TR-DESCRIPTION                PIC X(20).
102
103        01   UPDATE-ERROR-FLAGS.
104             05   BAD-TRANS-CODE                PIC X.
105             05   OUT-OF-STOCK                  PIC X.
106             05   BAD-ADJ-CODE                  PIC X.
107
108
109        PROCEDURE DIVISION.
110        A000-UPDATE-FILE.
111        *          INITIALIZE WORK AREAS
112             MOVE ZERO                          TO ERROR-COUNT.
113             MOVE LOW-VALUES                    TO OM-KEY-PREVIOUS.
114             MOVE LOW-VALUES                    TO TR-KEY-PREVIOUS.
115             OPEN INPUT TRANSACTION-FILE
116                        OLD-MASTER-FILE
117                 OUTPUT NEW-MASTER-FILE
118                        LOG-FILE
119                        ORDER-FILE.
120        *          GET PRIMING RECORDS
121             PERFORM X010-GET-VALID-TRANSACTION.
122             PERFORM X020-GET-VALID-MASTER.
123        *          PROCESS THE FILES
124             PERFORM B010-UPDATE-LOGIC
125                 UNTIL (OM-KEY = HIGH-VALUES  AND  TR-KEY = HIGH-VALUES)
126                        OR ERROR-COUNT IS GREATER THAN 10.
127             IF ERROR-COUNT IS GREATER THAN 10
128                 WRITE LOG-RECORD FROM TERMINATION-MSG
129                        AFTER ADVANCING 1 LINE.
130             CLOSE TRANSACTION-FILE
131                   OLD-MASTER-FILE
132                   NEW-MASTER-FILE
133                   LOG-FILE
134                   ORDER-FILE.
135             STOP RUN.
136
137        B010-UPDATE-LOGIC.
138             IF OM-KEY IS LESS THAN TR-KEY
139                 PERFORM C040-CHECK-QUANTITY
140                 WRITE NEW-MASTER FROM OLD-MASTER
141                 PERFORM X020-GET-VALID-MASTER
142             ELSE
143                 IF OM-KEY = TR-KEY
144                     PERFORM C010-APPLY-TRANSACTION
145                     PERFORM X010-GET-VALID-TRANSACTION
```

```
146                     ELSE
147                         IF ADDITION
148                             PERFORM C020-ADD-MASTER
149                             PERFORM X010-GET-VALID-TRANSACTION
150                         ELSE
151                             PERFORM C030-INVALID-TRANSACTION
152                             PERFORM X010-GET-VALID-TRANSACTION.
153
154         C010-APPLY-TRANSACTION.
155             IF DELETION
156                 PERFORM D010-DELETE-MASTER
157                 PERFORM X020-GET-VALID-MASTER
158             ELSE
159                 IF ADDITION
160                     PERFORM D030-INVALID-ADDITION
161                 ELSE
162                     MOVE SPACES TO UPDATE-ERROR-FLAGS
163                     CALL 'UPDATE-MASTER' USING OLD-MASTER
164                                                TRANSACTION
165                                                UPDATE-ERROR-FLAGS
166                     IF UPDATE-ERROR-FLAGS NOT = SPACES
167                         PERFORM D020-PRINT-UPDATE-ERRORS.
168
169         C020-ADD-MASTER.
170             MOVE TR-KEY                     TO NM-KEY.
171             MOVE TR-QUANTITY                TO NM-QUANTITY.
172             MOVE TR-QUAN-ON-ORDER           TO NM-QUAN-ON-ORDER.
173             MOVE TR-REORDER-POINT           TO NM-REORDER-POINT.
174             MOVE TR-REORDER-QUAN            TO NM-REORDER-QUAN.
175             MOVE TR-DESCRIPTION             TO NM-DESCRIPTION.
176             WRITE NEW-MASTER.
177
178         C030-INVALID-TRANSACTION.
179             MOVE TRANSACTION TO LOG-RECORD.
180             MOVE UNMATCHED-TRANS-MSG TO LOG-MESSAGE.
181             WRITE LOG-RECORD AFTER ADVANCING 1 LINE.
182             ADD 1 TO ERROR-COUNT.
183
184         C040-CHECK-QUANTITY.
185             IF OM-QUAN-ON-ORDER + OM-QUAN-ON-HAND  OM-REORDER-POINT
186                 MOVE SPACES                  TO ORDER-RECORD
187                 MOVE OM-KEY                  TO OR-KEY
188                 MOVE OM-DESCRIPTION          TO OR-DESCRIPTION
189                 MOVE OM-REORDER-QUAN         TO OR-QUANTITY
190                 WRITE ORDER-RECORD AFTER ADVANCING 1 LINE
191                 ADD OM-REORDER-QUAN TO OM-QUAN-ON-ORDER.
192
193         D010-DELETE-MASTER.
194             MOVE OLD-MASTER TO LOG-RECORD.
195             MOVE DELETE-MSG TO LOG-MESSAGE.
196             WRITE LOG-RECORD AFTER ADVANCING 1 LINE.
197
198         ***********************************
199         *D020-UPDATE-MASTER HAS BEEN CHANGED TO A SUBPROGRAM
200         ***********************************
201
202         D020-PRINT-UPDATE-ERRORS.
203             IF BAD-TRANS-CODE = 'X'
204                 MOVE TRANSACTION TO LOG-RECORD
205                 MOVE BAD-TRANS-CODE-MSG TO LOG-MESSAGE
```

```
206                         WRITE LOG-RECORD AFTER ADVANCING 1 LINE
207                         ADD 1 TO ERROR-COUNT.
208                 IF OUT-OF-STOCK = 'X'
209                     MOVE TRANSACTION TO LOG-RECORD
210                     MOVE OUT-OF-STOCK-MSG TO LOG-MESSAGE
211                     WRITE LOG-RECORD AFTER ADVANCING 1 LINE
212                     ADD 1 TO ERROR-COUNT.
213                 IF BAD-ADJ-CODE = 'X'
214                     MOVE TRANSACTION TO LOG-RECORD
215                     MOVE BAD-ADJ-CODE-MSG TO LOG-MESSAGE
216                     WRITE LOG-RECORD AFTER ADVANCING 1 LINE
217                     ADD 1 TO ERROR-COUNT.
218
219         D030-INVALID-ADDITION.
220             MOVE TRANSACTION TO LOG-RECORD.
221             MOVE BAD-ADDITION-MSG TO LOG-MESSAGE.
222             WRITE LOG-RECORD AFTER ADVANCING 1 LINE.
223             ADD 1 TO ERROR-COUNT.
224
225         X010-GET-VALID-TRANSACTION.
226             MOVE '?' TO SEQUENCE-ERROR-FLAG.
227             PERFORM Y010-READ-TRANSACTION
228                     UNTIL SEQUENCE-ERROR-FLAG = 'N'
229                         OR ERROR-COUNT IS GREATER THAN 10.
230
231         X020-GET-VALID-MASTER.
232             MOVE '?' TO SEQUENCE-ERROR-FLAG.
233             PERFORM Y020-READ-MASTER
234                     UNTIL SEQUENCE-ERROR-FLAG = 'N'
235                         OR ERROR-COUNT IS GREATER THAN 10.
236
237         Y010-READ-TRANSACTION.
238             READ TRANSACTION-FILE INTO TRANSACTION
239                     AT END MOVE HIGH-VALUES TO TR-KEY.
240             IF TR-KEY IS LESS THAN TR-KEY-PREVIOUS
241                 MOVE TRANSACTION TO LOG-RECORD
242                 MOVE TRANS-SEQUENCE-ERROR-MSG TO LOG-MESSAGE
243                 WRITE LOG-RECORD AFTER ADVANCING 1 LINE
244                 ADD 1 TO ERROR-COUNT
245             ELSE
246                 MOVE 'N' TO SEQUENCE-ERROR-FLAG.
247             MOVE TR-KEY TO TR-KEY-PREVIOUS.
248
249         Y020-READ-MASTER.
250             READ OLD-MASTER-FILE INTO OLD-MASTER
251                     AT END MOVE HIGH-VALUES TO OM-KEY.
252             IF OM-KEY IS LESS THAN OM-KEY-PREVIOUS
253                 MOVE OLD-MASTER TO LOG-RECORD
254                 MOVE MASTER-SEQUENCE-ERROR-MSG TO LOG-MESSAGE
255                 WRITE LOG-RECORD AFTER ADVANCING 1 LINE
256                 ADD 1 TO ERROR-COUNT
257             ELSE
258                 MOVE 'N' TO SEQUENCE-ERROR-FLAG.
259             MOVE OM-KEY TO OM-KEY-PREVIOUS.
260
261         ******************* END OF PROGRAM *************************
```

FIGURE 19.1   A main program to update a sequential file, which calls the subroutine of Figure 19.2 to do part of the actual file update processing.

The changes are minor. In the Data Division we added a structure containing three error flags. In the Procedure Division, we removed **D020-UPDATE-MASTER** (the paragraph that updated master records) and the subordinate paragraphs that it performed, and added a new paragraph to print some error messages. In **C010-APPLY-TRANSACTION**, the paragraph that is used to perform **D020-UPDATE-MASTER**, we removed the **PERFORM** statement and replaced it with a **CALL** and a few additional statements. The basic strategy is this. For reasons we will discuss shortly, we cannot print error messages from within the subprogram. Therefore, if any errors are found, we set an appropriate flag within the subprogram, then test the flag in the main program and, if necessary, print error messages in the main program. The function of the error flags is self-explanatory, as is the code to print the error messages.

Part of the reason we do not print the error messages in the subprogram is that to do so would complicate the subprogram and the parameter list; we would need to identify the file on which the messages are to be written, the format and text of the messages, the error count, and so on. However, if necessary these problems could be overcome. A more serious problem, however, is that a file can only be used in the program or subprogram that contains the **FD** defining the file. If we try to write the same **FD** in two or more subprograms, **COBOL** will treat the **FD**s as different files, each of which happens to have the same name as another file. The result would be chaos. Putting it another way, file names may not be used as parameters in the **USING** phrase, and a file may not be declared in more than one unit of the program.

19.4 THE SUBPROGRAM

The subprogram is shown in Figure 19.2. We observe that although it has an Environment Division header, nothing is in the division. This is because the subprogram does not deal with any files as such. In the Data Division there is no File Section and no Working-Storage Section. This is an accident of the processing to be done here; subprograms certainly may have these sections.

```
 1        IDENTIFICATION DIVISION.
 2        PROGRAM-ID.
 3            UPDATE-MASTER.
 4        DATE-WRITTEN.
 5            JULY 16, 1989.
 6
 7        ENVIRONMENT DIVISION.
 8
 9        DATA DIVISION.
10
11        LINKAGE SECTION.
12
13        01  OLD-MASTER.
14            05  OM-KEY                  PIC X(5).
15            05  OM-QUAN-ON-HAND         PIC 9(5).
16            05  OM-QUAN-ON-ORDER        PIC 9(5).
17            05  OM-REORDER-POINT        PIC 9(5).
18            05  OM-REORDER-QUAN         PIC 9(5).
19            05  OM-DESCRIPTION          PIC X(20).
20
```

```
21    01   TRANSACTION.
22         05   TR-KEY                          PIC X(5).
23         05   TR-QUANTITY                     PIC 9(5).
24         05   TR-TRANSACTION-CODE             PIC X.
25              88   ADDITION                             VALUE '1'.
26              88   ADJUSTMENT                           VALUE '2'.
27              88   RECEIPT                              VALUE '3'.
28              88   SHIPMENT                             VALUE '4'.
29              88   DELETION                             VALUE '5'.
30         05   TR-ADJUSTMENT-CODE              PIC 9.
31         05   TR-QUAN-ON-ORDER                PIC 9(5).
32         05   TR-REORDER-POINT                PIC 9(5).
33         05   TR-REORDER-QUAN                 PIC 9(5).
34         05   TR-DESCRIPTION                  PIC X(20).
35
36    01   UPDATE-ERROR-FLAGS.
37         05   BAD-TRANS-CODE                  PIC X.
38         05   OUT-OF-STOCK                    PIC X.
39         05   BAD-ADJ-CODE                    PIC X.
40
41
42    PROCEDURE DIVISION USING OLD-MASTER
43                             TRANSACTION
44                             UPDATE-ERROR-FLAGS.
45    A000-UPDATE-MASTER.
46         IF      SHIPMENT
47             PERFORM B010-PROCESS-SHIPMENT
48         ELSE IF RECEIPT
49             PERFORM B020-PROCESS-RECEIPT
50         ELSE IF ADJUSTMENT
51             PERFORM B030-PROCESS-ADJUSTMENT
52         ELSE
53             MOVE 'X' TO BAD-TRANS-CODE.
54
55    A999-EXIT.
56         EXIT PROGRAM.
57
58    B010-PROCESS-SHIPMENT.
59         IF OM-QUAN-ON-HAND IS NOT LESS THAN TR-QUANTITY
60             SUBTRACT TR-QUANTITY FROM OM-QUAN-ON-HAND
61         ELSE
62             MOVE 'X' TO OUT-OF-STOCK.
63
64    B020-PROCESS-RECEIPT.
65         ADD TR-QUANTITY TO OM-QUAN-ON-HAND.
66         SUBTRACT TR-QUANTITY FROM OM-QUAN-ON-ORDER.
67
68    B030-PROCESS-ADJUSTMENT.
69         IF      TR-ADJUSTMENT-CODE = 1
70             MOVE TR-QUANTITY TO OM-QUAN-ON-HAND
71         ELSE IF TR-ADJUSTMENT-CODE = 2
72             MOVE TR-QUANTITY TO OM-QUAN-ON-ORDER
73         ELSE IF TR-ADJUSTMENT-CODE = 3
74             MOVE TR-QUANTITY TO OM-REORDER-POINT
75         ELSE IF TR-ADJUSTMENT-CODE = 4
76             MOVE TR-QUANTITY TO OM-REORDER-QUAN
77         ELSE IF TR-ADJUSTMENT-CODE = 5
78             MOVE TR-DESCRIPTION TO OM-DESCRIPTION
79         ELSE
80             MOVE 'X' TO BAD-ADJ-CODE.
```

FIGURE 19.2 A subprogram called by the program of Figure 19.1 to perform file update processing.

The main paragraph of this subprogram has a somewhat unusual appearance, since it does not have an OPEN or CLOSE statement. Furthermore, instead of a STOP RUN statement, there is a new statement called EXIT PROGRAM, which must appear in a paragraph by itself. When this statement is encountered, execution simply returns to the calling program at the point immediately following the CALL statement.

As with STOP RUN, you may have any number of EXIT PROGRAM statements in the subprogram. The logic of the subprogram is much easier to understand, however, if we make a policy of never having more than one STOP RUN or EXIT PROGRAM in a program unit.

The code in the subprogram is essentially the same as in the corresponding paragraphs of UPDATE5 in Figure 13.11. We have changed the prefix codes of the paragraphs to reflect the structure of the subprogram and we have set error flags instead of writing messages; the remaining code is unchanged.

There is one feature of the subprogram that is not at all apparent from looking at the code, but which is very important to the execution of subprograms in general. There is no data storage contained within the Linkage Section of the subprogram! In spite of the fact that the Linkage Section looks very much like the Working-Storage Section of the main program, they are distinctly different in terms of data storage. In the Working-Storage Section of a program unit, whether in a main program or a subprogram, any data declaration causes the compiler to allocate space within the program unit to store the data. In the Linkage Section, the compiler simply uses the data definitions to determine what the parameters to the subprogram will look like. The data that is manipulated by the subprogram is actually located within the calling program. When the subprogram is called, a connection is made between the data described in the Linkage Section and the parameters used in the CALL statement to determine what data is being used by the subprogram. If we have several CALL statements with different parameters, the subprogram could be working with different data each time it is executed. This gives us tremendous flexibility and is a great advantage over using a paragraph, which must always work with the same data. However, because the data in the Linkage Section is actually located in another program unit, you may never use the VALUE clause in the Linkage Section except in level 88 entries.

The connection between a variable in the USING phrase of a CALL statement and a variable in the USING phrase of the Procedure Division header in the subprogram is made on the basis of position, not name. The first parameter in the CALL statement is matched to the first parameter in the subprogram, the second parameter in the CALL is matched to the second parameter in the subprogram, and so on. COBOL has no way of knowing whether the two parameter lists are actually in the same order. For example, if the subprogram had the parameter list in the order shown in Figure 19.2 but the CALL statement were written as

```
CALL 'UPDATE-MASTER' USING TRANSACTION
                           UPDATE-ERROR-FLAGS
                           OLD-MASTER
```

the main program and the subprogram would both compile correctly, they would link together correctly, but the results of execution would be totally incorrect and might even cause an abend.

19.5 EXECUTION RESULTS

When the program was compiled and run, the results were identical to those produced by **UPDATE5** in Chapter 13, shown below for easy reference.

NEW MASTER

```
000002001010004000120000040BOLT, 3 INCH X 1/2
000008000230004000060000040BOLT, 4 INCH X 1/2
00011002000020000350000100NUT, 1/2 INCH
000150099900888800777006666A CORRECT ADDITION
00021003100000000300000100BUSHING, 2 INCH OD
000240050901000020000050000500WASHER, 2 INCH
00036012340000000100000001000PIN, 1 INCH
000371230000000010000001000PIN, 1-1/2 INCH
00059422100000010000001000GADGET, RED
00061308750000001000001000WIDJET, GREEN
00070222220000010000001000WIDJET, PURPLE
0008000010000520005000030SAMPLE
000810010000000000008000005DRILL, 6 SPINDLE
000820100000030001200000200COTTER PINS, 2 IN
000840086200200010000000200COTTER PINS, 3 IN
```

LOG REPORT

```
000010001021                              THIS TRANSACTION IS OUT OF SEQUENCE
00011987651 111112222233333ERROR ENTRY    THIS ADDITION MATCHES AN EXISTING MASTER
00024012004                               INSUFFICIENT STOCK TO SHIP AMOUNT SPECIFIED
00036000005                               THIS TRANSACTION IS OUT OF SEQUENCE
0005154321000001000001000GADGET, BLUE     THIS MASTER RECORD HAS BEEN DELETED
00052000005                               THERE IS NO MASTER FOR THIS TRANSACTION
00059001230                               TRANSACTION CODE ILLEGAL
0006833333000001000001000MIS-FILE, RED-FACED  THIS MASTER IS OUT OF SEQUENCE
000810000029                              BAD ADJUSTMENT CODE
```

ORDER REPORT

```
00008      40    BOLT, 4 INCH X 1/2
00011     100    NUT, 1/2 INCH
00024     500    WASHER, 2 INCH
00080      30    SAMPLE
00082     200    COTTER PINS, 2 IN
00084     200    COTTER PINS, 3 IN
```

19.6 LINKING SUBPROGRAMS

When we use subprograms, the linking process becomes slightly more complicated than before. Up to now, the process for preparing a program for execution has been to compile it, then link it. For example, if we were working with the program MYPROG, we would execute

```
COBOL MYPROG;
LINK MYPROG;
```

However, if the program uses subprograms the procedure is slightly different. Suppose that **MYPROG** uses three subprograms, **SUB1**, **SUB2**, and **SUB3**; and that the four program units are stored in files MYPROGM.CBL, MYPROGS1.CBL, MYPROGS2.CBL, and MYPROGS3.CBL, respectively. The statements needed to create an executable program for MYPROG are the following:

```
COBOL MYPROGM;
COBOL MYPROGS1;
COBOL MYPROGS2;
COBOL MYPROGS3;
LINK MYPROGM+MYPROGS1+MYPROGS2+MYPROGS3,MYPROG;
```

Notice what these statements do. The first four commands compile the main program and the three subprograms; as always, the name passed to the compiler is the name of the file containing the program unit, not the name in the **PROGRAM-ID** paragraph. After all program units have been compiled we call the linker. The LINK statement contains two parameters. The first parameter is a list of the program units being linked. It begins with the main program then lists the subprograms, with the program names connected by plus signs. The second parameter is the name we wish to give to the executable program. Again, the names are the names of the files containing the program units, not the PROGRAM-ID names.

It is important to realize that if you are only changing one or two program units, you do not have to recompile everything. For example, if you discover an error in **SUB2**, you need only execute

```
COBOL MYPROGS2;
LINK MYPROGM+MYPROGS1+MYPROGS2+MYPROGS3,MYPROG;
```

This is one of the major advantages of using subprograms.

COBOL-85

19.7 COBOL-85 SUBPROGRAMS

One of the most significant areas of change in **COBOL-85** is in the way it deals with subprograms. Some of these changes, such as the use of internal subprograms (subprograms that lie within the bounds of the main program or another subprogram), offer the possibility of bringing **COBOL** much closer to the state of the art in software design. Others make **COBOL** much easier to use for certain problems. Most of changes are beyond the scope of our present discussion, but a few points are worth discussing briefly.

The first point involves the addition of the **EXTERNAL** phrase for file definition. We said before that a file cannot be defined in more than one program unit because **COBOL** will simply treat this as defining two separate files that happen to have the same name. In **COBOL-85**, however, you can define a file as follows:

```
FD  MASTER-FILE
    IS EXTERNAL
    LABEL RECORDS ARE STANDARD.
```

The **EXTERNAL** phrase tells **COBOL** that **MASTER-FILE** may be defined in more than one program unit; that is, in the main program and a subprogram, or in several subprograms. In this case all of these definitions refer to the same file, which allows you, for example, to open and close the file in one program unit and read from it or write to it in another program unit.

Another feature of **COBOL-85** subprograms of interest to us relates to the way in which program units are compiled. In earlier versions of **COBOL**, subprograms were required to be compiled separately from the main program and no two subprograms could be compiled together. **COBOL-85** includes a feature called the *end program header*, which allows you to chain a main program and its subprograms together as a single stream of code and compile them all at once. The format of the end program header is

> **END PROGRAM** program-name

For example, the program shown in Figures 19.1 and 19.2 normally would be compiled as two separate units. However, in **COBOL-85** we could write the following:

```
IDENTIFICATION DIVISION.
PROGRAM-ID.
   UPDATE6.
     .
     .
     .

END PROGRAM UPDATE6.
IDENTIFICATION DIVISION.
PROGRAM-ID.
   UPDATE-MASTER.
     .
     .
     .

END PROGRAM UPDATE-MASTER.
```

This file of code could then be submitted to the **COBOL** compiler and both program units would be compiled. In effect, the end program header simply serves to mark the end of one program unit and the start of another. Aside from the fact that both program units are compiled at once, the result is essentially the same as separate compilation. There is one important difference, however. Since the source code for all program units is contained in a single file, the compiler must create new files for the object code (the output from the compiler) for all but the first program. For example, suppose that the source code was contained in the file UPDATE6.CBL. The object code for the first program would be stored in UPDATE6.CBL, while the object code for the second program would be stored in UPDATE-M.OBJ. In otherwords, the file name for the second and all successive programs is based on the first eight characters in each program's **PROGRAM-ID**. This generally causes no problem, but you should know what file names to expect, and what names must be used in the LINK statement.

The last **COBOL-85** feature we will look at is the format for using nested subprograms. We can treat the main program and all its subprograms as a single program unit. For example, we could take the subprogram **UPDATE-MASTER** and nest it within **UPDATE6** as follows:

```
IDENTIFICATION DIVISION.
PROGRAM-ID.
   UPDATE6.
   .
   .
   .

*    BEGIN NESTED SUBPROGRAM
IDENTIFICATION DIVISION.
PROGRAM-ID.
   UPDATE-MASTER.
   .
   .
   .

END PROGRAM UPDATE-MASTER.
END PROGRAM UPDATE6.
```

Notice the difference between these two program skeletons. In the first, the **END PROGRAM** statement for **UPDATE6** comes *before* the beginning of the subprogram. In the second, we simply begin **UPDATE-MASTER** immediately after the last statement of **UPDATE6**. **UPDATE-MASTER** ends with its **END PROGRAM** statement, then the **END PROGRAM** statement for the main program comes at the very end. This program can now be processed with the single compile and link statements that we used before this chapter. That is,

```
COBOL UPDATE6;
LINK UPDATE6;
```

However, although the compilation and linking is somewhat simpler, we have lost the advantages of working with separate program files.

The subprogram features that have been added to **COBOL-85**, and which are available in Microsoft **COBOL**, go far beyond the brief examples we have shown here. A programmer interested in the more advanced features available with **COBOL-85** should study the Microsoft **COBOL** manual.

END COBOL-85

19.8 CONCLUSION

Subprograms offer flexibility, efficiency, and design sophistication far beyond what can be accomplished using only paragraphs. However, using subprograms effectively requires study and practice. What we have presented in this chapter is sufficient to enable you to begin using subprograms but, as with many aspects of **COBOL**, we recommend continued study of advanced subprogram concepts.

REVIEW QUESTIONS

1. Give several reasons for using subprograms.
2. What is the function of the Linkage Section?

3. Is it possible to place the **OPEN** and **CLOSE** statements for a file in a calling program and the **READ** or **WRITE** statements for it in a subprogram?

4. How many bytes of data are allocated within **SUBPROG** by the following code?

```
IDENTIFICATION DIVISION.
PROGRAM-ID.  SUBPROG.

ENVIRONMENT DIVISION.

DATA DIVISION.
LINKAGE SECTION.
77  ERROR-FLAG            PIC X.
01  DATA-REC.
    05  FLD-1             PIC S9(5).
    05  FLD-2             PIC X(10).
    05  FLD-3             PIC S9(8) COMP SYNC.

PROCEDURE DIVISION USING ERROR-FLAG, DATA-REC.
    .
    .
    .
```

5. Suppose you are given the following subprogram:

```
IDENTIFICATION DIVISION.
PROGRAM-ID.  SIMPLE.
ENVIRONMENT DIVISION.
DATA DIVISION.
LINKAGE SECTION.
77  XYZ                   PIC 9 VALUE 0.
PROCEDURE DIVISION USING XYZ.
    MOVE 9 TO XYZ.
EXIT-PARAGRAPH.
    EXIT PROGRAM.
```

What would happen if the program were called by the following statement?

```
CALL 'SIMPLE' USING 7.
```

ANSWERS TO REVIEW QUESTIONS

1. If a processing function is needed at several points in a program, it saves space to specify that function once in a subprogram and then call the subprogram into action whenever the function is needed. Another reason is that subprograms provide one good way to divide the effort of a project that is too large for one programmer to do in the available time. A third reason is that subprograms provide a way to separate the details of processing functions from the logic that controls them, which can often clarify program relations and improve understandability. Finally, subprograms provide a way to separate use of data between program modules so that one module cannot accidentally alter some data being used by another module.

2. It provides a subprogram with a description of the data from the calling program that the subprogram is to process.

3. No, unless you are using the **COBOL-85** options and specify **IS EXTERNAL** in the **FD** entries for the file.

4. Zero. There is never any data allocated within the Linkage Section. The definitions in the Linkage Section describe the format of parameters located within the calling program.

5. Nothing, since the program would not compile. The subprogram **SIMPLE** contains an error in that data in the Linkage Section may not have a **VALUE** clause. The calling program contains an error in that parameters in a **USING** clause must always be data names, not literals.

EXERCISES

1. Modify the seed catalog program in Figure 11.1 so that the functions of **C010-EDIT-LINE** are implemented in a subprogram instead of in the main program.

2. Modify the program in Figure 19.1 so that as much as possible of **X010-GET-VALID-TRANSACTION** and **X020-GET-VALID-MASTER** are implemented in separate subprograms instead of in the main program. There are several points to remember in carrying out this change. First, the **SELECT** and **FD** statements for each file must be contained within the appropriate subprogram and removed from the main program. Second, the subprograms must open and close the files at the proper time and at no other time. Third, in addition to having a data record as a parameter, each subprogram must return various flags and counts to the calling program. Finally, instead of printing error messages within the subprograms, you must pass a flag to the calling program that prints the error messages.

3. If you are using **COBOL-85**, write the program for Exercise 2 so that *all* of **X010-GET-VALID-TRANSACTION** and **X020-GET-VALID-MASTER** are implemented as subprograms. Use the **EXTERNAL** clause on file definitions where appropriate so that error messages can be printed within the subprograms.

4. (This exercise is suitable for use as a small project.)

   Make the following changes to the program described in Exercise 4 of Chapter 18. Instead of coding the municipality codes and tax rates directly into the program, the program should read a municipality tax file, load the data into a table, and search the table to find the entry that matches the municipality code in an employee pay record.

   The records in the municipality tax file have the following format:

   | Columns 1-2 | municipality code | PIC 99 |
   | Columns 3-6 | tax rate | PIC 99V99 |

   Design an appropriate table to hold this data. If the table overflows when it is being loaded, count the total number of records in the municipality file, print a message telling the user what happened and how large the table needs to be to hold the entire file, and stop the run. When you are processing the payroll records, if a record contains a municipality code that is not in the table print an appropriate error message and go on the the next payroll record.

The table loading process and the searching process should be performed in two separately compiled subprograms. The table itself must be defined in the main program (so that it can be used in both subprograms), but the file containing the municipality tax data must be defined in the loading subprogram. The call for the first subprogram should look something like the following:

```
CALL 'LOADTAX' USING TAX-TABLE-AREA, RECORD-COUNT,
                     OVERFLOW-FLAG.
```

RECORD-COUNT contains the number of records in the input file. If no overflow occurs this is equal to the number of records loaded into the table. **OVERFLOW-FLAG** indicates whether or not table overflow occurred during the loading process. In a well-designed system the subprogram should not report any errors, nor should its operation depend on any knowledge of how the table will be used or what the main program will do if overflow occurs. The function of the subprogram is to load records into the table, and to return to the calling program a count of the number of records in the input file and an indication of whether or not overflow occurred. The calling program is to determine whether the flag indicates that an error has occurred, and what should be done if it has.

The call for the second subprogram should look like the following:

```
CALL 'FINDTAX' USING TAX-TABLE-AREA, MUNICIPALITY-CODE,
                     TAX-RATE, NOT-FOUND-FLAG.
```

MUNICIPALITY-CODE contains the code for the municipality to be found in the table, **TAX-RATE** contains the tax rate for the specified municipality, and **NOT-FOUND-FLAG** contains a flag indicating whether or not the desired entry actually was found. Inside the subprogram use **SEARCH ALL** to locate the appropriate entry in the table. Note, however, that the method used to search the table is not visible from the main program.

CHAPTER 20

ADDITIONAL COBOL TOPICS

20.1   INTRODUCTION

In this chapter we discuss a number of **COBOL** features that remain to be considered. Some of them are widely used, but could not be studied appropriately until now. Others are infrequently or even rarely used in current programming practice, but should be discussed for the benefit of readers who will be maintaining programs that use them.

20.2   THE GO TO STATEMENT

The **GO TO** statement transfers control to the start of a named paragraph. It differs from the **PERFORM** statement in that the **PERFORM** executes a paragraph, then returns to the current location in the program, while the **GO TO** simply jumps to some new point in the program, then continues execution from this location. Current programming practice strongly discourages the use of **GO TO** statements. A detailed discussion of why **GO TO** statements add complexity to programs is beyond the scope of our present discussion, but most studies of software design techniques made since the late 1960s agree that **GO TO** statements tend to detract from the quality of a program. However, they do exist in some programs and can even prove useful in a few specific circumstances.

The **GO TO** statement has the following form:

<u>GO</u> **TO** paragraph-name

The paragraph name may be the same one in which the **GO TO** appears, a paragraph that appears earlier in the program, or a paragraph that appears later in the program. Generally, however, we recommend that **GO TO** statements refer to paragraphs that appear later in the program.

One of the situations in which a **GO TO** can simplify code is when execution of a task depends on a set of complex conditions all being true. For example, you might have a function which is performed on a data record only if the record can pass all of a number of edits. If the ability to perform one of these edits requires all previous edits to be successful, the code can look something like the following:

```
IF condition-1
    IF condition-2
        IF condition-3
              .
              .
              .
            IF condition-n
                process data
            ELSE
                process error-n
              .
              .
              .
        ELSE
            process error-3
    ELSE
        process error-2
ELSE
    process error-1.
```

Clearly, we would like to avoid all these nested **IF** statements. We can do this with the **GO TO** statement:

```
IF NOT condition-1
    process error-1
    GO TO PROCESS-EXIT.
IF NOT condition-2
    process error-2
    GO TO PROCESS-EXIT.
IF NOT condition-3
    process error-3
    GO TO PROCESS-EXIT.
    .
    .
    .
IF NOT condition-n
    process error-n
    GO TO PROCESS-EXIT.
*   AT THIS POINT THE DATA MUST BE VALID
    process data.
PROCESS-EXIT.
    EXIT.
```

The last two lines of this example demonstrate the use of a new **COBOL** statement called **EXIT**. **EXIT** must be the only statement in its paragraph, and it does not do anything but mark a location in a program. Execution will continue with the paragraph immediately following the **EXIT** paragraph. However, notice what we have accomplished. We test the conditions one at a time. Although we have only shown simple conditions in this example, each condition could be determined by extensive data analysis and calculation. If the condition is not valid, we process the error, then skip around all the remaining processing. However, if all conditions are true, that is, if no errors are found, we eventually reach the point where we process the data. In spite of the fact that we are using GO TO statements, this simple structure is easier to follow than if we had used the corresponding nested IF statements.

Note that it is permissible under COBOL syntax to complete the actions of one paragraph and the "fall through" to the beginning of the next paragraph; this is the way that execution reaches PROCESS-EXIT when the data is valid, and this is the way that execution reaches the paragraph following PROCESS-EXIT. Under the guidelines of structured programming used for this book, this never happens in any other circumstance. All paragraphs in this book—other than in this example—are entered through PERFORM statements, with the very rare exception of a paragraph entered through a GO TO.

There is a variation on the GO TO statement which can be used to implement the case structure, again as an alternative to the nested IF. This format of the GO TO is

---

GO TO paragraph-name-1 . . . paragraph-name-n DEPENDING ON identifier

---

The paragraph names may be any paragraph names in the program, while the identifier must be an elementary numeric item. To demonstrate the use of the GO TO . . . DEPENDING ON in the case structure, we will use the sequentia file update program. Recall that the transaction record has this format:

```
01  TRANSACTION.
    05  TR-KEY                   PIC X(5).
    05  TR-QUANTITY              PIC 9(5).
    05  TR-TRANSACTION-CODE      PIC X.
        88  ADDITION                 VALUE '1'.
        88  ADJUSTMENT               VALUE '2'.
        88  RECEIPT                  VALUE '3'.
        88  SHIPMENT                 VALUE '4'.
        88  DELETION                 VALUE '5'.
    05  TR-ADJUSTMENT-CODE       PIC X.
    05  TR-QUAN-ON-ORDER         PIC 9(5).
    05  TR-REORDER-POINT         PIC 9(5).
    05  TR-REORDER-QUAN          PIC 9(5).
    05  TR-DESCRIPTION           PIC X(20).
```

If the transaction is an adjustment, the data in the transaction is used to update one of five fields in the master record, depending on the value of TR-ADJUSTMENT-CODE. In previous versions of the program we used a nested IF statement to implement the case statement that controlled which of the five fields was updated. However, with the GO TO . . . DEPENDING ON we can use the following code:

```
IF ADJUSTMENT
    PERFORM E030-PROCESS-ADJUSTMENT
        THRU E039-PROCESS-ADJUSTMENT-EXIT.
    .
    .
    .
```

```
E030-PROCESS-ADJUSTMENT.
    GO TO
        E031-ADJUST-QUAN-ON-HAND
        E032-ADJUST-QUAN-ON-ORDER
        E033-ADJUST-REORDER-POINT
        E034-ADJUST-REORDER-QUAN
        E035-ADJUST-DESCRIPTION
            DEPENDING ON TR-ADJUSTMENT-CODE.
    MOVE 'X' TO BAD-ADJ-CODE.
    GO TO E039-PROCESS-ADJUSTMENT-EXIT.

E031-ADJUST-QUAN-ON-HAND.
    MOVE TR-QUANTITY TO OM-QUAN-ON-HAND.
    GO TO E039-PROCESS-ADJUSTMENT-EXIT.

E032-ADJUST-QUAN-ON-ORDER.
    MOVE TR-QUANTITY TO OM-QUAN-ON-ORDER.
    GO TO E039-PROCESS-ADJUSTMENT-EXIT.

E033-ADJUST-REORDER-POINT.
    MOVE TR-QUANTITY TO OM-REORDER-POINT.
    GO TO E039-PROCESS-ADJUSTMENT-EXIT.

E034-ADJUST-REORDER-QUAN.
    MOVE TR-QUANTITY TO OM-REORDER-QUAN.
    GO TO E039-PROCESS-ADJUSTMENT-EXIT.

E035-ADJUST-DESCRIPTION.
    MOVE TR-DESCRIPTION TO OM-DESCRIPTION.
    GO TO E039-PROCESS-ADJUSTMENT-EXIT.

E039-PROCESS-ADJUSTMENT-EXIT.
    EXIT.
```

The **PERFORM** statement under the **IF** uses **THRU** to specify a range of paragraphs to be performed. Complete rules governing the use of the **PERFORM** . . . **THRU** option may be found in the Microsoft **COBOL** manual. Since we only use the feature to simulate the case statement, we need not be concerned with these details.

The **GO TO** at the start of the example uses the **DEPENDING ON** option. As the format before the examples indicates, we list a number of paragraph names, five in this example. The variable named in the **DEPENDING ON** phrase must be a positive or unsigned integer, and its value should be in the range of one to the number of paragraph names. The execution of the statement results in a transfer to the first-named paragraph if the value of the **DEPENDING ON** variable is one, to the second-named paragraph if the value of the **DEPENDING ON** variable is two, and so on. If the value of the **DEPENDING ON** variable is less than one or greater than the number of paragraph names, there is no transfer and, instead, the statement after the **GO TO** . . . **DEPENDING ON** is executed. In our example, if **TR-ADJUSTMENT-CODE** is out of range, we set an error flag, then transfer control to the **EXIT** paragraph.

It is only accidental that the paragraphs named in the **GO TO** . . . **DEPEND-ING ON** appear in the same order as their names are written within the range of the case structure. In fact, it is not even necessary that the names in the **GO TO** all be distinct. To see how this could be useful, suppose that we had inherited the adjustment code from a previous file design that we were not permitted to change. Assume that adjustment codes of 1 or 3 specified an adjustment of the quantity on hand, a code of 2 or 5 specified an adjustment of a quantity on order, a code of 4 specified a description change, a code of 6 a reorder point change, and a code of 7 a reorder quantity change. Anything else is an error as before. The desired processing could be carried out with the following GO TO statement.

```
GO  TO
    E031-ADJUST-QUAN-ON-HAND
    E032-ADJUST-QUAN-ON-ORDER
    E031-ADJUST-QUAN-ON-HAND
    E035-ADJUST-DESCRIPTION
    E032-ADJUST-QUAN-ON-ORDER
    E033-ADJUST-REORDER-POINT
    E034-ADJUST-REORDER-QUAN
        DEPENDING ON TR-ADJUSTMENT-CODE.
```

Nothing else in the case structure need be changed.

Since there are only five cases to be considered in this example, the case structure can be implemented just as effectively with a nested IF statement as with the structure shown above. The GO TO ... DEPENDING ON implementation is really needed, however, when the number of cases becomes large. It is not uncommon in some applications to have a two-digit code, with most or all of the 100 combinations having to be handled by separated routines. In such a situation a nested IF is not practical, and writing 100 separate IF statements to test all of the possibilities is terribly inefficient. Of course, if you are using COBOL-85 the EVALUATE statement should be used.

20.3   THE COPY STATEMENT

It often happens that there are program segments that are needed in many different programs. An example would be a paragraph that prints a line of text to a report file and, when appropriate, prints a heading at the top of the page. Another very common situation is that many programs in a system process the same files or produce the same output records; all such programs will require identical record descriptions in their Data Divisions. It is time-consuming and error prone for all the programmers needing such program segments to write them out in a program, and for Data Division entries we are likely to wind up with many different descriptions for the same records. A much better solution is available through use of the COBOL COPY statement.

To use the COPY statement it is necessary to place the program segment that is to be copied into a text file that can be accessed by the COBOL compiler. Generally this file is created with the same text editor used to write the COBOL program. A collection of these text files is generally called a *library*. With the library available we are able to write programs in which we simply specify that sections of code are to be retrieved from the library and inserted at specified points in the program. This insertion is done before compilation, and compilation then proceeds just as through we had written out everything that was obtained from the library. In the program listing we are given the copy statement as we wrote it plus all the lines that were obtained from the library.

A simple example from programs used in previous chapters appears in Chapter 19, in the discussion of subprograms. In both the main program and the subprogram we need a definition of the old master record and the transaction record. It is easy to imagine that in an actual data processing installation, particularly one which uses subprograms frequently, there would be many other programs processing the same files that would also need the same record descriptions. After preparing the library entries for the two records under the names of **OMLIB** and **TRLIB**, we can simplify the writing of either of the programs using **COPY** statements. Figure 20.1 contains the first portion of the subprogram from Figure 19.2, written in this way.

The source program listing produced when this program was compiled is shown in Figure 20.2. So you can see how the inserted lines of code are marked, Figure 20.2 shows the listing from the Microsoft **COBOL** compiler—but we have removed some spaces to make the lines fit on the page here. As far as the compiler is concerned, this program is identical to the one in Figure 19.2.

There are several points to notice about the code in Figures 20.1 and 20.2. First, although it may seem strange to see what looks like procedural code in the Data Division, the **COPY** statement is indeed a *statement*, not just a clause in the record description. The record name is followed by a period and, in keeping with our convention never to put two statements on the same line, we begin the **COPY** statement on the next line. The name following the word **COPY** is the name of the library file containing the code to be copied.

The second point is that the included code does not contain a **01** level entry. The copied code replaces the **COPY** statement exactly and must make

```
IDENTIFICATION DIVISION.
PROGRAM-ID.
    UPDATE-MASTER.
DATE-WRITTEN.
    JULY 17, 1989.

ENVIRONMENT DIVISION.

DATA DIVISION.

LINKAGE SECTION.

01   OLD-MASTER.
     COPY OMLIB.

01   TRANSACTION.
     COPY TRLIB.

01   UPDATE-ERROR-FLAGS.
     05   BAD-TRANS-CODE        PIC X.
     05   OUT-OF-STOCK          PIC X.
     05   BAD-ADJ-CODE          PIC X.
```

FIGURE 20.1 An example of source code using the **COPY** statement to copy standard record definition.. (Some space has been removed to make the lines fit on the page of this book.)

```
Microsoft COBOL Version 3.00      L2.0 revision 053 17-Jul-89 17:05 Page    1
*                                        CH20P01.CBL
* Options: GNT(CH20P01.OBJ) NOLIST NOASMLIST  LIST"ch20p01.lst"  LW"132"
      1 IDENTIFICATION DIVISION.                                         1
      2 PROGRAM-ID.                                                      2
      3     UPDATE-MASTER.                                               3
      4 DATE-WRITTEN.                                                    4
      5     JULY 17, 1989.                                               5
      6                                                                  6
      7 ENVIRONMENT DIVISION.                                            7
      8                                                                  8
      9 DATA DIVISION.                                                   9
     10                                                                 10
     11 LINKAGE SECTION.                                                11
     12                                                                 12
     13 01  OLD-MASTER.                                                 13
*    14     COPY OMLIB.                                                 14
     15     05  OM-KEY             PIC X(5).           OMLIB    1
     16     05  OM-QUAN-ON-HAND    PIC 9(5).           OMLIB    2
     17     05  OM-QUAN-ON-ORDER   PIC 9(5).           OMLIB    3
     18     05  OM-REORDER-POINT   PIC 9(5).           OMLIB    4
     19     05  OM-REORDER-QUAN    PIC 9(5).           OMLIB    5
     20     05  OM-DESCRIPTION     PIC X(20).          OMLIB    6
     21                                                         15
     22 01  TRANSACTION.                                        16
*    23     COPY TRLIB.                                         17
     24     05  TR-KEY             PIC X(5).           TRLIB    1
     25     05  TR-QUANTITY        PIC 9(5).           TRLIB    2
     26     05  TR-TRANSACTION-CODE PIC X.             TRLIB    3
     27         88  ADDITION           VALUE '1'.      TRLIB    4
     28         88  ADJUSTMENT         VALUE '2'.      TRLIB    5
     29         88  RECEIPT            VALUE '3'.      TRLIB    6
     30         88  SHIPMENT           VALUE '4'.      TRLIB    7
     31         88  DELETION           VALUE '5'.      TRLIB    8
     32     05  TR-ADJUSTMENT-CODE  PIC 9.            TRLIB    9
     33     05  TR-QUAN-ON-ORDER   PIC 9(5).          TRLIB   10
     34     05  TR-REORDER-POINT   PIC 9(5).          TRLIB   11
     35     05  TR-REORDER-QUAN    PIC 9(5).          TRLIB   12
     36     05  TR-DESCRIPTION     PIC X(20).         TRLIB   13
     37                                                        18
     38 01  UPDATE-ERROR-FLAGS.                                19
     39     05  BAD-TRANS-CODE     PIC X.                      20
     40     05  OUT-OF-STOCK       PIC X.                      21
     41     05  BAD-ADJ-CODE       PIC X.                      22
```

FIGURE 20.2 A section of a program illustrating the appearance of the compiler source program when the **COPY** feature is used.

sense in that context. If we had started the library entries with **01** level lines of text, the code in Figure 20.2 would have had two sequential **01** level lines, the first of which has no **PICTURE** clause and no subordinate entries; this is, of course, an error in **COBOL**.

Finally, notice the format of the included code in Figure 20.2. At the left margin, all statements—including the copied statements—are numbered sequentially. The only mark to indicate the use of the COPY statement is the asterisk at the left of lines 14 and 23. However, in the right margin, copied lines of code are given a different sequence of line numbers from code in the main program. Thus, the statement COPY OMLIB is line 14 in both margins, but the blank line following this in the source code is line 21 in the left margin but is line 15 in the right margin. Furthermore, to help identify the library file, the first eight characters of the file name are printed on each copied line at the right side of the listing. The library file name and the right-hand column of line numbers only appear if you specify a line width of more than 115 characters, using the line width compiler directive; for example, LW"116".

A useful option of the COPY statement is the replacing phrase. For example, if we wanted the record key fields to be called MASTER-KEY and XACT-KEY, we could write the COPY statements as follows.

```
IDENTIFICATION DIVISION.
PROGRAM-ID.
    UPDATE-MASTER.
DATE-WRITTEN.
    JULY 17, 1989.

ENVIRONMENT DIVISION.

DATA DIVISION.

LINKAGE SECTION.

01  OLD-MASTER.
    COPY OMLIB
        REPLACING OM-KEY BY MASTER-KEY.

01  TRANSACTION.
    COPY TRLIB
        REPLACING TR-KEY BY XACT-KEY.

01  UPDATE-ERROR-FLAGS.
    05   BAD-TRANS-CODE         PIC X.
    05   OUT-OF-STOCK           PIC X.
    05   BAD-ADJ-CODE           PIC X.
```

The result would be as shown in Figure 20.3. Again, we have used the listing from the Microsoft compiler.

The **REPLACING** phrase of the COPY statement has several other options, which can be found in the Microsoft COBOL manual. We should mention that although the COPY statement is still used in many COBOL installations, the source code processors available on many computers provide their own built-in equivalent of the COPY statement, making the COPY statement unnecessary in these cases. Nonetheless, whether the result is obtained from the COPY statement or a source code processor, most data processing installations keep copies of common data records and other frequently used code in libraries and simply copy them into COBOL programs.

```
Microsoft COBOL Version 3.00      L2.0 revision 053 17-Jul-89 16:46 Page   1
*                                      CH20P02.CBL
* Options: GNT(CH20P02.OBJ) NOLIST NOASMLIST  LIST"ch20p02.lst"  LW"132"
      1 IDENTIFICATION DIVISION.                                            1
      2 PROGRAM-ID.                                                         2
      3     UPDATE-MASTER.                                                  3
      4 DATE-WRITTEN.                                                       4
      5     JULY 17, 1989.                                                  5
      6                                                                     6
      7 ENVIRONMENT DIVISION.                                               7
      8                                                                     8
      9 DATA DIVISION.                                                      9
     10                                                                    10
     11 LINKAGE SECTION.                                                   11
     12                                                                    12
     13 01  OLD-MASTER.                                                    13
*    14     COPY OMLIB                                                     14
*    15         REPLACING OM-KEY BY MASTER-KEY.                            15
     16     05                                               OMLIB         1
     17                         MASTER-KEY                   OMLIB         1
     18                              PIC X(5).               OMLIB         1
     19     05  OM-QUAN-ON-HAND     PIC 9(5).               OMLIB         2
     20     05  OM-QUAN-ON-ORDER    PIC 9(5).               OMLIB         3
     21     05  OM-REORDER-POINT    PIC 9(5).               OMLIB         4
     22     05  OM-REORDER-QUAN     PIC 9(5).               OMLIB         5
     23     05  OM-DESCRIPTION      PIC X(20).              OMLIB         6
     24                                                                   16
     25 01  TRANSACTION.                                                  17
*    26     COPY TRLIB                                                    18
*    27         REPLACING TR-KEY BY XACT-KEY.                             19
     28     05                                               TRLIB         1
     29                         XACT-KEY                     TRLIB         1
     30                              PIC X(5).               TRLIB         1
     31     05  TR-QUANTITY         PIC 9(5).               TRLIB         2
     32     05  TR-TRANSACTION-CODE PIC X.                  TRLIB         3
     33         88   ADDITION              VALUE '1'.       TRLIB         4
     34         88   ADJUSTMENT            VALUE '2'.       TRLIB         5
     35         88   RECEIPT               VALUE '3'.       TRLIB         6
     36         88   SHIPMENT              VALUE '4'.       TRLIB         7
     37         88   DELETION              VALUE '5'.       TRLIB         8
     38     05  TR-ADJUSTMENT-CODE  PIC 9.                  TRLIB         9
     39     05  TR-QUAN-ON-ORDER    PIC 9(5).               TRLIB        10
     40     05  TR-REORDER-POINT    PIC 9(5).               TRLIB        11
     41     05  TR-REORDER-QUAN     PIC 9(5).               TRLIB        12
     42     05  TR-DESCRIPTION      PIC X(20).              TRLIB        13
     43                                                                   20
     44 01  UPDATE-ERROR-FLAGS.                                           21
     45     05  BAD-TRANS-CODE      PIC X.                                22
     46     05  OUT-OF-STOCK        PIC X.                                23
     47     05  BAD-ADJ-CODE        PIC X.                                24
```

FIGURE 20.3 A section of a program illustrating the result of using the **COPY** statement with the **REPLACING** option.

20.4 THE COMPUTE STATEMENT

The **COMPUTE** statement provides a way to specify operations that are sometimes more cumbersome or even impossible to express otherwise. The general format is

$$\text{\underline{COMPUTE} identifier-1 [\underline{ROUNDED}]} = \begin{Bmatrix} \text{identifier-2} \\ \text{literal-1} \\ \text{arithmetic-expression} \end{Bmatrix}$$

[ON **SIZE ERROR**] imperative-statement

COBOL-85
___

As with other verbs, **COBOL-85** allows an optional **END-COMPUTE** phrase at the end of the statement.

END COBOL-85
___

Literal-1 must be numeric; identifier-2 must be an elementary numeric item; identifier-1 must be an elementary numeric item, which may or may not specify editing, as the circumstances require. The identifier-2 and literal-1 combinations provide an alternative to using the **MOVE** statement to assign identifier-1 a value; this is seldom done.

The arithmetic-expression option permits one to write formulas, from very simple to quite complex, for expressing operations, rather than writing sequences of arithmetic statements. It also permits the use of exponentiation (raising to a power) that cannot be done any other way in **COBOL**.

20.5 ARITHMETIC EXPRESSIONS

An arithmetic expression is made up of combinations of identifiers and literals, separated by arithmetic operators and parentheses. Although the simplest arithmetic expression consists of a single literal or identifier such as the following

```
COMPUTE TOTAL = 0.00.
COMPUTE TOTAL = FIRST-VALUE.
```

the most common arithmetic expression consists of literals and/or identifiers combined by the following arithmetic operators:

Operator	Meaning
+	add
–	subtract
*	multiply
/	divide
**	exponentiate

Each arithmetic operator must be preceded and followed by a space. Here are examples of the use of the four basic arithmetic operators, followed in each case by a statement expressing the same meaning using arithmetic verbs.

```
COMPUTE C = A + B.
ADD A, B GIVING C.

COMPUTE D = A + B + C + D.
ADD A B C TO D.

COMPUTE D = C - A - B.
SUBTRACT A B FROM C GIVING D.

COMPUTE B = B - A.
SUBTRACT A FROM B.

COMPUTE C = B / A.
DIVIDE B BY A GIVING C.

COMPUTE B = B / A.
DIVIDE A INTO B.

COMPUTE C = A * B.
MULTIPLY A BY B GIVING C.

COMPUTE B = A * B.
MULTIPLY A BY B.
```

Here are some examples of the use of arithmetic expressions in COMPUTE statements to carry out familiar data processing operations.

```
COMPUTE NET-PAY = GROSS-PAY - DEDUCTIONS.
COMPUTE MONTH-AVERAGE = YEAR-TOTAL / 12.
COMPUTE MARGIN = QTY-ON-HAND + QTY-ON-ORDER - QTY-RESERVED.
COMPUTE GROSS-PAY = HOURS-WORKED * PAY-RATE.
```

Exponentiation can be used to raise a quantity to a power like this:

```
COMPUTE B = A ** 4.
```

Most commonly, however, exponentiation is used to get roots, which cannot be done any other way in COBOL. For example, we could used the following to compute a square root:

```
COMPUTE B = A ** 0.5.
```

When there are a number of arithmetic operators in an expression, it is necessary to know the order in which they are carried out. The answer to this question is given by the following *operator hierarchy rule*:

In the absence of parentheses, all exponentiations are evaluated first, then all multiplications and divisions (from left to right), then all additions and subtractions (from left to right).

Thus, in the following example the division is carried out first, then the multiplication. The result of the division is added to A and the result of the multiplication is subtracted from the result of the addition.

```
A + B / C - D * E
```

In the next example, we take the square root of B, divide it by the square of C, and subtract the result of the division from A.

```
A - B ** 0.5 / C ** 2
```

If there is any doubt about what a given expression means, it can always be made explicit by the use of parentheses. Subexpressions within parentheses are always evaluated first, regardless of what the operator hierarchy rule would otherwise dictate. There should not be a space following a left parenthesis or preceding a right parenthesis, and left and right parentheses must be matched in meaningful pairs. Consider a few examples.

```
A * (B + C)
```

Parentheses are used to force the addition to be done before the multiplication.

```
(A * B / C) ** 0.5
```

Without the parentheses we would have **A** times **B**, divided by the square root of **C**, instead of taking the square root of the entire expression.

```
A / (B * C)
```

The parentheses here force **A** to be divided by the product of **B** and **C**. Without them, **A** would be divided by **B** and the result of the division would be multiplied by **C**. Similarly, in the following example the parentheses cause **C** to be subtracted from **B**, then the result subtracted from **A**. This gives **E** the value 2, while **D** has the value 0.

```
MOVE 3 TO A.
MOVE 2 TO B.
MOVE 1 TO C.
COMPUTE D = A - B - C.
COMPUTE E = A - (B - C).
```

A special arithmetic operator, which will find only specialized use, is the *unary minus sign*. The "unary" means that it applies to a single operand, rather than combining two operands as the binary minus does. As you would expect, the unary minus reverses the sign of the expression it precedes.

20.6 EXAMPLES OF THE USE OF THE COMPUTE STATEMENT

In the payroll programs in Chapters 6 and 7 we computed an employee's total exemptions and then, if the gross pay exceeded the exemptions, found the tax (See Figure 6.3). This can be done a bit more directly with a COMPUTE statement:

```
IF W-GROSS-PAY IS GREATER THAN W-EXEMPTION-TOTAL
    COMPUTE W-TAX ROUNDED =
            (W-GROSS-PAY - W-EXEMPTIONS-TOTAL) * C-TAXRATE
ELSE
    MOVE ZERO TO W-TAX.
```

Using the COMPUTE statement, we can also condense the computation of a worker's gross pay, including overtime, with this statement:

```
IF HOURS-WORKED NOT > 40
    COMPUTE W-GROSS-PAY ROUNDED = I-HOURS-WORKED * I-PAYRATE
ELSE
    COMPUTE W-GROSS-PAY ROUNDED =
            40 * I-PAYRATE
        + 1.5 * (I-HOURS-WORKED - 40) * I-PAYRATE.
```

This arranges the computation differently from the way it was done in the programs given earlier in the book. Since it is a simple matter to put the entire computation into one **IF** statement, we make entirely separate computations of the two cases, with and without overtime. As always, there are many other ways the calculations could be arranged, and the choice between them should be based on simplicity and clarity.

Both of the examples above could have been done using ordinary arithmetic verbs (and indeed were, in earlier chapters). Here is one example that cannot be done that way. In an inventory control application we wish to compute the *economic order quantity,* which is defined to be the number of units of an item that a firm should order at one time to minimize the sum of the cost of ordering and the cost of storing the item. In its simplest form, this is given by

$$\sqrt{\frac{2RS}{CI}}$$

where:

R = number of units used annually
S = cost of placing one order
C = cost of one unit
I = inventory carrying cost, expressed as a fraction of the value of the average inventory.

Since a square root is involved, this computation must be done with the **COMPUTE** statement, which could be as follows:

```
COMPUTE ECONOMIC-ORDER-QUANTITY =
(2 * ANNUAL-UNITS * ORDER-COST / (UNIT-COST * INV-COST)) ** 0.5.
```

20.7   LIMITATIONS ON THE USE OF THE COMPUTE STATEMENT

As in other arithmetic in **COBOL**, no numeric quantity may exceed 18 digits.

The **ON SIZE ERROR** clause may be used, but the test applies only to the final result. This gets us into what can be a serious problem with the free use of the **COMPUTE** statement: the programmer has no control over—or knowledge of—the intermediate results that are developed during the course of a computation. Although some **COBOL** manuals define how the **PICTURE**s of intermediate results are determined, the Microsoft manual does not, and even when the information is available many programmers don't use it. As a result, a program that works correctly for most data values may, on rare occasions, give a totally wrong result *with no warning whatsoever.*

In view of these problems and because of the relative unfamiliarity of many **COBOL** programmers with the mathematical rules involved, some installations make minimum use of the **COMPUTE** statement. Some, in fact, prohibit its use for anything except exponentiation. To balance the picture, however, it should be noted that some installations strongly encourage the free use of **COMPUTE** for all arithmetic.

20.8 ARITHMETIC EXPRESSIONS IN RELATION CONDITIONS

Arithmetic expressions may be used in relation conditions anywhere that an identifier or literal is permitted, letting us write statements such as

```
IF (JAN-USE + FEB-USE + MAR-USE) / 3 > PREV-AVERAGE-USE
    ADD 1 TO GROWTH-QUARTER-COUNT.

IF B ** 2 - 4 * A * C < ZERO
    PERFORM IMAGINARY-ROOTS-ROUTINE
ELSE
    PERFORM REAL-ROOTS-ROUTINE.
```

We have seen in earlier chapters how this type of expression can be useful.

Arithmetic expressions used in this way are subject to the same warnings about the lack of control over intermediate results that apply to the COMPUTE statement. Arithmetic expressions are not heavily used in this way.

20.9 THE RENAMES CLAUSE

The RENAMES clause, which must have the level 66 and which must follow the record description to which it applies, associates a new name with a prior grouping of data. Although this sounds something like REDEFINES clauses, there are important differences. As an example let us consider once more the OLD-MASTER and TRANSACTION records from the file update program in Chapter 13; this record, along with two RENAMES entries, is shown in Figure 20.4.

```
01   OLD-MASTER.
     05   OM-KEY                 PIC X(5).
     05   OM-QUAN-ON-HAND        PIC 9(5).
     05   OM-QUAN-ON-ORDER       PIC 9(5).
     05   OM-REORDER-POINT       PIC 9(5).
     05   OM-REORDER-QUAN        PIC 9(5).
     05   OM-DESCRIPTION         PIC X(20).

01   TRANSACTION.
     05   TR-KEY                 PIC X(5).
     05   TR-QUANTITY            PIC 9(5).
     05   TR-TRANSACTION-CODE    PIC X.
          88   ADDITION                      VALUE '1'.
          88   ADJUSTMENT                    VALUE '2'.
          88   RECEIPT                       VALUE '3'.
          88   SHIPMENT                      VALUE '4'.
          88   DELETION                      VALUE '5'.
     05   TR-ADJUSTMENT-CODE     PIC 9.
     05   TR-QUAN-ON-ORDER       PIC 9(5).
     05   TR-REORDER-POINT       PIC 9(5).
     05   TR-REORDER-QUAN        PIC 9(5).
     05   TR-DESCRIPTION         PIC X(20).
66   TR-GROUP-1 RENAMES TR-KEY THRU TR-QUANTITY.
66   TR-GROUP-2 RENAMES TR-QUAN-ON-ORDER THRU TR-DESCRIPTION.
```

FIGURE 20.4 An example of record definitions using the RENAMES clause.

The first **RENAMES** clause in this example makes **TR-GROUP-1** the name of an item consisting of **TR-KEY** and **TR-QUANTITY**. The second one makes **TR-GROUP-2** the name of an item consisting of everything from **TR-QUAN-ON-ORDER** through **TR-DESCRIPTION**. Suppose that instead of defining **NEW-MASTER** using the same structure we have used for **OLD-MASTER**, we define it as follows:

```
01   NEW-MASTER.
     05   NM-GROUP-1              PIC X(10).
     05   NM-GROUP-2              PIC X(35).
```

Then in the Procedure Division we could write, for example,

```
MOVE TR-GROUP-1 TO NM-GROUP-1.
MOVE TR-GROUP-2 TO NM-GROUP-2.
```

and get the two elementary items at the start of the transaction record and the four elementary items at the end of the transaction record moved to the new master record, thus eliminating the two codes from the middle of an addition record.

How does **RENAMES** differ from **REDEFINES**? The key to answering that question is the word **THRU** in the **RENAMES** clause. Using the **RENAMES**, we can make a name apply to a whole set of items rather than just one elementary or group item, which is all **REDEFINES** can do. Furthermore, there can be as many **RENAMES** clauses as are useful, and there are no restrictions concerning how the groupings they define may or may not overlap. It would be perfectly legal for us to have a third **RENAMES** like this:

```
66   TR-GROUP-3 RENAMES TR-QUANTITY THRU TR-REORDER-POINT.
```

The fact that **TR-GROUP-3** would overlap parts of the other two would make no difference at all.

In the simple example above we could have handled the problem by making the two groupings into ordinary group items. The **RENAMES** clause, however, can handle situations that could not be dealt with in this way. For example, suppose we had the following record description:

```
01   SAMPLE.
     05   A.
          10   B              PIC X.
          10   C              PIC X.
     05   D.
          10   E              PIC X.
          10   F.
               15   G         PIC X.
               15   H         PIC X.
          10   I.
               15   J         PIC X.
               15   K         PIC X.
```

The following **RENAMES** clause would be legal and meaningful, and what it accomplishes could not be done with group items except by restructuring the entire record

```
66   CG-GROUP RENAMES C THRU G.
```

Using the same record description, we could also write things like

```
66   BH  RENAMES A THRU F.
```

The letter **A** is a group item; **RENAMES** begins with the first elementary item in it. The letter **F** is also a group item, and renaming ends with the last elementary item in it.

Having shown some of what the **RENAMES** clause can do, we must ask why one would want to use it. One of the fundamental concepts of structured software design is that data, as well as procedural code, has an intrinsic hierarchy. The **RENAMES** clause completely ignores this hierarchy and the logical structure of the data. In almost all cases, you will find that the only motive for using the **RENAMES** clause is to save a few lines of code in the Procedure Division; this is almost always done at the expense of program clarity.

We have shown the **RENAMES** clause not because we recommend its use, but because maintenance programmers may encounter it in old programs. We strongly urge that the **RENAMES** clause be avoided, and in fact many installations forbid programmers to use it.

20.10 THE ALTER STATEMENT AND WHY IT SHOULD NEVER BE USED

The **ALTER** statement makes it possible to change the transfer point specified in a **GO TO** statement. Here is the general format:

```
ALTER procedure-name-1 TO [PROCEED TO] procedure-name-2

      [procedure-name-3 TO [PROCEED TO] procedure-name-4] . . .
```

Procedure-name-1, Procedure-name-3, etc., must be the names of paragraphs that contain only one sentence: a **GO TO** statement without the **DEPENDING ON** option. Procedure-name-2, Procedure-name-4, etc., must be the names of paragraphs or sections in the Procedure Division. The effect is to change the **GO TO**s so that, instead of whatever they said before, they now specify a transfer to the paragraphs named in the **ALTER** statement. A **GO TO** can be **ALTER**ed many times during the course of a program execution.

For an illustration of what the **ALTER** statement does, consider the program in Figure 20.5. Its purpose is to read a file of records, form the sum of the numbers found in the first three bytes of each record, and produce a count of the number of records. The program is written to take an alternative approach to getting the loop started, other than using **VALUE** clauses in the definitions of **RECORD-COUNT** and **TOTAL-A**. The scheme is that there is a paragraph named **FIRST-TIME-PARAGRAPH** that puts a 1 in **RECORD-COUNT** and moves the contents of the first record to the total. An **ALTER** statement within that paragraph is used to assure that it is executed only once. The paragraph must end with a **GO TO** statement to skip around the paragraph named **AFTER-FIRST-PARAGRAPH**. (We have avoided using the normal prefix conventions on the paragraph names, because any program that contains code like this one does is not likely to have any meaningful hierarchy or paragraph sequence.)

```
1              IDENTIFICATION DIVISION.
2              PROGRAM-ID.
3                  ALTER-DEMO.
4              DATE-WRITTEN.
5                  JULY 17, 1989.
6
7          *    THIS PROGRAM, WHICH USES THE ALTER STATEMENT, IS PRESENTED
8          *    ONLY TO SHOW FUTURE MAINTENANCE PROGRAMMERS WHAT THE
9          *    STATEMENT DOES, SINCE SOME EXISTING PROGRAMS DO USE IT.
10         *    USE OF THE ALTER STATEMENT IS TO BE STRONGLY DISCOURAGED.
11         *    --- -- --- ----- --------- -- -- -- -------- -----------
12
13
14             ENVIRONMENT DIVISION.
15             INPUT-OUTPUT SECTION.
16             FILE-CONTROL.
17                 SELECT INPUT-FILE            ASSIGN TO 'CH20P04.IN'.
18                 SELECT OUTPUT-FILE           ASSIGN TO 'CH20P04.OUT'.
19
20             DATA DIVISION.
21             FILE SECTION.
22
23             FD  INPUT-FILE
24                 LABEL RECORDS ARE STANDARD.
25             01  INPUT-RECORD                 PIC 999.
26
27             FD  OUTPUT-FILE
28                 LABEL RECORDS ARE STANDARD.
29             01  OUTPUT-RECORD.
30                 05   RECORD-COUNT            PIC 9(4).
31                 05   TOTAL-A                 PIC 9(6).
32
33             WORKING-STORAGE SECTION.
34
35             01  MORE-DATA-REMAINS-FLAG       PIC X.
36                 88  NO-MORE-DATA-REMAINS         VALUE 'N'.
37
38
39             PROCEDURE DIVISION.
40             MAIN-LINE-ROUTINE.
41                 OPEN INPUT INPUT-FILE
42                     OUTPUT OUTPUT-FILE.
43                 MOVE 'Y' TO MORE-DATA-REMAINS-FLAG.
44                 PERFORM READ-ROUTINE.
45                 PERFORM PROCESS-ONE-RECORD THRU PROCESS-ONE-RECORD-EXIT
46                     UNTIL NO-MORE-DATA-REMAINS.
47                 WRITE OUTPUT-RECORD.
48                 CLOSE INPUT-FILE
49                     OUTPUT-FILE.
50                 STOP RUN.
51
52             PROCESS-ONE-RECORD.
53         *
54         * THIS GO TO IS ALTERED IN FIRST-TIME-PARAGRAPH
55         *
56                 GO TO FIRST-TIME-PARAGRAPH.
57
```

```
58        FIRST-TIME-PARAGRAPH.
59            MOVE 1 TO RECORD-COUNT.
60            MOVE INPUT-RECORD TO TOTAL-A.
61            ALTER PROCESS-ONE-RECORD TO PROCEED TO AFTER-FIRST-PARAGRAPH.
62            GO TO READ-ROUTINE.
63
64        AFTER-FIRST-PARAGRAPH.
65            ADD 1 TO RECORD-COUNT.
66            ADD INPUT-RECORD TO TOTAL-A.
67
68        READ-ROUTINE.
69            READ INPUT-FILE
70                AT END MOVE 'N' TO MORE-DATA-REMAINS-FLAG.
71
72        PROCESS-ONE-RECORD-EXIT.
73            EXIT.
74
75        ********************** END OF PROGRAM *************************
```

FIGURE 20.5 A program using the **ALTER** statement to modify the effect of a **GO TO** statement.

Observe that the **PERFORM...UNTIL** in the main line routine is written with the **THRU** option. Because of the **GO TO**s involved here, there is no way to get all of the actions into one paragraph. Observe also, that the paragraph named **READ-ROUTINE** is entered in *three* different ways. It is executed first by a **PERFORM** in the main line routine, then there is a transfer to it with the **GO TO** in the paragraph executed for the first record, and in all other cases control falls through from the end of the previous paragraph.

This program does work, but even in something this elementary we readily see how much more complex the program is and how much more difficult it is to understand than if it were written in the style that is employed elsewhere in the book. The difficulty in understanding programs that have **ALTER** statements and many **GO TO**s is that to understand how a statement works, we have to know the complete sequence of prior program execution. The characteristic we have striven for throughout has been that to understand how a statement works, we need to know only a few other statements—all physically close by. Sometimes we have come closer to reaching that goal than others, but that has always been the goal. The **GO TO** and especially the **ALTER** statement destroy this "locality of context."

In programs of realistic size the extensive use of **GO TO**s and **ALTER**s can make a program extremely difficult to understand. This is especially true in the maintenance situation, where someone who has never seen the program before must become familiar with it as quickly as possible, sometimes under critical time pressure because the program has failed. In such a circumstance the sight of a **GO TO** statement in a paragraph by itself, signaling as it does the existence of an unknown number of **ALTER** statements at unknown locations throughout the program, strikes fear in the heart of the bravest programmer.

It is recommended most strongly that the **ALTER** statement never be used. (In fact, the **COBOL-85** standard promises that the **ALTER** statement will be removed from the *next* **COBOL** revision.) Nothing that it does cannot be done in other ways, very much more understandably. The subject is presented here solely for the benefit of those who may at some time be involved with existing programs that have **ALTER** statements in them. The maintenance of such programs can be materially simplified by adding comments to them (as in Figure 20.5) showing, for each altered **GO TO** statement, the location of all the **ALTER** statements that refer to it. This in no way converts use of the **ALTER** statement into acceptable programming practice, but it may help a bad situation a little. A better solution, if the use of the **ALTER** is not too extensive, is to recode parts of the program so that the **ALTER** is removed from the program entirely.

COBOL RESERVED WORDS

The following appendix lists the words that are reserved in the Microsoft **COBOL** compiler. In some cases, whether or not a word is treated as a reserved word depends on the compiler options you have selected through your directives. Words that are reserved in the 1974 American National Standard are not otherwise marked. Words unique to **COBOL-85** are underlined. Words taken from other dialects are shown in italics; the dialect is indicated to the right of the word by showing the relevant directive. Words marked as MSC are reserved in Microsoft **COBOL** but are not part of the 1974 American National Standard. If a word is reserved in both **COBOL-85** and another dialect, it is underlined and italicized.

		ASSIGN	
ACCEPT		AT	
ACCESS		AUTHOR	
ACTUAL	OSVS	AUTO	MSC
ADD		AUTO-SKIP	MSC
ADDRESS	VSC2	AUTOMATIC	MSC
ADVANCING			
AFTER		BACKGROUND-COLOR	MSC
ALL		BACKGROUND-COLOUR	MSC
ALPHABET	VSC2	BACKWARD	MSC
ALPHABETIC		BASIS	OSVS
ALPHABETIC-LOWER	VSC2	BEEP	MSC
ALPHABETIC-UPPER	VSC2	BEFORE	
ALPHANUMERIC	VSC2	BEGINNING	OSVS, VSC2
ALPHANUMERIC-EDITED	VSC2	BELL	MSC
ALSO		BINARY	VSC2
ALTER		BLANK	
AND		BLINK	MSC
ANY	VSC2	BLOCK	
APPLY	OSVS	BOTTOM	
ARE		BY	
AREA			
AREAS		C01	OSVS
ASCENDING		C02	OSVS

C03	**OSVS**	**COMPUTE**	
C04	**OSVS**	**CONFIGURATION**	
C05	**OSVS**	*CONSOLE*	**OSVS**
C06	**OSVS**	*CONTAINED*	**VSC2**
C07	**OSVS**	**CONTAINS**	
C08	**OSVS**	*CONTENT*	**VSC2**
C09	**OSVS**	*CONTINUE*	**VSC2**
C10	**OSVS**	**CONTROL**	
C11	**OSVS**	**CONTROLS**	
C12	**OSVS**	*CONVERTING*	**VSC2**
CALL		**COPY**	
CANCEL		*CORE-INDEX*	**OSVS**
CBL	**VSC2**	**CORR**	
CD		**CORRESPONDING**	
CF		**COUNT**	
CH		*CRT*	**MSC**
CHAINED	**MSC**	*CRT-UNDER*	**MSC**
CHAINING	**MSC**	*CSP*	**OSVS**
CHANGED	**OSVS**	**CURRENCY**	
CHARACTER		*CURRENT-DATE*	**OSVS**
CHARACTERS		*CURSOR*	**MSC**
CLASS	**VSC2**		
CLOCK-UNITS		**DATA**	
CLOSE		**DATE**	
COBOL		**DATE-COMPILED**	
CODE		**DATE-WRITTEN**	
CODE-SET		**DAY**	
COL	**MSC**	*DAY-OF-WEEK*	**VSC2**
COLLATING		**DE**	
COLOR	**MSC**	**DEBUG-CONTENTS**	
COLUMN		**DEBUG-ITEM**	
COM-REG	**VSC2**	**DEBUG-LINE**	
COMMA		**DEBUG-NAME**	
COMMAND-LINE	**OSVS**	**DEBUG-SUB-1**	
COMMIT	**MSC**	**DEBUG-SUB-2**	
COMMON	**VSC2**	**DEBUG-SUB-3**	
COMMUNICATION		**DEBUGGING**	
COMP		**DECIMAL-POINT**	
COMP-0	**MSC**	**DECLARATIVES**	
COMP-1	**VSC2**	**DELETE**	
COMP-3	**OSVS,VSC2**	**DELIMITED**	
COMP-4	**OSVS,VSC2**	**DELIMITER**	
COMP-5	**MSC**	**DEPENDING**	
COMP-X	**MSC**	**DESCENDING**	
COMPUTATIONAL		**DESTINATION**	
COMPUTATIONAL-0	**MSC**	**DETAIL**	
COMPUTATIONAL-1	**VSC2**	**DISABLE**	
COMPUTATIONAL-3	**OSVS,VSC2**	*DISK*	**MSC**
COMPUTATIONAL-4	**OSVS,VSC2**	*DISP*	**OSVS**
COMPUTATIONAL-5	**MSC**	**DISPLAY**	
COMPUTATIONAL-X	**MSC**	*DISPLAY-ST*	**OSVS**

DISPLAY-1	**VSC2**	*EXCLUSIVE*	**MSC**
DIVIDE		*EXEC*	**MSC**
DIVISION		*EXECUTE*	**MSC**
DOWN		*EXHIBIT*	**OSVS**
DUPLICATES		**EXIT**	
DYNAMIC		**EXTEND**	
		EXTERNAL	**VSC2**
EGCS	**VSC2**		
EGI		*FALSE*	**VSC2**
EJECT	**OSVS,VSC2**	**FD**	
ELSE		**FILE**	
EMI		**FILE-CONTROL**	
EMPTY-CHECK	**MSC**	*FILE-ID*	**MSC**
ENABLE		*FILE-LIMIT*	**OSVS**
END		*FILE-LIMITS*	**OSVS**
END-ACCEPT	**MSC**	**FILLER**	
END-ADD	**VSC2**	**FINAL**	
END-CALL	**VSC2**	**FIRST**	
END-COMPUTE	**VSC2**	*FIXED*	**MSC**
END-DELETE	**VSC2**	**FOOTING**	
END-DIVIDE	**VSC2**	**FOR**	
END-EVALUATE	**VSC2**	*FOREGROUND-COLOR*	**MSC**
END-IF	**VSC2**	*FOREGROUND-COLOUR*	**MSC**
END-MULTIPLY	**VSC2**	**FROM**	
END-OF-PAGE		*FULL*	**MSC**
END-PERFORM	**VSC2**		
END-READ	**VSC2**	**GENERATE**	
END-RECEIVE	**VSC2**	**GIVING**	
END-RETURN	**VSC2**	*GLOBAL*	**VSC2**
END-REWRITE	**VSC2**	**GO**	
END-SEARCH	**VSC2**	*GOBACK*	**OSVS,VSC2**
END-START	**VSC2**	*GREATER*	
END-STRING	**VSC2**	*GRID*	**MSC**
END-SUBTRACT	**VSC2**	**GROUP**	
END-UNSTRING	**VSC2**		
END-WRITE	**VSC2**	**HEADING**	
ENDING	**OSVS,VSC2**	**HIGH-VALUE**	
ENTER		**HIGH-VALUES**	
ENTRY	**OSVS,VSC2**	*HIGHLIGHT*	**MSC**
ENVIRONMENT			
EOP		**I-O**	
EQUAL		**I-O-CONTROL**	
ERASE	**MSC**	*ID*	**OSVS,VSC2**
ERROR		**IDENTIFICATION**	
ESCAPE	**MSC**	**IF**	
ESI		**IN**	
EVALUATE	**VSC2**	**INDEX**	
EVERY		**INDEXED**	
EXAMINE	**OSVS**	**INDICATE**	
EXCEPTION		**INITIAL**	
EXCESS-3	**MSC**	*INITIALIZE*	**VSC2**

INITIATE		*NAME*	**MSC**
INPUT		*NAMED*	**OSVS**
INPUT-OUTPUT		**NATIVE**	
INSERT	**OSVS**	**NEGATIVE**	
INSPECT		**NEXT**	
INSTALLATION		**NO**	
INTO		*NO-ECHO*	**MSC**
INVALID		*NOMINAL*	**OSVS**
IS		**NOT**	
		NOTE	**OSVS**
JAPANESE	**MSC**	*NULL*	**VSC2**
JUST		*NULLS*	**VSC2**
JUSTIFIED		**NUMBER**	
		NUMERIC	
KEPT	**MSC**	*NUMERIC-EDITED*	**VSC2**
KEY			
KEYBOARD	**MSC**	**OBJECT-COMPUTER**	
		OCCURS	
LABEL		**OF**	
LAST		**OFF**	
LEADING		**OMITTED**	
LEAVE	**OSVS**	**ON**	
LEFT		**OPEN**	
LEFT-JUSTIFY	**MSC**	**OPTIONAL**	
LEFTLINE	*MSC*	**OR**	
LENGTH		*ORDER*	**VSC2**
LENGTH-CHECK	**MSC**	**ORGANIZATION**	
LESS		*OTHER*	**VSC2**
LIMIT		*OTHERWISE*	**OSVS**
LIMITS		**OUTPUT**	
LINAGE		**OVERFLOW**	
LINAGE-COUNTER		*OVERLINE*	**MSC**
LINE			
LINE-COUNTER		*PACKED-DECIMAL*	**VSC2**
LINES		*PADDING*	**VSC2**
LINKAGE		**PAGE**	
LOCK		**PAGE-COUNTER**	
LOW-VALUE		*PALETTE*	**MSC**
LOW-VALUES		*PASSWORD*	**OSVS,VSC2**
		PERFORM	
MANUAL	**MVS**	**PF**	
MEMORY		**PH**	
MERGE		**PIC**	
MESSAGE		**PICTURE**	
MODE		**PLUS**	
MODULES		**POINTER**	
MORE-LABELS	**OSVS,VSC2**	**POSITION**	
MOVE		*POSITIONING*	**OSVS**
MULTIPLE		**POSITIVE**	
MULTIPLY		*PREVIOUS*	**MSC**
		PRINT-SWITCH	**OSVS**

PRINTER	**MSC**	*REVERSE-VIDEO*	**MSC**
PRINTER-1	**MSC**	**REVERSED**	
PRINTING		**REWIND**	
PROCEDURE		**REWRITE**	
PROCEDURES		**RF**	
PROCEED		**RH**	
PROCESSING	**VSC2**	**RIGHT**	
PROGRAM		*RIGHT-JUSTIFY*	**MSC**
PROGRAM-ID		*ROLLBACK*	**MSC**
PROMPT	**MSC**	**ROUNDED**	
PROTECTED	**MSC**	**RUN**	
PURGE	**VSC2**		
		S01	**OSVS**
QUEUE		*S02*	**OSVS**
QUOTE		**SAME**	
QUOTES		*SCREEN*	**MSC**
		SD	
RANDOM		**SEARCH**	
RANGE	**MSC**	**SECTION**	
RD		*SECURE*	**MSC**
READ		**SECURITY**	
READY	**OSVS**	*SEEK*	**OSVS**
RECEIVE		**SEGMENT**	
RECORD		**SEGMENT-LIMIT**	
RECORD-OVERFLOW	**OSVS**	**SELECT**	
RECORDING	**OSVS,VSC2**	*SELECTIVE*	**OSVS**
RECORDS		**SEND**	
REDEFINES		**SENTENCE**	
REEL		**SEPARATE**	
REFERENCE	**VSC2**	**SEQUENCE**	
REFERENCES		**SEQUENTIAL**	
RELATIVE		*SERVICE*	**OSVS,VSC2**
RELEASE		**SET**	
RELOAD	**OSVS,VSC2**	**SIGN**	
REMAINDER		**SIZE**	
REMARKS	**OSVS**	*SKIP-1*	**OSVS,VSC2**
REMOVAL		*SKIP-2*	**OSVS,VSC2**
RENAMES		*SKIP-3*	**OSVS,VSC2**
REORG-CRITERIA	**OSVS**	**SORT**	
REPLACE	**VSC2**	*SORT-CONTROL*	**VSC2**
REPLACING		*SORT-CORE-SIZE*	**OSVS**
REPORT		*SORT-FILE-SIZE*	**OSVS**
REPORTING		**SORT-MERGE**	
REPORTS		*SORT-MESSAGE*	**OSVS**
REQUIRED		*SORT-MODE-SIZE*	**OSVS**
REREAD	**OSVS**	*SORT-RETURN*	**OSVS,VSC2**
RERUN		**SOURCE**	
RESERVE		**SOURCE-COMPUTER**	
RESET	**OSVS**	**SPACE**	
RETURN		*SPACE-FILL*	**MSC**
RETURN-CODE	**OSVS,VSC2**	**SPACES**	

SPECIAL-NAMES		TRAILING	
STANDARD		*TRAILING-SIGN*	**MSC**
STANDARD-1		*TRANSFORM*	**OSVS**
STANDARD-2	**VSC2**	*TRUE*	**VSC2**
START		TYPE	
STATUS			
STOP		*UNDERLINE*	**MSC**
STORE	**OSVS**	UNIT	
STRING		*UNLOCK*	**MSC**
SUB-QUEUE-1		UNSTRING	
SUB-QUEUE-2		UNTIL	
SUB-QUEUE-3		UP	
SUBPROGRAM	**MSC**	*UPDATE*	**MSC**
SUBTRACT		UPON	
SUM		USAGE	
SUPPRESS	**OSVS,VSC2**	USE	
SYMBOLIC		*USER*	**MSC**
SYNC		USING	
SYNCHRONIZED			
SYSIN	**OSVS**	VALUE	
SYSIPT	**OSVS**	VALUES	
SYSLIST	**OSVS**	*VARIABLE*	**MSC**
SYSLST	**OSVS**	VARYING	
SYSOUT	**OSVS**		
SYSPNCH	**OSVS**	WHEN	
SYSPUNCH	**OSVS**	*WHEN-COMPILED*	**OSVS,VSC2**
		WITH	
TABLE		WORDS	
TALLY	**OSVS**	WORKING-STORAGE	
TALLYING		WRITE	
TAPE		*WRITE-ONLY*	**OSVS**
TERMINAL			
TERMINATE		ZERO	
TEST	**VSC2**	*ZERO-FILL*	**MSC**
TEXT		ZEROES	
THAN		ZEROS	
THEN	**OSVS,VSC2**		
THROUGH		.	
THRU		(	
TIME		)	
TIME-OF-DAY	**OSVS**	;	
TIMES		+	
TITLE	**VSC2**	–	
TO		*	
TOP		/	
TOTALED	**OSVS**	**	
TOTALING	**OSVS**	>	
TRACE	**OSVS**	<	
TRACK-AREA	**OSVS**	=	
TRACK-LIMIT	**OSVS**	>=	
TRACKS	**OSVS**	<=	

APPENDIX II

COMPOSITE LANGUAGE SKELETON

This appendix shows the general formats for all COBOL language elements, in the form of the general formats introduced in Section 3.14.

For ease of use in varying circumstances, both COBOL-74 and COBOL-85 formats are shown. See the running heads on the left hand pages to know which you are reading.

The main typographical conventions used may be found on pages 41-43. Two other conventions are employed in the COBOL-85 formats:

- The combination of braces and vertical bars means to select one or more of the options so enclosed.
- The appearance of the italic letter *S, R, I,* or *W* to the left of the format for the verbs OPEN, CLOSE, READ, and WRITE verbs in the COBOL-85 formats indicates that the Sequential I-O module, the Relative I-O module, the Indexed I-O module, or the Report Writer I-O module in which that general format is used.

Commas and semicolons, which are always optional, are not shown. The rules are simple: a comma may be used to separate members of a series, and a semicolon may be used after any clause. Each must be followed by a space.

The COBOL-74 standard (which can no longer be obtained from ANSI) made less extensive use of the series ellipsis than does COBOL-85; we have elected to show most of the COBOL-74 formats using the more condensed form. The rule is: to determine what element the ellipsis applies to, find the brace or bracket that matches the brace or bracket immediately preceding the ellipsis; the enclosed material may be repeated, generally as many times as desired although in some cases there are limits.

Local variations are always possible. For serious programming you need access to the reference manual for the particular compiler you are using.

In particular, you need the Microsoft COBOL manual. This book is not in any way an attempt to make that manual unnecessary.

GENERAL FORMAT FOR IDENTIFICATION DIVISION

IDENTIFICATION DIVISION.

PROGRAM-ID. program-name.

[AUTHOR. [comment-entry] ...]

[INSTALLATION. [comment-entry] ...]

[DATE-WRITTEN. [comment-entry] ...]

[DATE-COMPILED. [comment-entry] ...]

[SECURITY. [comment-entry] ...]

GENERAL FORMAT FOR ENVIRONMENT DIVISION

ENVIRONMENT DIVISION.

CONFIGURATION SECTION.

SOURCE-COMPUTER. computer-name [WITH DEBUGGING MODE].

OBJECT-COMPUTER. computer-name

$$\left[\text{MEMORY SIZE integer-1} \left\{ \begin{array}{l} \text{WORDS} \\ \text{CHARACTERS} \\ \text{MODULES} \end{array} \right\} \right]$$

[PROGRAM COLLATING SEQUENCE IS alphabet-name]

[SEGMENT-LIMIT IS segment-number].

[SPECIAL-NAMES. [implementor-name

$$
\begin{Bmatrix}
\text{\underline{IS} mnemonic-name-1 [\underline{ON} STATUS \underline{IS} condition-name-1} \\
\text{[\underline{OFF} STATUS \underline{IS} condition-name-2]]} \\
\text{\underline{IS} mnemonic-name-2 [\underline{OFF} STATUS \underline{IS} condition-name-2} \\
\text{[\underline{ON} STATUS \underline{IS} condition-name-1]]} \\
\text{\underline{ON} STATUS \underline{IS} condition-name-1 [\underline{OFF} STATUS \underline{IS} condition-name-2]} \\
\text{\underline{OFF} STATUS \underline{IS} condition-name-2 [\underline{ON} STATUS \underline{IS} condition-name-1]}
\end{Bmatrix}
\Bigg] \quad \dots
$$

[ALPHABET alphabet-name IS

$$
\begin{Bmatrix}
\text{\underline{STANDARD-1}} \\
\text{\underline{NATIVE}} \\
\text{implementor-name} \\
\begin{Bmatrix}
\text{literal-1} \begin{bmatrix} \begin{Bmatrix} \underline{\text{THROUGH}} \\ \underline{\text{THRU}} \end{Bmatrix} \text{literal-2} \\ \{\underline{\text{ALSO}}\ \text{literal-3}\}\ \dots \end{bmatrix} \end{Bmatrix} \dots
\end{Bmatrix}
\Bigg] \quad \dots
$$

[CURRENCY SIGN IS literal-4]
[DECIMAL-POINT IS COMMA].]

[INPUT-OUTPUT SECTION.

FILE-CONTROL.

    {file-control-entry} ...

[I-O-CONTROL.

$$
\begin{bmatrix}
\text{\underline{RERUN}} \begin{bmatrix} \underline{\text{ON}} \begin{Bmatrix} \text{file-name-1} \\ \text{implementor-name} \end{Bmatrix} \end{bmatrix} \\
\underline{\text{EVERY}} \begin{Bmatrix} \begin{Bmatrix} [\underline{\text{END}} \text{ OF}] \begin{Bmatrix} \underline{\text{REEL}} \\ \underline{\text{UNIT}} \end{Bmatrix} \\ \text{integer-1 \underline{RECORDS}} \end{Bmatrix} \text{OF file-name-2} \\ \text{integer-2 \underline{CLOCK-UNITS}} \\ \text{condition-name} \end{Bmatrix}
\end{bmatrix} \quad \dots
$$

$$
\begin{bmatrix}
\underline{\text{SAME}} \begin{bmatrix} \underline{\text{RECORD}} \\ \underline{\text{SORT}} \\ \underline{\text{SORT-MERGE}} \end{bmatrix} \text{AREA FOR file-name-3 \{file-name-4\} } \dots
\end{bmatrix} \quad \dots
$$

[MULTIPLE FILE TAPE CONTAINS file-name-5 [POSITION integer-3] ...] ... .]

GENERAL FORMAT FOR FILE CONTROL ENTRY

FORMAT 1:

SELECT [OPTIONAL] file-name

   ASSIGN TO implementor-name-1 [implementor-name-2] ...

$$\left[\text{RESERVE integer-1} \left[\begin{array}{l} \text{AREA} \\ \text{AREAS} \end{array} \right] \right]$$

   [ORGANIZATION IS SEQUENTIAL]

   [ACCESS MODE IS SEQUENTIAL]

   [FILE STATUS IS data-name-1].

FORMAT 2:

SELECT file-name

   ASSIGN TO implementor-name-1 [implementor-name-2] ...

$$\left[\text{RESERVE integer-1} \left[\begin{array}{l} \text{AREA} \\ \text{AREAS} \end{array} \right] \right]$$

   [ORGANIZATION IS] RELATIVE

$$\left[\text{ACCESS MODE IS} \left\{ \begin{array}{l} \text{SEQUENTIAL [RELATIVE KEY IS data-name-1]} \\ \left\{ \begin{array}{l} \text{RANDOM} \\ \text{DYNAMIC} \end{array} \right\} \text{RELATIVE KEY IS data-name-1} \end{array} \right\} \right]$$

   [FILE STATUS IS data-name-2].

FORMAT 3:

SELECT file-name

> ASSIGN TO implementor-name-1 [implementor-name-2] ...
>
> $\left[\underline{\text{RESERVE}} \text{ integer-1} \left[\begin{array}{l} \text{AREA} \\ \text{AREAS} \end{array} \right] \right]$
>
> [ORGANIZATION IS] INDEXED
>
> $\left[\underline{\text{ACCESS}} \text{ MODE IS} \left\{ \begin{array}{l} \text{SEQUENTIAL} \\ \text{RANDOM} \\ \text{DYNAMIC} \end{array} \right\} \right]$
>
> RECORD KEY IS data-name-1
>
> [ALTERNATE RECORD KEY IS data-name-2 [WITH DUPLICATES]] . . .
>
> [FILE STATUS IS data-name-3] .

FORMAT 4:

SELECT file-name-1 ASSIGN TO implementor-name-1 [implementor-name-2] ...

GENERAL FORMAT FOR DATA DIVISION

DATA DIVISION.

[FILE SECTION.

[FD file-name-1

$$\left[\text{BLOCK CONTAINS [integer-1 } \underline{\text{TO}} \text{] integer-2} \left\{ \begin{array}{l} \underline{\text{RECORDS}} \\ \text{CHARACTERS} \end{array} \right\} \right]$$

[RECORD CONTAINS [integer-3 TO] integer-4 CHARACTERS]

$$\underline{\text{LABEL}} \left\{ \begin{array}{l} \underline{\text{RECORD}} \text{ IS} \\ \underline{\text{RECORDS}} \text{ ARE} \end{array} \right\} \left\{ \begin{array}{l} \underline{\text{STANDARD}} \\ \underline{\text{OMITTED}} \end{array} \right\}$$

$$\left[\underline{\text{VALUE OF}} \left\{ \text{implementor-name-1 IS} \left\{ \begin{array}{l} \text{data-name-1} \\ \text{literal-1} \end{array} \right\} \right\} \cdots \right]$$

$$\left[\underline{\text{DATA}} \left\{ \begin{array}{l} \underline{\text{RECORD}} \text{ IS} \\ \underline{\text{RECORDS}} \text{ ARE} \end{array} \right\} \{\text{data-name-2}\} \cdots \right]$$

$$\left[\underline{\text{LINAGE}} \text{ IS} \left\{ \begin{array}{l} \text{data-name-3} \\ \text{integer-5} \end{array} \right\} \text{ LINES} \right.$$

$$\left[\text{WITH } \underline{\text{FOOTING}} \text{ AT} \left\{ \begin{array}{l} \text{data-name-4} \\ \text{integer-6} \end{array} \right\} \right]$$

$$\left[\text{LINES AT } \underline{\text{TOP}} \left\{ \begin{array}{l} \text{data-name-5} \\ \text{integer-7} \end{array} \right\} \right]$$

$$\left. \left[\text{LINES AT } \underline{\text{BOTTOM}} \left\{ \begin{array}{l} \text{data-name-6} \\ \text{integer-8} \end{array} \right\} \right] \right]$$

[CODE-SET IS alphabet-name-1].

$$\left[\left\{ \begin{array}{l} \underline{\text{REPORT}} \text{ IS} \\ \underline{\text{REPORTS}} \text{ ARE} \end{array} \right\} \text{ report-name} \quad \cdots \right] \quad .$$

[record-description-entry]...] ...

[SD file-name

    [RECORD CONTAINS [integer-1 TO] integer-2 CHARACTERS]

$$\left[\text{DATA} \quad \left\{ \begin{array}{l} \underline{\text{RECORD}} \text{ IS} \\ \underline{\text{RECORDS}} \text{ ARE} \end{array} \right\} \quad \{\text{data-name-2}\} \dots \right]$$

    [record-description-entry] ...] ...

[WORKING-STORAGE SECTION.

$$\left[\begin{array}{l} \text{77-level-description-entry} \\ \text{record-description-entry} \end{array} \right] \quad \dots \quad]$$

[LINKAGE SECTION.

$$\left[\begin{array}{l} \text{77-level-description-entry} \\ \text{record-description-entry} \end{array} \right] \quad \dots \quad]$$

[COMMUNICATION SECTION.

[communications-description-entry

[record-description-entry] ...] ...]

[REPORT SECTION.

[RD report-name

    [CODE literal-1]

$$\left[\left\{ \begin{array}{l} \underline{\text{CONTROL}} \text{ IS} \\ \underline{\text{CONTROLS}} \text{ ARE} \end{array} \right\} \quad \left\{ \begin{array}{l} \{\text{data-name-1}\} \dots \\ \underline{\text{FINAL}} \text{ [data-name-1]} \dots \end{array} \right\} \right]$$

$$\left[\underline{\text{PAGE}} \left[\begin{array}{l} \text{LIMIT IS} \\ \text{LIMITS ARE} \end{array} \right] \text{ integer-1} \left[\begin{array}{l} \text{LINE} \\ \text{LINES} \end{array} \right] \text{ [\underline{HEADING} integer-2]} \right.$$

      [FIRST DETAIL integer-3] [LAST DETAIL integer-4]

      $\left. \text{[\underline{FOOTING} integer-5]} \dots \right] \quad \cdot$

    {report-group-description-entry} ...] ...]

GENERAL FORMAT FOR DATA DESCRIPTION ENTRY

FORMAT 1:

level-number $\begin{bmatrix} \text{data-name-1} \\ \underline{\text{FILLER}} \end{bmatrix}$

[REDEFINES data-name-2]

$\left[\left\{ \begin{array}{l} \underline{\text{PICTURE}} \\ \underline{\text{PIC}} \end{array} \right\} \text{IS character-string} \right]$

$\left[[\underline{\text{USAGE}} \text{ IS}] \left\{ \begin{array}{l} \underline{\text{COMPUTATIONAL}} \\ \underline{\text{COMP}} \\ \underline{\text{DISPLAY}} \\ \underline{\text{INDEX}} \end{array} \right\} \right]$

$\left[[\underline{\text{SIGN}} \text{ IS}] \left\{ \begin{array}{l} \underline{\text{LEADING}} \\ \underline{\text{TRAILING}} \end{array} \right\} [\underline{\text{SEPARATE}} \text{ CHARACTER}] \right]$

$\left[\begin{array}{l} \underline{\text{OCCURS}} \text{ integer-2 TIMES} \\ \quad \left[\left\{ \begin{array}{l} \underline{\text{ASCENDING}} \\ \underline{\text{DESCENDING}} \end{array} \right\} \text{KEY IS } \{\text{data-name-3}\} \dots \right] \dots \\ \qquad [\underline{\text{INDEXED}} \text{ BY } \{\text{index-name-1}\} \dots] \\ \underline{\text{OCCURS}} \text{ integer-1 } \underline{\text{TO}} \text{ integer-2 TIMES } \underline{\text{DEPENDING}} \text{ ON data-name-4} \\ \quad \left[\left\{ \begin{array}{l} \underline{\text{ASCENDING}} \\ \underline{\text{DESCENDING}} \end{array} \right\} \text{KEY IS } \{\text{data-name-3}\} \dots \right] \dots \\ \qquad [\underline{\text{INDEXED}} \text{ BY } \{\text{index-name-1}\} \dots] \end{array} \right]$

$\left[\left\{ \begin{array}{l} \underline{\text{SYNCHRONIZED}} \\ \underline{\text{SYNC}} \end{array} \right\} \left[\begin{array}{l} \underline{\text{LEFT}} \\ \underline{\text{RIGHT}} \end{array} \right] \right]$

$\left[\left\{ \begin{array}{l} \underline{\text{JUSTIFIED}} \\ \underline{\text{JUST}} \end{array} \right\} \text{RIGHT} \right]$

[BLANK WHEN ZERO]

[VALUE IS literal-1].

FORMAT 2:

66 data-name-1 <u>RENAMES</u> data-name-2 $\left[\left\{ \begin{array}{c} \underline{THROUGH} \\ \underline{THRU} \end{array} \right\} \text{data-name-3} \right]$.

FORMAT 3:

88 condition-name-1 $\left\{ \begin{array}{c} \underline{VALUE} \text{ IS} \\ \underline{VALUES} \text{ ARE} \end{array} \right\}$ $\left\{ \text{literal-1} \left[\left\{ \begin{array}{c} \underline{THROUGH} \\ \underline{THRU} \end{array} \right\} \text{literal-2} \right] \right\} \dots$.

GENERAL FORMAT FOR COMMUNICATION DESCRIPTION ENTRY

FORMAT 1:

<u>CD</u> cd-name-1

FOR [<u>INITIAL</u>] <u>INPUT</u>

$\left[\begin{array}{l} [[\text{SYMBOLIC } \underline{QUEUE} \text{ IS data-name-1}] \\[4pt] [\text{SYMBOLIC } \underline{SUB\text{-}QUEUE\text{-}1} \text{ IS data-name-2}] \\[4pt] [\text{SYMBOLIC } \underline{SUB\text{-}QUEUE\text{-}2} \text{ IS data-name-3}] \\[4pt] [\text{SYMBOLIC } \underline{SUB\text{-}QUEUE\text{-}3} \text{ IS data-name-4}] \\[4pt] [\underline{MESSAGE} \ \underline{DATE} \text{ IS data-name-5}] \\[4pt] [\underline{MESSAGE} \ \underline{TIME} \text{ IS data-name-6}] \\[4pt] [\text{SYMBOLIC } \underline{SOURCE} \text{ IS data-name-7}] \\[4pt] [\underline{TEXT} \ \underline{LENGTH} \text{ IS data-name-8}] \\[4pt] [\underline{END} \ \underline{KEY} \text{ IS data-name-9}] \\[4pt] [\underline{STATUS} \ \underline{KEY} \text{ IS data-name-10}] \\[4pt] [\underline{MESSAGE} \ \underline{COUNT} \text{ IS data-name-11}]] \\[6pt] [\text{data-name-1, data-name-2, data-name-3,} \\ \quad \text{data-name-4, data-name-5, data-name-6,} \\ \quad \text{data-name-7, data-name-8, data-name-9,} \\ \quad \text{data-name-10, data-name-11}] \end{array} \right]$

FORMAT 2:

CD cd-name-1 FOR OUTPUT

    [DESTINATION COUNT IS data-name-1]

    [TEXT LENGTH IS data-name-2]

    [STATUS KEY IS data-name-3]

    [DESTINATION TABLE OCCURS integer-1 TIMES

        [INDEXED BY {index-name-1} ...]]

    [ERROR KEY IS data-name-4]

    [SYMBOLIC DESTINATION IS data-name-5] .

GENERAL FORMAT FOR REPORT GROUP DESCRIPTION ENTRY

FORMAT 1:

01 [data-name-1]

$$\left[\text{LINE NUMBER IS} \left\{ \begin{array}{l} \text{integer-1 [ON NEXT PAGE]} \\ \text{PLUS integer-2} \end{array} \right\} \right]$$

$$\left[\text{NEXT GROUP IS} \left\{ \begin{array}{l} \text{integer-3} \\ \text{PLUS integer-4} \\ \text{NEXT PAGE} \end{array} \right\} \right]$$

$$\text{TYPE IS} \left[\begin{array}{l} \left\{ \begin{array}{l} \text{REPORT HEADING} \\ \text{RH} \end{array} \right\} \\ \left\{ \begin{array}{l} \text{PAGE HEADING} \\ \text{PH} \end{array} \right\} \\ \left\{ \begin{array}{l} \text{CONTROL HEADING} \\ \text{CH} \end{array} \right\} \left\{ \begin{array}{l} \text{data-name-2} \\ \text{FINAL} \end{array} \right\} \\ \left\{ \begin{array}{l} \text{DETAIL} \\ \text{DE} \end{array} \right\} \\ \left\{ \begin{array}{l} \text{CONTROL FOOTING} \\ \text{CF} \end{array} \right\} \left\{ \begin{array}{l} \text{data-name-3} \\ \text{FINAL} \end{array} \right\} \\ \left\{ \begin{array}{l} \text{PAGE FOOTING} \\ \text{PF} \end{array} \right\} \\ \left\{ \begin{array}{l} \text{REPORT FOOTING} \\ \text{RF} \end{array} \right\} \end{array} \right]$$

    [[USAGE IS] DISPLAY].

FORMAT 2:

level-number [data-name-1]

$$\left[\quad \underline{\text{LINE}} \text{ NUMBER IS} \quad \left\{ \begin{array}{l} \text{integer-1} \quad [\text{ON } \underline{\text{NEXT}} \underline{\text{PAGE}}] \\ \underline{\text{PLUS}} \text{ Integer-2} \end{array} \right\} \quad \right]$$

[[<u>USAGE</u> IS] <u>DISPLAY</u>] .

FORMAT 3:

level-number [data-name-1]

$$\left\{ \begin{array}{l} \underline{\text{PICTURE}} \\ \underline{\text{PIC}} \end{array} \right\} \text{ IS character-string}$$

[[<u>USAGE</u> IS] <u>DISPLAY</u>]

$$\left[\quad \left\{ \begin{array}{l} \underline{\text{JUSTIFIED}} \\ \underline{\text{JUST}} \end{array} \right\} \text{ RIGHT} \quad \right]$$

[<u>BLANK</u> WHEN <u>ZERO</u>]

$$\left[\quad \underline{\text{LINE}} \text{ NUMBER IS} \quad \left\{ \begin{array}{l} \text{integer-1} \quad [\text{ON } \underline{\text{NEXT}} \underline{\text{PAGE}}] \\ \underline{\text{PLUS}} \text{ integer-2} \end{array} \right\} \quad \right]$$

[<u>COLUMN</u> NUMBER IS integer-3]

$$\left\{ \begin{array}{l} \underline{\text{SOURCE}} \text{ IS identifier-1} \\[1em] \underline{\text{VALUE}} \text{ IS literal-1} \\[1em] \{\underline{\text{SUM}} \text{ \{identifier-2\}} \ldots [\underline{\text{UPON}} \text{ \{data-name-2\}} \ldots]\} \ldots \\ \qquad \left[\quad \underline{\text{RESET}} \text{ ON} \quad \left\{ \begin{array}{l} \text{data-name-3} \\ \underline{\text{FINAL}} \end{array} \right\} \quad \right] \end{array} \right\}$$

[<u>GROUP</u> INDICATE] .

GENERAL FORMAT FOR PROCEDURE DIVISION

FORMAT 1:

[PROCEDURE DIVISION [USING {data-name-1} ...].

[DECLARATIVES.

{section-name SECTION [segment-number].   declarative-sentence

[paragraph-name.

    [sentence] ...] ...} ...

END DECLARATIVES.]

{section-name SECTION [segment-number].

[paragraph-name.

    [sentence] ...] ... } ...]

FORMAT 2:

PROCEDURE DIVISION [USING   {data-name-1} ...].

{paragraph-name.

    [sentence] ... } ...

GENERAL FORMAT FOR COBOL VERBS

<u>ACCEPT</u> identifier [<u>FROM</u> mnemonic-name]

<u>ACCEPT</u> identifier <u>FROM</u>
$\left\{ \begin{array}{l} \underline{DATE} \\ \underline{DAY} \\ \underline{TIME} \end{array} \right\}$

<u>ACCEPT</u> cd-name MESSAGE <u>COUNT</u>

<u>ADD</u>
$\left\{ \begin{array}{l} identifier\text{-}1 \\ literal\text{-}1 \end{array} \right\}$ ... <u>TO</u> {identifier-2 [<u>ROUNDED</u>]} ...

    [ON <u>SIZE</u> <u>ERROR</u> imperative-statement]

<u>ADD</u>
$\left\{ \begin{array}{l} identifier\text{-}1 \\ literal\text{-}1 \end{array} \right\}$ ...

    <u>GIVING</u> {identifier-2 [<u>ROUNDED</u>]} ...

    [ON <u>SIZE</u> <u>ERROR</u> imperative-statement]

<u>ADD</u>
$\left\{ \begin{array}{l} \underline{CORRESPONDING} \\ \underline{CORR} \end{array} \right\}$ identifier-1 <u>TO</u> identifier-2 [<u>ROUNDED</u>]

    [<u>ON</u> <u>SIZE</u> <u>ERROR</u> imperative-statement]

<u>ALTER</u> {procedure-name-1 <u>TO</u> [<u>PROCEED</u> <u>TO</u>] procedure-name-2} ...

<u>CALL</u>
$\left\{ \begin{array}{l} identifier\text{-}1 \\ literal\text{-}1 \end{array} \right\}$ [<u>USING</u> data-name-1 [data-name-2] ...]

    [ON <u>OVERFLOW</u> imperative-statement]

<u>CANCEL</u>
$\left\{ \begin{array}{l} identifier\text{-}1 \\ literal\text{-}1 \end{array} \right\}$ ...

<u>CLOSE</u>
$\left\{ file\text{-}name\text{-}1 \left[\begin{array}{l} \left\{ \begin{array}{l} \underline{REEL} \\ \underline{UNIT} \end{array} \right\} \left\{ \begin{array}{l} WITH\,\underline{NO}\,\underline{REWIND} \\ FOR\,\underline{REMOVAL} \end{array} \right\} \\ WITH \left\{ \begin{array}{l} \underline{NO}\,\underline{REWIND} \\ \underline{LOCK} \end{array} \right\} \end{array} \right] \right\}$ ...

<u>CLOSE</u> file-name-1 [WITH <u>LOCK</u>]} ...

COMPUTE {identifier-1 [ROUNDED]} ... = arithmetic-expression

    [ON SIZE ERROR imperative-statement]

DELETE file-name RECORD

    [INVALID KEY imperative-statement]

DISABLE $\left\{ \begin{array}{l} \text{INPUT [TERMINAL]} \\ \text{OUTPUT} \end{array} \right\}$ cd-name WITH KEY $\left\{ \begin{array}{l} \text{identifier-1} \\ \text{literal-1} \end{array} \right\}$

DISPLAY $\left\{ \begin{array}{l} \text{identifier-1} \\ \text{literal-1} \end{array} \right\}$ ... [UPON mnemonic-name]

DIVIDE $\left\{ \begin{array}{l} \text{identifier-1} \\ \text{literal-1} \end{array} \right\}$ INTO {identifier-2 [ROUNDED]} ...

    [ON SIZE ERROR imperative-statement]

DIVIDE $\left\{ \begin{array}{l} \text{identifier-1} \\ \text{literal-1} \end{array} \right\}$ INTO $\left\{ \begin{array}{l} \text{identifier-2} \\ \text{literal-2} \end{array} \right\}$

    GIVING {identifier-3 [ROUNDED]} ...

    [ON SIZE ERROR imperative-statement]

DIVIDE $\left\{ \begin{array}{l} \text{identifier-1} \\ \text{literal-1} \end{array} \right\}$ BY $\left\{ \begin{array}{l} \text{identifier-2} \\ \text{literal-2} \end{array} \right\}$

    GIVING {identifier-3 [ROUNDED]} ...

    [ON SIZE ERROR imperative-statement]

DIVIDE $\left\{ \begin{array}{l} \text{identifier-1} \\ \text{literal-1} \end{array} \right\}$ INTO $\left\{ \begin{array}{l} \text{identifier-2} \\ \text{literal-2} \end{array} \right\}$ GIVING identifier-3 [ROUNDED]

    REMAINDER identifier-4

    [ON SIZE ERROR imperative-statement-1]

DIVIDE $\left\{ \begin{array}{l} \text{identifier-1} \\ \text{literal-1} \end{array} \right\}$ BY $\left\{ \begin{array}{l} \text{identifier-2} \\ \text{literal-2} \end{array} \right\}$ GIVING identifier-3 [ROUNDED]

    REMAINDER identifier-4

    [ON SIZE ERROR imperative-statement]

ENABLE $\left\{ \begin{array}{l} \underline{\text{INPUT}} \text{ [TERMINAL]} \\ \underline{\text{OUTPUT}} \end{array} \right\}$ cd-name $\left[\text{ WITH } \underline{\text{KEY}} \left\{ \begin{array}{l} \text{identifier-1} \\ \text{literal-1} \end{array} \right\} \right]$

ENTER language-name-1 [routine-name].

EXIT [PROGRAM]

GENERATE $\left\{ \begin{array}{l} \text{data-name} \\ \text{report-name} \end{array} \right\}$

GO TO [procedure-name-1]

GO TO {procedure-name-1} ... procedure-name-n DEPENDING ON identifier

IF condition $\left\{ \begin{array}{l} \text{statement-1} \\ \underline{\text{NEXT SENTENCE}} \end{array} \right\} \left\{ \begin{array}{l} \underline{\text{ELSE}} \text{ statement-2} \\ \underline{\text{ELSE NEXT SENTENCE}} \end{array} \right\}$

INITIATE {report-name-1} ...

INSPECT identifier-1 TALLYING

$\left\{ \text{identifier-2 } \underline{\text{FOR}} \left\{ \left\{ \begin{array}{l} \left\{ \begin{array}{l} \underline{\text{ALL}} \\ \underline{\text{LEADING}} \end{array} \right\} \left\{ \begin{array}{l} \text{identifier-3} \\ \text{literal-1} \end{array} \right\} \\ \underline{\text{CHARACTERS}} \end{array} \right\} \left[\left\{ \begin{array}{l} \underline{\text{BEFORE}} \\ \underline{\text{AFTER}} \end{array} \right\} \text{INITIAL} \left\{ \begin{array}{l} \text{identifier-4} \\ \text{literal-2} \end{array} \right\} \right] \right\} ... \right\}$

INSPECT identifier-1 REPLACING

$\left\{ \begin{array}{l} \underline{\text{CHARACTERS}} \underline{\text{BY}} \left\{ \begin{array}{l} \text{identifier-5} \\ \text{literal-3} \end{array} \right\} \left[\left\{ \begin{array}{l} \underline{\text{BEFORE}} \\ \underline{\text{AFTER}} \end{array} \right\} \text{INITIAL} \left\{ \begin{array}{l} \text{identifier-4} \\ \text{literal-2} \end{array} \right\} \right] ... \\ \left\{ \begin{array}{l} \underline{\text{ALL}} \\ \underline{\text{LEADING}} \\ \underline{\text{FIRST}} \end{array} \right\} \left\{ \left\{ \begin{array}{l} \text{identifier-3} \\ \text{literal-1} \end{array} \right\} \underline{\text{BY}} \left\{ \begin{array}{l} \text{identifier-5} \\ \text{literal-3} \end{array} \right\} \left[\left\{ \begin{array}{l} \underline{\text{BEFORE}} \\ \underline{\text{AFTER}} \end{array} \right\} \text{INITIAL} \left\{ \begin{array}{l} \text{identifier-4} \\ \text{literal-2} \end{array} \right\} \right] ... \right\} \end{array} \right\} .$

INSPECT identifier-1 TALLYING

$$\left\{ \text{identifier-2} \ \underline{\text{FOR}} \left\{ \left[\left\{ \begin{matrix} \underline{\text{ALL}} \\ \underline{\text{LEADING}} \end{matrix} \right\} \left\{ \begin{matrix} \text{identifier-3} \\ \text{literal-1} \end{matrix} \right\} \right] \left[\left\{ \begin{matrix} \underline{\text{BEFORE}} \\ \underline{\text{AFTER}} \end{matrix} \right\} \text{INITIAL} \left\{ \begin{matrix} \text{identifier-4} \\ \text{literal-2} \end{matrix} \right\} \right] \right\} \dots \right\}$$

CHARACTERS (within the first brace, below ALL/LEADING)

REPLACING

$$\left\{ \begin{matrix} \underline{\text{CHARACTERS}} \ \underline{\text{BY}} \left\{ \begin{matrix} \text{identifier-5} \\ \text{literal-3} \end{matrix} \right\} \left[\left\{ \begin{matrix} \underline{\text{BEFORE}} \\ \underline{\text{AFTER}} \end{matrix} \right\} \text{INITIAL} \left\{ \begin{matrix} \text{identifier-4} \\ \text{literal-2} \end{matrix} \right\} \right] \\ \left\{ \begin{matrix} \underline{\text{ALL}} \\ \underline{\text{LEADING}} \\ \underline{\text{FIRST}} \end{matrix} \right\} \left\{ \left\{ \begin{matrix} \text{identifier-3} \\ \text{literal-1} \end{matrix} \right\} \underline{\text{BY}} \left\{ \begin{matrix} \text{identifier-5} \\ \text{literal-3} \end{matrix} \right\} \left[\left\{ \begin{matrix} \underline{\text{BEFORE}} \\ \underline{\text{AFTER}} \end{matrix} \right\} \text{INITIAL} \left\{ \begin{matrix} \text{identifier-4} \\ \text{literal-2} \end{matrix} \right\} \right] \right\} \dots \end{matrix} \right\} .$$

$$\underline{\text{MERGE}} \ \text{file-name-1} \left\{ \text{ON} \left\{ \begin{matrix} \underline{\text{ASCENDING}} \\ \underline{\text{DESCENDING}} \end{matrix} \right\} \text{KEY \{data-name-1\}} \ \dots \right\} \ \dots$$

[COLLATING $\underline{\text{SEQUENCE}}$ IS alphabet-name-1]

$\underline{\text{USING}}$ file-name-2 {file-name-3} ...

$$\left\{ \begin{matrix} \underline{\text{OUTPUT}} \ \underline{\text{PROCEDURE}} \ \text{IS procedure-name-1} \left[\left\{ \begin{matrix} \underline{\text{THROUGH}} \\ \underline{\text{THRU}} \end{matrix} \right\} \text{procedure-name-2} \right] \\ \underline{\text{GIVING}} \ \text{file-name-4} \end{matrix} \right\}$$

$$\underline{\text{MOVE}} \left\{ \begin{matrix} \text{identifier-1} \\ \text{literal-1} \end{matrix} \right\} \underline{\text{TO}} \text{ \{identifier-2\}} \ \dots$$

$$\underline{\text{MOVE}} \left\{ \begin{matrix} \underline{\text{CORRESPONDING}} \\ \underline{\text{CORR}} \end{matrix} \right\} \text{identifier-1} \ \underline{\text{TO}} \text{ identifier-2}$$

$$\underline{\text{MULTIPLY}} \left\{ \begin{matrix} \text{identifier-1} \\ \text{literal-1} \end{matrix} \right\} \underline{\text{BY}} \text{ \{identifier-2 [}\underline{\text{ROUNDED}}\text{]\}} \ \dots$$

[ON $\underline{\text{SIZE}}$ $\underline{\text{ERROR}}$ imperative-statement]

MULTIPLY $\left\{\begin{array}{l}\text{identifier-1}\\\text{literal-1}\end{array}\right\}$ BY $\left\{\begin{array}{l}\text{identifier-2}\\\text{literal-2}\end{array}\right\}$

GIVING {identifier-3 [ROUNDED]} ...

[ON SIZE ERROR imperative-statement]]

OPEN $\left\{\begin{array}{l}\text{INPUT}\left\{\begin{array}{l}\text{file-name}\\\text{-1}\end{array}\quad\left[\begin{array}{l}\underline{\text{REVERSED}}\\\text{WITH }\underline{\text{NO}}\underline{\text{REWIND}}\end{array}\right]\right\}...\\\text{OUTPUT \{file-name-2 [WITH \underline{NO} \underline{REWIND}]\} ...}\\\text{\underline{I-O} \{file-name-3\} ...}\\\text{\underline{EXTEND} \{file-name-4\} ...}\end{array}\right\}$ ...

OPEN $\left\{\begin{array}{l}\underline{\text{INPUT}}\text{ \{file-name-1\} ...}\\\underline{\text{OUTPUT}}\text{ \{file-name-2\} ...}\\\underline{\text{I-O}}\text{ \{file-name-3\} ...}\end{array}\right\}$ ...

PERFORM $\left[\text{procedure-name-1}\left[\left\{\begin{array}{l}\underline{\text{THROUGH}}\\\underline{\text{THRU}}\end{array}\right\}\text{procedure-name-2}\right]\right]$

PERFORM $\left[\text{procedure-name-1}\left[\left\{\begin{array}{l}\underline{\text{THROUGH}}\\\underline{\text{THRU}}\end{array}\right\}\text{procedure-name-2}\right]\right]$
$\left\{\begin{array}{l}\text{identifier-1}\\\text{integer-1}\end{array}\right\}$ TIMES

PERFORM $\left[\text{procedure-name-1}\left[\left\{\begin{array}{l}\underline{\text{THROUGH}}\\\underline{\text{THRU}}\end{array}\right\}\text{procedure-name-2}\right]\right]$
UNTIL condition-1

$$\underline{\text{PERFORM}} \left[\text{procedure-name-1} \left[\left\{ \genfrac{}{}{0pt}{}{\underline{\text{THROUGH}}}{\underline{\text{THRU}}} \right\} \text{procedure-name-2} \right] \right]$$

$$\underline{\text{VARYING}} \left\{ \genfrac{}{}{0pt}{}{\text{identifier-2}}{\text{index-name-1}} \right\} \underline{\text{FR}\atop\text{OM}} \left\{ \genfrac{}{}{0pt}{}{\text{identifier-3}}{\genfrac{}{}{0pt}{}{\text{index-name-2}}{\text{literal-1}}} \right\}$$

$$\underline{\text{BY}} \left\{ \genfrac{}{}{0pt}{}{\text{identifier-4}}{\text{literal-2}} \right\} \underline{\text{UNTIL}} \text{ condition-1}$$

$$\left[\underline{\text{AFTER}} \left\{ \genfrac{}{}{0pt}{}{\text{identifier-5}}{\text{literal-3}} \right\} \underline{\text{FROM}} \left\{ \genfrac{}{}{0pt}{}{\text{identifier-6}}{\genfrac{}{}{0pt}{}{\text{index-name-3}}{\text{literal-4}}} \right\} \right.$$

$$\left. \underline{\text{BY}} \left\{ \genfrac{}{}{0pt}{}{\text{identifier-7}}{\text{literal-5}} \right\} \underline{\text{UNTIL}} \text{ condition-2} \right]$$

$$\left[\underline{\text{AFTER}} \left\{ \genfrac{}{}{0pt}{}{\text{identifier-8}}{\text{literal-6}} \right\} \underline{\text{FROM}} \left\{ \genfrac{}{}{0pt}{}{\text{identifier-9}}{\genfrac{}{}{0pt}{}{\text{index-name-4}}{\text{literal-7}}} \right\} \right.$$

$$\left. \underline{\text{BY}} \left\{ \genfrac{}{}{0pt}{}{\text{identifier-10}}{\text{literal-8}} \right\} \underline{\text{UNTIL}} \text{ condition-3} \right]$$

$\underline{\text{READ}}$ file-name RECORD [$\underline{\text{INTO}}$ identifier]

    [AT $\underline{\text{END}}$ imperative-statement]

$\underline{\text{READ}}$ file-name [$\underline{\text{NEXT}}$] RECORD [$\underline{\text{INTO}}$ identifier]

    [AT $\underline{\text{END}}$ imperative-statement]

$\underline{\text{READ}}$ file-name RECORD [$\underline{\text{INTO}}$ identifier]

    [$\underline{\text{INVALID}}$ KEY imperative-statement]

$\underline{\text{READ}}$ file-name RECORD [$\underline{\text{INTO}}$ identifier-1]

    [$\underline{\text{KEY}}$ IS data-name]

    [$\underline{\text{INVALID}}$ KEY imperative-statement]

$\underline{\text{RECEIVE}}$ cd-name $\left\{ \genfrac{}{}{0pt}{}{\underline{\text{MESSAGE}}}{\underline{\text{SEGMENT}}} \right\}$ $\underline{\text{INTO}}$ identifier

    [$\underline{\text{NO}}$ $\underline{\text{DATA}}$ imperative-statement]

$\underline{\text{RELEASE}}$ record-name [$\underline{\text{FROM}}$ identifier]

RETURN file-name RECORD [INTO identifier] AT END imperative-statement

REWRITE record-name [FROM identifier]

REWRITE record-name [FROM identifier] [INVALID KEY imperative-statement]

SEARCH identifier-1 $\left[\ \text{VARYING}\ \left\{\begin{array}{l}\text{identifier-2}\\\text{index-name-1}\end{array}\right\}\right]$

   [AT END imperative-statement-1]

$\left\{\ \text{WHEN condition-1}\ \left\{\begin{array}{l}\text{imperative-statement-2}\\\text{NEXT SENTENCE}\end{array}\right\}\right\}$ ...

SEARCH ALL identifier-1 [AT END imperative-statement-1]

$\text{WHEN}\ \left\{\begin{array}{l}\text{data-name-1}\left\{\begin{array}{l}\text{IS EQUAL TO}\\\text{IS} =\end{array}\right\}\left\{\begin{array}{l}\text{identifier-3}\\\text{literal-1}\\\text{arithmetic-expression-1}\end{array}\right\}\\\text{condition-name-1}\end{array}\right\}$

$\left[\ \text{AND}\ \left\{\begin{array}{l}\text{data-name-2}\left\{\begin{array}{l}\text{IS EQUAL TO}\\\text{IS} =\end{array}\right\}\left\{\begin{array}{l}\text{identifier-4}\\\text{literal-2}\\\text{arithmetic-expression-2}\end{array}\right\}\\\text{condition-name-2}\end{array}\right\}\right]$ ...

$\left\{\begin{array}{l}\text{imperative-statement-2}\\\text{NEXT SENTENCE}\end{array}\right\}$

SEND cd-name FROM identifier-1

SEND cd-name $\left[\text{FROM identifier-1}\ \left\{\begin{array}{l}\text{WITH identifier-2}\\\text{WITH ESI}\\\text{WITH EMI}\\\text{WITH EGI}\end{array}\right\}\right.$

$\left[\left\{\begin{array}{l}\text{BEFORE}\\\text{AFTER}\end{array}\right\}\ \text{ADVANCING}\ \left\{\begin{array}{l}\left\{\begin{array}{l}\text{identifier-3}\\\text{integer-1}\end{array}\right\}\left[\begin{array}{l}\text{LINE}\\\text{LINES}\end{array}\right]\\\left\{\begin{array}{l}\text{mnemonic-name-1}\\\text{PAGE}\end{array}\right\}\end{array}\right\}\right]$

$$\underline{\text{SET}} \quad \left\{ \begin{array}{l} \text{index-name-1} \\ \text{identifier-1} \end{array} \right\} \quad \dots \quad \underline{\text{TO}} \quad \left\{ \begin{array}{l} \text{index-name-2} \\ \text{identifier-2} \\ \text{integer-1} \end{array} \right\}$$

$$\underline{\text{SET}} \quad \{\text{index-name-3}\} \quad \dots \quad \left\{ \begin{array}{l} \underline{\text{UP BY}} \\ \underline{\text{DOWN}} \ \underline{\text{BY}} \end{array} \right\} \quad \left\{ \begin{array}{l} \text{identifier-3} \\ \text{integer-2} \end{array} \right\}$$

$$\underline{\text{SORT}} \ \text{file-name-1} \left\{ \text{ON} \left\{ \begin{array}{l} \underline{\text{ASCENDING}} \\ \underline{\text{DESCENDING}} \end{array} \right\} \text{KEY} \ \{\text{data-name-1}\} \ \dots \right\} \ \dots$$

[COLLATING $\underline{\text{SEQUENCE}}$ IS alphabet-name-1]

$$\left\{ \begin{array}{l} \underline{\text{INPUT}} \ \underline{\text{PROCEDURE}} \ \text{IS section-name-1} \\ \underline{\text{USING}} \quad \{\text{file-name-2}\} \ \dots \end{array} \right. \left[\left\{ \begin{array}{l} \underline{\text{THROUGH}} \\ \underline{\text{THRU}} \end{array} \right\} \text{section-name-2} \right] \right\}$$

$$\left\{ \begin{array}{l} \underline{\text{OUTPUT}} \ \underline{\text{PROCEDURE}} \ \text{IS section-name-3} \\ \underline{\text{GIVING}} \quad \{\text{file-name-3}\} \ \dots \end{array} \right. \left[\left\{ \begin{array}{l} \underline{\text{THROUGH}} \\ \underline{\text{THRU}} \end{array} \right\} \text{section-name-4} \right] \right\}$$

$$\underline{\text{START}} \ \text{file-name} \left[\text{KEY} \left\{ \begin{array}{l} \text{IS} \ \underline{\text{EQUAL}} \ \text{TO} \\ \text{IS} = \\ \text{IS} \ \underline{\text{GREATER}} \ \text{THAN} \\ \text{IS} > \\ \text{IS} \ \underline{\text{NOT}} \ \underline{\text{LESS}} \ \text{THAN} \\ \text{IS} \ \underline{\text{NOT}} < \end{array} \right\} \text{data-name} \right]$$

[$\underline{\text{INVALID}}$ KEY imperative-statement]

$$\underline{\text{STOP}} \quad \left\{ \begin{array}{l} \underline{\text{RUN}} \\ \text{literal} \end{array} \right\}$$

$$\underline{\text{STRING}} \quad \left\{ \left\{ \begin{array}{l} \text{identifier-1} \\ \text{literal-1} \end{array} \right\} \ \dots \ \underline{\text{DELIMITED}} \ \text{BY} \left\{ \begin{array}{l} \text{identifier-2} \\ \text{literal-2} \\ \underline{\text{SIZE}} \end{array} \right\} \right\} \ \dots$$

$\underline{\text{INTO}}$ identifier-3

[WITH $\underline{\text{POINTER}}$ identifier-4]

[ON $\underline{\text{OVERFLOW}}$ imperative-statement]

SUBTRACT $\left\{ \begin{array}{l} \text{identifier-1} \\ \text{literal-1} \end{array} \right\}$ ... <u>FROM</u> {identifier-3 [<u>ROUNDED</u>]} ...

    [ON <u>SIZE</u> <u>ERROR</u> imperative-statement]

SUBTRACT $\left\{ \begin{array}{l} \text{identifier-1} \\ \text{literal-1} \end{array} \right\}$ .... <u>FROM</u> $\left\{ \begin{array}{l} \text{identifier-2} \\ \text{literal-2} \end{array} \right\}$

    <u>GIVING</u> {identifier-3 [<u>ROUNDED</u>]} ...

    [ON <u>SIZE</u> <u>ERROR</u> imperative-statement]

SUBTRACT $\left\{ \begin{array}{l} \underline{\text{CORRESPONDING}} \\ \underline{\text{CORR}} \end{array} \right\}$ identifier-1 <u>FROM</u> identifier-2 [<u>ROUNDED</u>]

    [ON <u>SIZE</u> <u>ERROR</u> imperative-statement]

<u>SUPPRESS</u> PRINTING

<u>TERMINATE</u> {report-name-1} ...

<u>UNSTRING</u> identifier-1

    $\left[\underline{\text{DELIMITED}} \text{ BY } [\underline{\text{ALL}}] \left\{ \begin{array}{l} \text{identifier-2} \\ \text{literal-1} \end{array} \right\} \left[\underline{\text{OR}} [\underline{\text{ALL}}] \left\{ \begin{array}{l} \text{identifier-3} \\ \text{literal-2} \end{array} \right\} \right] ... \right]$

    <u>INTO</u> {identifier-4 [<u>DELIMITER</u> IN identifier-5] [<u>COUNT</u> IN identifier-6]} ...

    [WITH <u>POINTER</u> identifier-7]

    [<u>TALLYING</u> IN identifier-8]

    [ON <u>OVERFLOW</u> imperative-statement]

<u>USE</u> <u>AFTER</u> STANDARD $\left\{ \begin{array}{l} \underline{\text{EXCEPTION}} \\ \underline{\text{ERROR}} \end{array} \right\}$ <u>PROCEDURE</u> ON $\left\{ \begin{array}{l} \text{\{file-name-1\} ...} \\ \text{INPUT} \\ \underline{\text{OUTPUT}} \\ \text{I-O} \\ \text{EXTEND} \end{array} \right\}$

<u>USE</u> <u>AFTER</u> STANDARD $\left\{ \begin{array}{l} \underline{\text{EXCEPTION}} \\ \underline{\text{ERROR}} \end{array} \right\}$ <u>PROCEDURE</u> ON $\left\{ \begin{array}{l} \text{\{file-name-1\} ...} \\ \text{INPUT} \\ \underline{\text{OUTPUT}} \\ \text{I-O} \end{array} \right\}$

USE <u>BEFORE</u> <u>REPORTING</u> identifier-1

<u>USE</u> FOR <u>DEBUGGING</u> ON $\left\{ \begin{array}{l} \text{cd-name-1} \\ \text{[\underline{ALL} REFERENCES OF] identifier-1} \\ \text{file-name-1} \\ \text{procedure-name-1} \\ \underline{\text{ALL}}\ \underline{\text{PROCEDURES}} \end{array} \right\}$ ...

<u>WRITE</u> record-name [<u>FROM</u> identifier-1]

$$\left[\left\{ \begin{array}{l} \underline{\text{BEFORE}} \\ \underline{\text{AFTER}} \end{array} \right\} \text{ADVANCING} \left\{ \begin{array}{l} \left\{ \begin{array}{l} \text{identifier-2} \\ \text{integer-1} \end{array} \right\} \left\{ \begin{array}{l} \text{LINE} \\ \text{LINES} \end{array} \right\} \\ \left\{ \begin{array}{l} \text{mnemonic-name-1} \\ \underline{\text{PAGE}} \end{array} \right\} \end{array} \right\} \right]$$

$$\left[\text{AT} \left\{ \begin{array}{l} \underline{\text{END-OF-PAGE}} \\ \underline{\text{EOP}} \end{array} \right\} \text{imperative-statement} \right]$$

<u>WRITE</u> record-name-1 [<u>FROM</u> identifier-1]

[<u>INVALID</u> KEY imperative-statement]

GENERAL FORMAT FOR CONDITIONS

RELATION CONDITION:

$$\left\{\begin{array}{l} \text{identifier-1} \\ \text{literal-1} \\ \text{arithmetic-expression-1} \\ \text{index-name-1} \end{array}\right\} \left\{\begin{array}{l} \text{IS [NOT] GREATER THAN} \\ \text{IS [NOT] >} \\ \text{IS [NOT] LESS THAN} \\ \text{IS [NOT] <} \\ \text{IS [NOT] EQUAL TO} \\ \text{IS [NOT] =} \end{array}\right\} \left\{\begin{array}{l} \text{identifier-2} \\ \text{literal-2} \\ \text{arithmetic-expression-2} \\ \text{index-name-2} \end{array}\right\}$$

CLASS CONDITION:

$$\text{identifier IS [NOT]} \left\{\begin{array}{l} \text{NUMERIC} \\ \text{ALPHABETIC} \end{array}\right\}$$

CONDITION-NAME CONDITION:

condition-name

SWITCH-STATUS CONDITION:

condition-name

SIGN CONDITION:

$$\text{arithmetic-expression IS [NOT]} \left\{\begin{array}{l} \text{POSITIVE} \\ \text{NEGATIVE} \\ \text{ZERO} \end{array}\right\}$$

NEGATED CONDITION:

NOT condition

COMBINED CONDITION:

$$\text{condition} \left\{\left\{\begin{array}{l} \text{AND} \\ \text{OR} \end{array}\right\} \text{condition-name}\right\} \dots$$

ABBREVIATED COMBINED RELATION CONDITION:

$$\text{relation-condition} \left\{\left\{\begin{array}{l} \text{AND} \\ \text{OR} \end{array}\right\} \text{[NOT] [relational-operator] object}\right\} \dots$$

MISCELLANEOUS FORMATS

QUALIFICATION:

$$\left\{ \begin{array}{l} \text{data-name-1} \\ \text{condition-name-1} \end{array} \right\} \quad \left[\left\{ \begin{array}{l} \underline{\text{IN}} \\ \underline{\text{OF}} \end{array} \right\} \text{data-name-2} \right] \ \dots$$

$$\text{paragraph-name} \quad \left[\left\{ \begin{array}{l} \underline{\text{IN}} \\ \underline{\text{OF}} \end{array} \right\} \text{section-name} \right]$$

$$\text{text-name} \quad \left[\left\{ \begin{array}{l} \underline{\text{IN}} \\ \underline{\text{OF}} \end{array} \right\} \text{library-name} \right]$$

SUBSCRIPTING:

$$\left\{ \begin{array}{l} \text{data-name} \\ \text{condition-name} \end{array} \right\} \quad (\text{subscript-1} \ [\ \text{subscript-2} \ [\ \text{subscript-3}]]\ )$$

INDEXING:

$$\left\{ \begin{array}{l} \text{data-name} \\ \text{condition-name} \end{array} \right\} \quad (\ \left\{ \begin{array}{l} \text{index-name-1} \ [\{\ \pm\ \}\ \text{literal-1}] \\ \text{literal-2} \end{array} \right\} \ \dots \ )$$

IDENTIFIER, FORMAT 1:

$$\text{data-name-1} \left[\left\{ \begin{array}{l} \underline{\text{IN}} \\ \underline{\text{OF}} \end{array} \right\} \text{data-name-2} \right] \dots \ (\text{subscript-1} \ [,\ \text{subscript-2} \ [,\ \text{subscript-3}]]\ )$$

IDENTIFIER, FORMAT 2:

$$\text{data-name-1} \left[\left\{ \begin{array}{l} \underline{\text{IN}} \\ \underline{\text{OF}} \end{array} \right\} \text{data-name-2} \right] \dots \left[(\left\{ \begin{array}{l} \text{index-name-1} \ [\{\ \pm\ \}\ \text{literal-1}] \\ \text{literal-2} \end{array} \right\} \right.$$

$$\left[\left\{ \begin{array}{l} \text{index-name-2} \ [\{\ \pm\ \}\ \text{literal-3}] \\ \text{literal-4} \end{array} \right\} \right] \left[\left\{ \begin{array}{l} \text{index-name-3} \ [\{\ \pm\ \}\ \text{literal-5}] \\ \text{literal-6} \end{array} \right\} \right] \right) \Big]$$

GENERAL FORMAT FOR COPY STATEMENT

$$\underline{\text{COPY}} \ \text{text-name-1} \left[\left\{ \begin{array}{l} \underline{\text{OF}} \\ \underline{\text{IN}} \end{array} \right\} \text{library-name} \right]$$

$$\left[\underline{\text{REPLACING}} \ \left\{ \left\{ \begin{array}{l} \text{==pseudo-text-1==} \\ \text{identifier-1} \\ \text{literal-1} \\ \text{word-1} \end{array} \right\} \underline{\text{BY}} \left\{ \begin{array}{l} \text{==pseudo-text-2==} \\ \text{identifier-2} \\ \text{literal-2} \\ \text{word-2} \end{array} \right\} \right\} \dots \right]$$

GENERAL FORMAT FOR IDENTIFICATION DIVISION

IDENTIFICATION DIVISION.

PROGRAM-ID. program-name $\left[\text{ IS } \left\{ \left| \begin{array}{l} \underline{\text{COMMON}} \\ \underline{\text{INITIAL}} \end{array} \right| \right\} \text{ PROGRAM } \right]$.

[AUTHOR. [comment-entry] ...]

[INSTALLATION. [comment-entry] ...]

[DATE-WRITTEN. [comment-entry] ...]

[DATE-COMPILED. [comment-entry] ...]

[SECURITY. [comment-entry] ...]

GENERAL FORMAT FOR ENVIRONMENT DIVISION

[ENVIRONMENT DIVISION.

[CONFIGURATION SECTION.

[SOURCE-COMPUTER. [computer-name [WITH DEBUGGING MODE].]]

[OBJECT-COMPUTER. [computer-name

$\left[\text{ MEMORY SIZE integer-1 } \left\{ \begin{array}{l} \underline{\text{WORDS}} \\ \underline{\text{CHARACTERS}} \\ \underline{\text{MODULES}} \end{array} \right\} \right]$

[PROGRAM COLLATING SEQUENCE IS alphabet-name-1]

[SEGMENT-LIMIT IS segment-number].]]

[SPECIAL-NAMES. [[implementor-name-1

$$\left\{ \begin{array}{l} \text{IS mnemonic-name-1 } [\underline{ON} \text{ STATUS IS condition-name-1} \\ \qquad\qquad\qquad [\underline{OFF} \text{ STATUS IS condition-name-2}]] \\ \text{IS mnemonic-name-2 } [\underline{OFF} \text{ STATUS IS condition-name-2} \\ \qquad\qquad\qquad [\underline{ON} \text{ STATUS IS condition-name-1}]] \\ \underline{ON} \text{ STATUS IS condition-name-1 } [\underline{OFF} \text{ STATUS IS condition-name-2}] \\ \underline{OFF} \text{ STATUS IS condition-name-2 } [\underline{ON} \text{ STATUS IS condition-name-1}] \end{array} \right\} \Big] \quad \cdots$$

[ALPHABET alphabet-name-1 IS

$$\left\{ \begin{array}{l} \underline{\text{STANDARD-1}} \\ \underline{\text{STANDARD-2}} \\ \underline{\text{NATIVE}} \\ \text{implementor-name-2} \\ \left[\left\{ \text{literal-1} \begin{array}{l} \left[\left\{ \begin{array}{l} \underline{\text{THROUGH}} \\ \underline{\text{THRU}} \end{array} \right\} \text{literal-2} \\ \{\underline{\text{ALSO}} \text{ literal-3}\} \cdots \end{array} \right] \end{array} \right\} \cdots \right] \end{array} \right\} \Big] \quad \cdots$$

$$\left[\underline{\text{SYMBOLIC}} \text{ CHARACTERS} \left\{ \left\{ \{\text{symbolic-character-1}\} \cdots \left\{ \begin{array}{l} \text{IS} \\ \text{ARE} \end{array} \right\} \{\text{integer-1}\} \cdots \right\} \cdots \right. \right.$$

$$\left. \left. [\underline{\text{IN}} \text{ alphabet-name-2}] \cdots \right\} \right] \cdots$$

$$\left[\underline{\text{CLASS}} \text{ class-name-1 IS} \left\{ \text{literal-4} \left[\left\{ \begin{array}{l} \underline{\text{THROUGH}} \\ \underline{\text{THRU}} \end{array} \right\} \text{literal-5} \right] \right\} \cdots \right] \cdots$$

[CURRENCY SIGN IS literal-6]
[DECIMAL-POINT IS COMMA].]]]

[INPUT-OUTPUT SECTION.

FILE-CONTROL.

 {file-control-entry} ...

[I-O-CONTROL.

$$\left[\left[\underline{\text{RERUN}} \left[\underline{\text{ON}} \left\{\begin{array}{l}\text{file-name-1}\\ \text{implementor-name-1}\end{array}\right\}\right]\right.\right.$$

$$\left.\underline{\text{EVERY}} \left\{\begin{array}{l}\left\{\begin{array}{l}[\underline{\text{END}}\text{ OF}] \left\{\begin{array}{l}\underline{\text{REEL}}\\ \underline{\text{UNIT}}\end{array}\right\}\\ \text{integer-1 }\underline{\text{RECORDS}}\end{array}\right\}\text{ OF file-name-2}\\ \text{integer-2 }\underline{\text{CLOCK-UNITS}}\\ \text{condition-name-1}\end{array}\right\}\left.\left.\right]\right]\ ...$$

$$\left[\underline{\text{SAME}} \left[\begin{array}{l}\underline{\text{RECORD}}\\ \underline{\text{SORT}}\\ \underline{\text{SORT-MERGE}}\end{array}\right]\text{AREA FOR file-name-3 \{file-name-4\} ...}\right]\ ...$$

[<u>MULTIPLE</u> <u>FILE</u> TAPE CONTAINS {file-name-5 [<u>POSITION</u> integer-3]} ...] ... .]]]]

GENERAL FORMAT FOR FILE CONTROL ENTRY

SEQUENTIAL FILE:

SELECT [OPTIONAL] file-name-1

ASSIGN TO $\left\{ \begin{array}{l} \text{implementor-name-1} \\ \text{literal-1} \end{array} \right\}$ ...

$\left[\underline{\text{RESERVE}} \text{ integer-1} \left[\begin{array}{l} \text{AREA} \\ \text{AREAS} \end{array} \right] \right]$

[[ORGANIZATION IS] SEQUENTIAL]

$\left[\underline{\text{PADDING}} \text{ CHARACTER IS} \left\{ \begin{array}{l} \text{data-name-1} \\ \text{literal-2} \end{array} \right\} \right]$

$\left[\underline{\text{RECORD}} \underline{\text{DELIMITER}} \text{ IS} \left\{ \begin{array}{l} \underline{\text{STANDARD-1}} \\ \text{implementor-name-2} \end{array} \right\} \right]$

[ACCESS MODE IS SEQUENTIAL]

[FILE STATUS IS data-name-2].

RELATIVE FILE:

SELECT [OPTIONAL] file-name-1

ASSIGN TO $\left\{ \begin{array}{l} \text{implementor-name-1} \\ \text{literal-1} \end{array} \right\}$ ...

$\left[\underline{\text{RESERVE}} \text{ integer-1} \left[\begin{array}{l} \text{AREA} \\ \text{AREAS} \end{array} \right] \right]$

[ORGANIZATION IS] RELATIVE

$\left[\underline{\text{ACCESS}} \text{ MODE IS} \left\{ \begin{array}{l} \underline{\text{SEQUENTIAL}} \text{ [RELATIVE KEY IS data-name-1]} \\ \left\{ \begin{array}{l} \underline{\text{RANDOM}} \\ \underline{\text{DYNAMIC}} \end{array} \right\} \underline{\text{RELATIVE}} \text{ KEY IS data-name-1} \end{array} \right\} \right]$

[FILE STATUS IS data-name-2].

INDEXED FILE:

SELECT [OPTIONAL] file-name-1

      ASSIGN TO $\left\{ \begin{array}{l} \text{implementor-name-1} \\ \text{literal-1} \end{array} \right\}$ ...

      $\left[\underline{\text{RESERVE}} \text{ integer-1} \left[\begin{array}{l} \text{AREA} \\ \text{AREAS} \end{array} \right] \right]$

      [ORGANIZATION IS] INDEXED

      $\left[\underline{\text{ACCESS}} \text{ MODE IS} \left\{ \begin{array}{l} \underline{\text{SEQUENTIAL}} \\ \underline{\text{RANDOM}} \\ \underline{\text{DYNAMIC}} \end{array} \right\} \right]$

      RECORD KEY IS data-name-1

      [ALTERNATE RECORD KEY IS data-name-2 [WITH DUPLICATES]] ...

      [FILE STATUS IS data-name-3].

SORT OR MERGE FILE:

SELECT file-name-1 ASSIGN TO $\left\{ \begin{array}{l} \text{implementor-name-1} \\ \text{literal-1} \end{array} \right\}$ ...

REPORT FILE:

SELECT [OPTIONAL] file-name-1

      ASSIGN TO $\left\{ \begin{array}{l} \text{implementor-name-1} \\ \text{literal-1} \end{array} \right\}$ ...

      $\left[\underline{\text{RESERVE}} \text{ integer-1} \left\{ \begin{array}{l} \text{AREA} \\ \text{AREAS} \end{array} \right\} \right]$

      [[ORGANIZATION IS] SEQUENTIAL]]

      $\left[\underline{\text{PADDING}} \text{ CHARACTER IS} \left\{ \begin{array}{l} \text{data-name-1} \\ \text{literal-2} \end{array} \right\} \right]$

      $\left[\underline{\text{RECORD}} \underline{\text{DELIMITER}} \text{ IS} \left\{ \begin{array}{l} \underline{\text{STANDARD-1}} \\ \text{implementor-name-2} \end{array} \right\} \right]$

      [ACCESS MODE IS SEQUENTIAL]

      [FILE STATUS IS data-name-2].

GENERAL FORMAT FOR DATA DIVISION

[DATA DIVISION.

[FILE SECTION.

$$
\left[
\begin{array}{l}
\text{file-description-entry \{record-description-entry\} ...} \\
\text{sort-merge-file-description-entry \{record-description-entry\} ...} \\
\text{report-file-description-entry}
\end{array}
\right]
\ ... \ \Bigg]
$$

[WORKING-STORAGE SECTION.

$$
\left[
\begin{array}{l}
\text{77-level-description-entry} \\
\text{record-description-entry}
\end{array}
\right]
\ ... \ \Bigg]
$$

[LINKAGE SECTION.

$$
\left[
\begin{array}{l}
\text{77-level-description-entry} \\
\text{record-description-entry}
\end{array}
\right]
\ ... \ \Bigg]
$$

[COMMUNICATION SECTION.

[communication-description-entry [record-description-entry] ...] ...]

[REPORT SECTION.

[report-description-entry {report-group-description-entry} ...] ...]]

GENERAL FORMAT FOR FILE DESCRIPTION ENTRY

SEQUENTIAL FILE:

<u>FD</u> file-name-1

    [IS <u>EXTERNAL</u>]

    [IS <u>GLOBAL</u>]

$$\left[\ \underline{BLOCK}\ CONTAINS\ [integer\text{-}1\ \underline{TO}]\ integer\text{-}2\ \left\{ \begin{array}{l} \underline{RECORDS} \\ CHARACTERS \end{array} \right\} \right]$$

$$\left[\ \underline{RECORD}\ \left\{ \begin{array}{l} CONTAINS\ integer\text{-}3\ CHARACTERS \\ IS\ \underline{VARYING}\ IN\ SIZE\ [[FROM\ integer\text{-}4]\ [\underline{TO}\ integer\text{-}5] \\ \qquad CHARACTERS]\ [\underline{DEPENDING}\ ON\ data\text{-}name\text{-}1] \\ CONTAINS\ integer\text{-}6\ \underline{TO}\ integer\text{-}7\ CHARACTERS \end{array} \right\} \right]$$

$$\left[\ \underline{LABEL}\ \left\{ \begin{array}{l} \underline{RECORD}\ IS \\ \underline{RECORDS}\ ARE \end{array} \right\} \left\{ \begin{array}{l} \underline{STANDARD} \\ \underline{OMITTED} \end{array} \right\} \right]$$

$$\left[\ \underline{VALUE\ OF}\ \left\{ implementor\text{-}name\text{-}1\ IS\ \left\{ \begin{array}{l} data\text{-}name\text{-}2 \\ literal\text{-}1 \end{array} \right\} \right\} \dots \right]$$

$$\left[\ \underline{DATA}\ \left\{ \begin{array}{l} \underline{RECORD}\ IS \\ \underline{RECORDS}\ ARE \end{array} \right\} \{data\text{-}name\text{-}3\} \dots \right]$$

$$\left[\ \underline{LINAGE}\ IS\ \left\{ \begin{array}{l} data\text{-}name\text{-}4 \\ integer\text{-}8 \end{array} \right\} LINES \right.$$

$$\left[\ WITH\ \underline{FOOTING}\ AT\ \left\{ \begin{array}{l} data\text{-}name\text{-}5 \\ integer\text{-}9 \end{array} \right\} \right]$$

$$\left[\ LINES\ AT\ \underline{TOP}\ \left\{ \begin{array}{l} data\text{-}name\text{-}6 \\ integer\text{-}10 \end{array} \right\} \right]$$

$$\left. \left[\ LINES\ AT\ \underline{BOTTOM}\ \left\{ \begin{array}{l} data\text{-}name\text{-}7 \\ integer\text{-}11 \end{array} \right\} \right] \right]$$

[<u>CODE-SET</u> IS alphabet-name-1].

RELATIVE FILE:

<u>FD</u> file-name-1

    [IS <u>EXTERNAL</u>]

    [IS <u>GLOBAL</u>]

$$\left[\ \underline{\text{BLOCK}} \ \text{CONTAINS} \ [\text{integer-1} \ \underline{\text{TO}}] \ \text{integer-2} \ \left\{ \begin{array}{l} \underline{\text{RECORDS}} \\ \text{CHARACTERS} \end{array} \right\} \right]$$

$$\left[\ \underline{\text{RECORD}} \ \left\{ \begin{array}{l} \text{CONTAINS integer-3 CHARACTERS} \\ \text{IS } \underline{\text{VARYING}} \text{ IN SIZE } [[\text{FROM integer-4}] \ [\underline{\text{TO}} \text{ integer-5}] \\ \qquad \text{CHARACTERS}] \ [\underline{\text{DEPENDING}} \text{ ON data-name-1}] \\ \text{CONTAINS integer-6 } \underline{\text{TO}} \text{ integer-7 CHARACTERS} \end{array} \right\} \right]$$

$$\left[\ \underline{\text{LABEL}} \ \left\{ \begin{array}{l} \underline{\text{RECORD}} \text{ IS} \\ \underline{\text{RECORDS}} \text{ ARE} \end{array} \right\} \left\{ \begin{array}{l} \underline{\text{STANDARD}} \\ \underline{\text{OMITTED}} \end{array} \right\} \right]$$

$$\left[\ \underline{\text{VALUE}} \ \underline{\text{OF}} \ \left\{ \text{implementor-name-1 IS} \ \left\{ \begin{array}{l} \text{data-name-2} \\ \text{literal-1} \end{array} \right\} \right\} \ \dots \ \right]$$

$$\left[\ \underline{\text{DATA}} \ \left\{ \begin{array}{l} \underline{\text{RECORD}} \text{ IS} \\ \underline{\text{RECORDS}} \text{ ARE} \end{array} \right\} \ \{\text{data-name-3}\} \ \dots \ \right] \ .$$

INDEXED FILE:

<u>FD</u> file-name-1

    [IS <u>EXTERNAL</u>]

    [IS <u>GLOBAL</u>]

$$\left[\ \underline{\text{BLOCK}} \ \text{CONTAINS} \ [\text{integer-1} \ \underline{\text{TO}}] \ \text{integer-2} \ \left\{ \begin{array}{l} \underline{\text{RECORDS}} \\ \text{CHARACTERS} \end{array} \right\} \right]$$

$$\left[\ \underline{\text{RECORD}} \ \left\{ \begin{array}{l} \text{CONTAINS integer-3 CHARACTERS} \\ \text{IS } \underline{\text{VARYING}} \text{ IN SIZE } [[\text{FROM integer-4}] \ [\underline{\text{TO}} \text{ integer-5}] \\ \qquad \text{CHARACTERS}] \ [\underline{\text{DEPENDING}} \text{ ON data-name-1}] \\ \text{CONTAINS integer-6 } \underline{\text{TO}} \text{ integer-7 CHARACTERS} \end{array} \right\} \right]$$

$$\left[\ \underline{\text{LABEL}} \ \left\{ \begin{array}{l} \underline{\text{RECORD}} \text{ IS} \\ \underline{\text{RECORDS}} \text{ ARE} \end{array} \right\} \left\{ \begin{array}{l} \underline{\text{STANDARD}} \\ \underline{\text{OMITTED}} \end{array} \right\} \right]$$

$$\left[\ \underline{\text{VALUE}} \ \underline{\text{OF}} \ \left\{ \text{implementor-name-1 IS} \ \left\{ \begin{array}{l} \text{data-name-2} \\ \text{literal-1} \end{array} \right\} \right\} \ \dots \ \right]$$

$$\left[\ \underline{\text{DATA}} \ \left\{ \begin{array}{l} \underline{\text{RECORD}} \text{ IS} \\ \underline{\text{RECORDS}} \text{ ARE} \end{array} \right\} \ \{\text{data-name-3}\} \ \dots \ \right] \ .$$

SORT-MERGE FILE:

<u>SD</u> file-name-1

$$
\left[\underline{\text{RECORD}} \left\{ \begin{array}{l} \text{CONTAINS integer-1 CHARACTERS} \\ \text{IS } \underline{\text{VARYING}} \text{ IN SIZE [[FROM integer-2] [\underline{TO} integer-3]} \\ \quad \text{CHARACTERS] [\underline{DEPENDING} ON data-name-1]} \\ \text{CONTAINS integer-4 } \underline{\text{TO}} \text{ integer-5 CHARACTERS} \end{array} \right\} \right]
$$

$$
\left[\underline{\text{DATA}} \left\{ \begin{array}{l} \underline{\text{RECORD}} \text{ IS} \\ \underline{\text{RECORDS}} \text{ ARE} \end{array} \right\} \{\text{data-name-2}\} \ldots \right] \quad .
$$

REPORT FILE:

<u>FD</u> file-name-1

[IS <u>EXTERNAL</u>]

[IS <u>GLOBAL</u>]

$$
\left[\underline{\text{BLOCK}} \text{ CONTAINS [integer-1 } \underline{\text{TO}} \text{] integer-2} \left\{ \begin{array}{l} \underline{\text{RECORDS}} \\ \underline{\text{CHARACTERS}} \end{array} \right\} \right]
$$

$$
\left[\underline{\text{RECORD}} \left\{ \begin{array}{l} \text{CONTAINS integer-3 CHARACTERS} \\ \text{CONTAINS integer-4 } \underline{\text{TO}} \text{ integer-5 CHARACTERS} \end{array} \right\} \right]
$$

$$
\left[\underline{\text{LABEL}} \left\{ \begin{array}{l} \underline{\text{RECORD}} \text{ IS} \\ \underline{\text{RECORDS}} \text{ ARE} \end{array} \right\} \left\{ \begin{array}{l} \underline{\text{STANDARD}} \\ \underline{\text{OMITTED}} \end{array} \right\} \right]
$$

$$
\left[\underline{\text{VALUE}} \text{ } \underline{\text{OF}} \left\{ \text{implementor-name-1 IS} \left\{ \begin{array}{l} \text{data-name-1} \\ \text{literal-1} \end{array} \right\} \right\} \ldots \right]
$$

[<u>CODE-SET</u> IS alphabet-name-1]

$$
\left\{ \begin{array}{l} \underline{\text{REPORT}} \text{ IS} \\ \underline{\text{REPORTS}} \text{ ARE} \end{array} \right\} \quad \{\text{report-name-1}\} \ldots \quad .
$$

GENERAL DESCRIPTION FOR DATA DESCRIPTION ENTRY

FORMAT 1:

level-number $\begin{bmatrix} \text{data-name-1} \\ \underline{\text{FILLER}} \end{bmatrix}$

[REDEFINES data-name-2]

[IS EXTERNAL]

[IS GLOBAL]

$\begin{bmatrix} \left\{ \begin{array}{l} \underline{\text{PICTURE}} \\ \underline{\text{PIC}} \end{array} \right\} \text{ IS character-string} \end{bmatrix}$

$\begin{bmatrix} [\underline{\text{USAGE}} \text{ IS}] \left\{ \begin{array}{l} \underline{\text{BINARY}} \\ \underline{\text{COMPUTATIONAL}} \\ \underline{\text{COMP}} \\ \underline{\text{DISPLAY}} \\ \underline{\text{INDEX}} \\ \underline{\text{PACKED-DECIMAL}} \end{array} \right\} \end{bmatrix}$

$\begin{bmatrix} [\underline{\text{SIGN}} \text{ IS}] \left\{ \begin{array}{l} \underline{\text{LEADING}} \\ \underline{\text{TRAILING}} \end{array} \right\} [\underline{\text{SEPARATE}} \text{ CHARACTER}] \end{bmatrix}$

$\begin{bmatrix} \underline{\text{OCCURS}} \text{ integer-2 TIMES} \\ \quad \begin{bmatrix} \left\{ \begin{array}{l} \underline{\text{ASCENDING}} \\ \underline{\text{DESCENDING}} \end{array} \right\} \text{ KEY IS } \{\text{data-name-3}\} \ldots \end{bmatrix} \ldots \\ \quad\quad [\underline{\text{INDEXED}} \text{ BY } \{\text{index-name-1}\} \ldots] \\ \underline{\text{OCCURS}} \text{ integer-1 } \underline{\text{TO}} \text{ integer-2 TIMES } \underline{\text{DEPENDING}} \text{ ON data-name-4} \\ \quad \begin{bmatrix} \left\{ \begin{array}{l} \underline{\text{ASCENDING}} \\ \underline{\text{DESCENDING}} \end{array} \right\} \text{ KEY IS } \{\text{data-name-3}\} \ldots \end{bmatrix} \ldots \\ \quad\quad [\underline{\text{INDEXED}} \text{ BY } \{\text{index-name-1}\} \ldots] \end{bmatrix}$

$\begin{bmatrix} \left\{ \begin{array}{l} \underline{\text{SYNCHRONIZED}} \\ \underline{\text{SYNC}} \end{array} \right\} \begin{bmatrix} \underline{\text{LEFT}} \\ \underline{\text{RIGHT}} \end{bmatrix} \end{bmatrix}$

$\begin{bmatrix} \left\{ \begin{array}{l} \underline{\text{JUSTIFIED}} \\ \underline{\text{JUST}} \end{array} \right\} \text{ RIGHT} \end{bmatrix}$

[BLANK WHEN ZERO]

[VALUE IS literal-1].

FORMAT 2:

66 data-name-1 <u>RENAMES</u> data-name-2 $\left[\left\{ \begin{array}{c} \underline{THROUGH} \\ \underline{THRU} \end{array} \right\} \text{data-name-3} \right]$.

FORMAT 3:

88 condition-name-1 $\left\{ \begin{array}{c} \underline{VALUE} \text{ IS} \\ \underline{VALUES} \text{ ARE} \end{array} \right\}$ $\left\{ \text{literal-1} \left[\left\{ \begin{array}{c} \underline{THROUGH} \\ \underline{THRU} \end{array} \right\} \text{literal-2} \right] \right\}$ ... .

GENERAL FORMAT FOR COMMUNICATION DESCRIPTION ENTRY

FORMAT 1:

<u>CD</u> cd-name-1

FOR [<u>INITIAL</u>] <u>INPUT</u>

[[SYMBOLIC <u>QUEUE</u> IS data-name-1]

[SYMBOLIC <u>SUB-QUEUE-1</u> IS data-name-2]

[SYMBOLIC <u>SUB-QUEUE-2</u> IS data-name-3]

[SYMBOLIC <u>SUB-QUEUE-3</u> IS data-name-4]

[<u>MESSAGE</u> <u>DATE</u> IS data-name-5]

[<u>MESSAGE</u> <u>TIME</u> IS data-name-6]

[SYMBOLIC <u>SOURCE</u> IS data-name-7]

[<u>TEXT</u> <u>LENGTH</u> IS data-name-8]

[<u>END</u> <u>KEY</u> IS data-name-9]

[<u>STATUS</u> <u>KEY</u> IS data-name-10]

[MESSAGE <u>COUNT</u> IS data-name-11]]

[data-name-1, data-name-2, data-name-3,
    data-name-4, data-name-5, data-name-6,
    data-name-7, data-name-8, data-name-9,
    data-name-10, data-name-11]

FORMAT 2:

<u>CD</u> cd-name-1 FOR <u>OUTPUT</u>

    [<u>DESTINATION</u> <u>COUNT</u> IS data-name-1]

    [<u>TEXT</u> <u>LENGTH</u> IS data-name-2]

    [<u>STATUS</u> <u>KEY</u> IS data-name-3]

    [<u>DESTINATION</u> <u>TABLE</u> <u>OCCURS</u> integer-1 TIMES

        [<u>INDEXED</u> BY {index-name-1} ...]]

    [<u>ERROR</u> <u>KEY</u> IS data-name-4]

    [SYMBOLIC <u>DESTINATION</u> IS data-name-5].

FORMAT 3:

<u>CD</u> cd-name-1

FOR [<u>INITIAL</u>] <u>I-0</u>

    [[<u>MESSAGE</u> <u>DATE</u> IS data-name-1]

      [<u>MESSAGE</u> <u>TIME</u> IS data-name-2]

      [SYMBOLIC <u>TERMINAL</u> IS data-name-3]

      [<u>TEXT</u> <u>LENGTH</u> IS data-name-4]

      [<u>END</u> <u>KEY</u> IS data-name-5]

      [<u>STATUS</u> <u>KEY</u> IS data-name-6]]

    [data-name-1, data-name-2, data-name-3,
        data-name-4, data-name-5, data-name-6]

GENERAL FORMAT FOR REPORT DESCRIPTION ENTRY

RD report-name-1

   [IS GLOBAL]

   [CODE literal-1]

   $\left[\left\{ \begin{array}{l} \text{CONTROL IS} \\ \text{CONTROLS ARE} \end{array} \right\} \left\{ \begin{array}{l} \text{\{data-name-1\} ...} \\ \text{FINAL [data-name-1] ...} \end{array} \right\} \right]$

   $\left[\text{PAGE} \left\{ \begin{array}{l} \text{LIMIT IS} \\ \text{LIMITS ARE} \end{array} \right\} \text{integer-1} \left[\begin{array}{l} \text{LINE} \\ \text{LINES} \end{array} \right] \text{[HEADING integer-2]} \right.$

   [FIRST DETAIL integer-3] [LAST DETAIL integer-4]

   $\left. \text{[FOOTING integer-5]} \right]$.

GENERAL FORMAT FOR REPORT GROUP DESCRIPTION ENTRY

FORMAT 1:

01 [data-name-1]

   $\left[\text{LINE NUMBER IS} \left\{ \begin{array}{l} \text{integer-1 [ON NEXT PAGE]} \\ \text{PLUS integer-2} \end{array} \right\} \right]$

   $\left[\text{NEXT GROUP IS} \left\{ \begin{array}{l} \text{integer-3} \\ \text{PLUS integer-4} \\ \text{NEXT PAGE} \end{array} \right\} \right]$

   TYPE IS $\left[\begin{array}{l} \left\{ \begin{array}{l} \text{REPORT HEADING} \\ \text{RH} \end{array} \right\} \\ \left\{ \begin{array}{l} \text{PAGE HEADING} \\ \text{PH} \end{array} \right\} \\ \left\{ \begin{array}{l} \text{CONTROL HEADING} \\ \text{CH} \end{array} \right\} \left\{ \begin{array}{l} \text{data-name-2} \\ \text{FINAL} \end{array} \right\} \\ \left\{ \begin{array}{l} \text{DETAIL} \\ \text{DE} \end{array} \right\} \\ \left\{ \begin{array}{l} \text{CONTROL FOOTING} \\ \text{CF} \end{array} \right\} \left\{ \begin{array}{l} \text{data-name-3} \\ \text{FINAL} \end{array} \right\} \\ \left\{ \begin{array}{l} \text{PAGE FOOTING} \\ \text{PF} \end{array} \right\} \\ \left\{ \begin{array}{l} \text{REPORT FOOTING} \\ \text{RF} \end{array} \right\} \end{array} \right]$

   [[USAGE IS] DISPLAY] .

FORMAT 2:

level-number [data-name-1]

$$\left[\ \underline{\text{LINE}} \text{ NUMBER IS } \left\{ \begin{array}{l} \text{integer-1 } [\text{ON } \underline{\text{NEXT}} \ \underline{\text{PAGE}}] \\ \underline{\text{PLUS}} \text{ Integer-2} \end{array} \right\} \ \right]$$

[[USAGE IS] DISPLAY].

FORMAT 3:

level-number [data-name-1]

$$\left\{ \begin{array}{l} \underline{\text{PICTURE}} \\ \underline{\text{PIC}} \end{array} \right\} \text{ IS character-string}$$

[[USAGE IS] DISPLAY]

$$\left[\ [\underline{\text{SIGN}} \text{ IS}] \ \left\{ \begin{array}{l} \underline{\text{LEADING}} \\ \underline{\text{TRAILING}} \end{array} \right\} \ \underline{\text{SEPARATE}} \text{ CHARACTER} \ \right]$$

$$\left[\ \left\{ \begin{array}{l} \underline{\text{JUSTIFIED}} \\ \underline{\text{JUST}} \end{array} \right\} \ \text{RIGHT} \ \right]$$

[BLANK WHEN ZERO]

$$\left[\ \underline{\text{LINE}} \text{ NUMBER IS } \left\{ \begin{array}{l} \text{integer-1 } [\text{ON } \underline{\text{NEXT}} \ \underline{\text{PAGE}}] \\ \underline{\text{PLUS}} \text{ integer-2} \end{array} \right\} \ \right]$$

[COLUMN NUMBER IS integer-3]

$$\left\{ \begin{array}{l} \underline{\text{SOURCE}} \text{ IS identifier-1} \\ \\ \underline{\text{VALUE}} \text{ IS literal-1} \\ \\ \{\underline{\text{SUM}} \ \{\text{identifier-2}\} \ \dots \ [\underline{\text{UPON}} \ \{\text{data-name-2}\} \ \dots \ ]\} \ \dots \\ \quad \left[\ \underline{\text{RESET}} \text{ ON } \left\{ \begin{array}{l} \text{data-name-3} \\ \underline{\text{FINAL}} \end{array} \right\} \ \right] \end{array} \right\}$$

[GROUP INDICATE].

GENERAL FORMAT FOR PROCEDURE DIVSION

FORMAT 1:

[PROCEDURE DIVISION [USING {data-name-1} ...].

[DECLARATIVES.

{section-name SECTION [segment-number].

    USE statement.

 [paragraph-name.

    [sentence] ...] ...} ...

END DECLARATIVES.]

{section-name SECTION [segment-number].

[paragraph-name.

    [sentence] ...] ... } ...]

FORMAT 2:

[PROCEDURE DIVISION [USING {data-name-1} ...].

{paragraph-name.

    [sentence] ... } ...]

602 COBOL-85 LANGUAGE SKELETON

GENERAL FORMAT FOR COBOL VERBS

ACCEPT identifier-1 [FROM mnemonic-name-1]

ACCEPT identifier-2 FROM $\left\{ \begin{array}{l} \underline{DATE} \\ \underline{DAY} \\ \underline{DAY\text{-}OF\text{-}WEEK} \\ \underline{TIME} \end{array} \right\}$

ACCEPT cd-name-1 MESSAGE COUNT

ADD $\left\{ \begin{array}{l} \text{identifier-1} \\ \text{literal-1} \end{array} \right\}$ ... TO {identifier-2 [ROUNDED]} ...

    [ON SIZE ERROR imperative-statement-1]

    [NOT ON SIZE ERROR imperative-statement-2]

    [END-ADD]

ADD $\left\{ \begin{array}{l} \text{identifier-1} \\ \text{literal-1} \end{array} \right\}$ ... TO $\left\{ \begin{array}{l} \text{identifier-2} \\ \text{literal-2} \end{array} \right\}$

    GIVING {identifier-3 [ROUNDED]} ...

    [ON SIZE ERROR imperative-statement-1]

    [NOT ON SIZE ERROR imperative-statement-2]

    [END-ADD]

ADD $\left\{ \begin{array}{l} \underline{CORRESPONDING} \\ \underline{CORR} \end{array} \right\}$ identifier-1 TO identifier-2 [ROUNDED]

    [ON SIZE ERROR imperative-statement-1]

    [NOT ON SIZE ERROR imperative-statement-2]

    [END-ADD]

ALTER {procedure-name-1 <u>TO</u> [<u>PROCEED</u> <u>TO</u>] procedure-name-2} ...

<u>CALL</u> $\left\{ \begin{array}{l} \text{identifier-1} \\ \text{literal-1} \end{array} \right\}$ $\left[\begin{array}{l} \underline{\text{USING}} \end{array} \right.$ $\left\{ \begin{array}{l} [\text{BY } \underline{\text{REFERENCE}}] \text{ {identifier-2} ...} \\ \text{BY } \underline{\text{CONTENT}} \text{ {identifier-2} ...} \end{array} \right\} \left. \cdots \right]$

  [ON <u>OVERFLOW</u> imperative-statement-1]

  [<u>END-CALL</u>]

<u>CALL</u> $\left\{ \begin{array}{l} \text{identifier-1} \\ \text{literal-1} \end{array} \right\}$ $\left[\begin{array}{l} \underline{\text{USING}} \end{array} \right.$ $\left\{ \begin{array}{l} [\text{BY } \underline{\text{REFERENCE}}] \text{ {identifier-2} ...} \\ \text{BY } \underline{\text{CONTENT}} \text{ {identifier-2} ...} \end{array} \right\} \left. \cdots \right]$

  [[ON <u>EXCEPTION</u> imperative-statement-1]

  [<u>NOT</u> ON <u>EXCEPTION</u> imperative-statement-2]

  [<u>END-CALL</u>]

<u>CANCEL</u> $\left\{ \begin{array}{l} \text{identifier-1} \\ \text{literal-1} \end{array} \right\}$

SW <u>CLOSE</u> $\left\{ \text{file-name-1} \left[\begin{array}{l} \left\{ \begin{array}{l} \underline{\text{REEL}} \\ \underline{\text{UNIT}} \end{array} \right\} [\text{FOR } \underline{\text{REMOVAL}}] \\ \text{WITH} \left\{ \begin{array}{l} \underline{\text{NO REWIND}} \\ \underline{\text{LOCK}} \end{array} \right\} \end{array} \right] \right\} \cdots$

RI <u>CLOSE</u>   file-name-1 [WITH <u>LOCK</u>]} ...

<u>COMPUTE</u> {identifier-1 [<u>ROUNDED</u>]} ... = arithmetic-expression-1

  [ON <u>SIZE</u> <u>ERROR</u> imperative-statement-1]

  [<u>NOT</u> ON <u>SIZE</u> <u>ERROR</u> imperative-statement-2]

  [<u>END-COMPUTE</u>]

<u>CONTINUE</u>

DELETE file-name-1 RECORD

    [INVALID KEY imperative-statement-1]

    [NOT INVALID KEY imperative-statement-2]

    [END-DELETE]

$$\text{DISABLE} \left\{ \begin{array}{l} \text{INPUT [TERMINAL]} \\ \text{I-O TERMINAL} \\ \text{OUTPUT} \end{array} \right\} \text{cd-name-1} \left[\text{WITH KEY} \left\{ \begin{array}{l} \text{identifier-1} \\ \text{literal-1} \end{array} \right\} \right]$$

$$\text{DISPLAY} \left\{ \begin{array}{l} \text{identifier-1} \\ \text{literal-1} \end{array} \right\} \dots \text{[UPON mnemonic-name-1]} \quad \text{[WITH NO ADVANCING]}$$

$$\text{DIVIDE} \left\{ \begin{array}{l} \text{identifier-1} \\ \text{literal-1} \end{array} \right\} \text{INTO \{identifier-2 [ROUNDED]\} } \dots$$

    [ON SIZE ERROR imperative-statement-1]

    [NOT ON SIZE ERROR imperative-statement-2]

    [END-DIVIDE]

$$\text{DIVIDE} \left\{ \begin{array}{l} \text{identifier-1} \\ \text{literal-1} \end{array} \right\} \text{INTO} \left\{ \begin{array}{l} \text{identifier-2} \\ \text{literal-2} \end{array} \right\}$$

    GIVING {identifier-3 [ROUNDED]} ...

    [ON SIZE ERROR imperative-statement-1]

    [NOT ON SIZE ERROR imperative-statement-2]

    [END-DIVIDE]

DIVIDE $\left\{ \begin{array}{l} \text{identifier-1} \\ \text{literal-1} \end{array} \right\}$ BY $\left\{ \begin{array}{l} \text{identifier-2} \\ \text{literal-2} \end{array} \right\}$

    GIVING {identifier-3 [ROUNDED]} ...

    [ON SIZE ERROR imperative-statement-1]

    [NOT ON SIZE ERROR imperative-statement-2]

    [END-DIVIDE]

DIVIDE $\left\{ \begin{array}{l} \text{identifier-1} \\ \text{literal-1} \end{array} \right\}$ INTO $\left\{ \begin{array}{l} \text{identifier-2} \\ \text{literal-2} \end{array} \right\}$ GIVING identifier-3 [ROUNDED]

    REMAINDER identifier-4

    [ON SIZE ERROR imperative-statement-1]

    [NOT ON SIZE ERROR imperative-statement-2]

    [END-DIVIDE]

DIVIDE $\left\{ \begin{array}{l} \text{identifier-1} \\ \text{literal-1} \end{array} \right\}$ BY $\left\{ \begin{array}{l} \text{identifier-2} \\ \text{literal-2} \end{array} \right\}$ GIVING identifier-3 [ROUNDED]

    REMAINDER identifier-4

    [ON SIZE ERROR imperative-statement-1]

    [NOT ON SIZE ERROR imperative-statement-2]

    [END-DIVIDE]

ENABLE $\left\{ \begin{array}{l} \text{INPUT [TERMINAL]} \\ \text{I-O TERMINAL} \\ \text{OUTPUT} \end{array} \right\}$ cd-name-1 $\left[\text{WITH KEY} \left\{ \begin{array}{l} \text{identifier-1} \\ \text{literal-1} \end{array} \right\} \right]$

ENTER language-name-1 [routine-name-1].

$$\underline{\text{EVALUATE}} \left\{ \begin{array}{l} \text{identifier-1} \\ \text{literal-1} \\ \text{expression-1} \\ \underline{\text{TRUE}} \\ \underline{\text{FALSE}} \end{array} \right\} \left[\underline{\text{ALSO}} \left\{ \begin{array}{l} \text{identifier-2} \\ \text{literal-2} \\ \text{expression-2} \\ \underline{\text{TRUE}} \\ \underline{\text{FALSE}} \end{array} \right\} \right] \dots$$

$$\{\{\underline{\text{WHEN}}$$

$$\left\{ \begin{array}{l} \underline{\text{ANY}} \\ \text{condition-1} \\ \underline{\text{TRUE}} \\ \underline{\text{FALSE}} \\ [\underline{\text{NOT}}] \left\{ \left\{ \begin{array}{l} \text{identifier-3} \\ \text{literal-3} \\ \text{arithmetic-expression} \end{array} \right\} \left[\left\{ \begin{array}{l} \underline{\text{THROUGH}} \\ \underline{\text{THRU}} \end{array} \right\} \left\{ \begin{array}{l} \text{identifier-4} \\ \text{literal-4} \\ \text{arithmetic-expression-2} \end{array} \right\} \right] \right\} \end{array} \right\}$$

$$[\underline{\text{ALSO}}$$

$$\left\{ \begin{array}{l} \underline{\text{ANY}} \\ \text{condition-2} \\ \underline{\text{TRUE}} \\ \underline{\text{FALSE}} \\ [\underline{\text{NOT}}] \left\{ \left\{ \begin{array}{l} \text{identifier-5} \\ \text{literal-5} \\ \text{arithmetic-expression-3} \end{array} \right\} \left[\left\{ \begin{array}{l} \underline{\text{THROUGH}} \\ \underline{\text{THRU}} \end{array} \right\} \left\{ \begin{array}{l} \text{identifier-6} \\ \text{literal-6} \\ \text{arithmetic-expression-4} \end{array} \right\} \right] \right\} \end{array} \right\} \dots \} \dots$$

imperative-statement

[<u>WHEN</u> <u>OTHER</u> imperative-statement-2]

[END-EVALUATE]

<u>EXIT</u>

<u>EXIT</u> <u>PROGRAM</u>

$$\underline{\text{GENERATE}} \left\{ \begin{array}{l} \text{data-name-1} \\ \text{report-name-1} \end{array} \right\}$$

<u>GO</u> TO [procedure-name-1]

<u>GO</u> TO {procedure-name-1} ... <u>DEPENDING</u> ON identifier-1

<u>IF</u> condition-1 THEN $\left\{ \begin{array}{l} \{\text{statement-1}\} \ \dots \\ \underline{\text{NEXT}} \ \underline{\text{SENTENCE}} \end{array} \right\}$ $\left\{ \begin{array}{l} \underline{\text{ELSE}} \ \{\text{statement-2}\} \ \dots \ [\underline{\text{END-IF}}] \\ \underline{\text{ELSE}} \ \underline{\text{NEXT}} \ \underline{\text{SENTENCE}} \\ \underline{\text{END-IF}} \end{array} \right\}$

<u>INITIALIZE</u> {identifier-1} ...

$\left[\underline{\text{REPLACING}} \left\{ \left\{ \begin{array}{l} \underline{\text{ALPHABETIC}} \\ \underline{\text{ALPHANUMERIC}} \\ \underline{\text{NUMERIC}} \\ \underline{\text{ALPHANUMERIC-EDITED}} \\ \underline{\text{NUMERIC-EDITED}} \end{array} \right\} \underline{\text{DATA}} \ \underline{\text{BY}} \left\{ \begin{array}{l} \text{identifier-2} \\ \text{literal-1} \end{array} \right\} \right\} \dots \right]$

<u>INITIATE</u> {report-name-1} ...

<u>INSPECT</u> identifier-1 <u>TALLYING</u>

$\left\{ \left\{ \text{identifier-2} \ \underline{\text{FOR}} \left\{ \begin{array}{l} \underline{\text{CHARACTERS}} \left[\left\{ \begin{array}{l} \underline{\text{BEFORE}} \\ \underline{\text{AFTER}} \end{array} \right\} \text{INITIAL} \left\{ \begin{array}{l} \text{identifier-4} \\ \text{literal-2} \end{array} \right\} \right] \dots \\ \left\{ \begin{array}{l} \underline{\text{ALL}} \\ \underline{\text{LEADING}} \end{array} \right\} \left\{ \left\{ \begin{array}{l} \text{identifier-3} \\ \text{literal-1} \end{array} \right\} \left[\left\{ \begin{array}{l} \underline{\text{BEFORE}} \\ \underline{\text{AFTER}} \end{array} \right\} \text{INITIAL} \left\{ \begin{array}{l} \text{identifier-4} \\ \text{literal-2} \end{array} \right\} \right] \dots \right\} \dots \end{array} \right\} \right\} \dots \right\} \dots$

<u>INSPECT</u> identifier-1 <u>REPLACING</u>

$\left\{ \begin{array}{l} \underline{\text{CHARACTERS}} \ \underline{\text{BY}} \left\{ \begin{array}{l} \text{identifier-5} \\ \text{literal-3} \end{array} \right\} \left[\left\{ \begin{array}{l} \underline{\text{BEFORE}} \\ \underline{\text{AFTER}} \end{array} \right\} \text{INITIAL} \left\{ \begin{array}{l} \text{identifier-4} \\ \text{literal-2} \end{array} \right\} \right] \dots \\ \left\{ \begin{array}{l} \underline{\text{ALL}} \\ \underline{\text{LEADING}} \\ \underline{\text{FIRST}} \end{array} \right\} \left\{ \left\{ \begin{array}{l} \text{identifier-3} \\ \text{literal-1} \end{array} \right\} \underline{\text{BY}} \left\{ \begin{array}{l} \text{identifier-5} \\ \text{literal-3} \end{array} \right\} \left[\left\{ \begin{array}{l} \underline{\text{BEFORE}} \\ \underline{\text{AFTER}} \end{array} \right\} \text{INITIAL} \left\{ \begin{array}{l} \text{identifier-4} \\ \text{literal-2} \end{array} \right\} \right] \dots \right\} . \end{array} \right\} \dots$

INSPECT identifier-1 TALLYING

$$
\left\{ \text{identifier-2} \underline{FOR} \left\{ \begin{array}{l} \underline{CHARACTERS} \left[\left\{ \begin{array}{l} \underline{BEFORE} \\ \underline{AFTER} \end{array} \right\} \text{INITIAL} \left\{ \begin{array}{l} \text{identifier-4} \\ \text{literal-2} \end{array} \right\} \right] \cdots \\ \left\{ \begin{array}{l} \underline{ALL} \\ \underline{LEADING} \end{array} \right\} \left\{ \left\{ \begin{array}{l} \text{identifier-3} \\ \text{literal-1} \end{array} \right\} \left[\left\{ \begin{array}{l} \underline{BEFORE} \\ \underline{AFTER} \end{array} \right\} \text{INITIAL} \left\{ \begin{array}{l} \text{identifier-4} \\ \text{literal-2} \end{array} \right\} \right] \cdots \right\} \cdots \end{array} \right\} \cdots \right\} \cdots
$$

REPLACING

$$
\left\{ \begin{array}{l} \underline{CHARACTERS} \underline{BY} \left\{ \begin{array}{l} \text{identifier-5} \\ \text{literal-3} \end{array} \right\} \left[\left\{ \begin{array}{l} \underline{BEFORE} \\ \underline{AFTER} \end{array} \right\} \text{INITIAL} \left\{ \begin{array}{l} \text{identifier-4} \\ \text{literal-2} \end{array} \right\} \right] \cdots \\ \left\{ \begin{array}{l} \underline{ALL} \\ \underline{LEADING} \\ \underline{FIRST} \end{array} \right\} \left\{ \left\{ \begin{array}{l} \text{identifier-3} \\ \text{literal-1} \end{array} \right\} \underline{BY} \left\{ \begin{array}{l} \text{identifier-5} \\ \text{literal-3} \end{array} \right\} \left[\left\{ \begin{array}{l} \underline{BEFORE} \\ \underline{AFTER} \end{array} \right\} \text{INITIAL} \left\{ \begin{array}{l} \text{identifier-4} \\ \text{literal-2} \end{array} \right\} \right] \cdots \right\} \end{array} \right\} \cdots
$$

INSPECT identifier-1 $\underline{CONVERTING}$ $\left\{ \begin{array}{l} \text{identifier-6} \\ \text{literal-4} \end{array} \right\}$ $\underline{TO}$ $\left\{ \begin{array}{l} \text{identifier-7} \\ \text{literal-5} \end{array} \right\}$

$\left[\left\{ \begin{array}{l} \underline{BEFORE} \\ \underline{AFTER} \end{array} \right\} \text{INITIAL} \left\{ \begin{array}{l} \text{identifier-4} \\ \text{literal-2} \end{array} \right\} \right] \cdots$

$\underline{MERGE}$ file-name-1 $\left\{ ON \left\{ \begin{array}{l} \underline{ASCENDING} \\ \underline{DESCENDING} \end{array} \right\} \text{KEY \{data-name-1\}} \cdots \right\} \cdots$

[COLLATING $\underline{SEQUENCE}$ IS alphabet-name-1]

$\underline{USING}$ file-name-2 {file-name-3} ...

$\left\{ \begin{array}{l} \underline{OUTPUT} \underline{PROCEDURE} \text{ IS procedure-name-1} \left[\left\{ \begin{array}{l} \underline{THROUGH} \\ \underline{THRU} \end{array} \right\} \text{procedure-name-2} \right] \\ \underline{GIVING} \text{ \{file-name-4\}} \cdots \end{array} \right\}$

$\underline{MOVE}$ $\left\{ \begin{array}{l} \text{identifier-1} \\ \text{literal-1} \end{array} \right\}$ $\underline{TO}$ {identifier-2} ...

$\underline{MOVE}$ $\left\{ \begin{array}{l} \underline{CORRESPONDING} \\ \underline{CORR} \end{array} \right\}$ identifier-1 $\underline{TO}$ identifier-2

$$\text{\underline{MULTIPLY}} \left\{ \begin{array}{l} \text{identifier-1} \\ \text{literal-1} \end{array} \right\} \text{\underline{BY}} \ \{\text{identifier-2 [\underline{ROUNDED}]}\} \ \dots$$

[ON <u>SIZE</u> <u>ERROR</u> imperative-statement-1]

[<u>NOT</u> ON <u>SIZE</u> <u>ERROR</u> imperative-statement-2]

[END-MULTIPLY]

$$\text{\underline{MULTIPLY}} \left\{ \begin{array}{l} \text{identifier-1} \\ \text{literal-1} \end{array} \right\} \text{\underline{BY}} \left\{ \begin{array}{l} \text{identifier-2} \\ \text{literal-2} \end{array} \right\}$$

<u>GIVING</u> {identifier-3 [<u>ROUNDED</u>]} ...

[ON <u>SIZE</u> <u>ERROR</u> imperative-statement-1]

[<u>NOT</u> ON <u>SIZE</u> <u>ERROR</u> imperative-statement-2]

[END-MULTIPLY]

S <u>OPEN</u> $\left\{ \begin{array}{l} \text{\underline{INPUT}} \left\{ \begin{array}{l} \text{file-name} \\ \text{-1} \end{array} \left[\begin{array}{l} \text{\underline{REVERSED}} \\ \text{WITH \underline{NO} REWIND} \end{array} \right] \right\} \dots \\ \text{\underline{OUTPUT}} \ \{\text{file-name-2 [WITH \underline{NO} REWIND]}\} \dots \\ \text{\underline{I-O}} \ \{\text{file-name-3}\} \dots \\ \text{\underline{EXTEND}} \ \{\text{file-name-4}\} \dots \end{array} \right\} \dots$

RI <u>OPEN</u> $\left\{ \begin{array}{l} \text{\underline{INPUT}} \ \{\text{file-name-1}\} \dots \\ \text{\underline{OUTPUT}} \ \{\text{file-name-2}\} \dots \\ \text{\underline{I-O}} \ \{\text{file-name-3}\} \dots \\ \text{\underline{EXTEND}} \ \{\text{file-name-4}\} \dots \end{array} \right\} \dots$

W <u>OPEN</u> $\left\{ \begin{array}{l} \text{\underline{OUTPUT}} \ \{\text{file-name-1 [WITH \underline{NO} REWIND]}\} \dots \\ \text{\underline{EXTEND}} \ \{\text{file-name-2}\} \dots \end{array} \right\} \dots$

$$\underline{\text{PERFORM}} \quad \left[\text{procedure-name-1} \left[\left\{ \begin{array}{l} \underline{\text{THROUGH}} \\ \underline{\text{THRU}} \end{array} \right\} \text{procedure-name-2} \right] \right]$$

[imperative-statement-1 <u>END-PERFORM</u>]

$$\underline{\text{PERFORM}} \quad \left[\text{procedure-name-1} \left[\left\{ \begin{array}{l} \underline{\text{THROUGH}} \\ \underline{\text{THRU}} \end{array} \right\} \text{procedure-name-2} \right] \right]$$

$$\left\{ \begin{array}{l} \text{identifier-1} \\ \text{integer-1} \end{array} \right\} \quad \underline{\text{TIMES}} \text{ [imperative-statement-1 } \underline{\text{END-PERFORM}}]$$

$$\underline{\text{PERFORM}} \quad \left[\text{procedure-name-1} \left[\left\{ \begin{array}{l} \underline{\text{THROUGH}} \\ \underline{\text{THRU}} \end{array} \right\} \text{procedure-name-2} \right] \right]$$

$$\left[\text{WITH } \underline{\text{TEST}} \left\{ \begin{array}{l} \underline{\text{BEFORE}} \\ \underline{\text{AFTER}} \end{array} \right\} \right] \underline{\text{UNTIL}} \text{ condition-1}$$

[imperative-statement-1 <u>END-PERFORM</u>]

$$\underline{\text{PERFORM}} \quad \left[\text{procedure-name-1} \left[\left\{ \begin{array}{l} \underline{\text{THROUGH}} \\ \underline{\text{THRU}} \end{array} \right\} \text{procedure-name-2} \right] \right]$$

$$\left[\text{WITH } \underline{\text{TEST}} \left\{ \begin{array}{l} \underline{\text{BEFORE}} \\ \underline{\text{AFTER}} \end{array} \right\} \right]$$

$$\underline{\text{VARYING}} \left\{ \begin{array}{l} \text{identifier-2} \\ \text{index-name-1} \end{array} \right\} \underline{\text{FR}}\underline{\text{OM}} \left\{ \begin{array}{l} \text{identifier-3} \\ \text{index-name-2} \\ \text{literal-1} \end{array} \right\}$$

$$\underline{\text{BY}} \left\{ \begin{array}{l} \text{identifier-4} \\ \text{literal-2} \end{array} \right\} \underline{\text{UNTIL}} \text{ condition-1}$$

$$\left[\underline{\text{AFTER}} \left\{ \begin{array}{l} \text{identifier-5} \\ \text{literal-3} \end{array} \right\} \underline{\text{FROM}} \left\{ \begin{array}{l} \text{identifier-6} \\ \text{index-name-3} \\ \text{literal-3} \end{array} \right\} \right.$$

$$\left. \underline{\text{BY}} \left\{ \begin{array}{l} \text{identifier-7} \\ \text{literal-4} \end{array} \right\} \underline{\text{UNTIL}} \text{ condition-2} \right] \dots$$

[imperative-statement-1 <u>END-PERFORM</u>]

<u>PURGE</u> cd-name-1

SRI <u>READ</u> file-name-1 [<u>NEXT</u>]   RECORD   [<u>INTO</u> identifier-1]

    [AT <u>END</u> imperative-statement-1]

    [<u>NOT</u> AT <u>END</u> imperative-statement-2]

    [END-READ]

R <u>READ</u> file-name-1 RECORD   [<u>INTO</u> identifier-1]

    [<u>INVALID</u> KEY imperative-statement-3]

    [<u>NOT</u> <u>INVALID</u> KEY imperative-statement-4]

    [<u>END-READ</u>]

I <u>READ</u> file-name-1 RECORD   [<u>INTO</u> identifier-1]

    [<u>KEY</u> IS data-name-1]

    [<u>INVALID</u> KEY imperative-statement-3]

    [<u>NOT</u> <u>INVALID</u> KEY imperative-statement-4]

    [<u>END-READ</u>]

<u>RECEIVE</u> cd-name-1 $\left\{ \begin{matrix} \underline{\text{MESSAGE}} \\ \underline{\text{SEGMENT}} \end{matrix} \right\}$ <u>INTO</u> identifier-1

    [<u>NO</u> <u>DATA</u> imperative-statement-1]

    [WITH <u>DATA</u> imperative-statement-2]

    [<u>END-RECEIVE</u>]

<u>RELEASE</u> record-name-1 [<u>FROM</u> identifier-1]

<u>RETURN</u> file-name-1 RECORD [<u>INTO</u> identifier-1]

    AT <u>END</u> imperative-statement-1

    [<u>NOT</u> AT <u>END</u> imperative-statement-2]

    [<u>END-RETURN</u>]

S REWRITE record-name-1 [FROM identifier-1]

RI REWRITE record-name-1 [FROM identifier-1]

    [INVALID KEY imperative-statement-1]

    [NOT INVALID KEY imperative-statement-2]

    [END-REWRITE]

SEARCH identifier-1 $\left[\text{VARYING} \left\{ \begin{array}{l} \text{identifier-2} \\ \text{index-name-1} \end{array} \right\} \right]$

    [AT END imperative-statement-1]

$\left\{ \text{WHEN condition-1} \left\{ \begin{array}{l} \text{imperative-statement-2} \\ \text{NEXT SENTENCE} \end{array} \right\} \right\} \ldots$

    [END-SEARCH]

SEARCH ALL identifier-1 [AT END imperative-statement-1]

$\text{WHEN} \left\{ \begin{array}{l} \text{data-name-1} \left\{ \begin{array}{l} \text{IS EQUAL TO} \\ \text{IS =} \end{array} \right\} \left\{ \begin{array}{l} \text{identifier-3} \\ \text{literal-1} \\ \text{arithmetic-expression-1} \end{array} \right\} \\ \text{condition-name-1} \end{array} \right\}$

$\left[\text{AND} \left\{ \begin{array}{l} \text{data-name-2} \left\{ \begin{array}{l} \text{IS EQUAL TO} \\ \text{IS =} \end{array} \right\} \left\{ \begin{array}{l} \text{identifier-4} \\ \text{literal-2} \\ \text{arithmetic-expression-2} \end{array} \right\} \\ \text{condition-name-2} \end{array} \right\} \right] \ldots$

$\left\{ \begin{array}{l} \text{imperative-statement-2} \\ \text{NEXT SENTENCE} \end{array} \right\}$

    [END-SEARCH]

SEND cd-name-1 FROM identifier-1

SEND cd-name-1 [FROM identifier-1] $\left\{ \begin{array}{l} \text{WITH identifier-2} \\ \text{WITH } \underline{\text{ESI}} \\ \text{WITH } \underline{\text{EMI}} \\ \text{WITH } \underline{\text{EGI}} \end{array} \right\}$

$\left[\left\{ \begin{array}{l} \underline{\text{BEFORE}} \\ \underline{\text{AFTER}} \end{array} \right\} \text{ADVANCING} \left\{ \begin{array}{l} \left\{ \begin{array}{l} \text{identifier-3} \\ \text{integer-1} \end{array} \right\} \left[\begin{array}{l} \text{LINE} \\ \text{LINES} \end{array} \right] \\ \left\{ \begin{array}{l} \text{mnemonic-name-1} \\ \underline{\text{PAGE}} \end{array} \right\} \end{array} \right\} \right]$

[REPLACING LINE]

SET $\left\{ \begin{array}{l} \text{index-name-1} \\ \text{identifier-1} \end{array} \right\}$ ... TO $\left\{ \begin{array}{l} \text{index-name-2} \\ \text{identifier-2} \\ \text{integer-1} \end{array} \right\}$

SET {index-name-3} ... $\left\{ \begin{array}{l} \underline{\text{UP}} \text{ BY} \\ \underline{\text{DOWN}} \text{ BY} \end{array} \right\}$ $\left\{ \begin{array}{l} \text{identifier-3} \\ \text{integer-2} \end{array} \right\}$

SET $\left\{ \text{{mnemonic-name-1}} \text{ ... } \underline{\text{TO}} \left\{ \begin{array}{l} \underline{\text{ON}} \\ \underline{\text{OFF}} \end{array} \right\} \right\}$ ...

SET {condition-name-1} ... TO TRUE

SORT file-name-1 $\left\{ \underline{\text{ON}} \left\{ \begin{array}{l} \underline{\text{ASCENDING}} \\ \underline{\text{DESCENDING}} \end{array} \right\} \text{KEY} \text{ {data-name-1} } ... \right\}$ ...

[WITH DUPLICATES IN ORDER]

[COLLATING SEQUENCE IS alphabet-name-1]

$\left\{ \begin{array}{l} \underline{\text{INPUT}} \text{ PROCEDURE IS procedure-name-1} \left[\left\{ \begin{array}{l} \underline{\text{THROUGH}} \\ \underline{\text{THRU}} \end{array} \right\} \text{procedure-name-2} \right] \\ \underline{\text{USING}} \text{ {file-name-2} } ... \end{array} \right\}$

$\left\{ \begin{array}{l} \underline{\text{OUTPUT}} \text{ PROCEDURE IS procedure-name-3} \left[\left\{ \begin{array}{l} \underline{\text{THROUGH}} \\ \underline{\text{THRU}} \end{array} \right\} \text{procedure-name-4} \right] \\ \underline{\text{GIVING}} \text{ {file-name-3} } ... \end{array} \right\}$

$$\underline{START}\text{ file-name-1 }\left[\underline{KEY}\left\{\begin{array}{l}\text{IS }\underline{EQUAL}\text{ TO}\\\text{IS }=\\\text{IS }\underline{GREATER}\text{ THAN}\\\text{IS }>\\\text{IS }\underline{NOT}\text{ }\underline{LESS}\text{ THAN}\\\text{IS }\underline{NOT}\text{ }<\\\text{IS }\underline{GREATER}\text{ THAN }\underline{OR}\text{ }\underline{EQUAL}\text{ TO}\\\text{IS }>=\end{array}\right\}\text{ data-name-1}\right]$$

[INVALID KEY imperative-statement-1]

[NOT INVALID KEY imperative-statement-2]

[END-START]

$$\underline{STOP}\left\{\begin{array}{l}\underline{RUN}\\\text{literal-1}\end{array}\right\}$$

$$\underline{STRING}\left\{\left\{\begin{array}{l}\text{identifier-1}\\\text{literal-1}\end{array}\right\}\text{ ... }\underline{DELIMITED}\text{ BY }\left\{\begin{array}{l}\text{identifier-2}\\\text{literal-2}\\\underline{SIZE}\end{array}\right\}\right\}\text{ ...}$$

<u>INTO</u> identifier-3

[WITH <u>POINTER</u> identifier-4]

[ON <u>OVERFLOW</u> imperative-statement-1]

[<u>NOT</u> ON <u>OVERFLOW</u> imperative-statement-2]

[<u>END-STRING</u>]

$$\underline{SUBTRACT}\left\{\begin{array}{l}\text{identifier-1}\\\text{literal-1}\end{array}\right\}\text{ ... }\underline{FROM}\text{ \{identifier-3 [\underline{ROUNDED}]\} ...}$$

[ON <u>SIZE</u> <u>ERROR</u> imperative-statement-1]

[<u>NOT</u> ON <u>SIZE</u> <u>ERROR</u> imperative-statement-2]

[<u>END-SUBTRACT</u>]

SUBTRACT $\left\{\begin{array}{l} \text{identifier-1} \\ \text{literal-1} \end{array}\right\}$ .... FROM $\left\{\begin{array}{l} \text{identifier-2} \\ \text{literal-2} \end{array}\right\}$

    GIVING {identifier-3 [ROUNDED]} ...

    [ON SIZE ERROR imperative-statement-1]

    [NOT ON SIZE ERROR imperative-statement-2]

    [END-SUBTRACT]

SUBTRACT $\left\{\begin{array}{l} \text{CORRESPONDING} \\ \text{CORR} \end{array}\right\}$ identifier-1 FROM identifier-2 [ROUNDED]

    [ON SIZE ERROR imperative-statement-1]

    [NOT ON SIZE ERROR imperative-statement-2]

    [END-SUBTRACT]

SUPPRESS PRINTING

TERMINATE {report-name-1} ...

UNSTRING identifier-1

    $\left[\text{DELIMITED BY [ALL]} \left\{\begin{array}{l} \text{identifier-2} \\ \text{literal-1} \end{array}\right\} \left[\text{OR [ALL]} \left\{\begin{array}{l} \text{identifier-3} \\ \text{literal-2} \end{array}\right\}\right]\right]$ ...

    INTO {identifier-4 [DELIMITER IN identifier-5] [COUNT IN identifier-6]} ...

    [WITH POINTER identifier-7]

    [TALLYING IN identifier-8]

    [ON OVERFLOW imperative-statement-1]

    [NOT ON OVERFLOW imperative-statement-2]

    [END-UNSTRING]

SRI USE [GLOBAL] AFTER STANDARD

$$\left\{ \begin{matrix} \text{EXCEPTION} \\ \text{ERROR} \end{matrix} \right\} \text{PROCEDURE ON} \left\{ \begin{matrix} \{\text{file-name-1}\} \ldots \\ \text{INPUT} \\ \text{OUTPUT} \\ \text{I-O} \\ \text{EXTEND} \end{matrix} \right\}$$

W USE AFTER STANDARD $\left\{ \begin{matrix} \text{EXCEPTION} \\ \text{ERROR} \end{matrix} \right\}$ PROCEDURE ON $\left\{ \begin{matrix} \{\text{file-name-1}\} \ldots \\ \text{OUTPUT} \\ \text{EXTEND} \end{matrix} \right\}$

USE [GLOBAL] BEFORE REPORTING identifier-1

$$\text{USE FOR DEBUGGING ON} \left\{ \begin{matrix} \text{cd-name-1} \\ \text{[ALL REFERENCES OF] identifier-1} \\ \text{file-name-1} \\ \text{procedure-name-1} \\ \text{ALL PROCEDURES} \end{matrix} \right\} \ldots$$

S WRITE record-name-1 [FROM identifier-1]

$$\left[\left\{ \begin{matrix} \text{BEFORE} \\ \text{AFTER} \end{matrix} \right\} \text{ADVANCING} \left\{ \begin{matrix} \left\{ \begin{matrix} \text{identifier-2} \\ \text{integer-1} \end{matrix} \right\} \left\{ \begin{matrix} \text{LINE} \\ \text{LINES} \end{matrix} \right\} \\ \left\{ \begin{matrix} \text{mnemonic-name-1} \\ \text{PAGE} \end{matrix} \right\} \end{matrix} \right\} \right]$$

$$\left[\text{AT} \left\{ \begin{matrix} \text{END-OF-PAGE} \\ \text{EOP} \end{matrix} \right\} \text{imperative-statement-1} \right]$$

$$\left[\text{NOT AT} \left\{ \begin{matrix} \text{END-OF-PAGE} \\ \text{EOP} \end{matrix} \right\} \text{imperative-statement-2} \right]$$

[END-WRITE]

RI WRITE record-name-1 [FROM identifier-1]

[INVALID KEY imperative-statement-1]

[NOT INVALID KEY imperative-statement-2]

[END-WRITE]

GENERAL FORMAT FOR COPY AND REPLACE STATEMENTS

COPY text-name-1 $\left[\left\{ \begin{array}{l} \underline{OF} \\ \underline{IN} \end{array} \right\} \text{library-name-1} \right]$

$\left[\underline{\text{REPLACING}} \left\{ \left\{ \begin{array}{l} \text{==pseudo-text-1==} \\ \text{identifier-1} \\ \text{literal-1} \\ \text{word-1} \end{array} \right\} \underline{BY} \left\{ \begin{array}{l} \text{==pseudo-text-2==} \\ \text{identifier-2} \\ \text{literal-2} \\ \text{word-2} \end{array} \right\} \right\} \dots \right]$

$\underline{\text{REPLACE}}$ {==pseudo-text-1== $\underline{BY}$ ==pseudo-text-2==} ...

$\underline{\text{REPLACE}}$ $\underline{\text{OFF}}$

GENERAL FORMAT FOR CONDITIONS

RELATION CONDITION:

$\left\{ \begin{array}{l} \text{identifier-1} \\ \text{literal-1} \\ \text{arithmetic-expression-1} \\ \text{index-name-1} \end{array} \right\} \left\{ \begin{array}{l} \text{IS [\underline{NOT}] \underline{GREATER} THAN} \\ \text{IS [\underline{NOT}] >} \\ \text{IS [\underline{NOT}] \underline{LESS} THAN} \\ \text{IS [\underline{NOT}] <} \\ \text{IS [\underline{NOT}] \underline{EQUAL} TO} \\ \text{IS [\underline{NOT}] =} \\ \text{IS \underline{GREATER} THAN \underline{OR} \underline{EQUAL} TO} \\ \text{IS >=} \\ \text{IS \underline{LESS} THAN \underline{OR} \underline{EQUAL} TO} \\ \text{IS <=} \end{array} \right\} \left\{ \begin{array}{l} \text{identifier-2} \\ \text{literal-2} \\ \text{arithmetic-expression-2} \\ \text{index-name-2} \end{array} \right\}$

CLASS CONDITION:

identifier-1 IS [\underline{NOT}] $\left\{ \begin{array}{l} \underline{\text{NUMERIC}} \\ \underline{\text{ALPHABETIC}} \\ \underline{\text{ALPHABETIC-LOWER}} \\ \underline{\text{ALPHABETIC-UPPER}} \\ \text{class-name-1} \end{array} \right\}$

CONDITION-NAME CONDITION:

      condition-name-1

SWITCH-STATUS CONDITION:

      condition-name-1

SIGN CONDITION:

$$\text{arithmetic-expression-1 IS [\underline{NOT}]} \left\{ \begin{array}{l} \underline{\text{POSITIVE}} \\ \underline{\text{NEGATIVE}} \\ \underline{\text{ZERO}} \end{array} \right\}$$

NEGATED CONDITION:

      $\underline{\text{NOT}}$ condition-1

COMBINED CONDITION:

$$\text{condition-1} \left\{ \left\{ \begin{array}{l} \underline{\text{AND}} \\ \underline{\text{OR}} \end{array} \right\} \text{condition-name-2} \right\} \dots$$

ABBREVIATED COMBINED RELATION CONDITION:

$$\text{relation-condition} \left\{ \left\{ \begin{array}{l} \underline{\text{AND}} \\ \underline{\text{OR}} \end{array} \right\} \text{[\underline{NOT}] [relational-operator] object} \right\} \dots$$

GENERAL FORMAT FOR QUALIFICATION

FORMAT 1:

$$
\left\{ \begin{array}{l} \text{data-name-1} \\ \text{condition-name-1} \end{array} \right\}
\left\{ \begin{array}{l} \left\{ \left\{ \begin{array}{l} \underline{\text{IN}} \\ \underline{\text{OF}} \end{array} \right\} \text{data-name-2} \right\} \dots \left[\left\{ \begin{array}{l} \underline{\text{IN}} \\ \underline{\text{OF}} \end{array} \right\} \left\{ \begin{array}{l} \text{file-name-1} \\ \text{cd-name-1} \end{array} \right\} \right] \\ \left\{ \begin{array}{l} \underline{\text{IN}} \\ \underline{\text{OF}} \end{array} \right\} \left\{ \begin{array}{l} \underline{\text{file-name-1}} \\ \text{cd-name-1} \end{array} \right\} \end{array} \right\}
$$

FORMAT 2:

$$
\text{paragraph-name-1} \left\{ \begin{array}{l} \underline{\text{IN}} \\ \underline{\text{OF}} \end{array} \right\} \text{section-name-1}
$$

FORMAT 3:

$$
\text{text-name-1} \left\{ \begin{array}{l} \underline{\text{IN}} \\ \underline{\text{OF}} \end{array} \right\} \text{library-name-1}
$$

FORMAT 4:

$$
\underline{\text{LINAGE-COUNTER}} \left\{ \begin{array}{l} \underline{\text{IN}} \\ \underline{\text{OF}} \end{array} \right\} \text{file-name-2}
$$

FORMAT 5:

$$
\left\{ \begin{array}{l} \underline{\text{PAGE-COUNTER}} \\ \underline{\text{LINE-COUNTER}} \end{array} \right\} \left\{ \begin{array}{l} \underline{\text{IN}} \\ \underline{\text{OF}} \end{array} \right\} \text{report-name-1}
$$

FORMAT 6:

$$
\text{data-name-3} \left\{ \begin{array}{l} \left\{ \begin{array}{l} \underline{\text{IN}} \\ \underline{\text{OF}} \end{array} \right\} \text{data-name-4} \left[\left\{ \begin{array}{l} \underline{\text{IN}} \\ \underline{\text{OF}} \end{array} \right\} \text{report-name-2} \right] \\ \left\{ \begin{array}{l} \underline{\text{IN}} \\ \underline{\text{OF}} \end{array} \right\} \text{report-name-2} \end{array} \right\}
$$

MISCELLANEOUS FORMATS

SUBSCRIPTING:

$$\left\{ \begin{array}{l} \text{condition-name-1} \\ \text{data-name-1} \end{array} \right\} \quad (\left\{ \begin{array}{l} \text{integer-1} \\ \text{data-name-2} [\{ \pm \} \text{ integer-2}] \\ \text{index-name-1} [\{ \pm \} \text{ integer-3}] \end{array} \right\} \quad \dots \quad)$$

REFERENCE MODIFICATION:

data-name-1 (leftmost-character-position: [length])

IDENTIFIER:

$$\text{data-name-1} \left[\left\{ \begin{array}{l} \underline{\text{IN}} \\ \underline{\text{OF}} \end{array} \right\} \text{data-name-2} \right] \quad \dots \quad \left[\left\{ \begin{array}{l} \underline{\text{IN}} \\ \underline{\text{OF}} \end{array} \right\} \left\{ \begin{array}{l} \text{cd-name-1} \\ \text{file-name-1} \\ \text{report-name-1} \end{array} \right\} \right]$$

[({subscript} ...)] [(leftmost-character-position: [length])]

GENERAL FORMAT FOR NESTED SOURCE PROGRAMS

IDENTIFICATION DIVISION

PROGRAM-ID. program-name-1 [IS INITIAL PROGRAM].

[ENVIRONMENT DIVISION. environment-division-content]

[DATA DIVISION. data-division-content]

[PROCEDURE DIVISION. procedure-division-content]

[[nested-source-program] ...

END PROGRAM program-name-1.]

GENERAL FORMAT FOR NESTED-SOURCE-PROGRAM

<u>IDENTIFICATION</u> <u>DIVISION</u>

<u>PROGRAM-ID</u>. program-name-2 $\left[\text{IS} \left\{ \left| \begin{array}{c} \underline{\text{COMMON}} \\ \underline{\text{INITIAL}} \end{array} \right| \right\} \text{PROGRAM} \right]$.

[<u>ENVIRONMENT</u> <u>DIVISION</u>. environment-division-content]

[<u>DATA</u> <u>DIVISION</u>. data-division-content]

[<u>PROCEDURE</u> <u>DIVISION</u>. procedure-division-content]

[nested-source-program] ...

<u>END</u> <u>PROGRAM</u> program-name-2.

GENERAL FORMAT FOR A SEQUENCE OF SOURCE PROGRAMS

{<u>IDENTIFICATION</u> <u>DIVISION</u>

<u>PROGRAM-ID</u>. program-name-3 [IS <u>INITIAL</u> PROGRAM].

[<u>ENVIRONMENT</u> <u>DIVISION</u>. environment-division-content]

[<u>DATA</u> <u>DIVISION</u>. data-division-content]

[<u>PROCEDURE</u> <u>DIVISION</u>. procedure-division-content]

[nested-source-program] ...

<u>END</u> <u>PROGRAM</u> program-name-3.} ...

<u>IDENTIFICATION</u> <u>DIVISION</u>

<u>PROGRAM-ID</u>. program-name-4 [IS <u>INITIAL</u> PROGRAM].

[<u>ENVIRONMENT</u> <u>DIVISION</u>. environment-division-content]

[<u>DATA</u> <u>DIVISION</u>. data-division-content]

[<u>PROCEDURE</u> <u>DIVISION</u>. procedure-division-content]

[[nested-source-program] ...

<u>END</u> <u>PROGRAM</u> program-name-4.]

APPENDIX III

PROGRAMMING STANDARDS

IDENTIFICATION DIVISION

1. The **AUTHOR** paragraph is required.
2. The **DATE-WRITTEN** and **DATE-COMPILED** paragraphs are not required, but are strongly recommended.
3. Include comments to describe the function of the program (briefly) and to clarify any code that is not self-explanatory.

ENVIRONMENT DIVISION

1. List **SELECT** statements in alphabetical order by file name.
2. If a **SELECT** statement cannot be written on one line indent continuation lines at least eight columns.

DATA DIVISION

1. File Description entries should appear in the same order as the corresponding **SELECT** statements.
2. All data names, including file names, should be functionally descriptive.
3. If possible, a data field that appears in more than one structure should have the same name in all structures. Use qualification where necessary to distinguish between occurrences.
4. If it is impractical to use the same name in all occurrences of a data field use similar names; for example:

   PRODUCT-WS: working storage
   PRODUCT-IN: input file
   PRODUCT-OUT: output file
   PRODUCT-PRINT: print record

5. Levels should either be numbered starting with **01** and then in steps of five (**01, 05, 10, 15**, etc.) or consecutively (**01, 02, 03, 04**, etc.). Whichever method you use, be consistent.
6. Successive levels should be indented four columns. For example, start level **05** in column 12, level **10** in column 16, level **15** in column 20, etc.
7. A given level number should always start in the same column.
8. Leave two blank columns between level numbers and data names.
9. Start all **PICTURE** clauses in the same column (such as column 40). Abbreviate **PICTURE** to **PIC**.

PROCEDURE DIVISION

1. A paragraph's name should be descriptive of the paragraph's function.
2. Each paragraph should be prefixed by a four-character sequence code. The purpose of this code is to relate the program code to the hierarchical structure of the program, and to help find referenced paragraphs easily. The sequence code should have the format **A999**. The driver paragraph, corresponding to the top level of the hierarchy chart, should begin with the letter **A**. Paragraphs corresponding to the second level of the hierarchy chart should begin with the letter **B**. Third level paragraphs should begin with **C**, and so on. No two sequence codes should be identical, and paragraphs should always be written in the program in order of increasing sequence code.
3. A paragraph name should be the only statement on its line.
4. Avoid the use of the **GO TO** statement if possible.
5. Do not ever under any circumstances use the **ALTER** verb.
6. Separate paragraphs by at least one blank line.
7. Any statement not covered by one of the following rules should begin in column 12.
8. Any statement not covered by one of the following rules should begin in the same column as the statement above it.
9. A statement that requires more than one line should have any continuation lines indented eight columns from the first line.
10. **AT END** or **INVALID KEY** clauses should be indented eight columns. For example,

```
        READ INPUT-FILE INTO INPUT-WS
                AT END MOVE 'N' TO MORE-DATA-FLAG.
```

11. **SIZE ERROR** clauses should be indented eight columns. For example,

```
        MULTIPLY QUANTITY BY COST GIVING VALUE-OF-SALE
                ON SIZE ERROR MOVE 'Y' TO ERROR-FLAG.
```

12. **PERFORM** statements should be formatted as follows:

```
        PERFORM B010-UPDATE-FILE
                UNTIL MORE-DATA-FLAG = 'N'.


        PERFORM C015-LOAD-TABLE
                VARYING X-TBL FROM 1 BY 1
                UNTIL X-TBL > TABLE-LIMIT.
```

13. In the `IF` statement, statements within the `IF` and `ELSE` clauses should be indented four columns. The `ELSE` is aligned under the corresponding `IF`. For example,

```
IF COST > CREDIT
    MOVE 'N' TO CREDIT-FLAG
ELSE
    MOVE 'Y' TO CREDIT-FLAG.
```

14. If you are using `COBOL-85`, `END` phrases should be aligned under the corresponding verb. For example,

```
READ INPUT-FILE INTO INPUT-WS
        AT END MOVE 'N' TO MORE-DATA-FLAG
END-READ.

MULTIPLY QUANTITY BY COST GIVING VALUE-OF-SALE
        ON SIZE ERROR MOVE 'Y' TO ERROR-FLAG
END-MULTIPLY.

PERFORM
    UNTIL MORE-DATA-FLAG = 'N'
    WRITE OUTPUT-RECORD FROM INPUT-RECORD
    READ INPUT-FILE
            AT END MOVE 'N' TO MORE-DATA-FLAG
    END-READ
END-PERFORM.

IF COST > CREDIT
    MOVE 'N' TO CREDIT-FLAG
ELSE
    MOVE 'Y' TO CREDIT-FLAG
END-IF.
```

15. All statements should end with a period unless they are part of a compound statement.

GENERAL

1. Start the Procedure Division at the top of a page. The Microsoft COBOL compiler contains two techniques for skipping to the top of a page within a listing. First, you can put a / in column seven. This causes the compiler to treat the line as a comment, but ejects a page before printing the line in the listing. Second, you can use the `EJECT` statement. The `EJECT` statement must be the only statement on the line, and its function is to cause a page eject at that point in the listing.
2. Design the program before you start to write code.
3. Implement the program to follow your design.
4. Simplify.
5. Clarify.
6. Make code self-explanatory.
7. If you cannot make a section of code self-explanatory, use comments to explain it.
8. *Write to be read by others!*

SAMPLE COBOL FORMATS

Note: **COBOL-85** statements are written in *italics*.

```
IDENTIFICATION DIVISION.
PROGRAM-ID.
    FORMAT-SAMPLE.
AUTHOR.
    D. GOLDEN.
DATE-WRITTEN.
    JULY 20, 1989.
DATE-COMPILED.

*    THIS PROGRAM PRESENTS SAMPLES OF COBOL CODING FORMATS.
*    IT IS NOT INTENDED TO MAKE SENSE AS A WORKING PROGRAM,
*    NOR DOES IT CONTAIN EXAMPLES OF EVERY COBOL STATEMENT.

ENVIRONMENT DIVISION.
INPUT-OUTPUT SECTION.
FILE-CONTROL.
    SELECT INPUT-FILE            ASSIGN TO 'SAMPLE.DAT'.
    SELECT REPORT-FILE           ASSIGN TO REPORT.

DATA DIVISION.
FILE SECTION.
FD  REPORT-FILE
    LABEL RECORDS ARE STANDARD.
01  REPORT-RECORD.
    05  EMPLOYEE-ID             PIC X(5).
    05  FILLER                  PIC XXX.
    05  HOURS-WORKED            PIC Z9.9.
    05  FILLER                  PIC XXX.
    05  GROSS-PAY               PIC $$,$$9.99.

WORKING-STORAGE SECTION.
01  TOTAL-SALARY                PIC S9(7)V99    VALUE ZERO.
01  MORE-DATA-REMAINS-FLAG      PIC X           VALUE 'Y'.
    88  MORE-DATA-REMAINS                       VALUE 'Y'.
    88  NO-MORE-DATA-REMAINS                    VALUE 'N'.

PROCEDURE DIVISION.
A000-STATEMENT-SAMPLES SECTION.
A010-PARAGRAPH-NAME.
    ACCEPT CATALOG-NUMBER AT 1070.
    ACCEPT TODAYS-DATE FROM DATE.
    ADD 1 TO LINE-NUMBER.
    ADD REGULAR-PAY OVERTIME-PAY GIVING GROSS-PAY.
    ADD DOLLARS TO SELLER-TOTAL ACCOUNT-TOTAL FINAL-TOTAL.
    CALL 'SUBPROG' USING PRODUCT-RECORD RESULT-FLAG.
    CLOSE INPUT-FILE
          REPORT-FILE.
    COMPUTE WEEKLY-SALARY ROUNDED = HOURLY-RATE * HOURS-WORKED.
    DELETE INDEX-PRODUCT-FILE
           INVALID KEY MOVE 'Y' TO ERROR-FLAG.
    DISPLAY 'DATA-FIELD = ' DATA-FIELD.
    DISPLAY SCREEN-DATA-NAME
            AT LINE 5  COLUMN 40.
```

```
DISPLAY DATA-FIELD
        AT LINE 5   COLUMN 40
        WITH BEEP BLINK HIGHLIGHT REVERSE-VIDEO
            FOREGROUND-COLOR 5
            BACKGROUND-COLOR 3
            BLANK LINE.
DIVIDE HOURS INTO MILES GIVING MILES-PER-HOUR
        ON SIZE ERROR MOVE 'Y' TO SIZE-ERROR-FLAG.
DIVIDE TOTAL-SALARY BY EMPLOYEE-COUNT GIVING AVERAGE-SALARY
        ON SIZE ERROR MOVE 'Y' TO SIZE-ERROR-FLAG
END-DIVIDE.
EVALUATE INPUT-CODE
    WHEN '1' PERFORM C010-FUNCTION-1
    WHEN '2' PERFORM C020-FUNCTION-2
    WHEN OTHER MOVE 'Y' TO ERROR-FLAG
END-EVALUATE.
EXIT.
GENERATE DETAIL-LINE.
GO TO Z999-EXIT.
IF W-GROSS-PAY IS GREATER THAN EXEMPTION
    SUBTRACT W-EXEMPTION FROM W-GROSS-PAY GIVING W-TAXABLE
    MULTIPLY W-TAXABLE BY C-TAXRATE GIVING W-TAX ROUNDED
ELSE
    MOVE ZERO TO W-TAX.
IF W-GROSS-PAY IS GREATER THAN EXEMPTION
    SUBTRACT W-EXEMPTION FROM W-GROSS-PAY GIVING W-TAXABLE
    MULTIPLY W-TAXABLE BY C-TAXRATE GIVING W-TAX ROUNDED
            ON SIZE ERROR MOVE 'Y' TO ERROR-FLAG
    END-MULTIPLY
ELSE
    MOVE ZERO TO W-TAX
END-IF.
INITIATE OVERTIME-REPORT.
INSPECT AMOUNT-FIELD
        TALLYING SPACE-COUNT FOR LEADING SPACES
        REPLACING LEADING SPACES BY '*'.
MOVE SPACES TO REPORT-RECORD.
MOVE QUANTITY OF TRANSACTION TO QUANTITY OF REPORT-RECORD.
MOVE ENROLLMENT TO SIZE-BY-GRADE-AND-YEAR (7, YEAR-SUBSCRIPT).
MULTIPLY UNIT-PRICE BY QUANTITY GIVING TOTAL-PRICE.
OPEN INPUT  ORDER-FILE
    OUTPUT NORMAL-HANDLING-FILE
            SPECIAL-HANDLING-FILE.
PERFORM C010-PROCESS-ONE-RECORD
        UNTIL MORE-DATA-REMAINS-FLAY = 'N'.
PERFORM B030-LOAD-TABLE
        VARYING X-TBL FROM 1 BY 1
        UNTIL X-TBL > TABLE-SIZE.
PERFORM
        VARYING X-TBL FROM 1 BY 1
        UNTIL X-TBL > TABLE-SIZE OR NO-MORE-DATA-REMAINS
    READ INPUT-FILE
            AT END MOVE 'N' TO MORE-DATA-REMAINS-FLAG
    END-READ
    IF MORE-DATA-REMAINS
        MOVE INPUT-RECORD TO TABLE-RECORD (X-TBL)
    END-IF
END-PERFORM.
```

```
READ INPUT-FILE
        AT END MOVE 'N' TO MORE-DATA-REMAINS-FLAG.
READ INDEXED-FILE
        INVALID KEY MOVE 'Y' TO KEY-ERROR-FLAG.
REWRITE EMPLOYEE-RECORD FROM EMPLOYEE-WS
        INVALID KEY MOVE 'Y' TO KEY-ERROR-FLAG.
SEARCH LOS-TABLE VARYING COL-INDEX
    WHEN LOS  LOS-TABLE (LOS-INDEX) NEXT SENTENCE.
SEARCH ALL PRODUCT-TABLE
    AT END MOVE 'N' TO PRODUCT-FOUND-FLAG
    WHEN CURRENT-PRODUCT = PRODUCT (PRODUCT-INDEX)
            MOVE 'Y' TO PRODUCT-FOUND-FLAG.
SET COL-INDEX UP BY 1.
SET COL-INDEX TO 1.
```
SET GREEN TO TRUE.
```
SORT SORT-FILE
    ON ASCENDING KEY CUSTOMER-NAME
        DESCENDING KEY PURCHASE-DATE
    USING PURCHASE-FILE
    GIVING SORTED PURCHASES.
SORT SORT-FILE
    ON ASCENDING KEY CUSTOMER-NAME
        DESCENDING KEY PURCHASE-DATE
    INPUT PROCEDURE B010-EDIT-INPUT
    OUTPUT PROCEDURE B020-PRODUCE-REPORT.
STOP RUN.
STRING  CUSTOMER-NAME DELIMITED BY SIZE
        SPACE
        CREDIT-AVAILABLE DELIMITED BY '.'
            INTO CREDIT-RECORD
            WITH POINTER INITIAL-POSITION.
SUBTRACT 40 FROM I-HOURS-WORKED GIVING W-HOURS-OVERTIME.
TERMINATE OVERTIME-REPORT.
UNSTRING ADDRESS-IN-RECORD DELIMITED BY '='
    INTO ADDRESS-LINE-1
        ADDRESS-LINE-2
        ADDRESS-LINE-3
    TALLYING IN FIELDS-FILLED
    ON OVERFLOW MOVE 'Y' TO OVERFLOW-FLAG.
WRITE NEW-MASTER-RECORD.
WRITE REPORT-RECORD AFTER ADVANCING 1 LINE.
```

APPENDIX IV

ANSWERS TO
STARRED EXERCISES

There are several acceptable answers to many of these exercises. The one shown here is sometimes better than other possibilities, but only occasionally is the test of goodness completely clear. For instance, it seldom makes any difference whether one writes **ADD A B GIVING C** or **ADD B A GIVING C**. In short, the answers given here are correct, but they often are not the *only* possible correct answers.

CHAPTER 3

```
1.  01   ACCOUNTS.
         05   RECEIVABLE          PIC 9(5)V99.
         05   PAYABLE             PIC 9(5)V99.
         05   PAST-DUE            PIC 9(5)V99.


3.  01   ALPHA-INPUT.
         05   A.
              10   B              PIC X(4).
              10   C              PIC X(5).
         05   D                   PIC X(6).
         05   E                   PIC X(7).


5.  01   NORMAL-LINE-OUT.
         05   IDENT               PIC XXX.
         05   FILLER              PIC XXX.
         05   COSTS.
              10   OUTGOING       PIC 9(4).99.
              10   FILLER         PIC XX.
              10   RETURNING      PIC 9(4).99.
              10   FILLER         PIC XX.
         05   TOTAL-MILES         PIC 9(5).
```

```
7. 01  INVENTORY.
       05  PART.
           10  PREFIX            PIC AA.
           10  BIN-NUMBER        PIC 9(4).
       05  YTD-USAGE.
           10  QTY               PIC 9(6).
           10  DOLLARS           PIC 9(5)V99.
       05  DESCRIPTION           PIC X(15).
       05  CODES.
           10  WHERE-MADE        PIC A.
           10  MFG-PURCH         PIC 9.
           10  HI-LO-USAGE       PIC 9.
       05  QOH                   PIC 9(5).
```

9. The record begins with a **POLICY-NUMBER** of seven alphanumeric characters, which is followed by a three-character **FILLER** item. Then there is a group item consisting of four amounts, each of which has six digits with two decimal places, and each of which is followed by a two-character **FILLER** item. The amounts, in order, are named **PREMIUM**, **DIVIDEND**, **INTEREST**, and **AMOUNT-DUE**. The record contains 46 characters, counting the **FILLER**s as character positions.

11. **a.** Add the values of the items named R and S to the value of T and replace the value of T with the sum.

   b. Add the values of R and S, and replace the value of T with the sum. The previous value of T does not enter into the calculation, and is destroyed by the action of this statement.

   c. Add the values of A, B, and C; subtract this sum from the value of D, and replace the value of D with the final result.

   d. Add the values of A, B, and C; subtract the sum from the value of D; replace the value of E with the final result. The value of D remains after the completion of the actions of the statement, but the old value of E is destroyed.

   e. The value of **FACTOR-9** is multiplied by 12.3; the product replaces the old value of **FACTOR-9**.

   f. The value of N is divided by the value of M; the old value of N is replaced by the result.

   g. The value of N is divided by the value of M and the rounded quotient is placed in Q.

13. **a.** ADD JAN FEB MAR GIVING 1-QUARTER.

   b. ADD YEAR-1 TO YEAR-2.

   c. ADD 13.45 ABC TO DEF.

   d. ADD 13.45 ABC DEF GIVING GHI.

   e. SUBTRACT 12 FROM Q-1.

   f. SUBTRACT Y-88 Y-89 FROM YEARS.

   g. MULTIPLY RATE-ADJUSTMENT BY FINAL-TOTAL ROUNDED.

   h. MULTIPLY MONTHLY-USAGE BY 12 GIVING YEAR-TOTAL.

   i. MULTIPLY MILES-PER-HOUR BY HOURS GIVING DISTANCE.

   j. DIVIDE YEAR-TOTAL BY 12 GIVING MONTHLY-AVERAGE.

    k. DIVIDE OVERLAP-FACTOR INTO MACHINE-UTILIZATION ROUNDED.

    l. DIVIDE TOTAL-TIME BY 60 GIVING HOURS REMAINDER MINUTES.

15. a. RESULT   PICTURE 9(4)V99.

   b. RESULT   PICTURE 9(5)V9.

   c. RESULT   PICTURE 9(5)V9(6).

17.

```
IDENTIFICATION DIVISION.
PROGRAM-ID.
    C03EX17.
*
*            THIS VERSION USES A FILE FOR INPUT
*
ENVIRONMENT DIVISION.
INPUT-OUTPUT SECTION.
FILE-CONTROL.
    SELECT EMPLOYEE-FILE           ASSIGN TO 'C03EX17.PAY'.
    SELECT PAY-REPORT-FILE         ASSIGN TO 'C03EX17.REP'.

DATA DIVISION.
FILE SECTION.
FD  EMPLOYEE-FILE
    LABEL RECORDS ARE STANDARD.
01  EMPLOYEE-RECORD.
    05 I-IDENT                     PIC X(5).
    05 I-HOURS-WORKED              PIC 99V9.
    05 I-PAY-RATE                  PIC 99V99.
    05 FILLER                      PIC X(68).

FD  PAY-REPORT-FILE
    LABEL RECORDS ARE STANDARD.
01  PAY-REPORT-RECORD.
    05 O-IDENT                     PIC X(5).
    05 FILLER                      PIC XXX.
    05 O-HOURS-WORKED              PIC 99.9.
    05 FILLER                      PIC XXX.
    05 O-PAY-RATE                  PIC 99.99.
    05 FILLER                      PIC XXX.
    05 O-PAY                       PIC 9(4).99.

WORKING-STORAGE SECTION.
    01 W-OUT-OF-DATA-FLAG          PIC X.

PROCEDURE DIVISION.
A000-MAIN-ROUTINE.
    OPEN INPUT  EMPLOYEE-FILE
         OUTPUT PAY-REPORT-FILE.
    MOVE 'N' TO W-OUT-OF-DATA-FLAG.
    READ EMPLOYEE-FILE
             AT END MOVE 'Y' TO W-OUT-OF-DATA-FLAG.
    PERFORM B010-PRODUCE-PAY-LINE
            UNTIL W-OUT-OF-DATA-FLAG = 'Y'.
    CLOSE EMPLOYEE-FILE
          PAY-REPORT-FILE.
    STOP RUN.
```

```
        B010-PRODUCE-PAY-LINE.
            MOVE SPACES TO PAY-REPORT-RECORD.
            MULTIPLY I-HOURS-WORKED BY I-PAY-RATE GIVING O-PAY ROUNDED.
            MOVE I-IDENT          TO O-IDENT.
            MOVE I-HOURS-WORKED   TO O-HOURS-WORKED.
            MOVE I-PAY-RATE       TO O-PAY-RATE.
            WRITE PAY-REPORT-RECORD.
            READ EMPLOYEE-FILE
                    AT END MOVE 'Y' TO W-OUT-OF-DATA-FLAG.



        IDENTIFICATION DIVISION.
        PROGRAM-ID.
            C03EX17.
        *
        *              THIS VERSION USES ACCEPT/DISPLAY FOR INPUT.
        *
        ENVIRONMENT DIVISION.
        INPUT-OUTPUT SECTION.
        FILE-CONTROL.
            SELECT PAY-REPORT-FILE        ASSIGN TO 'C03EX17.REP'.

        DATA DIVISION.
        FILE SECTION.
        FD  PAY-REPORT-FILE
            LABEL RECORDS ARE STANDARD.
        01  PAY-REPORT-RECORD.
            05  O-IDENT                PIC X(5).
            05  FILLER                 PIC XXX.
            05  O-HOURS-WORKED         PIC 99.9.
            05  FILLER                 PIC XXX.
            05  O-PAY-RATE             PIC 99.99.
            05  FILLER                 PIC XXX.
            05  O-PAY                  PIC 9(4).99.

        WORKING-STORAGE SECTION.
        01  W-IDENT                    PIC X(5).
        01  W-HOURS-WORKED             PIC 99V9.
        01  W-PAY-RATE                 PIC 99V99.

        PROCEDURE DIVISION.
        A000-MAIN-ROUTINE.
            OPEN OUTPUT PAY-REPORT-FILE.
            PERFORM B010-GET-PAY-DATA.
            PERFORM B020-PRODUCE-PAY-LINE
                    UNTIL W-IDENT = 'ZZZZZ'.
            CLOSE PAY-REPORT-FILE.
            STOP RUN.

        B010-GET-PAY-DATA.
            DISPLAY 'Enter identification number:  ' WITH NO ADVANCING.
            ACCEPT W-IDENT.
            DISPLAY 'Enter hours worked:           ' WITH NO ADVANCING.
            ACCEPT W-HOURS-WORKED.
            DISPLAY 'Enter pay rate:               ' WITH NO ADVANCING.
            ACCEPT W-PAY-RATE.
            DISPLAY ' '.
```

```
B020-PRODUCE-PAY-LINE.
    MOVE SPACES TO PAY-REPORT-RECORD.
    MULTIPLY W-HOURS-WORKED BY W-PAY-RATE GIVING O-PAY ROUNDED.
    MOVE W-IDENT          TO O-IDENT.
    MOVE W-HOURS-WORKED   TO O-HOURS-WORKED.
    MOVE W-PAY-RATE       TO O-PAY-RATE.
    WRITE PAY-REPORT-RECORD.
    PERFORM B010-GET-PAY-DATA.
```

Sample output:

```
12345   40.0   03.00   0120.00
23456   43.3   12.34   0534.32
23457   43.3   12.36   0535.19
55555   01.0   01.00   0001.00
```

CHAPTER 4

1. **a.** IF AGE is 18 or greater THEN
    add 1 to LEGAL-ADULT
    ENDIF

   b. IF PART-1-A contains the letter "S" THEN
    print STOCK-ITEM
    ENDIF

   c. IF SIZE-A is greater than 800 THEN
    add 1 to BIG
    ELSE
    add 1 to LITTLE
    ENDIF

   d. IF NAME-A is greater than NAME-B THEN
    move NAME-A to TEMPORARY
    ELSE
    move NAME-B to TEMPORARY
    ENDIF

   e. IF HOURS-WORKED is not equal to 40 THEN
    print "NON-STANDARD HOURS"
    ENDIF

4.   PRODUCE COMMISSION FILE:
    initialize more-data to 'y'
    get sale record
    PERFORM-UNTIL more-data = 'n'
        set up commission record
        write commission record
        get sale record
    ENDPERFORM
    stop

    Get a sale record:
        read a SALE-RECORD; at end move 'n' to more-data

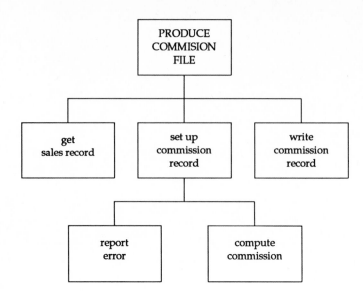

Hierarchy chart for Exercise 4.

Set up commission record:
    move SELLER to commission record
    move SALE-PRICE to commission record
    move BASE-PRICE to commission record
    IF PRODUCT-CODE is less than 1 or greater than 5 THEN
        report the error
    ELSE
        compute the commission
    ENDIF

Report error:
    set the commission to zero
    move "ERRONEOUS PRODUCT CODE" to commission record

Compute commission:
    EVALUATE PRODUCT-CODE
        WHEN 1
            commission = 0.15 * SALE-PRICE
        WHEN 2
            commission = 0.40 * (SALE-PRICE - BASE-PRICE)
        WHEN 3
            commission = 0.10 * BASE-PRICE +
                    0.50 * (SALE-PRICE - BASE-PRICE)
        WHEN 4
            commission = 25 + 0.05 * BASE-PRICE
        WHEN 5
            commission = 75
    ENDEVALUATE

We have intentionally omitted a specification for the module "write commission record" because the name of the module is the same as its specification. You may include or omit specification of a module this simple as you choose, but it should always be clear that the module was omitted by intent and not by oversight.

6. Produce tax file:

```
initialize more-data to 'y'
get pay record; at end move 'n' to more-data
PERFORM-UNTIL more-data = 'n'
  move identification to tax record
  move gross pay to tax record
  IF gross pay is greater than 2000 THEN
    tax = 0.04 * (gross pay - 2000)
  ELSE
    tax = 0
  ENDIF
  write tax record
  get pay record; at end move 'n' to more-data
ENDPERFORM
stop
```

8. Report file information:

```
move zero to total
initialize more-data to 'y'
get input record; at end move 'n' to more-data
PERFORM-UNTIL more-data = 'n'
  move IDENT to output record
  move DOLLARS to output record
  move OTHER-INFO to output record
  print output record
  add DOLLARS to total
  get input record; at end move 'n' to more-data
ENDPERFORM
print total
stop
```

CHAPTER 5

1. a.
```
IF AGE IS NOT LESS THAN 18
    ADD 1 TO LEGAL-ADULT.
```

b.
```
IF PART-1-A = 'S'
    PERFORM D050-PROCESS-STOCK-ITEM.
```

c.
```
IF SIZE-A IS GREATER THAN 800
    ADD 1 TO BIG
ELSE
    ADD 1 TO LITTLE.
```

d.
```
IF NAME-A IS GREATER THAN NAME-B
    MOVE NAME-A TO TEMPORARY
ELSE
    MOVE NAME-B TO TEMPORARY.
```

```
e.  IF HOURS-WORKED IS NOT EQUAL TO 40
        PERFORM C035-NON-STANDARD.


f.  IF CODE-X IS NOT NUMERIC
        PERFORM X020-BADE-CODE.
```

3.
```
ADD ON-HAND ON-ORDER GIVING TEMPORARY.
IF TEMPORARY IS LESS THAN REORDER-POINT
    MOVE REORDER-QTY TO ORDER-AMOUNT
ELSE
    MOVE ZERO TO ORDER-AMOUNT.
```

5.
```
IF      PRODUCT-CODE IS EQUAL TO '1'
    MULTIPLY 0.15 BY SALE-PRICE GIVING COMMISSION
ELSE IF PRODUCT-CODE IS EQUAL TO '2'
    SUBTRACT BASE-PRICE FROM SALE-PRICE GIVING TEMPORARY
    MULTIPLY 0.40 BY TEMPORARY GIVING COMMISSION
ELSE IF PRODUCT-CODE IS EQUAL TO '3'
    MULTIPLY 0.10 BY BASE-PRICE GIVING TEMP1
    SUBTRACT BASE-PRICE FROM SALE-PRICE GIVING TEMP2
    MULTIPLY 0.50 BY TEMP2
    ADD TEMP1 TEMP2 GIVING COMMISSION
ELSE IF PRODUCT-CODE IS EQUAL TO '4'
    MULTIPLY 0.05 BY BASE-PRICE GIVING TEMPORARY
    ADD 10.00 TEMPORARY GIVING COMMISSION
ELSE IF PRODUCT-CODE IS EQUAL TO '5'
    MOVE 35.00 TO COMMISSION
ELSE
    MOVE ZERO TO COMMISSION
    MOVE 'X' TO BAD-PRODUCT-CODE-FLAG.
```

COBOL-85

If you are using **COBOL-85** you can use the following **EVALUATE** statement.

```
EVALUATE PRODUCT-CODE
    WHEN '1'  MULTIPLY 0.15 BY SALE-PRICE
    WHEN '2'  SUBTRACT BASE-PRICE FROM SALE-PRICE GIVING TEMPORARY
              MULTIPLY 0.40 BY TEMPORARY GIVING COMMISSION
    WHEN '3'  MULTIPLY 0.10 BY BASE-PRICE GIVING TEMP1
              SUBTRACT BASE-PRICE FROM SALE-PRICE GIVING TEMP2
              MULTIPLY 0.50 BY TEMP2
              ADD TEMP1 TEMP2 GIVING COMMISSION
    WHEN '4'  MULTIPLY 0.05 BY BASE-PRICE GIVING TEMPORARY
              ADD 10.00 TEMPORARY GIVING COMMISSION
    WHEN '5'  MOVE 35.00 TO COMMISSION
    WHEN OTHER
              MOVE ZERO TO COMMISSION
              MOVE 'X' TO BAD-PRODUCT-CODE-FLAG
END-EVALUATE.
```

END COBOL-85

7.

```
IDENTIFICATION DIVISION.
PROGRAM-ID.
    C05EX07.
*
*              THIS VERSION USES A FILE FOR INPUT
*
ENVIRONMENT DIVISION.
INPUT-OUTPUT SECTION.
FILE-CONTROL.
    SELECT SERVICE-FILE          ASSIGN TO 'C05EX07.SER'.
    SELECT REPORT-FILE           ASSIGN TO 'C05EX07.REP'.

DATA DIVISION.
FILE SECTION.
FD  SERVICE-FILE
    LABEL RECORDS ARE STANDARD.
01  SERVICE-RECORD.
    05  EMP-NAME                 PIC X(20).
    05  FILLER                   PIC X(5).
    05  YEARS-OF-SERVICE         PIC 99.
    05  FILLER                   PIC X(53).

FD  REPORT-FILE
    LABEL RECORDS ARE STANDARD.
01  REPORT-RECORD.
    05  NAME-OUT                 PIC X(20).
    05  FILLER                   PIC X(5).
    05  YEARS-OF-SERVICE-OUT     PIC 99.
    05  FILLER                   PIC XXX.
    05  VETERAN-MESSAGE          PIC X(22).

WORKING-STORAGE SECTION.
01  OUT-OF-DATA-FLAG             PIC X VALUE 'N'.

PROCEDURE DIVISION.
A000-MAIN-ROUTINE.
    OPEN INPUT  SERVICE-FILE
         OUTPUT REPORT-FILE.
    READ SERVICE-FILE
         AT END MOVE 'Y' TO OUT-OF-DATA-FLAG.
    PERFORM B010-PROCESS-SERVICE-RECORDS
         UNTIL OUT-OF-DATA-FLAG = 'Y'.
    CLOSE SERVICE-FILE
         REPORT-FILE.
    STOP RUN.

B010-PROCESS-SERVICE-RECORDS.
    MOVE SPACES TO REPORT-RECORD.
    MOVE EMP-NAME TO NAME-OUT.
    MOVE YEARS-OF-SERVICE TO YEARS-OF-SERVICE-OUT.
    IF YEARS-OF-SERVICE IS GREATER THAN 40
        MOVE 'AN ABC COMPANY VETERAN' TO VETERAN-MESSAGE.
    WRITE REPORT-RECORD.
    READ SERVICE-FILE
         AT END MOVE 'Y' TO OUT-OF-DATA-FLAG.
```

```
        IDENTIFICATION DIVISION.
        PROGRAM-ID.
            C05EX07.
        *
        *               THIS VERSION USES ACCEPT/DISPLAY FOR INPUT
        *
        ENVIRONMENT DIVISION.
        INPUT-OUTPUT SECTION.
        FILE-CONTROL.
            SELECT REPORT-FILE          ASSIGN TO 'C05EX07.REP'.

        DATA DIVISION.
        FILE SECTION.
        FD  REPORT-FILE
            LABEL RECORDS ARE STANDARD.
        01  REPORT-RECORD.
            05  NAME-OUT                PIC X(20).
            05  FILLER                  PIC X(5).
            05  YEARS-OF-SERVICE-OUT    PIC 99.
            05  FILLER                  PIC XXX.
            05  VETERAN-MESSAGE         PIC X(22).

        WORKING-STORAGE SECTION.
        01  EMP-NAME                    PIC X(20).
        01  YEARS-OF-SERVICE            PIC 99.

        PROCEDURE DIVISION.
        A000-MAIN-ROUTINE.
            OPEN OUTPUT REPORT-FILE.
            PERFORM B010-GET-SERVICE-DATA.
            PERFORM B020-PROCESS-SERVICE-DATA
                    UNTIL EMP-NAME = SPACES.
            CLOSE REPORT-FILE.
            STOP RUN.


        B010-GET-SERVICE-DATA.
            DISPLAY 'Enter employee name:     ' WITH NO ADVANCING.
            ACCEPT EMP-NAME.
            DISPLAY 'Enter years of service:  ' WITH NO ADVANCING.
            ACCEPT YEARS-OF-SERVICE.
            DISPLAY ' '.

        B020-PROCESS-SERVICE-DATA.
            MOVE SPACES TO REPORT-RECORD.
            MOVE EMP-NAME TO NAME-OUT.
            MOVE YEARS-OF-SERVICE TO YEARS-OF-SERVICE-OUT.
            IF YEARS-OF-SERVICE IS GREATER THAN 40
                MOVE 'AN ABC COMPANY VETERAN' TO VETERAN-MESSAGE.
            WRITE REPORT-RECORD.
            PERFORM B010-GET-SERVICE-DATA.


            9.

        IDENTIFICATION DIVISION.
        PROGRAM-ID.
            C05EX09.
        *
        *               THIS VERSION USES A FILE FOR INPUT
        *
```

```
ENVIRONMENT DIVISION.
INPUT-OUTPUT SECTION.
FILE-CONTROL.
    SELECT EMPLOYEE-FILE          ASSIGN TO 'C05EX09.EMP'.
    SELECT REPORT-FILE            ASSIGN TO 'C05EX09.REP'.


DATA DIVISION.
FILE SECTION.
FD  EMPLOYEE-FILE
    LABEL RECORDS ARE STANDARD.
01  EMPLOYEE-RECORD.
    05  FILLER                    PIC X(44).
    05  IDENT                     PIC X(6).
    05  FILLER                    PIC X(19).
    05  GROSS-PAY                 PIC 9(5)V99.
    05  FILLER                    PIC X(4).


FD  REPORT-FILE
    LABEL RECORDS ARE STANDARD.
01  REPORT-RECORD.
    05  IDENT-OUT                 PIC X(6).
    05  FILLER                    PIC XXX.
    05  GROSS-PAY-OUT             PIC 9(5).99.
    05  FILLER                    PIC XXX.
    05  TAX                       PIC 9(5).99.

WORKING-STORAGE SECTION.
01  OUT-OF-DATA-FLAG              PIC X VALUE 'N'.
01  TEMPORARY-STORAGE            PIC 9(5)V99.

PROCEDURE DIVISION.
A000-MAIN-ROUTINE.
    OPEN INPUT  EMPLOYEE-FILE
         OUTPUT REPORT-FILE.
    READ EMPLOYEE-FILE
            AT END MOVE 'Y' TO OUT-OF-DATA-FLAG.
    PERFORM B010-COMPUTE-TAX
            UNTIL OUT-OF-DATA-FLAG = 'Y'.
    CLOSE EMPLOYEE-FILE
          REPORT-FILE.
    STOP RUN.


B010-COMPUTE-TAX.
    MOVE SPACES TO REPORT-RECORD.
    IF GROSS-PAY IS GREATER THAN 2000.00
        SUBTRACT 2000.00 FROM GROSS-PAY
                GIVING TEMPORARY-STORAGE
        MULTIPLY TEMPORARY-STORAGE BY 0.02 GIVING TAX ROUNDED
    ELSE
        MOVE ZERO TO TAX.
    MOVE IDENT TO IDENT-OUT.
    MOVE GROSS-PAY TO GROSS-PAY-OUT.
    WRITE REPORT-RECORD.
    READ EMPLOYEE-FILE
            AT END MOVE 'Y' TO OUT-OF-DATA-FLAG.
```

```
        IDENTIFICATION DIVISION.
        PROGRAM-ID.
            C05EX09.
        *
        *                THIS VERSION USES ACCEPT/DISPLAY FOR INPUT
        *
        ENVIRONMENT DIVISION.
        INPUT-OUTPUT SECTION.
        FILE-CONTROL.
            SELECT REPORT-FILE          ASSIGN TO 'C05EX09.REP'.

        DATA DIVISION.
        FILE SECTION.
        FD  REPORT-FILE
            LABEL RECORDS ARE STANDARD.
        01  REPORT-RECORD.
            05   IDENT-OUT              PIC X(6).
            05   FILLER                 PIC XXX.
            05   GROSS-PAY-OUT          PIC 9(5).99.
            05   FILLER                 PIC XXX.
            05   TAX                    PIC 9(5).99.

        WORKING-STORAGE SECTION.
        01  IDENT                       PIC X(6).
        01  GROSS-PAY                   PIC 9(5)V99.
        01  TEMPORARY-STORAGE           PIC 9(5)V99.

        PROCEDURE DIVISION.
        A000-MAIN-ROUTINE.
            OPEN OUTPUT REPORT-FILE.
            PERFORM B010-GET-PAY-DATA.
            PERFORM B020-COMPUTE-TAX
                    UNTIL IDENT = SPACES.
            CLOSE REPORT-FILE.
            STOP RUN.

        B010-GET-PAY-DATA.
            DISPLAY 'Enter employee identification: ' WITH NO ADVANCING.
            ACCEPT IDENT.
            DISPLAY 'Enter gross pay:                ' WITH NO ADVANCING.
            ACCEPT GROSS-PAY.
            DISPLAY ' '.

        B020-COMPUTE-TAX.
            MOVE SPACES TO REPORT-RECORD.
            IF GROSS-PAY IS GREATER THAN 2000.00
                SUBTRACT 2000.00 FROM GROSS-PAY
                        GIVING TEMPORARY-STORAGE
                MULTIPLY TEMPORARY-STORAGE BY 0.02 GIVING TAX ROUNDED
            ELSE
                MOVE ZERO TO TAX.
            MOVE IDENT TO IDENT-OUT.
            MOVE GROSS-PAY TO GROSS-PAY-OUT.
            WRITE REPORT-RECORD.
            PERFORM B010-GET-PAY-DATA.
```

11.

```
IDENTIFICATION DIVISION.
PROGRAM-ID.
    C05EX11.
*
*            THIS VERSION USES A FILE FOR INPUT
*
ENVIRONMENT DIVISION.
INPUT-OUTPUT SECTION.
FILE-CONTROL.
    SELECT INPUT-FILE           ASSIGN TO 'C05EX11.INP'.
    SELECT REPORT-FILE          ASSIGN TO 'C05EX11.REP'.

DATA DIVISION.
FILE SECTION.
FD  INPUT-FILE
    LABEL RECORDS ARE STANDARD.
01  INPUT-RECORD.
    05  IDENT                   PIC X(8).
    05  DOLLARS                 PIC 9(5)V99.
    05  OTHER-INFO              PIC X(65).

FD  REPORT-FILE
    LABEL RECORDS ARE STANDARD.
01  REPORT-RECORD.
    05  IDENT-OUT               PIC X(8).
    05  FILLER                  PIC XXX.
    05  DOLLARS-OUT             PIC 9(7).99.
    05  FILLER                  PIC XXX.
    05  OTHER-INFO-OUT          PIC X(65).

WORKING-STORAGE SECTION.
01  OUT-OF-DATA-FLAG            PIC X VALUE 'N'.
01  DOLLAR-TOTAL               PIC 9(7)V99 VALUE ZERO.

PROCEDURE DIVISION.
A000-MAIN-ROUTINE.
    OPEN INPUT  INPUT-FILE
         OUTPUT REPORT-FILE.
    READ INPUT-FILE
         AT END MOVE 'Y' TO OUT-OF-DATA-FLAG.
    PERFORM B010-PRINT-INPUT
         UNTIL OUT-OF-DATA-FLAG = 'Y'.
    MOVE SPACES TO REPORT-RECORD.
    MOVE 'TOTAL = ' TO IDENT-OUT.
    MOVE DOLLAR-TOTAL TO DOLLARS-OUT.
    WRITE REPORT-RECORD.
    CLOSE INPUT-FILE
          REPORT-FILE.
    STOP RUN.


B010-PRINT-INPUT.
    MOVE SPACES TO REPORT-RECORD.
    MOVE IDENT TO IDENT-OUT.
    MOVE DOLLARS TO DOLLARS-OUT.
    MOVE OTHER-INFO TO OTHER-INFO-OUT.
    WRITE REPORT-RECORD.
    ADD DOLLARS TO DOLLAR-TOTAL.
    READ INPUT-FILE
         AT END MOVE 'Y' TO OUT-OF-DATA-FLAG.
```

```
IDENTIFICATION DIVISION.
PROGRAM-ID.
    C05EX11.
*
*              THIS VERSION USES ACCEPT/DISPLAY FOR INPUT
*
ENVIRONMENT DIVISION.
INPUT-OUTPUT SECTION.
FILE-CONTROL.
    SELECT REPORT-FILE            ASSIGN TO 'C05EX11.REP'.

DATA DIVISION.
FILE SECTION.
FD  REPORT-FILE
    LABEL RECORDS ARE STANDARD.
01  REPORT-RECORD.
    05  IDENT-OUT                 PIC X(8).
    05  FILLER                    PIC XXX.
    05  DOLLARS-OUT               PIC 9(7).99.
    05  FILLER                    PIC XXX.
    05  OTHER-INFO-OUT            PIC X(65).

WORKING-STORAGE SECTION.
01  IDENT                         PIC X(8).
01  DOLLARS                       PIC 9(5)V99.
01  OTHER-INFO                    PIC X(65).
01  DOLLAR-TOTAL                  PIC 9(7)V99 VALUE ZERO.

PROCEDURE DIVISION.
A000-MAIN-ROUTINE.
    OPEN OUTPUT REPORT-FILE.
    PERFORM B010-GET-DATA.
    PERFORM B020-PRINT-INPUT
            UNTIL IDENT = SPACES.
    MOVE SPACES TO REPORT-RECORD.
    MOVE 'TOTAL = ' TO IDENT-OUT.
    MOVE DOLLAR-TOTAL TO DOLLARS-OUT.
    WRITE REPORT-RECORD.
    CLOSE REPORT-FILE.
    STOP RUN.

B010-GET-DATA.
    DISPLAY 'Enter identification:  ' WITH NO ADVANCING.
    ACCEPT IDENT.
    DISPLAY 'Enter dollar amount:   ' WITH NO ADVANCING.
    ACCEPT DOLLARS.
    DISPLAY 'Enter other information on following line:'
    ACCEPT OTHER-INFO.
    DISPLAY ' '.

B020-PRINT-INPUT.
    MOVE SPACES TO REPORT-RECORD.
    MOVE IDENT TO IDENT-OUT.
    MOVE DOLLARS TO DOLLARS-OUT.
    MOVE OTHER-INFO TO OTHER-INFO-OUT.
    WRITE REPORT-RECORD.
    ADD DOLLARS TO DOLLAR-TOTAL.
    PERFORM B010-GET-DATA.
```

```
    2.
IDENTIFICATION DIVISION.
PROGRAM-ID.
    C06EX02.

DATA DIVISION.
WORKING-STORAGE SECTION.
01   AN-FLD-1                    PIC X(5).
01   N-FLD-2                     PIC 9(5).
01   N-FLD-3                     PIC 999V99.
01   N-FLD-4                     PIC 999.99.

PROCEDURE DIVISION.
A000-MAIN.
    DISPLAY 'Enter a 5 character value:' AT 0101.
    ACCEPT AN-FLD-1 AT 0129.
    DISPLAY AN-FLD-1 AT 0201.
    ACCEPT AN-FLD-1 AT 0301.
    DISPLAY AN-FLD-1 AT 0310.
    DISPLAY 'Enter a 5 digit value:' AT 0501.
    ACCEPT N-FLD-2 AT 0525.
    DISPLAY N-FLD-2 AT 0601.
    ACCEPT N-FLD-2 AT 0701.
    DISPLAY N-FLD-2 AT 0710.
    MOVE 999.99 TO N-FLD-3.
    PERFORM B010-GET-NUMERIC
            UNTIL N-FLD-3 = ZERO.
    STOP RUN.

B010-GET-NUMERIC.
    DISPLAY 'Enter a PIC 999V99 value:'  AT 1001.
    ACCEPT N-FLD-3 AT 1028.
    DISPLAY N-FLD-3 AT 1101.
    MOVE N-FLD-3 TO N-FLD-4.
    DISPLAY N-FLD-4 AT 1201.


    3.
IDENTIFICATION DIVISION.
PROGRAM-ID.
    PAYROLL1.
DATE-WRITTEN.
    AUGUST 10, 1989.

ENVIRONMENT DIVISION.
INPUT-OUTPUT SECTION.
FILE-CONTROL.
    SELECT REPORT-FILE        ASSIGN TO 'C06EX03.REP'.

DATA DIVISION.
FILE SECTION.
FD   REPORT-FILE
     LABEL RECORDS ARE STANDARD.
01   REPORT-RECORD.
     05   O-PAYROLL-NUMBER     PIC X(5).
     05   FILLER               PIC XX.
     05   O-NAME               PIC X(20).
     05   FILLER               PIC XX.
     05   O-HOURS-WORKED       PIC 99.9.
```

```
    05  FILLER                PIC XX.
    05  O-PAYRATE             PIC 99.999.
    05  FILLER                PIC XX.
    05  O-DEPENDENTS          PIC 99.
    05  FILLER                PIC XX.
    05  O-GROSS-PAY           PIC 999.99.
    05  FILLER                PIC XX.
    05  O-TAX                 PIC 999.99.
    05  FILLER                PIC XX.
    05  O-NET-PAY             PIC 999.99.

WORKING-STORAGE SECTION.
01  C-EXEMPTION           PIC 99V99       VALUE 50.00.
01  C-TAXRATE             PIC   V999      VALUE   .210.
01  W-DEPENDENTS          PIC 99.
01  W-EXEMPTION-TOTAL     PIC 999V99.
01  W-GROSS-PAY           PIC 999V99.
01  W-HOURS-WORKED        PIC 99V9.
01  W-NAME                PIC X(20).
01  W-NET-PAY             PIC 999V99.
01  W-OVERTIME-HOURS      PIC   99V9.
01  W-OVERTIME-PAY        PIC 999V99.
01  W-PAYROLL-NUMBER      PIC X(5)        VALUE '00000'.
01  W-PAYRATE             PIC 99V999.
01  W-TAX                 PIC 999V99.
01  W-TAXABLE             PIC 999V99.


PROCEDURE DIVISION.
A000-PRODUCE-PAYROLL-CALC.
    OPEN OUTPUT REPORT-FILE.
    DISPLAY 'Enter payroll number:'        AT 0101
            WITH BLANK SCREEN.
    ACCEPT W-PAYROLL-NUMBER                 AT 0127.
    IF W-PAYROLL-NUMBER IS NOT EQUAL TO '99999'
        DISPLAY 'Enter employee name:'      AT 0201
        ACCEPT W-NAME                       AT 0227
        DISPLAY 'Enter hours worked:'       AT 0301
        ACCEPT W-HOURS-WORKED               AT 0327
        DISPLAY 'Enter pay rate:'           AT 0401
        ACCEPT W-PAYRATE                    AT 0427
        DISPLAY 'Enter number dependents:'  AT 0501
        ACCEPT W-DEPENDENTS                 AT 0527
    ELSE
        DISPLAY 'Run Terminated'            AT 0301.
    PERFORM B010-CALC-EMP-PAYROLL
        UNTIL W-PAYROLL-NUMBER = '99999'.
    CLOSE REPORT-FILE.
    STOP RUN.


B010-CALC-EMP-PAYROLL.
    MULTIPLY W-HOURS-WORKED BY W-PAYRATE
            GIVING W-GROSS-PAY ROUNDED.
    IF W-HOURS-WORKED IS GREATER THAN 40
        SUBTRACT 40 FROM W-HOURS-WORKED GIVING W-OVERTIME-HOURS
        MULTIPLY 0.5 BY W-OVERTIME-HOURS
        MULTIPLY W-OVERTIME-HOURS BY W-PAYRATE
                GIVING W-OVERTIME-PAY ROUNDED
        ADD W-OVERTIME-PAY TO W-GROSS-PAY.
    MULTIPLY C-EXEMPTION BY W-DEPENDENTS
            GIVING W-EXEMPTION-TOTAL.
```

```
      IF W-GROSS-PAY IS GREATER THAN W-EXEMPTION-TOTAL
          SUBTRACT W-EXEMPTION-TOTAL FROM W-GROSS-PAY
                  GIVING W-TAXABLE
          MULTIPLY C-TAXRATE BY W-TAXABLE GIVING W-TAX ROUNDED
      ELSE
          MOVE ZERO TO W-TAX.
      SUBTRACT W-TAX FROM W-GROSS-PAY GIVING W-NET-PAY.
      MOVE SPACES               TO REPORT-RECORD.
      MOVE W-PAYROLL-NUMBER      TO O-PAYROLL-NUMBER.
      MOVE W-NAME               TO O-NAME.
      MOVE W-HOURS-WORKED        TO O-HOURS-WORKED.
      MOVE W-PAYRATE            TO O-PAYRATE.
      MOVE W-DEPENDENTS          TO O-DEPENDENTS.
      MOVE W-TAX                TO O-TAX.
      MOVE W-GROSS-PAY          TO O-GROSS-PAY.
      MOVE W-NET-PAY            TO O-NET-PAY.
      WRITE REPORT-RECORD.
      DISPLAY 'Enter payroll number:'       AT 0101
              WITH BLANK SCREEN.
      ACCEPT W-PAYROLL-NUMBER               AT 0127.
      IF W-PAYROLL-NUMBER IS NOT EQUAL TO '99999'
          DISPLAY 'Enter employee name:'    AT 0201
          ACCEPT W-NAME                     AT 0227
          DISPLAY 'Enter hours worked:'     AT 0301
          ACCEPT W-HOURS-WORKED             AT 0327
          DISPLAY 'Enter pay rate:'         AT 0401
          ACCEPT W-PAYRATE                  AT 0427
          DISPLAY 'Enter number dependents:' AT 0501
          ACCEPT W-DEPENDENTS               AT 0527
      ELSE
          DISPLAY 'Run Terminated'          AT 0301.
```

5.

```
IDENTIFICATION DIVISION.
PROGRAM-ID.
    PAYROLL1.
DATE-WRITTEN.
    AUGUST 10, 1989.


ENVIRONMENT DIVISION.
INPUT-OUTPUT SECTION.
FILE-CONTROL.
    SELECT REPORT-FILE         ASSIGN TO 'C06EX05.REP'.

DATA DIVISION.
FILE SECTION.
FD  REPORT-FILE
    LABEL RECORDS ARE STANDARD.
01  REPORT-RECORD.
    05  O-PAYROLL-NUMBER       PIC X(5).
    05  FILLER                 PIC XX.
    05  O-NAME                 PIC X(20).
    05  FILLER                 PIC XX.
    05  O-HOURS-WORKED         PIC 99.9.
    05  FILLER                 PIC XX.
    05  O-PAYRATE              PIC 99.999.
    05  FILLER                 PIC XX.
    05  O-DEPENDENTS           PIC 99.
    05  FILLER                 PIC XX.
    05  O-GROSS-PAY            PIC 999.99.
```

```
        05  FILLER                PIC XX.
        05  O-TAX                 PIC 999.99.
        05  FILLER                PIC XX.
        05  O-NET-PAY             PIC 999.99.


    WORKING-STORAGE SECTION.
    01  C-EXEMPTION               PIC 99V99       VALUE 50.00.
    01  C-TAXRATE                 PIC V999        VALUE    .210.
    01  W-DEPENDENTS              PIC 99.
    01  W-EXEMPTION-TOTAL         PIC 999V99.
    01  W-GROSS-PAY               PIC 999V99.
    01  W-HOURS-WORKED            PIC 99V9.
    01  W-NAME                    PIC X(20).
    01  W-NET-PAY                 PIC 999V99.
    01  W-OVERTIME-HOURS          PIC 99V9.
    01  W-OVERTIME-PAY            PIC 999V99.
    01  W-PAYROLL-NUMBER          PIC X(5)        VALUE ZERO.
    01  W-PAYRATE                 PIC 99V999.
    01  W-RECORD-COUNT            PIC 9(5)        VALUE ZERO.
    01  W-TAX                     PIC 999V99.
    01  W-TAXABLE                 PIC 999V99.


    PROCEDURE DIVISION.
    A000-PRODUCE-PAYROLL-CALC.
        OPEN  OUTPUT REPORT-FILE.
        PERFORM C010-GET-PAYROLL-DATA.
        PERFORM B010-CALC-EMP-PAYROLL
                UNTIL W-PAYROLL-NUMBER = '99999'.
        MOVE SPACES TO REPORT-RECORD.
        MOVE W-RECORD-COUNT TO O-PAYROLL-NUMBER.
        MOVE 'RECORDS PROCESSED' TO O-NAME.
        WRITE REPORT-RECORD.
        CLOSE REPORT-FILE.
        STOP RUN.


    B010-CALC-EMP-PAYROLL.
        ADD 1 TO W-RECORD-COUNT.
        PERFORM C020-COMPUTE-GROSS-PAY.
        PERFORM C030-COMPUTE-EXEMPTIONS.
        PERFORM C040-COMPUTE-TAX.
        PERFORM C050-COMPUTE-NET-PAY.
        PERFORM C060-PRINT-OUTPUT.
        PERFORM C010-GET-PAYROLL-DATA.


    C010-GET-PAYROLL-DATA.
        DISPLAY 'Enter payroll number:'        AT 0101
            WITH BLANK SCREEN.
        ACCEPT W-PAYROLL-NUMBER                AT 0127.
        IF W-PAYROLL-NUMBER IS NOT EQUAL TO '99999'
            DISPLAY 'Enter employee name:'     AT 0201
            ACCEPT W-NAME                      AT 0227
            DISPLAY 'Enter hours worked:'      AT 0301
            ACCEPT W-HOURS-WORKED              AT 0327
            DISPLAY 'Enter pay rate:'          AT 0401
            ACCEPT W-PAYRATE                   AT 0427
            DISPLAY 'Enter number dependents:' AT 0501
            ACCEPT W-DEPENDENTS                AT 0527
        ELSE
            DISPLAY 'Run Terminated'           AT 0301.
```

```
C020-COMPUTE-GROSS-PAY.
    MULTIPLY W-HOURS-WORKED BY W-PAYRATE
            GIVING W-GROSS-PAY ROUNDED.
    IF W-HOURS-WORKED IS GREATER THAN 40
        SUBTRACT 40 FROM W-HOURS-WORKED GIVING W-OVERTIME-HOURS
        MULTIPLY 0.5 BY W-OVERTIME-HOURS
        MULTIPLY W-OVERTIME-HOURS BY W-PAYRATE
                GIVING W-OVERTIME-PAY ROUNDED
        ADD W-OVERTIME-PAY TO W-GROSS-PAY.

C030-COMPUTE-EXEMPTIONS.
    MULTIPLY C-EXEMPTION BY W-DEPENDENTS
            GIVING W-EXEMPTION-TOTAL.

C040-COMPUTE-TAX.
    IF W-GROSS-PAY IS GREATER THAN W-EXEMPTION-TOTAL
        SUBTRACT W-EXEMPTION-TOTAL FROM W-GROSS-PAY
            GIVING W-TAXABLE
        MULTIPLY C-TAXRATE BY W-TAXABLE GIVING W-TAX ROUNDED
    ELSE
        MOVE ZERO TO W-TAX.

C050-COMPUTE-NET-PAY.
    SUBTRACT W-TAX FROM W-GROSS-PAY GIVING W-NET-PAY.

C060-PRINT-OUTPUT.
    MOVE SPACES              TO REPORT-RECORD.
    MOVE W-PAYROLL-NUMBER    TO O-PAYROLL-NUMBER.
    MOVE W-NAME              TO O-NAME.
    MOVE W-HOURS-WORKED      TO O-HOURS-WORKED.
    MOVE W-PAYRATE           TO O-PAYRATE.
    MOVE W-DEPENDENTS        TO O-DEPENDENTS.
    MOVE W-TAX               TO O-TAX.
    MOVE W-GROSS-PAY         TO O-GROSS-PAY.
    MOVE W-NET-PAY           TO O-NET-PAY.
    WRITE REPORT-RECORD.

    7.
IDENTIFICATION DIVISION.
PROGRAM-ID.
    PAYROLL2.
DATE-WRITTEN.
    AUGUST 10, 1989.

ENVIRONMENT DIVISION.
INPUT-OUTPUT SECTION.
FILE-CONTROL.
    SELECT PAYROLL-FILE     ASSIGN TO 'C06EX07.DAT'.
    SELECT REPORT-FILE      ASSIGN TO 'C06EX07.REP'.

DATA DIVISION.
FILE SECTION.
FD  PAYROLL-FILE
    LABEL RECORDS ARE STANDARD.
01  PAYROLL-RECORD.
    05  I-PAYROLL-NUMBER    PIC X(5).
    05  I-NAME              PIC X(20).
    05  I-HOURS-WORKED      PIC 99V9.
    05  FILLER              PIC X(3).
    05  I-PAYRATE           PIC 99V999.
    05  I-DEPENDENTS        PIC 99.
    05  FILLER              PIC X(42).
```

```
FD  REPORT-FILE
    LABEL RECORDS ARE STANDARD.
01  REPORT-RECORD            PIC X(69).

WORKING-STORAGE SECTION.
01  NORMAL-OUTPUT-LINE.
    05  O-PAYROLL-NUMBER      PIC X(5).
    05  FILLER                PIC XX.
    05  O-NAME                PIC X(20).
    05  FILLER                PIC XX.
    05  O-HOURS-WORKED        PIC 99.9.
    05  FILLER                PIC XX.
    05  O-PAYRATE             PIC 99.999.
    05  FILLER                PIC XX.
    05  O-DEPENDENTS          PIC 99.
    05  FILLER                PIC XX.
    05  O-GROSS-PAY           PIC 999.99.
    05  FILLER                PIC XX.
    05  O-TAX                 PIC 999.99.
    05  FILLER                PIC XX.
    05  O-NET-PAY             PIC 999.99.

01  ERROR-RECORD.
    05  BAD-DATA              PIC X(38).
    05  FILLER                PIC X(4)       VALUE SPACES.
    05  ERROR-MESSAGE         PIC X(27)
        VALUE 'INVALID DATA IN THIS RECORD'.

01  C-EXEMPTION              PIC 99V99      VALUE 50.00.
01  C-TAXRATE                PIC  V999      VALUE  .210.
01  W-EXEMPTION-TOTAL        PIC 999V99.
01  W-GROSS-PAY              PIC 999V99.
01  W-NET-PAY                PIC 999V99.
01  W-OUT-OF-RECORDS-FLAG    PIC X          VALUE 'N'.
01  W-OVERTIME-HOURS         PIC  99V99.
01  W-OVERTIME-PAY           PIC 999V99.
01  W-TAX                    PIC 999V99.
01  W-TAXABLE                PIC 999V99.
01  W-VALID-RECORD-FLAG      PIC X.

PROCEDURE DIVISION.
A000-PRODUCE-PAYROLL-CALC.
    OPEN  INPUT PAYROLL-FILE
        OUTPUT REPORT-FILE.
    PERFORM C010-GET-VALID-PAY-REC.
    PERFORM B010-CALC-EMP-PAYROLL
        UNTIL W-OUT-OF-RECORDS-FLAG = 'Y'.
    CLOSE PAYROLL-FILE
        REPORT-FILE.
    STOP RUN.


B010-CALC-EMP-PAYROLL.
    PERFORM C020-COMPUTE-GROSS-PAY.
    PERFORM C030-COMPUTE-EXEMPTIONS.
    PERFORM C040-COMPUTE-TAX
    PERFORM C050-COMPUTE-NET-PAY.
    PERFORM C060-PRINT-OUTPUT.
    PERFORM C010-GET-VALID-PAY-REC.
```

```
C010-GET-VALID-PAY-REC.
    MOVE 'N' TO W-VALID-RECORD-FLAG.
    PERFORM UNTIL    W-VALID-RECORD-FLAG = 'Y'
                 OR W-OUT-OF-RECORDS-FLAG = 'Y'
        READ PAYROLL-FILE
                AT END MOVE 'Y' TO W-OUT-OF-RECORDS-FLAG
        END-READ
        IF W-OUT-OF-RECORDS-FLAG = 'N'
            IF      I-PAYROLL-NUMBER IS NOT NUMERIC
                OR  I-HOURS-WORKED   IS NOT NUMERIC
                OR  I-PAYRATE        IS NOT NUMERIC
                OR  I-DEPENDENTS     IS NOT NUMERIC
                MOVE PAYROLL-RECORD TO BAD-DATA
                WRITE REPORT-RECORD FROM ERROR-RECORD
            ELSE
                MOVE 'Y' TO W-VALID-RECORD-FLAG
            END-IF
        END-IF
    END-PERFORM.


C020-COMPUTE-GROSS-PAY.
    MULTIPLY I-HOURS-WORKED BY I-PAYRATE
            GIVING W-GROSS-PAY ROUNDED.
    IF I-HOURS-WORKED IS GREATER THAN 40
        SUBTRACT 40 FROM I-HOURS-WORKED GIVING W-OVERTIME-HOURS
        MULTIPLY 0.5 BY W-OVERTIME-HOURS
        MULTIPLY W-OVERTIME-HOURS BY I-PAYRATE
                GIVING W-OVERTIME-PAY ROUNDED
        ADD W-OVERTIME-PAY TO W-GROSS-PAY.


C030-COMPUTE-EXEMPTIONS.
    MULTIPLY C-EXEMPTION BY I-DEPENDENTS
            GIVING W-EXEMPTION-TOTAL.


C040-COMPUTE-TAX.
    IF W-GROSS-PAY IS GREATER THAN W-EXEMPTION-TOTAL
        SUBTRACT W-EXEMPTION-TOTAL FROM W-GROSS-PAY
            GIVING W-TAXABLE
        MULTIPLY C-TAXRATE BY W-TAXABLE GIVING W-TAX ROUNDED
    ELSE
        MOVE ZERO TO W-TAX.


C050-COMPUTE-NET-PAY.
    SUBTRACT W-TAX FROM W-GROSS-PAY GIVING W-NET-PAY.


C060-PRINT-OUTPUT.
    MOVE SPACES              TO NORMAL-OUTPUT-LINE.
    MOVE I-PAYROLL-NUMBER    TO O-PAYROLL-NUMBER.
    MOVE I-NAME              TO O-NAME.
    MOVE I-HOURS-WORKED      TO O-HOURS-WORKED.
    MOVE I-PAYRATE           TO O-PAYRATE.
    MOVE I-DEPENDENTS        TO O-DEPENDENTS.
    MOVE W-TAX               TO O-TAX.
    MOVE W-GROSS-PAY         TO O-GROSS-PAY.
    MOVE W-NET-PAY           TO O-NET-PAY.
    WRITE REPORT-RECORD FROM NORMAL-OUTPUT-LINE.


D010-VALID-RECORD-LOOP.
    READ PAYROLL-FILE
            AT END MOVE 'Y' TO W-OUT-OF-RECORDS-FLAG.
```

```
IF W-OUT-OF-RECORDS-FLAG = 'N'
     IF      I-PAYROLL-NUMBER IS NOT NUMERIC
        OR   I-HOURS-WORKED   IS NOT NUMERIC
        OR   I-PAYRATE        IS NOT NUMERIC
        OR   I-DEPENDENTS     IS NOT NUMERIC
        MOVE PAYROLL-RECORD TO BAD-DATA
        WRITE REPORT-RECORD FROM ERROR-RECORD
     ELSE
        MOVE 'Y' TO W-VALID-RECORD-FLAG.
```

CHAPTER 7

1. a. ZZ999

   b. $(6)

   c. $ZZ9.99

   d. +(5)

   e. Z9BB999

3.
```
01  I-RECORD.
    05  I-CUST-NO          PIC 9(5).
    05  I-CUST-NAME        PIC X(20).
    05  I-AMT-SALE         PIC S9(4)V99.
    05  I-PRODUCT-CODE     PIC X(6).
    05  FILLER             PIC X(42).
    05  I-RECORD-CODE      PIC X.

01  O-DETAIL-LINE.
    05  O-CUST-NO          PIC 99B999.
    05  FILLER             PIC X(5).
    05  O-CUST-NAME        PIC XBX(19).
    05  FILLER             PIC X(5).
    05  O-AMT-SALE         PIC $$,$$$.99-.
    05  FILLER             PIC X(5).
    05  O-PROD-CODE        PIC X(6).
    05  FILLER             PIC X(5).
    05  O-RECORD-CODE      PIC A.
```

5.
```
01  OUTPUT-LINE.
    05  ID-NUMBER-OUT          PIC X(6).
    05  REQUISITION-OUT        PIC X(6).
    05  FUND-OUT               PIC X(4).
    05  DEPARTMENT-OUT         PIC X(4).
    05  B-OUT                  PIC XX.
    05  PURCHASE-ORDER-OUT     PIC X(6).
    05  REFERENCE-OUT          PIC X(18).
    05  FILLER                 PIC X.
    05  GROSS-OUT              PIC ZZ,ZZZV99.
    05  FILLER                 PIC X.
    05  DISC-OR-DEDUC-OUT      PIC ZZZV99.
    05  FILLER                 PIC XX.
    05  AMOUNT-PAYABLE-OUT     PIC ZZZ,ZZV99.
```

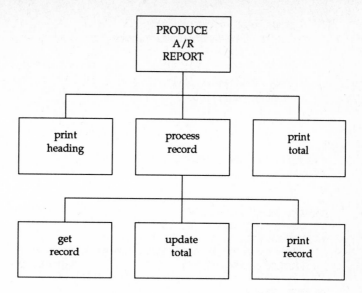

Hierarchy chart for Exercise 5.

7.

Produce A/R Report:
    print the heading
    PERFORM-UNTIL there are no more invoice records
       process one invoice record
    ENDPERFORM
    print the total

Print Heading:
    print "ACCOUNTS RECEIVABLE" line
    print blank line
    print first column heading line
    print second column heading line
    print blank line

Process Record:
    get the next invoice record
    IF there is a record to process THEN
      update the total
      print the output record
    ENDIF

Print Total:
    print a blank line
    move "TOTAL" to the output line
    move the total to the output line
    print the output line

Get Record:
    get an invoice record; at end set the end of file flag

Update Total:
add the invoice amount to the total

Print Record:
move the invoice fields to the output record
print the output record

In the following program several of the smaller modules have been
implemented as in-line code rather than as separate paragraphs.

```
IDENTIFICATION DIVISION.
PROGRAM-ID.
    C07EX07.

ENVIRONMENT DIVISION.
INPUT-OUTPUT SECTION.
FILE-CONTROL.
    SELECT ACCOUNTS-RECEIVABLE-FILE ASSIGN TO 'C07EX07.AR'.
    SELECT INVOICE-FILE            ASSIGN TO 'C07EX07.INV'.

DATA DIVISION.
FILE SECTION.
FD  ACCOUNTS-RECEIVABLE-FILE
    LABEL RECORDS ARE STANDARD.
01  ACCOUNTS-RECEIVABLE-RECORD      PIC X(60).

FD  INVOICE-FILE
    LABEL RECORDS ARE STANDARD.
01  INVOICE-RECORD.
    05  CUSTOMER-NUMBER             PIC X(5).
    05  CUSTOMER-NAME               PIC X(20).
    05  INVOICE-NUMBER              PIC X(5).
    05  INVOICE-DATE                PIC X(6).
    05  INVOICE-AMOUNT              PIC 9(4)V99.

WORKING-STORAGE SECTION.
01  HEADING-LINE-1                  PIC X(60)
        VALUE '            ACCOUNTS RECEIVABLE'.
01  HEADING-LINE-2.
    05  FILLER                      PIC X(31)
        VALUE 'CUSTOMER CUSTOMER'.
    05  FILLER                      PIC X(29)
        VALUE 'INVOICE   INVOICE   INVOICE'.
01  HEADING-LINE-3.
    05  FILLER                      PIC X(31)
        VALUE 'NUMBER    NAME'.
    05  FILLER                      PIC X(29)
        VALUE 'NUMBER    DATE     AMOUNT'.

01  INVOICE-LINE.
    05  CUSTOMER-NUMBER-OUT         PIC X(5).
    05  FILLER                      PIC X(4).
    05  CUSTOMER-NAME-OUT           PIC X(20).
    05  FILLER                      PIC XX.
    05  INVOICE-NUMBER-OUT          PIC X(5).
    05  FILLER                      PIC XXX.
    05  INVOICE-DATE-OUT            PIC XXBXXBXX.
    05  FILLER                      PIC XXX.
    05  INVOICE-AMOUNT-OUT          PIC ZZZ9.99.
```

```
01  TOTAL-LINE.
    05  FILLER                      PIC X(36) VALUE SPACES.
    05  FILLER                      PIC X(10) VALUE 'TOTAL'.
    05  INVOICE-TOTAL-OUT           PIC $$$$,$$9.99.

01  INVOICE-TOTAL                   PIC S9(6)V99 VALUE ZERO.

01  MORE-DATA-REMAINING-FLAG        PIC X VALUE 'Y'.
    88  NO-MORE-DATA-REMAINING              VALUE 'N'.
    88  MORE-DATA-REMAINING                 VALUE 'Y'.

PROCEDURE DIVISION.
A000-PRODUCE-AR-REPORT.
    OPEN INPUT  INVOICE-FILE
         OUTPUT ACCOUNTS-RECEIVABLE-FILE.
    WRITE ACCOUNTS-RECEIVABLE-RECORD FROM HEADING-LINE-1.
    MOVE SPACES TO ACCOUNTS-RECEIVABLE-RECORD.
    WRITE ACCOUNTS-RECEIVABLE-RECORD.
    WRITE ACCOUNTS-RECEIVABLE-RECORD FROM HEADING-LINE-2.
    WRITE ACCOUNTS-RECEIVABLE-RECORD FROM HEADING-LINE-3.
    MOVE SPACES TO ACCOUNTS-RECEIVABLE-RECORD.
    WRITE ACCOUNTS-RECEIVABLE-RECORD.
    PERFORM B010-PROCESS-RECORD
            UNTIL NO-MORE-DATA-REMAINING.
    MOVE SPACES TO ACCOUNTS-RECEIVABLE-RECORD.
    WRITE ACCOUNTS-RECEIVABLE-RECORD.
    MOVE INVOICE-TOTAL TO INVOICE-TOTAL-OUT.
    WRITE ACCOUNTS-RECEIVABLE-RECORD FROM TOTAL-LINE.
    CLOSE INVOICE-FILE
          ACCOUNTS-RECEIVABLE-FILE.
    STOP RUN.

B010-PROCESS-RECORD.
    READ INVOICE-FILE
            AT END MOVE 'N' TO MORE-DATA-REMAINING-FLAG.
    IF MORE-DATA-REMAINING
        ADD INVOICE-AMOUNT TO INVOICE-TOTAL
        PERFORM C010-PRINT-RECORD.

C010-PRINT-RECORD.
    MOVE SPACES TO INVOICE-LINE.
    MOVE CUSTOMER-NUMBER TO CUSTOMER-NUMBER-OUT.
    MOVE CUSTOMER-NAME   TO CUSTOMER-NAME-OUT.
    MOVE INVOICE-NUMBER  TO INVOICE-NUMBER-OUT.
    MOVE INVOICE-DATE    TO INVOICE-DATE-OUT.
    MOVE INVOICE-AMOUNT  TO INVOICE-AMOUNT-OUT.
    WRITE ACCOUNTS-RECEIVABLE-RECORD FROM INVOICE-LINE.
```

9. Add the following declarations to the Working-Storage Section:

```
77  W-GROSS-PAY-ERROR.
01  ERROR-RECORD.
    05  E-PAYROLL-NUMBER    PIC X(5).
    05  E-NAME              PIC BX(20).
    05  E-HOURS-WORKED      PIC BZ9.9.
    05  E-PAYRATE           PIC BZ9.999.
    05  E-GROSS-PAY         PIC B$$$9.99.
    05  E-MESSAGE           PIC X(29)
            VALUE ' GROSS PAY SUSPICIOUSLY LARGE'.
```

Modify paragraphs **B020-CALC-EMP-PAYROLL** and **C020-COMPUTE-GROSS-PAY**, and add paragraph **C070-PRINT-ERROR-MESSAGE** as shown below.

```
B020-CALC-EMP-PAYROLL.
    PERFORM C020-COMPUTE-GROSS-PAY.
    IF W-GROSS-PAY-ERROR = 'N'
        PERFORM C030-COMPUTE-EXEMPTIONS
        PERFORM C040-COMPUTE-TAX
        PERFORM C050-COMPUTE-NET-PAY
        PERFORM C060-PRINT-OUTPUT
    ELSE
        PERFORM C070-PRINT-ERROR-MESSAGE.
    PERFORM C010-GET-PAYROLL-DATA.


C020-COMPUTE-GROSS-PAY.
    MOVE 'N' TO W-GROSS-PAY-ERROR.
    MULTIPLY W-HOURS-WORKED BY W-PAYRATE
            GIVING W-GROSS-PAY ROUNDED.
    IF W-HOURS-WORKED IS GREATER THAN 40
        SUBTRACT 40 FROM W-HOURS-WORKED GIVING W-OVERTIME-HOURS
        MULTIPLY 0.5 BY W-OVERTIME-HOURS
        MULTIPLY W-OVERTIME-HOURS BY W-PAYRATE
                GIVING W-OVERTIME-PAY ROUNDED
        ADD W-OVERTIME-PAY TO W-GROSS-PAY.
    IF W-GROSS-PAY IS GREATER THAN 600.00
        MOVE 'Y' TO W-GROSS-PAY-ERROR.


C070-PRINT-ERROR-MESSAGE.
    MOVE W-PAYROLL-NUMBER      TO E-PAYROLL-NUMBER.
    MOVE W-NAME                TO E-NAME.
    MOVE W-HOURS-WORKED        TO E-HOURS-WORKED.
    MOVE W-PAYRATE             TO E-PAYRATE.
    MOVE W-GROSS-PAY           TO E-GROSS-PAY.
    WRITE REPORT-RECORD FROM ERROR-RECORD.
```

10. Fields must be set up in the Working-Storage Section for the counter (number of employees) and the three totals (gross pay, tax, and net pay); they should all be initialized with **VALUE ZERO** clauses. The **IF** statement in **C010-GET-PAYROLL-DATA** should be modified to look something like

```
IF NOT END-OF-DATA
    ADD 1 TO W-EMPLOYEE-COUNT
    .
    .
    .
```

Statements to accumulate the total gross pay, tax, and net pay can be placed at the end of **B020-CALC-EMP-PAYROLL**, just before **PERFORM C010-GET-PAYROLL-DATA**. To print all these counts and totals, define appropriate output lines in Working-Storage, then place **WRITE** statements in **A000-PRODUCE-PAYROLL-CALC** just before the **CLOSE** statement.

11.
```
05  STATE-CODE            PIC XX.
    88   ALABAMA               VALUE '01'.
    88   ALASKA                VALUE '02'.
    88   ARIZONA               VALUE '03'.

    Etc.
```

13.

```
IDENTIFICATION DIVISION.
PROGRAM-ID.
    C07EX13.

ENVIRONMENT DIVISION.
INPUT-OUTPUT SECTION.
FILE-CONTROL.
    SELECT OUTPUT-FILE            ASSIGN TO 'C07EX13.PIC'.

DATA DIVISION.
FILE SECTION.
FD  OUTPUT-FILE
    LABEL RECORDS ARE STANDARD.
01  OUTPUT-RECORD                 PIC X(80).

WORKING-STORAGE SECTION.
01  SENDING-1                     PIC 9(4) VALUE 1234.
01  SENDING-2                     PIC 9(4) VALUE 23.
01  SENDING-3                     PIC 9(4) VALUE 23.
01  SENDING-4                     PIC 9(4) VALUE 4.
01  SENDING-5                     PIC 9(4) VALUE 50.
01  SENDING-6                     PIC 9(4) VALUE ZERO.
01  SENDING-7                     PIC 9(4) VALUE 123.
01  SENDING-8                     PIC 9(4) VALUE 2.
01  SENDING-9                     PIC 9(4) VALUE 1234.
01  SENDING-10                    PIC 9(4) VALUE ZERO.
01  SENDING-11                    PIC 9(4) VALUE ZERO.
01  SENDING-12                    PIC 9(4) VALUE 102.

01  LINE-1.
    05  FILLER                    PIC X(50)
        VALUE '9(4)        1234                    $9(4)'.
    05  RECEIVING-1               PIC $9(4).
01  LINE-2.
    05  FILLER                    PIC X(50)
        VALUE '9(4)        0023                    $9(4)'.
    05  RECEIVING-2               PIC $9(4).
01  LINE-3.
    05  FILLER                    PIC X(50)
        VALUE '9(4)        0023                    $ZZ99'.
    05  RECEIVING-3               PIC $ZZ99.
01  LINE-4.
    05  FILLER                    PIC X(50)
        VALUE '9(4)        0004                    $ZZ99'.
    05  RECEIVING-4               PIC $ZZ99.
01  LINE-5.
    05  FILLER                    PIC X(50)
        VALUE '9(4)        0050                    $Z(4)'.
    05  RECEIVING-5               PIC $Z(4).
01  LINE-6.
    05  FILLER                    PIC X(50)
        VALUE '9(4)        0000                    $Z(4)'.
    05  RECEIVING-6               PIC $Z(4).
01  LINE-7.
    05  FILLER                    PIC X(50)
        VALUE '9(4)        0123                    $$999'.
    05  RECEIVING-7               PIC $$999.
```

```
01  LINE-8.
    05  FILLER                    PIC X(50)
        VALUE '9(4)        0002                   $$999'.
    05  RECEIVING-8               PIC $$999.
01  LINE-9.
    05  FILLER                    PIC X(50)
        VALUE '9(4)        1234                   $(5)'.
    05  RECEIVING-9               PIC $(5).
01  LINE-10.
    05  FILLER                    PIC X(50)
        VALUE '9(4)        0000                   $$$99'.
    05  RECEIVING-10              PIC $$$99.
01  LINE-11.
    05  FILLER                    PIC X(50)
        VALUE '9(4)        0000                   $(5)'.
    05  RECEIVING-11              PIC $(5).
01  LINE-12.
    05  FILLER                    PIC X(50)
        VALUE '9(4)        0102                   $$$99'.
    05  RECEIVING-12              PIC $$$99.


01  HEADING-1                     PIC X(60) VALUE
    '      SENDING ITEM                      RECEIVING ITEM'.
01  HEADING-2.
    05  FILLER                    PIC X(35)
        VALUE 'PICTURE    SAMPLE DATA'.
    05  FILLER                    PIC X(25)
        VALUE 'PICTURE EDITED RESULT'.
01  BLANK-LINE                    PIC X(60) VALUE SPACES.


PROCEDURE DIVISION.
A000-MAIN-ROUTINE.
    OPEN OUTPUT OUTPUT-FILE.
    WRITE OUTPUT-RECORD FROM HEADING-1.
    WRITE OUTPUT-RECORD FROM HEADING-2.
    WRITE OUTPUT-RECORD FROM BLANK-LINE.
    MOVE SENDING-1 TO RECEIVING-1.
    WRITE OUTPUT-RECORD FROM LINE-1.
    WRITE OUTPUT-RECORD FROM BLANK-LINE.
    MOVE SENDING-2 TO RECEIVING-2.
    WRITE OUTPUT-RECORD FROM LINE-2.
    WRITE OUTPUT-RECORD FROM BLANK-LINE.
    MOVE SENDING-3 TO RECEIVING-3.
    WRITE OUTPUT-RECORD FROM LINE-3.
    WRITE OUTPUT-RECORD FROM BLANK-LINE.
    MOVE SENDING-4 TO RECEIVING-4.
    WRITE OUTPUT-RECORD FROM LINE-4.
    WRITE OUTPUT-RECORD FROM BLANK-LINE.
    MOVE SENDING-5 TO RECEIVING-5.
    WRITE OUTPUT-RECORD FROM LINE-5.
    WRITE OUTPUT-RECORD FROM BLANK-LINE.
    MOVE SENDING-6 TO RECEIVING-6.
    WRITE OUTPUT-RECORD FROM LINE-6.
    WRITE OUTPUT-RECORD FROM BLANK-LINE.
    WRITE OUTPUT-RECORD FROM BLANK-LINE.
    WRITE OUTPUT-RECORD FROM BLANK-LINE.
    WRITE OUTPUT-RECORD FROM BLANK-LINE.
    WRITE OUTPUT-RECORD FROM BLANK-LINE.
    WRITE OUTPUT-RECORD FROM HEADING-1.
    WRITE OUTPUT-RECORD FROM HEADING-2.
```

```
WRITE OUTPUT-RECORD FROM BLANK-LINE.
MOVE SENDING-7 TO RECEIVING-7.
WRITE OUTPUT-RECORD FROM LINE-7.
WRITE OUTPUT-RECORD FROM BLANK-LINE.
MOVE SENDING-8 TO RECEIVING-8.
WRITE OUTPUT-RECORD FROM LINE-8.
WRITE OUTPUT-RECORD FROM BLANK-LINE.
MOVE SENDING-9 TO RECEIVING-9.
WRITE OUTPUT-RECORD FROM LINE-9.
WRITE OUTPUT-RECORD FROM BLANK-LINE.
MOVE SENDING-10 TO RECEIVING-10.
WRITE OUTPUT-RECORD FROM LINE-10.
WRITE OUTPUT-RECORD FROM BLANK-LINE.
MOVE SENDING-11 TO RECEIVING-11.
WRITE OUTPUT-RECORD FROM LINE-11.
WRITE OUTPUT-RECORD FROM BLANK-LINE.
MOVE SENDING-12 TO RECEIVING-12.
WRITE OUTPUT-RECORD FROM LINE-12.
CLOSE OUTPUT-FILE.
STOP RUN.
```

CHAPTER 8

1. The **ADD** statement in **E010-GET-PAYROLL-RECORD** is executed even when the end-of-file is encountered, so **VALID-RECORD-COUNT** will be one greater than it should be. To correct the problem make the **ADD** statement subordinate to an **IF** statement like the following:

   ```
   IF W-OUT-OF-RECORDS-FLAG = 'N'
       ADD 1 TO VALID-RECORD-COUNT.
   ```

2. In addition to the syntax errors found by the compiler, the program contains the following errors:

   a. There is no **STOP RUN** statement.

   b. There are no periods at the end of the **IF** and **ADD** statements in **B010-PROCESS-INPUT-RECORD**. The result is that the **ADD** and **READ** statements are subject to the **IF**. As soon as the **IF** because false, a fairly common situation in this program, no more data will be read and the program will go into an infinite loop.

   c. **MORE-DATA-REMAINS-FLAG** is not initialized. Since it is unlikely that its initial value will be equal to **YES** by accident, the **IF** statement on line 63 will almost certainly be false and no data will be processed.

   d. Not only is there no period at the end of line 91 (which was caught by the compiler as a syntax error), there are no periods anywhere in **C010-PROCESS-ACCOUNT-TOTAL**. However, this would not cause any problems in this particular program.

```
4. IF      MARRIED
        PERFORM D020-MARRIED-ROUTINE
   ELSE IF SINGLE
        PERFORM D010-SINGLE-ROUTINE
   ELSE IF DIVORCED
        PERFORM D030-DIVORCED-ROUTINE
   ELSE IF WIDOWED
        PERFORM D040-WIDOWED-ROUTINE
   ELSE
        PERFORM D050-ERROR-ROUTINE.


6. IF SALARY-CODE = 'W'
       IF GROSS-PAY IS GREATER THAN 500
           PERFORM E050-EXCESSIVE-PAY-POSSIBLE
       ELSE
           NEXT SENTENCE
   ELSE
       IF SALARY-CODE = 'S'
           IF GROSS-PAY IS GREATER THAN 1400
               PERFORM E050-EXCESSIVE-PAY-POSSIBLE
           ELSE
               NEXT SENTENCE
       ELSE
           IF SALARY-CODE = 'M'
               IF GROSS-PAY IS GREATER THAN 4500
                   PERFORM E050-EXCESSIVE-PAY-POSSIBLE
               ELSE
                   NEXT SENTENCE
           ELSE
               PERFORM X030-ERROR-ROUTINE.


8.
IDENTIFICATION DIVISION.
PROGRAM-ID.
    C08EX08.

ENVIRONMENT DIVISION.
INPUT-OUTPUT SECTION.
FILE-CONTROL.
    SELECT ACCOUNTS-RECEIVABLE-FILE ASSIGN TO 'C08EX08.AR'.
    SELECT INVOICE-FILE             ASSIGN TO 'C08EX08.INV'.

DATA DIVISION.
FILE SECTION.
FD  ACCOUNTS-RECEIVABLE-FILE
    LABEL RECORDS ARE STANDARD.
01  ACCOUNTS-RECEIVABLE-RECORD     PIC X(60).

FD  INVOICE-FILE
    LABEL RECORDS ARE STANDARD.
01  INVOICE-RECORD.
    05  CUSTOMER-NUMBER            PIC X(5).
    05  CUSTOMER-NAME              PIC X(20).
    05  INVOICE-NUMBER             PIC X(5).
    05  INVOICE-DATE               PIC X(6).
    05  INVOICE-AMOUNT             PIC 9(4)V99.

WORKING-STORAGE SECTION.
01  HEADING-LINE-1                 PIC X(60)
        VALUE '              ACCOUNTS RECEIVABLE'.
```

```
01  HEADING-LINE-2.
    05  FILLER                      PIC X(31)
        VALUE 'CUSTOMER CUSTOMER'.
    05  FILLER                      PIC X(29)
        VALUE 'INVOICE   INVOICE   INVOICE'.
01  HEADING-LINE-3.
    05  FILLER                      PIC X(31)
        VALUE 'NUMBER   NAME'.
    05  FILLER                      PIC X(29)
        VALUE 'NUMBER   DATE      AMOUNT'.

01  INVOICE-LINE.
    05  CUSTOMER-NUMBER-OUT         PIC X(5).
    05  FILLER                      PIC X(4).
    05  CUSTOMER-NAME-OUT           PIC X(20).
    05  FILLER                      PIC XX.
    05  INVOICE-NUMBER-OUT          PIC X(5).
    05  FILLER                      PIC XXX.
    05  INVOICE-DATE-OUT            PIC XXBXXBXX.
    05  FILLER                      PIC XXX.
    05  INVOICE-AMOUNT-OUT          PIC ZZZ9.99.

01  TOTAL-LINE.
    05  FILLER                      PIC X(36) VALUE SPACES.
    05  FILLER                      PIC X(10) VALUE 'TOTAL'.
    05  INVOICE-TOTAL-OUT           PIC $$$$,$$9.99.

01  INVOICE-TOTAL                   PIC S9(6)V99 VALUE ZERO.

01  MORE-DATA-REMAINING-FLAG        PIC X VALUE 'Y'.
    88  NO-MORE-DATA-REMAINING              VALUE 'N'.
    88  MORE-DATA-REMAINING                 VALUE 'Y'.

01  TOTAL-OVERFLOW-FLAG             PIC X VALUE 'N'.

01  TOTAL-OVERFLOW-MESSAGE          PIC X(52)
    VALUE '    ***** OVERFLOW OCCURRED.   TOTAL INVALID. *****'.

PROCEDURE DIVISION.
A000-PRODUCE-AR-REPORT.
    OPEN INPUT  INVOICE-FILE
         OUTPUT ACCOUNTS-RECEIVABLE-FILE.
    WRITE ACCOUNTS-RECEIVABLE-RECORD FROM HEADING-LINE-1.
    MOVE SPACES TO ACCOUNTS-RECEIVABLE-RECORD.
    WRITE ACCOUNTS-RECEIVABLE-RECORD.
    WRITE ACCOUNTS-RECEIVABLE-RECORD FROM HEADING-LINE-2.
    WRITE ACCOUNTS-RECEIVABLE-RECORD FROM HEADING-LINE-3.
    MOVE SPACES TO ACCOUNTS-RECEIVABLE-RECORD.
    WRITE ACCOUNTS-RECEIVABLE-RECORD.
    PERFORM B010-PROCESS-RECORD
            UNTIL NO-MORE-DATA-REMAINING.
    MOVE SPACES TO ACCOUNTS-RECEIVABLE-RECORD.
    WRITE ACCOUNTS-RECEIVABLE-RECORD.
    IF TOTAL-OVERFLOW-FLAG = 'Y'
        WRITE ACCOUNTS-RECEIVABLE-RECORD
                FROM TOTAL-OVERFLOW-MESSAGE
    ELSE
        MOVE INVOICE-TOTAL TO INVOICE-TOTAL-OUT
        WRITE ACCOUNTS-RECEIVABLE-RECORD FROM TOTAL-LINE.
    CLOSE INVOICE-FILE
          ACCOUNTS-RECEIVABLE-FILE.
    STOP RUN.
```

```
B010-PROCESS-RECORD.
    READ INVOICE-FILE
            AT END MOVE 'N' TO MORE-DATA-REMAINING-FLAG.
    IF MORE-DATA-REMAINING
        PERFORM C020-PROCESS-INVOICE.


C010-PRINT-RECORD.
    MOVE SPACES TO INVOICE-LINE.
    MOVE CUSTOMER-NUMBER TO CUSTOMER-NUMBER-OUT.
    MOVE CUSTOMER-NAME   TO CUSTOMER-NAME-OUT.
    MOVE INVOICE-NUMBER  TO INVOICE-NUMBER-OUT.
    MOVE INVOICE-DATE    TO INVOICE-DATE-OUT.
    MOVE INVOICE-AMOUNT  TO INVOICE-AMOUNT-OUT.
    WRITE ACCOUNTS-RECEIVABLE-RECORD FROM INVOICE-LINE.


C020-PROCESS-INVOICE.
    ADD INVOICE-AMOUNT TO INVOICE-TOTAL
            ON SIZE ERROR MOVE 'Y' TO TOTAL-OVERFLOW-FLAG.
    PERFORM C010-PRINT-RECORD.
```

CHAPTER 9

1. In A000-PRODUCE-AR-REPORT delete all lines between the OPEN statement and PERFORM B010-PROCESS-RECORD. Define a line counter field and initialize it to any value greater than 45. Modify C010-PRINT-RECORD to something like the following:

```
C010-PRINT-RECORD.
    IF LINE-COUNT IS NOT LESS THAN 45
        PERFORM D010-PRINT-HEADING.
    MOVE SPACES TO INVOICE-LINE.
    MOVE CUSTOMER-NUMBER TO CUSTOMER-NUMBER-OUT.
    MOVE CUSTOMER-NAME   TO CUSTOMER-NAME-OUT.
    MOVE INVOICE-NUMBER  TO INVOICE-NUMBER-OUT.
    MOVE INVOICE-DATE    TO INVOICE-DATE-OUT.
    MOVE INVOICE-AMOUNT  TO INVOICE-AMOUNT-OUT.
    WRITE ACCOUNTS-RECEIVABLE-RECORD FROM INVOICE-LINE
            AFTER ADVANCING 1 LINE.
    ADD 1 TO LINE-COUNT.


D010-PRINT-HEADING.
    WRITE ACCOUNTS-RECEIVABLE-RECORD FROM HEADING-LINE-1
            AFTER ADVANCING PAGE.
    WRITE ACCOUNTS-RECEIVABLE-RECORD FROM HEADING-LINE-2
            AFTER ADVANCING 2 LINES.
    WRITE ACCOUNTS-RECEIVABLE-RECORD FROM HEADING-LINE-3
            AFTER ADVANCING 1 LINE.
    MOVE SPACES TO ACCOUNTS-RECEIVABLE-RECORD.
    WRITE ACCOUNTS-RECEIVABLE-RECORD AFTER ADVANCING 1 LINE.
    MOVE 0 TO LINE-COUNT.
```

2. Put two additional MOVEs at the end of D010-PROCESS-ACCOUNT-GROUP and one additional MOVE at the end of C010-PROCESS-SELLER-GROUP, just before PERFORM X010-LINE-OUT. Actually, this is probably a preferable format for general use, since if there are a great many minor totals in each intermediate group it could become clumsy looking ahead to see what the intermediate level is.

4. Define an error message and a sequence error flag in Working-Storage, and initialize the flag with **VALUE 'N'**. Modify **A000-PREPARE-SALES-REPORT** as follows:

```
PERFORM B010-PROCESS-ACCOUNT-GROUP
    UNTIL NO-MORE-DATA OR SEQUENCE-ERROR-FLAG = 'Y'.
IF SEQUENCE-ERROR-FLAG = 'Y'
    MOVE SEQUENCE-ERROR-MESSAGE TO DETAIL-LINE
ELSE
    MOVE SPACES TO DETAIL-LINE
    MOVE FINAL-TOTAL TO FINAL-TOTAL-OUT.
```

Modify **B010-PROCESS-ACCOUNT-GROUP** to the following:

```
B010-PROCESS-ACCOUNT-GROUP.
    MOVE ZERO TO ACCOUNT-TOTAL.
    MOVE ACCOUNT-NUMBER TO PREVIOUS-ACCOUNT-NUMBER.
    PERFORM C010-PROCESS-ACCOUNT-RECORD UNTIL
            ACCOUNT-NUMBER IS NOT EQUAL TO PREVIOUS-ACCOUNT
        OR  NO-MORE-DATA
        OR  SEQUENCE-ERROR-FLAG = 'Y'.
    IF SEQUENCE-ERROR-FLAG = 'N'
        MOVE SPACES TO DETAIL-LINE
        MOVE PREVIOUS-ACCOUNT-NUMBER TO ACCOUNT-NUMBER-OUT
        MOVE ACCOUNT-TOTAL TO ACCOUNT-TOTAL-OUT
        PERFORM X010-LINE-OUT
        ADD ACCOUNT-TOTAL TO FINAL-TOTAL.
```

Finally, at the end of **C010-PROCESS-ACCOUNT-RECORD** add the following statement:

```
IF MORE-DATA-FLAG = 'Y'
    IF ACCOUNT-NUMBER IS LESS THAN PREVIOUS-ACCOUNT-NUMBER
        MOVE 'Y' TO SEQUENCE-ERROR-FLAG.
```

CHAPTER 10

1.

Decimal	Binary	Hexadecimal
7	111	7
8	1000	8
19	10011	13
23	10111	17
34	100010	22

3.

Hexadecimal	Binary	Decimal
4	100	4
B	1011	11
10	10000	16
14	10100	20

5. +123

   Packed: 0001 0010 0011 1100
   Display: 0011 0001 0011 0010 0011 0011

+1234

Packed: 0000 0001 0010 0011 0100 1100
Display: 0011 0001 0011 0010 0011 0011 0011 0100

-90345

Packed: 1001 0000 0011 0100 0101 1101
Display: 0011 1001 0011 0000 0011 0011 0011 0100 0111 0101

-6

Packed: 0110 1101
Display: 0111 0110

7.

Graphic Symbol	EBCDIC Code	ASCII Code
2	1111 0010	0011 0010
B	1100 0010	0100 0010
M	1101 0100	0100 1101
W	1110 0110	0101 0111
+	0100 1110	0010 1011
(	0100 1101	0010 1000

9.

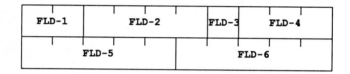

CHAPTER 11

1. Two possibilities:

```
IF COLUMN-23-CODE NOT = '1' AND NOT = '2' AND NOT = '3'
    MOVE 'X' TO INVALID-CODE-FLAG.

IF COLUMN-23-CODE = '1' OR '2' OR '3'
    NEXT SENTENCE
ELSE
    MOVE 'X' TO INVALID-CODE-FLAG.
```

3.
```
IF (SIZE-A   13 AND SIZE-A   37) AND SIZE-B   50
    ADD 1 TO REGULAR-COUNT
ELSE
    ADD 1 TO SPECIAL-COUNT.
```

5.

Modify C010-GET-ORDER-NUMBER as follows:

```
C010-GET-ORDER-NUMBER.
    MOVE 'N' TO VALID-ORDER-NUMBER.
    PERFORM D005-GET-VALID-ORDER-NUMBER
        UNTIL VALID-ORDER-NUMBER = 'Y'.
      .
      .
      .
```

```
    D005-GET-VALID-ORDER-NUMBER.
        DISPLAY 'Enter order number:'          AT 0101
            WITH BLANK SCREEN.
        ACCEPT ORDER-NUMBER OF ORDER-DATA      AT 0125.
        IF ORDER-NUMBER OF ORDER-DATA IS NOT NUMERIC
            DISPLAY 'ORDER NUMBER CONTAINS '   AT 0225
            DISPLAY 'A NON-NUMERIC CHARACTER' AT 0247
            DISPLAY 'PLEASE RE-ENTER THE ORDER NUMBER'
                                               AT 0325
        ELSE
            DISPLAY '                        '  AT 0225
            DISPLAY '                       '  AT 0247
            DISPLAY '                              '
                                               AT 0325
        MOVE 'Y' TO VALID-ORDER-NUMBER.


 9.
IDENTIFICATION DIVISION.
PROGRAM-ID.
    C11EX09.


ENVIRONMENT DIVISION.
INPUT-OUTPUT SECTION.
FILE-CONTROL.
    SELECT ORDER-FILE                 ASSIGN TO 'C11EX09.ORD'.
    SELECT NORMAL-HANDLING-FILE        ASSIGN TO 'C11EX09.NOR'.
    SELECT SPECIAL-HANDLING-FILE       ASSIGN TO 'C11EX09.SPE'.


DATA DIVISION.


FILE SECTION.
FD  ORDER-FILE
    LABEL RECORDS ARE STANDARD.
01  ORDER-RECORD.
    05  ORDER-NUMBER              PIC X(6).
    05  RECORD-TYPE               PIC X.
    05  CATALOG-NUMBER.
        10  CATALOG-FIRST-DIGIT   PIC X.
        10  CATALOG-REMAINING     PIC X(4).
    05  SIZE-CODE                 PIC X.
    05  QUANTITY                  PIC 99.
    05  ITEM-DESCRIPTION          PIC X(40).
    05  X-PRICE                   PIC X(5).
    05  9-PRICE REDEFINES X-PRICE PIC 999V99.
    05  FILLER                    PIC X(20).


FD  NORMAL-HANDLING-FILE
    LABEL RECORDS ARE STANDARD.
01  NORMAL-LINE                   PIC X(132).


FD  SPECIAL-HANDLING-FILE
    LABEL RECORDS ARE STANDARD.
01  SPECIAL-LINE                  PIC X(132).


WORKING-STORAGE SECTION.
01  ERROR-FLAGS.
    88  RECORD-OK                            VALUE SPACES.
```

```
        05  CAT-NO-NOT-NUMERIC              PIC X.
        05  FIRST-DIGIT-INVALID            PIC X.
        05  SIZE-CODE-NOT-PERMITTED        PIC X.
        05  NO-SUCH-SIZE-CODE              PIC X.
        05  QUANTITY-AND-PRICE-CODES.
            88  QTY-AND-PRICE-OK                      VALUE SPACES.
            10  QTY-NOT-NUMERIC            PIC X.
            10  PRICE-NOT-NUMERIC          PIC X.
        05  INVALID-PRICE-OR-QTY           PIC X.
        05  LARGE-PRICE                    PIC X.

    01  ERROR-MESSAGES.
        05  CAT-NO-NOT-NUMERIC-MSG         PIC X(50)
            VALUE ' CATALOG NUMBER CONTAINS AN IMPROPER CHARACTER'.
        05  FIRST-DIGIT-INVALID-MSG        PIC X(50)
            VALUE ' FIRST DIGIT OF CATALOG NUMBER INVALID'.
        05  SIZE-CODE-NOT-PERMITTED-MSG    PIC X(50)
            VALUE ' THIS ITEM DOES NOT TAKE A SIZE CODE'.
        05  NO-SUCH-SIZE-CODE-MSG          PIC X(50)
            VALUE ' THERE IS NO SUCH SIZE CODE'.
        05  QTY-NOT-NUMERIC-MSG            PIC X(50)
            VALUE ' QUANTITY CONTAINS AN IMPROPER CHARACTER'.
        05  PRICE-NOT-NUMERIC-MSG          PIC X(50)
            VALUE ' PRICE CONTAINS AN IMPROPER CHARACTER'.
        05  INVALID-PRICE-OR-QTY-MSG       PIC X(50)
            VALUE ' EITHER PRICE OR QUANTITY IS WRONG'.
        05  LARGE-PRICE-MSG                PIC X(50)
            VALUE ' PRICE LARGE - SHOULD BE CHECKED'.

    01  MORE-DATA-REMAINS-FLAG             PIC X     VALUE 'Y'.
        88  NO-MORE-DATA-REMAINS                     VALUE 'N'.

    01  OUTPUT-LINE.
        05  ORDER-NUMBER                   PIC Z(5)9.
        05  CATALOG-NUMBER.
            10  CATALOG-FIRST-DIGIT        PIC BBX.
            10  CATALOG-REMAINING          PIC BX(4).
        05  SIZE-CODE                      PIC BX.
        05  QUANTITY                       PIC BBZ9.
        05  OUTPUT-PRICE                   PIC BB$$$$9.99.
        05  ITEM-DESCRIPTION               PIC BBX(40).
        05  FILLER                         PIC X(59) VALUE SPACES.

    01  PRICE-LIMIT                        PIC  999V99 VALUE 150.00.
    01  TEST-REMAINDER                     PIC S999V99 COMP-3.
    01  UNIT-PRICE                         PIC S999V99 COMP-3.

    PROCEDURE DIVISION.
    A000-VALIDATE-ORDERS.
        OPEN INPUT  ORDER-FILE
             OUTPUT NORMAL-HANDLING-FILE
                    SPECIAL-HANDLING-FILE.
        READ ORDER-FILE
             AT END MOVE 'N' TO MORE-DATA-REMAINS-FLAG.
        PERFORM B010-VALIDATE-ONE-LINE
             UNTIL NO-MORE-DATA-REMAINS.
        CLOSE ORDER-FILE
             NORMAL-HANDLING-FILE
             SPECIAL-HANDLING-FILE.
        STOP RUN.
```

```
B010-VALIDATE-ONE-LINE.
    MOVE SPACES TO ERROR-FLAGS.
    PERFORM C010-EDIT-LINE.

    IF QTY-AND-PRICE-OK
        MOVE CORRESPONDING ORDER-RECORD TO OUTPUT-LINE
        MOVE 9-PRICE TO OUTPUT-PRICE
        IF RECORD-OK
            WRITE NORMAL-LINE FROM OUTPUT-LINE
                    AFTER ADVANCING 2 LINES
        ELSE
            WRITE SPECIAL-LINE FROM OUTPUT-LINE
                    AFTER ADVANCING 2 LINES
            PERFORM C020-WRITE-MESSAGES
    ELSE
        WRITE SPECIAL-LINE FROM ORDER-RECORD
                AFTER ADVANCING 2 LINES
        PERFORM C020-WRITE-MESSAGES.

    READ ORDER-FILE
            AT END MOVE 'N' TO MORE-DATA-REMAINS-FLAG.

C010-EDIT-LINE.
    IF CATALOG-NUMBER OF ORDER-RECORD IS NOT NUMERIC
        MOVE 'X' TO CAT-NO-NOT-NUMERIC.

    IF CATALOG-FIRST-DIGIT OF ORDER-RECORD = '0' OR '2'
        MOVE 'X' TO FIRST-DIGIT-INVALID.

    IF (CATALOG-FIRST-DIGIT OF ORDER-RECORD = '1' OR '8' OR '9')
        AND SIZE-CODE OF ORDER-RECORD IS NOT EQUAL TO SPACES
        MOVE 'X' TO SIZE-CODE-NOT-PERMITTED.

    IF SIZE-CODE OF ORDER-RECORD = 'A' OR 'D' OR 'G' OR 'J'
        OR 'K' OR 'L' OR 'S' OR 'T' OR 'U' OR ' '
        NEXT SENTENCE
    ELSE
        MOVE 'X' TO NO-SUCH-SIZE-CODE.

    IF QUANTITY OF ORDER-RECORD IS NOT NUMERIC
        MOVE 'X' TO QTY-NOT-NUMERIC.

    IF X-PRICE NOT NUMERIC
        MOVE 'X' TO PRICE-NOT-NUMERIC.

    IF QTY-AND-PRICE-OK
        DIVIDE 9-PRICE BY QUANTITY OF ORDER-RECORD
                GIVING UNIT-PRICE REMAINDER TEST-REMAINDER
                ON SIZE ERROR MOVE 'X' TO INVALID-PRICE-OR-QTY.
    IF QTY-AND-PRICE-OK AND TEST-REMAINDER NOT EQUAL TO ZERO
        MOVE 'X' TO INVALID-PRICE-OR-QTY.

    IF X-PRICE IS NUMERIC AND 9-PRICE GREATER THAN PRICE-LIMIT
        MOVE 'X' TO LARGE-PRICE.

C020-WRITE-MESSAGES.
    IF CAT-NO-NOT-NUMERIC = 'X'
        WRITE SPECIAL-LINE FROM CAT-NO-NOT-NUMERIC-MSG
                AFTER ADVANCING 1 LINES.
    IF FIRST-DIGIT-INVALID = 'X'
        WRITE SPECIAL-LINE FROM FIRST-DIGIT-INVALID-MSG
                AFTER ADVANCING 1 LINES.
```

```
                IF SIZE-CODE-NOT-PERMITTED = 'X'
                    WRITE SPECIAL-LINE FROM SIZE-CODE-NOT-PERMITTED-MSG
                                AFTER ADVANCING 1 LINES.
                IF NO-SUCH-SIZE-CODE = 'X'
                    WRITE SPECIAL-LINE FROM NO-SUCH-SIZE-CODE-MSG
                                AFTER ADVANCING 1 LINES.
                IF QTY-NOT-NUMERIC = 'X'
                    WRITE SPECIAL-LINE FROM QTY-NOT-NUMERIC-MSG
                                AFTER ADVANCING 1 LINES.
                IF PRICE-NOT-NUMERIC = 'X'
                    WRITE SPECIAL-LINE FROM PRICE-NOT-NUMERIC-MSG
                                AFTER ADVANCING 1 LINES.
                IF INVALID-PRICE-OR-QTY = 'X'
                    WRITE SPECIAL-LINE FROM INVALID-PRICE-OR-QTY-MSG
                                AFTER ADVANCING 1 LINES.
                IF LARGE-PRICE = 'X'
                    WRITE SPECIAL-LINE FROM LARGE-PRICE-MSG
                                AFTER ADVANCING 1 LINES.


      *************** END OF PROGRAM *********************************
```

CHAPTER 12

1. Change paragraphs B010-MAIN-MENU-DRIVER and C010-UPDATE--PRODUCT-CODE as shown. Add C005-GET-VALID-SELECTION and D005-GET-VALID-UPDATE-SELECT.

```
    B010-MAIN-MENU-DRIVER.
    *       DISPLAY THE MAIN MENU SCREEN
            DISPLAY MAIN-MENU.
    *       GET THE SELECTION VARIABLE
            MOVE 'N' TO VALID-SELECTION-FLAG.
            PERFORM C005-GET-VALID-SELECTION
                  UNTIL VALID-SELECTION.
    *       EXECUTE THE SELECTED TASK
            IF      SELECTION = '1'
                MOVE 'N' TO END-PRODUCT-UPDATE-FLAG
                PERFORM C010-UPDATE-PRODUCT-FILE
                      UNTIL END-PRODUCT-UPDATE-FLAG = 'Y'
            ELSE IF SELECTION = '2'
                PERFORM C020-UPDATE-MAILING-FILE
            ELSE IF SELECTION = '3'
                PERFORM C030-SPECIAL-HANDLING
            ELSE IF SELECTION = '4'
                PERFORM C040-SHIP-ORDERS
            ELSE IF SELECTION = '5'
                PERFORM C050-PRODUCE-REPORTS
            ELSE IF SELECTION = '6'
                PERFORM C060-VALIDATE-ORDERS
            ELSE
                MOVE 'Y' TO TERMINATE-FLAG.

    C005-GET-VALID-SELECTION.
            ACCEPT SELECTION                 AT 2048
                                        WITH REVERSE-VIDEO.
            IF SELECTION = '1' OR '2' OR '3' OR '4' OR '5' OR '6' OR
                        'Q' OR 'q' THEN
                MOVE 'Y' TO VALID-SELECTION-FLAG
```

```
            ELSE
                DISPLAY MAIN-SELECTION-ERROR
                                          AT 2228
                                          WITH BACKGROUND-COLOR 5
                                               FOREGROUND-COLOR 7.


    C010-UPDATE-PRODUCT-FILE.
        DISPLAY UPDATE-PRODUCT-MENU.
        MOVE 'N' TO VALID-SELECTION-FLAG.
        PERFORM D005-GET-VALID-UPDATE-SELECT
                UNTIL VALID-SELECTION.
        IF        SELECTION = '1'
            PERFORM D010-ADD-PRODUCT-RECORD
        ELSE IF SELECTION = '2'
            PERFORM D020-CHANGE-PRODUCT-RECORD
        ELSE IF SELECTION = '3'
            PERFORM D030-DELETE-PRODUCT-RECORD
        ELSE
            MOVE 'Y' TO END-PRODUCT-UPDATE-FLAG.


    D005-GET-VALID-UPDATE-SELECT.
        ACCEPT SELECTION              AT 1748
                                      WITH REVERSE-VIDEO
        IF SELECTION = '1' OR '2' OR '3' OR 'Q' OR 'q' THEN
            MOVE 'Y' TO VALID-SELECTION-FLAG
        ELSE
            DISPLAY UPDATE-PRODUCT-SELECTION-ERROR
                                      AT 1928
                                      WITH BACKGROUND-COLOR 5
                                           FOREGROUND-COLOR 7.



    3.
    IDENTIFICATION DIVISION.
    PROGRAM-ID.
        C12EX03.


    ENVIRONMENT DIVISION.
    INPUT-OUTPUT SECTION.
    FILE-CONTROL.
        SELECT REPORT-FILE        ASSIGN TO 'C12EX03.REP'.


    DATA DIVISION.
    FILE SECTION.
    FD  REPORT-FILE
        LABEL RECORDS ARE STANDARD.
    01  REPORT-RECORD             PIC X(75).


    WORKING-STORAGE SECTION.
    77  C-EXEMPTION              PIC  S99V99  VALUE +50.00.
    77  C-TAXRATE                PIC    SV999 VALUE +.210.
    77  W-DEPENDENTS             PIC 99.
    77  W-EXEMPTION-TOTAL        PIC S999V99.
    77  W-GROSS-PAY              PIC S999V99.
    77  W-GROSS-PAY-FLAG         PIC X.
        88  GROSS-PAY-VALID                    VALUE 'Y'.
        88  GROSS-PAY-INVALID                  VALUE 'N'.
        88  GROSS-PAY-REJECTED                 VALUE 'R'.
    77  W-HOURS-WORKED           PIC 99V9.
    77  W-NAME                   PIC X(20).
    77  W-NET-PAY                PIC S999V99.
```

```
77  W-OVERTIME-HOURS                 PIC  S99V99.
77  W-OVERTIME-PAY                   PIC  S999V99.
77  W-PAYROLL-NUMBER                 PIC  9(5).
    88  END-OF-DATA                                  VALUE 99999.
77  W-PAYRATE                        PIC  99V999.
77  W-SELECTION                      PIC  X.
77  W-TAX                            PIC  S999V99.
77  W-TAXABLE                        PIC  S999V99.
77  W-TODAYS-DATE                    PIC  9(6).
77  W-VALID-SELECTION                PIC  X.


01  HEADING-LINE-1.
    05  FILLER                       PIC X(26)
        VALUE 'PAYROLL CALCULATION REPORT'.
    05  FILLER                       PIC X(41)     VALUE SPACES.
    05  REPORT-DATE                  PIC 99/99/99 VALUE ZERO.


01  HEADING-LINE-2.
    05  FILLER                       PIC X(42)
        VALUE 'NUMBER           NAME              HOURS  RATE '.
    05  FILLER                       PIC X(29)
        VALUE ' DEP   GROSS      TAX     NET'.


01  PAYROLL-LINE.
    05  O-PAYROLL-NUMBER             PIC X(5).
    05  O-NAME                       PIC BBX(20).
    05  O-HOURS-WORKED               PIC BBZ9.9.
    05  O-PAYRATE                    PIC BBZ9.999.
    05  O-DEPENDENTS                 PIC BBZ9.
    05  O-GROSS-PAY                  PIC BB$$$9.99.
    05  O-TAX                        PIC BB$$$9.99.
    05  O-NET-PAY                    PIC BB$$$9.99.

SCREEN SECTION.
01  PAYROLL-DATA-SCREEN
        BACKGROUND-COLOR IS 1
        FOREGROUND-COLOR IS 7.
    05  VALUE 'PAYROLL DATA ENTRY'
        BLANK SCREEN
        HIGHLIGHT
        LINE 5    COLUMN 32.
    05  VALUE 'pay number:'
        LINE 8    COLUMN 11.
    05  SCREEN-PAYROLL-NUMBER    PIC 9(5)
        TO W-PAYROLL-NUMBER
        REVERSE-VIDEO
        COLUMN + 3.
    05  VALUE 'name:'
        COLUMN 34.
    05  SCREEN-NAME              PIC X(20)
        TO W-NAME
        REVERSE-VIDEO
        COLUMN + 3.
    05  VALUE 'hours:'
        LINE + 2    COLUMN 11.
    05  SCREEN-HOURS-WORKED      PIC Z9.9
        TO W-HOURS-WORKED
        REVERSE-VIDEO
        COLUMN + 3.
```

```
      05   VALUE 'rate:'
           COLUMN 28.
      05   SCREEN-PAYRATE              PIC Z9.999
           TO W-PAYRATE
           REVERSE-VIDEO
           COLUMN + 3.
      05   VALUE 'dependents:'
           COLUMN 46.
      05   SCREEN-DEPENDENTS           PIC Z9
           TO W-DEPENDENTS
           REVERSE-VIDEO
           COLUMN + 3.

 01   OVERFLOW-SCREEN
           BACKGROUND-COLOR IS 1
           FOREGROUND-COLOR IS 7.
      05   VALUE "Employee's gross pay is too large."
           LINE 12    COLUMN 11.
      05   VALUE 'Select one of the following options:'
           LINE + 1   COLUMN 11.
      05   VALUE 'A - accept data as entered and continue'
           LINE + 2   COLUMN 16.
      05   VALUE "R - reject this employee's data"
           LINE + 1   COLUMN 16.
      05   VALUE '(employee will not be processed)'
                      COLUMN + 2.
      05   VALUE 'H - change the hours worked'
           LINE + 1   COLUMN 16.
      05   VALUE 'P - change the pay rate'
           LINE + 1   COLUMN 16.
      05   VALUE 'B - change both hours worked and pay rate'
           LINE + 1   COLUMN 16.


 PROCEDURE DIVISION.
 A000-PRODUCE-PAYROLL-CALC.
     OPEN OUTPUT REPORT-FILE.
     PERFORM B010-PRINT-COLUMN-HEADINGS.
     PERFORM C010-GET-PAYROLL-DATA.
     PERFORM B020-CALC-EMP-PAYROLL
         UNTIL END-OF-DATA.
     CLOSE REPORT-FILE.
     STOP RUN.


 B010-PRINT-COLUMN-HEADINGS.
     ACCEPT W-TODAYS-DATE FROM DATE.
     MOVE W-TODAYS-DATE TO REPORT-DATE.
     WRITE REPORT-RECORD FROM HEADING-LINE-1.
     MOVE SPACES TO REPORT-RECORD.
     WRITE REPORT-RECORD.
     WRITE REPORT-RECORD FROM HEADING-LINE-2.
     MOVE SPACES TO REPORT-RECORD.
     WRITE REPORT-RECORD.
     MOVE SPACES TO REPORT-RECORD.
     WRITE REPORT-RECORD.


 B020-CALC-EMP-PAYROLL.
     MOVE '?' TO W-GROSS-PAY-FLAG.
     PERFORM C020-COMPUTE-GROSS-PAY
             UNTIL    GROSS-PAY-VALID
                   OR GROSS-PAY-REJECTED.
```

```
        IF GROSS-PAY-VALID
            PERFORM C030-COMPUTE-EXEMPTIONS
            PERFORM C040-COMPUTE-TAX
            PERFORM C050-COMPUTE-NET-PAY
            PERFORM C060-PRINT-OUTPUT.
        PERFORM C010-GET-PAYROLL-DATA.


    C010-GET-PAYROLL-DATA.
        DISPLAY PAYROLL-DATA-SCREEN.
        ACCEPT SCREEN-PAYROLL-NUMBER.
        IF NOT END-OF-DATA
            ACCEPT SCREEN-NAME
            ACCEPT SCREEN-HOURS-WORKED
            ACCEPT SCREEN-PAYRATE
            ACCEPT SCREEN-DEPENDENTS
        ELSE
            DISPLAY 'Run Terminated'           AT 1432
                                               WITH HIGHLIGHT.


    C020-COMPUTE-GROSS-PAY.
        MOVE 'Y' TO W-GROSS-PAY-FLAG.
        MULTIPLY W-HOURS-WORKED BY W-PAYRATE
                GIVING W-GROSS-PAY ROUNDED
                    ON SIZE ERROR MOVE 'N' TO W-GROSS-PAY-FLAG.
        IF GROSS-PAY-INVALID
            PERFORM D010-BASE-PAY-OVERFLOW
        ELSE
            PERFORM D020-COMPUTE-OVERTIME
            IF GROSS-PAY-INVALID
                PERFORM D030-OVERTIME-PAY-OVERFLOW.


    C030-COMPUTE-EXEMPTIONS.
        MULTIPLY C-EXEMPTION BY W-DEPENDENTS
                GIVING W-EXEMPTION-TOTAL.


    C040-COMPUTE-TAX.
        IF W-GROSS-PAY IS GREATER THAN W-EXEMPTION-TOTAL
            SUBTRACT W-EXEMPTION-TOTAL FROM W-GROSS-PAY
                    GIVING W-TAXABLE
            MULTIPLY C-TAXRATE BY W-TAXABLE GIVING W-TAX ROUNDED
        ELSE
            MOVE ZERO TO W-TAX.


    C050-COMPUTE-NET-PAY.
        SUBTRACT W-TAX FROM W-GROSS-PAY GIVING W-NET-PAY.


    C060-PRINT-OUTPUT.
        MOVE SPACES                TO PAYROLL-LINE.
        MOVE W-PAYROLL-NUMBER      TO O-PAYROLL-NUMBER.
        MOVE W-NAME                TO O-NAME.
        MOVE W-HOURS-WORKED        TO O-HOURS-WORKED.
        MOVE W-PAYRATE             TO O-PAYRATE.
        MOVE W-DEPENDENTS          TO O-DEPENDENTS.
        MOVE W-TAX                 TO O-TAX.
        MOVE W-GROSS-PAY           TO O-GROSS-PAY.
        MOVE W-NET-PAY             TO O-NET-PAY.
        WRITE REPORT-RECORD FROM PAYROLL-LINE.


    D010-BASE-PAY-OVERFLOW.
        DISPLAY OVERFLOW-SCREEN.
```

```
        MOVE 'N' TO W-VALID-SELECTION.
        PERFORM E010-GET-VALID-SELECTION
              UNTIL W-VALID-SELECTION = 'Y'.
        IF      W-SELECTION = 'A' OR 'a'
           PERFORM D020-COMPUTE-OVERTIME
           MOVE 'Y' TO W-GROSS-PAY-FLAG
        ELSE IF W-SELECTION = 'R' OR 'r'
           MOVE 'R' TO W-GROSS-PAY-FLAG
        ELSE IF W-SELECTION = 'H' OR 'h'
           DISPLAY 'hours:'                  AT 1011 WITH BLINK
           ACCEPT SCREEN-HOURS-WORKED
           DISPLAY 'hours:'                  AT 1011
        ELSE IF W-SELECTION = 'P' OR 'p'
           DISPLAY 'rate:'                   AT 1028 WITH BLINK
           ACCEPT SCREEN-PAYRATE
           DISPLAY 'rate:'                   AT 1028
        ELSE IF W-SELECTION = 'B' OR 'b'
           DISPLAY 'hours:'                  AT 1011 WITH BLINK
           ACCEPT SCREEN-HOURS-WORKED
           DISPLAY 'hours:'                  AT 1011
           DISPLAY 'rate:'                   AT 1028 WITH BLINK
           ACCEPT SCREEN-PAYRATE
           DISPLAY 'rate:'                   AT 1028.

   D020-COMPUTE-OVERTIME.
        IF W-HOURS-WORKED IS GREATER THAN 40
           SUBTRACT 40 FROM W-HOURS-WORKED GIVING W-OVERTIME-HOURS
           MULTIPLY 0.5 BY W-OVERTIME-HOURS
           MULTIPLY W-OVERTIME-HOURS BY W-PAYRATE
                 GIVING W-OVERTIME-PAY ROUNDED
           ADD W-OVERTIME-PAY TO W-GROSS-PAY
                 ON SIZE ERROR MOVE 'N' TO W-GROSS-PAY-FLAG.

   D030-OVERTIME-PAY-OVERFLOW.
        DISPLAY OVERFLOW-SCREEN.
        MOVE 'N' TO W-VALID-SELECTION.
        PERFORM E010-GET-VALID-SELECTION
              UNTIL W-VALID-SELECTION = 'Y'.
        IF      W-SELECTION = 'A' OR 'a'
           MOVE 'Y' TO W-GROSS-PAY-FLAG
        ELSE IF W-SELECTION = 'R' OR 'r'
           MOVE 'R' TO W-GROSS-PAY-FLAG
        ELSE IF W-SELECTION = 'H' OR 'h'
           DISPLAY 'hours:'                  AT 1011 WITH BLINK
           ACCEPT SCREEN-HOURS-WORKED
           DISPLAY 'hours:'                  AT 1011
        ELSE IF W-SELECTION = 'P' OR 'p'
           DISPLAY 'rate:'                   AT 1028 WITH BLINK
           ACCEPT SCREEN-PAYRATE
           DISPLAY 'rate:'                   AT 1028
        ELSE IF W-SELECTION = 'B' OR 'b'
           DISPLAY 'hours:'                  AT 1011 WITH BLINK
           ACCEPT SCREEN-HOURS-WORKED
           DISPLAY 'hours:'                  AT 1011
           DISPLAY 'rate:'                   AT 1028 WITH BLINK
           ACCEPT SCREEN-PAYRATE
           DISPLAY 'rate:'                   AT 1028.
```

```
E010-GET-VALID-SELECTION.
    ACCEPT W-SELECTION                          AT 2111
            WITH BACKGROUND-COLOR 1.
    IF W-SELECTION = 'A' OR 'a' OR 'R' OR 'r' OR 'H' OR 'h' OR
                     'P' OR 'p' OR 'B' OR 'b'
        MOVE 'Y' TO W-VALID-SELECTION
    ELSE
        DISPLAY 'Selection must be one of the options above.'
                                                AT 2311.
```

CHAPTER 13

1.

open files
set KEY-1, KEY-2, PREVIOUS-KEY-1, and PREVIOUS-KEY-2 to low values
set sequence error flag and duplicate key flag to false
get FILE-1 record
get FILE-2 record
PERFORM-UNTIL (KEY-1 = high values and KEY-2 = high values)
        or a sequence error is detected
        or duplicate keys are detected
    IF KEY-1 = KEY-2 THEN
        set duplicate key flag
    ELSE
        IF KEY-1 is less than KEY-2 THEN
            write the FILE-1 record
            get FILE-1 record
        ELSE
            write the FILE-2 record
            get FILE-2 record
        ENDIF
    ENDIF
ENDPERFORM
IF a sequence error was detected THEN
    write an error message
ENDIF
IF duplicate keys were detected THEN
    write an error message
ENDIF
close files
stop

GET FILE-X RECORD:
    read a record from FILE-X; at end set KEY-X to high values
    IF KEY-X is less than PREVIOUS-KEY-X THEN
        set the sequence error flag
    ELSE
        move KEY-X to PREVIOUS-KEY-X
    ENDIF

3. The main work is in **B010-MERGE-RECORD**. This logic can be accomplished in many other ways, but make sure that your solution processes duplicates correctly. Try it on the following data. (Since the data is defined as **PIC X(5)**, be sure that the numbers are right-justified.)

```
      KEY-1    KEY-2    KEY-3
        1        1        2
        1        3        2
        4        3        3
        4        5        5
        6        5        6
        8        8        7
        8        9       10
       10       10       10
       11       11       11
```

```
   IDENTIFICATION DIVISION.
   PROGRAM-ID.
       C13EX03.

*      MERGE WITH SEQUENCE CHECKING

   ENVIRONMENT DIVISION.
   INPUT-OUTPUT SECTION.
   FILE-CONTROL.
       SELECT IN-FILE-1            ASSIGN TO FILE1.
       SELECT IN-FILE-2            ASSIGN TO FILE2.
       SELECT IN-FILE-3            ASSIGN TO FILE3.
       SELECT OUT-FILE             ASSIGN TO OUTFILE.

   DATA DIVISION.
   FILE SECTION.

   FD  IN-FILE-1
       LABEL RECORDS ARE STANDARD.
   01  IN-RECORD-1                 PIC X(80).

   FD  IN-FILE-2
       LABEL RECORDS ARE STANDARD.
   01  IN-RECORD-2                 PIC X(80).

   FD  IN-FILE-3
       LABEL RECORDS ARE STANDARD.
   01  IN-RECORD-3                 PIC X(80).

   FD  OUT-FILE
       LABEL RECORDS ARE STANDARD.
   01  OUT-RECORD                  PIC X(80).

   WORKING-STORAGE SECTION.

   01  W-IN-RECORD-1.
       05  KEY-1                   PIC X(5).
       05  REST-OF-RECORD-1        PIC X(75).

   01  W-IN-RECORD-2.
       05  KEY-2                   PIC X(5).
       05  REST-OF-RECORD-2        PIC X(75).

   01  W-IN-RECORD-3.
       05  KEY-3                   PIC X(5).
       05  REST-OF-RECORD-3        PIC X(75).
```

```
01    PREVIOUS-KEY-1              PIC X(5) VALUE LOW-VALUES.
01    PREVIOUS-KEY-2              PIC X(5) VALUE LOW-VALUES.
01    PREVIOUS-KEY-3              PIC X(5) VALUE LOW-VALUES.

01    SEQUENCE-ERROR-FLAG         PIC X VALUE 'N'.
      88  SEQUENCE-ERROR              VALUE 'Y'.


PROCEDURE DIVISION.
A000-MERGE-3-FILES.
    OPEN INPUT IN-FILE-1
               IN-FILE-2
               IN-FILE-3
        OUTPUT OUT-FILE.
    PERFORM X010-READ-1.
    PERFORM X020-READ-2.
    PERFORM X030-READ-3.
    PERFORM B010-MERGE-RECORD
        UNTIL  (KEY-1 = HIGH-VALUES
            AND KEY-2 = HIGH-VALUES
            AND KEY-3 = HIGH-VALUES)
            OR  SEQUENCE-ERROR.
    IF SEQUENCE-ERROR
        DISPLAY 'SEQUENCE ERROR - JOB ABORTED'.
    CLOSE IN-FILE-1
          IN-FILE-2
          IN-FILE-3
          OUT-FILE.
    STOP RUN.

B010-MERGE-RECORD.
    IF (KEY-1 > KEY-2 AND KEY-1 > KEY-3)
        WRITE OUT-RECORD FROM W-IN-RECORD-1
        PERFORM X010-READ-1
    ELSE
        IF (KEY-2 NOT > KEY-1 AND KEY-2 > KEY-3)
            WRITE OUT-RECORD FROM W-IN-RECORD-2
            PERFORM X020-READ-2
        ELSE
            WRITE OUT-RECORD FROM W-IN-RECORD-3
            PERFORM X030-READ-3.

X010-READ-1.
    READ IN-FILE-1 INTO W-IN-RECORD-1
        AT END MOVE HIGH-VALUES TO KEY-1.
    IF KEY-1 IS LESS THAN PREVIOUS-KEY-1
        MOVE 'Y' TO SEQUENCE-ERROR-FLAG
    ELSE
        MOVE KEY-1 TO PREVIOUS-KEY-1.

X020-READ-2.
    READ IN-FILE-2 INTO W-IN-RECORD-2
        AT END MOVE HIGH-VALUES TO KEY-2.
    IF KEY-2 IS LESS THAN PREVIOUS-KEY-2
        MOVE 'Y' TO SEQUENCE-ERROR-FLAG
    ELSE
        MOVE KEY-2 TO PREVIOUS-KEY-2.

X030-READ-3.
    READ IN-FILE-3 INTO W-IN-RECORD-3
        AT END MOVE HIGH-VALUES TO KEY-3.
```

```
        IF KEY-3 IS LESS THAN PREVIOUS-KEY-3
            MOVE 'Y' TO SEQUENCE-ERROR-FLAG
        ELSE
            MOVE KEY-3 TO PREVIOUS-KEY-3.
```

5.

```
IDENTIFICATION DIVISION.
PROGRAM-ID.
    C13EX05.


ENVIRONMENT DIVISION.
INPUT-OUTPUT SECTION.
FILE-CONTROL.
    SELECT TRANSACTION-FILE            ASSIGN TO TRANS.
    SELECT OLD-MASTER-FILE             ASSIGN TO OLDMAST.
    SELECT NEW-MASTER-FILE             ASSIGN TO NEWMAST.
    SELECT DELETION-FILE               ASSIGN TO DELETION.


DATA DIVISION.

FILE SECTION.

FD  TRANSACTION-FILE
    LABEL RECORDS ARE STANDARD.
01  TRANSACTION-BUFFER                 PIC X(80).


FD  OLD-MASTER-FILE
    LABEL RECORDS ARE STANDARD.
01  OLD-MASTER-BUFFER                  PIC X(80).


FD  NEW-MASTER-FILE
    LABEL RECORDS ARE STANDARD.
01  NEW-MASTER.
    05  NM-KEY                         PIC X(5).
    05  NM-QUANTITY                    PIC 9(5).
    05  FILLER                         PIC X(70).


FD  DELETION-FILE
    LABEL RECORDS ARE STANDARD.
01  DELETION-REPORT.
    05  CARRIAGE-CONTROL               PIC X.
    05  DELETION-LINE                  PIC X(132).


WORKING-STORAGE SECTION.

01  OLD-MASTER.
    05  OM-KEY                         PIC X(5).
    05  OM-QUANTITY                    PIC 9(5).
    05  FILLER                         PIC X(70).


01  TRANSACTION.
    05  TR-KEY                         PIC X(5).
    05  TR-QUANTITY                    PIC 9(5).
    05  TR-TRANSACTION-CODE            PIC X.
        88  ADDITION                               VALUE '1'.
        88  ADJUSTMENT                             VALUE '2'.
        88  RECEIPT                                VALUE '3'.
        88  SHIPMENT                               VALUE '4'.
        88  DELETION                               VALUE '5'.
    05  FILLER                         PIC X(69).
```

```
01   HOLD-MASTER                          PIC X(80).

01   NEED-MASTER-FLAG                     PIC X VALUE 'Y'.
     88   NEED-MASTER                           VALUE 'Y'.


PROCEDURE DIVISION.
A000-UPDATE-FILE.
    OPEN INPUT TRANSACTION-FILE
              OLD-MASTER-FILE
         OUTPUT NEW-MASTER-FILE
              DELETION-FILE.
    PERFORM C010-GET-TRANSACTION.
    PERFORM C020-GET-MASTER.
    PERFORM B010-UPDATE-LOGIC
        UNTIL OM-KEY = HIGH-VALUES  AND  TR-KEY = HIGH-VALUES.
    CLOSE TRANSACTION-FILE
          OLD-MASTER-FILE
          NEW-MASTER-FILE
          DELETION-FILE.
    STOP RUN.

B010-UPDATE-LOGIC.
    IF OM-KEY IS LESS THAN TR-KEY
        WRITE NEW-MASTER FROM OLD-MASTER
        PERFORM C020-GET-MASTER
    ELSE
        IF OM-KEY = TR-KEY
            IF DELETION
                MOVE OLD-MASTER TO DELETION-LINE
                WRITE DELETION-REPORT AFTER ADVANCING 1 LINE
                PERFORM C010-GET-TRANSACTION
                PERFORM C020-GET-MASTER
            ELSE
                PERFORM C030-UPDATE-MASTER
                PERFORM C010-GET-TRANSACTION
        ELSE
            PERFORM D010-ADD-MASTER
            PERFORM C010-GET-TRANSACTION.

C010-GET-TRANSACTION.
    READ TRANSACTION-FILE INTO TRANSACTION
        AT END MOVE HIGH-VALUES TO TR-KEY.

C020-GET-MASTER.
    IF NEED-MASTER
        READ OLD-MASTER-FILE INTO OLD-MASTER
            AT END MOVE HIGH-VALUES TO OM-KEY
    ELSE
        MOVE HOLD-MASTER TO OLD-MASTER
        MOVE 'Y' TO NEED-MASTER-FLAG.

C030-UPDATE-MASTER.
    DISPLAY ' OM ', OM-KEY, ' TR ', TR-KEY.

D010-ADD-MASTER.
    MOVE OLD-MASTER TO HOLD-MASTER.
    MOVE 'N' TO NEED-MASTER-FLAG.
    MOVE  TR-KEY TO OM-KEY.
    MOVE TR-QUANTITY TO OM-QUANTITY.
    DISPLAY ' OM ', OM-KEY, ' NM ', TR-KEY.


******************* END OF PROGRAM ****************************
```

Notice what the changes involve. In the Working-Storage Section we define a place to hold a master record temporarily, and a flag to tell whether there is anything in this storage area. In the Procedure Division, instead of automatically writing the new master we execute **D010-ADD-MASTER** when an **ADDITION** transaction is processed. This paragraph saves the old master, sets the flag so that we know there is something in the hold area, and creates a new master. If the next transaction has the same key as this master, it is applied to the new master. Eventually, when the program gets another master record, we get the record from the hold area instead of reading one from the file and the flag is reset. Code such as this can be used to apply as many transaction records as necessary (including none) to a newly created master record.

6. In the Working-Storage Section, rename **SEQUENCE-ERROR-FLAG** as **MASTER-SEQUENCE-ERROR-FLAG** and initialize it to 'N'; add definitions for **XACT-SEQUENCE-ERROR-FLAG** and **XACT-SEQUENCE-ERROR-COUNT**, initialized to zero; change **TERMINATION-MSG** to show 100 errors; and add appropriate definitions for **MASTER-SEQUENCE-MSG** and **XACT-SEQUENCE-MSG**. Then make the following changes in the Procedure Division.

```
PERFORM B010-UPDATE-LOGIC
     UNTIL (OM-KEY = HIGH-VALUES  AND  TR-KEY = HIGH-VALUES)
             OR ERROR-COUNT IS GREATER THAN 100
             OR MASTER-SEQUENCE-ERROR-FLAG = 'Y'
             OR XACT-SEQUENCE-ERROR-COUNT IS GREATER THAN 10.
IF      ERROR-COUNT IS GREATER THAN 100
     WRITE LOG-RECORD FROM TERMINATION-MSG
             AFTER ADVANCING 1 LINE
ELSE IF MASTER-SEQUENCE-ERROR-FLAG = 'Y'
     WRITE LOG-RECORD FROM MASTER-SEQUENCE-MSG
             AFTER ADVANCING 1 LINE
ELSE IF XACT-SEQUENCE-ERROR-COUNT IS GREATER THAN 10
     WRITE LOG-RECORD FROM XACT-SEQUENCE-MSG
             AFTER ADVANCING 1 LINE.
```

Change **X010-GET-VALID-TRANSACTION** to test **XACT-SEQUENCE-ERROR-COUNT** instead of **ERROR-COUNT**.

Change **X020-GET-VALID-MASTER** as follows:

```
X020-GET-VALID-MASTER.
     READ OLD-MASTER-FILE INTO OLD-MASTER
         AT END MOVE HIGH-VALUES TO OM-KEY.
     IF OM-KEY IS LESS THAN OM-KEY-PREVIOUS
         MOVE 'Y' TO MASTER-SEQUENCE-ERROR-FLAG
     ELSE
         MOVE OM-KEY TO OM-KEY-PREVIOUS.
```

Change **Y010-READ-TRANSACTION** to increment **XACT-SEQUENCE-ERROR-COUNT** instead of **ERROR-COUNT**.

Delete **Y020-READ-MASTER**.

CHAPTER 14

```
1. ADD SET-UP (13) UNIT-TIME (13) GIVING JOB-TIME.

3. ADD AMOUNT TO SALES (SELLER-NUMBER).

5.      MOVE ZERO TO TOTAL.
        PERFORM D030-TOTALLER
            VARYING S-DAY FROM 1 BY 1
                    UNTIL S-DAY  5.
        DIVIDE TOTAL BY 5 GIVING AVERAGE-TIME.
        .
        .
        .

    D030-TOTALLER.
        ADD A-TIME (S-DAY) TO TOTAL.

7.      MOVE 1 TO BIG-SELLER.
        MOVE SALES (1) TO BIG-SALES.
        PERFORM C020-FIND-BIG
            VARYING SELLER FROM 2 BY 1
                    UNTIL SELLER  50.
        DISPLAY BIG-SELLER, ' ', BIG-SALES.
        .
        .
        .

    C020-FIND-BIG.
        IF SALES (SELLER)  BIG-SALES
            MOVE SELLER TO BIG-SELLER
            MOVE SALES (SELLER) TO BIG-SALES.

9.

WORKING-STORAGE SECTION.
01   STUDENT-NAME-VALUES.
     05   FILLER  PIC X(25) VALUE 'ANDERSON, JAMES G.       '.
     05   FILLER  PIC X(25) VALUE 'BRIDGES, SUSAN H.        '.
     05   FILLER  PIC X(25) VALUE 'BROWN, JUDITH F.         '.
     05   FILLER  PIC X(25) VALUE 'CASHMAN, FREDERICK P.    '.
     .
     .
     .

01   STUDENT-NAME-TABLE REDEFINES STUDENT-NAME-VALUES.
     05   STUDENT-NAME   PIC X(25) OCCURS 40 TIMES.

11.

    PERFORM C050-WRITE-A-LINE
        VARYING GRADE FROM 1 BY 1
                UNTIL GRADE  12.
        .
        .
        .

C050-WRITE-A-LINE.
    MOVE GRADE TO GRADE-OUT.
    MOVE SIZE-BY-GRADE-AND-YEAR (GRADE, 3) TO ENROLLMENT-OUT.
    WRITE OUTPUT-LINE.
```

13.

```
    PERFORM C050-WRITE-A-LINE
        VARYING GRADE FROM 1 BY 1
                UNTIL GRADE > 12.
     .
     .
     .

C050-WRITE-A-LINE.
    MOVE GRADE TO GRADE-OUT.
    ADD SIZE-BY-GRADE-AND-YEAR (GRADE, 1)
        SIZE-BY-GRADE-AND-YEAR (GRADE, 2)
        SIZE-BY-GRADE-AND-YEAR (GRADE, 3)
        SIZE-BY-GRADE-AND-YEAR (GRADE, 4)
        GIVING TOTAL-ENROLLMENT.
    DIVIDE TOTAL-ENROLLMENT BY 4
        GIVING AVERAGE-ENROLLMENT-OUT ROUNDED.
    WRITE OUTPUT-LINE.
```

15.

```
    READ YEAR-IN-FILE
        AT END MOVE 'N' TO MORE-DATA-REMAINS-FLAG.
    SUBTRACT 1987 FROM YEAR.
    MOVE 1 TO BIG-GRADE.
    MOVE SIZE-BY-GRADE-AND-YEAR (1, YEAR) TO BIG-ENROLLMENT.
    PERFORM C030-FIND-BIG
        VARYING GRADE FROM 2 BY 1
                UNTIL GRADE > 12.
    ADD 1987 TO YEAR.
    MOVE YEAR TO YEAR-OUT.
    MOVE BIG-GRADE TO BIG-GRADE-OUT.
    MOVE BIG-ENROLLMENT TO BIG-ENROLLMENT-OUT.
    WRITE OUTPUT-LINE.
     .
     .
     .

C030-FIND-BIG.
    IF SIZE-BY-GRADE-AND-YEAR (GRADE, YEAR) > BIG-ENROLLMENT
        MOVE GRADE TO BIG-GRADE
        MOVE SIZE-BY-GRADE-AND-YEAR (GRADE, YEAR)
                TO BIG-ENROLLMENT.
```

17. Add the following to Working-Storage.

```
01  OVERFLOW-FLAG               PIC X VALUE 'N'.
    88   NO-OVERFLOW                  VALUE 'N'.

01  OVERFLOW-MESSAGE.
    05  FILLER                  PIC X(34)
        VALUE 'TABLE OVERFLOW.  RUN TERMINATED.  '.
    05  FILLER                  PIC X(37)
        VALUE 'MODIFY PROGRAM TO ALLOW FOR AT LEAST '.
    05  NEW-TABLE-SIZE          PIC ZZ,ZZ9.
    05  FILLER                  PIC X(8) VALUE 'ENTRIES.'.
```

Change the Procedure Division as follows.

```
A000-VALIDATE-ORDERS.
    PERFORM B020-LOAD-VALID-NUMBER.
    IF NO-OVERFLOW
        PERFORM A010-CONTINUE-VALIDATION.
    STOP RUN.

A010-CONTINUE-VALIDATION.
    OPEN INPUT  ORDER-FILE
         OUTPUT NORMAL-HANDLING-FILE
                SPECIAL-HANDLING-FILE.
    MOVE 'Y' TO MORE-DATA-REMAINS-FLAG.
    READ ORDER-FILE
            AT END MOVE 'N' TO MORE-DATA-REMAINS-FLAG.
    PERFORM B010-VALIDATE-ONE-LINE
            UNTIL NO-MORE-DATA-REMAINS.
    CLOSE ORDER-FILE
          NORMAL-HANDLING-FILE
          SPECIAL-HANDLING-FILE.
    .
    .
    .

B020-LOAD-VALID-NUMBER.
    OPEN INPUT CATALOG-FILE.
    MOVE 'Y' TO MORE-DATA-REMAINS-FLAG.
    MOVE ZERO TO X-CATALOG.
    READ CATALOG-FILE
            AT END MOVE 'N' TO MORE-DATA-REMAINS-FLAG.
    PERFORM C030-LOAD-CATALOG-RECORD
            UNTIL  NO-MORE-DATA-REMAINS.
    CLOSE CATALOG-FILE.
    IF X-CATALOG  VALID-NUMBER-MAX
        MOVE X-CATALOG TO NEW-TABLE-SIZE
        DISPLAY OVERFLOW-MESSAGE
        MOVE 'Y' TO OVERFLOW-FLAG
    ELSE
        MOVE X-CATALOG TO VALID-NUMBER-MAX.
    .
    .
    .

C030-LOAD-CATALOG-RECORD.
    ADD 1 TO X-CATALOG.
    IF X-CATALOG NOT  VALID-NUMBER-MAX
        MOVE MASTER-CATALOG-NUMBER TO VALID-NUMBER (X-CATALOG).
    READ CATALOG-FILE
            AT END MOVE 'N' TO MORE-DATA-REMAINS-FLAG.
```

CHAPTER 16

1. Items **c** and **d** assume that **STRING-TALLY** and **COUNTER** have the initial values of zero.

   a. INSPECT ITEM-A REPLACING ALL ' ' BY '0'.

   b. INSPECT ITEM-B REPLACING FIRST 'A' BY '2'.

   c. INSPECT ITEM-C TALLYING STRING-TALLY FOR LEADING '*'.

   d. INSPECT ITEM-D TALLYING COUNTER FOR LEADING '*'
                   REPLACING LEADING '*' BY '0'.

   e. INSPECT ITEM-E@PGTXT SUB IN = REPLACING CHARACTERS BY
          '9' BEFORE INITIAL 'X'.

3.

```
IDENTIFICATION DIVISION.
PROGRAM-ID.
    C16EX03.

ENVIRONMENT DIVISION.
INPUT-OUTPUT SECTION.
FILE-CONTROL.
    SELECT CUSTOMER-FILE        ASSIGN TO CUSTFILE.
    SELECT LETTER-FILE          ASSIGN TO LETTERS.

DATA DIVISION.
FILE SECTION.
FD  CUSTOMER-FILE
    LABEL RECORDS ARE STANDARD.
01  CUSTOMER-RECORD.
    05  CUSTOMER-NAME.
        10  LAST-NAME           PIC X(15).
        10  FIRST-NAME          PIC X(15).
        10  CUS-TITLE           PIC X(5).
    05  CUSTOMER-ADDRESS.
        10  HOUSE-NUMBER        PIC X(5).
        10  STREET-NAME         PIC X(15).
        10  CITY                PIC X(15).
        10  STATE               PIC X(15).
        10  ZIP                 PIC X(5).
    05  REST-OF-RECORD          PIC X(110).

FD  LETTER-FILE
    LABEL RECORDS ARE STANDARD.
01  LETTER-RECORD               PIC X(80).

WORKING-STORAGE SECTION.

01  MORE-DATA-REMAINS-FLAG      PIC X.
    88  NO-MORE-DATA-REMAINS            VALUE 'N'.

PROCEDURE DIVISION.
A000-PRINT-LETTERS.
    OPEN INPUT  CUSTOMER-FILE
         OUTPUT LETTER-FILE.
    MOVE 'Y' TO MORE-DATA-REMAINS-FLAG.
    READ CUSTOMER-FILE
            AT END MOVE 'N' TO MORE-DATA-REMAINS-FLAG.
    PERFORM B010-PRINT-HEADING
            UNTIL NO-MORE-DATA-REMAINS.
    CLOSE CUSTOMER-FILE
          LETTER-FILE.
    STOP RUN.

B010-PRINT-HEADING.
    MOVE SPACES TO LETTER-RECORD.
    STRING
        CUS-TITLE       DELIMITED BY SPACE
        SPACE           DELIMITED BY SIZE
        FIRST-NAME      DELIMITED BY SPACE
        SPACE           DELIMITED BY SIZE
        LAST-NAME       DELIMITED BY SPACE
            INTO LETTER-RECORD.
```

```
        WRITE LETTER-RECORD AFTER ADVANCING 5 LINES.
        MOVE SPACES TO LETTER-RECORD.
        STRING
            HOUSE-NUMBER   DELIMITED BY SPACE
            SPACE          DELIMITED BY SIZE
            STREET-NAME    DELIMITED BY SPACE
                INTO LETTER-RECORD.
        WRITE LETTER-RECORD AFTER ADVANCING 1 LINE.
        MOVE SPACES TO LETTER-RECORD.
        STRING
            CITY           DELIMITED BY SPACE
            ', '           DELIMITED BY SIZE
            STATE          DELIMITED BY SPACE
            SPACE          DELIMITED BY SIZE
            ZIP            DELIMITED BY SIZE
                INTO LETTER-RECORD.
        WRITE LETTER-RECORD AFTER ADVANCING 1 LINE.
        MOVE SPACES TO LETTER-RECORD.
        STRING
            'Dear '        DELIMITED BY SIZE
            CUS-TITLE      DELIMITED BY SPACE
            SPACE          DELIMITED BY SIZE
            LAST-NAME      DELIMITED BY SPACE
                INTO LETTER-RECORD.
        WRITE LETTER-RECORD AFTER ADVANCING 3 LINES.
        READ CUSTOMER-FILE
                AT END MOVE 'N' TO MORE-DATA-REMAINS-FLAG.
```

CHAPTER 17

2.

```
        IDENTIFICATION DIVISION.
        PROGRAM-ID.
            C17EX02.

        ENVIRONMENT DIVISION.
        INPUT-OUTPUT SECTION.
        FILE-CONTROL.
            SELECT ACCOUNT-FILE        ASSIGN TO 'C17EX02.ACC'.
            SELECT REPORT-FILE         ASSIGN TO 'C17EX02.REP'.

        DATA DIVISION.

        FILE SECTION.

        FD  ACCOUNT-FILE
            LABEL RECORDS ARE STANDARD.
        01  ACCOUNT-RECORD.
            05  ACCOUNT-NUMBER         PIC X(5).
            05  SALE-AMOUNT            PIC 9(5)V99.
            05  FILLER                 PIC X(68).

        FD  REPORT-FILE
            LABEL RECORDS ARE OMITTED
            REPORT IS SALES-REPORT.
```

```
WORKING-STORAGE SECTION.

01   MORE-DATA-FLAG                  PIC X.
     88  NO-MORE-DATA                        VALUE 'N'.

REPORT SECTION.

RD   SALES-REPORT
     CONTROLS ARE FINAL
                 ACCOUNT-NUMBER
     PAGE LIMIT IS 60 LINES
          HEADING       1
          FIRST DETAIL  4
          LAST DETAIL   55
          FOOTING       60.
01   TYPE IS PAGE HEADING LINE IS 1.
     05  COLUMN 1                    PIC X(48)
         VALUE 'ACCOUNT      TOTAL   AMOUNT   FINAL TOTAL'.
     05  COLUMN 45                   PIC X(04) VALUE 'PAGE'.
     05  COLUMN 49                   PIC Z(6)9
              SOURCE IS PAGE-COUNTER.


01   ACCOUNT-LINE TYPE DETAIL LINE PLUS 1.
     05  COLUMN 1                    PIC Z(4)9
             SOURCE IS ACCOUNT-NUMBER
             GROUP INDICATE.
     05  COLUMN 16                   PIC $$$,$$9.99
             SOURCE IS SALE-AMOUNT.
01   TYPE CONTROL FOOTING ACCOUNT-NUMBER LINE PLUS 1
                 NEXT GROUP PLUS 1.
     05  COLUMN 1                    PIC Z(4)9
             SOURCE IS ACCOUNT-NUMBER.
     05  COLUMN 7                    PIC $$$$,$$9.99 SUM SALE-AMOUNT.

01   TYPE CONTROL FOOTING FINAL LINE PLUS 3.
     05  COLUMN 26                   PIC $$$$,$$9.99 SUM SALE-AMOUNT.


PROCEDURE DIVISION.
A000-PREPARE-SALES-REPORT.
     OPEN INPUT  ACCOUNT-FILE
          OUTPUT REPORT-FILE.
     MOVE 'Y' TO MORE-DATA-FLAG.
     INITIATE SALES-REPORT.
     READ ACCOUNT-FILE
          AT END MOVE 'N' TO MORE-DATA-FLAG.
     PERFORM B010-PROCESS-ACCOUNT-GROUP
          UNTIL NO-MORE-DATA.
     TERMINATE SALES-REPORT.
     CLOSE ACCOUNT-FILE
          REPORT-FILE.
     STOP RUN.

B010-PROCESS-ACCOUNT-GROUP.
     GENERATE ACCOUNT-LINE.
     READ ACCOUNT-FILE
          AT END MOVE 'N' TO MORE-DATA-FLAG.
```

APPENDIX V

LOADING THE MICROSOFT COBOL COMPILER

Because microcomputers come with a variety of different data storage options, and because the Microsoft COBOL compiler has many options that control the way it operates, there are many different ways in which the compiler can be configured for use, far too many to discuss in detail. The installation procedure described in this appendix is sufficient to run the examples presented in this book. We assume that your computer has a hard disk drive installed as drive C, and a floppy disk drive installed as drive A. We will describe how to load the COBOL compiler into a subdirectory on the C drive and how to configure your operating system to use the compiler. Before you begin installation, be sure that you have about 2.5M bytes of space available on your hard disk. (Actually, you will probably want more space than this since you will need to have work space available when you compile your programs.) When you compile programs, the COBOL source files can be either on the hard disk or on floppy disks.

We assume that your operating system is DOS, version 3.00 or later. If you are using OS/2, some of the installation procedures vary slightly from what we will describe; see the Microsoft *Operating Guide* for details.

The task of loading the compiler is controlled by a program called SETUP, provided by Microsoft as part of the compiler software. SETUP will tell you which disks to use at varying points in the installation process, ask you questions about the options you wish to select, load files onto your hard disk, and configure the operating system to use the COBOL compiler.

Begin by loading the floppy disk labelled SETUP into drive A, then type

A:
SETUP

The first line makes the A drive the default disk drive, and the second line begins execution of SETUP.

When SETUP begins execution, you will first see several introductory screens, then one that asks whether you wish to continue with the installation process. If you are indeed ready to install the **COBOL** compiler, type Y.

The next screen will ask you to select the compiler components you wish to install. There are ten choices, numbered 1-0 (0 represents 10); you can toggle a selection on or off by typing its number. To select the component needed for the material covered in this book, you will need items 1, 3, 4, and 6. If you have made the proper selections, the screen should look like Figure 1.

```
                        Component Selection

This section allows you to select the components you wish to be installed on
your fixed disk. To avoid using more space than necessary, you are advised to
select only those components you know you have a need for. Others can be loaded
at a later time, as required, using SETUP. A default selection has been made to
guide you.

      1.  DOS specific compiler and libraries             Selected
      2.  OS/2 specific compiler and libraries            Not selected
      3.  Microsoft Utilities (LINK.EXE, etc.)            Selected
      4.  Demonstration programs.                         Selected
      5.  Message Control System.                         Not selected
      6.  Accept/Display configuration utilities.         Selected
      7.  File REBUILD utility.                           Not selected
      8.  Conversion Series 3 (for RM compatability)      Not selected
      9.  Conversion Series 5 (for DG compatability)      Not selected
      0.  Inter language communication support            Not selected

 You can select/reject components by pressing the associated number.

 When you have made your selection, please press ENTER to continue
```

FIGURE 1 The Component Selection screen.

The next screen tells you how to load the Microsoft Editor; if you wish to use this editor, see the *Microsoft Editor User's Guide*.

The following screen gives you the choice of using the default configuration for the **COBOL** compiler or selecting your own options. Since we will be selecting our own options, press the Enter key to continue. This brings us to the Dialect Selection screen. For the programs in this book, we have selected ANSI 74, IBM VS **COBOL** II Release 2, and ANSI 85 (options 1, 5, and 7). This gives compatibility with the current version of IBM **COBOL**, as well as compatibility with the 1974 and 1985 **COBOL** standards. As with the Component Selection screen, type an option number to toggle that option on or off.

The next screen controls compilation options. Since our objective is still to maintain compatibility with IBM mainframe compilers, we select options 4 and 5 and turn off all others. The resulting screen looks like the one shown in Figure 2.

The next five screens tell the SETUP program what size floppy disks you are using (3-1/2" or 5-1/4"), what drive will contain the **COBOL** installation

```
                        Default Compilation Options

    This screen allows you to select certain default compilation options. You
    should refer to the Operating Guide for details of the effect of these options.

        1. Bound checking on subscripts                    Not selected

        2. Ignore the picture size on unsigned COMP fields Not selected

        3. COMP fields are not truncated                   Not selected

        4. OS/VS and VS COBOL II PERFORM behaviour          Selected

        5. OS/VS COMP data storage allocation scheme        Selected

        6. Microsoft COBOL 2.2 run-time emulation          Not selected

        7. ANSI 85 Nested call support                     Not selected


    You can select/reject options by pressing the associated number.

    When you have made your selection, please press ENTER to continue
```

FIGURE 2 The Compilation Options screen after appropriate options have been selected.

disks, and the subdirectory on your hard disk where you want the programs installed. We recommend that you install all programs in the same subdirectory, so the options become fairly simple. First enter 3 or 5 to select the disk size appropriate for your system, then specify the drive identifier, generally drive A. If you want to use the default directory name recommended by Microsoft (C:\COBOL) simply press the Enter key for each of the following screens. Otherwise, supply the subdirectory name you want to use.

At this point, SETUP has all the information it needs to begin loading files onto your hard disk. You are given the choice of continuing the installation, previewing the installation but not actually loading files, changing some of the choices you made, or terminating installation. To continue, type 1 on the action screen. If you do so, SETUP will compute how much disk space is needed to load all the files and will tell you if your hard disk has enough space.

Your next choice is whether or not you want SETUP to create a default COBOL.DIR file, and we recommend that you do so. If you wish to modify this file later you may, but selecting this option gives you a good starting point. Based on the options we have selected, you would see the following result shown in Figure 3.

SETUP is now ready to copy files from the floppy disks to the hard disk. This will involve as many as nine different floppy disks for the options we

```
          Do you want to create a COBOL.DIR file [Y/N] ? y

          Creating C:\COBOL\COBOL.DIR ...

          Compiler directives included in COBOL.DIR ...

          MF(4)
          ANS85
          NOBOUND
          PERFORM-TYPE(OSVS)
          IBMCOMP
          VSC2
          ASSIGN(EXTERNAL)

          Press ENTER to continue ...
```

FIGURE 3 The COBOL.DIR file created by SETUP.

have suggested—more if you have chosen additional options—so be patient. SETUP will lead you through several screens, prompting you to insert the proper floppy disks in drive A one at a time.

At this point all the files needed for the Microsoft **COBOL** compiler have been copied to the hard disk. However, since the operating system does not yet know where to find the compiler when you call for it, it would still not be possible to use the compiler unless you kept all your **COBOL** programs in the compiler's subdirectory. To tell the operating system to look in the new subdirectory when you call for the **COBOL** compiler, you need to add the subdirectory's name to the end of the *path* used by your system.

The operating system path is a list of subdirectory names that tells DOS where to look for programs being executed. When you execute a program, DOS searches through the subdirectories listed in the path one by one until the program is found. Normally, the path list is defined as part of your AUTOEXEC.BAT file, a file that is automatically executed when you start your computer. The last task that SETUP performs is to ask you whether you want it to add the **COBOL** subdirectory name to your path. For example, suppose that AUTOEXEC.BAT looks like this:

prompt Date: d_Time: t_
prompt pg
path=c:\;c:\bat;c:\dos;c:\msword

This file will print the date and time when you start your computer, then set the system prompt so that it prints the name of the current subdirectory. (If you are not familiar with the prompt statement, look in your DOS manual or in a textbook describing how DOS operates.)

The path statement tells the operating system to look for program files first in the root directory of the C drive, then in a subdirectory called "BAT," then in the subdirectory "DOS," and finally in the directory "MSWORD." We assume that batch files are kept in BAT, operating system files are kept in DOS, and that we use Microsoft Word, which is kept in MSWORD.

If you tell SETUP that you want to modify AUTOEXEC.BAT to use **COBOL**, the resulting file will look like this:

```
prompt Date: $d$_Time: $t$_
prompt $p$g
path=c:\;c:\bat;c:\dos;c:\msword;C:\COBOL
SET COBDIR=C:\COBOL
SET LIB=C:\COBOL
```

The **COBOL** subdirectory has been added to the path statement, and two system parameter variables, COBDIR and LIB, have been defined. These variables tell the **COBOL** compiler where to find various files and libraries that it needs during compilation. (By the way, your original AUTOEXEC.BAT file has not been lost; SETUP automatically saves a backup copy.)

SETUP has now finished its job and you get the message "Installation complete." However, you still have one task to perform. In order to make the ACCEPT/DISPLAY modules and the indexed sequential file processing modules as flexible as possible, you need to link several object (.OBJ) modules to create executable (.EXE) files. The statements needed are

```
LINK @ADIS.LNK;
LINK IXSIO;
```

Before you execute these link statements you should define the **COBOL** subdirectory to be the current default directory. If you have just finished executing SETUP you can do this by executing

```
C:
CD C:\COBOL
```

The first statement makes C the default drive, and the second statement makes C:\COBOL the current subdirectory.

You have now completed installation of the Microsoft **COBOL** compiler. However, part of the operating environment needed by the compiler is not established until you reboot your computer, so you may wish to reboot immediately.

INDEX

Programming, 1
Programming standards, 74
Programming style, 170-171
Program specification, 118-119, 121, 232
Program structure, 16, 23, 25, 81-106
Program stub, 329
Program testing, 125, 188-189
Project exercise, 63, 105-106, 127-128, 241, 360-362, 409, 457-459
Prompt, 38, 310
Pseudocode, 65, 69-71, 75, 109, 174
Punched card, 8

Qualification, of data name, 256-257
Quantity on hand, 348
Quantity on order, 348
Query function, in ANIMATOR, 202
Quotation mark, 4

RAM, 244
Random access file, 421
Random access memory, 244
RD, 488
READ, 20, 23-24, 26
READ...INTO, 324
Receipt, in file updating, 342
Receiving item, 131
Record, 17, 26
RECORD CONTAINS, 415-416, 486
RECORD KEY, 422, 432
Record sequential file, 420
Recursion, 181
REDEFINES, 252-253, 283, 367-368
Relational operator, 86, 272
Relation condition, 85-86, 354, 550
RELATIVE KEY, 443
Relative record file, 421, 441, 443-445
Relative record number, 447
REMAINDER, 48
RENAMES, 550-551
Reorder point, 348
Reorder quantity, 348
REPLACING, 463
REPORT FOOTING, 489
REPORT HEADING, 489
REPORT IS, 486
Report section, 482, 486-487, 489, 491
Report writer, 477-502
Reserved word, 5, 41
RETURN, 511
REVERSE-VIDEO, 292
REWRITE, 439
ROUNDED, 43

Rounding, 43, 50
Run diagram, 323
Run-time error, 169, 188

S, in PICTURE, 130
Sales statistics application, 215-242, 484-492
Save item, 326
Scaling, 140
Screen definition, 288, 290-292
Screen Section, 287
SD, 505
SEARCH, 382-383, 385, 387, 389, 393
SEARCH ALL, 390-391
Section, 5
SECURE, 311
Seed catalog application, 267-314, 417-455
SELECT, 18, 274
Selection, 70
Selection object, 98
Selection subject, 98
Semantics, 177
Sending item, 131
Sentence, 3, 21
Sequence, 70
Sequence area, 9
Sequence checking, 326-328
Sequence error, 341
Sequential file, 323
Sequential file processing, 217-239, 317-362, 412, 417-421, 521-532
SET, 380-381
Shipment, in file updating, 342
Short-circuiting, 270
Sign, 49, 130, 153, 246
SIZE ERROR, 43-44, 50
Slack byte, 251, 400
Slash, 9, 224
    in PICTURE, 139
SORT, 503-518
Sorting, 217, 503-518
SOURCE, 491
Source code, 6, 169
Space, See Blank
SPACES, 39
Spacing of lines, 224-226, 477-482
SPECIAL-NAMES, 225
Specification, program, 118-119, 121, 232
Square bracket, 42
Square root, 549
Standards, See Programming standards